ENGLISH HERITAGE
PRACTICAL BUILDING CONSERVATION

BUILDING ENVIRONMENT

ASHGATE

© English Heritage 2014

All rights reserved. No part of this publication may be reproduced, stored in a retrieval system or transmitted in any form or by any means, electronic, mechanical, photocopying, recording or otherwise without the prior permission of the publisher.

English Heritage has asserted their right under the Copyright, Designs and Patents Act 1988 to be identified as the author and editor of this work.

English Heritage
1 Waterhouse Square
138–142 Holborn
London EC1N 2ST

Published by
Ashgate Publishing Limited
Wey Court East
Union Road
Farnham
Surrey GU9 7PT
England

Ashgate Publishing Company
Suite 420
101 Cherry Street
Burlington
VT 05401-4405
USA

www.ashgate.com

British Library Cataloguing in Publication Data

Practical building conservation.
    Building environment.
    1. Building materials–Environmental aspects.
    2. Weathering of buildings. 3. Historic buildings–
    Conservation and restoration.
    I. English Heritage.
    720'.288-dc22

Library of Congress Control Number: 2001012345

ISBN-13: 9780754645580

Printed in the United Kingdom by Henry Ling Limited, at the Dorset Press, Dorchester, DT1 1HD

To the memory of John Ashurst (1937–2008), an inspiration and friend to all the editors, whose encouragement and support was a great motivation for this new series of Practical Building Conservation.

ENGLISH HERITAGE
PRACTICAL BUILDING CONSERVATION

BUILDING ENVIRONMENT

Series Editors: Bill Martin and Chris Wood

Volume Editors: Robyn Pender, Brian Ridout, Tobit Curteis

NOTES ON VOLUME EDITORS & CONTRIBUTORS

Volume Editors & Principal Authors:
Robyn Pender, Brian Ridout, Tobit Curteis

Dr Robyn Pender is a Senior Architectural Conservator in the Building Conservation and Research Team at English Heritage, and serves on the Cathedrals Fabric Commission for England. A physicist specialising in moisture transport in building materials and systems, she studied wall-painting conservation at the Courtauld Institute of Art.

Dr Brian Ridout is also a Senior Architectural Conservator in English Heritage's Building Conservation and Research Team. He is a biologist and building scientist who has worked for many years as an international expert on timber decay and damp problems.

Tobit Curteis, who studied history of art at Warwick University and the conservation of wall paintings at the Courtauld Institute of Art, is a fellow of the International Institute of Conservation, and runs a private conservation practice specialising in environmental issues in historic buildings and monuments. He is a consultant to English Heritage, the Church Building Council and the National Trust.

Principal Contributors:
Paul Beckett, Bill Bordass, Iain McCaig, Sarah Pinchin, Nicholas Warns

Paul Beckett is a conservation surveyor who has worked on historic buildings of all periods; he has reviewed many of the volumes in this series of *Practical Building Conservation*.
Bill Bordass is a building scientist studying the technical and environmental performance of new, existing and historic buildings in operation, and has contributed to over 200 publications on energy and building performance. **Iain McCaig** is a Senior Architectural Conservator in the Building Conservation and Research Team, and studied architecture before specialising in building conservation; he is currently concentrating on issues concerning energy use in the historic built environment. **Sarah Pinchin** is an archaeologist with postgraduate training in wall-painting conservation from the Courtauld Institute of Art; her expertise includes preventive conservation and the deterioration of *in-situ* building stone. **Nicholas Warns**, a former Scholar with the Society for the Protection of Ancient Buildings, is inspecting architect for almost 90 churches in England.

The volume editors would like to take this opportunity to thank all their contributors for their help and support with this book, as well as for the information and images they have so generously provided.

Other Contributors:

Paul Baker, Sharon Cather, Caroline Cattini, Vicky Curteis, Jo Deeming, David Drewe, Steve Emery, Pedro Gaspar, Sophie Godfraind, Alison Henry, Arthur McCallum, Tracy Manning, Will Marshall, Edith Mueller, Andrew More, Geraldine O'Farrell, Peter Rumley, John Stewart, Amanda White, Clara Willett, Chris Wood

CONTENTS

The Practical Building Conservation Series v
About This Book vii
Using These Books viii

INTRODUCTION 1
The Building Environment 3
The Building Itself 11
    The Building Envelope 13
    Failure of the Envelope 14

BUILDING SCIENCE 17
Conservation of Energy 19
Understanding Failures 32
    Failure Under Load 32
    Thermal Behaviour 35
    Moisture in Building Materials 37

INTERACTIONS WITH THE ENVIRONMENT 51
The Building Envelope 53
    Functions of the Building Envelope 54
    Interior Parts of the Envelope 99
How the Envelope Modifies the Interior Conditions 103
    The Effect of Building Occupation 109

CONTROLLING THE INTERIOR ENVIRONMENT 113
Environments for Users 115
    Ventilation 117
    Heating 121
    Cooling 128
    Lighting 131
    Service Supplies 139

DETERIORATION & DAMAGE	145
Environmental Deterioration	147
Deterioration of Materials	149
Deterioration of the Envelope	161
ASSESSING THE BUILDING ENVIRONMENT	211
Environmental Assessment	213
Background Research	218
Building Performance Surveys	221
Specialist Investigations	256
DIAGNOSIS	309
CARE & REPAIR	325
Day-to-Day Care	327
Treatment & Repair	350
Dealing with Persistent Issues	351
Planning Interventions	354
Interventions on the Envelope	362
Modifying the Interior Environment	408
Assessing Interventions	443
SPECIAL TOPICS	445
Buildings & Human Health	447
Dealing with Disasters	461
Improving Energy & Carbon Performance	503
GLOSSARY	601
INDEX	629
ACKNOWLEDGEMENTS & PICTURE CREDITS	647

THE PRACTICAL BUILDING CONSERVATION SERIES

This series of *Practical Building Conservation* technical handbooks supersedes the original five volumes written by John and Nicola Ashurst, and published in 1988.

The series is aimed primarily at those who look after historic buildings, or who work on them. The ten volumes should be useful to architects, surveyors, engineers, conservators, contractors and conservation officers, but also of interest to owners, curators, students and researchers.

The contents reflect the work of the Building Conservation and Research Team, their colleagues at English Heritage, and their consultants and researchers, who together have many decades of accumulated experience in dealing with deteriorating building materials and systems of all types. The aim has been to provide practical advice by advocating a common approach of firstly understanding the material or building element and why it is deteriorating, and then dealing with the causes. The books do not include detailed specifications for remedial work, neither do they include a comprehensive coverage of each subject. They concentrate on those aspects which are significant in conservation terms, and reflect the requests for information received by English Heritage.

Building conservation draws on evidence and lessons from the past to help understand the building, its deterioration and potential remedies; this encourages a cautious approach. New techniques, materials and treatments often seem promising, but can prove disappointing and sometimes disastrous. It takes many years before there is sufficient experience of their use to be able to promote them confidently. Nonetheless, understanding increases with experience and building conservation is a progressive discipline, to which these books aim to contribute.

The volumes also establish continual care and maintenance as an integral part of any conservation programme. Maintenance of all buildings, even of those that have deteriorated, must be a priority; it is a means of maximising preservation and minimising costs.

Most of the examples shown in the books are from England: however, English Heritage maintains good relations with conservation bodies around the world, and even where materials and techniques differ, the approach is usually consistent. We therefore hope the series will have a wider appeal.

Dr Simon Thurley
Chief Executive, English Heritage

BUILDING ENVIRONMENT

ABOUT THIS BOOK

Any book that tries to deal with the vast topic of 'the building environment' must necessarily cover a great deal of ground, from the weather, the physics of heat and moisture, and the basics of architecture and engineering, to the building's use and the maintenance and repair of complex materials and systems. *Building Environment* is the product of the many years spent observing buildings by the volume editors and their contributors: buildings of all kinds, modern as well as traditional in construction, in all uses and under all conditions. It presents a comprehensive overview of building performance, and aims to equip anyone responsible for a building's care with sufficient knowledge to be able to recognise fundamental problems, and to either confidently deal with those that are straightforward themselves or successfully delegate those that are more difficult to specialists.

Many patterns of deterioration appear repeatedly, and familiarity with these patterns makes it possible to recognise and even predict common causes of problems, such as the inevitable blocked gutters and drains. Even so, every building environment is essentially unique, and the underlying causes may not always be as they first seemed. We therefore aim to steer readers away from 'symptoms-led' thinking: the same patterns of deterioration can arise from many different problems, and it is important to always approach the situation with an open mind. This is why the book is structured to present a coherent and logical picture of first what the building environment is, then how it works, how it fails, and finally how problems can best be remediated.

After a short **Introduction**, the **Building Science** chapter describes the physical processes that explain the many links between the building and its environment. **Interactions with the Environment** shows how these links affect the way building envelopes are designed to work, and the impact of their surroundings. The role played by the building occupants – particularly when trying to adjust the interior conditions – is covered in **Controlling the Interior Environment**. **Deterioration & Damage** looks first at the environmental degradation of individual building materials, before proceeding to consider how the envelope as a whole can fail. **Assessing the Building Environment** covers the actions needed to understand how a particular building is functioning and how it is failing, including specialist investigations such as environmental monitoring. A short chapter discussing approaches to **Diagnosis** is followed by **Care & Repair**, which introduces the various maintenance and remedial works designed to address environmental problems. Finally, the **Special Topics** at the end of the book address three important issues associated with the building environment: human health; disasters such as floods and fires; and reducing energy use and carbon emissions.

At times the conclusions we have drawn will be familiar to most readers, at others they may be at variance with accepted wisdom; but we have taken the decision to contest familiar notions which we have good reason to believe to be wrong. Too many problems can be traced back to the repetition of misconceived ideas about how building environments operate.

The audience for this volume of *Practical Building Conservation* is certain to be diverse: not only architects and surveyors with many years of experience dealing with historic buildings, but also students, building managers and homeowners who wish to keep their houses in the best possible condition. For this reason a good deal of introductory material is included; we hope that this will prove helpful even to experienced readers when they need to explain to their clients and colleagues exactly how building envelopes work.

USING THESE BOOKS

For accessibility and ease of use, the information given in the text has not been footnoted, and rather than references, short lists of further reading are given at the end of the appropriate chapters. References to other sections within the text are given in **bold**, and references to other publications in ***bold italics***.

Links to other books in the *Practical Building Conservation* series are indicated throughout the text by the relevant volume symbol, showing that more information on the topic will be found in that volume.

- Conservation Basics   ➲ BASICS
- Concrete   ➲ CONCRETE
- Earth, Brick & Terracotta   ➲ EARTH & BRICK
- Glass & Glazing   ➲ GLASS
- Metals   ➲ METALS
- Mortars, Renders & Plasters ➲ MORTARS
- Roofing   ➲ ROOFING
- Stone   ➲ STONE
- Timber   ➲ TIMBER

Although every attempt has been made to explain terms as they first occur in the text, a glossary has also been included, and this can be found just before the index.

INTRODUCTION

This short preface divides into two sections: the first describing the building environment in its broadest sense; and the second introducing the concept of environmental deterioration, and explaining how this book should be used to help those responsible for the preservation of buildings to understand, assess and deal with environmental deterioration.

Buildings come in many shapes and sizes, and may be constructed from a range of different materials. They might be very simple and functional, or elaborately complex and decorative, but all share one principal purpose: that is, to create an interior space protected from the extremes of the weather, and with conditions suitable for the building's function (be that living, working or storage). For instance, a barn must stay dark and cool as well as dry, whereas an office building needs to be warm in winter and cool in summer, and have plenty of light by which to work.

The structure that separates the interior space from the exterior world is commonly called the 'building envelope'. At its simplest this comprises a roof, walls and floor, but most also incorporate features intended to increase weather-resistance (such as rainwater disposal systems) or to make the building more usable (such as windows).

In most buildings, the 'natural' interior environment created by the interaction of the exterior conditions with the envelope is altered by various systems controlled by the occupants, such as ventilation, heating, cooling and artificial lighting. Over the past century or so there have been vast changes in the way that buildings are being used, and to this list must therefore be added services such as plumbing and electrical wiring.

The sum of all these inputs – external and internal, natural and artificial – is known as the 'building environment', and it has the greatest possible impact on the behaviour of any built structure and on its survival. To conserve a building it is vital to have a good working knowledge of its environment, of the ways the building envelope might interact with that environment, and of how this interaction could cause deterioration or even failure.

THE BUILDING ENVIRONMENT

INFLUENCES ON THE BUILDING

THE EXTERIOR ENVIRONMENT

The primary influence on a building is always the environment to which it is exposed. This is typically very complex, since it includes not only the weather, but perhaps also pollution, runoff patterns, the water table, ground movements and many other factors of this type. Every building environment will depend to some extent on the local terrain, and crucially on the way the surrounding land is being used.

The exterior environment has no predefined geographical limit, but extends out as far as any factor that might be affecting the building condition. In some circumstances this could be quite considerable distances: for example, winds can carry sea salts far inland, which means that an assessor trying to understand a problem related to chlorides may be forced to take the maritime environment into account, even though the structure may be some way from the coast.

The building itself will alter the exterior environment in its near vicinity, such as windiness or runoff. To try to understand patterns of complex environmental problems (for example, storm damage, pollution, flooding or traffic vibration), the position, construction and even the materials of the building will need to be taken into account.

As a result, the exterior environment of every building will always be unique.

COMPONENTS OF THE EXTERIOR ENVIRONMENT

AIR QUALITY

The air may contain gases and particulates – 'pollutants' – able to interact adversely with building materials. Pollutants can be in the form of particles, droplets of liquid or gases, and may be 'primary pollutants' emitted directly into the air by some process such as volcanic eruption or combustion; or 'secondary pollutants', which will form when two or more primary pollutants interact.

WEATHER

'Weather' is the term used to describe the state of the local atmosphere: that is, hot or cold, wet or dry, calm or stormy, clear or cloudy ('climate' is the term used for the average atmospheric conditions over longer periods of time).

The components of the weather that have the most impact on buildings include rain and snow, the temperature and humidity of the air, the direction, strength and gustiness of the wind, and the patterns of sunlight. These all will vary locally and according to exposure, and may well have different impacts on different parts of the building.

What Causes Weather

Almost all the familiar weather phenomena – including winds, clouds, 'precipitation' (rain, snow and fog) and extreme events such as storms – occur in the 'troposphere', the lowest zone of the atmosphere, where the air can interact with the Earth's surface. This interaction produces the local variations in air temperature and humidity from which the weather largely derives.

A warm surface will heat the air above it, decreasing its density and causing it to rise. The principal influence on ground temperature is the angle at which sunlight strikes the atmosphere, which varies with latitude; in northern countries such as England, sunlight strikes at an oblique angle, but in the tropics the sun is directly overhead and the ground is heated strongly. Since the Earth's axis of rotation is slightly tilted, in England the sun is at its most acute angle in June, warming the ground, which in turn warms the air over the following months, producing summer conditions. The exact orbital parameters alter very slightly over time, so over thousands of years the northern hemisphere has had spells of temperate climate interspersed with the very cold conditions that produced the Ice Ages.

The temperature to which the Earth's surface heats depends on the nature of the surface, particularly its ability to absorb solar energy, or to be cooled by wind. As a result, neighbouring areas of ground may be at very different temperatures. The air above them will be warmed or cooled accordingly, and it is this that produces winds, as areas of high-pressure air move into areas of lower pressure.

As winds pass over the surface, they help to evaporate water from sea and ground, and to carry it away as vapour (see the **Building Science** chapter for a detailed description of the processes involved in evaporation and condensation). The moist air is less dense, and will travel upwards towards areas where the pressure is lower and the air cooler, and there may condense to form clouds. If conditions are suitable for condensation close to the surface, the result is a fog.

Clouds may also develop at the boundaries where air pockets of different pressure meet, and it is at these 'weather fronts' that some condensed vapour may coalesce to form droplets large enough to be affected by gravity. These fall as rain, hail or snow; the size and shape of the raindrops or snowflakes is determined by the temperature and humidity of the air. Hail forms under extreme conditions: during storms when a low freezing level is combined with a strong updraught. Tiny ice crystals form and are drawn upwards through zones in the storm clouds where they accrete more ice; eventually they become so large that their mass can no longer be supported by the updraught, and they fall as hailstones.

Surface conditions strongly affect precipitation: for example, on the windward side of hills and mountains (especially near the coast), water-laden air will be forced upwards to form clouds and rain; on the leeward side, conditions are often very dry.

Weather systems are extremely complex, not least since local cloudiness and precipitation will cause uneven surface heating. Small changes can be self-feeding, eventually producing much wider weather patterns such as hurricanes and cyclones, and in some cases very robust climate patterns (such as the wind-driven Gulf Stream, which by carrying warm water northeast across the Atlantic makes western Europe considerably warmer than it would otherwise be).

TOPOGRAPHY

In classical literature the term 'topography' was used for writing about places, and included all aspects of place: not only geological features, but also vegetation and man-made structures, and even local history and culture. In the USA, topography is reserved for the study of terrain (the 'relief' of the land surface, including elevation, slope, and orientation), but in the UK and many other parts of the world, it is still used in its classical sense.

The topography will affect the local environment, sometimes very strongly. It will modify or even control local precipitation and windiness, the soil characteristics and ground drainage patterns, and therefore the local vegetation. The positioning and even the design of buildings may need to respond to these very local conditions, so neighbouring villages may show very different types of construction.

Terrain

The terrain is mostly the result of natural actions, with land built up by geological processes being worn down by steady erosion, or by more sudden changes such as landslips. This eventually leads to rivers and streams running through hollows and valleys and deepening over time, and to very local patterns of weather. Human activities such as agriculture, mining and transport can also alter the local terrain, and often have particularly strong impacts on buildings.

Lead tetraoxide staining
The conversion of exposed lead to lead tetraoxide causes a pinkish surface discolouration. This alteration has recently become common and widespread, especially in rural areas; metal specialists are tentatively linking it to wind-blown fertilisers.

Local Land Use

As well as affecting the terrain, local land use can be critical to other aspects of the exterior environment. For example, rainwater runoff patterns will depend on the land cover: in built-up areas, surfaces such as tarmac and cement may prevent rainwater soaking into the earth. Many pollutants can also be traced back to land use, from airborne particulates and gases traceable to transport and industry, to contaminants in groundwater coming from agricultural biocides and fertilisers.

BUILDING ENVIRONMENT
INTRODUCTION

The situation of a building – the topology, geology and hydrology of its surroundings – are a principal influence on its environment.

GEOLOGY

Soil Characteristics

The characteristics of the soil are one of the most important factors governing local drainage, and hence the stability of buildings. Soil is for the most part eroded rock, composed of particles in a range of sizes.

Broadly speaking – definitions vary slightly and the type of material can also have an effect – the coarsest grains (0.0625–2 mm) are known as 'sand', grains 0.0039–0.0625 mm as 'silt' and the finest grains (with diameters smaller than 2 μm) as 'clay'. The ratio of these sizes determines the basic soil type and characteristics such as permeability: for example, the sand content determines aeration and drainage, whilst the clay particles, which are chemically active, are able to bind with water and plant nutrients. Organic inclusions such as plant materials are also important, and the soil may also be mixed with pebbles and gravel. Many different classification systems are used for soil, depending on the intention of the analysis: the International Union of Soil Sciences recommends the *World Reference Base for Soil Resources*.

Well-drained sandy soils move very little as moisture contents change, but certain clay-rich soils are apt to expand and contract. This can affect the stability of buildings constructed on them, especially where there are seasonal extremes of wetness and dryness leading to cracking as well as swelling.

Soil characteristics such as elasticity and swellability are also important for those building materials made from them: earthen construction systems such as cob and rammed earth, or the fired bricks and tiles that are made from clay. ⊖EARTH & BRICK ⊖ROOFING

HYDROLOGY

Hydrology is the study of the movement, distribution and quality of water; for understanding the building environment, this means the water distribution and movement through the ground and across its surface. As well as rainwater, runoff, and groundwater, the local hydrology usually also includes artificial components (water running through the mains and waste water running through the sewers, for example).

Water Table

Water from rain, and from reservoirs such as rivers and lakes, may seep down through the soil and through cracks in rock formations. Eventually a layer of porous earth at some depth may begin to saturate, forming an 'aquifer'. The highest point of an aquifer is called the local 'water table'. 'Groundwater' is a wider term that includes the water table, other water locked in bedrock or deeper in the earth, the moisture in the soil, and (in very cold areas) permafrost.

The water table is of special importance to buildings constructed on wooden pilings, as was once common practice in marshy areas. The saturated timber can survive for centuries, because being immersed in the water table prevents its decay. ⊝TIMBER

Hydrology can be complex and very poorly understood. In particular, many towns and cities have watercourses or drains that have been enclosed and built over in the past, and the exact location of these has often not been recorded. In this case, trees planted too close to a hidden culvert eventually caused it to collapse without warning.

BUILDING ENVIRONMENT
INTRODUCTION

THE INTERIOR ENVIRONMENT

The basic interior environment is set by the way the building modifies the exterior conditions, not only preventing the penetration of wind, rain and sunlight, but also buffering the extremes of temperature and humidity.

The nature and extent of this buffering depends on the materials and construction of the building. For temperature, the important criteria are thermal inertia and radiant heat transfer: the exterior of the building will be heated and cooled by the changing weather, but these temperature changes will be transferred through the fabric more slowly, so that the interior may never reach the exterior maxima and minima. The greater the thermal mass of the envelope, and the less able it is to transfer radiant energy (sunlight), the more the temperature will be buffered. The buffering of ambient humidity depends on the permeability of the building materials, and how readily they can absorb water vapour from the air and release it again when conditions change.

The fabric will also buffer the changes in the interior conditions that arise from the way the building is being used: for example, the introduction of water from respiration and wet materials, as well as from cooking and cleaning.

Building use is the other principal component of the interior environment, especially in buildings where the users attempt intensive control by heating, cooling, ventilation and lighting.

THE BUILDING ITSELF

THE BUILDING ENVELOPE

The building is essentially a shell that separates the exterior from the interior. To be effective, this shell – or 'envelope' – must be able to prevent the weather harming the building fabric or contents, buffer changes in temperature and humidity, deflect rainwater and groundwater, and absorb ground movements and wind stresses.

Traditional systems for coping with the weather were basically quite straightforward, although they had many local variants. Roofs were covered with materials such as tiles and thatch that were layered to prevent rainwater penetrating, or sometimes with sheets of waterproof materials such as lead or copper. Pitches evolved to encourage the rain to run off, and systems were developed to collect it and channel it safely away, keeping the fabric dry and in good condition. Timber frames absorbed changes in humidity levels and could cope with most minor leaks. Roofs also shaded the interior and kept to a minimum the interior temperature rises due to sunlight exposure. To further resist the rain and the changing exterior temperatures, traditional buildings had solid walls, and were constructed using permeable materials such as earth, stone, brick and lime mortar, sometimes on frameworks of timber. ROOFING

In isolated buildings surrounded by open ground that sloped away from the building, wide eaves and the natural permeability of the wall materials were all that was needed to keep the rain from penetrating the fabric. As buildings began to be constructed taller and closer together, however, it became necessary to develop systems to collect rain as it fell from the eaves and channel it safely away. If the ground around the building was unsuitable, rain and runoff needed to be controlled with a drainage system.

One essential element of any building is a doorway, and most also need windows to let in light and air. Since these openings puncture the envelope and so could let in less desirable aspects of the exterior environment, elements such as hood mouldings and cornices were developed to deflect the rain, and doors and shutters were added to keep out the weather, provide security and give the users control over the amount of ventilation.

The advantages of covering the opening with a translucent material that let through the light whilst stopping the wind and rain were obvious, and many materials (including oiled paper and thin slices of horn or mica) were tried before sheet glass became affordable enough to be used for functional windows.

During the Industrial Revolution, sheet glass began to be made in quantity, together with structural and sheet steel, and cement. These are essentially impermeable materials, and with their introduction the concept of the building envelope began to change radically, with a new emphasis on waterproofing rather than on permeability. Glass began to be popular for roofs that allowed natural lighting of large interior spaces, and by the end of the 20th century, entire walls were being constructed with multiple layers of glass and other waterproof sheet materials. The introduction of building services such as electricity and plumbing led to other radical changes in construction. MORTARS
EARTH & BRICK GLASS METALS CONCRETE

BUILDING ENVIRONMENT
INTRODUCTION

FAILURE OF THE ENVELOPE

Once the envelope can no longer provide conditions that are suitable for the way it must be used, the building can quickly become unfit for purpose and will therefore have 'failed'.

Failures can have many causes, but will commonly have their roots in problems with the building environment. The basic problem for the building envelope is that the very materials and systems that are intended to deal with the exterior environment are necessarily exposed to it, and will eventually deteriorate as a result. Most envelopes can work well even under severe weather conditions; but problems may begin if parts of the fabric begin to break down, or if poorly considered alterations are made.

Water is directly implicated in the many ways in which building materials deteriorate, including the decay of timber, the corrosion of metal, the decohesion of unfired earthen construction, and the freeze-thaw breakdown of mortar, stone and brick. It can also be an indirect factor: changing moisture contents can lead to the physical breakdown of renders and masonry, by mechanisms including salt cycling. Water can also combine with pollutants to produce acids and alkalis that can attack common building materials such as stone and metals.

Wind can cause both gradual erosion and sudden mechanical damage, and it is also the primary agent in both driven rain and evaporation (which is one of the main mechanisms underlying the movement of water through the building fabric).

Temperature variations caused by solar heating or evaporative cooling can lead to localised dimensional change in composite components. In metal roofs, for example, this may stress the joints, and over time eventually cause sheets to crack and tear. Exposure to the ultraviolet components of sunlight will break down organic materials such as timber, paints, and sealants such as putties and mastics.

Sunlight will encourage the growth of both microscopic organisms and plants. Higher plants and animals can also cause damage, and leaves, urine, droppings and dead birds are common sources of damaging nitrate salts.

The other volumes in this series all contain detailed information about the many ways by which the exterior environment can cause the deterioration of particular building materials.
MORTARS **METALS** **EARTH & BRICK** **ROOFING** **GLASS** **STONE** **TIMBER** **CONCRETE**

Buildings are complex systems composed of many different materials, and trouble in one area or with one material or component can lead to failures elsewhere. Fortunately, traditional buildings tended to be over-engineered, and many can be rescued even after prolonged periods of neglect. Modern construction methods take a rather different approach to isolating the interior from the exterior, and this can sometimes lead to more complex and severe failures (see **Interactions with the Environment**). But whatever the materials or type of construction, finding ways of slowing or preventing deterioration depends on a good understanding of the building environment.

EXAMINING THE BUILDING ENVIRONMENT

The usual motivation for trying to understand how the environment of a building is working is that signs of local or general failure have been noticed by the building users or manager.

The most common issue they might seek to address, often by calling in outside expertise, is 'damp': a vague term that describes a symptom rather than the cause of a poor building environment. Indeed, moisture problems can have many causes, including rainwater penetration through holes and cracks, blocked drains or faulty runoff, inappropriate interventions, condensation because of thermal bridging, interior plumbing leaks, or the operation of heating systems. Often there will be more than one factor at work, and causes may well interact. Since similar patterns of failure can arise from very different causes, a symptom-led approach to care and repair is fraught with danger: trying to 'damp-proof' without a proper understanding of the building environment can trigger a whole range of ill-considered interventions – such as applying waterproof renders or plasters – that in practice may not solve the problem but could easily exacerbate it.

The environment of every building is unique, but behaviour will nonetheless follow certain general patterns. For example, liquid water will move through all types of permeable building material from any persistent source, but the source could be anything from a leaking drainpipe or gutter to the water table or a watercourse.

BUILDING ENVIRONMENT
INTRODUCTION

Environmental investigations may also be needed should a building manager wish to adjust the interior conditions, often again because a problem has been noticed: perhaps the atmosphere is stuffy or feels cold. Just as is the case when dealing with failure, leaping into solutions (increasing the ventilation, perhaps, or installing heating) is apt to backfire if the environment is not well understood first.

Thus the key to all building conservation is to try to characterise the way the building is behaving in the context of its environment (including its use), taking account of all the many processes that could be involved in deterioration and the many ways these might interact.

Although this sounds complex, in many cases it is actually quite straightforward: a good basic understanding can be derived quickly from an environmental assessment that takes account of the building's unique characteristics. To design and implement an assessment, however, a building manager must have a reasonable working knowledge of the ways building materials and systems function. Being comfortable with the basic building science covered in the next chapter will help building owners or their advisers to solve many everyday issues of care and repair themselves, and perhaps more importantly to recognise when a problem is unusually complex and therefore demands special expertise if it is to be dealt with successfully.

BUILDING
SCIENCE

This chapter introduces some simple concepts of building physics to help building practitioners better understand complex deterioration processes, and determine the most reliable methods of assessment, treatment and ongoing care.

Buildings are complicated systems constructed of very complex materials, and the environments to which they are exposed vary continually. Nevertheless, by observation it is possible to see that they do behave in some very predictable ways, and this makes it possible to use some basic scientific concepts (particularly those describing how moisture and heat behave in air and in porous materials) to better understand how building systems and materials react to the environment, and to determine the best means of dealing with any problems.

An exterior wall made up of permeable materials, with a blocked gutter leaking water into the wall at the top and a cement render on the exterior, is a good example of the power of a scientific approach, but also of its limitations. The basic physics behind the movement of water in the wall – for example, how it is controlled by moisture transfer rates through the materials, and the relative rates of evaporation from the interior and exterior surfaces – is all-important when it comes to interpreting the resulting deterioration and deciding what best to do about it. To the observer with a working knowledge of the underlying processes driving moisture movement, the pattern of damage may even point towards hidden causes: that the wall could have internal voids, for example, or that air movement in the room may be of critical importance. On the other hand, the complexities of any real wall or real environment make it unwise to try to use scientific principles to model a particular building, or predict an exact pattern of deterioration: here, observation will always be a much more powerful tool than theory.

A scientific approach is at its most practical when it is aimed at understanding which information will be needed to confidently plan the preservation or repair of a complex building envelope. Arguably, the most useful tool is 'conservation of energy', a simple physical law that makes it straightforward to not only make an intelligent guess about how the building environment might be working as a whole, but also to break down a very complex picture into its essential components, allowing problems and remedial solutions to be considered in a logical way.

CONSERVATION OF ENERGY

In a famous series of introductory lectures to young American college students, the physicist Richard Feynman began by explaining what seems to be the fundamental law of the universe: *"There is a fact, or if you wish, a law, governing all natural phenomena that are known to date. There is no known exception to this law—it is exact so far as we know. The law is called the conservation of energy. It states that there is a certain quantity, which we call 'energy', that does not change in the manifold changes which nature undergoes. That is a most abstract idea, because it is a mathematical principle; it says that there is a numerical quantity which does not change when something happens. It is not a description of a mechanism, or anything concrete; it is just a strange fact that we can calculate some number and when we finish watching nature go through her tricks and calculate the number again, it is the same."*

This law of conservation of energy – which says that in an isolated system, energy is neither created nor destroyed, but can only be changed from one form to another – is by no means merely abstract: it is of the greatest possible practicality when it comes to trying to make sense of real physical behaviour of all kinds, not least in buildings.

Stott Park Bobbin Mill

Energy can be transformed into many different forms, including heat, friction, light and sound.

The mill at Stott Park was originally powered by a water wheel, which converted the potential energy of falling water into mechanical energy, driving a line shaft that ran along the apex of the roof. This was used to power the equipment for cutting the timber, turning the lathes and spinning the waxing barrels. The water wheel was later replaced by a horizontal steam engine.

BUILDING ENVIRONMENT
BUILDING SCIENCE

FORCE, WORK & ENERGY

To understand why the conservation of energy is the most generally useful (as well as the most far-reaching) law of physics, a few definitions are needed: although the words used to describe energy – 'force' and 'work' – are familiar in everyday language, their meanings are subtly different in science.

- *Force*
  Any physical influence that could potentially cause an object to undergo a certain change, either altering its movement (how fast it is travelling, or in what direction) or its dimensions (compressing it or stretching it, for example). To describe a force, not only its strength but also the direction in which it is acting must be specified; for instance, the force of gravity is always towards the centre of the Earth.

- *Work*
  If a force acting on an object causes a change, no matter how small, it is said to have performed 'work' on the system. By definition, work is the force applied multiplied by the dimension of the change, so more work is done to carry a box three metres than to carry it for one metre in the same direction. A system's capacity to do work is its 'energy': by definition, energy is "*the property of matter and radiation which is manifest as a capacity to perform work (such as causing motion or the interaction of molecules)*".

There are two basic forms of energy:

- 'Kinetic energy', which is the ability of an object to do work because it is moving; for example, by colliding with another object and setting that moving as well. If work is done on an object to start it moving, stop it moving, or change its direction, its kinetic energy will be changed.
- 'Potential energy', which is the ability of an object to do work because of its position or its structure; it is associated with an energy field of some kind acting on the object (gravity on an object with mass, for example, or an electric field on a charged molecule, or the molecular bonds holding a solid object together). If an object is moved from one location to another inside the field acting on it (say, a brick is lifted from the ground up to the top of some scaffolding, or a spring is pulled open), then its potential energy will be changed.

FORMS OF ENERGY

Conservation of energy is a universal law because all things, including mass, are essentially composed of energy. Theoretically everything could be described as some combination of kinetic and potential energy, but in practice this approach is not nearly as helpful as defining some more general forms of energy based on some of the familiar patterns of macroscopic behaviour. For example, although the behaviour of a rubber ball could be explained in terms of the kinetic and potential energy of the molecules and chemical bonds within the rubber, it is usually easier and more helpful to speak of the 'elastic forces' that cause it to bounce. The following table describes the main forms of energy likely to be met within building materials and systems.

COMMON FORMS OF ENERGY ENCOUNTERED IN BUILDING SCIENCE

TYPE OF ENERGY	DESCRIPTION
ELECTROMAGNETIC	The energy emitted and absorbed by charged particles; it travels as a transverse wave, with various amplitudes (strength) and frequencies
	The term 'radiant energy' is commonly used in radiometry, solar energy, heating and lighting
GRAVITATIONAL POTENTIAL	The potential energy due to height, and equal to the work that would be needed to lift an object of a certain mass to that height
	A brick will have much less gravitational potential energy at the bottom of a wall than it does at the top of a tower, and a single brick will have much less gravitational potential energy than a load of bricks
CHEMICAL	The energy associated with the atomic, molecular or aggregate structure of a material; in chemistry, it refers to the potential of a material to be altered by a chemical reaction, or to alter other materials
	Breaking chemical bonds releases energy, often in the form of heat (an 'exothermic' reaction); and energy will need to be added to a system to break chemical bonds (hot water will more easily dissolve most salt crystals than cold water, for example)
SURFACE	The cohesion of the molecules in a liquid where it meets a dissimilar material (such as air or another liquid) produces a surface film that is under tension
	This 'meniscus' is critical to the moisture uptake and transfer in building materials
MECHANICAL	The sum of all the potential and kinetic energies in a mechanical system, which depends on the motion and position of its parts
	The mechanical energy of the thrown ball is composed of the kinetic energy imparted to it when thrown, the gravitational potential energy due to the ball's height, and the interaction of the ball with the air (for the most part, this means frictional forces impeding its flight)
ELASTIC	The potential mechanical energy stored in an object when it is compressed, stretched or twisted, but is able to recover its shape when the distorting force is removed
	For some solid objects, distortion may generate thermal energy, causing its temperature to rise
THERMAL	The kinetic and potential energy associated with the random motion of the atoms and molecules in an object; as these move, they collide and release thermal energy
	All molecules in all materials warmer than absolute zero (0 K on the Kelvin scale and −273.15°C on the Celsius scale) are in constant motion, as heat energy transforms into kinetic energy
	If energy is added to the system (for instance, the object is heated), they will move faster and collide more often, and the object's temperature will rise; the increase will depend on the internal structure of the material, and how free the particles making it up are to move (most metals heat more effectively than most ceramics, for example)
	In materials, thermal energy is often transferred by internal elastic waves called 'phonons'
ACOUSTIC	The energy associated with phonons caused by vibrations travelling into a material (travelling as a compression wave: sound energy cannot travel through a vacuum)
	Used to describe all vibrational energy, even when the frequency is well outside the human range of hearing

BUILDING ENVIRONMENT
BUILDING SCIENCE

The Electromagnetic Spectrum

Energy in the form of electromagnetic radiation ('radiant energy') travels as photons, which can move through a vacuum. The movement is in the form of a transverse wave (that is, the change in strength, or amplitude, is at right angles to the direction of travel, like a wave in water). There is a simple linear relationship between the energy of radiation and the length of the wave – the energy is inversely proportional to the wavelength – which is shown in the 'electromagnetic spectrum'; radiation with long wavelengths (such as radio waves) is less energetic than radiation with short wavelengths (such as gamma rays). The electromagnetic spectrum is a continuum, most of which is covered by the energy output of the sun, though this has peaks in certain wavelengths. The tiny part of the spectrum to which human eyes have evolved to be sensitive is what we call 'visible' light.

For buildings, the various wavelengths of solar radiation not only produce heat, but drive other critical processes, from the weather to plant growth and the chemical breakdown of materials.

The electromagnetic spectrum

The electromagnetic spectrum is a common and useful model for understanding the interaction between electromagnetic energy and matter. There is a direct relationship between the energy of the wave and its frequency (the inverse of its wavelength): so, for example, ultraviolet light has a smaller wavelength than infrared light, but much greater energy.

Depending on the situation being assessed, physicists decide to describe the interactions of electromagnetic energy using wave mechanics, or an alternative model – no less valid – where the interaction is considered instead in terms of colliding particles ('photons'; a photon is the smallest unit of electromagnetic radiation).

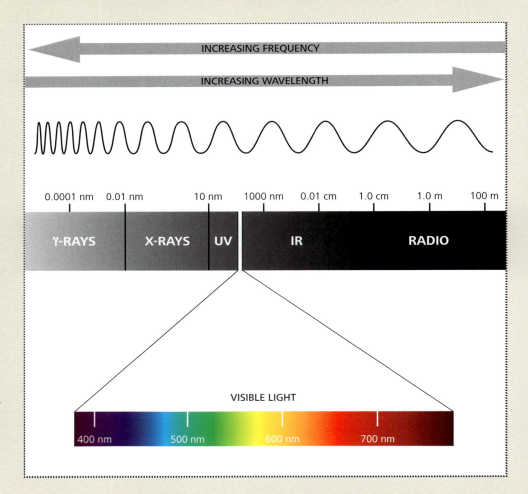

EXCHANGE OF ENERGY

The total energy in the universe is constant, but where it is and what form it takes is continually changing; and much of physics is devoted to understanding the processes by which this transformation takes place. For example, gravitational energy in the heart of the sun transforms partly into nuclear energy, which transforms partly into radiation. The radiation travelling to the earth may interact with a solar cell and be transformed partly into electrical energy; the electrical energy may be used to boil a kettle. When the kettle boils some of the energy may be transformed into heat, some into kinetic energy (the convection of the water), some into chemical energy (turning liquid water into steam) and some into sound (the bubbling and the kettle whistle).

Energy exchange is driven largely by differences in energy levels. When an object with a higher energy meets an object with a lower energy, energy will be transferred from the higher to the lower until they reach a stable state ('equilibrium'), where there is no longer any energy difference between them to drive exchange. The classic case of this is heat transfer: heat will pass from a hot object to a colder object, but not vice versa. When hot tea is poured into a cup, some of the heat will be transferred to the china, and some to the air, so the water will become cooler, and the cup hotter. Over time, the heat in the water and cup will transfer into the air, until everything comes to the same temperature.

Exactly how the energy is transferred depends on the system. Kinetic energy, for example, is most often transferred by collision: if two objects collide, the speed and direction with which they were travelling will be changed. This depends on the mass of the objects: if one object is much lighter, its path will be changed much more. For example, if a water molecule collides with a wall, it will rebound, but the wall will be essentially unchanged.

Energy exchange is almost never 'perfect': some energy is always dissipated in other ways, such as sound or friction. If a ball is thrown through a window, some of the original kinetic and gravitational potential energy will be transformed into chemical energy (breaking the bonds holding the glass together and releasing latent chemical energy in the glass as well), some will be lost in the sound of the breaking glass, and some will be transferred to the sherds of glass, causing them to fly apart.

Energy exchange

In any interaction where energy is exchanged, the total amount of energy in the system remains the same: in other words, energy will neither be created nor destroyed, but may well be changed into other forms.

For example, if a ball is thrown through a window, the original mechanical energy in the ball is partly converted into potential energy; the shattering of the glass will also release some of its latent chemical energy. The output includes the potential energy of the flying sherds of glass and the noise of the breakage. The general pattern of such behaviour is predictable and easy to understand, but it would be impractical to try to calculate exactly how the glass will break, or exactly where the sherds and the ball will eventually come to rest.

BUILDING ENVIRONMENT
BUILDING SCIENCE

THE INTERACTION OF ENERGY WITH MATERIALS

Because the total energy of the system must stay constant, conservation of energy can be used to analyse any situation where energy is changing form.

CHANGES IN MATERIAL STRUCTURE

When external forces are applied to materials, the energy is transferred into material properties such as elastic energy and thermal energy, and these in turn can affect the behaviour of the material itself, and even the shape of components made from it. The observations of 17th-century scientist Robert Hooke of the way materials behave under 'loads' (the engineering term for applied forces) – how their shape is altered, and to what extent the original form is recovered when the load was removed – were the beginning of the science of structural engineering.

Elasticity

Hooke, who was Surveyor to the City of London after the Great Fire in 1666, coined the terms 'plasticity' and 'elasticity' to describe a material's resistance to being permanently deformed (a material that can be permanently changed by a load is 'plastic'; one which returns to shape when the load is removed is 'elastic').

Unfortunately the relationship between load and deformation is not a simple one, since it also depends on the shape of the object being loaded: a thin bar is much easier to bend than a block, and a steel wire is much more rigid than a steel spring. A century after Hooke, Swiss mathematician Leonhard Euler used the concept of elasticity to develop a way of calculating the deflection of a loaded beam, but it was not until 1822 that the way loads act on objects was first broken down into workable concepts by Augustin-Louis Cauchy, a professor at the Ecole Polytechnique in Paris. He introduced the term 'stress', which he defined to be the load divided by the area over which it is acting. His simple formula took account of the way a small load acting over a small area (such as the point of a nail being hammered into a surface) could have a much greater impact than a larger load that is spread over a wide area. Cauchy also introduced the concept of 'strain' to describe the effect of the stress on the shape of the object: the strain is the extent to which it is compressed or stretched.

The twin concepts of stress and strain allowed the 19th-century scientist Thomas Young to develop an experimental method for determining the elasticity of any material: the 'Young's modulus' is the stress needed to stretch a standardised test piece out to twice its original length. This means that the load-bearing behaviour of materials can be measured in terms of the 'pulling' loads that cause lengthening (the 'tensile strength') and the 'pushing' loads that lead to compression (the 'compressive strength').

Strength

Material strength is a rather nebulous concept, not least since it is defined by failure. The main difficulty is that different types of stress will cause different types of failure, so any material may be strong exposed to one type of load, and weak when exposed to another.

The basic characteristics of a material are its reaction to being compressed or stretched (that is, compressive and tensile strength), but there are others such as yield and fatigue strength, and brittleness and plasticity.

None of these concepts can be defined simply, and it is certainly not possible to determine the suitability of a building material for a particular purpose solely on its 'strength'. Brittle materials such as cement, stone and glass can be very strong in compression, but will fail under tension because they cannot store the energy from the load by changing shape elastically. Although the tensile strengths of wrought iron and glass are almost the same, it takes a million times more energy to break iron (which is plastic) than glass (which is brittle). On top of this, environmental conditions are also important: for example, many plastic materials will become more brittle as the temperature drops.

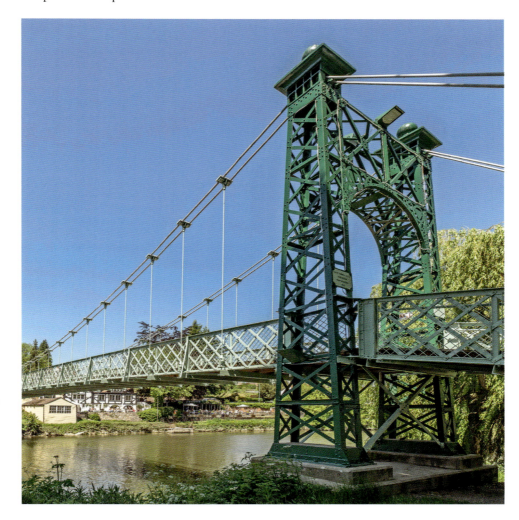

The direction in which a load is being applied is just as important as its magnitude. For example, twisted-steel cables (such as these supporting the Porthill Bridge in Shrewsbury, Shropshire) are extremely strong in tension. They are also strong in compression, so long as the compressive force is applied across the cable: crushing a twisted-steel cable is almost impossible. If, however, the compressive force is applied to the ends, the cable will immediately buckle and bend.

BUILDING ENVIRONMENT
BUILDING SCIENCE

Types of Failure

Materials 'fail' when the forces acting on them cause either permanent deformation ('yield', or 'ductile fracture') or breakage at some point ('fracture', or 'brittle failure').

- *Yield*
  Under an applied force, the material will first begin to deform elastically, returning to its original shape when the stress is released. Once the 'yield point' of the material is passed, however, the distortion becomes plastic: some deformation will remain even when the load is removed.

- *Fracture*
  Under an applied force, the material will begin to crack; eventually the crack will propagate right through the object, breaking it apart. Cracks form more-or-less at right angles to the force, although the way they develop depends on whether the material is ductile or brittle, crystalline or amorphous. In granular materials, for example, the crack may travel either through the grains or along the boundaries between them. Crack formation in some materials, such as glass, is very complex and still not completely understood.

Most materials can both yield or fracture, depending on conditions such as temperature and the type of force applied, but for practical purposes it can be useful to classify materials into those that are 'brittle' (tending to fracture) and those that are 'ductile' (tending to yield). This depends on the microstructure: cast iron is brittle, for example, but wrought iron is ductile. ⊖METALS

Brittle Fracture

Brittle materials under load will show little or no plastic deformation before the moment of fracture, but once cracking has begun, it will continue to grow even if the load is then removed.

The way failure occurs depends largely on whether the material is crystalline or amorphous. In crystalline brittle materials, tensile stress applied at right angles to the crystallographic planes will cause them to cleave apart. In amorphous brittle materials, cracks will develop at right angles to the applied tension; these can spread very rapidly, and will result in a characteristic 'conchoidal fracture'.

Ductile Fracture

If an object made of a ductile material is stretched, it will deform plastically before it finally breaks: indeed, it does not precisely crack under the stress, but rather is slowly stretched, becoming thinner and thinner ('necking') until it finally pulls apart. If the stress is removed before fracture, the object may well remain distorted, but remain in one piece. This is partly because the plastic distortion absorbs so much of the applied stress; if the loading and environmental conditions are suitable, many ductile metals can deform to twice their original length or more without actually breaking.

The more ductile the material, the more energy will be needed to make a crack grow until it reaches a critical length, characteristic of the material, after which it becomes self-propagating. Very elastic materials such as sprung steel (which are able to return to their original shape or position after deformation under load) will fail when even very short cracks begin to appear, since they cannot dissipate the energy from the applied load: that is, the critical crack length is very short. On the other hand, objects made from more ductile materials can survive intact with even quite long cracks.

Critical crack length also explains metal fatigue and work-hardening: as A. A. Griffiths showed in the 1920s, all materials accumulate microscopic cracks as they are worked; these relieve stress and the object remains stable until they reach critical length; at which point it will suddenly fracture.

Patterns of fracture

The stress that causes a particular component to fail is called its 'fracture strength' or 'breaking strength'. This is usually determined in the laboratory by a tensile test that plots the relationship between stress and strain when a specimen is stretched to fracture point in a device that is designed to exert a pure pulling force, with absolutely no bending. The appearance of the resulting fracture depends on the microstructure of the material.

Left: Brittle materials (such as hardened carbon steel) break with a clean sharp fracture.

Top right: Ductile materials (such as copper) will distort before fracturing. When the tensile load is applied the material will begin to 'neck', stretching out at its weakest point. Small holes begin to form within the neck, and just before fracture these coalesce to form a larger void, from which cracks propagate out to the surface. The resulting break face is therefore usually quite rough.

Middle right: Crystalline materials (such as cast iron) will fracture between the crystal planes, leaving smooth breaks.

Bottom right: Amorphous materials (such as glass or flint) develop 'conchoidal' fractures.

Many materials can exhibit several different material characteristics at the same time, perhaps showing some ductile behaviour before undergoing crystalline fracture, or may show different characteristics at different temperatures or humidities.

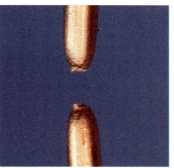

BUILDING ENVIRONMENT
BUILDING SCIENCE

Basic Structural Characteristics

Most structural characteristics depend as much on the size and shape of the component made from the material as on the material itself. Moreover, whether structural characteristics are good or bad will depend on the use to which the component is being put.

STRUCTURAL CHARACTERISTICS OF MATERIALS

BRITTLENESS

When subjected to stress, breaks without significant strain (deformation)	Brittle materials absorb relatively little energy before fracturing
	Often release energy as sound ('snapping') as they fracture

ELASTICITY

Exposure to stress causes temporary strain	Elastic materials absorb substantial amounts of the load energy before reaching the yield point; this is released when load is removed
The material recovers its original shape when the load is removed	If the stress is high enough, at the 'yield point' elasticity will give way to plasticity (permanent strain)

PLASTICITY

Exposure to stress causes permanent strain	Plastic materials absorb substantial amounts of the load energy before fracturing
The material remains deformed even if the load is removed before fracture	

MALLEABILITY
Material deforms under compressive stress

A metal that can be hammered or rolled to produce a sheet is 'malleable'

DUCTILITY
Material deforms under tensile stress

A metal that can be stretched out to form a wire is 'ductile'

STRENGTH

COMPRESSIVE STRENGTH
Lowest compressive stress that leads to brittle or ductile failure

TENSILE STRENGTH
Lowest tensile stress that leads to ductile failure

YIELD STRENGTH
Lowest stress that produces permanent deformation

IMPACT STRENGTH
Smallest suddenly applied load that will cause the material to break; depends on the yield strength and the elasticity of the material, but also on the volume of the component

FATIGUE STRENGTH
Lowest cyclic load that will cause the material to harden and break; depends on the size and shape of component, and on its microscopic characteristics, as well as the environmental conditions

THERMAL ENERGY IN MATERIALS

The transfer of heat, which is particularly important for understanding building systems, can occur by radiation, conduction or convection, or a combination of these processes.

Radiation

The transfer of thermal energy as electromagnetic radiation does not require a medium: by radiation, heat can transfer through a vacuum (solar energy, for example). The interaction of radiative energy with matter depends on the wavelengths of which it is composed. The ultraviolet component of sunlight can break down organic molecules, whereas longer wavelengths generally penetrate further (although this will depend on the material). Infrared light, for example, will penetrate objects and energise their molecules, causing heating.

Like the sun, all hot objects radiate energy (the ability of an object to emit radiation of a particular wavelength is known as its 'emissivity'). Although the energy emitted from very hot objects such as molten metal is intense enough to be visible, most heat radiation is at longer wavelengths, invisible to the human eye but detectable with an infrared camera. The absorption of radiant heat also depends on the chemical and physical characteristics of the object being radiated: dull metal surfaces will absorb more energy than white-painted timber.

Conduction

Conduction is the transfer of thermal energy by direct contact between molecules; this is strongest in solid materials (where the atoms are close together), and depends on the characteristics of the material. Materials that do not readily conduct heat, such as brick, plaster and stone, are said to have high 'thermal inertias'. Metals readily absorb and conduct heat, and are therefore said to have low thermal inertias.

Convection

Convection is the transfer of thermal energy by fluid circulation (a form of kinetic energy), together with some conduction; it is most important in gases (such as air) and in liquids (such as water). Convection is a more complex form of transfer than simple radiation or conduction, but is very effective at transferring heat throughout a volume of liquid. In gases and vapours, the driving force for natural convection is 'buoyancy' (the effect of gravity on areas of different density): hot air is less dense, and so will rise.

BUILDING ENVIRONMENT
BUILDING SCIENCE

Chemical Reactions

The basic building block of matter is the atom, which is composed of a cloud of negatively charged electrons surrounding a positively charged nucleus.

Atoms can gain and lose electrons from the electron cloud, and the result will be an 'ion': an atom that has an overall positive or negative charge, and is therefore electrically active and in a higher energy state. For many atoms this happens quite easily, and most of these are commonly found in stable compounds with other charged particles; the element iron, for example, is usually found in nature as an oxide (combined with oxygen to form ferrous oxide [FeO], or rust).

Certain atoms are naturally very stable, and so tend not to be found as compounds in nature: gold is an element of this type.

CHEMICAL ENERGY IN MATERIALS

Chemical reactions will also absorb or release energy; and the more stable the material, the more energy will be needed to make it react. A good example is the carbonation cycle for lime mortar. To create mortar from limestone (calcium carbonate, $CaCO_3$), which is very stable, it is necessary to add a great deal of energy in the form of heat; this process (called 'calcining') breaks the chemical bonds and releases carbon dioxide gas, leaving a very unstable compound known as 'quicklime' (calcium oxide, CaO). Quicklime contains so much of the initial heat energy that it is famously aggressive, reacting violently with many other materials. To form a more workable material for plasters, the excess energy is deliberately released by 'slaking' (combining the quicklime with copious quantities of water), to produce a much less active compound (calcium hydroxide, $CaOH_2$). The reaction produces a great deal of heat. In the final step of the process, calcium hydroxide is allowed to combine with carbon dioxide again, to form the stable compound calcium carbonate once more.

Action of Reagents

There are many different types of chemical reaction possible, including oxidation and reduction (where atoms lose or gain electrons), neutralisation, disassociation and molecular rearrangement. Since they all involve molecular bonds being broken or created, an input of energy is essential: it may be chemical energy provided by introducing a solvent such as water, or it may be heat or even kinetic energy. Many molecular bonds are weak and easily broken, and even crystals can be dissolved if they take up enough energy.

ACOUSTIC ENERGY IN MATERIALS

Electromagnetic waves are transverse waves, which (like a wave in water) vibrate at right angles to the direction in which they are travelling, but sound propagates as a 'longitudinal' mechanical wave: the affected particles move parallel to the direction of travel. The incoming acoustic energy moves through a material as a 'compression' wave that pushes the molecules in the material together so that they transfer kinetic energy to each other (this is why sound cannot travel in a vacuum).

In a solid object, transmission of acoustic energy can be very complex: it will be affected by many things, including the shape of the object and the materials of which it is composed, and all the interfaces between those materials. The wave may be reflected by some materials, and absorbed by others (those able to dissipate the incoming energy in other ways, such as heat). It may be refracted at interfaces between different materials, or wherever the temperature or pressure or moisture content changes.

In enclosed spaces, reflected or refracted acoustic energy may 'reverberate', reflecting again and again ('echoing'). This can give rise to 'resonance': certain frequencies may cause a particular object or space to oscillate between two or more different but fairly stable states. Resonance is likely whenever a system is able to transfer energy easily between two or more different types of storage (for example, as a pendulum swings, its kinetic energy is transferred to potential energy and back again). At resonant frequencies, the system can store energy so efficiently that even very small vibrations can quickly amplify into large oscillations. Resonance can occur with any type of wave, transverse as well as longitudinal, but it is sound waves that provide the most familiar day-to-day examples, such as building windows beginning to vibrate loudly in response to the idling of a nearby truck.

Chemical energy
Facing page: An excellent example of chemical energy in construction is the production of lime. Thermal energy is added to break apart the chemical bonds in limestone, producing calcium oxide or 'quicklime', which is extremely reactive: lime pits were used to safely destroy the bodies of plague victims, for example.

Acoustic energy
Right: Musical instruments are designed to be extremely resonant. In string instruments, the elastic energy in the strings is released by vibration, and then transferred to acoustic energy via a sound-box; woodwind instruments produce sound from the oscillation of air trapped in a tube of some resonant material such as wood or metal. The same principles govern the transmission of sound into and through a building.

Audible sound has a frequency of anything from 10 to 20,000 vibrations per second, but the line between audible and inaudible is blurred: deep bass sounds can be felt physically even when they cannot strictly be 'heard'. Acoustics, which is the science of mechanical waves in gases, liquids and solids, covers all types of vibration, including those that are inaudible to humans.

BUILDING ENVIRONMENT
BUILDING SCIENCE

UNDERSTANDING FAILURES

To preserve a building, it is vital to understand the many ways in which it might fail.

Building envelopes and environments are invariably complicated, so it is always useful to be able to draw on a simple concept such as energy conservation to help dissect what may be occurring, and decide which of the many possible factors are the most important to perceived – or potential – deterioration. By taking into account the ways in which energy may be transferring through the fabric, it becomes easier to understand and assess the impact of complex processes such as heat exchange, thermal movement, chemical attack, sound and vibration, structural failure, and most importantly the movement of moisture.

FAILURE UNDER LOAD

The behaviour of a building under an applied mechanical force, or 'load', is critical to its survival. 'Overloading' can cause local breakdown of materials and components, or even major failings of the building structure itself.

Damage to a building envelope as a result of structural failures such as overloading can lead to environmental problems such as water ingress. These in turn can cause material breakdown, and hence further deterioration of the structure.

FORCES ACTING ON BUILDINGS

The forces acting on a building include the permanent or 'fixed' loads (such as the weight of the roof and the walls and floors, or of the fixed furniture), together with a whole range of time-varying loads (from wind pressures, to occupants moving around inside). They can change very slowly but steadily, or cyclically over the course of the day or the working week or the season, or suddenly as a result of a one-off event. The ability of the structure to withstand a load will invariably depend on where that load is being applied, and whether it is fixed or variable, steady or sudden. Sudden forces can transmit a great deal of energy, and can cause the failure of systems that would be perfectly capable of supporting much greater loads when these are applied more gradually.

There are multiple levels of complexity; to list a few of the most important factors:
- The impact of a load will vary according to the nature of the force it is applying to the fabric: for instance, the force of a roof may be constant and steady (the weight of the covering, for example), or persistent but variable (the wind pressure), or transient (a tree falling on the roof during a storm)
- The same load will affect different materials and components differently
- The way materials behave under load usually depends on temperature and humidity (amongst other environmental variables)
- The effect of a load on a building component will depend on the shape of the component as well as on the materials from which it is made
- Buildings are composed of many different components and many different materials, so the total effect of a load will depend on how these interact.

The transfer of mechanical energy through a building will depend not only on the material of which it is made, but all those aspects of its shape or composition that might interrupt the way stress passes through it. This includes material flaws or discontinuities, deliberate features such as holes and corners, and even cuts and scratches: in short, any locations where a component might fracture or collapse under load long before the load is sufficient to cause the failure of the materials themselves.

TYPES OF BUILDING STRUCTURE

Traditional Construction Systems

Traditional building systems were developed empirically rather than theoretically (many experimental designs must have failed and been lost along the way). Building craftsmen and the makers of building materials learnt by experience, and passed their skills and knowledge on through the apprenticeship and guild systems. By no means all traditional building was 'best practice', but vernacular building styles did tend to be robust, and well suited to local materials, climate and use. Until the 19th century, the difficulties of predicting the behaviour of complex structures of this type were usually dealt with by adding excess bulk; in this way, stresses were more widely distributed through the building, making catastrophic failure less likely.

Modern Construction Systems

With the Industrial Revolution, a number of important changes in building practice occurred: most particularly, transport became much cheaper and easier (so it was no longer necessary to build from local materials), and new manufacturing methods were introduced. Iron and glass began to be produced in sufficient quantities to take on a structural role, and new materials appeared such as concrete, laminated and compressed wood products, and (later) plastics. These materials were considered more homogeneous and reliable than traditional materials such as timber and stone, and easier to model mathematically. Engineers therefore developed algorithms that attempted to predict behaviour of structures made from these materials, and this was one of the most important factors leading to vast changes in building technology.

Building systems became much less dependent on local materials and skills, and by the beginning of the 21st century many traditional approaches to construction had almost disappeared. Rather than over-engineering by bulk, building systems have increasingly relied on minimal frameworks supporting light weatherproof coverings. This allows buildings with multiple storeys: something that would be almost impossible with traditional construction systems, and which has different modes of failure.

STRUCTURAL FAILURE OF BUILDINGS

The behaviour of any structure made up of multiple components – especially those between different materials that react differently to changes in environmental factors such as fluctuating temperatures – depends on the joints and interfaces between those components. As well as being the likeliest spots to be sensitive to overloading, building joints of all kinds are also the points most likely to be weakened by exposure: for example, water may seep into joints and cause local decay or corrosion, and differential movement can stress glues and other systems for fixing components together. Unsurprisingly, structural analysis of buildings is always very complex, although these general principles can be used to help building owners and managers better understand risks, and interpret existing failures.

LOADS FROM SOUND & OTHER VIBRATION

Sound and other sources of vibration can result from outside the building (from passing traffic, for example) or from within (most typically from day-to-day use and from building works).

The forces induced in the fabric will be transmitted through the building both directly and indirectly: they may travel through the air, through the materials, or through hollows and voids in the fabric (including service pipes and conduits). Forces can rebound from hard surfaces with little or no reduction in intensity, and indeed may be amplified by reverberation or resonance. Analysis can be extremely complex: the loudest noise or strongest vibration in a particular space will not always be that which originated closest, or was loudest to begin with.

THERMAL BEHAVIOUR

In many interactions at least some of the energy will be transferred as heat: many chemical reactions are 'exothermic', for example. Building materials can gain heat by exposure to solar radiation or simply to warm air, and can lose heat to cooler air or air that is moving across the surface. Thermal transfer is strongest if the material is wet, since water is an excellent conductor of heat.

PHYSICAL EFFECT OF HEATING & COOLING

Changing the temperature of a material will often alter its physical nature: gases may change in volume, for example, and solids may become more plastic as they heat, or more brittle as they cool. Some of these changes are gradual; others may be sudden transitions, occurring when the temperature reaches a certain point (the characteristic 'glass transition' temperature of an amorphous material such as a plastic resin is the point where it changes from being relatively hard and brittle into being soft and deformable).

Many objects will change dimension with temperature, and these changes may not be uniform, but depend on the material's structure or the shape of the object. Complex objects composed of two or more materials fixed together can be subject to high stresses at the interfaces where the materials meet.

The familiar phenomena of a zone of dirt deposition above a heater is easily explained by thinking in terms of energy conservation: air warmed by contact with the radiator has enough energy to support quite heavy particles of dust against gravity, and to carry these upwards at it rises through buoyancy. As the warm air meets the wall above, however, it loses heat both through conduction to the cold surface and to friction. Eventually it will no longer be warm enough to support the dust, which is then deposited.

Heavier particles will be found at the base of the zone, and finer particles higher up the wall. The zone will begin lower if it is above a smaller radiator, if the wall is very cold, or if its surface is very rough.

BUILDING ENVIRONMENT
BUILDING SCIENCE

HEAT TRANSFER

'Thermal conductivity' describes the ability of a material or system to conduct heat, but this is far from straightforward.

Looking at a single material, heat transfer can involve all types of mechanism (radiation, conduction and convection) in ways that can be hard to predict, especially when the materials are permeable and contain some water. The moisture distribution – and hence the patterns of heat transfer – will itself change with temperature (see **Moisture in Building Materials**). This means that thermal conductivity is not a single value, but one that depends on the material's properties, its moisture content, the temperatures involved, and whether the temperature differences that are driving heat through the material are steady or changing. Measurement is therefore not straightforward either. There are many different methods, and some are better suited than others to certain materials. Most measurements are of energy transfer per thickness of material per degree [W/(mK)]. The inverse of thermal conductivity, the 'thermal resistivity', is the resistance of a material to the transfer of heat through it (that is, its ability to act as a thermal insulator).

THERMAL TRANSFER COEFFICIENTS

Measurement and interpretation become even more complex for systems composed of more than one material. In the construction industry, several different measurements are commonly used, including 'thermal resistance', 'thermal conductance' and 'thermal transmittance'. The broad definitions of these are:

- *Thermal resistance*
  The property of a material to resist the flow of heat through it.

- *Thermal conductance*
  The quantity of heat that passes in a given period of time through a plate of a particular area and thickness when the temperatures of its two faces differ by 1 K.

- *Thermal transmittance (also called the 'U-value')*
  The rate of transfer of heat through a given area of material or structure under the impetus of a temperature difference between the two faces of the structure.

It is very important to be aware that these are not tight definitions, and that they do not describe any fundamental characteristic of the material or system. For example, if the external conditions mean that the heat is being transferred through a particular building component primarily via conduction, the thermal transmittance will not be the same as when transfer involves a greater degree of convection. This makes it very difficult to directly compare measurements from different sources.

MOISTURE IN BUILDING MATERIALS

Water – especially an excess of water – is involved in most of the processes that break down building materials, from timber decay to metal corrosion. To understand these deterioration processes, it is first necessary to understand how water behaves in liquid, vapour and solid form, and how it interacts with building materials.

INTRODUCTION TO WATER

Both chemically and physically, water behaves in some very unusual ways, although most are so familiar to us that we tend to overlook them and forget just how odd they really are. For example, the majority of materials are densest when they are in their solid form, but ice is lighter than liquid water (and so floats). All other small molecules – carbon dioxide, for example – are usually gaseous at room temperature, but water has such high freezing and boiling temperatures that it is usually found as a liquid.

Most of these peculiar properties are a result of the unusual structure of water molecules. The two hydrogen atoms and a single oxygen atom that make up the molecule are arranged not linearly but in a V-shape, with an electron cloud that is displaced towards the oxygen atom. This means that water molecules are 'polar': that is, the oxygen end has a slightly negative charge, and the hydrogen end a slightly positive charge. Opposite charges attract, so water molecules will tend to stick to each other. This is not only why the liquid state is so common, but also why liquid water has a high surface tension. Both these qualities are vital to many natural processes.

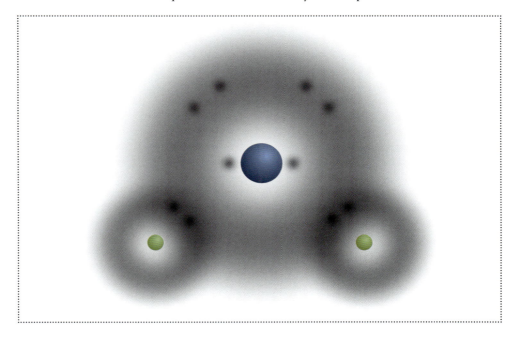

A single water molecule

Water molecules are composed of one oxygen and two hydrogen atoms, and are small (0.275 nm across). The single electron of each hydrogen atom bonds with one of the six electrons on the outermost shell of the oxygen to form two 'bonded pairs' that repel the two remaining pairs of oxygen electrons; this distorts the shape of the charge cloud, so instead of the hydrogen atoms being on opposite sides of the oxygen, they form a V-shape with an angle of around 104° for an isolated water vapour molecule, or 106° for molecules bonded together to form liquid water. This means that a water molecule is 'polar': it has a negative electric charge on the oxygen side and a positive charge on the hydrogen side.

BUILDING ENVIRONMENT
BUILDING SCIENCE

Multiple water molecules

Hydrogen bonds are weak, and will constantly form and reform to create the partially ordered structures that characterise liquid water (*top*). In ice, each molecule bonds rigidly to four others (*bottom*).

Recent research shows that where water meets a solid surface, some molecules are ordered like ice, even though the temperature and pressure are that of liquid water.

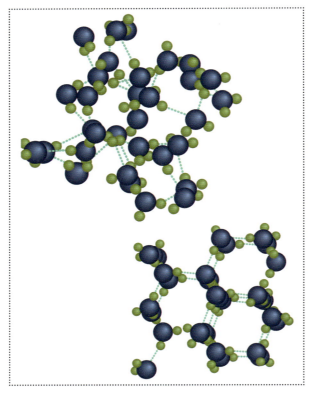

Although 'liquid water' may at first sound like a tautology, distinguishing clearly between water as a liquid and water as a vapour is absolutely critical to being able to predict the paths it may take into and through a building structure. Water vapour molecules will interact with each other only if they happen to collide, but all the molecules in liquid water will cling together, so that it flows as a single entity.

Water can bond to other charged molecules as well, and so can dissolve many different compounds (it is often called 'the universal solvent'). It will also tend to attach itself to charged surfaces, and this is one of the most important reasons why so many materials are hydrophilic ('water-loving').

The polarity of the molecules also makes water very responsive to any external electrical forces. Molecules will align with an electrical field, so water is a strong dielectric (that is, it strongly affects the overall strength of an applied electric field). Electricity does not travel very easily through pure liquid water, but absolutely pure water is actually rather rare in nature, since – being such a good solvent – it more usually contains dissolved charged molecules. These charged solutions, or electrolytes, are excellent conductors of electricity, and they are usually what is meant by 'water'.

To increase the heat of water by just a single degree requires more energy than for any other compound except ammonia, and water's heat of vaporisation (that is, how much heat is needed at boiling point to convert a liquid to a gas or vapour) is also high. What this means in practice is that water vapour in the atmosphere can buffer sizeable changes in air temperature. This characteristic moderates not just local microclimates, but the earth's climate as a whole.

Terms such as vapour pressure, absolute humidity and relative humidity are convenient shorthand ways of describing the complex interactions between water and air. The following sections give an introduction to what these shorthand terms really mean, and how they are best used.

WATER AS A VAPOUR

Water vapour, the gaseous phase of water, is a small but significant component of the earth's atmosphere. It is taken up through a continuous process of evaporation, leaving the atmosphere again via condensation, in the form of clouds, rain, snow and dew (for example). Water vapour is less dense than dry air and so will rise, but liquid water will fall under the action of gravity.

The amount of water vapour in the air at any one time is usually expressed as a pressure (the vapour pressure), and is so measured in pascals (or newtons per square metre). One rather helpful way of envisaging vapour pressure is to imagine a 1-cubic-metre 'box' of air and water vapour. The ambient heat energises the water molecules so that they are in continual motion, colliding with the imaginary 'walls' of the box (and more rarely with the other molecules in the air). This exerts an outwards force on the walls: the 'water vapour pressure'. The more collisions there are, the greater the vapour pressure, so it is easy to see that the vapour pressure must increase whenever more water molecules are added to the same volume of air or the temperature is raised (increasing the energy of the molecules).

It is most common to describe the actual quantity of water vapour in terms of the 'absolute humidity' [AH]; the actual number of water molecules suspended in the air at any one time (usually measured as weight per volume: for example, grams of water per cubic metre of air). It is also possible to determine the ratio of the mass of water vapour in the air to the mass of the air as a whole, including the water vapour; this is known as the 'specific humidity', but it is not a parameter commonly used in discussions about moisture in buildings.

Water vapour has a very low density; water in the air will only become visible as it condenses and coalesces to form mist, fog or steam.

BUILDING ENVIRONMENT
BUILDING SCIENCE

Condensation on surfaces

Condensation on cold surfaces may collect to form liquid water. If the surface is of sufficiently low permeability (glass or metal, for example, or as here, polished marble), the water may run down the surface.

CONDENSATION & EVAPORATION

In almost every collision a molecule of water vapour makes, whether with another water molecule, or some other molecule in the air, or a surface, it will lose a little of its energy, until eventually it may be left with too little energy to break away again the next time it collides. A molecule which can no longer break away is said to have 'condensed'.

The more water molecules there are in the air, the more likely they are to collide, losing so much energy that they are forced to condense. If the vapour pressure of air near a surface is very high, eventually the surface may be covered in a film of liquid water: that is, by 'condensation'.

The colder the surface, the more energy the vapour molecules will lose each time they collide with it, so condensation is more likely on a cool surface. How cold the surface would have to be to cause a film of condensation depends on the air's absolute humidity and temperature (that is, on the vapour pressure). The vapour pressure can be used to calculate a 'dew-point temperature' [DPT]; if a surface exposed to air at that vapour pressure drops below this temperature, then water will begin to condense onto it.

Condensation is not a permanent state. A condensed water molecule will absorb heat energy from the surface and from the air, and occasionally from vapour molecules colliding with it. Eventually it may gain enough energy to break free of the surface once more: that is, to 'evaporate'. Heating a surface will cause some of the water molecules condensed upon it to evaporate again.

SATURATION & RELATIVE HUMIDITY

Returning for a moment to the image of an imaginary box of air, it is easy to see that if more water molecules are added to the box, eventually there will come a point where the number of water molecules condensing exactly equals the number of molecules evaporating: beyond this point, adding more water molecules to the air will simply cause the same number of molecules to condense out. The vapour pressure therefore remains steady, and the air is said to be 'saturated': that is, it is holding as much moisture as it possibly could at that temperature.

If the number of water molecules in the imaginary box were kept constant, but the air was heated, each molecule would have more energy to lose before it would be forced to condense: in other words, hotter air can hold more water molecules.

If there is a source of liquid water in a sealed container, the air in the container will take up water molecules by evaporation until the air is saturated. This can take some time, depending on the size of the container and the surface area of the source (the greater the surface area, the faster the evaporation).

Free air is rarely saturated, but instead will be holding only a fraction of the water molecules it could potentially hold. The actual extent of saturation is usually expressed as a percentage, and is called the 'relative humidity' [RH] (relative to saturation, in other words). By definition, the RH of saturated air is 100 %, so air at 50 % RH is holding half of the number of water molecules it potentially could hold at that temperature. Air with an RH of 50 % at 25 °C will be holding much more moisture (that is, it will have a much higher AH) than air of 50 % RH at 15 °C.

Condensation in voids

Because so very few water molecules are needed to saturate air, if the air in a void or hollow exposed to some sink of liquid water is allowed to equilibrate, its relative humidity will reach 100 % no matter how small that sink of moisture may be. In a closed container even a single drop of water will be ample to cause the air within to saturate: the condensation in these bottles shows that each is at 100 % RH, regardless of the quantity of liquid water present.

For this reason, measuring the relative humidity in a void in a wall can only show that the wall is dry or that it has some moisture within it: it cannot indicate how much moisture is actually present.

BUILDING ENVIRONMENT
BUILDING SCIENCE

Standard Nomenclature

ASHRAE

The American Society of Heating, Refrigerating and Air-Conditioning Engineers [ASHRAE] updates its publication *Handbook: Fundamentals* every four years. This includes the latest equations and definitions for concepts such as relative humidity, and is the accepted standard source for such information.

BRITISH STANDARDS

BS 1339–1: Humidity. Terms, definitions and formulae gives British Standard definitions and formulae for humidity, and humidity measurement.

The relationship between temperature and water vapour content is not a simple one, however, since raising the temperature also causes the vapour molecules to move faster. This increases the number of collisions (and the vapour pressure) and makes condensation more likely. It also increases the chances of a condensed molecule acquiring enough energy from collisions to break free of the surface again; that is to say, evaporation is also increased. In a similar way, adding water vapour increases both condensation and evaporation. Other complications arise when the air approaches the freezing point or boiling point of water.

As a result, the equations for calculating relative humidity, absolute humidity or dew-point temperature are very complex, and have to be confirmed against meticulous experiments. Using these studies, tables, psychrometric charts and computer programs have been generated that make it possible for users to use two critical measurements – such as air temperature together with RH or DPT – to look up the other various 'thermohygrometric' parameters of the air, including the vapour pressure and the AH.

MOVEMENT OF WATER VAPOUR

All natural systems eventually equilibrate, moving towards their most stable state, where all the forces acting on them are in balance with each other. In free air, water molecules will therefore travel from areas of high vapour pressure towards areas of lower vapour pressure, until the pressures are even.

Inside a permeable material, by contrast, air pressure has little effect. The forces acting upon a vapour molecule in a pore will be dominated by the exchange of kinetic energy, friction, and the electrical attraction (or repulsion) of the polar molecule to the pore surfaces and to other charged particles (including other water molecules). It will therefore travel randomly, bouncing off the pore walls. The more convoluted the pore system, the more energy will be lost in collisions and the more likely the molecule is to condense.

The result is that, deeper than a few millimetres from the surface, the behaviour of water vapour inside pores is to all intents and purposes independent of the exterior environmental conditions. Normal pressure differences on either side of a slice of material will have no influence on the behaviour of water vapour within; indeed, testing vapour permeability by pulling water vapour through a sample demands vacuum pumps capable of imposing extremely high pressure differences.

Porous & Permeable Materials

Any material which is made up of a solid matrix interspersed with voids (or 'pores') is by definition 'porous', but not all porous materials are 'permeable': for that, liquids or gases must be able to travel through the pores. This means that at least some of the pores must connect both with each other and with the surface, to produce a pathway through the material. Permeability depends on the chemical and physical characteristics of not only the material, but also the liquid or gas. For building conservation, this is usually water, and the term 'permeability' is usually a shorthand for 'water permeability'. Permeability depends on many things, including how many pathways exist, and how narrow and convoluted they are, the many microscopic physical and chemical interactions between the pore walls and the water, and whether the pores contain any soluble materials such as salts and clays which might interact with the water (as is common with building materials).

Various laboratory tests are used to try to assess permeability – for example, mercury porosimetry – but no single test can provide a definitive measurement, and all have significant errors. Tests using inert gases, for example, give misleading results for water, which will react with the pore walls and contaminants. One common and simple approach is to impregnate the material with a coloured resin to replicate the paths water might take, and then make thin sections to allow a two-dimensional visual assessment of the area of the material given over to possible pathways. The benefits of this type of measurement can be seen by looking at the example of the oölitic limestones, Portland Stone and Bath Stone. Although to the naked eye Bath Stone appears very open and porous, water sorption tests show it to be much less permeable than Portland Stone. Blue resin-impregnated thin sections suggest why: in Portland Stone (*below left*), the water can travel through the cement between the oöliths (the rounded particles), but in Bath Stone (*below centre*) this cement is impermeable, and so the water must travel through the oöliths themselves; water pathways can exist only where these touch.

The problems with using thin sections to predict permeability arise partly from the difficulty of getting the viscous resin into the pores, but more importantly from the interpretation of the results. Applying the same test to York sandstone (*below right*), little if any blue can be seen, which might suggest that York Stone is not very permeable. In fact, it is easy to show by experiment that it transfers liquid water very readily indeed: much more so than either of the limestones, because it wicks through the tiny capillary spaces between the tightly packed grains, which are all but invisible in the thin section. The scale is very important in all materials, since moisture transfer is believed to proceed largely through the 'micropores' (pores and capillaries with diameters of 1–2 nm).

Interpretation of thin sections is also affected by the fact they are a two-dimensional slice, but moisture transfer is a three-dimensional process. Great care must be taken to make sure the section is representative of the material as a whole and does not neglect the natural asymmetries in the material being examined, such as layering. Recent progress in X-ray scanning equipment raises the possibility of imaging three-dimensional pore structures down to micropore level.

Portland Limestone

Bath Limestone

York Sandstone

BUILDING ENVIRONMENT
BUILDING SCIENCE

WATER AS A LIQUID

Like water vapour, liquid water will also travel towards the lowest pressure, but it will do so much more efficiently, since the molecules behave not independently (as they do in water vapour), but rather flow as a continuum. Water molecules in a liquid are close enough to be held together by electric forces, so that when one molecule moves, it entrains (or drags along with it) all the neighbouring molecules. As liquid water flows through a permeable material, the water molecules coming up against the pore walls may be attracted to them as well (if they are charged or are holding other charged materials), and there will also be frictional forces. This can slow down the movement, but it is almost never enough to stop the overall flow, even in the smallest pores.

The most important result of flow is that liquid water can quickly find the shortest path of travel through the most convoluted pore structure, even when the pressure difference or other force driving it is very small. Flow can also be driven by gravity, which would be too weak to have any effect on a single molecule of water vapour in the air, but is significant when it acts on the many molecules that are bonded together in a liquid.

In liquid water, the molecules are sufficiently close together to form polar bonds. This causes them to move more or less coherently, although (unlike in a solid) bonds between individual molecules are breaking and forming all the time. The bonding is just strong enough to allow water to flow under the action of forces such as gravity.

The effects of surface tension

The mutual bonding of water molecules means that the surface of liquid water forms a curved 'meniscus', with the liquid pressure inside the liquid being at equilibrium with the vapour pressure in the air above it.

The shape of the meniscus of a drop of water on a surface depends not only on the vapour pressure of the air, but on the interaction between water and the surface. A 'hydrophobic' surface such as a surface smeared with grease resists wetting, and so produces beads of water with sharply curved menisci (*top left*); a 'hydrophilic' surface produces much flatter beads (*bottom left*).

The curvature itself affects the vapour pressure in the air above it: if the meniscus is convex (as it is in a bead of water on a surface), the vapour pressure above it will be increased.

Water in a tube (such as a straw) will have a concave meniscus, and this lowers the vapour pressure above. The water level will therefore be forced to rise up the tube to equilibrate the liquid and vapour pressures. Since the curvature is greater in a narrow tube, the water will rise higher (*right*).

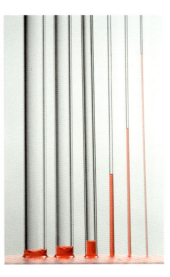

WETTING OF PERMEABLE MATERIALS

Surface Tension & Wetting

The molecules in liquid water are all attracted to each other, but this means the molecules at the surface (the 'meniscus') do not have a force pulling at them equally in all directions, but instead are under tension. To minimise the resulting 'surface tension', the water beads: in the absence of gravity or any other forces, a droplet of water will be perfectly spherical, so that the surface area is as small as possible. A water droplet on a surface interacts with gravity, but also with the surface itself, and this affects the curvature of the meniscus. If the surface attraction is very strong, the curvature will be much less than if the surface is hydrophobic (the water is said to 'wet' the surface). If the surface is tilted, the droplet will move down the surface, but when it meets an edge, the attraction to the surface may still be strong enough to compete with gravity, and the liquid will cling in place; it may even flow uphill under the edge if it has sufficient momentum.

Capillarity (Wicking)

Surface tension is also the principal reason for 'capillarity', the phenomenon which causes liquid water to rise higher in a straw than it does in a cup, which is fundamental to understanding how moisture behaves in a building material. In 1871, J. J. Thompson (Lord Kelvin) showed that the curvature of a meniscus alters the vapour pressure above it: if the meniscus is convex (as it is with a droplet on a surface), the pressure is increased, but if it is concave, the vapour pressure is reduced; the extent of the change is directly related to the degree of curvature. In a straw, the meniscus will be curved because the water clings to the walls, so the water must travel upwards until the force exerted by the vapour pressure difference is balanced out by the weight of liquid. The thinner the straw (or 'capillary'), the higher the water will rise. Kelvin pointed out that this was a partial explanation of why permeable materials spontaneously absorb water.

BUILDING ENVIRONMENT
BUILDING SCIENCE

Liquid flow paths within permeable materials

Experiments suggest that liquid water in permeable materials travels principally through the 'micropore system', composed of pores up to about a micrometre in diameter. As water condenses or is drawn in from a liquid water source by capillary action, it drains from larger pores and collects in the finer capillaries, through which it can readily flow, so the material does not have to be saturated for liquid flow to occur.

Water-vapour movement within permeable materials is largely independent of the external temperature and humidity, but if 'liquid flow paths' exist and are linked to the surface, then changes in exterior conditions will be able to drive liquid water movement through the material, and this movement can be very rapid.

This has many implications for understanding how water travels through building materials. To give just two important examples: surface evaporation can cause bulk drying; and water vapour condensing or rain falling onto a wall may be drawn in if the materials contain enough water to have formed liquid flow paths.

This diagram indicates the way in which liquid water may collect on the surfaces of larger pores, or fill fine capillaries, even though many other voids remain dry.

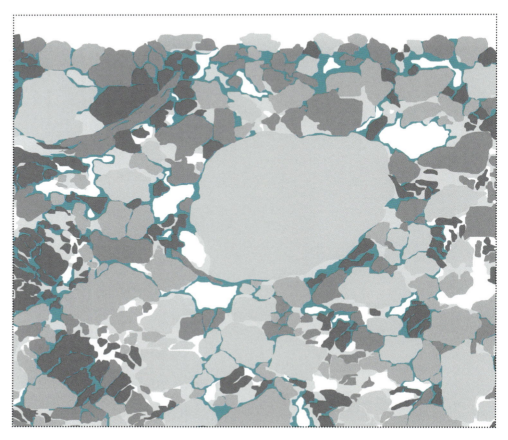

Hygroscopicity

Most permeable materials will spontaneously absorb water vapour from the ambient air. Permeable materials tend to be 'hygroscopic' because inside the pores there are many factors to lower the vapour pressure, and thus draw moisture into the material. These include the condensation of vapour on the pore walls, which reduces the absolute humidity. Condensation will be greatest where the pore system is very convoluted or includes many dead-end pores, or where the pore surfaces are very rough. There may be chemical interactions as well: contaminants such as some soluble salts will also attract and hold water molecules, increasing hygroscopicity.

A molecule attached to a pore wall will attract more molecules to itself, so eventually (if there is enough moisture in the air) a film of condensation will begin to line the pore. As Lord Kelvin realised when he described capillarity, the curvature of these liquid films will itself lower the vapour pressure in the pore, drawing in more vapour. Eventually there may be so much condensed water that it will begin to flow as a liquid into the neighbouring pores, entraining any vapour molecules it touches, and lowering the vapour pressure still further.

Capillary Absorption

Permeable building materials always contain some water even when they are 'dry', and if they come into contact with a reservoir of liquid water, they can quickly absorb moisture and become wet. Capillary absorption describes the ways in which permeable materials take up liquid water, and there are many laboratory tests that record how this happens for building materials. The simplest and most useful is to place a sample (for example, a single brick) in contact with the surface of a reservoir of water. Liquid will rise up through the pores, and it is often possible to see the water front as it advances.

It is interesting to consider the way a more complex material system – say two bricks joined together with mortar – absorbs liquid water. Flow slows at every interface (brick to mortar, and mortar to brick). This is because although in a single material the liquid water can quickly find efficient paths through which to flow, at interfaces these flow paths will be severed. If there is any air gap between the materials, then it will have to cross the gap and enter the pores of the next material as a vapour, at least until enough water has accumulated in the gap to fill it with liquid. This vapour transfer will be very slow and inefficient, and even joints between layers of mortar that are all but invisible to the naked eye can be shown to impede water movement.

Hydraulic Pressure

As water fills the pores, it will push ahead of it the air inside them. The increase in air pressure ahead of the moving water front equates to the hydraulic pressure: the force driving the uptake of water. This has been shown to be more than 100 kPa inside a brick at 20°C (that is, about the pressure required to inflate a car tyre). Indeed, the pressure building up ahead of the hydration front can be so high that the pore walls may be fractured, and if the element has a surface coating, this may be blown off. Air pressure may be one reason why coatings applied to plaster, stone and brick are often seen to cause surface spalling, even in the absence of significant quantities of salt.

Evaporation

Evaporative drying – water molecules leaving liquid water to become water vapour – is the process which prevents hygroscopic materials continuing to take up moisture from the air until they are completely saturated.

Still air in contact with a source of moisture will quickly equilibrate with that source (a damp wall, for example). After a short time, the absolute humidities of the wall and of the air in immediate contact with the wall will no longer change, unless some other factor such as the temperature changes as well.

Air moving across the surface has a great deal of energy and is never at equilibrium, and so can very easily carry water molecules from the surface, which maintains a high vapour-pressure difference between the surface and the ambient air. Moving air has a very much greater capacity for evaporation than still air of the same absolute humidity and temperature. Quadrupling the air speed across a wall surface will double the rate of drying.

DRYING OF PERMEABLE MATERIALS

The wetting of permeable materials is fairly straightforward, in macroscopic terms at least, and fairly well understood. This is not the case for drying, which is more complex, and moreover much more difficult to study. It is much easier to get water into a permeable material than it is to get it out again. The difference between the speed and effectiveness of wetting and drying, called the 'hysteresis', depends not only on the prevailing environmental conditions, but also on the characteristics of the material – its pore structure and chemistry, for example – and on the nature of the liquid being considered (usually water, together with any contaminants).

Essentially, drying means water molecules passing out from the material and into the ambient air, via evaporation at the surface. For this to be possible, the drivers for evaporation must be strong enough to overcome the many forces drawing moisture into the fabric. The ambient relative humidity is certainly important, but the most significant driver is the flow of air across the surface.

At first, drying can be very fast, as long as evaporation is carrying away water molecules that have travelled through the material and arrived at the surface as a liquid. Once there is insufficient moisture left in the material to maintain a liquid flow from the wet material in the centre to the evaporative surface, the water molecules will have to travel some part of the way as vapour, and so the rate of drying from then on will depend almost entirely on the pore structure and the chemistry of the material: the ambient air movement, humidity and temperature have very little effect on the movement of vapour molecules in pores. This means that drying slows dramatically.

These two separate phases of drying are sometimes called Stage I and Stage II:

- *Stage I*
  Drying mainly by liquid transfer. This is very fast, and is governed mostly by the ambient environmental conditions.

- *Stage II*
  Drying mainly by vapour transfer. This is very slow, and to all intents and purposes independent of the ambient environmental conditions.

In practical terms, this means that if the surface layers of a wet material are dried very quickly, the bulk of the material will actually stay wet for longer. To remove the maximum amount of water, Stage I drying must be prolonged. Wet building walls that are force-dried using high temperatures and very low humidities until they appear dry (while the bulk of the wall remains wet) will develop wet surfaces again after a few weeks, as liquid flow paths slowly re-establish themselves through to the surface.

Facing page: Detail of *Laundry Drying on the Bank of the Seine*, by Gustave Caillebotte, c.1892.

Evaporation is driven largely by the movement of air. This is why a cool and overcast day that is breezy is better for drying laundry than a still day, no matter how sunny it may be.

Further Reading

Arpaci, V. S., Kao, S-H., Selamet, A. (2000); *Introduction to Heat Transfer*; New Jersey: Prentice Hall

Eisenberg, D. S., Kauzmann, W. (2005); *The Structure and Properties of Water*; Oxford: Oxford University Press

Feynman, R., Leighton, R., Sands, M. (1970); *The Feynman Lectures on Physics (3-Volume Edition)*; Boston: Addison Wesley

Gordon, J. E. (2003); *Structures: Or Why Things Don't Fall Down (2nd Edition)*; Cambridge, MA: Da Capo Press

Hall, C., Hoff, W. D. (2012); *Water Transport in Brick, Stone and Concrete (2nd Edition)*; London: Spon

Innocent, C. F. (2011); *The Development of English Building Construction (Reprint of 1916 Edition)*; Cambridge: Cambridge University Press

McMullan, M. (2012); *Environmental Science in Building (7th Edition)*; Basingstoke: Palgrave Macmillan

Moncrieff, A., Weaver, G. (1992); *An Introduction to Materials (2nd Edition)*; *The Science For Conservators Series, Volume 1*; Museums and Galleries Commission Conservation Unit; London: Routledge

INTERACTIONS WITH THE ENVIRONMENT

This chapter gives a brief introduction to the critical components of a building envelope, looking at how these function to keep the weather out, and specifically to keep the building dry. It finishes with a discussion about how the envelope modifies the extremes of the exterior conditions, providing an interior microclimate suitable for the building's use.

The environment of every structure is unique, since it depends on the precise interaction between the fabric, and the exterior and interior conditions. Indeed, a structure will itself have a certain amount of impact on its external environment: for example, some elements may shade others from sunlight or protect them from rain, and the presence of a building will certainly affect local wind turbulence.

The building environment is never static, since the exterior conditions will fluctuate with the time of day, the seasons and the weather, and the interior conditions will vary according to the way the building is being used. The building envelope must therefore be able to successfully respond to small changes in structural load, and in exterior and interior ambient conditions.

As long as these changes are not so severe that they cause failure, the result is a 'dynamic' equilibrium: that is, the building is stable in the broader sense, although on closer examination it is always moving and changing. For example, each time the sun is hidden by a cloud, the metal roof sheets will cool and shrink slightly, warming and expanding again when the sun reappears; and the joints on a well-designed metal roof covering are designed to cope with these movements. Timber rafters in the roof will absorb water vapour rising from washing or cooking, and release it again as the humidity drops.

A dynamic equilibrium takes some time to form after a building is constructed, as the new structure slowly settles: wet materials will dry, and some dry materials will take up moisture from the air and the surrounding structure to become a little wetter; structural elements may distort or even crack until all the loads are well distributed. Once this settling process is completed, however, a good building will be able to cope with its environment without significant alteration or deterioration. The ways in which it does this are critical to understanding how the envelope is intended to function.

THE BUILDING ENVELOPE

The role of a building is to protect the interior from the exterior environment: the fabric must reduce the impact of the sun and wind, modifying the exterior extremes of temperature and humidity so that the interior is relatively stable; and it must be able to stop rainwater from penetrating not only into the interior, but into the construction itself. To do this, all buildings have some form of roof, and almost all also have walls; and onto this basic plan are superimposed other features that help make it usable for its intended purpose, such as windows and internal partitions.

Successful buildings are, by definition, those that cope well with the weather conditions to which they are exposed. Vernacular architecture demonstrates this most clearly: it developed in response to local climate, and was for the most part built using local materials and local labour that made construction and maintenance straightforward.

Vernacular architecture

Vernacular building designs vary according to the materials available, and the weather with which the building must cope. Villages in clay-rich areas may be composed of houses constructed largely from brick, with clay roof tiles; and areas rich in stone may have many slate roofs. Where rainfall is heavy or winters harsh, roofs may be more steeply pitched and walls may be rendered. The design and materials of tried-and-tested architecture of this type will tell the alert visitor much about the local environment.

BUILDING ENVIRONMENT
INTERACTIONS WITH THE ENVIRONMENT

FUNCTIONS OF THE BUILDING ENVELOPE

To determine how a building envelope might be operating, a clear picture must be developed of the purpose and action of each of its components, of how they work together as a whole, and of how the ensemble interacts with the exterior and interior environments. Even apparently decorative elements often have functional purposes, which must be understood if repairs and alterations are not to endanger the operation of the envelope.

IMPORTANT ELEMENTS OF THE BUILDING ENVELOPE

- Chimneys, vents and other elements of the heating and/or cooling systems
- Attics and other roof spaces, including those converted to living space
- Roofs and elements that pierce them, such as chimneys and dormers
- Bathrooms, kitchens and other sources of water vapour and liquid water
- Exterior walls and elements that shed water, such as string courses and hood mouldings
- Patterns of occupation and use
- Plumbing
- Artificial lighting and other energy supplies
- Rainwater goods
- Partition walls and floors, especially between areas of the building that have different interior environments
- Ground drainage
- Foundations and below-ground walls and floors
- Ground floors
- Elements that pierce the exterior walls, such as windows and doors

The building envelope

Every building envelope is unique. It will be composed of elements deliberately intended to serve a weatherproofing function (such as the roof and exterior walls), elements intended to control interior conditions (such as the fireplaces and other heating systems), and elements which are primarily intended to serve other purposes, but which will still have a strong impact on the interior environmental conditions (such as interior partitions and plumbing). Even apparently minor elements such as wallpapers can have a significant effect on the envelope's condition and behaviour.

KEEPING THE BUILDING DRY

In any climate that is not extremely arid, the fundamental demand on any building envelope is that it should be able to handle water. This function is critical to the way the building envelope is detailed and constructed.

Water meets the envelope in many forms, and from many sources, of which rainfall and groundwater are the most important. Almost all the familiar detailing of buildings stems from the need to move water from these sources safely away from the fabric, and especially to keep it from penetrating to the interior.

Water can be taken up by the building fabric in different ways: absorbed as a vapour, drawn up as a liquid into the pores or through fine cracks, joints and interfaces between building elements, condensed from the air onto cold surfaces, or by a combination of any or all of these (see **Building Science**). It can then travel through the structure, driven a little by gravity and very much by the ambient conditions, especially those causing evaporation. As it moves, it will transfer heat, and it can often transport contaminants as well.

The phase in which water is found (liquid, vapour or ice) is critical to its behaviour, and will also affect building materials in different ways. Phases may be very localised, since they will depend on so many factors: not only the temperature, but also (amongst others) the flow of air across the surface, the chemical and physical nature of the material, and the nature and concentration of any contaminants.

DEALING WITH RAINWATER

Like light falling on glass, rainwater meeting the envelope can be deflected from it, absorbed and held by it, or transmitted through it, and the ways in which the building does this are a marker of how successful it is at fulfilling this primary role:

- *Deflection*
  Good envelopes deflect as much rainwater as possible, by using features such as drips and overhangs. Water may be collected and channelled away in gutters and drains.
- *Absorption*
  Traditional building materials such as brick, stone and lime mortar are permeable, and can absorb rainwater in surface pores, from which it can later evaporate.
- *Transmission*
  Modern rainscreen building systems allow a degree of transmission, with penetrating water being collected in internal drainage systems, but in both modern and traditional systems transmission of rainwater right through the envelope is a sign of failure.

How rainwater interacts with the envelope depends on other environmental factors as well, most notably windiness, air temperature and solar radiation. The risk of failure, and therefore the need for good detailing, increases with exposure to all these factors.

Handling Precipitation

The form precipitation takes will affect the way the structure deals with water. Rain can fall as soft showers, steady rain, heavy downpours and storms, or – in cold conditions – as sleet and snow. Water also collects as dew and ice, and the building envelope must handle these as well. Other climate factors are also very important, most particularly wind, since they mean that some parts of the building will be much more exposed to the weather than others.

Precipitation must be described as depth per time, and is usually measured in millimetres per hour (with locations being described in millimetres per year), but most of these time frames are much too long to effectively describe storms, during which the total quantity of rain might fall in just a few minutes. This distinction is important, since it is intense downpours that can overwhelm otherwise effective water-disposal systems.

Water accumulates as it travels down the building: relatively little rain will hit the ridge of the roof, but the overall volume per area will increase as it runs down the fall, and the incident rain is added to it. For a sizeable roof, even light rain may generate significant quantities of water at the eaves. Since precipitation depends on local climate, including local wind patterns, successful detailing is always site-specific, and may well be different for different parts of the building, depending on their exposure.

Many characteristic features of the building envelope are intended principally to keep the fabric and contents dry. These include not only the roof and the walls, but also the rainwater disposal systems (which bring rainwater at height safely down to the ground), the drains (which deal with water at ground level), and any water-shedding features such as eaves, copings and cornices. Chimneys, doors, windows and any other openings in the envelope are weak points, and so would be positioned with care, and often protected with details such as porches and hood mouldings.

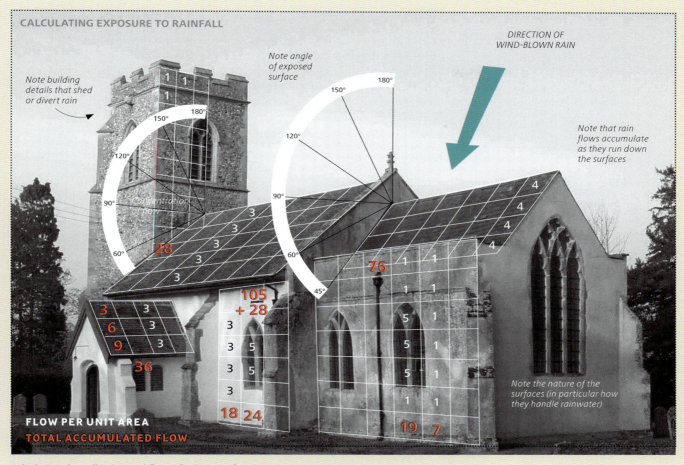

Calculating the collection and flow of rainwater for sizing rainwater goods

The impact of rain depends on both its strength and its direction relative to the building; since this depends on the wind speed and direction, which can be extremely variable, buildings must be constructed to cope with conditions that can vary greatly from season to season, or even from storm to storm. The amount of water collected by a surface such as a roof pitch or wall will depend on its angle relative to the rain.

Rain collects as it travels down the building: the load of water at the roof ridge is much smaller than at the eaves. This must be taken into account when calculating the volume of water with which the rainwater goods and drains will have to cope. The way the flow is concentrated will also be important: for example, if a downpipe discharges onto a roof, the ability of the cover to withstand the extra load of water will depend on whether the flow is quickly spread, or is concentrated by the design of the roof (perhaps a metal roof having narrow bays that trap the discharged water in a small area). Good roofs are designed to reduce potential problems such as those posed by valley gutters, which take the load from two slopes. Pitch is important for water disposal systems and drains, as well as for gutters and roofs.

A critical factor is the nature of the surfaces, particularly their water-resistance. The surface pores of permeable materials such as lime mortar, brick or stone will temporarily absorb much of the water falling on them, greatly reducing runoff in comparison to water-resistant materials such as cement renders, glass and metal. Water-shedding features such as cornices and hood mouldings will scatter water away from the walls; these tend to be less common in modern architecture, and may have been lost from earlier buildings during renovations.

Most drains must cope not only with the water from the rainwater goods, but also with runoff at ground level. In urban areas, or wherever water-resistant surfaces surround the building, runoff and splashback may add considerably to the load of water hitting the base of the walls during storms.

BUILDING ENVIRONMENT
INTERACTIONS WITH THE ENVIRONMENT

Roofs

The roof is the building's first line of defence against rain, and this is one of the primary factors governing their design. For example, in rainy locations, roofs are more likely to be steep to facilitate runoff, although pitch will also depend on the materials of which the roof is made. At the same time, roofs may serve other important functions such as reducing solar heating, or preventing the loss of warmth generated in the interior: a glass roof on a Victorian shopping arcade is designed to protect against the rain and the exterior air, but to admit sunlight. ⊖ROOFING ⊖GLASS

The two basic components of the roof are the supporting structure and the covering.

Supporting Structures

The supporting structure of a roof must be able to handle both the dead load of the cover and the live loads of the wind. Most traditional structures use a framework of long, strong beams as a roof support, made of a fairly rigid material with sufficient tensile and compressive strength. This rests upon the top of the walls. In traditional structures, the load is transferred to massive walls or to a timber frame, which in turn transfer it to the ground.

Timber was probably the first material to be used for roof supports, and it remains the most popular choice, though since the Industrial Revolution, iron and steel have become common for large buildings, and since the 20th century beams have also been made from concrete reinforced with steel to give the necessary tensile strength. At times, beams of stone have also been used, but these are very heavy and very difficult to handle, and can bridge only short distances.

Many traditional roofs relied on structures made of large quantities of timber, which also served to buffer the internal humidity.

Changes to Roofing Practice

Traditionally, roof coverings such as tiles and slates were supported by horizontal laths or battens fixed to the rafters, which allowed air to pass freely between the exterior and the roof space. In more exposed areas roof slopes were sometimes boarded, but 'penny' gaps would often be left between the boards to allow ventilation, and sometimes on steep pitches gaps were wider again.

It was not until the 20th century that underlays were introduced. Reinforced bitumen felt ('sarking' felt) was laid beneath the battens on pitched roofs to provide a temporary waterproof covering during re-roofing, reduce dirt and dust ingress, and act as a second line of defence against defects in the roof covering. It was also believed to cut wind uplift. Underlays reduced the air permeability of the roof, making it necessary to provide ventilation at the eaves level. Current practice favours semi-permeable underlays. ➔ROOFING

The Romans pioneered the use of masonry to make arched roof structures, where the load was passed through the arch or vault, and hence onto the supporting walls. This type of roof could span 40 m or more, and stone arches and vaults remained popular for large prestigious buildings throughout the Middle Ages. The most recent innovation is the tensile roof, where the load is taken not by the walls, but by cables and posts set away from the building envelope. These are more complex versions of the tent roof, and are commonly used with plastic or fabric coverings. ➔ROOFING ➔GLASS ➔STONE ➔TIMBER ➔CONCRETE

Roof Coverings

Roof coverings provide the waterproofing, and must be able to send rain down to the eaves with minimal penetration into the roof space. A covering must be durable, not only because of its critical importance to the building envelope, but because the roof is usually the least accessible part of the building. It must be able to survive poor weather with minimal care and maintenance, and must therefore be detailed according to the material being used. The pitch is critical in this regard: certain coverings (such as thatch and small clay tiles) will fail if the pitch is not steep enough to force rain to flow quickly enough down to the eaves.

The simplest covering would be made of a single piece of waterproof material, placed at an angle to ensure that rainwater could not pool; and, indeed, some very small outbuildings are roofed in exactly this way, using perhaps a single large stone slab or a sheet of corrugated iron. Other than this, there are two options:

- *'Water-resistant' coverings*

  Coverings composed of multiple small units (such as tiles or bundles of straw), laid overlapping so that the rainwater penetrating between two units is stopped by a third positioned underneath the joint; in areas where very small slates are used there may even be another layer again. In this way the rain runs down through the covering towards the eaves. To be effective, such a roof must usually be quite steeply pitched.

- *'Waterproof' coverings*

  Coverings made of sheet materials such as metal, asphalt or glass, which are intended to completely prevent all water penetration, and will fail if they are punctured. There must be as few joints as possible, and these must be dealt with carefully, but the roof can be laid almost flat.

BUILDING ENVIRONMENT
INTERACTIONS WITH THE ENVIRONMENT

How roof coverings handle rain

Roof coverings can either be 'water-resistant' (resisting rain by deflecting it through multiple layers), or 'waterproof' (using a single layer of material that blocks all water from entering the covering).

Top: A water-resistant roof: examples include thatch and clay tiles, as well as slates. Rainwater that succeeds in penetrating through a gap between two 'units' (which could be reeds or straw, or tiles or slates) will be deflected by a third unit below, which stops further vertical penetration. In this way rain is channelled down through the cover and out at the eaves. Since the system depends on gravity to move the water downwards as quickly as possible, water-resistant roofs must be pitched.

Bottom: A waterproof roof: examples include glass and asphalt, as well as sheet metal. Rainwater flows over the waterproof surface and down to the eaves. The major difference with water-resistant roofs is that waterproof roofs will fail if they are perforated: there must be no vertical penetration at all. For this reason any joints in the cover must be detailed to prevent leakage. One advantage of waterproof coverings, however, is that they can be used on roofs with very low pitches.

The earliest covers were overlapping, and were probably made of cut turf or sod, with thatch appearing soon after. Thatch could not only be made of materials that were widely available, such as wheat straw and rye, but these were comparatively light. The supporting structure did not therefore have to be very robust, which was a great advantage. The next technological step introduced covers made of small flat panels – or 'tiles' – hung (just like thatch) from horizontal battens fastened across the rafters. Tiles could be made of any suitable local material: timber shingles, fired clay, or stone in areas where suitable fissile stones such as slate were available. Systems for laying tiles were developed that reflected the local climate, as well as the quality of the materials available: in areas with strong wind-driven rain, for example, they could be laid with three or more 'laps'.

Continuous roofs require particular materials and careful detailing, but they have the great advantage that they can be laid at low pitch. The earliest used sheet metals – mostly lead or copper – were expensive but very durable, and proved popular for churches. Sheets had to be supported on wooden boards laid across the rafters, to prevent sagging or cracking. Asphalt, which also needed support, began to be used for coverings in the 19th century, coinciding with the increasing use of flat roofs (for which it remains a popular choice).

After metals became cheaper during the Industrial Revolution, roofs began to be covered in corrugated iron and steel or zinc, and more recently sheet aluminium and stainless steel have both become important. Corrugation stiffens sheets so that they do not need additional support. The other introduction was glass, as new production methods made large sheets possible and dramatically cut cost. Special supporting structures were developed that also served to hold the glazing. →ROOFING →METALS →GLASS

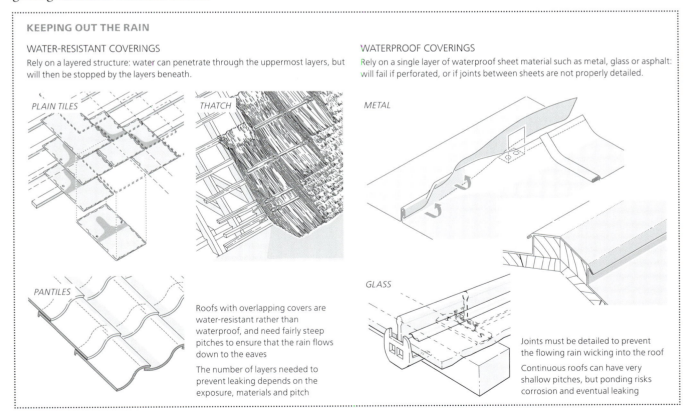

KEEPING OUT THE RAIN

WATER-RESISTANT COVERINGS
Rely on a layered structure: water can penetrate through the uppermost layers, but will then be stopped by the layers beneath.

WATERPROOF COVERINGS
Rely on a single layer of waterproof sheet material such as metal, glass or asphalt: will fail if perforated, or if joints between sheets are not properly detailed.

PLAIN TILES

THATCH

METAL

PANTILES

Roofs with overlapping covers are water-resistant rather than waterproof, and need fairly steep pitches to ensure that the rain flows down to the eaves

The number of layers needed to prevent leaking depends on the exposure, materials and pitch

GLASS

Joints must be detailed to prevent the flowing rain wicking into the roof

Continuous roofs can have very shallow pitches, but ponding risks corrosion and eventual leaking

BUILDING ENVIRONMENT
INTERACTIONS WITH THE ENVIRONMENT

Roof Design

The shape and construction of the roof is critical to how it sheds water. Every joint – whether between the elements of the cover or between different pitches – must be thought through.

Wherever two planes of the roof meet, such as at the ridges and the valleys, or at the points where vertical elements such as chimneys or dormer windows pierce the covering, there will be weak spots that are prone to leaking. These must be protected with special covers (such as ridge or hip tiles), or by waterproofing with flashing or mortar fillets. ⇒MORTARS ⇒METALS ⇒ROOFING

The design also needs to take the prevailing weather into account, especially the wind: flatter roofs may be more prone to lifting especially on the lee side, and ridges must be made wind-resistant as well as waterproof.

The relationship between roof pitch and covering material

Pitch is critical to the effectiveness of any roof, but it will depend not only on the choice of covering system, but also on the type of building and its exposure. For example, although lead can be laid at very low pitches, it is also found on prestigious buildings such as cathedrals with steeply pitched and very exposed roofs, because it is so long-lasting and relatively low-maintenance.

Detailing of Joints

Ideally, all roofs and joints would be sloped so that rainwater never pooled, but in practice, roofs are often so complex that there are many places where water can collect, such as horizontal joints where two pitched surfaces meet. These must be well detailed, and 'weathered' (sealed in some way) if they are not to leak. ⊖ROOFING

Joints or interfaces of all types are weak places liable to water penetration, and so must also be weathered. The sealing system must be able to cope with differential movement, and be formed in such a way as to deflect water away from the joint. 'Fillets' in lime mortar (often including hair to increase flexibility and reduce cracking) have been used for this purpose from the earliest periods, although they require regular maintenance. Nowadays, cement mortars are often used for filleting, but these are very brittle and tend to crack and let in water, so lime remains a better choice. ⊖MORTARS

The alternative to filleting is 'flashing': thin sheets of metal – typically lead – covering the joint, and usually chased into masonry on the most exposed edge to prevent water running in behind. Flashing became an increasingly popular alternative to mortar fillets as metals decreased in price. ⊖METALS

To weather joints between tiled coverings and abutments, 'soakers' are often used: small pieces of lead or zinc that run under the tile and curve up the abutment. They are protected either with a cover flashing chased into the abutment, or with mortar.

Ridges, hips, valleys and joints

No matter how decorative some roof detailing may appear, most are a direct result of the need to keep the joints watertight. This is true of ridge cappings on tiled and thatched roofs, the detailing of hips and valleys, and the rolled joints on metal roofs.

BUILDING ENVIRONMENT
INTERACTIONS WITH THE ENVIRONMENT

Protecting Openings in Roofs

The most familiar openings in roof coverings are chimneys, but dormer windows and skylights are also very common. Since any opening in a roof will be vulnerable to leaking, they need to incorporate weathering details such as flashing or mortar fillets to channel water back down the roof. ⊖ROOFING

Openings in roofs

Where elements such as chimneys, dormers or roof lights penetrate a covering, the joints must be waterproofed with mortar fillets or metal flashings.

Roof Ventilation

As far as ventilation is concerned, there are five basic roof configurations. ➔ROOFING

ROOF VENTILATION CONFIGURATIONS			
ROOF SPACE	DESCRIPTION	EXAMPLES	TYPICAL PERFORMANCE
OPEN	No separation between the roof space and the interior	Barns; churches where the ceiling has been removed	This functions well as long as the interior absolute humidity is not too high
WELL-VENTILATED	Largely air-impermeable ceiling between roof space and interior; roof is very permeable to the exterior air	Traditional well-ventilated attic over lath-and-plaster ceiling in good condition	Most moisture comes from the exterior (as rain or vapour) and readily evaporates as conditions change; functions well since drying exceeds wetting
BUFFERED	Sealed roof space containing large amounts of timber, with little air exchange either with the interior or the exterior	Attic over lath-and-plaster ceiling; roof space over a stone vault	Heating by the sun drives cycles of condensation and evaporation; functions well as long as there is no added source of moisture such as a leak
CONNECTED	Ceiling is very permeable, allowing air to rise from the interior into the roof space	Ceiling is a poor air barrier, or perforated by fittings	Can fail if moisture load from interior is high; increasing ventilation through the roof will pull more moist air up from below
UNDERDRAWN	Ceiling is between or just below the structural members of the roof	Halls, churches, converted loft spaces	Can be problematic because penetrating liquid water or water vapour may accumulate in a localised area

As the moisture content of the interior air has increased as a result of more cooking, washing and cleaning, condensation has become a greater problem (see **Deterioration & Damage**); it may be exacerbated by the introduction of underlays, and the reduction in air exchange between the interior and exterior. Modern roofs may therefore incorporate ventilators at the eaves and ridge. ➔ROOFING

In more extreme climates, ventilation detailing could be quite complex. In the tropics, roofs were given extra ventilators to remove hot air rising from the interior, as well as air in the roof space that was being heated by sunlight on the roof. In climates cold enough to have substantial snowfall during the winter, roofs were specially detailed to prevent melting snow forming ice dams, or wicking into the roof through the tiles and slates.

BUILDING ENVIRONMENT
INTERACTIONS WITH THE ENVIRONMENT

Rainwater Disposal Systems

The earliest roofs had projecting eaves, which not only protected the top of the wall, but also helped to shed water away from its base. This simple approach to rain disposal works only if the surrounding ground is able to absorb the water, and does not slope back towards the wall. It will be counterproductive if there are other buildings nearby, and indeed water disposal can be a serious problem in towns and cities. It is certainly not surprising that the earliest buildings we know of in the British Isles – at Skara Brae, on the island of Orkney – also have the earliest known drains. These buildings were probably thatched, with wide eaves to keep the rainwater away from the walls and the footings. Taller buildings required more elaborate ways of collecting water and channelling it safely away from the fabric.

Disposing of Water from the Roof

From the earliest period, gutters and pipes must have been made from timber and fired clay, but metal was much more reliable and long-lived, and will have been introduced for this purpose wherever it was available (particularly lead, which could easily be worked by bossing). Unfortunately, we actually know surprisingly little about early rainwater disposal (especially on utilitarian buildings): timber and poorly fired clay elements can both deteriorate quickly when exposed to water, and metal piping was scavenged and reused (for example, in 1750 building statutes introduced in London to prevent theft banned lead for the lowest 6 foot (1.8 m) of downpipes, which were instead made of wood). Nevertheless, it seems reasonable to assume early rainwater disposal resembled modern systems fairly closely, and what little evidence remains confirms this theory.

The earliest known mention of downpipes being used on buildings in England comes in an account of works to the White Tower at the Tower of London, undertaken in 1240. Nevertheless, rainwater goods are likely to have been extensively used on many buildings, wherever the design or the location of the building made it impossible to rely on having eaves that projected far enough to prevent rainwater runoff damaging the envelope.

Very few examples of Roman gutters and downpipes remain, perhaps because many were made of materials like wood that decayed, or metals such as lead which were reused. This surviving terracotta downpipe is in Pompeii.

Ancient masonry buildings do retain some features that allow us to guess at how rainwater was probably controlled. In Greek temples, for example, a channel was cut into the back of the cornices to serve as a gutter, and the water was discharged at regular spouts, often decorated with lion masks with tongues of protective tile. If the cornice did not continue along the sides of the roof, the water was allowed to fall off the eaves. These ideas were copied later by the Romans for their own temples.

Although the earliest solid evidence of downpipes being used in England is a mention in the 1240 accounts for the Tower of London (which describes their installation to protect the newly whitewashed walls), it must be presumed that the Romans used downpipes and gutters of some type for such buildings as the multistorey *insulae* they built in cities such as Canterbury (*Durovernum Cantiacorum*). Clay downpipes do survive in some Roman sites, notably Pompeii.

By the Middle Ages, gutters on grand buildings were being supported partly on corbels and partly on the top of the wall. Occasionally a parapet was provided to conceal the gutter, and this was often made into an important decorative feature. On structures that were less important, the parapet was often a continuation of the wall itself, and the gutter was set into a trough that rested on the lower end of the roof timbers. Spouts, in the form of gargoyles, are one of the most recognisable elements of the architecture of this period.

After the Dissolution of Monasteries in 1539, large quantities of lead were stripped from abbey roofs and recast as rainwater goods. Hoppers and pipes became fashionably eye-catching, with cast and painted decoration.

Cast-iron water supply pipes began to be laid in London during the mid-1700s, and over the course of the 19th century iron largely replaced lead for downpipes. In the period after the Second World War cast iron was itself mostly superseded by aluminium, steel and asbestos cement; in the 1950s plastics began to be used, and were common by the 1970s. Some current plastic rainwater systems are designed to replicate the appearance of cast iron and lead, not least because metal theft has again become a serious problem. Modern materials and production systems allow gutters and pipes to be made with fewer joints, which can be a significant advantage where regular maintenance is difficult. ⊖METALS

BUILDING ENVIRONMENT
INTERACTIONS WITH THE ENVIRONMENT

Gutters

Overhanging eaves and cornices are designed to deflect water away from the walls below, shedding it from the roof onto the surrounding ground. This is how thatched roofs must shed water, and if a building is isolated and the ground slopes away, this may be all that is needed. In most cases, however, it is necessary to collect the rainwater running off at the eaves into open gutters that then direct the water to a discharge point or outlet.

Eaves gutters, which are set away from the wall on brackets or secured to the ends of the rafters, can theoretically be laid level rather than on a slope, in which case the force driving the water along to the discharge points will not be gravity, but rather the pressure head built up along their length; but most are laid on a slope down to the outlet. The edge of the roof must overlap the gutter, but not so far that water overshoots in heavy rain.

Box gutters are used between vertical surfaces, most typically at the junction between a sloping roof and a parapet wall. Most are lined with lead, with numerous expansion joints, and are designed to allow foot traffic. They must be wider than an eaves gutter, and be straight with a uniform slope of at least 1 in 80. Parapets have often been popular for buildings even though the risks to the fabric from blocked or leaking parapet gutters is very high, since leaking water will travel directly into the wall head.

If roof pitches meet at a more-or-less horizontal intersection, the junction will need to be protected with a valley gutter. Like box gutters, valley gutters must be sloped, and will need to be deep enough to take the entire load of rainwater from both pitches if they are not to cause problematic leaks.

Outlets

The accumulated water from the gutters must be diverted away from the building. The simplest way of doing this is with a spout, which throws the water outwards away from the walls. Medieval buildings with gutters hidden behind parapets made a feature of spouts, enclosing them in elaborate stone gargoyles.

Spouts can be very effective so long as the ground below is able to absorb the discharged water without trouble, and is sloped away from the footings of the building so that runoff cannot cause problems, although the wind can still sometimes blow the jet of water back against the building. If, however, the ground is paved or otherwise poorly absorbent, or the land slopes back towards the walls, or nearby buildings are very close, then spouts will not be effective and the water from the gutters will instead need to be channelled through vertical pipes running down to the ground ('rainwater downpipes'), and hence into drains.

During the Gothic Revival, gargoyles once again became important features of the architecture, this time as purely decorative elements; the rainwater did not travel through their mouths, but through downpipes below.

For eaves gutters, downpipes can be made to run directly from the base of the gutter at its discharge point, and a similar approach is taken to concealed downpipes, which travel through the walls from the lowest point of the box gutter above. The risk is that sudden downpours may seal the mouth of the air-filled downpipe, causing the gutter to overflow. For this reason, the discharge point of a box gutter is formed as a 'box' able to fill with water, allowing time for the back pressure of the air to dissipate.

Post-medieval parapet gutters drained through the parapet used the same remedy, in the form of 'hopper' heads: metal reservoirs at the top of the downpipe, fed with the water from the gutters by 'scuppers'. Hoppers rapidly became a decorative feature of the building, with 17th- and 18th-century lead versions often being elaborately cast and painted. To ensure against overflow, hoppers very occasionally incorporated spouts as well, and this approach has recently seen a revival.

Spouts and hoppers

The water collected in gutters could be discharged through spouts, or diverted into downpipes, often by way of hoppers.

As well as being functional, these features often became important parts of the building decoration. Gargoyles were used to decorate spouts in the medieval period, and later, lead was cast to make elaborate hoppers, which were often also tinned or painted.

BUILDING ENVIRONMENT
INTERACTIONS WITH THE ENVIRONMENT

Rainwater Downpipes

Downpipes carry the water collected in the gutters to gulleys or drains, or sometimes to storage tanks where it can be collected for later use. They must be positioned correctly, and be sufficiently large and numerous to be able to handle the entire load of water from the gutters.

Ideally, downpipes would run straight from the gutters to the ground – any bend is a potential site for blockages – and would be set away from the wall to reduce the risk from leaks and to allow maintenance, but in practice they may be tucked into corners or even concealed inside the walls to make them less conspicuous. They may also be very decorative, or partly embedded into the wall. Instead of emptying into a gulley or drain, they may sometimes discharge into a lower gutter or even onto a roof. In this case, the end of the pipe must be detailed to prevent problems: it may need a 'shoe' (an angled pipe to divert the discharge away from sensitive parts of the fabric), or perhaps a distributor to spread the water so that the gutter is not overwhelmed.

The simplest downpipe of all is a chain, down which the water can run. It should not be fixed at the bottom. Chains will not protect the wall from wind-blown spray or splash-back at ground level, but neither will they block. They are more common in regions with cold winters, since they will continue to direct water even during freezing conditions (when pipes would block, and perhaps burst).

Gulleys & Drains

The way the water is handled as it discharges from the downpipes is critical, since they carry the load of rain from the roof perilously close to the footings. In very old buildings, downpipes often ended in a shoe that simply directed the water away from the foot of the building, perhaps into a channel or ditch. A safer method, and one that is needed if the topography and ground conditions are not ideal, is to run the water into a gully, and hence a drain that can carry it safely away. Although the downpipe could be connected directly to the drain, this risks blocking it with debris washed down from the roof and gutters, so it is better that the pipe discharges over a grille. Most gulleys will also collect some of the water running across the surface back towards the footings, and channel it into the rainwater disposal drainage.

Together with the discharge from the downpipes, drains must sometimes handle runoff from the ground as well as other forms of waste water. They are described in more detail in **Controlling Water from the Ground**.

Soakaways

In its simplest form, a soakaway is a deep hole or trench, set some distance from the building and connected to the drains. This is used to collect excess rainwater and store it as it slowly seeps into the surrounding ground. Soakaways must be large enough to cope with successive downpours, and positioned well away from the building (preferably where the land is lower or is sloping away). The base of the soakaway must be above the top of the water table at all times of the year.

A soakaway for a small house may be no more than a hole about one metre square and 1.5-m deep, filled with rubble, though most modern soakaways have empty chambers to increase capacity. Larger buildings require much bigger soakaways, and these are often lined with dry-jointed or honeycomb brickwork. Most are given an impervious cover (often concrete or plastic sheeting) so that water can only enter through the drainpipe, which is usually around 100 mm in diameter and positioned to enter the soakaway about 100 mm below the top.

After some time soakaways will fill up with mud and debris, gradually becoming less effective. In this case they will need to be excavated. Modern designs often incorporate cellular concrete or plastic boxes that are reasonably easy to remove and clean or replace.

Below-ground drains are always prone to blocking, and so should incorporate rodding points and inspection hatches, especially wherever two or more pipes meet.

Sewage Systems

Sewers are the network of ground pipes that are used to collect and carry rain runoff and waste water away for treatment and disposal. There are three types of system:

- *Surface water or storm sewers*

    These carry runoff from roofs, roads, paved areas, together with seepage from soakaways, usually into streams, rivers or watercourses.

- *Foul sewers*

    These carry water that has been used for cooking and washing, waste from toilets, and from industrial processing to treatment works.

- *Combined sewers*

    These are single-pipe systems that carry both foul and surface water to treatment works, and are no longer constructed.

Sewers and other groundwater systems are discussed in more detail in **Controlling Water from the Ground**.

BUILDING ENVIRONMENT
INTERACTIONS WITH THE ENVIRONMENT

PRINCIPAL ELEMENTS OF A RAINWATER DISPOSAL SYSTEM

GUTTERS

NONE (WIDE OVERHANGS)	EAVES GUTTER	BOX GUTTER	VALLEY GUTTER

OUTLETS

SPOUT	DIRECTLY INTO DOWNPIPE	HOPPER	OVERFLOW SPOUT

RAINWATER DOWNPIPES

EXTERNAL	PARTLY EMBEDDED	CONCEALED	CHAINS

PRINCIPAL ELEMENTS OF A RAINWATER DISPOSAL SYSTEM

GULLEYS

Ditches or channels that connect the downpipe to a drain, and may also carry any overflow of rainwater from the eaves or gutters and direct it towards the drains

DRAINPIPES

Buried pipes leading to falls, designed to carry away or divert groundwater, rainwater discharged from roof, or waste water (sewage) away from the footing of the building

DRAINS

Watercourses, culverts and other sumps able to hold excess water (for example, rainwater during a storm), releasing either into the ground away from the building into soakaways or the sewerage system

SOAKAWAYS

Artificial sumps to collect excess water

Also used to slow the discharge of stormwater into watercourses or sewers

BUILDING ENVIRONMENT
INTERACTIONS WITH THE ENVIRONMENT

Walls

Walls have many functions, including buffering the fluctuating exterior conditions and providing security, but equally important is keeping out the rain. This is especially true for modern construction systems such as curtain walling, where the walls rather than the roof are the primary defence against the weather. Traditional and modern walls differ in materials and construction, and thus in how they handle rainwater.

Traditional Wall Construction

Traditional wall construction is water-resistant rather than waterproof: 'storage' or 'mass' systems, in which the ability to resist rain depends on the permeability of the materials. Permeable materials such as stone, brick and lime mortar temporarily absorb rain in the near-surface pores, but since even the strongest rain is not a continuous stream of water, air resistance will prevent it penetrating more than a millimetre or so. As soon as the rain eases off or the wind increases, this surface water will evaporate again (indeed, in driving rain conditions there will be strong airflow across the surface, so evaporation can be very effective even in the worst weather). Because the rain cannot accumulate to the point where it begins to flow as a liquid, traditional construction in good condition is an excellent rain barrier.

Rain can penetrate a permeable material only if it is already wet from some other more constant source of water (such as a faulty drain or a blocked gutter). In wet walls, there will be liquid flow paths between the surface and the interior which could wick in the rain as it hits. Traditional building design was therefore intended to prevent liquid water penetration, by details that included projecting eaves to protect the wall head, and cills and hood mouldings with drip edges to protect the wall around doors and windows.

Pitched roofs and projecting eaves can halve the quantity of rain deposited on walls. A study of timber-framed buildings in British Columbia found that there was a perfect inverse correlation between rain-related wall damage and the depth of roof overhang.

Protective wall finishes

Protective finishes of many kinds were traditionally used to prevent water penetration, especially where the building was exposed to extreme weather: in hilly regions or near the coast, for example.

Common finishes included limewash, slates or tiles hung from battens, timber weatherboarding, and renders based on lime mortar such as 'rough cast' (where coarse aggregate was thrown or pressed into a fresh render). Even stone and brick buildings were commonly rendered, and in some areas the renders incorporated pargetting, painting or other decoration. Most were limewashed for durability.

Often only traces of such finishes now remain, and many renders on early buildings were deliberately removed at a later period to reveal the underlying masonry. In the 20th century, many lime-based renders and rough casts were replaced with cement-based finishes.

A traditional wall might be only 100-mm thick, or as deep as a metre or more. A single type of construction will probably include several very different materials: soft porous chalk and hard impervious flint, for example, or earth and timber lath. On top of this, older buildings may well incorporate several types of construction, reflecting years of alterations and repairs. The inevitable irregularities – bonding patterns, voids, concealed timbers, or metal cramps and the like – add to the complexity of a wall and how it handles moisture.

Some materials needed additional protection, as did some types of construction, especially in very exposed conditions. Water-sensitive materials such as rammed earth are best protected with permeable lime-based renders and coats of lime wash, and rendering was also used to protect very exposed elements such as towers, where rain might otherwise enter around joints. Being very permeable, these finishes did not interfere with the way the wall handled moisture. They did have to be kept well maintained, so yearly limewashing, regular repointing and regular re-rendering were features of building care for many centuries. Lime mortars and limewashes could fill small cracks in the finish, and when used on stone were believed to 'feed' the wall and keep it in good condition. ⊖MORTARS ⊖EARTH & BRICK ⊖STONE ⊖TIMBER

Wind-Driven Rain

In England, walls facing south and west are likely to be the most affected by driving rain. This will vary considerably with local conditions, and the situation can be very complicated: for example, exposed walls meet with more rain, but also more wind and often more sunlight, both of which increase drying. In practice it is often north walls that stay colder, and ultimately wetter. Turbulence is also important: in general, corners and projecting structures such as porches or extensions tend to be damper and colder than the main body of the building.

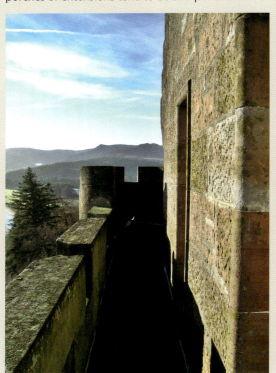

Theoretically, since rain is not a continuous source of water, it should not be able to penetrate deeper than a millimetre or so into a traditionally constructed wall (such as brick or stone masonry, or a wall with a lime render). Nevertheless, many reliable records do exist of water appearing on the inside of solid masonry walls during rainstorms.

The debate caused by these two conflicting observations continued for many years, and it was postulated that the observed moisture was in fact due to condensation on wind-chilled walls, rather than the rain being carried through the wall.

Experiments have now shown that penetration of driving rain is indeed possible, but the critical factor is whether or not the wall has an existing moisture problem. If a traditionally constructed wall is basically dry, then – just as a dry sponge will not soak up water – even the strongest driven rain will not be able to penetrate. If, on the other hand, the wall contains enough liquid moisture for there to be flow paths from the exterior to the interior (usually because of a problem with the building envelope, such as faulty downpipes or drains, faulty pointing, and poor renders), then rain hitting the wall will be drawn in (as into a wet sponge), and can be carried right through even the thickest masonry.

Driving rain can penetrate through a wet wall

At Brodick, on the Isle of Arran in Scotland, the driving rain is some of the strongest measured in the British Isles. Moisture monitoring of the tower room of Brodick Castle revealed that rainwater was passing through only one of the four walls: not the most exposed, but the wall which was already wet because the flashing on the exterior walkway had failed.

Finishes for Harsh Climates & Exposed Locations

A form of rendering called 'rough cast' ('harling' in Scotland) developed to protect walls from harsh climates: small pebbles or fine stone chips were thrown onto a fresh lime render using a specially shaped trowel, and the whole was then limewashed. ⊖MORTARS

A number of other building traditions use cladding systems rather than permeable renders. In England the most common of these are tile-hanging and weatherboarding. In most cases the tiles are hung from wooden battens fixed to the walls, just as they would be on a roof. Weatherboarding generally incorporates a wooden frame fixed to the wall, and covered with overlapped planks of timber. In both cases it was important that the cover was not so tightly laid nor the boards or tiles so flat that rainwater would be wicked in. Loose laying also allowed the evaporation of any water that did penetrate. The corners were weak points, and required extra protection.

When walls are given protective cladding, the corners and edges will be susceptible to water penetration, and must be detailed accordingly.

BUILDING ENVIRONMENT
INTERACTIONS WITH THE ENVIRONMENT

Modern Wall Construction

Modern construction is based on what can be called 'hollow-wall' systems, which use multiple layers of material to prevent the penetration of wind-driven rain. The main hollow-wall systems are:

- *Cavity walls*
  Introduced in the middle of the 19th century, and popular for constructing houses.

- *Cladding systems*
  Systems such as the 'rainscreen'; essentially a development of weatherboarding and tile-hanging, making particular use of waterproof materials such as sheet metal and glass.

Cavity Walls

Cavity walls are something of a hybrid between traditional and modern construction systems, being made up of two layers (or 'leaves') of brick, stone or concrete block masonry, usually stretcher-bonded. This gives thin inner and outer walls, with a narrow air gap between them that seems to have been originally intended to prevent water penetration, but offered a degree of heat insulation and perhaps also cut material costs. The leaves are held together at intervals, originally by bricks and later using metal 'ties'.

Although in 1877, **Building Construction** stated, *"Walls are now constructed to a very large extent in such a way that they present a hollow space or vacuity in the interior this not only affecting a considerable saving on bricks but tending to keep the interior face of the wall dry or damp proof and this to a very considerable degree of completeness"*, this type of building did not in fact become very popular in England until after the First World War, when traditional lime mortars were largely replaced by cement. Between the 1920s and 1970s it was the dominant form of brick masonry construction, and was especially popular for low-rise and domestic architecture.

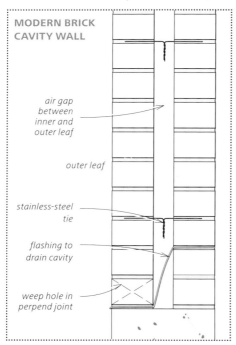

MODERN BRICK CAVITY WALL

air gap between inner and outer leaf

outer leaf

stainless-steel tie

flashing to drain cavity

weep hole in perpend joint

Early systems used bricks as ties, but these were found to transmit water across the cavity either through the joints, or across the bricks. To prevent this, perforated bricks were introduced, but soon metal ties (made with a slight bend in the middle to act as a drip, preventing moisture transfer) became the preferred option. The width of the gap between the leaves varied.

In the early days of cavity construction, whether or not the cavity should be ventilated was much debated, but by the end of the 19th century the prevailing consensus was that there should be a small amount of ventilation to the exterior, similar to that which was being provided under floors with air bricks, but that the cavity should be sealed well around doors and windows and other openings, and beneath the roof line. Much later such vents were largely replaced by 'weep holes', made by omitting mortar from some of the vertical (perpend) joints in a course at the base of the wall. As well as providing ventilation, these were meant to drain metal gutters or flashing at the bottom of the cavity, inserted to collect moisture travelling down the interiors of the leaves (there is little practical evidence that they achieved either of these aims). Cavities also became wider, to give more tolerance during construction, and allow for more air movement.

Rainscreen Walls & Other Cladding Systems

Modern construction is based on walls which are not massive, but instead are – like roofs – composed of a supporting frame which is sealed by a water-resistant covering of some kind. This favours rapid construction, and allows buildings to be made much taller. Non-load-bearing 'curtain' walls, for example, are made by hanging thin panels of largely impermeable materials (such as metals, glass, high-fired ceramics and concrete) from a load-bearing framework of timber, steel, aluminium or reinforced concrete.

The first buildings to be constructed in this way were Oriel Chambers and 16 Cork Street in Liverpool, designed by local engineer Peter Ellis in the 1860s. Ellis' revolutionary ideas were taken across the Atlantic by visiting American John Wellborn Root, and it was in Chicago and New York that the revolutionary new construction systems were used to build the first multistorey 'skyscrapers'. Curtain-wall construction is now ubiquitous for offices and factories, and the principles behind it are being used increasingly for low-rise domestic construction as well. ⊖GLASS

In this theory of building, a perfect wall cover would be 'face-sealed': that is, it would be completely waterproof. In practice, it proved virtually impossible to prevent all water penetration, especially when the sealants used on the joints between the individual components of the cladding aged and began to fail.

Glass walling

Left: Oriel Chambers, in Liverpool, was the world's first glass curtain-wall building, where the walls take little or no structural load, but serve only to keep out the weather.

Right: Modern glazing systems depend on sealants to protect the joints between panels.

BUILDING ENVIRONMENT
INTERACTIONS WITH THE ENVIRONMENT

Rainscreens

'Rainscreen' wall systems keep rainwater out with multiple layers of waterproof materials, with drains between and sometimes ventilation to remove any water able to penetrate through the joints.

A. Inner panel made of moisture-resistant and insulating material.

B. Support system for cladding (rails fixed to the primary structure).

C. Ventilation cavity; allows drying by air movement and vapour diffusion.

D. Support for outer panel.

E. Outer panel; stops most rain. Any penetrating water runs down the cavity, and out from the wall via cills and weep holes.

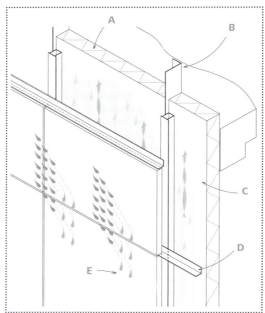

The materials used for cladding are largely or completely impermeable, so rainwater is not absorbed, but rather runs down the surface and accumulates below. For tall buildings in particular, the resulting flow of water can be intense, and will quickly be wicked into any unsealed joints or other flaws in the building skin. Face-sealed walls were found to leak badly, so the 'rainscreen' façade was developed. The walls of rainscreen buildings are composed of a number of different layers, each as waterproof as possible in itself, but with drains at the base to collect and remove any rainwater that is able to penetrate. ⊝EARTH & BRICK ⊝GLASS

Rainscreens may also include ventilation ('pressure-moderated' systems) to help drying, and most also incorporate layers of water-resistant membrane, although including any form of vapour barrier can sometimes lead to condensation problems.

The most recent type of curtain wall is 'structural glazing', where glass panels form the main water-resistant layer, joined together with sealants (usually silicone) rather than being held in a frame. There are three principal systems: the simplest has the panels supported by glass fins or beams set at right-angles to the façade; in 'structural sealant' glazing the panels are glued to an aluminium carrier frame; and in 'planar glazing' they are held by bolts. The movement of the glass (under wind pressure, for example) is allowed for, with washers or by making the bolts articulated. The bolts attach to a complex connecting plate, often called a 'spider'.

The *Glass & Glazing* volume in this series describes curtain-walling systems in more detail. ⊝GLASS

WINDOWS & DOORS

A building envelope is of little practical use without a means of entry and exit, and most also need some means of letting in natural light and fresh air, or perhaps for letting out the smoke generated in the interior by cooking and heating. Openings such as windows and chimneys make buildings usable, but piercing the envelope creates weak points that must be specially protected from the rain. ⊖GLASS ⊖TIMBER

The first priority with doors and windows is to stop the rain and wind coming through by adding some form of covering or seal that can be opened or shut as required. Early door and window openings were closed with hinged panels of timber: doors and shutters, which could also be fixed shut with bars and locks, to provide security as well as weather protection.

The disadvantage of wooden shutters for sealing windows was that, when closed, they let in little or no natural light. Many translucent materials, from oiled parchment to horn and alabaster, were used to protect early window openings, but the ideal material was found to be glass, which was both transparent and very resistant to water. Even when glass was extremely expensive, it was used for windows by joining small pieces together in a framework of lead; as its price dropped dramatically over the 19th and 20th centuries, it became available in larger sheets and was used increasingly as a building material. Modern construction often uses glass for roof coverings and walling, as well as for conventional windows.

Shutters

Wooden shutters were used to protect window voids before glass became widely available.

Left: An original shutter on a Saxon church window in Berkshire.

Right: Shutters remained in use even after glass windows became common, giving a secondary layer of protection. Some were pierced to let in sunlight even when closed.

BUILDING ENVIRONMENT
INTERACTIONS WITH THE ENVIRONMENT

Protection of openings

As openings in the building envelope, windows and doors must be protected from rain penetration.

Protection often takes the form of some sort of overhang or canopy, which, in the case of doors, also serve to protect waiting visitors. Traditional architectural details such as copings, cornices and hood mouldings were designed to throw or direct rainwater away from the openings. Often the openings were also set well back into the wall for added protection.

The junction between the window and the wall is a weak point, which should be detailed to prevent rainwater entering the fabric. Much of the familiar detailing of traditional buildings is primarily intended to deflect as much rainwater as possible from openings: although features such as porches, cornices, hood mouldings and window frames can certainly be very decorative, protection is their primary purpose.

Masonry buildings often used stone to frame windows and doors, since well-selected stone was very resistant to erosion. 'Stucco' (strong mortar, modelled to shape) could be used as a cheaper alternative, although it required good maintenance, including regular repair and at times replacement.

Although details vary with the period and type of building, early windows were generally set into wooden frames fitted into the opening, often with some form of flashing to prevent moisture in the wall rotting the timber. Any gaps between the wall and the window needed to be waterproofed with mortar or in some other way. ⊝GLASS

The detailing on traditional buildings was often ornate, but each element served a practical as well as a decorative purpose.

For example, the chapel of Keble College (a Victorian Gothic building) incorporates many features to protect the windows from rain: cornices, string courses, hood moulding with stops, and a sloped cill with mouldings to cast water running down the glass away from the wall below.

BUILDING ENVIRONMENT
INTERACTIONS WITH THE ENVIRONMENT

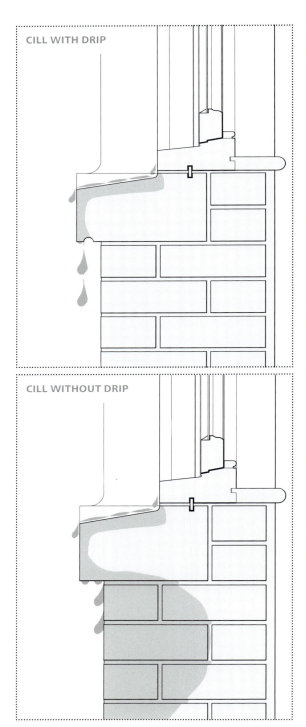

Windows are a considerable problem for modern buildings constructed to a minimalist aesthetic. These structures often aim for a perfectly flush façade, with no visible elements to deflect rainwater. It is not possible to rely completely on sealants, since even if a seal is perfect when installed, it will eventually start to age and leak, especially if it is under any stress or subjected to frequent movements. Successful detailing demands integrated drainage to move any moisture that is able to enter back to the exterior. Sealants and rain-deflecting elements such as cills must be as water-resistant as possible, and the designs also incorporate capillary breaks to prevent liquid water travelling right through the system.

●GLASS ●TIMBER

The window cill is a critical component, preventing water penetrating around the base of a window, and directing water that has run down the glass away from the wall. Traditionally, cills were made from stone or hardwood (often left unpainted), and had drips cut just under the lower edge to prevent water running back along the underside.

Drips

Top: Functioning drips are critical to overhanging water-shedding features such as window cills.

Bottom: If the drip is absent or blocked, surface tension can cause rainwater to run back along the underside of the element, allowing it to wick into the joints with the wall.

Structure of Window & Door Openings

Lintels (*top*) and relieving arches (*bottom*) both serve to direct the load of the fabric above to either side of the opening.

Timber elements such as lintels and bressumer beams may be subject to decay if water is allowed to enter the wall, but they were often robust enough to continue to function effectively even when considerably weakened. Many windows and doors were provided with at least two lintels: one set flush into the outer wall; and another 'safe lintel' set behind it.

In a traditional massive structure, the load of the building above the opening must be transferred in some way to the surrounding walls and hence down to the ground. One approach is to make the horizontal component into an arch, which can direct even very heavy loads outwards. Rectangular openings, which are easier to construct and much more common, rely instead on beams or 'lintels': bars of some material with good tensile and compressive strength, embedded into the wall on either side of the opening.

Since the lintel is of the greatest importance to the structure, often at least two were provided for each opening: an outer lintel set flush into the wall face (and often exposed), together with an inner lintel (or 'safe lintel') set behind, and often concealed by the interior wall finishes.

Lintels have usually been made of timber, though more recently steel or reinforced concrete have become common. Stone has also been used from time to time, but its weakness in tension means that openings with stone lintels often also have 'relieving arches' set into the masonry above the opening to take some of the load. Extra protection may also be provided by using mortars that are as elastic as possible (these may be based on earth rather than lime).

In massive walls, very large windows (such as those used for shop fronts) and projecting windows (bay windows, bow windows and oriel windows) require special reinforcement, which is provided by large 'bressumer' beams able to span the entire gap. Bressumers require a certain amount of vertical support, which is often provided by timber uprights framing the windows.

BUILDING ENVIRONMENT
INTERACTIONS WITH THE ENVIRONMENT

Traditionally, flood-sensitive buildings were located whenever possible on higher ground to take advantage of natural slopes away from the footings. Landscaping (including contouring and planting) was used to divert runoff, or reduce its severity.

CONTROLLING WATER FROM THE GROUND

The building envelope must also be able to deal with water entering at ground level. As well as true groundwater from the water table, or rain running over and through the ground surface, this can mean water from leaking drains, running off from the building, or falling rain splashing back onto the base of the walls.

The systems for dealing with groundwater can be loosely divided into those that prevent surface water wetting the footings, and those that stop water entering the fabric from the ground (that is, from the water table or the drains, or some similar source).

Protection from Surface Water

Preventing Splashback

Splashback is a risk wherever rainwater or runoff strikes a more-or-less flat surface abutting a wall, heavily enough that it bounces back and wets the wall. Most commonly the flat surface is the ground surrounding the building, but problems can also occur wherever a wall abuts any suitable exposed element (for example, a portico or a flat-roofed extension). Splashing can also occur under eaves if the gutters are missing, or undersized. To prevent splashback, ideally roofs would have projecting eaves or effective gutters and downpipes, and the ground or other surrounding surfaces would slope away from the wall and not be covered with hard surfacing (such as concrete or stone paving). In practice, such ideal situations are uncommon.

Any moisture-sensitive materials on the wall, such as timber, need to be kept well above the zone of splashing, or else protected with flashing or a permeable render.

Preventing Runoff Towards the Building

Whenever the ground is unable to absorb all the rain or other water falling on it, the water will 'run off' (flow across the surface); this is more common – and more severe – where the terrain is steep. Underlying environmental reasons for significant runoff are many, including unusually heavy downpours, soil that is already saturated, soil that is very dry and so resists moisture uptake, and sealed surfaces such as roads and paving. It is often serious in built-up areas, where there may be little or no exposed ground, and almost all the rainfall must be handled by storm drains. This has the knock-on effect of steadily reducing the moisture content of the soil, to the point where subsidence may become a problem.

Ground Drainage

Storm drains and culverts are by no means new – they were certainly used in most if not all early townships and cities across the world – and they remain the principal way of dealing with heavy runoff, especially in urban areas.

Since the 1950s, water management practice has sought to keep the foul water and stormwater drainage systems separate. This stops the stormwater overwhelming sewage treatment works, discharging it into watercourses, the sea, or occasionally soakaways or other holding systems such as ponds. In England, mains drainage and culverts are still combined in many areas, although in new developments they must now be separated.

The 12th-century drains at Monk Bretton Priory in Yorkshire are among the oldest still surviving in England.

Some form of drainage channel was needed wherever buildings were constructed close together, or wherever it was necessary to bring in fresh water or discard dirty water.

BUILDING ENVIRONMENT
INTERACTIONS WITH THE ENVIRONMENT

Ground drains may also be used to slow or stop runoff across sloped open ground. Most are based on the 'French' drain, which American engineer Henry French developed for agricultural land. These were originally simple sloped trenches filled with gravel, set across hillsides to catch the water as it ran down; later they incorporated perforated pipes and geotextile linings to stop them silting up too quickly.

The drains around building perimeters, intended to collect and dispose of both surface runoff towards the building and rainwater from the downpipes, are usually modified French drains that direct the collected water towards a discharge point (commonly a private soakaway or a public sewer). In England, there has been a fashion for backfilling perimeter drains with coarse gravel rather than capping with clay, especially if the drainage was installed specifically to deal with moisture problems. This, however, is counter-productive, since the gravel lets water run in easily, but prevents it evaporating; it also makes maintenance difficult (see **Deterioration & Damage** and **Care & Repair**).

Protection from Capillary Rise

If a wall made of permeable materials has water at its base, it will rise up the wall to the point where the rate at which water is being removed by evaporation equals the rate at which it is being drawn up through the material. This process is governed by the permeability of the wall and the speed of evaporation, which means it is affected by the ambient conditions (the temperature, humidity, and especially the air movement), the porosity of the materials and the structure of the wall (the thickness and nature of the joints between materials being particularly important).

Although some theoretical models have suggested that in a thick homogeneous wall water could rise several metres, real buildings present a very different picture. In a brick wall with lime-mortar joints, for example, moisture almost never rises higher than one or two courses, except where the wall has been given an impermeable coating such as a cement render, which prevents evaporation. Even in the laboratory, it has proved almost impossible to make realistic walls with significant rising damp.

Capillary rise

If a sample of permeable material is exposed to a continuous source of moisture at its base, water will rise up to the point where the rate of uptake equals the rate of evaporation.

Increasing the rate of evaporation (for example, by increasing the airflow across the sample) reduces the maximum height of capillary rise, whilst partially coating the sample to reduce the evaporation will make the water rise higher. Capillary rise will also be lower in a thin wall, where the greater surface area-to-volume ratio makes evaporation more effective.

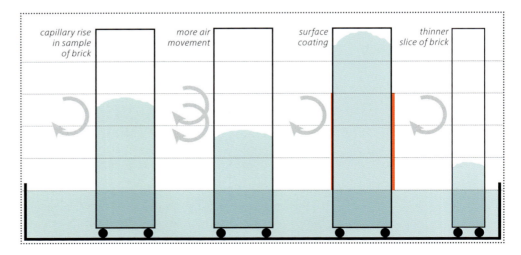

Rising damp?

The pattern of damage over the length of this run of brick masonry demonstrates why 'rising damp' – capillary rise from the water table – is unlikely to be a cause of serious moisture problems.

The classic pattern of decay and salt staining that is often attributed to rising damp is visible only on the exposed section of wall to the right, where it is clear that the true cause is water percolating down from the top of the wall. To the left, where the top of the masonry is protected, only the very base shows any sign of moisture damage, as would be expected where the source of moisture is the water table.

Serious problems from groundwater seem to have begun when sewers and mains water supplies were introduced in the mid-19th century; this was when the term 'rising damp' was invented and damp-proof coursing introduced. Leaking pipes are a much more serious source of persistent water than the water table, and the problems seem to have been exacerbated when cement renders were introduced (these prevent evaporation and so drive moisture further up the wall). Often the render will have been applied in response to a moisture problem, and thus have made the situation worse rather than better. Impermeable finishes may also make it difficult to locate the true source of the water.

One reason for the resistance of real walls to moisture rising from the base is their inherent inhomogeneity, and particularly the many interfaces between the different materials; every joint between mortar and brick will hinder the passage of water through the wall. Fundamentally, however, capillary rise is limited by evaporation, and this is far more effective in a real wall than is assumed in most theoretical models. The model most often used to calculate potential capillary rise assumes the wall to be like a bundle of fine long straws, each having a single entrance and exit. This is a reasonable analogy for water uptake in a tree, but not for building materials, where the pore structure is multi-directional and branching, with many links to surface pores through which moisture can evaporate. In practice, moisture problems from groundwater tend to occur when the wall has an impermeable finish such as a cement render that prevents the water from evaporating.

Interestingly, there is no evidence of any technology to prevent rising groundwater until the late Victorian period. The first 'damp-proof course' was a system of interlocking vitrified stoneware tiles laid through the depth of the wall a little way above ground level to deal with infiltration from poor early sewers, which tended to back up and flood cellars. This was developed and christened in 1859 by John Taylor; other builders used bituminous materials, but slate quickly became the popular choice. By the late 1870s damp-proof coursing had been incorporated into English building legislation, and although sewers and water supply systems are now much less problematic, it is still required for new build. For existing buildings, alternatives such as injected damp-proofing are sometimes used, although there is little or no evidence that these are effective (see **Deterioration & Damage**). The original cause of the problem appears to have been forgotten, and 'rising damp' has become a catch-all phrase for all moisture problems in walls, even when the water is percolating down from above.

Although the water table will not in fact be a source of problems for most types of construction, water-sensitive materials such as timber and cob will still need to be protected from ground moisture. The traditional approach has been to construct walls made primarily of these materials onto a masonry plinth made of stone or brick.

BUILDING ENVIRONMENT
INTERACTIONS WITH THE ENVIRONMENT

Below-Ground Walls (Lateral Penetration)

Subterranean rooms such as cellars can suffer from moisture travelling horizontally through the exterior walls from the ground, where it evaporates inside the room. Cellars were often used only for non-moisture-sensitive storage, but there have been many attempts to find ways of waterproofing buried walls on the exterior, to prevent groundwater entering.

There are several medieval records of waterproofing repair 'mortars' being made with water-resistant materials such as pitch, rosin and wax, and applied hot to line wells and cisterns, and to repair masonry walls with serious moisture ingress problems, although these are sparse and there are no known survivals. A material of this type was said to have been used in the 14th century on the old Westminster Palace in London, on a buttress which seems to have sat either in or very near the river, although whether it proved successful is not recorded (the buttress seems to have been repaired in this way twice, first in 1319 and again in 1340). In the 19th century, bitumen renders were used from time to time, though their lifespan was limited (being organic, bitumen will gradually break down on exposure to wet earth). By the 20th century, renders based on artificial cements had become popular for dealing with lateral penetration, which was seen as an increasingly important issue.

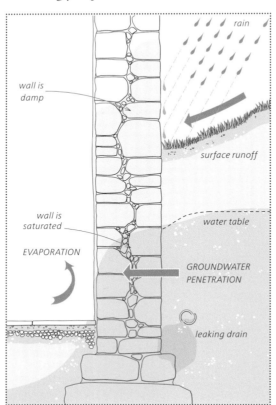

Lateral penetration

Where the level of the interior floor is below that of the ground, the wall will always have a high moisture content: as well as rain running down the walls, it will receive rain running off the ground surface, groundwater, and water from any faulty pipes or drains.

More recently, more sophisticated materials have appeared, such as vertical 'geodrains'. These are stiff sheets of corrugated plastic wrapped in a geotextile; the corrugations provide an air gap that prevents water penetration (although it is sometimes believed they are channels to divert water, or that they help drying by increasing ventilation). Geodrains must be sealed at the top to prevent rainwater entering the corrugations.

No intervention on the wall alone can entirely prevent moisture penetration in a below-ground wall, since some water will still be able to travel under the bottom edge of the barrier, and rise up through the wall and the ground from below. For this reason, where damp-proofing is required by regulation, the chosen membrane or other material must usually be continued under or through the footings, as well as through the walls.

DEALING WITH OTHER WEATHER PARAMETERS

How water interacts with the building envelope also depends heavily on other aspects of the weather, such as temperature, wind and solar radiation. Evaporation, for example, is largely driven by air movement. The structure must be able to withstand these parameters in their own right as well: it must not only provide security and keep out wind and wind-blown rain, but also buffer the exterior variations in temperature and humidity to make the interior conditions more acceptable.

The way the envelope copes with the weather depends on its materials, its structure and its exposure (the way it is orientated to the prevailing weather conditions, or protected from them by surrounding vegetation or buildings, for example).

TEMPERATURE

The characteristic speed with which a material changes bulk temperature in response to heating or cooling energy is known as its 'thermal inertia'. The thermal inertia of a material that heats or cools slowly (such as wood or stone) is high, and that of a material which changes temperature quickly (say, a metal such as copper) is low.

Radiative heating is a particular issue for materials with low thermal inertias, especially if the result is significant changes in material characteristics. For example, many materials with low thermal inertias will tend to change dimension over the course of the day, expanding as they are heated by the sun and shrinking again as they cool in the shade. Building design must take such changes into account: for example, the joints that connect metal roof sheets must permit considerable differential movement, if they are not to crack or tear at fixing points. Another material characteristic that will change with temperature is brittleness: materials that are malleable at ordinary summer temperatures may become brittle in the winter.

Heat Exchange Through the Envelope

The other aspect of the thermal inertia of the building fabric is the effect this has on heat exchange through the envelope. Traditional building systems and materials with high thermal inertias (such as timber or thick solid brick masonry) will transfer heat from the exterior to the interior, or vice-versa, much more slowly than materials such as metal and glass. Building elements that (due to their material, design and position) can cause heat to travel between the interior and exterior are known as 'thermal bridges', and they can have a significant effect on the way the envelope as a whole behaves.

Windows

Glass windows can easily become thermal bridges, but are such useful parts of the building envelope that, over the history of building technology, there have been many methods introduced to improve their resistance to heat transfer. Until the second half of the 20th century, they were commonly equipped with wooden shutters, or blinds and thick curtains, which could be drawn across the glass to prevent heat exchange whenever it was not absolutely necessary to allow light in or to see out.

As glass became cheaper, 'secondary glazing' (a second complete window set into the same frame) was introduced, and this remains a very effective way of reducing heat transfer – especially heat loss from the interior to the exterior – whilst maintaining transparency. For most buildings the secondary glazing is set on the inside of the original window, but for churches (where the additional window is principally intended to protect stained glass from rain, sunlight and vandalism) it is usually placed on the exterior.

Early secondary glazing in houses often took the form of a second sash window, which (like sash shutters) sometimes slid into pockets below or to the side of the window, but casement-style secondary glazing is also found, especially in colder regions. Most modern versions have frames made of metal (usually aluminium), and are either fixed, hinged or sliding casements. Some types are designed to be entirely removed during summer. ⊖GLASS

More recently, it has become popular to replace window glass or the glass in curtain-wall panels with Insulated Glazing Units, or IGUs (commonly called 'double glazing', although IGUs may in fact be triple-glazed). These are sandwiched panels of glass spaced apart in a frame; the voids between the panes are either evacuated, or filled with a dehydrated air or some other gas intended to reduce heat transfer.

Approaches to secondary glazing

Secondary glazing has a history as long as the use of glass in windows, and is used to cut noise penetration as well as reduce heat loss.

Traditional systems were simply second sliding or casement windows set into the same embrasure, usually timber-framed, which could be opened and shut in the same manner (*top and middle*).

Later systems have tended to use horizontal sliding sashes set in metal frames (*bottom*), or demountable systems which can be removed and stored in summer.

Thermal bridges

To keep the interior temperature from being too strongly affected by the exterior conditions, building frames must not be able to transfer heat between the interior and exterior. Common weak points include balconies supported on cantilevered parts of the frame, as shown here in thermal images taken of a recent construction in Chicago.

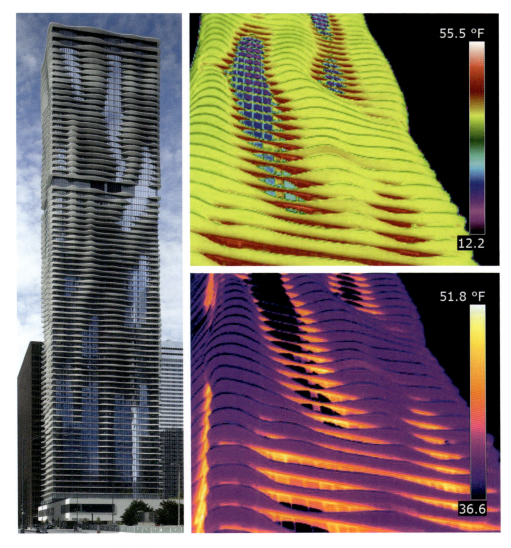

Other Thermal Bridges

Thermal bridging is a serious issue for much modern construction, which uses large quantities of metals and glass, and other materials with low thermal inertias. For example, in winter, a wind-cooled steel-framed balcony connected to the steel frame of a curtain-wall building will draw heat from the interior; in summer, it will transfer solar heat to the interior.

Modern structures often incorporate sophisticated 'thermal breaks' to try to prevent bridging. These cut the links between building elements on the interior and exterior by introducing an insulating material in-between them. ⊝GLASS

BUILDING ENVIRONMENT
INTERACTIONS WITH THE ENVIRONMENT

Effect of Temperature on Wet Materials

Temperature is also very important for permeable materials or building systems that might hold moisture, and the designs of building envelopes must address local weather extremes if they are to be successful. For example, changes in temperature that alter moisture contents may change the dimensions of permeable materials such as timber, and radiative heating can cause large changes in vapour pressure that can drive moisture through building systems. This is a particularly important consideration for the design of hollow-wall construction systems.

Freeze-thaw damage is another potential hazard of exterior temperatures. This can cause the rapid breakdown of wet permeable materials, so great precautions must be taken by the builder to ensure that any element at risk of saturation (such as a hood moulding over a door or window) is designed so that as little water as possible can collect. In particular, there should be no place that rainwater can pool, or wick into a joint.

Freeze-thaw damage to stone

Freeze-thaw damage is not well understood; the freezing point depends on the size of the pore, so in a real material with multiple pore sizes there should always be spaces into which the water can move as it freezes. The essential cause may be a build up of air pressure in the pores.

Whatever the exact mechanism, it is known that freeze-thaw damage occurs only in materials that have a very high water content, such as poorly fired bricks exposed to rain, or (as here) stone that is in contact with a source of liquid water.

Coping with Ice & Snow

In climates cold enough for water to freeze, building envelopes must be designed to cope with numerous additional dangers.

Structures may need to be able to support heavy loads of snow, with detailing to prevent the snow avalanching from roofs or melting and forming ice dams. Even in less extreme conditions, problems will occur if water freezes, since this increases its volume and may damage the surrounding materials. Building systems must be therefore designed to trap as little water as possible, either in the materials themselves or in the joints between them.

If a warm roof is covered in snow, the underside will melt, causing the snow cover to slide down the roof. Snow falling from a roof is easily heavy enough to damage the gutters and eaves, and any roofs below; or for that matter, any passers-by. In snowy areas, roofs often have hooks or 'snow boards' to keep the snow in place.

Melting snow and ice are not otherwise a great problem for steeply pitched roofs, but they can cause numerous problems for flatter roofs. The centres of roof bays may begin to bow under the weight of snow, causing an uneven distribution that makes the problem steadily worse. If this happens, when the snow melts it will not be able to drain away (most drains are located at the supports, and so will be higher than the bay centres). As the snow melts, the roof may begin to leak.

Snow can build up on a roof until the weight becomes a problem. Loads can be hard to predict, because the characteristics of the snow can vary so much (it can be dry and powdery, or wet and sticky).

Top: The cover of snow on a roof is rarely even, since it depends on the wind and the roof structure; moreover, wind-speed higher than about 20 km/h will cause 'drift' (the movement of fallen snow). Drifted snow will often accumulate in the valleys, and on the downwind side of pitched and arched roofs.

Bottom: Snow sliding off a roof can be very dangerous, and in areas where heavy snowfall is common roofs are usually equipped with hooks or (as here) with snowguards to keep the snow in place.

BUILDING ENVIRONMENT
INTERACTIONS WITH THE ENVIRONMENT

ICE DAMS

Snow is an excellent insulator, but transmits solar radiant heat energy easily, and the result is that snow-covered roofs will warm up, even if they are well insulated from the interior. Meltwater runs down under the snow, and then freezes at the colder gutters and overhanging eaves, chilled by the wind; moreover, the soffits are in the shade (and so are not heated by the sun). In modern construction, heating can also be caused by thermal plumes rising from cladding. The resulting icicles and 'ice dams' often lead to roof leakages, and are a common cause of damage to gutters and the edges of roofs when snow is able to stay on the roof for prolonged spells.

To avoid these problems, roofs in snowy climates must be kept below freezing when the outside temperature drops below zero. Heat from the interior must therefore be stopped from reaching the roof covering, by making ceilings airtight and well-insulated, and avoiding placing heat-producing equipment and ducting in the attic space; if thermal plumes are a problem, overhangs must be insulated. Most importantly, the underside of the roof must be very well ventilated. One common traditional solution was to have a double roof, with the lower roof sealed, and the upper roof left open on all sides so that it would be washed by the cold air; this is still recommended practice. ⊃ROOFING

If snow is able to remain on roofs for a prolonged period, ice dams will be a common sight, occurring wherever the roof is inadequately ventilated: especially where the ceiling is poorly air-sealed or poorly insulated as well, or where heat-producing equipment such as a hot-water tank has been located in the roof space.

WIND

The wind impacts on building envelopes in a number of different ways. It will drive rain against the fabric, but will also be the major agent of evaporative drying and cooling (and thus one of the most important factors governing the movement of moisture through the building materials and systems).

Wind produces a positive (compressive) load where it meets the envelope on the windward face, but a negative suction (tensile) load elsewhere. This simple basic pattern is complicated by turbulence, which is the result not only of the landscape that surrounds the building, but of the building itself. For example, the pressure on roofs with low pitches tends to be negative, causing uplift, especially on the leading edge, whereas roofs with pitches steeper than about 25° tend to have positive pressures on the windward face, and suction pressures on the leeward. Wind loading is a particularly important consideration for tall buildings, especially those of curtain-wall construction.

Wind is also the principal factor driving the exchange of air between the building interior and the exterior. Air is also exchanged through the building envelope because of buoyancy (warmer air is less dense, and will tend to rise: this is known as the 'stack effect'). In practice, the exchange of interior and exterior air is the result of the complex interactions between wind pressure, building design and buoyancy. For example, the 'drawing' of a chimney is driven by the pressure difference between the bottom and top of the flue, which is governed partly by the chimney's height, partly by the heating of the air by the fire, and partly by the wind across the top of the flue.

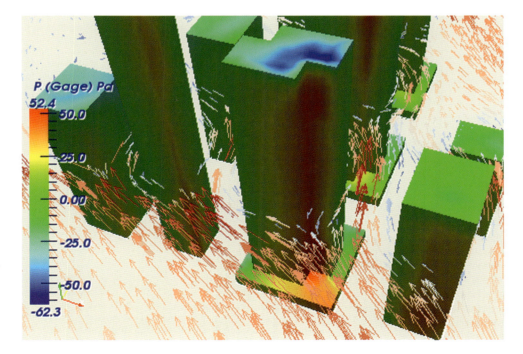

Wind loading can be extremely complex and variable, and is difficult to predict even using sophisticated modelling systems or experiments in wind tunnels.

Conditions will change with a change of wind direction, and may be permanently altered by alterations in the surrounding topography, including the construction of other buildings nearby.

BUILDING ENVIRONMENT
INTERACTIONS WITH THE ENVIRONMENT

Stack Effect

The 'stack effect' is driven largely by buoyancy: hot air rises through the upper floors and out through the roof, which draws exterior air in through windows and other gaps in the envelope on the lower floors. Where the exterior air pressure is greater than the interior air pressure, air will be drawn into the building; where the pressure is greater in the interior, indoor air will be drawn outwards.

The strength of the stack effect depends largely on the temperature difference between the exterior and interior air, together with the strength and direction of the wind. At some height (the 'neutral pressure point' [NPP]) the internal and external air pressures will be equal, so below this point the air will be drawn in from the exterior; above, it will be drawn outwards.

For a building of only two or three storeys, the NPP may be well above the roof line; even so, the stack effect can be an important driver of internal airflow, especially in winter in cold climates, where heating may create temperature differences as great as 25°C. In summer the indoor air may be cooler than the exterior, so flow would be in the opposite direction, but the temperature difference is likely to be much smaller and the stack effect ventilation much weaker.

For very tall buildings, the stack effect may well mean that air flows in opposite directions on different floors. Below the NPP, the exterior air will be drawn in; above the NPP, the interior air will tend to be drawn outwards. On those floors around the height of the NPP, airflow may reverse whenever weather conditions change.

The other pertinent factor governing the impact of the stack effect is the design of the building, especially the location of openings and vents. If the floors are leakier than the walls, the NPP will be lower; where the upper floors are leakier than the lower floors, it will be higher. Chimneys, leaky ceilings and fans can therefore easily bring the NPP down close to ceiling level, making air exchange in the roof space hard to predict.

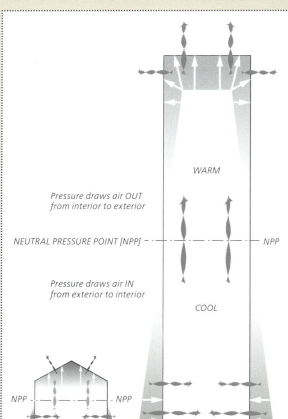

The direction in which air travels between the building interior and exterior as a result of the stack effect depends on the height of the neutral pressure point [NPP], at which the internal and external pressures are equal. The NPP will in turn depend on the construction of the building and on its exposure; it will change with changes in weather conditions.

INTERIOR PARTS OF THE ENVELOPE

The internal structure of the building is also a critical part of the envelope. Buildings are almost never simple single-roomed boxes, but are usually divided into smaller spaces (often having different uses) by partition walls, floors and ceilings. These dividers can interact with the exterior parts of the envelope in complex ways; for example, in a steel-framed curtain-wall building without thermal breaks, the steel supports of the floors may be significant thermal bridges.

For many buildings, too, the division between interior and exterior can be quite ambiguous. Verandas, draught lobbies, vented attics and subfloor spaces, for example, all combine elements of both the exterior and the interior environments, and can interact with both.

Internal partitions

A ruined building shows the traces of plaster (here and there protected with lead flashing) that indicate how the interior of the envelope was once partitioned with walls and floors. In general, the central dividing walls were load-bearing, and helped to carry the floor and ceiling joists, and the landings of the staircases.

Another important aspect of internal partitions, whether or not they are load-bearing, is the role they play in preventing the spread of fire. In most modern buildings, and increasingly for many older buildings as well, fire-safety requirements have a critical impact on how the internal divisions (including doors and stairs) are detailed, and how air is allowed to flow through the interior spaces.

BUILDING ENVIRONMENT
INTERACTIONS WITH THE ENVIRONMENT

INTERNAL STRUCTURES

GROUND FLOORS

The floor that rests on or just above the ground is one of the most important interior parts of the envelope, since it connects the interior spaces with the ground (which is essentially part of the exterior). A 'ground floor' can have a significant impact on the interior environment of a room, that depends not only on its material and construction, but on whether it is suspended or placed directly against the earth. In the latter case, the floor will tend to be damp, both from rising groundwater and from condensation developing on the cold surface.

Finishes for Ground Floors

The earliest ground floors were probably simply the existing earth rammed down hard, a system that was later improved by laying down a layer of selected earth, clay or chalk (or some similar locally available material) either directly onto the ground, or else onto sand or clay rammed to form a solid layer 50–100-mm thick. These types of earthen floors continued to be used until the beginning of the 20th century, although by this time they were to be found only in basements, kitchens and outhouses. From the 16th century to the Victorian period, lime-plaster floors were popular, the plaster being laid onto the earth. 'Lime-ash' floors, as their name suggests, were made of layers of lime and ash and also laid directly on to the ground. ➔MORTARS

From the medieval period until the early 19th century, floors in grander houses were more usually covered with plain stone flags or tiles of fired clay.

The ground temperature under and next to the building will be very close to annual average air temperature, but solid floors absorb radiant heat from the building users, and so feel cold. Chills are also a problem with draughty timber suspended floors, although the draught keeps the timber in good condition.

In both cases, the traditional solution was to cover the floors with rushes and herbs, or with mats and carpets, as shown here in Plas Mawr town house in Conwy, North Wales.

Air bricks

Air bricks could function quite well if a timber floor was fairly leaky, and was not covered by too much in the way of carpets or furniture, since the draught pulled air through the bricks. Otherwise it was difficult to obtain a flow of air sufficient to keep the timber dry. The air bricks could themselves be an excellent conduit for insects and, if set too low in the wall, for floodwater, and so sometimes exacerbated decay problems rather than solving them.

By the early 18th century, new methods of floor construction appeared. 'Strip foundations' provided the frame between which timber floor structures could be suspended (sometimes with 'chamber' walls as extra support). Floorboards were also sometimes laid on timber joists that rested directly on the ground. These approaches were not consistent, even in a single building. A Victorian house may be found to have mostly solid floors, but timber floors over deep voids in just one or two of the rooms: typically the dining and drawing rooms, which suggests that the underlying intention was to provide a relatively warm floor. Deep voids under suspended floors may also sometimes be a way of building on a sloping site.

If moisture builds up under a suspended floor, the joists can begin to decay, causing unpleasant smells in the room and eventually leading to structural damage. It is probably for this reason that, in the later 19th century, 'air bricks' began to be retrofitted into outer walls underneath suspended ground floors to try to ventilate wet spaces. Since it is difficult to ventilate through air bricks unless conditions are ideal, air bricks did not always work, but eventually they became a standard part of new construction (see **Care & Repair: Cavity Ventilation**).

Between the two World Wars all these types of flooring were largely replaced by concrete, usually (but not always) incorporating a damp-proof membrane. Many new concrete floors now incorporate embedded heating (see **Conditioning the Indoor Environment**).

BASEMENTS

Subterranean rooms (crypts, cellars and basements) of traditional buildings were often not used as habitable space, but for storing materials resistant to moisture and cold.

Where basement rooms were excavated so that the ground directly abutted the exterior walls, the walls would be intractably wet with water travelling through from the exterior. One effective solution to this was to dig the earth away, making a narrow trench through which water could not pass. Trenches were sometimes covered with grilles, or with tiles or flags to prevent debris from collecting in the gap.

Where space permitted, a more flexible solution was to make a wide 'area'. Georgian and Victorian townhouses commonly included full-height basements with windows, used for service rooms, and having a separate service entrance. Steps over the area were used to connect the pavement to the front door and the principal rooms, which were found on the 'raised ground' floor and first floor, rather than the true ground floor.

BUILDING ENVIRONMENT
INTERACTIONS WITH THE ENVIRONMENT

UPPER FLOORS

Until the 20th century, upper floors in buildings were made either of wooden boarding on timber joists, or of gypsum supported on reeds or laths laid above the joists. Timber joists are still common for houses, covered sometimes with timber but more commonly with composite panels, and finished with parquet or carpet. For large commercial buildings, reinforced-concrete floors are now typical.

To cut down sound from the rooms above and the transmission of odours through the building, intermediate timber floors were sometimes 'pugged'. 'Pugging boards' were laid in the spaces between the joists, and the cavities were filled with some material that provided sound insulation (usually a lime mortar). ⊖MORTARS ⊖TIMBER

PARTITION WALLS

Partition walls separate the internal spaces from one another; they are generally of much lighter construction than external walls (often traditional lath and plaster), and if the environments they separate are very different, they may be able to transfer a great deal of heat and moisture. Wall coverings add another level of complexity to the way moisture and heat transfer. This is particularly important for materials that significantly impede heat or moisture movement, such as modern impermeable paints and vinyl wallpapers.

CEILINGS

Very early buildings were basically single spaces heated with open fires, and rarely had ceilings; instead, the smoke was allowed to seep through the roof (the timbers and thatch of buildings of this date are sometimes smoke-blackened). The introduction of fireplaces and chimneys allowed the construction of multilevel buildings, and ceilings and upper-level floors began to be introduced, constructed from timber boards or lath-and-plaster attached to the joists. Ceilings had numerous advantages, most notably that they reduced heat loss through the roof and provided an attic space for storage. Another important benefit was the exclusion of dirt and dust; in particular, birds or bats roosting in the rafters caused much less nuisance.

By the 16th century, decorative plaster ceilings had become fashionable for larger houses, but from the 20th century onwards ceilings began to be made from plasterboard, in many cases sealed and insulated to prevent heat loss, and air and moisture transfer. The most recent important change in structure has been the introduction of recessed lighting and other services that puncture the ceiling.

ATTICS

Traditionally, the space under a pitched roof was often inaccessible, although in larger houses it was used for storage. It was cold, and although rain would sometimes penetrate, a high rate of air exchange made for quick evaporation. If the roof and rainwater goods were in good condition, the space remained dry. In the 20th century, it became popular to convert attics into habitable space, which has had an enormous effect on the structure and behaviour of the building envelope.

HOW THE ENVELOPE MODIFIES THE INTERIOR CONDITIONS

103

The exterior environment is constantly changing and will on occasions be extreme, with seasonal, daily and even hourly variations in temperature and humidity, as well as rain and wind. The building envelope modifies these changes so that the interior conditions are less extreme and less variable, not only by physically preventing the ingress of rain and wind, but by limiting the exchange of air between the interior and exterior, by buffering the changes in temperature and humidity, and by reducing air movement (which drives evaporation).

Since the resulting interior conditions are characteristic of the fabric and construction, as well as its condition, they will not be the same at all points within the building, or at all times, or at all seasons.

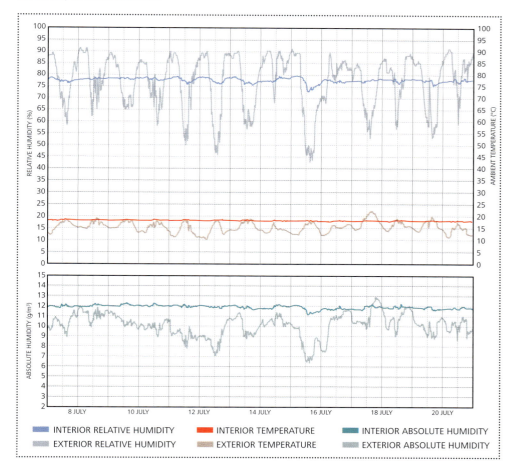

Buffering

In St Gabriel's Chapel, in the crypt of Canterbury Cathedral, the extremes of the exterior climate – the relative humidity, temperature and absolute humidity – are greatly modified by the building envelope.

BUILDING ENVIRONMENT
INTERACTIONS WITH THE ENVIRONMENT

BUFFERING

Buffering is one of the most important functions of the building envelope. The building fabric modifies the fluctuations in the exterior conditions in several important ways:

- limiting air exchange
- storing heat when the weather is hot or when solar radiation levels are high, and emitting it again when exterior temperatures drop
- absorbing water vapour when the exterior relative humidity is high, and emitting it again when conditions become drier.

The use of permeable materials and mass construction in traditional building make it particularly efficient at buffering.

REDUCING AIR EXCHANGE

Because so much heat energy and water vapour is carried by the external air, the degree to which that air is able to enter the building (and how much the internal air is able to leave) is critical to how much the interior conditions differ from those in the exterior.

In the past, buildings generally allowed a fair amount of air exchange, particularly through windows, fireplaces and roofs, though exterior walls tended to be massive with little air leakage, and air movement in the interior was often restricted by internal partition walls and floors.

Air is exchanged between interior and exterior through openings in the building envelope, such as chimneys and windows.

Modern buildings – or traditional buildings adapted to modern standards – are usually designed to be airtight (although they do lack many of the older systems of draughtproofing, such as heavy door curtains and shutters). This airtightness is intended to prevent the escape of artificial heating or cooling energy, but it does increase the risk of high internal moisture contents. Modernised buildings may be 'open plan', with relatively few internal divisions to prevent air exchange between interior spaces such as kitchens and living areas.

BUFFERING THE EXTERIOR TEMPERATURE

As the exterior air and the building envelope come into thermal equilibrium, the fabric will be heated or cooled in response to the difference between its own temperature and the temperature of the air. Since the fabric has a much greater thermal inertia than the air, it will change temperature much more slowly, and this alone smooths out the temperature variations so that the interior climate is more stable than the exterior.

The exchange of heat between the exterior air and the fabric involves every form of transfer:

- *Conduction and convection*

  Conduction transfers heat between the fabric and the exterior air, and the resultant warming or cooling is governed by convection. Air movement will also drive evaporative cooling. Thermal exchange depends not only on the thermal inertia of the individual materials, but also on the building's 'thermal mass' (that is, the thermal inertia of the entire structure). Voids in the roof space or the walls that let in air can rapidly cool the fabric, but trapped air is an excellent insulator. A thatched roof, for example, is made up not only of the straw itself, but also the air trapped within and between the individual straws, and so thatch can keep a building warm in winter and cool in summer.

- *Radiation*

  Sunlight heats the fabric directly, and the fabric radiates some of this heat back into the environment to a degree governed by its 'emissivity'; this depends on the type of material, and especially on its surface texture and reflectivity. For example, in hot climates, roofs are often made of reflective materials or painted in light colours, since this keeps the interior cooler. Radiative transfer also greatly affects how the building conditions feel to the occupants. For example, a large window will make occupants feel overheated if the sun is shining on the glass, and chilled at night or when the wind is blowing, even though the indoor air temperature has remained more or less constant. A stone masonry wall will conduct little or no heat between exterior and interior, but radiative heat loss from the body into the mass of the stone will make occupants feel colder.

Thermal buffering will depend on the materials and structure of the envelope, but also on its condition, particularly whether or not the permeable fabric is wet: wet walls will transfer heat very effectively no matter how thick they are, especially if exterior wind movement is driving evaporative cooling. Another important consideration is whether the envelope includes any significant 'thermal bridges' (elements made of materials with low thermal inertias that transfer heat easily, such as metal or glass, and which connect the exterior to the interior: metal window frames, for example). Thermal bridging not only interferes with buffering, but creates local cold spots on the interior, which will be prone to condensation and other problems.

Windows are a weak point in any structure, not only having a low thermal mass (especially when they had metal frames), but also tending to transfer radiant heat. A glass window in sunlight, for example, may heat a room during the day via radiative transfer, and then cool it at night by transferring room heat outwards. When glass was expensive, windows were generally small, and to prevent heat exchange were usually protected with internal and external shutters and blinds.

Traditional buildings usually provide good thermal buffering, since both the materials and the construction have a great deal of thermal mass. Metal and glass were used sparingly, and serious thermal bridges were therefore uncommon. Radiative transfer into massive walls and floors was reduced with wall and floor coverings of timber or fabric (panelling, tapestries and carpets).

By contrast, materials with low thermal inertias are critical to modern architecture. In response, engineers have been forced to develop sophisticated ways of increasing thermal mass, such as thermal breaks, multilayered insulation systems for walls and IGUs [Insulated Glazing Units] to replace single sheets of glass in windows and curtain walls. Glass may also be covered with plastic filters to reduce radiative uptake.

Thermal buffering

Like many medieval churches, St Botolph's, at Hardham in Sussex, has massive masonry walls. These have an extremely high thermal inertia and are therefore excellent temperature buffers. During the day, their external surfaces are warmed by the sun and the air; this heat transfers through the wall slowly, so that by evening – when the exterior conditions have begun to cool – the interior will still be warming. If the building is not heated, maximum interior temperatures will be reached well after the hottest part of the day, and although the interior will always be cooler than the exterior maxima, it will also stay warmer than the coldest exterior conditions. In other words, the interior temperatures will be both more stable and less extreme than the exterior.

In a building of this type, thermal buffering is enhanced by the small amount of surface area taken up by windows and other components of low thermal inertia.

If such a building is heated or cooled, buffering will reduce the amount of energy that must be used to achieve the desired temperatures.

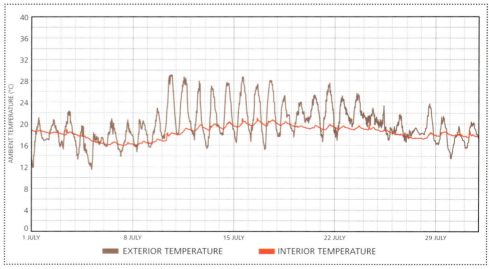

BUFFERING THE EXTERIOR HUMIDITY

The primary mechanism for humidity buffering is air exchange: buildings that are very 'leaky' tend to have internal relative humidities that closely follow those of the exterior air. The secondary mechanism is permeable materials absorbing and releasing water vapour in response to changing relative humidities. If the interior vapour pressure is constant, the fabric and the interior air will be at equilibrium, but if the vapour pressure of the air changes, then hygroscopic materials such as brick, stone, lime plaster and especially timber will respond by either taking up or giving up moisture until a new equilibrium is reached.

Every permeable building material will have its own characteristic hygroscopicity, taking up moisture from the air in a way that depends on (amongst other factors) the structure of its pore system and the presence of contaminants such as salts. Moisture absorption and desorption depends on the ambient conditions: for example, plotting a hygroscopic material's moisture content against changing ambient relative humidity generates a characteristic curve, showing the 'equilibrium relative humidity' of the material.

Some degree of existing moisture is important to the material's buffering capacity, since very dry materials absorb moisture much less effectively (just as a sponge will not absorb water when dry, but becomes very absorbent indeed once slightly wetted: the reasons for this are discussed in **Building Science**). It has been shown experimentally that an oven-dried lime plaster will absorb very little water vapour from the air, but after several months or years of exposure, even plaster in perfect condition will be holding some moisture in its pores, and will therefore be an excellent buffer. Materials such as timber will usually be holding significant amounts of moisture (as much as 15 % by weight for wood in good condition), and this acts as a sink of water when, say, a temperature increase causes the ambient relative humidity to drop. It also helps the wood to take up water vapour when the humidity rises again (that is, when the temperature drops, or wetter air enters the building).

The envelope will also have its own characteristic 'hygric mass': the way it buffers humidity will depend not only on the permeability of single materials, but on the behaviour of complex groups of materials. Discontinuities, interfaces, joints, surface finishes and coatings may all have a significant impact. For example, moisture-resistant coatings such as vinyl paints will hinder evaporation much more than they hinder moisture uptake, so painted plaster may steadily become wetter (see **Building Science**).

The average absolute humidity in the interior will be steadier, but typically slightly higher, than the exterior.

All parts of the building can contribute to the humidity buffering, including the interior and the contents such as timber furniture. The floor is one of the largest surfaces for moisture exchange; traditional solid floors, which do not incorporate damp-proof membranes but are bedded directly onto the earth or onto a permeable lime-based mortar, can account for more than half the moisture content of the fabric. So long as there is plentiful air movement and air exchange this does not damage the building, and indeed it prevents groundwater being driven up the walls.

BUILDING ENVIRONMENT
INTERACTIONS WITH THE ENVIRONMENT

Air movement and air exchange both tend to encourage evaporation, helping the ambient air pick up moisture from the fabric under all conditions. Humidity buffering is considerably more effective in traditional buildings, where permeable materials make up much of the envelope.

Humidity buffering

In most buildings, the primary influence on the interior relative humidity is the exterior weather. The rapid fluctuations and wide-ranging humidities characteristic of the exterior are modified in the interior by two principal factors: the degree to which the envelope prevents the air exchange; and the hygroscopicity of the materials within the space.

Although it is most common to compare interior and exterior relative humidities, in buildings where temperature is not rigidly controlled it is more revealing to look at the absolute humidities, which reveal differences that are masked by the variations in temperature.

Top: Buffering by limiting air exchange: comparing the absolute humidity of the exterior with that of the interior shows the excellent humidity buffering within St Gabriel's Chapel, in the crypt of Canterbury Cathedral. This is the pattern to be expected of any space with thick solid walls and small windows, where very little air is being exchanged with the exterior.

Bottom: Buffering by hygroscopicity: the cathedral's archive store in the south-west porch has thick stone walls, but it also has a roof that is far from airtight. Here the temperature is steady, but the absolute humidity changes rapidly in response to the exterior. Even so, the degree of change is modified by the moisture absorption and desorption from the stone and structural timber, and the papers, wood and other hygroscopic materials in the store.

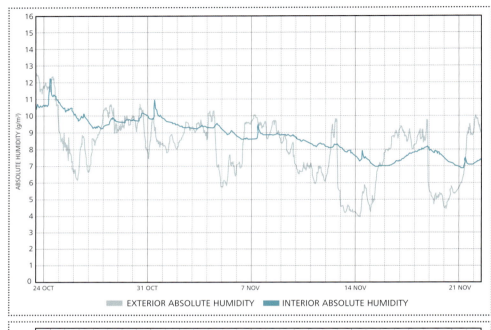

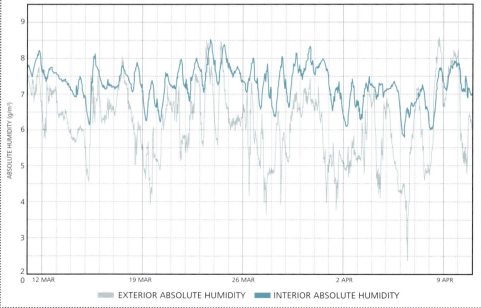

THE EFFECT OF BUILDING OCCUPATION

As well as causing general wear and tear, building use alters the internal environment. For example, simply by exhaling and perspiring, each occupant adds some 50 g of water to the air every hour. People also bring in moisture from other sources – for example, on wet coats and umbrellas – as well as via the tasks they undertake in the building, such as cooking and cleaning.

Superimposed on these sources are the changes caused by systems intended to make internal conditions suitable for use. This includes not only heating and cooling, but services such as plumbing and lighting. In the past there were few of these, but most buildings are now connected to public supplies of water, gas and electricity. Partly as a result, the envelope must now cope with many more functions which can affect the environment – laundering as well as washing and cooking, for example – being undertaken indoors. Running any services into the building structure will have significant implications for the envelope, especially for very 'low-carbon' buildings which attempt to be completely airtight.

The use of the building greatly affects the interior conditions, otherwise set by the way the fabric buffers the exterior conditions.

As well as the changes to humidity and temperature due to the building occupants themselves, and the services they introduce, fittings and furnishings can dramatically alter air-flow patterns and evaporation. Materials such as wood, cloth and paper will all contribute significantly to humidity buffering.

BUILDING ENVIRONMENT
INTERACTIONS WITH THE ENVIRONMENT

The Building Interior & Contents

The building contents – that is, those temporary and permanent parts of the interior that do not form part of the basic envelope – can have a significant impact on the interior environment.

The ways in which contents interact with the interior conditions are complex and often very interesting. First and foremost, the furniture and fittings may alter the transfer of moisture through the envelope. To give some common examples:

- wallpapers and paints will affect evaporation from the wall surfaces; in the worst case this can lead to condensation problems and mould growth
- the position of furniture will affect the flow of air through the space; in the worst case, this too may lead to stagnant areas and problems of mould growth
- impermeable floor coverings (such as carpet underlays), or even large items of furniture, can prevent air passing through floors of timber and other permeable materials; by limiting evaporative drying this can lead to localised decay if there is sufficient moisture from a leak or from condensation
- cleaning regimes that involve significant quantities of water can be a source of deterioration.

In addition, many materials are permeable, acting as a source and sink for moisture, and thus buffering the changes in ambient humidity that would otherwise occur when the indoor air temperature fluctuates (perhaps because the building is heated).

As well as their direct effect on the buffering of exterior conditions, and the impact on air movement, contents have an indirect effect on the environment, which may well be artificially adjusted to suit their preservation.

The care of building contents is a special subject, and well beyond the remit of this book, but it can be useful to consider certain traditional care regimes for what they can tell us about the way past occupants used their buildings, and by implication what they expected their interior environments to be like. For example, until the Victorian period, English houses were usually rather sparsely furnished, and the furniture was often quite simple. Seating was mostly in the form of benches and chests ranged against walls, together with three-legged stools that could be taken from room to room as required. Because bedrooms were commonly cold, modest homes sometimes had beds set into cupboards, with doors that could be closed if necessary; ventilation was provided by panels of fretwork or spindles. Wealthier households had four-poster beds with curtains that could be drawn to keep in the warmth.

Heavy curtains, wall tapestries and carpets were also invaluable for keeping living rooms comfortable in winter. These were often taken down and stored over summer, when they were both less useful and at greater risk of damage from humidity. Sometimes there were seasonal alternatives, such as light summer curtains that helped reduce light penetration, but did not affect heat transfer.

Close control of temperature and humidity

Close control with heating or air-conditioning can constrain conditions to fairly tight bands, but this is at the cost of stability. The feedback systems controlling the conditioning will cause the temperature and humidity to fluctuate rapidly.

Here, graphs of interior and exterior temperature, and relative humidity, in the same church before and after the installation of a humidistat-controlled heating system show this effect. The strong drops in humidity associated with occasional heating have been largely removed, but otherwise the conditions are in fact more variable with close control than without.

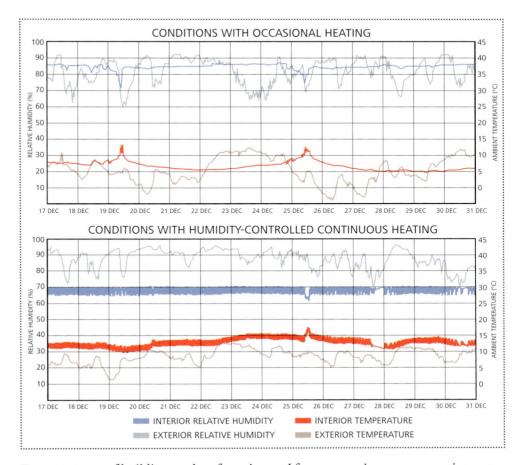

For some types of building, such as factories used for very precise processes, strict boundaries may need to be set for the interior conditions; and controls are increasingly common for other types of building as well. This is always challenging, since it effectively means fighting against the natural behaviour of the building. As many links as possible between the interior and exterior environments must be broken by drastically cutting natural ventilation, and increasing the thermal buffering (for example, heavily insulating the walls and roof, or even creating a room-within-a-room to ensure that there are no exterior walls at all). Moisture buffering often proves especially difficult, especially if the use of the space is adding moisture. Mechanical ventilating and conditioning systems may be an option, but while these can deliver conditions that are held within a tight range, they do this by causing rapid small fluctuations in temperature and humidity, and condensation often remains a serious problem.

The ways building users may attempt to control the interior conditions, and the effect this has on the building environment, are discussed in detail in the next chapter.

BUILDING ENVIRONMENT
INTERACTIONS WITH THE ENVIRONMENT

Further Reading

British Standards Institution (2000); *BS EN 12056–3:2000 Gravity drainage systems inside buildings. Roof drainage, layout and calculation*; London: BSI

British Standards Institution (2002); *BS460:2002+A2:2007 Cast iron rainwater goods. Specification*; London: BSI

British Standards Institution (2007); *BS8490:2007 Guide to siphonic roof drainage systems*; London: BSI

British Standards Institution (2008); *BS EN 752:2008 Drain and sewer systems outside buildings*; London: BSI

Brunskill, R. W. (2000); *Vernacular Architecture: An Illustrated Handbook (4th Edition)*; London: Faber

Clifton-Taylor, A., Simmins, J. (eds) (1987); *The Pattern of English Building (4th Edition)*; London: Faber

Grant, N., Moodie, M. (2001); *Waste Water from Churches*; Report commissioned from Elemental Solutions for the Gloucester DAC; available at www.gloucester.anglican.org/content/pages/documents/1352755360.pdf

Hawkes, D. (2012); *Architecture and Climate: An Environmental History of British Architecture 1600–2000*; London & New York: Routledge

Lstiburek, J. W., Carmody, J. (1993); *Moisture Control Handbook: Principles and Practices for Residential and Small Commercial Buildings*; New York: Van Nostrand Reinhold

National Trust (2006); *Manual of Housekeeping: The Care of Collections in Historic Houses Open to the Public*; London: Elsevier Butterworth Heinemann

Office of the Deputy Prime Minister (2002); *Part H: Drainage and Waste Disposal*; Approved Document of the Building Regulations 2000; available at www.planningportal.gov.uk/uploads/br/BR_PDF_ADH_2002.pdf

Oliver, P. (2007); *Dwellings: The Vernacular House Worldwide*; London: Phaidon

Penoyre, J., Penoyre, J. (1978); *Houses in the Landscape: Regional Study of Vernacular Building Styles in England and Wales*; London: Faber

Peters, R. J., Smith, B. J., Hollins, M. (2011); *Acoustics and Noise Control (3rd Edition)*; New Jersey: Prentice Hall

Torraca, G. (2009); *Lectures on Materials Science for Architectural Conservation*; Los Angeles: Getty Conservation Institute; also available at www.getty.edu/conservation/publications_resources/pdf_publications/materials_science_architectural_conserv.html

Weber, W., Yannas, S. (2014); *Lessons from Vernacular Architecture: Achieving Climatic Buildings by Studying the Past*; Abingdon, Oxon: Routledge Earthscan

Useful Websites

English Heritage: www.english-heritage.org.uk

The Environment Agency: www.environment-agency.gov.uk

The Building Science Corporation produces a wide range of useful free publications covering all aspects of the building environment and building design, including *Building Science Insights* and *Building Science Digests*: www.buildingscience.com

CONTROLLING THE INTERIOR ENVIRONMENT

This chapter looks at some of the many ways building users attempt to alter the 'natural' interior conditions to make their building more comfortable or utilitarian. The idea of what constitutes an acceptable building environment has changed dramatically since the Industrial Revolution, first as new materials and technology made it possible to design much more elaborate building services, and then as expectations of comfort and ease of use increased.

Even in the best-buffered buildings with the thickest walls and the best-insulated roofs, it is often necessary to artificially intervene to improve the interior microclimate, not only for the comfort and health of users, but for the safe storage of their belongings. The extent and type of artificial control depends largely on the type of building and its use: barns and other storage structures generally have simple passive systems, and houses and working spaces the most complex and energy-intensive systems.

For occupied buildings, the level of control also depends on the user's definition of 'comfort', which is apt to depend on circumstances, personal tastes and, to some extent, fashion. Over the course of the 20th century, comfort came to be seen as a technical issue to be solved by interventions on the building fabric, with central services such as central heating, cooling, humidification and forced ventilation becoming increasingly common. These services, and others such as plumbing and electrical wiring, have effects on the interior environment that are superimposed on the conditions created by the way the envelope buffers the exterior conditions. The resulting microclimate is likely to be very complex, not least because the various components will not be independent of each other.

ENVIRONMENTS FOR USERS

In the cold and dark northern countries, the simplest and earliest modifications to building environments were improved heating, lighting and ventilation. Open hearths were installed to warm the interior during winter, and to enable cooking indoors in poor weather. This increased the need for ventilation, so holes were cut into walls to let air enter, with wooden shutters to keep out the rain in poor weather. These improvements gradually became more sophisticated, with the invention of flues and chimneys that could extract smoke more efficiently, and systems of transparent materials that allowed windows to be used to let in sunlight as well as air.

Provision of artificial lighting and plumbing was also hugely advantageous, although for most buildings such systems remained rudimentary until very recent times.

Adjusting the 'natural' interior environment of the building

Lighting, heating, cooling and ventilation are all ways in which users can adapt the interior environment to better suit themselves. Many of these 'services' are now electronic, and powered from central supplies, but traditionally all control and all power was at point of source.

BUILDING ENVIRONMENT
CONTROLLING THE INTERIOR ENVIRONMENT

With the arrival of cheap energy in the 19th century, and especially after the introduction of centralised supplies of gas and electricity, artificial control of the environment became a dominant feature of construction technology, replacing many of the functions hitherto catered for by modifying the building envelope. The range of possibilities for conditioning the interior environment broadened, and the demands of building users and the level of control steadily increased, with dramatic changes since the inventions of central heating and air conditioning. Within the second half of the 20th century in England, central heating and interior bathrooms changed from being an exception to being the rule in housing. Spaces such as cellars and lofts in houses, which had once been left more or less unused to help stabilise the building envelope, were widely converted into habitable spaces, sometimes with the aid of heating or fans, or other climate controls. Even very early buildings were being fitted with sophisticated heating, humidification and lighting systems. In modern construction, services became the principal source of light and ventilation, as well as heating and cooling. Most curtain-wall office buildings, for example, have such large floor plates that even during the day they depend on electrical lamps rather than their extensive windows for lighting.

These changes to building construction and use have significant implications for the longevity of buildings, and for the extent to which they consume energy, that are only just beginning to be understood. It is useful in this regard to examine the history of the various buildings services, how they operate, and how and why they were introduced.

The Industrial Revolution not only led to a wider range of cheaper fuels such as coal, but also the development of new technology for controlling the interior environment, such as this coal-fired Victorian 'Gurney' stove in Peterborough Cathedral (which once powered an extensive heating system, but has now been incorporated into a new system as a radiator).

VENTILATION

The term 'ventilation' is generally used to describe the combination of air exchange and air movement that occurs through windows, doors, chimneys and other points that allow exterior air into the interior. This is required to prevent condensation problems, as well as for the building users' health. A building envelope can buffer the changes in exterior humidity and temperature only if the exchange of air between the exterior and interior is limited. If there is a great deal of ventilation, even the thickest walls will be unable to buffer fluctuations in relative humidity and air temperature.

Air Exchange or Air Movement?

Although air exchange and air movement are often conflated when examining the behaviour of a building, there are important differences between them.

AIR EXCHANGE

The total volume of air being swapped between two locations: for example, between the interior and the exterior through open doors or windows, or between a room and a roof space via leaks in the ceiling. Air exchange is assessed by pressure testing or by monitoring the dissipation of tracer gases, and expressed either as litres per second, or as air changes per hour [ach]: that is, the fraction of the total volume of air in the room that could be exchanged in one hour. Air exchange measurements give little idea of the air's capacity for evaporation, which depends mostly on the air circulation, or flow.

AIR MOVEMENT

Air movement arises from air exchange, from building use, from forced ventilation, and from convection from the hot and cold surfaces in rooms (especially heaters and windows). Air movement can be measured by an anemometer, but this is not easy, since the pattern of flow is likely to be both changeable and turbulent, and it is of course invisible. It is possible to reveal flow patterns over a short period by smoke tests and other visualisation methods, and there are computer models that attempt to derive patterns from data about the shape of the room and the temperatures of the surfaces.

Types of Air Exchange

Natural Air Exchange

Natural air exchange is produced by wind pressure and gravity, and takes place through the existing structure: through weaknesses such as loosely fitting roofs, doors or windows, or through chimneys and doors and windows left ajar; or through the way the building is being used. Wind enters on the windward side of the building and leaves on the leeward, whilst air passing over chimneys and other apertures creates suction, and sometimes a measurable stack effect.

For chimneys, studies from the 1940s concluded that an increase in wind speed of 16 km/h increased the natural air exchange by about 1.5 ach [air changes per hour]. With doors and windows closed, but with a fire burning in the grate, the average ventilation rate was found to be 4.5 ach. This dropped to 1.6 ach when the fire was out and the flue cold, and to 0.6 ach when the flue was sealed.

Artificial Air Exchange

Artificial air exchange is an intentional attempt to change the interior environment by opening windows, fitting ducts and grilles, or installing forced ventilation such as fans. These days many artificial systems preheat or precool the air coming into the building.

BUILDING ENVIRONMENT
CONTROLLING THE INTERIOR ENVIRONMENT

HISTORY OF ARTIFICIAL VENTILATION

Until the 19th century, most rooms had opening windows to provide both light and ventilation, and some had their own source of heat as well. Even where fireplaces became redundant for heating, they still provided an important source of ventilation. Chimneys gave a strong draught, especially when a fire was lit in the grate. Thus control was in the hands of the building users, who could open and close the windows and the grate, or choose to light a fire.

The dramatic increase in medical knowledge during the 19th century coincided with ever more unhealthy living conditions in cities. For occupied buildings, some ventilation is necessary, if only to prevent mould growth and the ensuing health problems. Health pioneers such as Florence Nightingale stressed the importance of clean air and excellent ventilation, and accordingly hospitals were built with large windows and fireplaces.

The history of artificial ventilation is also a history of central heating, as the two developed in parallel. Forced ventilation was known to be crucial for environments with insufficient natural airflow, such as mines and ships, and the common solution in these cases was to use the drawing power of a fire (for example, at the top of mine shafts). In the early 19th century, William Strutt designed a heating system for a new infirmary in Derbyshire, which depended on incoming air being carried to the stove through a 70-metre underground passage (preheating it slightly in winter, and cooling it in summer). The driving force for the airflow was the heat passing up through a masonry duct near the centre of the building.

The heating system designed in 1819 by William Strutt, for a new infirmary in Derbyshire, was one of the first of many innovative approaches to temperature conditioning that depended on complex ventilation systems.

The octagonal Central Tower of the Palace of Westminster is not merely decorative, but was intended by the engineer David Boswell Reid to draw air out from the interior. It was a critical part of his complex and ambitious design for artificially ventilating the new building.

In 1818 the Marquis de Chabannes, who had installed central heating in the House of Commons, published *On Conducting Air by Forced Ventilation and Regulating the Temperature in Dwellings*, and six years later Thomas Tredgold wrote his *Principles of Warming and Ventilating Public Buildings*. Chabannes also tried using the heat from chandeliers to ventilate the Covent Garden Theatre, and artificial ventilation of theatres soon became common.

The earliest systems all depended on slight differences in air temperature and pressure, and so could be defeated by an open window or door. One solution was to seal all the openings, but this approach remained unpopular until the late 20th century. Instead, air pumps and fans were introduced. The principles of mechanical ventilation were well understood from other fields (such as metal refining, which used bellows to blow air), but finding a reliable power source proved difficult until the invention of steam engines.

In 1833, David Boswell Reid, a fellow of the Royal College of Surgeons, began experimenting with a new system to ventilate the House of Commons, which used a fire at the base of a stack to draw air through holes in the floor and out through a specially designed ceiling. A man with a product to sell, his *Illustrations of the Theory and Practice of Ventilation*, written in 1844, asserted: "…*after [mental anxiety and defective nutriment] no other cause, at least in modern times, appears to have inflicted so great an evil upon the human race as defective Ventilation…*".

There was considerable opposition to forced ventilation and central heating, with critics such as Florence Nightingale questioning both its efficacy and its cost-effectiveness. In *Notes on Hospitals*, published in 1863, she wrote: "*The doors, windows and fire-places should be the chief means of ventilation for properly constructed wards. If a ward must be ventilated artificially, it betrays a defect of original construction which no artificial ventilation can compensate; it is an expensive means of doing that which can be done cheaply and efficiently by constructing your building to admit the open air around.*" Reid himself had found it difficult to ensure that the incoming air was pure, and Nightingale also questioned the wisdom of striving for constant room conditions, regardless of time of day or time of year.

BUILDING ENVIRONMENT
CONTROLLING THE INTERIOR ENVIRONMENT

Problems and criticisms notwithstanding, by the second half of the 19th century artificial ventilation had been completely accepted by architects, and increasingly complex systems were being developed. In highly polluted cities it usually gave a better interior air-quality, and, most importantly, it allowed the development of taller, deeper buildings with lower ceiling heights and more floors, which could also be built more closely together. Bathrooms and kitchens, which had previously to be housed separately or at least away from the main living areas, could be integrated into the main structure. It became easier to standardise designs, since the architect was not obliged to take into account the building orientation and the local climate (addressing any resulting problems with the internal environment by adapting the artificial heating and ventilation). New buildings were designed around the necessary elements of heating and ventilation: giant air towers, fixed windows and entrance vestibules.

The need to conceal ducting helped increase the popularity of hollow-wall construction, which in turn led to the development of curtain-wall building with double-glazing, metal panels and integrated ducting. By a certain irony, such buildings – with their low thermal inertia, deep floor plates, and absence of fireplaces and opening windows – require artificial heating, cooling and ventilation if they are to be usable.

New approaches to construction also changed perceptions about how buildings could be used. With automatic controls and fixed windows, the occupants were no longer the primary controllers of the interior environment, and it became very difficult to provide different conditions for different rooms. The buildings themselves became much less autonomous, since the control systems were connected to external energy sources.

The demand for natural ventilation decreased over the second half of the 20th century: the deadly London smog of 1952, and the consequent first *Clean Air Act* of 1956, drew attention to the problems of air pollution, and building statutes that demanded flues or vents or night ventilators in windows were gradually abandoned. In climates where heating was common in winter, reducing air exchange was encouraged to cut energy losses. In super-insulated buildings, which aimed for extremely high energy efficiency, natural air exchange was drastically reduced or even eliminated, and artificial ventilation systems used to filter or even recycle the interior air.

Reduced ventilation and air movement began to cause noticeable problems such as mould and condensation (which was made worse by the increasing use of impermeable building materials: 19th-century books on building construction and health do not mention condensation at all). A 1984 report from the World Health Organisation suggested that the occupants of as many as 30 % of new and remodelled buildings were suffering from 'sick building syndrome', which they linked to poor ventilation, air-conditioning, heating, moulds, chemical outgassing and inadequate filtration of incoming air. More recent studies in the UK and elsewhere have suggested that asthma rates are higher in some modern housing, but there is still considerable dispute about the links between health and ventilation (see **Special Topic: Buildings & Human Health**).

With so many conflicting points of view about the advantages and disadvantages of ventilation, it is not surprising that there is no agreement on ideal ventilation rates, although public buildings may be obliged to meet particular requirements set by legislation.

HEATING

The effect of heating on building envelopes depends on the type of heating being used, and the way in which it is managed. It also depends on the way in which the heat is distributed. Two models are commonly used: general heating, which aims to control the temperature of the complete internal air space and provide comfortable conditions for users throughout the building; and localised heating, which aims to generate heat only in occupied areas and only whilst the building is being used.

It is useful to make a broad division between convective systems and radiant systems, although in practice radiant heaters will always have some convective effect, and most convective heaters will radiate slightly. For example, 'radiators' connected to a wet heating system transfer only about a third of their heat by radiation, with the rest being transferred into a room by convection. Conductive heating systems are not significant for buildings: underfloor heating systems do incorporate a very small component of conduction by directly heating the feet of occupants walking on the floor, but most of the heat they generate is transferred by radiation and convection.

Radiant Heating Systems

Radiant heating transmits energy directly to the surface of the person or object, without noticeably heating the air between; to do this effectively, heaters must develop very high surface temperatures. Typical systems transmitting the greater part of the heat they generate via radiation include open fires, gas and paraffin heaters, electric pew-back heaters, wall-mounted panel heaters, and electrical radiant units (including infrared and electric-bar heaters).

Systems burning paraffin or gas, particularly calor gas, produce substantial quantities of water vapour as a by-product, and so must always be externally vented to avoid problems such as condensation and mould growth. Unvented combustion heaters can also introduce chemical pollutants to the interior, and so are not suitable for heating historic buildings or buildings with fragile contents.

Sulphate pollution
Early coal-fired heaters were a common source of various interior pollutants, particularly sulphates, which can react with the building materials. This macro-photograph of the surface of the medieval wall paintings at Hardham Church in Sussex shows the type of damage that could result.

Convective Heating Systems

Convective heating warms the air, which in turn warms the person or object. Typical systems transmitting the greater part of the heat they generate via convection include hot-water central heating systems, electric convective heaters (both passive and fan-assisted), under-pew convective heaters, and hot-air blower systems. There are also the many types of small portable heater used for temporary heating, including oil-filled convective radiators and electric fan heaters.

BUILDING ENVIRONMENT
CONTROLLING THE INTERIOR ENVIRONMENT

HISTORY OF ARTIFICIAL HEATING

In most places, not least England, the earliest and most common building service was heating. Until the 19th century – and beyond for the poorest households – an open fireplace was the only means of heating, cooking and drying inside a building. The earliest fireplaces were simply fire pits on a central hearth in the middle of the building; smoke would billow around the inside of the building before finally escaping through gaps or primitive louvres in the roof.

The occupying Romans brought with them very sophisticated services. By about 100 AD, air heated by central furnaces was being channelled through open spaces under floors (called hypocausts), and out through flues set into the building walls. Although such comforts were all but forgotten after the Romans withdrew from Britain, by the 12th century Cistercian monks were including very similar systems in monasteries such as Rufford.

About this time flues also began to reappear in northern Europe, in the form of chimneys. These were cylindrical and built of stone, and as well as channelling away the smoke and gases, actively drew air through the fire, ensuring that it burnt well. The earliest existing example of a chimney in England is said to be that in the keep of Conisbrough Castle in Yorkshire, which dates to 1185. Often they were located centrally, toward the lower end of the open hall, where the opposing doors could be used to control the draught, but sometimes they were set against walls. From the early 15th century, this arrangement came to be the norm. Smoke rose to the roof and found its way out through the roof coverings, or the unglazed windows, or openings provided at the ridge or gablets.

The earliest heating systems were simply open fires in the middle of a principal room, used also for cooking (*top left*). Smoke found its way out of the interior through windows, doors and other gaps in the building envelope, and carbon monoxide poisoning was an ever-present risk.

Early fireplaces were postioned near the centre of the building, and later into an alcove on a gable end (*bottom left*). These had simple smoke outlets in the gablets (*right*).

Chimneys are a surprisingly late addition to domestic architecture (*left*). Early examples were simple shafts of masonry, usually brick, in the centre of the house (*top centre*). This example (Pendean farmhouse, originally from West Lavington in Sussex, but now rebuilt in the Weald and Downland Open Air Museum) is dated to the early 17th century; it serves back-to-back fireplaces in the centre of the building (*bottom centre*).

As was usual in such buildings, a cupboard for smoking bacon is built into the chimney upstairs (*right*).

As the open hall gave way to houses with upper floors during the 16th century, some way had to be found for channelling the smoke. This led to the development first of the 'smoke bay', and then of the 'smoke hood' (a timber structure infilled with wattle and daub). These were quickly superseded by fireplaces and chimneys built of brick, as this most suitable of materials became increasingly available. The dates for these advances vary with the status, size and type of house, and depend on its whereabouts; for example, in some parts of England, houses with smoke hoods were still being built during the late 17th century, and brick fireplaces were not introduced until the late 18th century.

Masonry flues needed to be lined to prevent gases escaping through joints and cracks, and the traditional method of doing this was to apply a mix of lime putty and fresh cow dung (known as 'parge') as the chimney was being built. Some later chimneys were constructed by placing the bricks around tile liners. From as early as the 13th century, they were topped with an additional superstructure which protected the flues from rain. At first this seems to have been a simple stone, but the advantages of extending the flues above any obstructions to the flow of air – and reducing downdraughts – were quickly recognised, and the 'chimney pot' evolved. Few of the simple early pots survive, but they seem to have been made, as they still are, of fired clay, and weathered with flaunching.

The fire created a draught through the house and up the chimney, which whilst it had the benefit of keeping the fabric and contents conditions dry, must have been rather uncomfortable. By the second half of the 15th century, very wealthy owners of grand properties such as castles and monasteries had begun to install 'inglenook' fireplaces; these were large enough to incorporate alcoves to the side of the fire, in which people could sit or even stand. The fireplace was plastered and limewashed to help reflect light and heat back into the room, and efficiency could also be increased by installing a 'fireback' (a piece of iron that sat behind the fire). During the winter the fire would be kept burning continuously to prevent downdraughts through the chimney; because burning this amount of fuel was expensive, inglenooks did not really begin to be widely used in houses until the second half of the 16th century.

BUILDING ENVIRONMENT
CONTROLLING THE INTERIOR ENVIRONMENT

In the 17th and 18th centuries, as incomes increased, a number of significant changes and improvements were introduced. Buildings became more compartmentalised, and small fireplaces began to be installed in different rooms. These often used charcoal or coal as a fuel, which burns much more efficiently than wood. In 1678, Prince Rupert (a nephew of Charles I, and a noted amateur scientist) suggested raising the grate of the fireplace to improve airflow and venting. Grates proved particularly useful for coal fires, as they allowed more oxygen to reach the fuel.

Chimneys were a high fire risk, since the deposits from combustion not only interfered with the airflow, but tended to be very flammable. By the close of the Georgian period, regular sweeping had become common to keep flues in good order.

At the very end of the 1700s, Benjamin Thompson (Count Rumford) designed a fireplace with a tall, shallow firebox that, by restricting the opening, drew smoke up and out of the building much more efficiently, and greatly increased the amount of heat radiated back into the room. Rumford showed how existing fireplaces could be improved by inserting bricks into the hearth to make angled side walls, and in the flue incorporating a metal choke, or 'damper', to stop draughts through the chimney when the fire was not being used. Soon many fashionable London houses had been modified according to Rumford's instructions, and inglenook fireplaces began to be filled to make them smaller and more efficient. By the 19th century most new fireplaces were made up of two parts: the surround (consisting of the mantelpiece and side supports, usually in wood or stone) and the insert where the fire burned, which was constructed of cast iron and often backed with decorative tiles.

Left: By the 18th century chimneys had become very complex, and often incorporated multiple flues.

Right: An illustration from an 1834 edition of the *Mechanics Magazine*, contrasting the use of child chimney sweeps against mechanical methods. This cut-away drawing gives some idea of how convoluted the multiple flue systems could be.

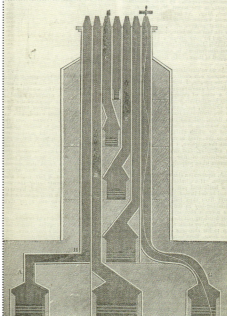

As fireplaces became smaller, so did chimneys: by the end of the 18th century most flues were no wider than a single brick. At the same time they also became more complex. A single 'stack' might incorporate several flues serving fireplaces on different floors, with separations between them that were sometimes slender enough to risk damage when the chimney was swept. Houses were sometimes built with two stacks: one at the front, and another at the back. A profusion of chimneys with elaborate pots became a characteristic of Victorian buildings, especially in the increasingly crowded towns.

But the heyday of the fireplace was nearing its end. The possibility of transforming the common closed stove to central heating – with the heat source outside, and warm air piped into the rooms – had first been suggested by John Evelyn in the early 17th century, but the idea was not seriously explored until the beginning of the Industrial Revolution. The enormous new industrial buildings proved difficult to heat, however, and by 1792, William Strutt had designed a system with a single hot-air furnace to heat a new fireproof mill in Derby.

Steam heating was also developed. Scottish engineer Neil Snodgrass, for example, used piped steam to heat a mill at Dornoch in 1799, by allowing the condensation to run down inside the same pipes. Steam heating proved increasingly popular for large buildings like the House of Commons, but nevertheless by the 1830s the most common means of warming small buildings was stove-based central heating.

Piping hot water through rooms to heat them had first been proposed in the 1770s, and systems were used in the early 19th century to heat Westminster Hospital and the Orangery at Windsor Castle. In 1829, Price Brothers of Bristol patented a hot-water boiler system, and within a decade such systems became widespread.

Early hot-water heating systems ran at low pressure, and so needed cumbersome pipe work with wide-diameter pipes. Although the first patent for a high-pressure system was granted to Angier Marsh Perkins in 1831, the early furnaces were notoriously unreliable and even dangerous: Perkins' was intended to run at a maximum of 177°C, but would sometimes reach much higher temperatures and pressures. High-pressure systems were also much more complex, requiring equipment such as governors, expansion tubes and valves. As a result, medium-pressure systems were introduced, and these remained the most popular choice until viable high-pressure systems were developed towards the end of the century. Thin pipes could be more easily integrated into smaller buildings; hot water systems with boilers and radiators became steadily more popular, and indeed ubiquitous after the *Clean Air Act* of 1956 made the burning of ordinary coal and wood illegal in large cities such as London.

The room heaters themselves also evolved. The earliest were simple coils of piping, although they were often given decorative housings. 'Radiators' (something of a misnomer, since 70 % of their heat transfer is by convection) were introduced in the 1880s, and were soon available in a myriad of styles. They were positioned under windows to encourage circulation of air around the room.

In 1930 engineer Oscar Faber introduced 'underfloor heating', using embedded pipes to carry warm water through the floors (the same system could be used to carry cooling water in summer instead, although this was less common in England). This quickly became popular, especially for large buildings, despite persistent problems with leakage in early systems.

In the latter part of the 20th century the introduction of electricity into homes led to numerous new approaches to domestic heating, as well as the development of more sophisticated controls. Thermostats could be used to set desirable air temperatures in wet heating systems, with the boiler running whenever the temperature dropped below the set point, and fans could be incorporated into heaters to circulate the warm air in a controlled manner. Electric bar radiators were introduced, and new underfloor heating systems appeared, based on embedded electrical cables rather than water. Ducted heated-air systems took air heated by gas and used fans to circulate it through conduits, and out through vents in the floors or walls (although ducted heating was never as popular in England as it became in the USA).

With the 21st century have come concerns about energy sources and sustainability, and more sophisticated boilers were introduced, some running on alternative fuels. Stoves have increased in popularity again, many burning a range of fuels including wood, wood pellets and coal. Direct heating systems have also become more common, from simple examples such as solar hot-water heaters to more sophisticated equipment designed to extract heat from the ground, the air or a nearby body of water. The latter are based on connecting the source of heat to a heat sink in the building (a system of radiators or underfloor heating, for example) via a 'heat pump', which – like an ordinary refrigerator – contains a loop of refrigerant, with a compressor which raises its pressure and thus its temperature, and an expansion valve and evaporator. The pressure difference created must be great enough to allow the refrigerant to condense on the hot side of the pump (where there is a heat exchanger to warm the building heating water), and to evaporate on the cool side (where the heat exchange is with the incoming supply of water from the source). This produces low-level constant heating, best suited to buildings with a large thermal mass. For ground-source and water-source heat pumps, the source can be 'open-loop' (the water is extracted directly from the environment) or 'closed-loop' (circulating a mixture of water and anti-freeze). More information about heat pumps can be found in the **Special Topic: Improving Energy & Carbon Performance**.

Although fireplaces have been almost entirely replaced by the many other forms of heating, they have never entirely lost their charm, and are often kept functional even when other mechanisms provide day-to-day heating. Parging was common until the 1965 *Building Regulations* introduced a requirement that new flues be equipped with a liner during construction. At first, clay pipes were chiefly used for this, but as regulations were tightened, concrete liners and metal liners became standard. Modern masonry fireplaces often have large windows of heat-proof glass, so that heat is provided after start-up by radiation through the glass, and then (as the masonry heats up) by radiation from the bricks.

Stoves

Open fires are very inefficient: the temperature at which they burn solid fuels such as wood – about 240°C – is too low for complete combustion, which also increases smoke emissions; and the damper must be closed as soon as the fire has burnt out to prevent heat loss. Stoves are a vast improvement, since they allow the supply of combustion air to be controlled.

Stoves evolved from fire chambers, in which the fire was enclosed on three sides by masonry walls, and covered by an iron plate. In water-heating 'back-boiler' open fires, commonly used in Ireland, the fire grate (which holds the fuel) is partly surrounded by a chamber filled with water, which is heated by the rising flue gases as well as by the fire itself. This allows as much as 80 % of the combustion potential to be realised as heat, and the circulating water prevents the boiler from overheating.

In 1735 a French architect, François Cuvilliés, developed the 'Castrol stove' (or 'stew stove'), which completely enclosed the fire in a sealed combustion chamber vented to a flue via a stovepipe. This allowed the airflow to be regulated, increasing the combustion temperature to 600°C, and virtually eliminating the loss of heat by convection. Stoves also stopped warm room air from being sucked up the chimney and lost, but were intended primarily for cooking, providing both a direct flame and an oven set to one side.

The earliest Castrol stoves were made of masonry, with fireholes covered by perforated iron plates, and were wood-fired, but by 1742, Benjamin Franklin had patented an all-metal version which quickly proved popular. Iron could withstand much higher temperatures, allowing coal to be used as a fuel instead of wood. Coal-fired iron stoves were mass-produced throughout the 19th and well into the 20th century, and were used for heating and boiling water as well as for cooking.

Modern stoves incorporate catalytic converters to burn any combustible products remaining in the gases and smoke coming from the main combustion chamber. This both increases heat output and decreases pollution. Some also incorporate firebox insulation, or large baffles to produce longer, hotter gas flow paths. Most also include a window to reveal some firelight, and to allow the user to see the state of the fire.

BUILDING ENVIRONMENT
CONTROLLING THE INTERIOR ENVIRONMENT

COOLING

The fundamental tool for cooling is the building itself: its design and its position, particularly its exposure to solar gain. For example, pitched glass roofs are a challenging feature in any climate, tending to overheat in summer (when the sun is high and sunlight strikes almost at 90°), and chilling in winter when the low angle of the sun means the incoming energy is mostly reflected away.

PASSIVE SYSTEMS

An existing building can be cooled passively (without the use of mechanical components such as fans) in one of two basic ways:

- by cutting the amount of heat travelling into the building by shading, or perhaps by insulation
- by moving hot air that has been generated in the interior out to the exterior.

CUTTING ENERGY INPUT

Options for shading are many, and aside from correct positioning and detailing of the building, include awnings over windows and other forms of protection for glass, such as blinds and shutters, or careful planting. Behavioural changes are also very helpful: avoiding sunlight penetration may mean drawing curtains or blinds in exposed parts of the building during certain hours of the day, and opening them again when the sun has moved.

VENTILATING TO THE EXTERIOR

The earliest windows primarily provided ventilation, and cross ventilation through open windows and windows remains the most effective means of passive cooling. If the openings are high up, this helps remove the hot air rising in the interior. 'Passive-stack ventilation' uses an extreme version of this principle, with warm air allowed to rise up though chimneys or towers, pulling in cooler air through an inlet at the bottom of the stack. Flow up the tower is helped by wind across the top. This makes the occupants more comfortable by evaporative cooling, and if the incoming air really is colder then the interior itself is cooled.

ACTIVE SYSTEMS

FANS

Fans do not in fact lower the temperature, but act by moving the air over the building occupants so that evaporative cooling can make them more comfortable. The earliest fan systems were all manual: swinging ceiling fans such as the 'punkahs' were used in India as early as 500 BC. With the introduction of electricity, a wide range of equipment became available, from rotating ceiling fans to free-standing oscillating units.

AIR COOLING

In the hot dry climates of the Middle East, 'wind-catchers' (tall, capped towers with one face open to the prevailing wind, which they channel into the building to cool the occupants) were sometimes combined with a *qanat*, or underground water channel, which cooled the air as it passed through.

A similar principle is used for modern evaporative air coolers, which pump water through a wick over which warm dry exterior air is blown; evaporation changes this to cool, moist air. Evaporative coolers are only effective if the difference between the air temperature and dew-point temperature is very high; they will not work well in humid climates.

Systems that dehumidify by first cooling the air below the dew-point and then re-heating it to the desired temperature were introduced only in the 20th century, and are very energy-intensive: 'air conditioning' controls not only the temperature and humidity, but also the filtration and distribution of the air using ducts and fans. The first electrical air-conditioning system was developed for industrial processing in 1902, and – like current systems – used the evaporation of liquefied gas to chill the air and remove water vapour from it. This proved useful for controlling the conditions for high-rise buildings with deep footplates (which could not depend on natural air exchange), and by the end of the 20th century air conditioning had become usual in offices. To be efficient, air conditioning relies on re-circulating the air, which usually means that the windows and other openings must be kept closed; the building must then rely entirely on forced rather than natural ventilation.

Despite the heavy energy demands of air-cooling and conditioning systems, both are becoming increasingly common in houses as well as commercial buildings, even in temperate climates such as England.

Although the idea of cooling is often associated with hot climates (these wind-catchers are in Yazd, Iran), from time to time, cooling is needed even in temperate climates. In England, cooling in traditional housing often relied on making best use of windows: sash windows could be opened to ventilate rooms very precisely, and blinds and awnings could be used to reduce solar gain.

BUILDING ENVIRONMENT
CONTROLLING THE INTERIOR ENVIRONMENT

OPTIONS FOR COOLING IN DIFFERENT CLIMATES

TEMPERATURE		HUMIDITY		
DAY	NIGHT	DAY	NIGHT	OPTIONS
Medium	Low	Dry	Dry	Cross ventilation Passive-stack ventilation
Medium	Low	Medium	Dry	Cross ventilation Passive-stack ventilation
High	Low	Low-High	Low-High	Decrease solar heating by shading, insulation Evaporative cooling
High	Medium	High	High	Ventilation will probably be counterproductive Fans Air conditioning
High	High	High	High	Fans Air conditioning

Dehumidification

Broadly speaking, there are two types of mechanical dehumidifiers: refrigerant systems and desiccant systems.

Refrigerant dehumidifiers work by passing the humid air over a surface – usually a refrigerating coil – so cold that the water vapour condenses out onto it. The cold dried air is then passed over a warm surface to be heated again, and is then expelled back into the room. Performance usually decreases at low temperatures, because ice tends to form on the coils.

Desiccant dehumidifiers work by exposing the moist air to the 'desiccant', which is some material able to quickly and effectively absorb water vapour (most commonly a microporous aluminosilicate, or 'zeolite'). This is impregnated onto a wheel which slowly revolves through two chambers. In the upper chamber, the top half of the wheel absorbs moisture from the input air; in the lower, the wheel is dried by heating.

Both systems require that the water storage container is emptied regularly, either by hand or by plumbing into the main water-disposal system.

LIGHTING

Of all the changes to building services, the most profound and far-reaching is surely lighting, and yet it is also arguably the least appreciated. We have become so accustomed to a world where all but the humblest in the worst districts of the poorest countries can flick the light switch to instantly illuminate a room as they walk into it, that it is hard to remember the technology and materials to make this possible became available only a century ago. It is certainly ironic that we now complain at the time it takes for some of the recent low-energy lamps to come to full strength, when we consider the much greater difficulties our very recent forebears met with when trying to light interior spaces.

For most of human history, in all cultures and climates, lighting was much the same and very simple: sunlight during the day, and at night perhaps the moon, coupled with fires, rush lights and lamps in the form of flat dishes filled with oil or animal fat. Even the candle is a comparative newcomer, and it always remained something of a luxury, especially when made with beeswax rather than tallow.

Detail of *Evening at Home*, 1867, by Johann Mengels Culverhouse

For most of history the main sources of light were the sun and the moon, supplemented by fires, oil lamps, rushlights or, more rarely, candles.

BUILDING ENVIRONMENT
CONTROLLING THE INTERIOR ENVIRONMENT

NATURAL LIGHTING

Since the sun was the main source of lighting, it was extremely important that buildings be designed to maximise natural illumination. In his books on architecture, the Roman engineer Vitruvius drew attention to the importance of windows not only for libraries and other working rooms, but for passages and staircases, and gave instructions about how the building should be positioned on its site so that the windows of the rooms needed in the morning should face east to catch the morning sun, and rooms such as kitchens which needed to be kept cool would not be heated by the sun in summer. Vitruvius also observed that surrounding buildings would complicate the positioning of windows, and that the angle of sunlight penetration would need to be determined with care.

Keeping out the weather whilst still admitting the light, glass was the ideal material, but it was far too expensive for most until production improvements were introduced in the Industrial Revolution. Elizabethan stately homes often had magnificent windows, but this was conspicuous consumption by the extremely wealthy: the windows were valued separately for probate, and were often detached and taken from house to house as their owners moved.

Sunlight was not benign, however, and its adverse impacts on fragile materials such as dyed fabric were soon recognised. Traditional means of limiting exposure included shutters, and by the 17th century curtains had been introduced. Window protection quickly became more complex, and began to be used for decoration and privacy as well as sun control. By the Victorian period a single window might have as many as six systems for controlling light: awnings, external shutters, internal shutters, roller blinds, light sun curtains, and heavy curtains which also kept in the warmth. ⊖GLASS

Awnings took many forms, from fixed metal covers to canvas awnings that could be drawn back when shading was not needed. Metal awnings (such as those shown here) were originally painted in bright colours, and sometimes striped to resemble canvas.

Many of these systems were removed in the 20th century, as simplicity and sunlight became fashionable again, and windows themselves became much larger. The resulting problems of light damage began to be handled by plastic films able to filter out many of the harmful wavelengths, either applied to the existing glazing or integrated within new laminated glass.

ARTIFICIAL LIGHTING

In early buildings, cooking fires (which were kept permanently alight) provided the main source of illumination after sunset. They also served to light the rush lights or candles by which all other evening work was done, and that were taken from room to room as needed. Householders were adept at making rush lights and trimming wicks to maximise light; but overall illumination would seem astonishingly dim to modern eyes.

By the 12th century, elaborate chandeliers and wall sconces had appeared, but even in grand houses these were reserved for special occasions, and were only rarely completely filled with candles even then.

Rush lights

Until the Industrial Revolution, rush lights were the most important form of domestic illumination. They were made (as shown here) by soaking the stripped pith of a reed in oil or fat, and were held in wrought-iron special stands that kept them at about 45° (the optimum angle for burning brightly and efficiently).

The 18th-century naturalist Gilbert White noted in his diary that a long rush light of 28.5 inches (72 cm) took just under an hour to burn; more typical examples around 30 cm long were said be consumed within 10 to 15 minutes.

BUILDING ENVIRONMENT
CONTROLLING THE INTERIOR ENVIRONMENT

OIL LAMPS & OTHER TECHNOLOGICAL ADVANCES

Like so many of the changes that separate traditional building from modern construction, the revolution in lighting can be traced back to the Industrial Revolution, when many materials that had hitherto been extremely expensive and difficult to make began to be mass-produced. ⊖METALS ⊖GLASS

It was the enormous cost of glass and metal that had probably inhibited the invention of closed lanterns, for these began to appear only in the late 18th century. In 1784, Aimé Argand, a Swiss chemist, patented a lamp in which a wide flat wick was wrapped around a central tube through which air could pass, coupled with a glass cover and chimney that created an updraught over the flame. The only oils available at the time were very thick, and were fed to the wick by gravity; this meant that the reservoir was above the flame and cast a shadow. Over the next few years, various improvements were introduced to try to overcome this, with some late variants using clockwork pumps so that the reservoir could be positioned at the bottom of the lamp instead.

In the 19th century, lamps were introduced; after kerosene replaced the vegetable oils originally used, such lamps became very popular.

Candles, lamps and rush lights could be made more effective by stands incorporating reflectors of polished metal or blown glass globes filled with water.

All lights with open flames, including gas lamps, had the significant disadvantage that they tended to create smoke as well as light.

Oil lamps became much more effective after 1859, when paraffin (kerosene) was introduced. In contrast to the vegetable oils like colza that were commonly used, this was light and volatile enough to be drawn up the wick. The reservoir could therefore be positioned in the base of the lamp, and so a myriad of elaborate pumps and control systems became obsolete at a stroke.

Although lamps became increasingly effective, candles continued to be used, often together with sophisticated holders incorporating mirrors and lenses to focus the light, and elaborate mechanisms that kept the candle at the correct height as it burned. Plaited wicks were introduced, which curled out of the flame as they burnt, lessening the need for regular trimming.

Surveyors required a light bright enough to be seen in the far distance, and for this purpose, 'limelight' was invented in the 1820s. Heating a cylinder of calcium oxide in an oxyhydrogen flame produced an extremely strong white light, which was tested for lighthouses and became very popular for theatres; but the operating temperatures were far too high for the system to be used in small lamps, and so limelight was never used for domestic buildings.

BUILDING ENVIRONMENT
CONTROLLING THE INTERIOR ENVIRONMENT

GAS LIGHTING

The Scottish engineer and inventor William Murdoch was the first to use gas to light a building: his own house in Redruth in Cornwall, in 1794. Moving back to Birmingham in 1798, Murdoch partially lit the Watt factory by gas, and in 1805 he fully lit a cotton mill in Manchester with a system that eventually had over 900 lamps.

The first public demonstration of gas lighting was conducted in London in 1807, when a number of lights and decorative flames were mounted along the wall of Carlton House Gardens. These were supplied by piping from a retort producing the gas, but by 1810 the world's first public gas supplier (the Gas Light and Coke Company) had been formed in Westminster. This led to the rapid spread of gas for street lighting, and within 10 years London had 30,000 gas lamps fed by almost 200 km of gas main. The Argand burner that had done so much to improve the performance of oil lamps was adapted by William Sugg for use with gas, and the 'London Argand' became the standard for measuring illumination.

The Victorian architect George Gilbert Scott made extensive use of gas lighting in his restoration of Hereford Cathedral. This early photograph shows one of Scott's standard lamps illuminated; the photographer has deliberately concealed the foot of the gasolier, together with its associated gas supply pipes.

It is interesting to compare the effect of gas lighting on eyes more used to rushlights and candles; *A Guide to the Restored Portions of the Cathedral Church of Hereford*, printed in 1863, observes that *"...the fullest effect is given to the mode of lighting peculiar to the present age; the ethereal character of which, as compared with that more material vehicle of light, the ordinary candle, is well exemplified."*

Nevertheless, it was not until 1852 that gas was used to light a major building – the new House of Commons – and only much later again did gas lighting start to be used in ordinary houses. On his website *williamsugghistory.co.uk*, recording the history of William Sugg's company, Chris Sugg observes: *"Domestic lighting was not considered as important because the existing oil lamps and candles provided sufficient light for the simple life that existed in most homes and most if not all dwellings had an open fire. The new street lighting had even provided additional light to the upstairs bedrooms of many houses so that the candlelight required to see the way to bed could be extinguished once the room was reached! In addition, the lighting in the largest of houses and mansions had by this stage achieved a sort of 'status' using oil with 'lamp rooms' for cleaning and filling the oil reservoirs and staff trained to the tasks. Gas was considered 'infra dig' as being for the masses and clearly unsuitable for the lighting of the interior in the 'better' houses."*

Gas fittings and fixtures

It took some time for electrical lighting to finally supplant gas, and even today some consider the light more pleasant. Fittings ranged from simple to highly elaborate, with ingenious mechanisms to direct light or increase ventilation.

Top left and top right: Remaining interior gas lights are now rare; on the left a wall fitting, and on the right a desk lamp. Almost all of these have now disappeared or been converted to electricity, although the supply piping and the taps may still be found (*bottom right*).

Bottom left: A magnificent ventilating 'sun burner' ceiling lamp, one of several still in place in the Victoria and Albert Museum in London. These too have been converted to electricity, but it is still possible to see original features such as ventilation slots in the ceiling support into which air at the ceiling level was drawn in and up by the temperature of the central flue, heated by the gas flames. As part of the conversion, hidden uplighters were introduced to illuminate the ceiling, but this is a modern conceit: as the name of these lamps suggests, they were intended to appear like miniature suns beaming light downwards.

Like chandeliers and sconces, gas fittings were positioned on walls or hung from the centre of the room. They tended to emit a great deal of heat, although they usually burnt quite cleanly. As lighting levels increased, the overheating became a problem, and in large public buildings, 'sun burner' or ventilating lamps were sometimes installed; these connected through the ceiling to a flue vented to the exterior, so that the fitting also provided room ventilation.

In 1885 the gas mantle was invented by chemist Carl Auer von Welsbach, who realised that rare earths such as thorium would luminesce when heated. To form filaments around the flame, he impregnated a bag of cotton mesh, which could be handled relatively easily, with a mixture of thorium dioxide and cerium dioxide. Once in place, illuminating the lamp would burn away the fibre, leaving behind a delicate framework of rare earths; the same basic process is still used today to make mantles for camping lanterns. The resulting light is intensely strong and white. The mantle allowed the gas lamp to retain its lead in lighting for many years, whilst electrical lighting was slowly developing.

BUILDING ENVIRONMENT
CONTROLLING THE INTERIOR ENVIRONMENT

With the advent of electric light, reaching for a light switch quickly became a reflex action when entering a room, with lighting often being used throughout the day as well as at night.

Left: The earliest commercial electrical lamps were produced by Swan in England and Edison in the USA.

Right: Early switches were turnkeys imitating those used for gas lighting, such as this example in the John Rylands Library in Manchester.

ELECTRIC LIGHTING

Building on research into the possibility of electrical lighting by Humphrey Davy, James Bowman Lindsay and Warren De la Rue amongst others, the first mass-produced electric 'light bulb' was introduced in 1879 by Joseph Swan in England, and refined by Thomas Edison in the USA.

General acceptance of electricity as a source of light had to wait until centralised power supplies, which in England were not introduced until the 1930s, but its advantages – in particular, safety and convenience – were soon clear. Electricity could be supplied easily to every room, turned on and off with a remote switch, and centrally controlled if necessary; a unique benefit was the ability to angle the light in any direction. Once the National Grid was in place, electricity quickly displaced all other forms of lighting for both domestic and commercial buildings.

The level of lighting considered necessary increased exponentially as people became accustomed to electric light, which at first had seemed shockingly bright. Lighting began to be used for decoration in its own right, rather than as illumination for particular tasks; coloured neon signs were used to advertise products and building features were picked out with external floodlighting. A multitude of lamps were introduced, from fluorescent strips to multicoloured LEDs, each producing different qualities of light, and service conduits were introduced to take the necessary wiring.

Electrical wiring and lighting is now so ubiquitous that it is almost impossible to imagine life without it. Office lighting is often designed to turn on automatically and run throughout the day, even in buildings with walls made of glass, and buildings are constructed with ever-larger floor plates; some have been constructed entirely without windows, relying on lighting for illumination and air-conditioning systems for fresh air.

SERVICE SUPPLIES

One of the greatest differences between buildings of the 20th and 21st centuries, and those built earlier, is the provision that must be made for the pipes and cables that transmit electricity, gas and water through the building (and usually to and from a public supply). This has transformed architecture in many ways, and the retrofitting of services invariably has impacts on earlier buildings.

WATER

The earliest sources of water for buildings were wells and pumps outside, or more rarely within the scullery. Water was carried by hand to where it was needed in the building, and dirty water was simply poured away outside.

SEWAGE

In cities, disposal of waste water soon proved to be a greater issue than water supply. The cholera outbreaks in London in the middle of the 19th century led to the construction of an underground sewer network, complete with pumping stations, to move the outfall further down the Thames away from the centres of habitation (treatment works were not introduced until the 20th century).

Crossness Pumping Station in south-east London was built between 1859 and 1865 as part of a scheme to divert sewage away from the Thames, which had become dangerously polluted. Designed by engineer Joseph Bazalgette and architect Charles Henry Driver, it used four steam engines to pump waste into a huge reservoir from which it could be released into the river when the tide was on the ebb. Crossness was one of four pumping stations connected to more than 130 km of new sewers constructed beneath London's streets.

BUILDING ENVIRONMENT
CONTROLLING THE INTERIOR ENVIRONMENT

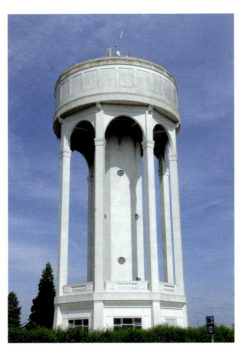

Tilehurst Water Tower, erected by Reading Borough Council in 1932, is still in use.

WATER SUPPLY

For supplying water, pressure is critical; most systems need around 300 kPa to function. Raising water uses potential energy: raising a water tank by just 102 mm produces a kilopascal of pressure.

The first modern water supply systems relied on water towers filled by pumps, and left to supply the surrounding buildings. These are still a common sight in many towns, and they remain a necessary adjunct to the supply system in cities. As the early skyscrapers began to dominate New York, for example, city ordinances were introduced to require all buildings taller than six storeys to have water towers on their roofs, since the pressure needed to supply the upper floors from the mains would have been strong enough to burst the pipes.

Water Supplies Within Houses

Within early Victorian houses, the only water supplies were through lead pipes to the scullery, or in rich houses perhaps to the water closet, which discharged into a night-soil collector. Later, when interior plumbing became more extensive and elaborate, steel tanks were placed as high in the house as possible (usually in the attic), from which water could run down through pipes to where it was needed. At first these tanks were filled by hand, then through lead pipes run from the scullery pump, and finally from the mains. Even long after most other countries had changed to mains water supplies for most houses, in England water tanks continued to be installed to supply hot water systems and toilets. 'Header' tanks (small feed-and-expansion tanks) were also placed in the attic to supply wet central heating systems. Both storage and header tanks began to disappear at the end of the 1980s, when 'combination' boilers capable of directly heating mains water were introduced. In new houses the entire water supply now comes from the mains, but older houses may use mains water only for the kitchen tap, with a tank supplying all other systems. High-rise buildings must still use water tanks, and Part B of the Building Regulations requires them to have pumps and tanks for fire-fighting.

The invention and rapid uptake of internal water services has had some unexpected side-effects. 'Plumbing' originally referred to the trade primarily dealing with rainwater disposal (the name comes from the Latin word for lead), but by the late 20th century it had come to refer largely to work on water and gas supplies, waste-water disposal systems, and other services within buildings; there is now no trade specifically devoted to the design or installation of rainwater goods.

GAS

Although Victorian streets, shops, offices and factories were often lit by gas, supplies were localised and often unreliable, as well as expensive. Gas was therefore not generally used in houses until after 1900, when central supplies were developed.

Gas began to be delivered into houses via lead piping, and remained popular for lighting until well into the century. By the middle of the century, electrical lighting had become more accessible, and the main uses for gas had switched to heating and cooking. This change in priorities is well illustrated by the 1920 *Gas Regulation Act*, which introduced standards for gas quality: when regulation had begun in the mid-19th century, gas was judged by illuminating power, but the Act changed the judging standard to heating power (calorific value).

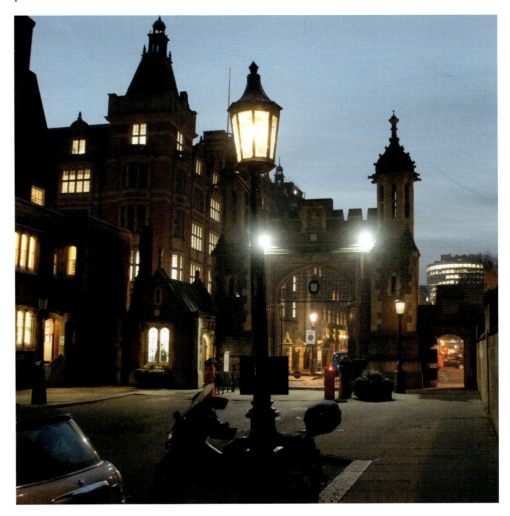

The streets of Lincoln's Inn Fields, like a number of other historic areas in London, are still lit by gas.

BUILDING ENVIRONMENT
CONTROLLING THE INTERIOR ENVIRONMENT

ELECTRICITY

Even more than gas, the acceptance of electricity as a system for providing industrial and household energy was dependent on the development of a robust supply system.

The earliest electrification systems were local: in 1881, for example, Godalming in Surrey became the first place in Britain to have electric street lighting, powered by a water-powered generator. London would wait many decades before power provision was organised enough to support more than the most well-to-do districts, but in the north of the country, metropolitan councils quickly saw the financial benefits of supplying electricity to shops, factories and homes at the same time as it was being generated for street lighting and electric trams. By 1893, Leeds' House-to-House Electric Light Supply Co Ltd had 139 private customers, but with a tram driver earning some 22 shillings a week, the quarterly minimum charge of 33 shillings made electricity prohibitively expensive for all but the wealthiest households. Electrical appliances such as irons began to appear in the 1890s, and indeed could be hired from municipal suppliers, but use was sparse: in 1910 no more than 7 % of homes in the UK had electric lighting.

Many attempts were made to try to persuade the government to allow large suppliers to develop, but it was not until 1926 that a report commissioned by the government from William Weir led to the first *Electricity (Supply) Act*, the appointment of the Central Electricity Board, and a commitment to construct a 'National Grid' supplying electricity to towns across the country, to a standardised voltage and frequency.

Constructing the National Grid was a mammoth enterprise. Electrification forever changed the way buildings across the world were serviced, which in turn led to dramatic changes in architecture.

Between 1927 and 1933, 6500 km of supply cable was laid to connect generators across the country, and the percentage of homes using electricity jumped from 20 % to 70 % in only six years. Uptake then slowed, however; electricity remained beyond the reach of working-class households, and in 1939 most smaller villages and 88 % of farms in Britain had still had no electrical supply to which they could connect. Much of the power was generated by coal-fed stations, which led to supply problems during and immediately after the Second World War.

In the end, it appears to have been the wish for televisions which encouraged the final 30 % of households without electricity to pay the cost of connection to the Grid. By 1965 more than 94 % of households had been electrified.

Trunking for early wiring

Bottom left: Early trunking was sometimes in the form of a surface-mounted wooden box with a flat lid. Grooves cut into the top of the lid indicated where the wiring underneath ran, preventing problems when the lid was fixed to the boxing with tacks.

Bottom right: An example of this type of trunking surviving *in situ* shows a fitting incorporated for a hanging ceiling light, the fibre flex of which still survives.

Top: In one of the first all-electric buildings, the 1900 John Rylands Library in Manchester, the trunking was made to this pattern, but in bronzed gunmetal rather than wood. The more expensive material was chosen to highlight the prestige of using cutting-edge technology for providing light, and for much the same reason the fittings were designed to leave the electric lamps exposed to view.

WIRING

Most early electrical wiring is of a kind to horrify a modern services engineer, but it was a revolution in safety compared to the open flames that had hitherto been used for lighting and cooking. The first wires were either bare or covered in cloth, and were stapled in place. Wiring at the end of the 19th century was insulated with impregnated paper in a sheath of lead, with soldered joints, but this proved prone to moisture problems. In 1908 vulcanised india-rubber insulation [VIR] was introduced. This was often enclosed in a strip metal sheath, which could be bonded to each metal wiring device to provide earthing.

Another popular approach was to run wires through conduits such as old gas pipes. One early type of conduit was made of wooden mouldings, with grooves to take single conductor wires, but this was soon recognised as very dangerous. Safer systems allowed wires to be run through building voids, or even chased into solid walls and floors. Conduits remain popular in certain instances, although they are now made of non-conducting materials such as plastic, and are most commonly used for the cables associated with ever-more-complicated telecommunications services.

BUILDING ENVIRONMENT
CONTROLLING THE INTERIOR ENVIRONMENT

Further Reading

Dillon, M. (2002); *Artificial Sunshine: A Social History of Lighting*; London: National Trust

English Heritage Building Services Engineering and Safety Team (2010); *BsEST Practice 5, Principles of Conservation Practice: Engineering the Past to Meet the Needs of the Future*; Swindon: English Heritage; available at *www.helm.org.uk/guidance-library/bsest5-principles-of-conservation-practice/*

Fryer, F. (1993); 'Antique light'; in *The Building Conservation Directory 1993*; also available from *www.buildingconservation.com/articles/antiquelight/antiquelight.htm*

Jeckyll, G. (1904); *Old West Surrey: Some Notes and Memories*; London: Longmans & Co

Leeds City Art Galleries, Rutherford, J. (1992); *Country House Lighting 1660–1890*; Temple Newsome Country House Studies No.4; Leeds: Leeds City Art Galleries

Nightingale, F. (1863); *Notes on Hospitals (3rd edition)*; London: Longman, Green, Longman, Roberts, and Green; also available at *www.archive.org/details/notesonhospital01nighgoog*

Roberts, B. (2008); *Historic Building Engineering Systems and Equipment: Heating and Ventilation*; London: English Heritage & the CIBSE Heritage Group; also available at *www.english-heritage.org.uk/content/publications/publicationsNew/heating-ventilation/heatingventilation.pdf*

Taylor, J. (1998); 'Light fittings in Georgian and early Victorian interiors'; in *The Building Conservation Directory 1998*; also available at *www.buildingconservation.com/articles/light98/light98.htm*

Taylor, J. (2000); 'Lighting in the Victorian home'; in *The Building Conservation Directory 2000*; also available at *www.buildingconservation.com/articles/lighting/lighting.htm*

Weightman, G. (2011); *Children of Light: How Electricity Changed Britain Forever*; London: Atlantic

Useful Websites

CIBSE Heritage Group: *www.hevac-heritage.org/*

English Heritage building services: *www.english-heritage.org.uk/professional/advice/advice-by-topic/buildings/services/*

William Sugg & Co: *www.williamsugghistory.co.uk*

DETERIORATION & DAMAGE

The building envelope must always remain intact and in good condition, not just to keep the internal spaces functional, but also to prevent the building itself from decaying and eventually failing. This chapter looks at the ways building envelopes deteriorate: firstly by considering the environmental deterioration of the building materials and then by looking at how such deterioration causes the envelope itself to fail.

Buildings can begin to fail for many reasons: it may be that a particular material has degraded, or a critical element has collapsed because of a faulty design or poor maintenance; perhaps a combination of materials or elements is deteriorating because of material interactions or poorly distributed loads. Even if a particular building element is not of historic significance, its deterioration may be of great concern if it could cause wider problems. For example, in a building with embedded timber framing the corrosion of a blocked downpipe could easily let water into the wall, leading first to timber decay and hence to structural problems.

The continued success of a building will depend on four major factors: the materials, the construction, the nature of the external environment, and the way it is being used.

In almost every case, failure can be traced back to the interactions between the building and its environment. Buildings and contents flourish with stability: rapidly changing temperatures and humidities tend to lead to problems. Condition often depends critically not only on whether it is artificially heated or cooled, but how it is ventilated.

Condition also depends on care: on whether the building is well looked after or neglected; busy, or used only sporadically. Sometimes the conditions best suited to the occupants may conflict with those best for preserving the fabric. Indeed, use may also determine what constitutes 'failure'. For example, a barn used for housing livestock will be perfectly functional even if the roof leaks quite considerably, but a museum housing important veneered furniture will not tolerate any water leakage at all, nor even much variation in interior air temperature or humidity.

ENVIRONMENTAL DETERIORATION

All the principal causes of deterioration – poor original design or construction, or inappropriate later alterations or additions, or material failure (whether because of ageing or wear and tear, or because of intrinsic inadequacies) – are, more often than not, fundamentally related to failures in the way the building envelope interacts with the exterior environment. Indeed, it is perhaps useful to begin with a general statement: in most forms of failure, water proves to be a critical factor. As a general rule, building systems are robust unless a substantial quantity of moisture is able to enter the fabric, or there are repeated cycles of wetting and drying. Except perhaps in the aftermath of a disaster such as a violent storm or an earthquake, even structural failure can usually be traced back to moisture ingress.

A certain amount of deterioration is unavoidable, since materials will degrade with age and exposure; for example, the carbonation of reinforced concrete will eventually lead to the corrosion of the steel reinforcement. Even so, in practice, most decay can be attributed to preventable causes, such as liquid water penetration.

The mixture of materials and structures making up a building is always very complex, and failure can result not only from the breakdown of an individual component, but also from adverse interactions between neighbouring materials. Moreover, the environment is likely to vary over a building's lifetime. Its current condition must be interpreted in the context of all these wider issues.

Buildings must cope with adverse weather, and most especially with rain: water is implicated in many forms of failure. A building that is poorly maintained or has fundamental flaws with the way it handles the exterior environment (such as this caponnier at Dover Western Heights, where the roof has been made of bricks) may begin to deteriorate exponentially.

BUILDING ENVIRONMENT
DETERIORATION & DAMAGE

Many buildings are able to continue in use with little more than basic care and maintenance. Much of the surviving traditional construction (especially vernacular buildings) has proved intrinsically robust, even when it was not especially well built. The materials themselves have aged extremely slowly, and the structures have benefited from some degree of over-engineering, which has allowed them to withstand a fair amount of deterioration and abuse. Local builders passed on methods that were found to work in local conditions, and if these were not always 'best practice', they were good enough to be effective with the available materials and labour. The construction was well understood, not only by the builders but by the users, as were the ways in which it could fail (and hence how it would need to be protected and maintained). There must have been many failures, but in the days before deliberate preservation, failed buildings were usually abandoned or replaced. Many experimental materials and techniques must have fallen by the wayside, but successful innovations were retained and incorporated into subsequent buildings.

Contemporary construction has tended to depend on specially developed materials rather than design to provide a robust envelope. For example, flat roofs may be constructed without any fall, relying on materials such as EPDM synthetic rubber to provide waterproofing. Buildings based on relatively new materials such as concrete and steel, and constructed with new techniques such as curtain walling, often have rather more intractable environmental issues than traditional construction, since these innovations have not yet withstood the test of time. Many are proving intrinsically problematic, and conservation can sometimes be a considerable test of ingenuity.

This chapter aims to guide the reader through the processes behind environmental deterioration, by looking briefly first at how environmental factors such as moisture or light can damage materials, and then in more detail at the way this damage can lead to failures of the building envelope.

If rainwater penetration leads to the decay and subsequent failure of supporting timbers, this may increase the stress on other parts of the fabric, and may also lead to accelerated water ingress. If such deterioration continues, the ultimate result could be structural collapse.

DETERIORATION OF MATERIALS

ENVIRONMENTAL AGENTS OF DAMAGE

Environmental factors that cause materials to deteriorate include:
- mechanical breakdown from overloading (stress and strain), or from wear and tear
- moisture (high and low moisture contents, changing moisture contents)
- light (mostly the ultraviolet components of sunlight)
- temperature (high and low temperatures, changing temperatures)
- chemical attack (from salts and other contaminants)
- biological attack (where the materials provide a nutrient source or a habitat).

The following is a very brief introduction to general processes by which deterioration occurs. The materials volumes in this series of *Practical Building Conservation* give detailed descriptions of failure mechanisms, and should be consulted for more information. ⊝MORTARS ⊝METALS ⊝EARTH & BRICK ⊝GLASS ⊝STONE ⊝TIMBER ⊝CONCRETE

MECHANICAL BREAKDOWN

Mechanical breakdown of materials ranges from slow attrition by steady processes such as salt decay or wind erosion, through shorter-term processes such as overloading, to the sudden damage caused by impact. Depending on the material, mechanical breakdown may occur more easily if it is wet, or unusually hot or cold, or if it has already been weakened by decay.

Facing page: The many materials making up a building envelope will necessarily be exposed to many environmental agents of deterioration, including wind, light and pollution, and especially rain.

Right: The failure of materials can be sudden, but in most cases it is a prolonged and gradual process. Salt decay of stone, for example, can cause dramatic surface erosion, but it would take decades or even centuries to destroy a wall by this process alone.

BUILDING ENVIRONMENT
DETERIORATION & DAMAGE: DETERIORATION OF MATERIALS

MOISTURE DAMAGE

Water is critical to most of the processes that break down materials, from timber decay to metal corrosion. The majority of building materials, especially traditional materials, are permeable, absorbing moisture both as a vapour and a liquid (see **Building Science**). Even non-permeable materials such as metal and glass may corrode if exposed to water for prolonged periods.

Although it is natural to ask what moisture contents are problematic for different materials, this simple question has no simple answer. For a very few materials it is possible to define 'acceptable' moisture contents according to how much damage is likely to occur – for example, timber should remain in good condition if its moisture content is between 10 % and 16 % of its dry weight – but for most, acceptable moisture contents have never been agreed. Part of the problem is that a moisture content that would be perfectly tolerable for the walls of a church may be far too high for a house. Indeed, high moisture contents prevent salt crystallisation, and so can be very desirable for many non-organic building materials such as stone masonry, but be unsuitable for associated organic components such as embedded timber, or for the comfort of users.

In the strict sense 'dry' would mean 'devoid of all water', but since all permeable materials are to some degree hygroscopic, none will never be absolutely dry. By the same token, a material might be defined as being 'wet' when it is holding as much water as it possibly can, but this is extremely rare: in practice, it would only happen to submerged materials, and indeed many materials will quite happily tolerate saturation: all salts will be in solution, and even most agents of organic decay will not be able to survive in anaerobic conditions. Deterioration is in fact more likely at rather lower moisture contents, especially when these fluctuate.

'Wet' & 'Dry'

For the purposes of building conservation, a sensible working definition of 'wet' and 'dry' can be derived from the function and performance of the individual building and its materials:

A building or building component is 'dry' when its moisture state causes no problems either for its preservation, or for the health or comfort of its occupants.

A component can be considered 'wet' when its water content is causing its deterioration or noticeably poor indoor conditions, even if its moisture content is below saturation.

Moisture contents will also change over time as the material responds to its environment. Exposed to liquid water, permeable materials will become wetter. The moisture content will vary according to the amount of water available, or as the conditions driving water transfer change; and the result will be problems such as salt crystallisation. Some materials swell and shrink according to moisture content, and clays and earths may turn to powder if they contain too little water, or lose cohesion if they contain too much.

Uptake of water vapour is governed by the ambient relative humidity, and as long as that changes quite slowly, materials such as stone, brick and mortar will be able to equilibrate without damage, absorbing moisture, and then giving it up again to the air when conditions become drier. By contrast, sudden changes (say, strong heating which rapidly reduces the ambient relative humidity) can induce severe deterioration, such as the cracking and distortion of joinery, the flaking of paints, and the powdering of salt-laden plaster. ⇒MORTARS ⇒METALS ⇒EARTH & BRICK ⇒GLASS ⇒STONE ⇒TIMBER ⇒CONCRETE

Moisture-related deterioration

High moisture contents are implicated in many types of material deterioration, including the decay of organic materials such as timber, the disaggregation of clays and earths, and the activation of damaging chemical reactions (such as the sulphation of limestone under polluted conditions).

Risks from high moisture levels are not confined to permeable materials: metal and glass, for example, will both corrode if exposed to water for prolonged periods.

Low moisture contents can also cause problems, particularly for timber (which may shrink) and unfired earthen materials (which may powder).

Varying moisture contents are often the most harmful of all, especially if the changes happen rapidly or repeatedly. This is especially true for permeable materials, where problems associated with fluctuating moisture levels include the powdering and flaking of stone, mortar and brick due to salt erosion or raised hydraulic pressures, and stresses from dimensional changes (in particular, the swelling and shrinking of wood and clay).

Water is also associated with many failures of minor building materials: for example, the breakdown of adhesives such as those used in joinery or to fix wallpapers.

BUILDING ENVIRONMENT
DETERIORATION & DAMAGE: DETERIORATION OF MATERIALS

LIGHT DAMAGE

Light can have a direct impact on materials, with the ultraviolet component of sunlight attacking organic materials, but can also have many indirect impacts, such as surface heating (see **Temperature-Related Deterioration**) and the encouragement of biological growth (see **Biological Decay**), with all its associated problems.

The effect of sunlight on organic materials is cumulative, increasing with increased exposure. Impact depends not only on the duration of exposure, but also on the wavelengths involved and the strength (or 'amplitude') of the radiation. The results depend on the type of material:

Silvering of exposed timber is caused by ultraviolet light oxidising lignin. For durable hardwoods such as oak this is not a problem, but for softwoods that must be painted to ensure longevity, silvering will prevent the paint adhering. The silvered surface must therefore be removed before the timber can be repainted.

- *Oil paints and varnishes*
  The long molecular chains on oil-based paints and varnishes become unstable when exposed to ultraviolet radiation; various reactions take place, including free-radical chain reactions (which lead to bleaching and an increase in transparency) and 'auto-oxidation' (which causes the drying oils to polymerise, leading to cracking, hazing, loss of gloss and yellowing).

- *Wood*
  Lignin will auto-oxidise when exposed to ultraviolet light, leading to some surface bleaching. Some of the long molecular chains may break up, lowering the degree of polymerisation and weakening the wood, but this reduces further light penetration. As a result, damage is limited to the surface of the timber and has little if any effect on the overall condition of joinery.

- *Textiles*
  Textiles such as woven cottons and wools are affected in much the same manner as wood, but prove far more fragile: with exposure, the fibres rapidly become brittle, and light-sensitive pigments such as dyes will fade.

TEMPERATURE DAMAGE

155

Like water and light, temperature affects materials in a number of important ways, and varying temperatures may cause more damage than temperatures that are very high or very low. Many materials – concrete, plastics, metals and glass, for example – will change dimensions if heated and cooled, putting stress on joints. If that movement is constrained, the material can fail; examples include the tearing of metal roof sheets at attachment points, and the cracking of glass window panes that have been cut too large.

Temperature also affects certain structural characteristics of materials (elasticity, for example). Materials such as cast iron, which are reasonably elastic at room temperature, can become brittle when chilled, and heating can cause materials such as asphalt and many plastics to soften, or even to melt.

There is a strong synergy between temperature and moisture-related damage. Cold surfaces may develop condensation, for example, and permeable materials which have a high water content may be in danger if they are exposed to freezing temperatures, especially if the temperature repeatedly fluctuates around freezing point.

Temperature-related damage

Changes in temperature can cause dimensional changes in materials with low thermal inertias, such as metal and glass. If the movement of such materials is constrained – for example, if metal roof sheets are too tightly fixed, or if glass panes are fitted too tightly into their frames – the resulting stress can cause them to crack or tear.

Some materials (asphalts, for example) may soften and lose strength and stability as their temperature rises (*top left*), and such materials may also become more brittle if temperatures drop.

Temperature also leads to damage because of its effect on moisture. Although timber has a high thermal inertia, changes in temperature will lead to changes in moisture content which can cause expansion and contraction (*top right*).

A combination of low temperatures and moisture can be particularly serious. If temperatures drop to the point that the water within a wet permeable material (such as the stone surround to a pond, shown *bottom left*) begins to freeze, there may be sudden and dramatic failure. Condensation on cold surfaces is another serious problem: if this is extensive or prolonged, the resulting runoff can cause liquid moisture problems such as the decay of timber window frames (*bottom right*).

BUILDING ENVIRONMENT
DETERIORATION & DAMAGE: DETERIORATION OF MATERIALS

CHEMICAL ATTACK

Contaminants can attack building materials wherever there is water to activate chemical reactions. Salts are the most common and most dangerous, although the link between the salts and the damage is not very well understood. Salt contamination can occur by deposition, or by the salts being dissolved and transported by liquid water.

Metal will corrode when there is a film of electrolyte (water containing dissolved salts) on the surface or trapped in crevices. ⊝METALS

Salts are also associated with the deterioration of permeable materials such as mortar, brick and stone; they are carried into the pores by liquid water, either from leaks or by rain dissolving pollution deposits on the surface. Areas of pitting, powdering and flaking will often also show salt efflorescences, and changing humidities that cause salts to repeatedly crystallise and dissolve are known to lead to material breakdown, although whether it is the salt crystals themselves that cause the damage, or some other associated mechanism such as air pressure, is still a matter for research and conjecture.
⊝MORTARS ⊝EARTH & BRICK ⊝STONE ⊝CONCRETE

An associated problem with encrustations of pollutants such as salts and dust is that they can attract and hold moisture, leading to chemical attack and other problems.

Sulphate pollutants are among the most obvious and damaging contaminants. They can react with the surface of exposed stone to form soluble compounds, which may then be washed away by rain; as this process continues, the surface loss accelerates.

Salts

'Salt' is the chemical name given to a crystalline material made up of two ions, one positively and one negatively charged (a 'cation' and an 'anion', respectively), so that the compound itself is neutral. The ions may be either charged atoms or charged molecules, and can be inorganic or organic.

Water can easily break the ionic bonds, dissolving the crystal to produce a salt solution. How easily a particular salt dissolves in liquid water depends not only on the strength of its bond, but also on the water's temperature and whether there are any other sources of energy. The humidity needed for the deliquescence of any particular salt is known as that salt's 'equilibrium relative humidity' [RHeq]. Many salts are so sensitive to dissolution by water that they will dissolve (or 'deliquesce') in humid air; indeed, some salts absorb atmospheric moisture so readily that they are never found as crystals under normal ambient conditions.

In free air, where no other forces are acting on the salt, the RHeq for most salts is very stable (only slightly dependent on ambient temperature). This is exploited by using salts such as calcium chloride as desiccants, to take up and trap excess humidity. In a confined space, a super-saturated solution of a salt can be used to set the humidity in the air above it: because the solution has the capacity to take up vapour until the air finally equilibrates with the solution, at equilibrium the relative humidity above the solution will be equivalent to the RHeq of the salt.

Things become more complicated where there are mixtures of salts, or where the salts are not in free air: in pores, for example, the bonding of the salts to the pore walls and the physical constraints on behaviour alter the sorption of water in ways that are impossible to predict. Sometimes salt analysis is used to try to determine which ambient relative humidities are most likely to drive crystallisation cycles, but in almost all cases materials contain not one but several salts, and the resulting salt mixtures have very complex equilibrium relative humidities.

SALTS IN BUILDING MATERIALS

Salt contamination is to be expected in buildings. Sources are many: pollutants, wind-blown sea salts and de-icing salts, decaying organic matter such as leaves, excrement and dead animals, preserving salts, gunpowders, and fertilisers that have been stored or used in the building. Some of the original materials will probably have included some salts, as will many materials added later, such as cements.

Soluble salts are carried into permeable building materials by water, often via leaks in water disposal systems. As the water travels through the pores, the salts are deposited according to their solubility and the conditions within the material, with the most soluble salts appearing where the water evaporates as crystal growths called 'efflorescences'. The structure of efflorescences, and of 'subflorescences' and 'cryptoflorescences' (salt deposits within the material rather than at the surface), vary widely depending on the conditions.

Ions that first travel into the fabric as part of one particular salt (perhaps as part of a treatment or repair material) may, once there, combine with other ions to form new salts. Because these new salts may be less soluble than the original species, they may be more damaging: for example, at normal ambient humidities, nitrates or chlorides of calcium and magnesium will usually remain in solution, but nitrates and chlorides of potassium and sodium can crystallise, as can sulphates of sodium and magnesium. The black crusts of gypsum on carbonate building stones caused by sulphate air pollution are much more soluble if certain other salts – especially sodium chloride de-icing salts – are present as well.

BUILDING ENVIRONMENT
DETERIORATION & DAMAGE: DETERIORATION OF MATERIALS

SOURCES OF SOME COMMON IONS

SALT	COMMON SOURCES
SULPHATES	Building stone, clay-based building materials such as brick, cement and concrete, gypsum-based building materials, groundwater, polluted air, sea spray, fertiliser
MAGNESIUM	Dolomitic limestone, de-icing salts, fertilisers, sea spray
CARBONATES	Limestone, groundwater, de-icing salts, wood ash, detergents
CHLORIDES	Groundwater (near source of sodium chloride), sea spray, de-icing salts, calcium-chloride concrete additives, pesticides, breakdown of plastics
NITRATES	Groundwater, biological decay, manufacture of gunpowder, nitrifying bacteria, fertilisers, explosives, food preservatives, chemical removal of tree stumps
CALCIUM	Building stone, mortar, groundwater, fertilisers
SODIUM	Groundwater, conservation treatments, cement, sea spray, de-icing salts, food preservatives, detergents
POTASSIUM	Groundwater, conservation treatments (particularly waterglass), manufacture of gunpowder, chemical removal of tree stumps
AMMONIUM	Groundwater, polluted air, conservation treatments, explosives, fertilisers
OXALATES	Formed by reaction of calcite in stone with oxalic acid from some types of microbiological growth or from hydrocarbon pollutants (the mechanism of formation is disputed)

DAMAGE MECHANISMS

When trying to understand salt-related damage, conservators are hampered by the fact that – despite a great deal of meticulous research – the mechanisms of damage remain unclear. Different ions will precipitate at different humidities, so various salt species will tend to crystallise in different locations in permeable materials. The very soluble salts tend to be found on or very near the surface, and are not usually associated with much physical damage (although they may be the most obvious, and therefore appear the most alarming). Similarly, very insoluble salts seem usually to be relatively benign, staying locked within the material, and rarely dissolving or moving. Damage is usually associated with semi-soluble species (those that tend to crystallise and dissolve repeatedly under typical building conditions). These deposit within the pores below the surface.

Salt crystals certainly expand as they absorb moisture (for example, a sodium-sulphate crystal will grow to more than three times its dry volume before finally deliquescing), but that alone should not be sufficient to cause the severe damage that is often apparent. The process is undoubtedly complicated, and may well involve a build-up of air pressure, high-energy non-crystalline growth, or energy released during phase changes between different forms of the salt. The macroscopic patterns of damage after interventions such as the installation of heating certainly suggest that, whatever the mechanisms, if the ambient conditions are changing rapidly – even if the actual degree of the changes is quite small – salt-contaminated building materials will begin to decay more quickly.

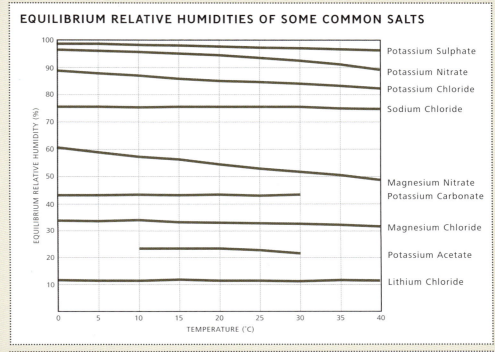

The equilibrium relative humidities and solubilities of salts depend on the ambient temperature; indeed, some salts (such as barium nitrate) show stepwise changes.

Laboratory studies have shown that even more complex behaviour results when mixtures of salts are involved: in these circumstances the solubilities and equilibrium relative humidities become almost impossible to predict.

All these results have been obtained for salts in free air: within the pores of a permeable material, behaviour will also depend on the interactions between the salts and the pore walls, which will differ from pore to pore. The exact salt mixture in each pore is also likely to vary, and may well change over time. Since the pore temperature and humidity will not be measurable either, it is essentially futile to try to model the exact response of a real salt-contaminated material to changing ambient humidity and temperature.

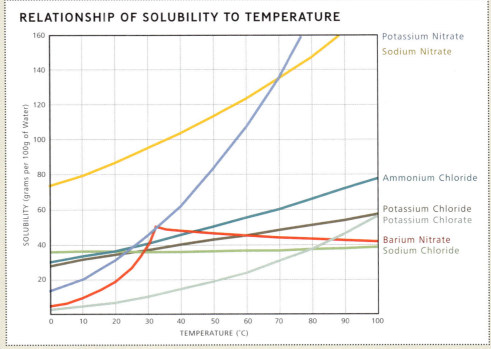

BUILDING ENVIRONMENT
DETERIORATION & DAMAGE: DETERIORATION OF MATERIALS

BIOLOGICAL ATTACK

There are many biological agents that attack building materials, ranging from microscopic growths such as fungi and bacteria (which can break down organic materials such as wood, and colonise many other materials including metal and glass), through smaller plants and insects, to higher plants and animals. The type and severity of damage varies greatly, from the purely aesthetic (lichens obscuring decorative stonework), to the decay of structural timber. Externally, lichens, mosses, algae and nitrifying bacteria can secrete acids, which can break down the matrix of stone and form surface crusts, and recent research has shown that bacteria and biofilms can change the surface tension of salt solutions, sometimes greatly increasing salt damage; but more commonly the damage is very slight. Organic acids – the product of metabolism – can also attack metals, removing the patina that protects them from corrosion.

TIMBER DECAY

The organisms which colonise and feed on building materials can often survive at a wide range of temperatures and humidities, but most require a reasonable supply of liquid water to thrive. To understand the conditions under which such organisms thrive, it is often best to discover their natural environment outside of buildings. For example, most rot fungi evolved to exploit dead wood on the forest floor, and require conditions that are continuously wet to survive and thrive. ➔TIMBER

Agents of timber decay

Timber with a high moisture content for a prolonged period of time can be attacked by fungi such as *Coprinus cinereus* (*top left*) and dry rot (*Serpula lacrymans*) (*top right*).

Fungal decay then allows insect pests such as the deathwatch beetle *Xestobium rufovillosum* to exploit the wet wood (*bottom left and right*).

DETERIORATION OF THE ENVELOPE

WHY BUILDING ENVELOPES FAIL

The building envelope is a complex structure of various components made up of a wide range of materials, so material deterioration is only part of the story of how buildings fail. Each material will react differently to environmental changes, and moreover the response of a single material might well depend on the shape and size of the component made from it. Problems will often begin at joints and interfaces.

The whole building system may have an impact: for example, the deterioration of a component might be exacerbated if it is also under stress from a structural load.

With so many variables, the behaviour of the building envelope is wide-ranging and complex. The fundamental issues that could lead to environmental failure include:

- the impact of the exterior environment
- problematic building designs or materials
- poor maintenance
- problematic building alterations (changes to the envelope that affect its function)
- other interventions such as thermal upgrading, or inappropriate treatments and repairs
- building use (both the wear and tear caused by the occupation of the building, and actions taken to alter the interior conditions)
- events such as floods, fires or impact.

There is considerable overlap between these issues – poor design may make maintenance difficult or exacerbate failure in a storm, for example – but it is nevertheless helpful to consider them independently.

IMPACT OF THE EXTERIOR ENVIRONMENT

Every building is embedded in its own unique exterior environment, which is the result not only of the local weather, but of the way that weather is affected by the surrounding landscape. It incorporates many factors that could affect the envelope, including not only the temperature and humidity of the air, but the direction, speed and gustiness of the wind, and the exposure to sunlight or to rain and snow. Local land use can lead to pollution, or problems such as traffic vibration; local plants and animals may cause various problems. The effective exterior environment might be be very localised, but could extend a considerable distance, according to its impact on the building.

The exterior environment is unlikely to be static over the lifetime of the building: ground levels may build up around the footings, for example; rural areas may become urbanised; open ground may be paved over (changing soil moisture contents and altering runoff patterns); planting or new buildings nearby may change the patterns of wind. Sewage and mains water post-date many of the buildings in England, so pipe leaks can expose envelopes to much higher quantities of groundwater than they would previously have encountered. Thus, a building of any antiquity may well be exposed to conditions very different from those for which it was originally designed.

Facing page: The small flint church at Coombes, on the South Downs in West Sussex, illustrates how a building's local environment can change dramatically over time.

When the church was built in the late 11th century, the village it served was earning a healthy income by harvesting salt from nearby pans fed by coastal marshes. As the marshes disappeared, the village declined, and today almost nothing of the original buildings remains. The church is now surrounded by a working farm. It overlooks a cement factory at Shoreham, once a source of atmospheric pollutants, but abandoned a decade ago.

The current state of the building envelope is the cumulative result of all the many impacts from these past environments, as well as from the conditions which are affecting the church today.

IMPACT OF RAIN

Traditional building systems based on permeable materials are very resilient, and can resist rain and even some degree of moisture penetration, but they will begin to fail if water enters in substantial quantities for prolonged periods of time, or if moisture contents vary repeatedly (leading to salt crystallisation damage, for example). A wall with a history of moisture issues will be more prone to taking up both liquid water and water vapour, so once problems begin they may take some time to resolve. ⊃MORTARS ⊃STONE ⊃EARTH & BRICK ⊃TIMBER

Hollow-wall construction systems have different weaknesses, which mostly centre around the joints. Face-sealed systems are particularly prone to moisture penetration, not only because they lack a secondary drainage system, but because the seals are exposed and thus more apt to deteriorate than the protected sealants in rainscreen systems. ⊃GLASS ⊃STONE

In all types of building, moisture can enter through and around openings such as windows and doors. Sealing around openings and diverting water away from them is always important, but is a particular challenge for construction systems that rely on rainscreens and interstitial drains. Doors and opening windows also usually rely to some extent on metal components such as hinges, which can easily trap water and corrode unless they are made from a very resistant material such as stainless steel. ⊃METALS ⊃GLASS

Problems often occur at joints between materials that differ in permeability, such as the boundary between bricks and Portland cement mortars. At this point, fine cracks often form that tend to wick up rainwater running down the façade. Lapped joints or cracks in flashing are also prone to water penetration. ⊃MORTARS ⊃EARTH & BRICK ⊃STONE

The junction between different building elements is also a potential point of failure. For example, porches fitted flush to the wall will need effective flashing if they are not to leak. Roof junctions can be problematic for the same reason, especially where two pitches meet in a valley gutter which itself has little or no fall. These tend to collect debris, exacerbating the risk. Hidden timber lintels are a weak point in many walls, since if water is able to enter, the wood may decay and lead to structural failure before the problem is noticed. ⊃ROOFING

IMPACT OF OTHER EXTERIOR SOURCES OF WATER

Although the water table is often cited when there are moisture problems in walls, in practice this is a very rare source, causing at most a low band of damp at the very base of the walls. More important sources of water at ground level include surface runoff, where the ground slopes back towards the building; splashback from rainfall; and leaking sewage or water mains. Moisture problems have also been found where flower beds have been dug near the wall, especially if these are being watered by irrigation systems.

Most often, serious moisture penetration will be traceable back to a failed drain or sewer, a faulty downpipe or gulley, or some similar defect. Unless the problem is of very long standing, damage will usually be localised near to the source, but 'damp' may be spread further, and rise higher in the wall, if there are exterior or interior finishes (such as cement renders) that reduce evaporation. Nor will all sources of apparent 'groundwater' be found at ground level, since rainwater will quickly percolate downwards through the fabric from problems such as blocked parapet gutters or faulty chimney flashings, before finally manifesting itself at the base of the wall where it may be identified as 'capillary rise'.

Water from any source can carry with it semi-soluble salts that will crystallise in the zone of evaporation associated with maximum height of the capillary rise. This will give rise to patches of salt efflorescence, and possibly surface deterioration.

Groundwater: Subsidence & Heave

The water in the soil under a building (whatever its source) exerts a hydraulic pressure that helps support the weight of both the overlying ground and the structure. If the amount of water changes, this can have dramatic results, particularly in clay-rich soils. Subsidence can lead to landslips and local collapses, and severe building damage: cracking and distortion of the foundation and structure, soil penetrating through service ducts, and water damage, for example. Bridges and large buildings on pile foundations may buckle or tilt.

If water is lost (perhaps pumped out into a well or used for irrigation, or occasionally taken up by large trees), the soil may shrink; and this shrinkage may not be fully reversed even if the water returns. Increasing water levels, on the other hand, can lead to heave, or subsidence via liquefaction: the water acts as a lubricant, causing the soil to lose its resistance to shear. One common cause of this is a soakaway too close to the building.

Cyclical loading – classically from earthquakes, though strong sources of vibration can produce a similar effect – can compound the load, and lead to the complete breakdown of the soil. Most at risk are loose soils with poor drainage and usually moderate water contents, especially sandy or silty soils that are not very plastic.

Subsidence is associated with significant and often sudden changes in the moisture content of the ground under the building. Common underlying causes include failed drains or culverts, or nearby building works that have altered the hydrogeology. Potential problems may lie concealed, and only manifest themselves in the aftermath of a sudden change in groundwater such as after a flood.

BUILDING ENVIRONMENT
DETERIORATION & DAMAGE: DETERIORATION OF THE ENVELOPE

IMPACT OF WIND

Wind is a critical element of the climate, and one that is very local. Loads are not typically distributed evenly, and may vary suddenly in both strength and direction; it is usually the suction loads that cause the most damage. Turbulence is just as important as the prevailing wind speeds and directions. Windows are particularly vulnerable to suction damage, especially if they are made of leaded glass. Chimney pots are subject to large wind forces, and may fly off and cause damage elsewhere if they are not fixed firmly in place. Branches or even uprooted trees thrown onto the building can also be a source of damage during storms, especially to roofs.

Wind causes erosion and (by increasing evaporation) can exacerbate salt decay. Evaporative cooling can cause condensation on the underside of roofs and sometimes on the interiors of walls. Occasionally, wind cooling can increase the number of freeze-thaw cycles.

Susceptibility to wind damage will probably be unique to the building, since exposure will depend critically on the surrounding landscape, as well as the prevailing local winds. The height, shape and orientation of the building will all be important, as will the surrounding terrain, and the neighbouring structures and vegetation. Wind can drive rain upwards against gravity: for instance, between slates or under flashing. It is also a major factor in building ventilation.

Even very exposed buildings may cope perfectly well with ordinary wind loadings, but fail in storms. A potential problem is damage from wind-blown branches or debris (sometimes called 'wind-throw'). Here, a section of the parapet of a tower has been dislodged in a storm, and has crashed through the roof of the church below.

IMPACT OF EXTERIOR TEMPERATURES

167

Temperature changes induced by air temperatures and solar heating can cause problems both directly and indirectly.

Direct Damage

The structural characteristics of many materials and components will alter over the temperature ranges common even in mild climates such as those characterising much of England: components that have been heated by the sun may soften and deform, but when cooled by low air temperatures or wind movement may become brittle.

Dimensional change is another common issue: components may expand when warm, and contract when cool. For this reason, metal roofing sheets that are fixed in place too tightly will tear, and elements made of susceptible materials such as concrete must include expansion joints if they are not to crack. Components made of several different materials – for example, windows, which have timber or metal frames combined with glass – must be designed to allow each to expand and contract at different rates; this is usually achieved by incorporating flexible materials such as putties and lime mortars at the interfaces.

Metal roofs must be detailed to prevent damage from differential heating. Expansion and contraction happen very rapidly: the roof sheets will respond even to the sun passing behind a cloud.

The impact of exposure to sunlight depends on the construction, and will change through the day and across the seasons. It will also be greatly affected by the topography of the surroundings, including light being reflected off nearby surfaces such as glass-clad façades.

BUILDING ENVIRONMENT
DETERIORATION & DAMAGE: DETERIORATION OF THE ENVELOPE

Freeze-thaw damage

Freeze-thaw damage can occur in any wet permeable material exposed to low temperatures, but is most commonly seen in masonry. Problems may be exacerbated by the use of cement-based mortars, which trap water. The pattern of deterioration reflects not only exposure, but also the variation in the quality of the bricks or stones, since it is the weaker units that will fail. So many factors can be at work that freeze-thaw is often hard to unequivocally pinpoint as a reason for deterioration.

Indirect Damage

Many of the problems indirectly caused by temperature involve its effect on moisture. For example, cooling may lead to condensation, and wet permeable materials may break down under freezing conditions, especially if subjected to repeated cycles of freezing and thawing.

Although the precise mechanism for freeze-thaw damage is not well understood, it may be related to the bursting of water pipes in cold weather. In this case at least, it is not actually the force exerted on the walls of the pipe by the expansion of the water as it freezes that does the damage: the pipe is much too strong, and instead forces the ice crystals to grow along the pipe. This compresses the air trapped ahead of the ice front, so air pressure will build up until eventually it is sufficient to split the pipe apart at the joints. Hot-water pipes are more prone to failure than cold-water pipes, since the cold-water system often includes toilet cisterns which act as expansion valves.

Roofs that are periodically covered in thick snow face other problems. If the ceilings are not insulated and the attic space above is not very well ventilated to the exterior, the roof covering may heat up, causing the snow to slide off, which can be a risk to building elements below. The meltwater may refreeze at the eaves, causing ice dams that endanger not only the eaves and gutters, but passers-by as well.

IMPACT OF SUNLIGHT

As with temperature, sunlight can cause damage both directly and indirectly, although in this case the direct damage is usually confined to superficial changes, and it is the indirect damage – chiefly localised heating – that is able to cause the most severe problems for most building envelopes. Since exposure depends on the building and its surroundings, this can change quite dramatically through the day and the year.

Direct Damage

Although the ultraviolet component of sunlight can break down organic materials in building components, this is usually superficial. It is of most importance for decorative surfaces such as wall paintings or wallpapers that incorporate dye pigments, where the appearance can be dramatically altered by fading. Exposed timberwork will change colour, but this will not affect its strength to any significant degree. Sunlight can also break down glues and sealants such as putties and silicones, which can be a serious issue for some modern curtain-wall construction, but the degree of damage will depend on the exposure. ⊖GLASS

Indirect Damage

Solar heating can cause materials to expand and contract, and can also act as a catalyst for chemical reactions. Solar heating can cause very high vapour pressures in surface pores and inside hollow-wall construction, and this can force moisture through the wall. Sunlight exposure is also a critical factor governing the growth of plants and microorganisms in and around the building.

Sunlight damage

Many plastics are very susceptible to damage from ultraviolet light.

In this railway station roof, the transluscent panels have severely discoloured. Even newer replacement panels (such as that at top left) are beginning to show signs of the same deterioration.

BUILDING ENVIRONMENT
DETERIORATION & DAMAGE: DETERIORATION OF THE ENVELOPE

IMPACT OF GROUND MOVEMENTS

Traditional buildings have a good deal of elasticity and plasticity, and so can absorb most daily and seasonal movements. Where there have been no major changes to the surroundings or the water table, and there have been no structural alterations or catastrophic events such as tremors, older buildings rarely develop structural problems.

Unfortunately, significant local changes are not that uncommon: new drains, the paving over of ground surfaces, and trees may all lead to lower soil moisture contents, which in the worst cases may cause subsidence (see **Groundwater: Subsidence & Heave** earlier in this section). Water-logged soil may heave as a result of winter frosts. There may be more dramatic changes if nearby excavations lead to earth slippages; and plasters, renders and even masonry can crack because of vibration from building works or traffic.

In traditionally constructed buildings (which include materials such as lime mortars, which have a great deal of elasticity and plasticity), it is not at all uncommon to find that significant distortions have occurred as the building has settled over time.

This may cause some problems for certain components – windows and doors may not open or shut correctly without rehanging, for example – but only very rarely does it lead to failure of the structure.

IMPACT OF POLLUTION

Airborne pollutants are a common source of contaminants such as salts, which in the presence of rain or condensation can attack building components. The most infamous chemical reaction is the transformation of calcium carbonate to calcium sulphate (gypsum), which forms a dark crust on limestones such as Portland Stone: gypsum is more soluble and so will be washed away by rain, producing the characteristic white, eroded surface on exposed areas of the building. For silicaceous sandstones, acidic rainwater may dissolve minerals and redeposit them on the surface, where they bind particulates and other dirt to form a rain-resistant black crust. This changes the permeability, and eventually the crust may spall off, causing very serious damage.

Industry and land-use changes are leading to new types of pollution, and hence new types of deterioration. For example, over the past 15 or more years, exposed lead has begun to be affected by a reddish discolouration, caused as lead carbonate alters to lead tetraoxide. This seems to be most common in rural areas, and it has been speculated that a major factor could be wind-blown fertilisers. Meanwhile, salt problems in masonry seem to be increasing with the widespread use of de-icing salts on roads. ⬢STONE ⬢METALS

The type and severity of pollution damage depends on the exposure, the type of pollutants and the building material. Water is a catalyst for many of the resulting reactions.

Left: Limestone (calcium carbonate) exposed in London displays the characteristic surface darkening that shows calcium carbonate has been transformed to calcium sulphate (gypsum), and the white streaking where the exposed gypsum has then been washed away by rainwater. This process steadily erodes the surface of the stone.

Top right: Alteration of the surface of lead sheet to pinkish lead tetraoxide is now common, especially in rural areas, and may be associated with wind-blown fertilisers. It does not decrease the longevity of the lead, but it can be very disfiguring.

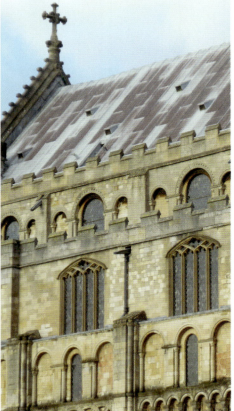

BUILDING ENVIRONMENT
DETERIORATION & DAMAGE: DETERIORATION OF THE ENVELOPE

BIOLOGICAL DETERIORATION

Many types of deterioration fall under this broad category, ranging from the microorganisms that feed on timberwork and other organic building components, to plants and animals that use the building for support or shelter. There is often a chain of damage; for example, a roof timber that is wet because of a persistent leak can be attacked by fungi, which in turn breaks the wood down sufficiently for it to be exploited by timber-consuming insects such as the deathwatch beetle. ➔TIMBER ➔BASICS

Timber Decay

Timber decay is often the critical material deterioration leading to failure of the building envelope: it has the most serious effects, and can lead to knock-on damage. For example, if a building flaw such as a blocked gutter allows enough water to penetrate that the rafter ends begin to decay, this can cause local failures of the roof, leading to more rainwater penetration and yet more deterioration of the timber.

Water ingress can lead to decay

Liquid water is the root cause of most problems with the building envelope. Here, for example, it has led to the deterioration of the timber bressumer beam supporting the wall and roof above a bow window.

Damaging plant growth

Certain plants will readily grow on building envelopes, wherever their seeds can lodge, and there is sufficient trapped water and debris: in gutters and on cornices, for example. In England the most ubiquitous of the plants found growing on buildings is the butterfly bush *Buddleia davidii*, a native of south-west China that was introduced to England in the 1890s (*top left*). Buddleia evolved to live on high rocky ground, and so can tolerate cool temperatures, disturbed ground and poor soil with a low moisture content; it also has small seeds that are spread by wind. Derelict building sites and neglected walls are ideal habitats (it was first noticed as a coloniser when it was found growing vigorously in bomb sites during the Second World War).

Some species are benign (*top centre*), but can still cause damage if they block rainwater goods or drains (*top left, centre right*). Others have woody roots that will cause severe damage if allowed to grow unchecked (*top right*).

Bottom left: Climbers of all types can cause problems if they are allowed to grow until they interfere with rainwater goods or force their way into roof spaces.

Bottom right: Trees growing near buildings can cause problems for drains and other water pipes, and during spring and autumn, shed flowers and leaves can block gutters. Wind-blown branches and falling trees will also be a greater risk in stormy weather.

Plants

Nearby trees can be a risk to buildings and especially roofs, not only because of potential wind damage, but because falling leaves and flowers can block rainwater goods. Trees should never be positioned with boughs overhanging a thatched roof: rainwater dripping from the branches hasten decay of the covering, as can dropped leaves and flowers; the sugary substances exuded by trees such as lime can also encourage breakdown. ⊕ROOFING

Plants growing on the envelope are a common source of building damage. Ivy can grow upwards, blocking gutters and sometimes sending adventitious roots into masonry (especially if the main stems have been severed close to the ground in an attempt to kill the plant). Woody shrubs that grow from wind-borne seeds, such as buddleia, can take root in nooks and crannies high on the façade: wind, rain, solar gain and freeze-thawing etching the surface of building stone can provide the niches for colonisation, whilst pollution from the combustion of fossil fuels can provide the necessary carbon-rich nutrients. Organic salts washing down from mosses and algae may encourage the salt decay of masonry, or the corrosion of critical metal components such as roof sheets and flashings.

BUILDING ENVIRONMENT
DETERIORATION & DAMAGE: DETERIORATION OF THE ENVELOPE

Climbers are often beautiful, and can sometimes help to protect the walls beneath them from rainwater or fluctuating temperatures, but they must be kept pruned to prevent them entering the roof space or damaging the gutters, or opening up mortar joints.

Climbers can also hide façade deterioration, delaying the recognition of problems until they are so advanced that symptoms begin to appear elsewhere.

Ferns and higher plants can grow on buildings where organic material has accumulated, and there is a good source of water. If they become established and grow, their roots can cause significant damage to the envelope.

The consequences of creepers growing on walls can be anything from beneficial to disastrous, depending on the type of creeper and its maturity. A covering of wisteria or ivy might protect a wall from the environment and keep it warm and dry, but if it does wet (perhaps because of problems with rainwater goods), then the creeper will inhibit drying. Climbers make maintenance difficult and more importantly they will cause severe damage if they are allowed to grow above gutter level, disrupting the rainwater goods, and forcing their way between the roof coverings and into the roof space. ⊖BASICS

Trees and other woody perennials can also cause problems if changes in drainage and runoff have desiccated the soil, forcing the plants to send out roots in search for alternative sources of moisture. Although tree roots cannot drive their way into intact drainage pipes, fine rootlets searching out moisture may find a route into drains through leaks or cracks, after which they will quickly proliferate and block the pipe. In the worst cases, roots might disturb foundations and floors. Certain species are considered of particular concern, such as Japanese knotweed (*Fallopia japonica*).

Animals

Organic building components can be a food source for higher animals as well as fungi and insects. On recently repaired windows, blue tits and other small songbirds can devour all the fresh linseed-oil putty before it is painted, and birds may also remove straw from thatch as nesting material. Insects living on the building will also be a food source: woodpeckers can cause severe damage to shingles when hunting for insects hiding underneath. ⊃GLASS ⊃ROOFING ⊃BASICS

The many creatures that make shelters and nests by burrowing into soft earth, or by exploiting holes and crevices in rocks, may find the wall of a building a very congenial environment. Open eaves, or damp and damaged roofs, make excellent habitats for many insects and higher animals, from mason bees (which nest in small holes they will excavate in mortar and even stone) to colonies of rats (which can entirely undermine earth walls by tunnelling to produce extensive 'runs'). ⊃EARTH & BRICK

Squirrels and other rodents such as mice and rats may shelter in roof spaces, and a common associated problem is that they will chew through wiring, which as well as causing direct damage, also creates a significant fire risk.

Roof spaces of roofs in poor repair are a common place to find bird nests; the nesting materials and debris host many insect pests, and these can migrate to the interior and attack the building contents. Birds will also nest in and around rainwater disposal systems, often blocking gutters and hoppers. Poorly maintained straw thatch will attract nesting birds as well as birds hunting for insects, and is similarly popular with squirrels. ⊃ROOFING

Pigeon infestation can be very localised, and different points will be used for roosting at night and for perching during the day (when the chosen location will usually be that which gives them the best view of a potential food source).

BUILDING ENVIRONMENT
DETERIORATION & DAMAGE: DETERIORATION OF THE ENVELOPE

Excreta can be a serious problem in buildings such as churches that support bat colonies.

Bat numbers have declined seriously as their natural habitats have disappeared, and with barns being converted for living space and woodland under stress, many country churches have become important roost sites. Bats do not roost in one place continually, but will always be seeking new sites in the building. They may enter gaps around the doors, windows or eaves; in churches, a common location for a roost is the gap between the chancel arch and the roof rafters. The greatest period of activity will be between June and September, with the bats hibernating from December until April.

Sadly, bats flying about and roosting inside can cause considerable damage. A colony can produce substantial quantities of droppings and urine, which can pit, stain and etch many materials; in churches, the outcome is usually damage to brasses, timberwork and wall paintings. The urine, which is 70% urea, decays to form dilute ammonia, and the droppings stick to the surface, making it very difficult to clean without causing further damage. Churches supporting large bat populations can quickly become unpleasant and unhygienic to use, setting the building users against those seeking to protect the bats. In the past, churches often had ceilings that protected the contents from damage, but many of these were removed when it became popular to reveal the timber roof supports.

Although many birds can make their homes in and around buildings, undoubtedly those that are most damaging for buildings in England are feral pigeons (*Columbia livia*) and herring gulls (*Larus argentatus*). The biggest problem with these birds is their guano, which is not only unsightly and a common source of salts, but a significant health hazard. Gulls may nest on roofs, occasionally in small but argumentative colonies; pigeons form large colonies and nest in protected spaces such as wooden soffits, where they can cause very considerable damage.

Jackdaws (*Corvus monedula*) may be a problem in large old chimneys: they will drop twigs down the chimney in the hope of forming a nesting platform, and if they do succeed in making a nest, this can be a source of a great deal of combustible material, as well as trapping moisture.

Not all animal damage is due to interlopers. Many buildings are, or were, intended to house livestock, and the urine of cattle, sheep and horses is a typical source of organic salts in barn walls. Wear caused by cattle licking the walls is a known problem for earthen byres.

PROBLEMATIC BUILDING DESIGN OR MATERIALS

Many design choices can have environmental consequences, particularly moisture problems. Materials may not be suitable for their location or exposure, or may have deteriorated over the lifetime of the building. It would be impossible to compose an exhaustive list of all the issues that could arise from a flawed choice of material or design; this is a short introduction to those that are most common and debilitating.

For humbler buildings of some antiquity, it is actually quite rare to find significant problems due to the original materials or building design, since any flaws will usually have been corrected long ago, or the building will have been abandoned. For these and other older buildings, recent deterioration can more usually be traced back to added materials or later alterations, which will often be introduced without an adequate understanding of how the building envelope is intended to operate, and the likely impact of changes (see **Building Alterations**).

Decorative design may conflict with function, and especially with good maintenance. Embedded downpipes are a common example of this type of problem: they prevent the regular repainting needed to prevent corrosion, reduce evaporative drying, and leaking water can readily travel into the body of the wall.

Fundamental issues may well occur wherever the envelope design has been led more by appearance than by practicality. For example, the downpipes of St Paul's Cathedral in London are concealed within its walls, where they are hard to maintain and where leaks can quickly cause severe problems. This is very often the case for any building type that follows a strict aesthetic, from Georgian terrace houses to minimalist glass office buildings. ⊖GLASS
⊖EARTH & BRICK

Faults in the original materials or design are most often met with in recent construction simply because these buildings have not been tested to the same degree by time. Many will also have been built using innovative materials or systems, which may not deliver the promised benefits, or may shorten lifespans or produce unforeseen problems.

BUILDING ENVIRONMENT
DETERIORATION & DAMAGE: DETERIORATION OF THE ENVELOPE

FLAWED WATER-HANDLING FEATURES

Faulty Roofs

Roof design and materials must both be fit-for-purpose if they are not to cause serious problems. Abutments and other vertical features piercing the coverings, such as chimneys and dormer windows, are a common site for rainwater penetration.

Valley gutters (which must carry the water from at least two pitches) are a typical source of leaks, especially if they have little or no fall, or are poorly supported: wherever debris can collect and water can pool or 'pond', water penetration is always a great risk. Parapet gutters are prone to leaking for much the same reason.

The lower the pitch of the roof, the greater the likelihood of ponding. This is a serious issue for modernist architecture, where the roof is often almost completely flat: flat roofs are intrinsically problematic; and since leaks can travel considerable distances before becoming visible on the interior, the exact source of the water can be very difficult to locate. Asphalt on low-pitched or flat roofs is particularly at risk, especially if aged and cracked, since it will be strongly affected by air temperature and solar heating. Differential thermal movement may break down the bond between the asphalt and the rim of embedded rainwater outlets, allowing rainwater to run down the outside of the downpipe. If an area of decking becomes saturated and begins to decay, it may well sag, causing further ponding. ⮕ROOFING

In areas with cold winters, parapet gutters bounding flat roofs are particularly susceptible to being blocked by ice and snow, which can lead to condensation problems on the underside of the metal (and subsequent rotting of the gutter sole or underside corrosion).

Horizontal valley gutters are a common cause of moisture problems. Standing water is always a danger, since it will very easily find its way downwards through any weak point in the fabric. Valleys also tend to fill with debris, blocking the drainage, trapping moisture and preventing evaporative drying.

Roofs covered by different materials, or with different underlying structures, may be prone to leaking at the interface, especially if the materials have very different characteristics of movement, or of thermal expansion and contraction. The most serious problems of this kind arise with glass atrium roofs, where differential movement can fracture the glazing. Bituminous felt coverings edged with metal or plastic trim often have problems, since the trim tends to shift and tear the edges of the covering. ⮕GLASS

Rainwater Disposal Expertise

According to the BRE, a fifth of all houses in the UK have defective rainwater disposal systems, and as many as one in 12 have problems with valley gutters or flashing. There is no argument about the importance of rainwater goods and drains to the longevity and performance of the building, so why should there be so much poor design, installation and maintenance? Part of the answer may lie in the current absence of a trade dedicated to rainwater disposal systems. In the past, this was the task of plumbers, who worked alongside other specialist building trades, and as their name implies, dealt largely with flashing, gutters, downpipes and drains that were so often made of lead (*plumbum* in Latin). The Worshipful Company of Plumbers is one of London's oldest livery companies.

With the introduction of sanitation and indoor water supplies, followed by gas central heating, the role of the plumber changed beyond recognition. Few if any plumbers would now claim to have any specialist knowledge of rainwater disposal, and design and execution is instead undertaken by architects, builders and roofers in an arguably *ad hoc* manner.

Faulty Rainwater Goods

Gutters

Eaves gutters carry a load of liquid water that can easily travel into the building fabric when there is a leak. Typical faults include insufficient capacity, kinks or blockages that allow water to collect, and ineffective outlets. When a gutter is too long or too small to cope with the load of rainwater from the roof, it may work well enough near the downpipe, but overflow further away from the outlet. If the end-stops are faulty or missing, rainwater will cascade onto the structure. A gutter set so that one side is lower than the other will have a reduced capacity, and the consequent overflowing will be particularly hazardous if the gutter tilts towards the wall rather than away from it.

Brackets can be a weak point: if there are too few, or they are incorrectly spaced, the gutter may sag, causing ponding or overflow. Heavy loads of ice and snow can cause brackets to bend or break.

Gutters may also be made of poor materials, have badly detailed joints, or be set too low below the eaves or too near to the wall plate (so that overflows wet the wall). The 'secret' gutters sometimes used at abutments are prone to blocking but difficult to maintain. Another 20th-century practice, now fortunately uncommon, was the use of precast concrete gutters. The linings of these tended to split, and most leaked badly.

Outlets

In a rainstorm, the flow of water into valley gutters can be so strong that it overshoots the outlet, especially if it has been poorly designed or inadequately sized. This can be particularly dangerous for timber-framed buildings.

Outlets often block with leaves and other debris, washed down from the roof and along the gutter. Even on a well-maintained building, this may occur during a bad storm, so good outlets must allow for an occasional overflow. As with gutters, this should be over the front of the outlet, where it is safer and will be more visible, rather than over the back, where it will be towards the wall.

Concealed outlets, such as those where the cheeks of dormer windows meet the roof, block easily but are difficult to inspect and clear. ⊖ROOFING

180 Loss of water-shedding features

Over time, water-shedding features may be lost as a result of deterioration or redecoration. The original purpose of features such as lime renders or cornices and hood mouldings may no longer be apparent to the building owner, and they may be perceived as purely decorative and sacrificed either to the whims of fashion, or because they are seen as a maintenance burden.

Downpipes

Downpipes may not be sufficiently large or numerous to handle the load of water from the gutters, and they are often positioned incorrectly. Turbulence at bends may interrupt flow, as it can with any pipe. Downpipes are sometimes discharged onto lower roofs, rather than into drains, and this can cause serious damage, especially if the discharge point is close to a wall, or the roof covering prevents the water from spreading out across the surface (as with pantiles or other ridged tiles, for example; or metal roof coverings, with their batten rolls and standing seams, and so forth).

The ideal downpipe – which would be round in cross-section, straight with few joints, and positioned well away from the wall with brackets to prevent leaks reaching the wall, encourage drying and allow easy maintenance – is, in practice, found very rarely. It is more usual to find that the pipes have been fastened close against the wall, often in corners where access and maintenance is difficult. Pipes may even have been partly or wholly embedded into the wall, where leaks will be particularly dangerous but could easily remain unnoticed until the resulting water damage has become very serious.

Aesthetic choices have often dominated over practicality when it comes to features designed to handle rainwater. Many large buildings and terraces have few downpipes on their front façades; instead, the rainwater is collected in a narrow parapet gutter that feeds into a trough or pipe running through the attic to the rear of the building. This arrangement is very dangerous should blockages or overflows occur, and there is usually very little access for maintenance.

Water-Shedding Features

Another problem is the removal of features designed to serve a practical purpose, such as hood mouldings and window surrounds intended to safely divert rainwater.

Faulty Ground Drainage

Often downpipes discharge to one side of the gully cover, and gaps and cracks in the surround may allow water to wick through. There may be a good deal of splashing onto the walls, and sometimes the gulley surround is only built up on three sides, which can channel water back into the wall.

All ground drainage will eventually block, so the worst designs are those that do not include easy access for inspection and maintenance. Blockages can be more troublesome if the downpipes pass directly into the ground without an intervening gulley; water can then back up the pipe, seeping out of joints and sometimes even overflowing the gutters.

Soakaways should generally operate efficiently for about 10 years before needing clearing, but many property owners are unaware of their existence, so maintenance is very poor. Luckily, the ground is often so porous and the soakaway sufficiently far from the building that the consequences of failure are not severe with ordinary rainfall, but problems may occur in severe storms.

Another important source of moisture problems is exterior ground levels that are higher than the interior floor levels, so moisture is inexorably drawn into the wall. This is a common problem for ancient churches, which once stood on mounds, but may now have churchyards that are feet higher than the floor level, but on a smaller scale it can trouble any building with recent landscaping.

Arguably the most common source of moisture problems is faulty drainage. It is not uncommon to find that although the roof has been repaired and all the gutters and downpipes have been replaced, the drainage at the foot of the wall remains blocked.

Even if the floor levels are higher than the ground around the walls, if the flow of runoff is towards the building rather than away from it, and there are no intervening drains, rainstorms will lead to wet walls. Rainwater runoff is an increasing problem for buildings now that so many external surfaces are covered with impermeable paving, as is splashback from rain.

The introduction of modern water services adds another potential source of moisture: leaking supply pipes and sewers.

BUILDING ENVIRONMENT
DETERIORATION & DAMAGE: DETERIORATION OF THE ENVELOPE

PROBLEMS WITH WALLS

Wall Thickness

The ability of traditional wall construction to buffer heat and to prevent moisture penetration depends on the thickness of the walls. This is not always adequate, especially if the exterior wall was once an internal wall (made external, for example, by the demolition of an adjoining building).

Vented hollow walls may develop condensation problems.

Condensation in Corners

Mould and other signs of condensation damage can often be found in corners, and there are a number of reasons for this, including in some cases poor detailing letting in water. The primary factors are the exposure of the corner to wind, and the geometry, however: at a corner, there is much more surface exposed to cooling and wetting on the exterior in comparison to the internal surface area exposed to evaporative drying.

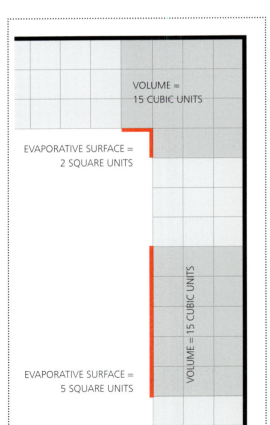

Mould growth in corners

There are a number of reasons why moulds and other microorganisms are most commonly found growing in the corners of rooms. Externally, corners have a greater area exposed to rain and wind, and internally, the ratio of surface area to volume is very low, reducing evaporation. Additionally, air movement may be restricted by local turbulence, and often also by the placement of furniture.

Mortar Joints

Pointing will eventually erode and need replacing if it is to continue to keep rain from penetrating masonry walls. Repointing must be done with skill and attention to detail, using the correct mortar and appropriate tools to prevent forming voids in which penetrating moisture can pool.

Moisture problems can easily occur in masonry that has been constructed with mortars based on cement rather than lime. Such mortars are hard, brittle and water-resistant; cracks can easily form between the joint and the brick or stone, allowing water to wick into the wall, but preventing it from drying out again. Similar problems occur when walls are repointed with cement-based mortars. ⊖MORTARS ⊖EARTH & BRICK

Infill Panels

Traditional infill panels in half-timbered construction were made of various materials, chiefly wattle-and-daub or wooden staves packed with hemp and lime, although brick masonry was popular in the 15th century, and again for construction and repairs in the 19th and 20th centuries.

The interface between the infill panel and the timber frame is a weak point that can let in rainwater if the joint is allowed to deteriorate. Penetrating moisture can be particularly serious if the materials or construction prevent this water evaporating, since this can lead to decay of the timber frame: for example, if the infill panels have been repaired with cement-based mortars. ⊖TIMBER ⊖EARTH & BRICK

Hollow-Wall Construction

Both modern curtain walling and traditional cladding – shingling, tile-hanging, weatherboarding and metal sheeting – depend not so much on the water-proofing of the exterior leaf as on the systems of ventilation, and particularly of drainage that are intended to remove any water that does penetrate. If such systems are inadequate, the wall will fail, and this can be serious because moisture ingress will happen within the wall, where it can do a great deal of damage before being noticed.

Ventilation will depend strongly on wind speed and direction, so problems may begin in a hitherto effective wall if the exterior environment changes. ⊖GLASS

Use of Semi-Permeable or Impermeable Vapour Barriers

'Vapour barriers' – sheet materials intended to retard or prevent the movement of water vapour – are a very recent addition to the lexicon of building technology.

After the Second World War, lightweight framed construction systems, and impermeable cladding materials such as glass, metal and asphalt, became popular, which greatly reduced the fabric's ability to buffer humidity. At the same time, ventilation rates were reduced, and the inevitable result was an increase in condensation problems. In response, vapour barriers were introduced: the idea was to provide a layer that stopped the water vapour generated in the building from travelling through the envelope, and condensing on colder parts of the roof, walls or floors.

BUILDING ENVIRONMENT
DETERIORATION & DAMAGE: DETERIORATION OF THE ENVELOPE

The belief that vapour transport was the principal culprit in moisture problems was based on theories developed by Frank Rowley, an American engineer, which assumed that most water vapour passing through the envelope was diffusing through the pores of the building materials. This was enthusiastically taken up by the manufacturers of materials such as polythene sheet, which was proposed as an ideal material for vapour barriers, though after many failures it was eventually replaced by various semi-permeable membranes. In the USA, vapour barriers became for some decades a standard part of the hollow-wall construction, despite considerable confusion about exactly where in a multilayered system they should be positioned: in colder climates, the theory held, they should be on the inner, 'warmer' side of the envelope, since this was assumed to be the side where the vapour pressure would be higher. This is not necessarily true, and indeed for most buildings diffusion is a negligible source of vapour transfer: virtually all the water vapour travelling between the exterior and interior will be carried by air infiltrating through openings and gaps.

The fabric can accumulate water not just from the condensation of moist indoor air, but from every kind of source and from every direction: above, from failures of the roof or rainwater control; below, from blocked drains or water mains or runoff; via the penetration of humid air or rain through exterior faults; or via plumbing leaks in the interior, to name just the most common examples. With luck, a wall with a vapour barrier in place will stay dry, and its presence will not be an issue, but there always is a danger that it could lead to mould or more serious moisture problems. As a result of widespread damage and some dramatic failures, the demand for vapour barriers has now been dropped from the US building codes (see **History of Vapour Barriers**). It should be noted that other water-resistant materials used on or within the wall surfaces, including impermeable paints and vinyl wallpapers, can have a very similar effect.

Although vapour barriers are no longer obligatory, they are still widely used in new construction, and in England they are increasingly incorporated during works to older buildings as well, often when insulation is installed or attics converted to living space but also increasingly as a precautionary measure in walls. Part of the reason for their continued popularity seems to be a confusion between vapour barriers and air barriers, which are intended to prevent air entering wall cavities (this does cause vapour transfer, as well as reducing the thermal mass of the envelope). Reducing air infiltration can be vital when it comes to making buildings energy-efficient. Vapour barriers are not necessarily air barriers as well, but manufacturers have begun to produce 'air-and-vapour control layers' [AVCLs] which are intended to retard the migration of both air and water vapour. Indeed, the 2011 edition of *BS 5250 Code of practice for control of condensation in buildings* has replaced the term 'vapour barrier' with 'AVCL'.

To be effective an air barrier must have no flaws or gaps, but it can be difficult to ensure the complete integrity of an AVCL membrane, especially at the joints between floors, roofs and walls, at windows, or around building services. Because the membrane will reduce evaporation from the fabric, any holes or gaps can lead to condensation problems. As it happens, traditional building materials are a safe and effective way of excluding both air and water: for example, renders and plasters of lime mortar have been shown to be excellent at preventing air leakage into cavity walls, but without increasing the risk of condensation. Permeable renders and plasters will also reduce moisture uptake from rain or condensation, but without impeding drying (see **Wall Finishes**, below).

History of Vapour Barriers

American building scientist William Rose first traced the history of vapour barriers in a paper for the Association for Preservation Technology in 1997, and his work was one of a number of studies which led to the requirement for vapour barriers to be used in construction being removed from building codes in the USA. This box draws strongly on Rose's highly recommended article.

Traditional construction did not use vapour barriers, but over the second half of the 20th century they became standard practice in modern building, and eventually came to be recommended practice for traditional structures as well. Their introduction has been closely tied to that of insulation, and also to an emphasis on the transfer of water vapour rather than liquid water (which is in fact the true source of building deterioration) that has dominated building design for the past half century.

Originally, thermal insulation was not used primarily for comfort or energy efficiency, but rather to prevent cold spots and mould growth in humidified industrial buildings such as mills. Unfortunately, the insulation itself absorbed moisture, and could eventually become saturated.

In the 19th century, American engineer Frank Rowley was asked by the National Mineral Wool Association to test mineral-wool insulation. Rowley had successfully applied the heat-transfer equations developed by French physicist Joseph Fourier to buildings, so he tried a very similar mathematical approach to model the transfer of moisture. His model attributed all moisture movement to the diffusion of water vapour through materials from areas of high pressure to areas of low pressure, and did not take into account moisture brought in to the system by air infiltration, nor liquid water penetration, nor the impact of moisture already within the system. Although Rowley did conduct a number of experiments on walls of light timber-frame construction insulated with mineral wool, since these eliminated all moisture sources other than diffusion, they served simply to confirm his theories.

Membranes that restrict the passage and evaporation of water can be innocuous, but they can also sometimes be the cause of serious problems. If quantities of moisture are introduced into the wall by rain penetration, leaks or severe condensation, or even during construction, it will be trapped, and the result can be mould problems and material deterioration. In the worst cases, affected buildings have had to be demolished: the social housing shown here was only 10 weeks old, but black mould has already covered the membrane, and the timber frames are saturated and beginning to decay. Although this example is in the USA, similar problems have occurred in the UK.

BUILDING ENVIRONMENT
DETERIORATION & DAMAGE: DETERIORATION OF THE ENVELOPE

One conclusion that Rowley might have drawn from his experiments was that mineral wool was not suitable as an insulation material, and that preference should be given instead to materials that were dense and not very permeable to air. He instead proposed that moisture problems be prevented by incorporating barriers to prevent the uptake of water vapour. He also supported the ventilation of attics and underfloor voids, and such was his influence that both practices were soon adopted as standard in new building construction, although they were so very different to the traditional approaches which had previously been considered best practice. Although problems arose almost immediately, these were attributed to faults with the workmanship rather than the theory. For example, insulation of timber-clad walls made the wood much colder, and hence led to raised moisture contents and the peeling of the paint, but this was blamed on vapour travelling through the cladding from inside the building.

American building regulations requiring vapour membranes in modern house construction seem to have been adopted with little or no critical assessment, perhaps because they first appeared during the Second World War. The key paper supporting the regulations, which William Rose describes as being 'obscure', required them to be incorporated in new walls and ceilings, and by 1951 this paper was being cited in regulations that covered not just modern multilayer hollow-wall construction systems, but buildings of all types.

Since water-resistant paints and other coatings can be used as vapour barriers, the new regulations were enthusiastically promoted by manufacturers of paints as well as of membranes, and it was soon forgotten that none of the approaches advocated had actually been proven. Much confusion resulted from the requirement to install barriers on the 'warm' side of the wall to avoid condensation problems: which is the warm side not only depends on the construction and the climate, but may well change with the seasons.

The earliest UK references to the use of 'vapour barriers' is in post-war editions of the Building Research Station's *The Principles of Modern Building*. Discussing the circumstance under which condensation could occur within the thickness of a construction element, the 1959 edition noted that (depending on the moisture load and the materials used) the condensed moisture might be absorbed and held by the fabric until the environmental conditions favoured evaporation. It did suggest that a vapour barrier might sometimes be considered for use on the warm side of a wall, where the capacity of the fabric to absorb moisture was small and the moisture content of the internal air was high (a humidified factory was given as an example), but observed that – since installing and maintaining a complete and perfect barrier was likely to be difficult – an alternative escape path for any vapour able to penetrate would need to be provided.

Inevitably, wider use led to many practical issues, and some memorable disasters. The impossibility of keeping moisture entirely out of building walls was soon more widely recognised, and impermeable materials such as polythene sheet were replaced by semi-permeable membranes that were said to be able to prevent liquid water penetration whilst permitting the passage of water vapour. It is not clear from the physics of moisture transfer how this could be possible (see **Building Science**), and in practice such materials have indeed been known to transmit rainwater under certain conditions. Notable failures associated with the use of vapour barriers have continued both in the USA and the UK.

The requirement for vapour barriers was removed from the US building code in 2010. The UK building regulations have never demanded their use, but they do state that *"any material that could be adversely affected by condensation, moisture from the ground, rain and snow will either resist the passage of moisture to the material, be treated or otherwise be protected from moisture"*. The British Standard **BS 5250 Code of practice for control of condensation in buildings** (first published in 2002) gives prescriptive recommendations on the use of 'vapour-control layers'; the 2011 edition replaces this with 'air- and-vapour control layers' [AVCLs]. As a result, vapour barriers have increasingly been incorporated under the impression that it would be dangerous to omit them.

It is, however, safer to assume that some water will always find its way into the building fabric, and avoid including any materials that might hinder it evaporating away again (including vinyl wallpapers and impermeable paints). If a vapour barrier does need to be used – for example, to protect water-sensitive insulation – the building maintenance regime will need to explicitly incorporate regular inspections of that area to catch any moisture problems before they can cause serious damage (see *Care & Repair*).

Faulty Wall Finishes

Problematic Renders

In the past, renders were a standard way of protecting exposed masonry walls from moisture, but many traditional lime renders were removed during the 19th and 20th centuries, when it became fashionable to expose the underlying masonry. Traditional lime-based renders require regular upkeep by limewashing, and this was another reason given for their removal.

From the early 19th century onwards, replacement renders were usually based on cement (first natural, or 'Roman' cement, and later by 'artificial' hydraulic cements, such as Ordinary Portland Cement), but these can be a source of problems rather than a remedy. Cement renders are almost impermeable, so rain will course down the surface (rather than being absorbed in the surface pores, as it is with a lime- or clay-based render). They are also more brittle than the wall, and so tend to form fine cracks, through which the water flowing down the surface can easily wick. This water – together with any moisture entering the walls from other sources – will be trapped, steadily increasing moisture levels. This is particularly dangerous for earthen buildings, where the eventual result can be such a high water content that the clay loses cohesion, causing the structure to collapse. ⊃MORTARS ⊃EARTH & BRICK

Cement renders and cement tanking can also push moisture problems further up the wall. ⊃MORTARS

Cement renders

Cement is an unsuitable material for renders, being brittle and of very low permeability. If water is able to penetrate behind a cement-based render, it cannot easily evaporate and will be trapped in the wall, or else travel through the wall to evaporate on the interior.

The cement render shown here demonstrates two typical problems: rainwater from a faulty downpipe is wicking in through a crack in the render; and water from a blocked drain is rising up behind the render at the base of the wall.

BUILDING ENVIRONMENT
DETERIORATION & DAMAGE: DETERIORATION OF THE ENVELOPE

188 Damage due to a cement render

By trapping penetrating water, cement renders can quickly lead to the deterioration of the wall behind: here the removal of the render has revealed extensive decay of the historic timber frame, and the decomposition of the original wattle-and-earth infill panels.

Problematic Claddings

Cladding functions very much like a roof covering. As with a tiled roof, there will be more penetration of water if the lapped units (slates or shingles or timber boards) lie absolutely flat against each other, since this creates the ideal conditions for wicking rainwater into the wall. ➔ROOFING ➔TIMBER

Curtain-Wall Systems

Many of the materials used for the outer leaf of modern curtain walls – glass and metal, for example – are waterproof, and like cement will cause rain to run down the surfaces, but will prevent the evaporation to the exterior of any water that penetrates. The weak point is therefore at the joints between panels of material, which must be very well detailed. Even so, moisture ingress is likely: early single-leaf curtain-wall systems tended to leak badly under certain weather conditions. Later rainscreen walls have internal drains and ventilation to remove incoming moisture, but these systems will be overwhelmed if too much rainwater is able to penetrate the outer leaf. ➔GLASS

Paints & Coatings

Paints and coatings are often applied simply for decoration, and traditional masonry and timber were often protected with limewash, which has also helped to keep lime renders and plasters in good condition. A number of other external building materials (such as many softwoods and ferrous metals) must also be protected with coatings.

Paints and coatings are not innocuous, however: although they may reduce the amount of water penetrating to the base material, they will limit the evaporation of any water that does get in (for example, through cracks in the paint layer at joints). Since it is impossible to entirely exclude water, successful coatings are permeable enough to allow moisture to escape before the underlying materials are damaged. This was a notable characteristic of the lead-based paints that were commonly used until the mid-20th century, and which tended to become chalky and increasingly permeable on exposure.

Impermeable Coatings

Most modern paint and coating systems are intended to be as impermeable as possible, to prevent moisture penetration, but in practice no coating is entirely waterproof, and permeable building materials are easily hygroscopic enough to overcome the barrier to absorption posed by the coating. On the other hand, evaporation will be inhibited, so moisture levels will gradually build up. Eventually this may lead to such problems as decay and corrosion, or the decohesion of plasters and clays, and even of stone and brick. ⊝TIMBER ⊝METALS ⊝MORTARS ⊝EARTH & BRICK ⊝STONE

Coatings generally degrade when they are exposed to sunlight. Hard or brittle coatings will also tend to crack and split where they run over joints (especially joints in moving elements such as windows and gates). Flaws of this type allow water to enter behind the coating, where it is then trapped.

Failed coatings on window frames

Windows are an excellent example of the benefits and dangers of waterproof coatings.

Paint prevents glazing putty drying out and failing, and also protects the frame from water damage, but if the paint is poorly chosen or poorly maintained, it will allow water to reach the frame. At the same time, it hampers evaporation, allowing moisture levels to build up. The outcomes include rotting of timber frames (*left*) and corrosion of metal frames (*right*).

BUILDING ENVIRONMENT
DETERIORATION & DAMAGE: DETERIORATION OF THE ENVELOPE

Faulty Treatments of Subterranean Spaces

Basements, cellars and subfloor voids are usually rather cold, and may feel somewhat damp due to lateral moisture penetration from the ground, but this is not a problem as long as the spaces are not used for living, and the walls can be left uninsulated and undecorated; the space can then serve to keep the rest of the envelope in good condition. Most underfloor spaces are actually quite dry unless the building has faulty peripheral drainage, poor runoff or some other liquid moisture problem.

A common remedial treatment for a subterranean space with moisture problems is to line the walls internally with an impermeable material, such as a cement-based plaster. This does not prevent water entering the wall, but it will reduce evaporation; if it is able to evaporate above the cement, it will be pushed upwards. Tanking a cellar or basement that is wet because of a serious moisture problem such as a leaking drain, without dealing with the source, has even been known to lead to moisture problems in the walls of the rooms above.

If subfloor walls are wet, then floor timbers – especially embedded joists – may begin to decay. Underfloor ventilation was first introduced in the early 19th century specifically to protect the timber from rot, because at the time the connection between wood-destroying fungus and the supply of moisture was not recognised, and it was thought that fresh air would prevent its growth. In practice, ventilation grilles often appear to serve little purpose – the ventilation achievable would not be sufficient to resolve a moisture problem significant enough to allow decay – and ground-level grilles may allow runoff and flood water to enter the underfloor space. ⊖TIMBER

Over time the ground levels around a building may change, and runoff may be directed towards, rather than away from, the base of the walls. In severe cases, walls intended to be exposed may end up partly buried, leading to problems with lateral moisture penetration.

The reduced evaporation to the exterior may also exacerbate damage if there is another source of liquid water affecting the wall, such as a blocked drain.

Serious decay problems have been noticed where underfloor insulation has been used to prevent heat loss, although it is not always clear whether this is a direct result of the insulation (associated, perhaps, with condensation), or due to the insulation materials trapping penetrating water from sources such as groundwater or faulty drains.

Where water penetration is a problem, decay will be worse if an impermeable floor covering has been laid (a vinyl sheet, for example; or a carpet with a rubber backing), or if solid furniture is preventing drying from an area of floor or wall.

Problems with Chimneys

Chimneys are very exposed, and so are prone to many environmental problems, including erosion and damage from high winds (especially where they have been used as a support for television antennae or – worse – micro wind turbines). Structural deterioration is also associated with use: thermal expansion of the flue lining can cause vertical cracking, for example. Structural problems are all the more likely since chimneys were often constructed with a single brick skin.

Salts from combustion gases will readily combine with water, and can attack the flue lining and the mortar joints and fillets. The water driving the salt deterioration comes from more than one source: rain penetration, certainly, but also condensation.

Rain can simply fall down the flue, or be wicked in around faulty flashing and mortar fillets (especially if these have been repaired in the past with cement-based mortars), or penetrate through the weakened masonry. Gable stacks and chimneys with offsets are particularly vulnerable to weather damage. Mortar used to anchor the chimney pots and to weather joints will be prone to frost decay.

Condensation occurs in chimneys which are still in use if the combustion gases travel upwards through the flue cool too quickly; this can happen if the fuels have a high water content, or if the flue is very wide or tall, or if it is cooled below the dew-point temperature by the exterior conditions. In disused flues, condensation will occur if either the fireplace or the chimney is sealed, or there is simply inadequate ventilation in the absence of a fire in the grate.

Damage is often worst at or immediately below the roof covering, since water in the upper part of the chimney will be drawn towards the drier area below the covering. Salt-jacking of mortar joints or the formation of ettringite in cement can cause bulging, and because rain wetting and drying are unlikely to be the same on all sides, afflicted chimneys may be bent away from the prevailing weather. ⊃MORTARS ⊃CONCRETE

The deposition of combustion products can lead to salt decay of the chimney masonry.

The failure of flue linings is often a critical factor in all these types of deterioration, but it can also cause direct damage: failed parging may fall and block a flue, or allow smoke to escape into neighbouring flues.

Problems may also be visible on the interior, particularly staining from hygroscopic salts accumulating at bends in the flue and then migrating through the chimney breast. Casting replacement liners *in situ* adds large amounts of water, and this can lead to staining or make existing stains worse. Stains can appear even after the chimney has fallen into disuse, if the flue is not kept dry by capping and ventilation.

Disuse can introduce other issues as well: for example, if a chimney breast has been removed without the stack being dismantled or otherwise supported, structural problems are a very likely result.

BUILDING ENVIRONMENT
DETERIORATION & DAMAGE: DETERIORATION OF THE ENVELOPE

FAULTY WINDOW & DOOR DESIGNS

Openings such as doors and windows must be protected from rainwater penetration, but unfortunately detailing and water-shedding features are often lost when windows are replaced. For example, it is common to find that the drips cut in the underside of cills have been filled with paint, and replacement cills may have no drips at all.

Moisture penetration can lead to the decay of timber lintels, but this only rarely causes structural failure. Decayed lintels would not need to be replaced unless there were clear signs of ongoing instability.

The traditional approach to controlling temperature and preventing light damage to the building contents was by blinds and awnings, but these have often been removed as fashions have changed. For float glass, solar films are a common alternative, but they have a relatively short lifespan, and will eventually start to blister and require replacement. For this reason they can cause considerable damage if applied to early glass, especially if the glass is already corroding ⊖GLASS

Modern windows are often designed to prevent all air leakage, and it is also increasingly common to draughtproof older windows. In both cases, if there is no other sufficient source of ventilation, this can lead to condensation problems in occupied rooms.

Modern window construction

For modern hollow-wall construction, the waterproofing of windows presents considerable difficulties. They must be sealed back to the wall leaf behind the cladding, which itself is designed to serve as a second layer of waterproofing.

POOR MAINTENANCE

Waterproofing components often have limited lifespans, especially when exposed, and if these are not checked regularly and replaced when necessary (before they have had a chance to fail), the result can be severe moisture penetration. Examples of materials needing regular inspection and repair include mortar fillets and renders, flashings, paints and other coatings, and sealants such as mastics. Since gutters collect any debris washed off the roof, they can easily block. Without regular maintenance, gutters have even been known to support quite sizeable shrubs. This build-up of vegetation can be great enough to bridge the gap between the gutter and the wall, making a conduit for rainwater to enter the wall head.

Outlets and hopper boxes are a major source of damp in buildings because they are easily blocked. If the outlet from a parapet gutter to a hopper box is through a thick wall, then the hopper might be set at a much lower level than the gutter. This produces a good fall for the outlet, but leaves a long length of angled pipe within the wall. It is always necessary to be aware of concealed outlets and pipes because water damage frequently does not become obvious until after there is significant concealed damage (perhaps the decay of a timber lintel, for example, which then manifests as cracking or even collapse).

It is common to find the hallmarks of faulty downpipes: water fanning out behind the pipe, often associated with salt staining, and even the growth of moisture-loving plants such as algae and ferns in eroded joints. Problems are often very obvious in the aftermath of rainstorms.

If a leak is allowed to continue, salt deterioration may appear on the interior of the wall, and internal surfaces may begin to powder and flake. Timber components such as skirting boards, as well as lintels, window linings, embedded joist ends and joist plates, will be at risk of decay.

Blockages in hoppers can usually be seen easily because water cascades over the edges. Overflow spouts may be added to make failure more obvious and move the excess water away from the walls, but this will only be effective if they are used as an early-warning system for blockages, and not as an alternative to clearance.

BUILDING ENVIRONMENT
DETERIORATION & DAMAGE: DETERIORATION OF THE ENVELOPE

194 Causes and results of poor maintenance

Failure to keep the rainwater disposal system in good working condition will quickly lead to problems in the interior, from staining and salt cystallisation to timber decay.

Blocked downpipes tend to overflow from the joints, or through splits and holes made by corrosion of cast-iron pipes where painting has been neglected. Unfortunately these flaws are often at the back of the pipe, where they are hidden from view and from maintenance: also precisely where a leak can do most damage to the wall, and where there is little evaporation to aid drying.

Drains inevitably block as silt is washed into them, so neglect of maintenance in the drainage systems can have serious repercussions.

In hollow-wall construction, any trays or other internal drains must be fixed to the internal leaf to stop water leaking behind, so moisture problems will begin if the adhesives begin to fail. The trays may have collected debris as the wall was being built, preventing them from operating correctly. Detritus may increase as insects such as nesting wasps enter through the ventilation holes.

PROBLEMATIC BUILDING ALTERATIONS

EXTERNAL ALTERATIONS

Building additions or alterations will often disturb the equilibrium of the building. Issues may arise if materials exert different loads, or if the way the building interacts with the weather, especially the wind and rain, is altered.

The intersections between the existing building and any new additions must be very well detailed, particularly if the extension requires the introduction of valley gutters, or if it compromises the existing rainwater disposal or drains. If alterations to traditional buildings are made using modern materials and building systems, there may be unexpected conflicts. For example, the runoff from large areas of glass or metal may erode masonry joints below.

A common external intervention in the Victorian period was the removal of exterior lime- and clay-based renders from masonry. This made moisture penetration more likely. More recently, permeable renders and washes have been replaced with cements and impermeable paints, which will cut evaporation and can therefore trap penetrating moisture in the wall; vapour membranes can have a very similar effect.

INTERNAL ALTERATIONS

It is even more common to rearrange or otherwise alter the interior spaces of buildings than it is to alter their exteriors. Assuming that alterations such as the removal of walls do not endanger the building structurally, the most important changes will be those that alter the air movement, ventilation, temperature or humidity, or the way the fabric interacts with the environment. For example, traditional solid and suspended-timber ground floors acted as a large surface for water from the ground to evaporate, keeping capillary rise under control. Since the Second World War, however, many of these floors have been replaced with impermeable concrete, often incorporating a damp-proof membrane for good measure. From then on, all evaporation must be through the walls (which remain in direct contact with the ground), and in combination with a source of moisture such as a leaking sewer or drain can result in capillary rise problems in the walls.

Subtle alterations can still produce significant environmental changes: even moving furniture can change patterns of airflow and drying. Problems are most likely to be acute where there is a substantial difference between the interior and exterior conditions because the building is being artificially heated or cooled. In snowy climates, insulated ceilings can lead to ice dams, especially where warmed interior air is able to travel upwards into the roof space around the edges of the ceiling, or through the voids made by recessed lights or ductwork.

One problem unique to traditional buildings with interesting roof framing has been the removal of ceilings to expose the attractive timberwork. This means there is no longer any roof space or attic space to act as a buffer, and it also removes the physical protection which a ceiling provides against leaks and dust, and against nesting birds and bats.

BUILDING ENVIRONMENT
DETERIORATION & DAMAGE: DETERIORATION OF THE ENVELOPE

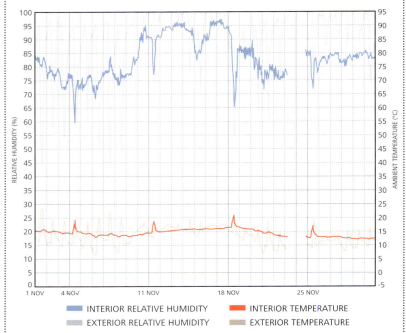

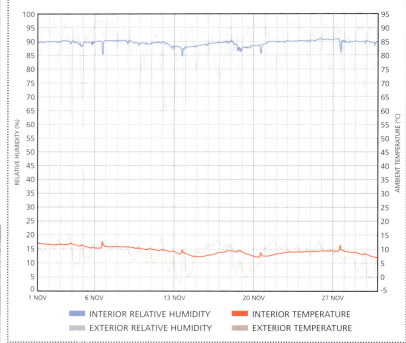

PROBLEMS DUE TO OTHER INTERVENTIONS

INSULATION

Roof Insulation

Adding insulation in an attic at ceiling level is an excellent way of preventing the loss of heating and cooling energy, but it prevents the roof space being dried by the warm air rising from the interior. The risk of condensation will be greater if the ventilation of the roof space has been reduced (perhaps by adding an underlay when re-roofing), or if humid air is infiltrating from the interior through the ceiling via holes for recessed lighting, access hatch, pipes and cables. That said, most spaces will perform perfectly well, since the roof timbers will act as an effective humidity buffer.

If attics are converted to living space, the insulation must be installed above, between or below the structural elements of the roof, and will therefore be more vulnerable to rain penetration. If the roof space is sealed from the exterior, penetrating rainwater or rising water vapour will be trapped, which could lead to serious problems such as timber decay, or the corrosion of metal coverings or fixings. For traditional roofs with no boards or other continuous linings, there is usually sufficient air exchange through the covering (and if not, there is sufficient humidity buffering in the timbers to prevent condensation); but modern roofs with underlays will sometimes fail without good eaves-to-ridge ventilation. ➔ROOFING

Wall Insulation

Insulating walls presents greater challenges: for example, some types of cavity-wall insulation may absorb moisture from leaks, or even from condensation on the internal face of the cool outer leaf. For historic buildings, installing wall insulation (whether on the interior or exterior) will almost certainly damage period features, and the proportions of the room or façade, but there are practical problems as well.

Insulating on the interior will stop the wall being warmed by the heated indoor air in cold weather, which as a result will tend to become colder. If humid indoor air is able to come into contact with it, condensation may result. If the wall surface is porous, the moisture will be absorbed, and provided it is not trapped behind the insulation but able to evaporate again when conditions change, problems would be unlikely. If, however, the condensation is collecting on impermeable surfaces, or if the rate at which water is entering exceeds the rate at which it is evaporating from the wall, then there may be problems. This risk is exacerbated if there are other sources of water, such as leaks or rain penetration. Wet materials will also conduct heat very effectively, so poorly designed insulation can prove counter-productive, increasing rather than decreasing the exchange of energy through the envelope (see also **Special Topic: Improving Energy & Carbon Performance**).

Insulating on the exterior is more effective, since it makes use of the thermal capacity of the wall. In theory it is also a lower-risk option, but it must be detailed and installed to prevent rain penetration, which can prove challenging (especially at openings and corners, or wherever the thickness of the insulation interferes with any water-shedding features such as eaves and cornices).

Facing page:
At St Botolph's Church in Hardham, West Sussex, the replacement of the original ceiling (removed during 19th-century renovations) dramatically improved the building's ability to buffer external conditions. This was vital to the preservation of the 11th-century wall paintings.

Top: The church before the reinstatement of the ceiling, together with a graph showing how the internal conditions closely corresponded to the exterior weather.

Bottom: After a new ceiling was installed, the interior conditions fluctuated much less quickly, and temperature and humidity changes were greatly reduced.

BUILDING ENVIRONMENT
DETERIORATION & DAMAGE: DETERIORATION OF THE ENVELOPE

INAPPROPRIATE TREATMENTS

Buildings will often have been treated for environmental problems in the past, with more or less success. Many or most proprietary treatments are not merely ineffective, but invasive; and some can lead to new problems. What is more, if limited funds are spent on an expensive proprietary remedial system rather than on works to fix the underlying cause (usually a straightforward moisture problem), the problem may well remain unresolved. What is more, many common treatments and repairs can have unintended adverse consequences.

Impermeable Interior Finishes for Rooms Partly Below Ground Level

Applying waterproof coatings or plasters to deal with water penetration from raised exterior ground levels is a good example of a treatment that fails, because it addresses the symptom rather than the underlying problem. Walls showing interior deterioration due to moisture problems are coated with a water-resistant plaster (usually cement), but by preventing evaporation this forces the water to move elsewhere. Applying an impermeable finish to an external wall that is partly below ground level, for example, will simply push the evaporation zone for water penetrating laterally through from the ground higher up the wall.

Backfilling Drains with Gravel or Pea Shingle

Land drains are often installed at the foot of exterior walls to address moisture problems. The correct way of detailing perimeter drains – capping with clay and grass – is shown in **Treatment & Repair**, but in England they are often constructed exactly like French field drains, and backfilled with gravel in the belief that this will aid evaporation. Instead, it allows rainwater and runoff to run down through the gravel and collect in the base of the drain, but the spaces between the stones are far too large to act as capillaries, so the water is trapped. By contrast, clay has very fine capillaries that resist water penetration from above, but can draw groundwater up to the surface, where it can evaporate.

Backfilling with gravel

In England, drains at the base of walls are often filled with gravel rather than being capped over with clay, the preferred material. This is poor practice, since the gravel prevents evaporation – indeed, pea shingle is often used as garden mulch for precisely this reason – and it also makes inspection and maintenance difficult, because it is more difficult to excavate than clay. Over time the trench will collect washed-in debris and topsoil. Eventually it becomes the ideal habitat for weeds and other self-seeding plants, the roots of which may grow into the pipes.

Proprietary Systems for 'Damp-Proofing'

Since moisture problems are ubiquitous, products for 'damp' remediation are always likely to be popular, especially if they promise infallible and permanent results. Treatments tend to be standardised: the same approach is used for every building moisture problem, regardless of the actual source. Moreover, it is usually difficult to see the proposed systems could possibly work, since they tend to be founded on basic misunderstandings of how moisture and heat behave. For example, the oldest and most famous proprietary system, the 'Knapen tube', apparently relies on the idea that the increase in buoyancy of moist air will be overcome by the wet air being colder, and therefore falling rather than rising, which is demonstrably not the case.

Companies often begin with good intentions and may even request testing from independent bodies. To date, such tests have all found any improvement to be related not to the proprietary product, but to other interventions made at the same time, such as clearing drains and repairing rainwater goods. As a result some companies have ceased selling products that have been shown not to function as advertised, but others have continued to promote them, sometimes quite aggressively. Sadly, many of these systems will actually damage the building, and some can make moisture problems worse rather than better. More importantly, all are expensive, and divert resources away from dealing with the primary causes of any real moisture problem: typically a blocked drain or downpipe, leaking plumbing or some other simple fault, often combined with a cement render that is trapping the moisture.

Some observers have noted that proprietary 'damp' systems are encouraged by the mortgage process, where the lender requires a survey, and the surveyor recommends a 'damp expert' to look at the possibility of problems. In practice such expertise is rarely independent, but usually comes from companies offering remedial systems.

WALL SIPHONS & OTHER EMBEDDED UNITS

Wall siphons are sold as a preventative measure, as well as a way of dealing with existing 'rising damp'. They are a common sight on buildings with a history of moisture problems, where the fundamental reasons for the problem have never been identified nor dealt with.

In about 1908, Achille Knapen, an engineer from Brussels, invented the 'knapen siphon', a system with which he claimed to have dried the walls of the Belgian Royal Palace in just two months. His product was subsequently installed in many important buildings, including the Palace of Versailles, and was internationally patented. British Knapen Ltd began to operate under licence in the UK and Ireland in 1928.

Similar proprietary systems for drying building fabric using 'ventilating' units, made of porous clay or plastic embedded in holes made in the wall, were introduced by various companies over subsequent decades, in many different shapes and materials.

BUILDING ENVIRONMENT
DETERIORATION & DAMAGE: DETERIORATION OF THE ENVELOPE

Knapen's system used units triangular in cross-section and about 3 cm in diameter. These were embedded into holes drilled upwards into the wall at a slight angle. Siphons were supposed to reach the centre of the wall, and were originally made to measure. They were placed in a straight line, about 13 inches (33 cm) apart in early installations, although later this varied considerably, according to the installer's practice. The theory behind their operation was that moist air within the wall would percolate into the siphons, where it would be swapped with dry air from the exterior, steadily drying the fabric. Knapen seems to have envisaged that the moist air would be cooled by contact with the siphon, and would then be denser and flow downwards out of the tube, as lighter dry air flowed in upwards. Since moist air is actually lighter than dry air and rises rather than falls, if the mechanism was to work the tubes would have to point upwards rather than downwards; this is not possible, since they would then fill with water whenever it rained. The action of the tubes would also depend on the construction and materials of the wall, and many other variables including wind direction and strength, solar gain, and seasonal changes in air temperature and humidity. Moisture transfer could arguably be in either direction: the siphons could just as easily let in moist air as dry air, and this could cause condensation, increasing rather than decreasing the amount of water in the wall. Increasing air circulation would also compromise the thermal buffering of the wall. In practice, though, there is probably little effect: studies of ventilation through grilles suggest that there is unlikely to be any significant airflow into a siphon, especially one positioned near the base of a wall.

Apart from the physical damage caused by installing siphons and similar devices, the real concern is that they could become entry points for insects and other pests, and conduits for rainwater and floodwater to penetrate deep into the wall.

In the 1930s, British Knapen Ltd commissioned the Building Research Station to test its system, using a protocol which Achille Knapen himself devised. The resulting report, which is now in the National Archive, has a note attached that says: *"Laboratory experiments have been carried out at the Building Research Station to test the effect of the Knapen tubes on the rate of drying of blocks of stone, and in addition, a test on the effect of Knapen tubes on the drying of brick walls standing in water in the open has been completed for British Knapen Limited. Visits of inspection have also been made to certain buildings in which the Knapen tube system has been applied. In no case has a significant effect attributed to the Knapen tubes been observed."*

These negative conclusions were supported by subsequent investigations, and indeed by observations over the intervening 80 years, but nevertheless these and similar systems continue to be marketed, and it is not uncommon to find rows of embedded siphons disfiguring building façades, whilst the obvious sources of the moisture problem remain.

Siphonic systems are sold as a means of preventing moisture rising through the walls from the water table, but may sometimes be found installed at levels far higher than any 'rising damp'.

INJECTED DAMP-PROOFING

The idea that some hydrophobic material could be injected into a masonry wall to prevent capillary rise came from a surprising source: not a buildings scientist, but an entomologist at Imperial College in London who was researching insect exoskeletons during the 1940s and early 1950s. Having noted that insect cuticles were waterproofed with an emulsion of wax, fat and protein stabilised with polyphenols, Dr H. Hurst set up Cambridge Timberproofing Laboratories, and developed a product called 'Actane' that consisted mainly of natural rubber latex and a stabiliser of sodium methyl siliconate. Once injected, this was supposed to transform into a silicone as carbon dioxide and other substances within the wall reduced its alkalinity (in fact, the environments in walls are usually themselves very alkaline).

Hurst injected his mixture at low pressure into the mortar joints of thin solid walls: a line of 10-mm holes was drilled right through the wall at 50-mm intervals. On the inner face of the wall the holes were sealed with a waterproof cement containing Actane, and a length of guttering filled with more Actane was temporarily attached to the outer face, positioned so that the additional fluid would also drain into the wall through the holes.

Eventually the latex component was omitted from the formula, but treating with a more miscible water-based methyl siliconate solution remained popular. Salt efflorescences proved a problem with sodium methyl siliconate, so potassium methyl siliconate was used instead, with catalysts added to speed curing and to reduce the risk of salt migration or leaching.

As time went on, the intervals between injection points became much greater, with holes being spaced 150–170 mm apart, and often drilled only part way through the wall. In the 1970s solvent-based solutions of silicone or stearate were introduced; both silicones and stearates were injected into the brick rather than the mortar, so that it was possible to use higher injection pressures. A more recent variant are thixotropic 'creams' (emulsions of silane or siloxane).

There are numerous flaws in the theory behind injected damp-proofing, most particularly the fact that the injected material travels into the larger voids, cracks and pores of the material, whereas moisture travels through the micropore system, which remains unchanged. This is coupled with the near impossibility of guaranteeing a continuous layer of material right through the entire heterogeneous wall, with no breaks or flaws, so it is not surprising that studies by researchers such as the BRE have found no evidence that even well-executed injected damp-proofing can do more than reduce moisture transfer under certain circumstances.

Injected damp-proofing cannot be supported on a number of conservation grounds:
- the damage caused by drilling
- the risk involved in injecting liquids deep into the wall
- most systems require a cement render to be applied.

A cement-based render in particular is likely to cause harm rather than good, especially in a wall that already has moisture problems.

OTHER SYSTEMS

Other common proprietary systems for 'damp-proofing' include electro-osmosis, but this is chiefly sold for drying wet walls rather than for preventing 'rising damp' (see **Care & Repair: Patent Systems for Drying Wet Walls**).

IMPACT OF BUILDING USE

For all the problems attributable to building use, buildings are known to stay in better condition when used, rather than when unoccupied. Nevertheless, the use of the building introduces a number of issues for the building environment, most obviously the intentional and unintentional changes to the interior temperature and humidity, but also plumbing and other services. Other factors which may need to be considered include building alterations, including such everyday changes as moving the furniture (which may affect the circulation of air) and more radical interventions such as installing a new heating or cooling system, or new ventilation.

Wear and tear is also important: the abrasion and denting of floor finishes, for example, or the loosening of window hinges. Cleaning also causes surface erosion, and can be a significant source of moisture as well; but it may be necessary because use introduces many pollutants, such as dust, or grease from touching and from activities such as cooking.

CONDITIONING OF THE INDOOR AIR

Undoubtedly the conditions best for building users are often in conflict with those best for the building fabric. Desirable indoor air conditions are strongly influenced by fashion and the availability of technology, and may well change when the building is sold, or when a new use is found for it.

For modern construction, the way the indoor air is conditioned is critical to the way the building is intended to function. For traditionally constructed buildings, conditions are usually more stable when the space is not conditioned, because of the way the building buffers the outdoor conditions. There is some buffering of indoor changes as well, but more typically it is possible to identify more or less regular cycles and fluctuations:

- *Fluctuations due to feedback control systems*

    Control systems will be set to respond to measured levels in humidity or temperature. The rapidity and efficacy of response depends on the measurement sensors chosen, and where these are positioned. In poorly designed systems, the result may be rapid small fluctuations, which may initiate damage mechanisms such as salt cycling.

- *Variations due to the exterior conditions*

    Condition systems may work differently at different times of the day, on different days of the week, and in different seasons.

Conditioning may also produce progressive and more or less permanent changes in the building equilibrium: for example, prolonged heating may begin to dry the fabric, steadily reducing the absolute humidity.

As well as temporal variations, there are likely to be spatial variations, according to the use of spaces in the building. Serious problems can arise if one space is highly controlled, and a connecting space is not; this can happen in single-occupancy buildings, but is of most concern in buildings under multiple occupancy, where spaces may be conditioned quite independently.

Ventilation

In the 19th century ventilation was primarily seen as a way of replacing *"foul or vitiated air"*, but with buildings now being much less draughty and central heating common, it is more typically used to relieve condensation problems.

Many buildings are now highly sealed to prevent heat loss, with little air exchanged between the interior and the exterior. At the same time, the internal moisture load from cooking, washing and cleaning has greatly increased, and the building surfaces finished with less permeable materials, which cannot buffer water vapour to the same extent as (for example) timber or lime plaster. This has made ventilation an important issue (see **Special Topic: Improving Energy & Carbon Performance**).

Increasing the exchange rate between the interior and exterior is now often seen as being a 'natural' way of preserving a building, and unequivocally good, but in practice the consequences can often be very complex and hard to predict. It will destabilise a stable environment, and if there is too much exchange between the interior and the exterior, the building fabric may not act as an efficient thermal or moisture buffer.

Since the exterior air humidity varies with the seasons and the weather, it could bring moisture into the room rather than removing it. Therefore, actions such as cutting permanent ventilation holes through walls could lead to problems, as well as encouraging salt crystallisation and giving a conduit for pests to enter.

Condensation on a wall painting in a church in Hertfordshire was the immediate result of the windows and doors being thrown open early in spring, when the exterior relative humidity was still very high.

Although water beading is clearly visible only on the surfaces coated in wax, condensation will also be occurring in the surface pores of the surrounding, more permeable, areas.

Even when ventilation is used only occasionally, it may not be benign, especially if it is controlled by human senses rather than by measurements of the exterior ambient humidity. For example, a common way of unwittingly causing condensation in churches with thick cold walls is to throw open the doors and windows in early spring, on the first sunny, breezy day. The exterior air feels very fresh under these conditions, but also it is usually very humid (with the solar heating and plenty of evaporation, moisture is taken up from the ground, which is damp after winter). On meeting cool surfaces in the interior of the building, it therefore condenses, sometimes quite dramatically.

BUILDING ENVIRONMENT
DETERIORATION & DAMAGE: DETERIORATION OF THE ENVELOPE

Control of Temperature & Humidity

Heating

Both natural and artificial air circulation may generate cold draughts, which means that heating can actually make conditions less comfortable. Certain systems can also damage the fabric: fan-forced heating, for example, can desiccate timberwork, and the coal-fired stoves once popular for heating churches deposited sulphate pollutants on the walls that may still be causing problems many decades later. Calor-gas heaters emit large quantities of water vapour, and leaking hot water pipes are another common source of moisture.
⊖TIMBER ⊖STONE ⊖MORTARS

Even radiator systems can lead to much higher relative humidities than an older building will have originally experienced. A room heated by a coal fire with a chimney will have had an air-exchange rate of 5–6 ach, and a relative humidity of 35–40 %. In the same room with the same number of occupants and the same furniture, but heated by a radiator, with no chimney and the windows closed, the relative humidity will quickly rise to 100 %.

Most modern heating systems use thermostatic controls to minimise temperature fluctuations, or to avoid extremes that could damage the fabric (for instance, freezing temperatures). For traditionally constructed buildings with a good deal of thermal buffering, this approach should theoretically be quite energy-efficient: once it has been brought to the desired temperature, the building fabric should act as a heat sink. Unfortunately, thermal stability may not in itself be beneficial to the building or its contents: sensitive materials usually respond far more to changes in humidity than they do to changes in temperature. A change of 10 °C may have little effect on wood or stone, but a variation of 10 % in the relative humidity can cause the timber to shrink and swell, and repeated changes in humidity can cause serious salt decay in masonry.

Solid ground floors have a very high thermal inertia, so although they take a long time to heat, they also take a long time to cool, and hence will buffer variations in indoor temperature. In summer, however, or whenever the air is warm and damp, they can be prone to condensation problems. In winter, when room heating warms the surface, interstitial condensation can sometimes occur.

Pollution damage from heating
Airborne pollutants may be found in the interior of the building as well as the exterior, with heating systems being the most common source. Structural roof timbers in older buildings will sometimes be found to have superficial damage from sulphur-dioxide fumes, emitted by the large coke stoves that were used to heat churches and public buildings in the Victorian period. The result is a characteristic yellowing and roughening of the surface, such as that found on the medieval oak ceiling timbers of Westminster Hall in London.

Condensation damage from heating

Heating can pull stored moisture from the fabric, and lead to condensation on cooler surfaces. These may be cold either because they have a very low thermal inertia, or because they have a very high thermal mass that takes a considerable time to heat: longer than the room heating is on.

Top: Staining and water damage at the bottom of windows is a common problem: the glass surface is cold because it readily loses heat to the exterior air, and because it is impermeable, the condensed water can collect and run down.

Bottom: It will take prolonged room heating to warm a solid ground floor, so in buildings such as parish churches that are used and heated only occasionally, flooring can suffer from condensation. Here, damage to tiles is exacerbated by a rubber-backed carpet that prevents the condensed water from drying.

In some cases, heating is installed to lower the ambient relative humidity, but in a traditionally constructed building this may not be what actually happens. Because of the vapour exchange between the ambient air and the permeable fabric, the interior humidity in traditional buildings tends to be very stable in the absence of other climate factors. If the interior air is suddenly heated, this drives down the vapour pressure, and moisture can be drawn very quickly from the fabric in considerable quantities. If the heating is then turned off, the extra load of moisture in the air cannot be immediately absorbed, and so will condense on cooler surfaces.

If the ambient absolute humidity is varying, perhaps because there is significant air exchange between the interior and the exterior, or because the fabric contains a great deal of moisture, then heating is likely to cause fluctuations in relative humidity even if the temperature is constant. A large increase in temperature, especially if it is quite sudden, can cause the ambient relative humidity to fall, but a slow change will largely be buffered by the building fabric, which will give up moisture to the air.

An excellent illustration of this is the heating of a medieval parish church for Sunday services. During the week, when the heating is not running and the relative humidity is high, water vapour will be absorbed into the fabric until the walls and the ambient air are at equilibrium. When the heating is turned on, the relative humidity of the air will begin to drop, but this will draw moisture out from the fabric. This evaporation can be efficient, because the heating induces convection currents. The net result is that the ambient relative humidity decreases slightly, but the ambient absolute humidity – the actual amount of water in the air – increases.

BUILDING ENVIRONMENT
DETERIORATION & DAMAGE: DETERIORATION OF THE ENVELOPE

Condensation events

Condensation becomes a risk whenever the ambient dew-point temperature nears or exceeds the temperature of the surfaces.

In buildings of traditional construction, a frequent cause of a sudden increase in dew-point temperature is intermittent heating of the air, which rapidly lowers the ambient relative humidity. This causes stored moisture to be drawn from the permeable fabric, increasing the absolute humidity (and thus the dew-point temperature). Since the fabric has a high thermal inertia and cannot change temperature nearly so quickly in response to the heating, the result is condensation events (such as those caught here by a time-of-wetness sensor).

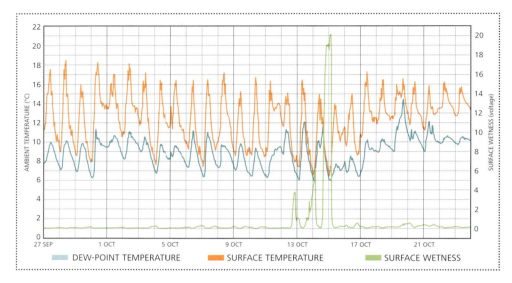

The Sunday service itself will be a source of more water vapour from the respiration of the congregation, and from the drying of their wet clothes. As soon as the heating is turned off once again, the temperature of the air drops quickly and the relative humidity increases; the fabric once again begins to absorb moisture, but this re-absorption is considerably slower than the original evaporation, which was helped by convection. As a result, as the temperature drops, the relative humidity often increases to the point where condensation is able to form on the internal surfaces.

Design & Control

The location of heating and the way it is managed over the year will also have an impact on how it behaves. A badly sited radiator can easily damage the surrounding fabric by local overheating, and potentially by leaking: it is sensible to anticipate that all wet systems could eventually leak.

Altering systems can have unexpected consequences. For example, it is common to position new gas boilers in existing chimneys, but if the flue is not made narrower at the same time, the gases will condense too quickly and patches of condensation will appear in the chimney.

Control regimes will have to change over the course of the year, but the weather can be so variable that it is usually very difficult to decide the most suitable times to turn the heating on and off. Postponing start-up until late in the season can actually be counter-productive; if the heat is turned on only in November, it will lead to a rapid rise in temperature and a drop in relative humidity that increases evaporation from walls, increasing the absolute humidity, which may well cause condensation.

Intermittent heating can have results that are difficult to predict, although condensation is a possible outcome. Materials do tend to respond poorly to sudden changes, and to cyclical changes.

Leaking

Like all internal plumbing, wet heating systems can be prone to leaking, and problems may be serious if the piping is concealed. Large cast-iron Victorian hot-water heating pipes have often been associated with localised heat and moisture damage.

Hydronic (water-based) underfloor heating and cooling has a history of problems. Early systems used copper pipes, but these quickly corroded when embedded in cement floors, and steel pipes also developed problems. In the 1970s plastics such as polybutylene and EDPM were introduced, but these also failed quickly. Current systems use cross-linked polyethylene [PE-x], extruded to minimise joints. A long lifespan is claimed for these materials, which were developed for military applications (such as heating the decks of naval ships and aircraft hanger aprons), but it would be wise to be cautious, and allow for future maintenance and repair in the design.

Dehumidification & Air Conditioning

Dehumidification is very difficult in practice, and there can be problems if systems flood. Drying out sensitive fabric may be a real risk.

Many dehumidification units form part of a more general air-conditioning system. These work by cooling the air to remove moisture and then reheating it again to comfort level, so they are very complex, and it is a general rule that air conditioning is installed for the benefit of the occupants, as it is never to the benefit of the building.

For the building fabric, the problem with air conditioning is that in attempting to create conditions that are stable over hours, it induces a great deal of short-term fluctuation. These fluctuations are worse if the control thermostats and humidistats are poorly positioned: the slower the feedback of the system, the greater the resulting changes in temperature and humidity. If used in warm, humid weather in buildings with thin walls or modern hollow-wall construction, air conditioning can pull water in through flaws in the fabric from the exterior, and this can cause moisture problems (especially if the walls also contain vapour-resistant membranes or finishes: mould growth behind vinyl wallpaper is a very common problem for air-conditioned hotel rooms, for instance).

Complex air-conditioning systems rely on ducting and forced ventilation, and these can be failure points. The air supply should be kept clean and fresh, but often it is run through dirty floor or ceiling spaces, and indeed in some cases the floor and ceiling voids are themselves used as part of the ducting system. The evaporators and water storage systems may develop moulds or support bacterial growth, potentially creating health risks (see **Special Topic: Buildings & Human Health**).

Another problem with air-conditioning systems is their sheer complexity, which makes them apt to fail. Failure can take many forms, and can be harmful and costly: the system may suddenly begin pumping in quantities of very hot and humid air, for example. It is therefore important that emergency shut-down systems be incorporated to cope with such eventualities.

NOISE PROBLEMS

Sound transfers into and through a building via both the air and the fabric, and the source of noise can therefore be the external environment, or the building itself, or a result of occupation.

This has become an increasingly important issue for a number of different reasons:
- more noise (and other vibrations) is coming from the wider environment
- more internal noise is coming from electrical and other equipment (including air control systems such as fans and air conditioners, as well as stereos and televisions)
- building materials and systems are being used that allow sound to propagate more easily (for example, hollow wall construction, service pipes and conduits, steel frames and smooth hard surfaces on floors, walls and furniture).

Problems are particularly serious for multi-occupancy buildings, especially those with mixed use. The building regulations in England now require buildings undergoing a material change of use to meet certain soundproofing conditions.

Noise from the Exterior

Noise from the exterior may be very directional, and can be affected by external conditions (particularly the direction of the wind). It will be able to enter through any gaps in the fabric, but may also interact with the fabric itself, sometimes causing amplification or resonance.

Noise from the Fabric

Vibrations of the building fabric, whatever their source, can lead to noise problems. For example, wind may cause metal roof sheets to resonate, causing an audible drumming. Hollow building elements such as pipes can cause particular problems; the 'knocking' of plumbing – 'water hammer' – is due to resonating trapped air. Stiffer and denser materials such as brick masonry are less likely to transmit sound than thin and flexible materials such as timber or glass, but the shape of the elements also counts, as does the way they are fixed: materials such as lime mortar which are able to absorb energy will deaden sound, but very elastic joints may lead to resonance. It is therefore important to locate the source of the vibration very exactly.

Noise from Occupation

Hollow building elements, such as typical partition walls, can transmit internal noise through the building. As well as the usual noises from occupation, such as footfalls or televisions, unwelcome sounds can arise from building services (for example, humming ventilation or lighting) or from the fabric itself (for example, windows rattling, or roof coverings resonating under certain wind conditions).

DAMAGE FROM DISASTROUS EVENTS

Sudden disasters often arise from the environment outside the building, as well as factors within. Often the immediate damage to the building envelope is only part of the story, and it is the subsequent water infiltration that causes the greatest problems. Great quantities of water are used to extinguish fires, for example; and the theft of metal roof sheets from parish churches is often noticed only during a subsequent rainstorm.

Another source of envelope damage is impact. Since the advent of roads, cars and trucks, this is no longer rare, and restricted largely to trees and other objects thrown by the wind during storms, but are becoming common. Stone archways are often damaged by delivery trucks (which are increasing in size), and buildings at busy crossroads may sustain severe impact damage not once, but repeatedly. Recently, significant problems have been attributed to the use of satellite navigation devices: the suggested routes may take heavy traffic down roads too narrow for it to pass without damaging roadside buildings and other important structures such as bridges.

Disastrous events, and how the damage caused by them should best be minimised, are discussed in detail in the **Special Topic: Dealing with Disasters**.

Environmental risks can be sudden and dramatic, as well as insidious and slow: here, a toll house has been badly damaged by a vehicle which has collided with it. Situated as they usually are at busy junctions, toll houses are a common victim of this type of disaster.

In the aftermath of any serious and sudden event, the first priority must be to stabilise and shore up, but the methods used for such emergency measures should be no less conservation-safe than those chosen for more permanent repairs: damage can easily be compounded by ill-considered actions such as stripping out, or temporary repair using inappropriate materials.

BUILDING ENVIRONMENT
DETERIORATION & DAMAGE: DETERIORATION OF THE ENVELOPE

Further Reading

Abouzeid, A., Channon, D., Sever, P. (2007); 'Bird damage to historic buildings'; in *The Building Conservation Directory, 2007*; also available at *www.buildingconservation.com/articles/birddamage/birddamage.htm*

Douglas, J., Ransom, B. (2007); *Understanding Building Failures (3rd Edition)*; London & New York: Routledge

Ellison, R. (2000); 'The effects of daylight'; in *The Building Conservation Directory, 2000*; also available at *www.buildingconservation.com/articles/daylight/daylight.htm*

Hall, F., Greeno, R. (2013); *Building Services Handbook (7th Edition)*; London & New York: Routledge

Honeybourne, D. (1983); 'Harmful interactions between building materials'; in *Transactions of the Association for Studies in the Conservation of Historic Buildings*; Vol. 8; pp.44–48

Johnson, A. (2006); *Understanding the Edwardian and Inter-War Houses (1920s & 1930s)*; Ramsbury, Wiltshire: The Crowood Press

Marshall, D., Worthing, D., Dann, N. (2009); *Understanding Housing Defects (3rd Edition)*; London & New York: Routledge

Rock, I. (2005); *The Victorian House Manual*; Yeovil, Somerset: J. H. Haynes & Co Ltd

Rock, I. (2005); *The 1930s House Manual*; Yeovil, Somerset: J. H. Haynes & Co Ltd

Rose, W. B. (1997); 'Moisture control in the modern building envelope: History of the vapor barrier in the U. S., 1923–52'; in *APT Bulletin*; Vol.28, *No.4 Mending the Modern*; pp.13–19

Rose, W. B. (2005); *Water in Buildings: An Architect's Guide to Moisture and Mold*; Hoboken: John Wiley & Sons

Royal Institution of Charted Surveyors (2011); *Japanese Knotweed and Residential Property (Consultation Draft 1st Edition)*; RICS Information Paper; available at *consultations.rics.org/consult.ti/japaneseknotweed/consultationHome*

Useful Websites

The Building Science Corporation produces a wide range of excellent publications covering all aspects of the building environment and deterioration, including *Building Science Insights* and *Building Science Digests*: *www.buildingscience.com*

The Royal Society for the Protection of Birds has extensive information about birds in buildings: *www.rspb.org*

ASSESSING THE BUILDING ENVIRONMENT

This chapter covers the processes and actions involved in assessing the building envelope and its environment, including historical research, surveys and specialist investigations. It introduces the reader to the principle tools for environmental assessment, from simple surveying to highly specialised techniques such as environmental monitoring.

The interaction between a building envelope and its exterior and interior environment is always dynamic: fluctuating with the daily and seasonal changes in the weather, changing slowly as materials wear or as maintenance needs accumulate, and occasionally altering suddenly as a result of more dramatic events such as storms, or because deterioration has reached a tipping point where a critical component can no longer support the structural loads acting on it.

Assessment is essentially an attempt to build a picture of the building environment, and to understand the particular interactions that are causing the envelope to succeed or fail. This can be done for many reasons, or a combination of reasons:

- to check whether there is any deterioration and decay
- to understand an observed pattern of deterioration
- to understand the behaviour of the building so that the likely impact of a proposed change can be estimated
- to build a detailed picture of the building's behaviour that can serve as a baseline for assessing the impact of future changes (whether these are intentional, or a result of natural wear and tear).

It is a critical part of general building care, intimately linked to maintenance, and just as important when a building has no apparent problems as when serious issues are evident. Well-designed assessment systems allow the building's behaviour under changing conditions to be understood, and problems to be identified before they cause damage.

ENVIRONMENTAL ASSESSMENT

Understanding the way a building is performing requires a holistic approach to investigation. Assessment ranges across disciplines: as well as surveying the state of the fabric, it will need to take into account the surrounding landscape and weather, the building services, and the ways it is being used. It therefore demands a clear strategy and good coordination: investigations must be undertaken with a goal in mind, and the results must not be interpreted in isolation.

The level of investigation required for an environmental assessment will vary: it depends on the significance of the building, the importance of the issues being investigated, and the type of problem. For example, roof damage caused by a falling branch will be obvious; but if the damaged area is left exposed for some time, it may take some effort to properly investigate the subsequent moisture penetration. Again, understanding the goal of the assessment is critical.

Assessment processes can be quick and simple, or prolonged and elaborate, depending on the nature and scale of the environmental problems as well as the importance of the building.

In all cases, though, assessment should be coordinated by a project leader with a clear plan and a clear goal in mind.

BUILDING ENVIRONMENT
ASSESSING THE BUILDING ENVIRONMENT

PLANNING ENVIRONMENTAL ASSESSMENT

Good planning is essential to ensure resources (which are always limited) are used to the best purpose. Otherwise, it may happen that critical investigations are forgotten, whilst others consume too much of the available time or money.

The essential first step is to clearly articulate the overall aim of the assessment, and the questions it is seeking to answer. Is it intended to give a general bill-of-health to the building, or to assess a known problem, or to support other works?

OPPORTUNITY POINT FOR ASSESSMENT	
TYPICAL QUESTIONS BEING ASKED	COMMENTS
ASSESSMENT TO INTERPRET PROBLEMS	
What are the critical problems, and what are their underlying causes? Is deterioration ongoing? Would any treatments or repairs be able to slow or even halt ongoing deterioration? Is it necessary or desirable to repair damage and losses?	Environmental problems must themselves be traced back to their origins: to faults in the building design or materials, or to their breakdown over time, or to sudden damage (due to storms or fires, for example) Diagnosis means understanding the sources of problems, but also determining ways of resolving them, and in fact in many cases identifying the source is enough to make the choice of remedial action obvious
ASSESSMENT AT A CHANGE OF OWNERSHIP	
What are the strengths and weaknesses of the building envelope? Are there any ongoing issues, and if so, what is their severity and how urgent is it to address them?	This is often the chance to gather good baseline data about the building It is vital to undertake a proper assessment: too often, for example, moisture problems are lumped together under the catch-all title 'damp', leading to interventions that are not only ineffective but could be harmful
ASSESSMENT TO PREPARE FOR ALTERATIONS	
What physical effect would the proposed interventions have on the building envelope? What are the potential benefits? What are the potential problems, and is there any way these can be mitigated? How can the impact of the alterations be assessed?	Often the aim has not been clearly articulated: for example, the scheme may call for 'heating', when the aim is comfort under certain conditions The clearer the intention of an alteration, the easier it is to design successfully (that is, achieving the desired effect with the minimum of risk to the fabric)

By following this process, it becomes possible to determine the scope and scale of the assessment.

Care and repair of the building environment could comprise anything from a straightforward localised repair, to the conservation of a particular material or building element, or an extensive programme of alterations or improvements. Each would demand different types of information, at different levels of detail.

The *Conservation Basics* volume of this series provides an overview of the techniques currently available for surveying and monitoring historic buildings, and discusses their use and their limitations. It covers measured surveys (which give the basic template onto which information about the building can be recorded), the use of documentary sources and structural archaeology (which can provide information about the origins, evolution and associations of the building), and the various condition surveys, specialist investigations and diagnostic techniques (which together help to build a picture of the building's construction and condition). ⊖BASICS

Building condition surveys are the basic means of understanding the current state of the fabric, and identifying problems. As discussed in *Conservation Basics*, there are four main types of condition survey:

- Preliminary surveys (also known as 'basic' or 'reconnaissance' surveys)
- Periodic surveys (also known as 'property management' surveys, and commonly carried out as quadrennial or quinquennial surveys)
- Building fabric surveys (also known as 'full', 'comprehensive' or 'detailed' surveys)
- Structural surveys.

There is no single standard approach to undertaking a building condition survey. The level of detail, and the methods of presentation, will largely depend on the experience of the building professionals involved and the brief to which they are working.

Where environmental problems are being encountered, or sometimes where a change of use is being considered, a more detailed environmental assessment may be necessary. This can and should be tailored to meet the specific requirements, and scaled up or down to suit the circumstances of the particular building or problem. It uses three basic tools:

- *Background research*
  Gathering together information from existing sources such as old building records and photographs concerning the history and significance of the building, and the history of problems and interventions.

- *Building performance surveys*
  In-situ assessment of the building envelope, of the environment and the building use, in order to understand the design and operation of the building, its current state of conservation, and the nature of any environmental problems.

- *Specialist investigations*
  Studies commissioned from specialists to better understand issues that have not been resolved by background research or the building performance survey; these might involve such activities as material testing, environmental monitoring and detailed archival research. Expertise should be called in as necessary to fulfil the project aims, and even with smaller projects it can be very helpful to seek advice from experienced specialists early on, since they may well be able to help in developing an effective approach to assessment. It is very important, however, that advice is independent, and is not sought solely from contractors who have products to sell.

The results of these investigations feed into an iterative process, where information is collected in as much detail as required to meet the needs of the building. Good management is vital to this: assessment may involve several specialists, and the results of an investigation in one area may well have ramifications in another, so information needs to be passed around and discussed as soon as it is collected.

ITERATIVE INVESTIGATION

The key to successful environmental assessment is to undertake just enough investigation to have confidence in the decisions being taken for care and repair. It is helpful to see investigation strategy as an iterative process, with investigations being undertaken in a logical order and regularly reviewed, as depicted in the diagram opposite.

Preliminary background research and site surveying will always be needed to be sure that the problem being investigated has been put into proper context, and it may be that this is sufficient to move forward with confidence. In other cases, more investigation will be needed to understand why the problem has occurred, and how it should best be dealt with; this could mean undertaking specialist investigations, or more background research, or a more detailed building-performance survey, or some combination of any or all of these. The outcome of each investigation may resolve the issue, or it may raise further important questions.

Investigations stop as soon as a decision can be taken with sufficient confidence. What this exactly means will depend very much on the building and the type of problems being studied; more detailed investigation will probably be required if the building is very significant, or if the problem is very complicated.

Reviewing the information gathered to date is a job for the whole project team, whether that comprises simply the building owner or manager, or a group of specialist advisers as well. It will include:

- *Risk assessment*
  Is it more dangerous to take immediate action (risking that the understanding of the problem may be incomplete, or even misguided), or to delay whilst further investigations are made (potentially allowing the problem to worsen)?

- *Cost-benefit assessment*
  Will the extra time and money needed to undertake further investigation be merited?

Each review must determine whether the information collected to date is sufficient to make a decision with the required confidence. This is a classic 'triage' question, where the answer – like a traffic light – could be red, green or amber.

DECISION-MAKING IN ENVIRONMENTAL INVESTIGATION & ASSESSMENT

DECISION		EXAMPLE: CONDENSATION IN CURTAIN-WALL IGU PANEL
🔴	**TAKE NO ACTION AT THIS TIME** Enough information has been collected to make it clear either that no work is currently needed, or that works would be unwise to undertake at this stage	Several aged IGUs (Insulated Glazing Units) are affected ACTION: Problem is mostly aesthetic, so action is not urgent, but repair or replacement of older units should be added to the list for actions when the next opportunity for building refurbishment arises
🟡	**INVESTIGATE FURTHER** There is currently insufficient information to make the decision either to stop, or to proceed with treatment or repair	Many relatively new IGUs are affected across a widespread area of the building ACTION: Check records to see exactly how long the problem has existed (additional background research); check state of seals and glass for cracking (additional surveying); if several glass panels are cracked, check for differential thermal movement (specialist investigation)
🟢	**TAKE ACTION** Enough information has been collected to understand the problem, and to know how it should best be dealt with	Only one IGU is affected; water has entered via a crack in one of the glass panels caused by impact ACTION: Replace glass or entire unit, and install protection to prevent future breakages

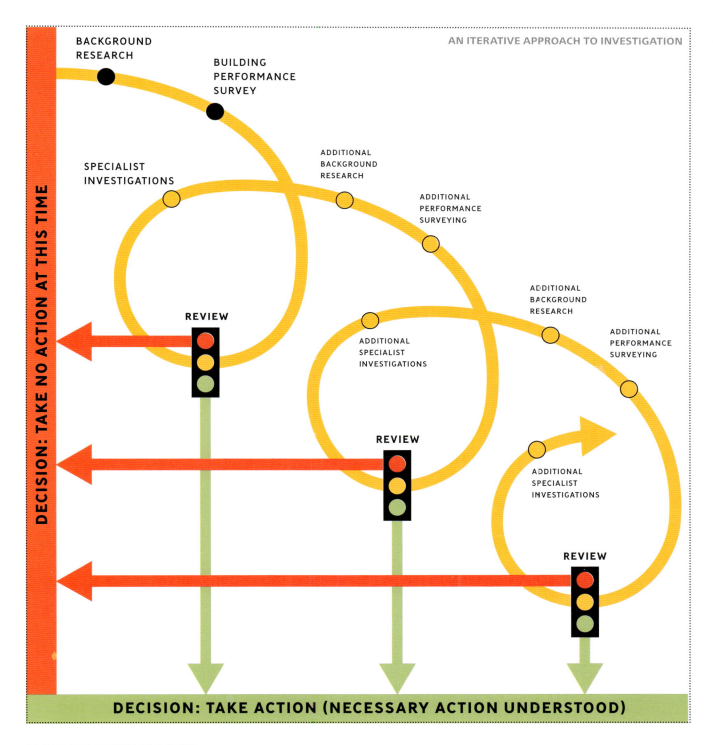

BUILDING ENVIRONMENT
ASSESSING THE BUILDING ENVIRONMENT

BACKGROUND RESEARCH

The way the building has been used over time will have shaped not only its internal microclimate, but how and why it has been altered, and how and why it has been damaged or has deteriorated over time. What must be dealt with today is the sum total of what has survived, what has been lost, and what has been added. Some changes will have been deliberate and some accidental; many will have occurred in the course of maintenance and repair (for example, the loss of water-shedding detailing).

Sources of Information

Sources are many and varied, from logbooks and records of works to conversations with owners and building staff. Old photographs, drawings and postcards are invaluable, and can help put approximate dates to alterations, or to the onset of deterioration. They may even reveal hitherto unknown stages in the building's evolution.

Historic maps are another very important resource, as are old construction manuals, the earliest of which date from the 18th century. Records of previous alterations, repairs and treatments are particularly important. Larger estates and buildings often hold records of works, and these can sometimes be extremely detailed. Additional material may be held by conservators, by previous owners, surveyors or architects, or by members of the local community (such as churchwardens). Local people will often be able to offer useful information and advice.

Technical and historical information can also be obtained from a wide range of sources, including public record offices, the National Monuments Record, local authority records (including Historic Environment Records), amenity and local building trust societies, and some specialist archives and libraries (such as those held by the Royal Institute of British Architects). The National Archives hold useful records of the Land Tax and Hearth Tax.

When using any source, it is important to take its reliability into account. Anecdotal comments and undated photos may still prove very helpful, but may need to be backed up by hard evidence.

The *Conservation Basics* volume in this series gives a detailed description of the sources and processes involved in background research. ➔BASICS

With good research, it may be possible to uncover some of the original intentions behind alterations. Certain changes will be traceable back to prevailing fashions, such as the Victorian passion for 'truth in materials' that led to the stripping of countless renders and plasters, or the current vogue for 'open-plan' living. There have been trends in treatment and repair as well, and these have caused a great many failures (the most cogent example of this is probably the change from lime-based mortars for repointing and rendering to cement, which has caused a great many moisture problems and solved very few). Changes in use are also important. For example, in the past, parish churches were used daily or even twice-daily, but many are now idle during the week, and heated only on Sunday mornings.

Research may also uncover records of disastrous events that may have affected the building, such as fires and floods.

Background research is vital for planning building surveys: it may even be possible to find evidence of early drains or maps showing services, which will help focus investigations. The building history may well give clues to areas that have persistently caused problems, and perhaps even some idea of the rate of decay. It may also be the best way to resolve the puzzle of why a problem has suddenly begun, perhaps after a long period of relative stability. Where the building is ancient enough to have revealed any fundamental weaknesses, the source of the problem will often be found in some change made to the fabric or environment (the heating, to name a common example).

As background information is collected, it must be stored in some logical way. One of the most useful tools is the timeline: entering information in chronological order can reveal unsuspected relationships between problems and building history.

Timelines

Timelines are a useful way of organising information as it is collected. Although dates should preferably be narrowed down as closely as possible, even putting important events into approximate chronological order can prove revealing. Dated photographs are particularly helpful in this regard, and may even be more reliable than some types of written record.

In the example shown here (Dymchurch Martello Tower, in Kent) a timeline was used to establish the relationship between a severe ongoing moisture problem and earlier works to the building, including changes to the roof and the application of a cement render. Old photographs allow otherwise unknown dates to be approximately filled in, such as when the cement is likely to have been applied, and when the hut on the roof was removed. In the future, newly discovered information may allow more missing dates to be filled in.

1927

1955

1992

TIMELINE: DYMCHURCH MARTELLO TOWER		
DATE	OCCURRENCE	COMMENTS
1805–12	Tower constructed	Original render of lime-ash-tallow (permeable)
1870s	Military use ceases; Coastal Blockade and Coastguard take over	Was this when the original gun was removed?
Late 19th century	Brick exterior staircase installed	Was this coeval with the installation of hut on roof?
Before 1927	Timber hut installed on roof	What was hut for? How was it fixed in place?
Before 1940s	Roof covered in asphalt	Was this coeval with the installation of the hut?
1940s	Occupied by Royal Artillery	Did this result in any lasting alterations?
1951	Coastguard leaves	Maintenance issues as a result?
After 1955	Timber hut on roof removed	Was this part of the 1960s works programme?
After 1955	Exterior rendered in cement, tooled to resemble stone	Impermeable render will lead to moisture problems
1959	Transferred from War Office to Ministry of Works	Becomes historic monument
1960s	Major works programme	Was this when the render was applied and the hut removed?
Post 1960s	Total replacement of all wooden joinery in interior	When? Suggests severe moisture problems have begun
Date still unknown	Brick exterior staircase removed	Was this part of the 1960s works programme?

BUILDING ENVIRONMENT
ASSESSING THE BUILDING ENVIRONMENT

Determining Significance

"The significance of a place embraces all the diverse cultural and natural heritage values that people associate with it, or which prompt them to respond to it. These values tend to grow in strength and complexity over time, as understanding deepens and people's perceptions of a place evolve."

English Heritage
Conservation Principles, Policies and Guidance
Principle 3.2

There are many reasons why buildings or places – heritage assets – may be of value to society and, therefore, worth keeping. They help us understand the past while adding to the richness of our environment in the present. The significance of a place is embodied not only in its physical material – its fabric – and its setting, but also in the artefacts and documents associated with it, and in the meanings it has for people through use, association and commemoration.

The values that give significance to heritage assets are wide-ranging and interrelated: buildings and places provide material evidence about the lives of past generations. For example, they may offer insights into developments in construction technology, reflecting the distribution of materials, skills, ideas, knowledge, money and power in particular localities, and at particular points in time.

Buildings and places connect us, intellectually and emotionally, with past events and people. They may also give us aesthetic pleasure. In addition, they bestow on communities a shared sense of place and identity, along with potential functional and economic benefits. These values are not inherent but are attributed by people. This means that significance – the reasons we value places, and the relative importance we give to these values – may change over time.

Understanding the significance of a place is fundamental to determining the best approach to its care and repair, or in making decisions about its future. It is the first stage in the conservation process. If the heritage values are not understood, it will be impossible to assess whether proposed works will have a beneficial or harmful effect on the place. This approach to conservation is now widely accepted, and underpins English Heritage's *Conservation Principles, Policies and Guidance*. The majority of grant-giving bodies require an assessment of significance as part of a conservation management plan to accompany funding applications. However, this process is as important for small conservation works as it is for large projects. Good practitioners should always seek an understanding of the heritage values of a place on which to base their proposals, even if they have not been required to articulate them formally. ➔BASICS

BUILDING PERFORMANCE SURVEYS

Surveys of building performance aim to establish the current state of the building, including the way it is being used. As such they are the primary tool for locating environmental problems, identifying their sources and understanding their effects.

Building-performance surveys can be brief or exhaustive, depending on the size and complexity of the building and its conservation issues. This chapter covers many of the investigations that could be involved, including such highly specialised investigations as environmental monitoring, but in practice in the vast majority of cases a very simple examination of the building may be enough to reveal the critical sources of most problems (identifying faulty water-disposal systems, or heating issues, for example).

The correct level to aim for is the simplest that can successfully answer the fundamental questions about how the building behaves, and what may be the causes of deterioration. It is rare indeed that there are sufficient resources for over-complicated surveying, and although it might be risky to begin complex building works or to attempt to remedy problems before the underlying issues are properly understood, it can be even more unwise to spend time and money on detailed examination if that is at the expense of making vital repairs (such as clearing drains or repairing roofs).

Almost inevitably, much of the effort of a building performance survey will be concentrated on understanding and assessing the envelope, and particularly the way it is handling water. Even though the underlying problems might involve many different environmental factors, in the final analysis, moisture is implicated in so many problems that it is almost always the impact on the water-resistance of the envelope that proves to be the critical issue. For example, roof sheets may be torn by wind lift or differential heat movement, but the important outcome is that the tear lets in rainwater. Problems with the building services often manifest themselves as condensation or mould, or moisture-related decay.

If the basic surveys needed to determine care and maintenance requirements, or to assess damage after (say) a storm, are usually the province of the building's owners or occupants, a full performance survey is more usually commissioned from a specialist surveyor or architect, or occasionally from a conservator. This may happen when a change of use is being considered, or when it has been noticed that the contents are deteriorating or the indoor conditions are becoming unpleasant for the building's users.

On the basis of a survey of building performance, a good surveyor should be able not only to identify faults and determine whether these are historic or ongoing, but be in a position to comment on the effectiveness of the building as a whole, and on how it is likely to be affected by wear-and-tear, or by the proposed alterations. They may recommend further investigations, such as materials testing or environmental monitoring, to better understand complex issues.

BASICS OF PERFORMANCE SURVEYING

For building owners or advisers, it is useful to make frequent rapid building condition surveys to see how the envelope is functioning, with particular attention being paid to water-disposal systems. These surveys will not only ensure that any problems are noticed soon after they appear (before they can cause major damage), but will help form a picture of the way the building environment works as a whole.

In addition to these everyday surveys, a quick check should be made after a storm or other severe weather, and occasionally at different times of the year, to see how the building is coping with seasonal drivers such as leaf fall, prolonged rain or changes in the heating regime.

These types of survey are fastest and most efficient when they are undertaken by someone very familiar with the building, such as the building owner or manager, or (in the case of historic buildings such as churches) the architect or surveyor to the fabric; it is easy for those with less understanding of the ordinary behaviour of the building to see evidence of old problems and assume these are still active.

It is also wise to schedule a thorough survey once every few years, to pick up those changes that have occurred so gradually that they might well be missed by those seeing the building every day. These too are often undertaken by a building professional, but that professional should be very familiar with the building and the way it is being used. A good example of this type of survey is the quinquennial inspection required of churches and many other historic buildings. The aim should be not only to assess defects that are already active, but to identify any potential trouble spots, and the survey will need to incorporate all the regular specialist checks required for the various building services and the other critical service components (such as lightning protection).

PERFORMANCE SURVEYS

If an environmental problem is noticed, or if building works are planned, a survey of building performance will be needed. The first step is to make a very basic inspection of the building, its environment and the way it is being used; and indeed this may be all that is needed to plan effective care and repair.

If the basic performance survey does not give sufficient information, further investigations may be required, and these may well demand a certain amount of special expertise or equipment. Indeed, in difficult and complex cases, it may be helpful to call in a specialist in building performance sooner rather than later, since they may well be able to help structure the most effective programme of study and assessment.

Good practice when dealing with environmental problems is to complete all the necessary and uncontroversial alterations or repairs to the envelope, or the services that have been identified in the performance survey, let the building settle for a reasonable period, and then re-survey to see whether the problems have been resolved. If they have not, more intensive investigation and assessment will be required.

Basic Performance Surveys

Basic building performance surveys aim to determine the fundamental characteristics of the building environment as a whole, including the building occupation and use of services. They should not require any special skills or tools. Although the extent of the survey may well be constrained by limited access, in a basic survey every attempt should be made to look at all parts of the building, including the roof spaces and basements, and all water-handling features and drainage. It may be possible to examine high points of the structure with binoculars, for example.

A primary intention is usually to investigate problems with the way the building handles water, so it is important to characterise any factor that could be influencing this, including the surrounding topography, the weather, the services such as plumbing and those uses of the building that generate water vapour. There may be several quite separate sources of water, and unless all of these can be identified and taken into consideration, treatment and control measures are unlikely to be completely effective and may even prove detrimental. That said, there can be a tendency to lump together all moisture problems (no matter how complex) under the blanket term 'damp', when other factors could be equally important, and should therefore be assessed with equal care. For example, condensation could be due to temperature factors such as solar gain or poor heating regimes rather than the ingress of water vapour.

Deterioration associated with environmental parameters other than water – such as temperature, pollution and light – can be more difficult to assess in a basic performance survey. As ever, for a building of any antiquity that is showing signs of such problems, it is helpful to begin by considering whether any recent changes to the building or its use might have upset a previous equilibrium.

Measured surveys

Measured performance surveys may demand the services of a specialist. Here, for example, the floor elevations inside St Peter's Church, in Barton-upon-Humber, were plotted in great detail for English Heritage by specialist surveyors using a laser scanner. Two sets of measurements were made a year apart, specifically to assess subsidence.

As with all investigations undertaken by contractors, the primary investigator or project leader must tightly define the intention and scope of the survey, working closely with the specialist to ensure that the required outcomes are clear, and that the work is directed towards problem-solving rather than simply the collection of information.

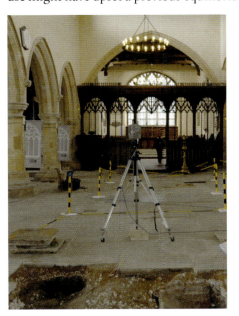

A measured survey may be needed to support a quantitative assessment of environmental issues. For example, if there seems to be a complex problem associated with runoff, the ground levels may need to be plotted with some accuracy. Measurements can be used to reveal spatial relationships between building elements or with the building services, which in a complex structure may be difficult to discern by eye. They can also help to clarify the relationships between different phases of construction (which can have a strong impact on behaviour).

Accurate measurements (including plans and elevations) are also likely to prove invaluable if detailed performance surveys are needed, and for the preparation of specifications for any remedial works.

BUILDING ENVIRONMENT
ASSESSING THE BUILDING ENVIRONMENT

Detailed Performance Surveys

To understand complex problems, a more detailed survey of performance may be needed. This is likely to require better access than the basic survey, and perhaps more expertise or a wider range of tools. Although it will sometimes be necessary to look at the building as a whole, more commonly a detailed survey will concentrate on a particular problem area or areas.

The information gathered during the basic survey and any measured surveys will be the basis for specifying the detailed performance survey, which may sometimes be outsourced to a building-performance specialist. If this is indeed the case, close consultation will be needed to define the issues to be covered, and it is not uncommon for the brief to change at this point: the specialist may well be able to suggest more effective approaches or more useful tools. It is the specialist's responsibility to clearly explain which methods of investigation will be able to deliver the required information.

Detailed surveys often incorporate *in-situ* tests, or the removal of samples for examination and analysis off site. The purpose of any such test would need to be clearly understood and agreed in advance; it is also important to bear in mind that, if the building is protected, some types of sampling will require statutory consent. ⊖BASICS

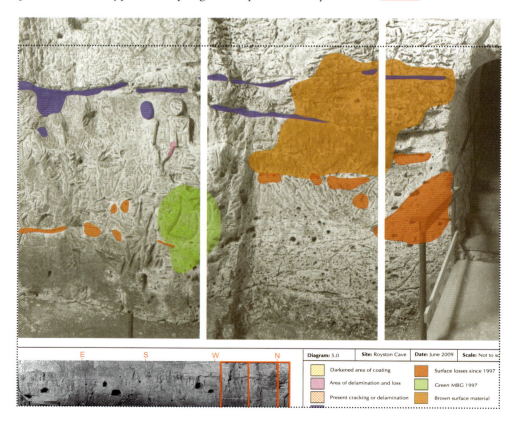

Condition mapping

Detail of a condition map of Royston Cave, in Hertfordshire.

Condition mapping is a powerful tool for investigating environmental problems. By recording the location and extent of different types of deterioration, it may be possible to distinguish patterns that would otherwise pass unnoticed. This can uncover relationships between different deterioration phenomena, and can also help to narrow down possible causes by quantifying the relationship between deterioration and location.

Health & Safety

SURVEYING HAZARDS

HAZARDOUS MATERIALS

Buildings may contain a number of hazardous materials, from toxic moulds to asbestos fibres, and it is important to be aware of as many of these as possible before beginning surveying if invasive investigations are not to prove dangerous. The materials of greatest concern are arguably lead paint and asbestos. The following is a brief introduction; the Health and Safety Executive should always be consulted for the latest advice and guidelines (*www.hse.gov.uk*).

Lead Paint

Lead is toxic to many organs, and because it interferes with the development of the nervous system, it is particularly dangerous to children. Although it has been known to be a health hazard since the earliest times, until the 1960s paints containing lead as a pigment or a drying agent were common, and at the time of press they could still be used in England for some listed buildings. The lead content was at its highest in paints made from the 1930s until about 1955; it is always wise to assume that some proportion of lead will be present in pre-1960s paintwork, especially on window and door frames, skirting boards, radiators and pipes, and indeed on walls. Specialist analytical companies can be called in to assess the extent of lead paint if necessary.

Intact paint is not a high risk, but dust and fumes from heated paint are, so it is important to take suitable precautions before undertaking invasive investigations such as drilling or opening-up.

Asbestos

Asbestos, a naturally occurring fibrous silicate mineral able to strongly resist heat and chemical damage, became very popular with builders and manufacturers of building products in the 19th century as a flame retardant, and to add tensile strength and flexibility. It was used extensively and widely: as a compound for dry walls and jointing, in sheeting and tiles, in cladding, roofing felts and shingles, as an additive for plasters, cements and textured coatings, and as lagging for pipes and for general heat and sound insulation.

Unfortunately, asbestos proved to be extremely dangerous, with inhalation causing malignant lung cancer, mesothelioma and asbestosis. Health concerns began to be raised in the early 1900s, and asbestosis was recognised as a work-related disease by the 1930s, but restrictions on use did not become common until much later. In 2006 the European Union finally banned all use of asbestos, together with any extraction, manufacture or processing.

Asbestos is a particular concern when surveying curtain walling, since dismantling is often required: likely locations to find the material include fire and smoke breaks at the interfaces between the walls and the floor slabs, and within opaque spandrel panels (which might have a fire protection function). Structural columns adjacent to the curtain wall were often protected against fire with materials containing asbestos, and asbestos was sometimes also incorporated within insulation materials. The project manager of any proposed works on a building that might contain asbestos should ask for a copy of the Asbestos Risk Register before works begin. If there is any possibility that asbestos could be encountered during dismantling, a specialist asbestos consultant should be called in.

BUILDING ENVIRONMENT
ASSESSING THE BUILDING ENVIRONMENT

ACCESS

SCAFFOLDING

To gain access to historic building façades for close inspection, 'independent tied' scaffolds should normally be provided. These derive no vertical support from the building, but they must be tied to it for horizontal stability. Ties can pass through window openings and 'hook' back against the internal surface of the external wall, or can grip the window reveals. In both cases, great care must be taken not to damage either the glass and glazing, or any internal finishes.

Where independent tied scaffolds are not practicable, the scaffold may need to be fixed to the stone or brickwork (provided it is adequate for the purpose). This will usually mean setting anchor sleeves into the masonry to take fixing bolts. Sleeves and bolts that are to remain in place following completion of the works should always be made of stainless steel, to reduce the risk of further damage to the building. Transom poles must be fitted with end caps to protect masonry surfaces.

If fixing into the masonry is not permitted, then a freestanding scaffold will have to be used. As these are self-supporting, they are necessarily more substantial than scaffolds restrained by the building, and are therefore much more expensive. Mobile scaffold towers are cheaper and quicker to erect, but they do not adapt so easily to confined spaces or to steeply sloping ground, and there are strict limits on safe working height and load capacity.

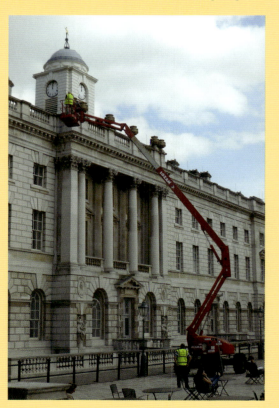

MOBILE ELEVATED PLATFORMS

Hydraulic platforms provide an almost instant means of access. Like mobile scaffold towers, scissor lifts are difficult to use in confined spaces, or if the ground is rough or steeply sloping.

'Cherry pickers' – machines with the working platform on an articulated telescopic boom – can operate at greater heights, and their good reach gives access to elements set back from the front line of the building, but they also require an access point sufficiently wide to accommodate the machine, and fairly flat and stable ground capable of bearing its weight. They are also comparatively expensive, although in some cases their cost may be offset by the speed of working they permit.

ROPE ACCESS

Rope access is becoming increasingly common, and can provide rapid, flexible and cost-effective access to many parts of a building not only for inspection, but also for works such as cleaning and painting.

Workers are suspended from the building on both a working rope and an independently anchored back-up rope. Small tools are attached to the worker's harness by means of a lanyard, and larger tools and equipment are suspended on an independent rope. Some buildings (such as churches) may have architectural features that are suitable for anchoring; on other buildings, eyebolts must be fixed in place to take the ropes.

Rope access requires suitably qualified personnel operating in accordance with the guidelines of the Industrial Rope Access Trade Association [IRATA], and the correct equipment; there are an increasing number of firms that specialise in rope access for historic building conservation.

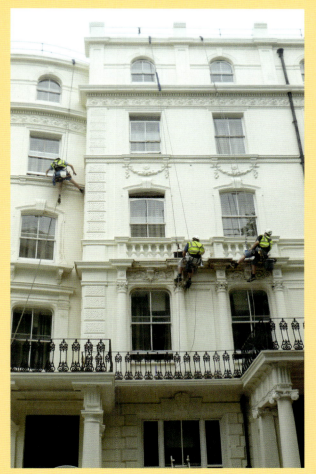

LADDERS

Ladders are comparatively cheap, easy to erect and can be used in many situations. On the whole they should be used only for reaching a working area rather than as a working platform. Ladders can be used for quick tasks (such as day-to-day inspections or cleaning debris from gutters) if, after assessing the risks, the use of other equipment is not justified because of the low risk and short duration of the works.

Ladders should be securely clipped or tied to prevent them slipping. Where regular access by means of a ladder is required (for example, to access a parapet gutter), it may be possible to fix an eyebolt to which the top of the ladder can be secured, to stop it falling sideways or slipping down. Ladders should never be leant against delicate historic surfaces.

The *Conservation Basics* volume in this series has more information about safety precautions for working on buildings. ⊖BASICS

BUILDING ENVIRONMENT
ASSESSING THE BUILDING ENVIRONMENT

RECORDING PERFORMANCE SURVEYS

Surveys must be adequately recorded, although the level of detail this demands will depend on the level of investigation and the reasons for it. Even a basic survey can be usefully entered into a building logbook (which may be no more than a computerised database). Fortunately, recording is rarely onerous, since it is often integral to the process of examination: the notes, photographs and sketches made during the survey will constitute its main record. As soon as possible after the survey has been completed, the notes should be summarised to highlight the principal findings, together with any recommendations for more detailed or specialist investigations which might be needed to cast light on particular problems.

For more detailed performance surveys, recording will need to be both meticulous and repeatable. For example, the materials, construction and condition of the area being examined will have to be recorded thoroughly, and any cracks or displacements recorded and measured so any changes can be seen in future surveys.

Good photographs are an invaluable adjunct to any survey of the building condition: images of deterioration and damage will provide the background detail to written observations, and be critical to the authority and effectiveness of any final report.

If possible, areas of damage should be mapped onto photographs or drawings, since the patterns of deterioration are often an excellent indicator of the nature of the underlying problems, and can help to identify underlying causes as well as any interactions between different decay processes. ➔BASICS

Survey Records

A survey is an invaluable baseline for later examinations, since changes between successive surveys may reveal progressive decay, and might even allow quantification of the rate of deterioration. It is therefore important that it is recorded in a precise and systematic manner, easily accessible to other surveyors in future.

PROFORMA FOR SURVEYING

It is good practice to develop a simple proforma or checklist to help structure the recording – and indeed the survey itself – and prevent anything being overlooked. As a minimum, the proforma should give space for recording:

- the name and location of the building
- the date of the survey, and the names, qualifications and contact details of all those involved
- what methods of inspection were used during the survey (including any constraints on access)
- general environmental information about the site, including the local weather, neighbouring structures and local land use, or nearby industries that may affect the building
- a description of the weather conditions at the time of the survey
- a description of the building, covering the basic materials and construction, and any features of special interest; the type or condition of original and added materials; the condition of the building envelope, including all water disposal systems, and any signs of moisture problems; the way the building is being used; and the building services, especially those that control the interior environment (heating and cooling systems), with a description of their settings, and the way they are being used.

UNDERTAKING A PERFORMANCE SURVEY

Although the level of accuracy and detail needed will differ greatly depending on the aims of the performance survey and the resources devoted to it, even the most rapid check after a storm will demand close observation and good recording.

The following is a detailed description of the basic logic that underlies all types of building performance survey, from the most simple and generic to the most specific and specialist.

PRELIMINARY WORK

The first step for the assessor is to bring together all the information gathered from previous surveys and from the background research (if the building is being surveyed in detail for the first time, this will consist largely of the latter). Any problem areas noted in earlier reports should be identified, so that these can be prioritised.

Documentary evidence of how the building appeared in the past, such as copies of old photographs, can help identify alterations or deterioration; if they are dated, they can sometimes be used to give a rough estimate of deterioration rates.

Building performance surveys of all types should follow a protocol to make sure all areas of are covered adequately, but any protocol must still be flexible enough to be adapted to the unique characteristics of the building and its environment. For the first survey, it will usually be necessary to develop a system of identification for those parts of the building being examined. Ideally, this is very simple and logical, so that if necessary it can easily be reconstructed by anyone consulting the survey record in the future, even if the key to the system has been lost.

A template for recording can often be prepared in advance. For all but the simplest surveys, this would include plans of all floors of the building, and elevations of all interior and exterior faces. For many buildings these may already exist, but it is rare that the existing drawings will be flawless, so corrections often need to be made as the survey proceeds. In addition, many surveyors will wish to draw rough plans and elevations as they work (as well as sketching interesting or peculiar details), since this demands close and systematic observation. Plans of building services are also extremely useful.

Most building performance surveys will incorporate some form of mapping, often not only to record the condition, but also to indicate areas where works will be needed. The base maps for this will usually have to be prepared in advance. What form they take will depend on the level of detail and accuracy required, and of course on the resources available; but they are often simply as rough sketches or photographs printed onto plain paper so that they can be easily annotated on site.

Tools for Surveying Building Performance

Good surveying requires effective equipment, but this does not have to be complex. The list below is not exhaustive, but it does include a range of tools that various professional assessors have found useful for surveying the building and its environment. Every assessor soon develops their own preferred kit, and indeed a tool one assessor finds invaluable, another may never use.

Proper clothing and protective gear should be included in every toolkit, not least good-quality dust masks. For investigating areas where there could be hazardous materials – extensive bird droppings, for example, or a risk of asbestos – current statutory guidance on protective equipment and procedures must be checked and followed. Details of the latest requirements are available from the Health and Safety Executive website (*www.hse.gov.uk*).

Recording equipment:
- marker pens and paper ('permatrace' drawing film is useful for surveying during wet weather)
- a dictaphone or other sound-recording device
- a camera with a range of lenses from wide-angle to macro.

Measuring equipment:
- long tape measures, a metre rule, a laser measure
- a spirit level
- a surveyor's rod or ranging pole.

Observational tools:
- a magnifying viewer, such as a ×10 hand lens
- binoculars (useful magnifications are 8 × 40 or 10 × 40)
- a powerful torch.

Other useful tools:
- a folding ladder or some other means of quick higher-level access
- a sharp bradawl to check for timber decay and other deterioration, especially under paint
- a small chisel and a hammer (a light hammer is also useful for assessing hollowness: for example, behind plasters or renders)
- wire, or a retractable car aerial, to check the depth of holes and voids
- a small spade and a crowbar for lifting access covers, for checking gulleys and drains
- a plumb bob, or billiard balls, for checking falls and levels
- a bucket or a hosepipe that can be connected to a tap, for checking the operation of water disposal systems
- hand-held resistance or capacitance moisture meters
- sampling tools and materials (including sharp scalpels, small stiff paint-brushes for taking samples of surface materials such as efflorescences, sealable plastic bags, glass or plastic tubes, and other airtight containers).

For investigating particular buildings or building issues, assessors may sometimes use more elaborate equipment such as hand-held temperature and relative humidity loggers able to give readings for dew point and absolute humidity, borescopes for investigating voids, infrared surface-temperature thermometers, thermal imaging cameras, 'Karsten tubes' for measuring the absorption of liquid water through surfaces, portable ultraviolet lamps to check for organic coatings and deposits, and metal detectors or handheld micropower impulse radar devices to look for embedded metal and other hidden elements.

GENERAL RULES FOR ON-SITE WORK

It is important to make a note of the weather conditions during the survey; and indeed, despite the discomfort, it can be very useful to survey during a rainstorm where possible.

Examination and recording must always be very systematic to avoid missing any features, especially those that typically cause problems (such as the rainwater and groundwater disposal systems). For this reason, experienced building assessors almost always prefer to follow a standard method of their own devising. Most begin by examining the surroundings and then the exterior of the envelope, working downwards from the top of the building (the roof ridges), and then going on to consider the interior.

Multiple sources of problems

A neglected building will accumulate problems from many sources, and so even if a major source is obvious, all other possible sources must be identified and taken into account.

In the case illustrated here, a church exhibits typical symptoms of poor maintenance, including blocked gutters, blocked and broken drains with splashback, broken and blocked downpipes, and a cracked cement render with localised losses that is trapping moisture in the walls.

These flaws in the envelope manifest themselves very clearly as damage on the interior (*bottom left*). The wall paintings have clearly been conserved in the fairly recent past, indicating that there have been moisture problems occuring for some time, but it is the recent stains and losses (post-dating the conservation) which show that those problems are ongoing, and indeed have become more serious.

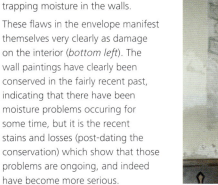

BUILDING ENVIRONMENT
ASSESSING THE BUILDING ENVIRONMENT

If there is exterior damage that is likely to let in water, corresponding deterioration should be looked for on the interior.

Similarly, interior problems should be associated with exterior faults wherever possible. Here, for example, slipped slates are the cause of decay in the roof beams.

Since any flaws with the exterior of the building envelope could well be affecting the interior, the problems should be marked onto the plan and elevations so that the condition of the interior at the same point can be assessed later. For example, if ivy is growing into a gutter, it indicates that the wall plate area should be checked inside for signs of moisture ingress, such as decay in the timber beam-ends.

If there are clear signs of damage and loss, but the current environmental conditions appear to be good, the aim must be to check whether the deterioration is a sign of past problems that have since been resolved, or whether it is continuing (in which case the source will need to be determined and dealt with). For example, a timber window frame may have decayed due to frequent condensation running down the glass, caused by high interior humidities generated by calor-gas heating that has since been removed. Although the damage remains and may need to be repaired, in this case the cause is no longer active so no other intervention will be needed.

The type of deterioration can be a helpful pointer to the answer to the fundamental question of whether the deterioration is dormant or active. For example, although salt crystallisation can still produce deterioration of plaster decades after a leak has been dealt with, if there is active woodworm in timber it suggests there is a 'live' source of liquid water. Another guide is recent losses, especially if these can be dated with the help of the background research.

Past treatments and repairs should be identified wherever possible, even where these are not mentioned in reports. They can themselves be a source of problems, but even more importantly they are also an excellent indicator of persistent issues.

If there are areas of concern that cannot be assessed fully for lack of access, equipment or particular expertise, the assessor should note these down for more detailed investigation at a later date.

UNDERTAKING A DETAILED SURVEY

SURVEYING THE SETTING

The first job when undertaking a detailed building performance survey is to form a picture of the building's setting and its wider environment. If the users of the building cannot summarise the local weather conditions, including the wind exposure, it may be possible to read clues from the landscape, and perhaps from the design of the building itself and the way the fabric has weathered.

The local topography is equally important: the slope of the terrain, the nature and location of any nearby structures, and the ways the surrounding ground is surfaced, will all have a significant impact on the building and should be noted onto a rough plan. Trees and other sizeable plants should be recorded, with measurements being taken of vegetation wherever it abuts the building, or could affect drainage systems. If tall trees are sited where they could endanger the building should branches fall or the tree be blown down by the wind, this too must be noted, so that inspections by a tree surgeon can be added to the schedule of regular maintenance tasks.

BUILDING ENVIRONMENT
ASSESSING THE BUILDING ENVIRONMENT

SURVEYING THE EXTERIOR

The appearance and structure of the building as a whole should be recorded, noting any visible alterations and extensions, and all the interfaces between different materials or different types of construction. These areas may need to be looked at more closely, to ensure that there are no associated problems.

STRUCTURE

The structure should be examined for evidence of recent instability, such as recent cracking, or cracks and displacements that are growing. Recent activity may be shown by fresh losses and debris. Since it is extremely helpful to compare current patterns to those on earlier photographs and drawings, good photographs and measurements should be taken of any areas of concern.

ROOFS

The roof is one of the most important parts of the building envelope, and so merits very close examination. For pitched roofs, although a certain amount of investigation can be done from the ground using binoculars – to make a quick examination after a storm, for example – a thorough survey will need full access. For flat roofs or roofs with parapet gutters, direct access will be essential.

Falls on flat roofs and parapet gutters can be checked with a spirit level, or by seeing if a marble or ball-bearing will roll in the direction of the outlets. Any areas where water can pool should be marked onto a plan for checking on the interior, as this is where leaks will be most likely.

On any type of roof, all joints between different parts of the structure will need to be checked, especially where the fall is shallow. The ridges and hips should be inspected to ensure that all cappings are intact, and all waterproofing features functioning correctly. The covering should then be looked over for any signs of trouble (see the *Roofing* volume in this series for detailed information on the types of problems that may occur with different types of covering). ⊖ROOFING

The waterproofing around elements that pierce the roof, such as upstands and dormer windows, or chimneys and other service exhausts, are other likely places to look for signs of failure. Faulty flashings and mortar fillets are a frequent cause of leaks, and deserve close examination. They will often be found to be in poor condition.

Chimneys damaged by salt-jacking (expansion of mortar joints due to sulphate attack causing the formation of expansive ettringite) often have a pronounced bend. This tends to be away from the wettest face; slower drying is believed to encourage the growth of the ettringite crystals.

WATER DISPOSAL SYSTEMS

All the other elements critical to water disposal systems on and around the building must be checked to see whether or not they are still operating correctly, since some blockages are more than likely (it is very rare indeed to find a system in perfect working order). Algae and moss, water staining and vegetation growing out of mortar joints are all very obvious signs of established problems, although surprisingly often they will not have been noticed by the building's users.

It is essential to identify every part of the water-handling systems, including those parts that are concealed (such as hidden downpipes, ground drains and soakaways). For properties that have been neglected, this can involve a certain amount of digging or investigation with equipment such as drain cameras (see **Specialist Investigations**). Again, good preliminary research can help, by locating likely drains and soakaways.

It is always easiest to understand how water-management systems operate in practice by observing what actually happens during a rainstorm. Where this is not possible, or would be too dangerous, a hosepipe or bucket can be used to pour water down gutters, downpipes and gulleys to check operation.

WALLS

The distribution of surface dirt and pollutants is a good indicator of how rainwater flows down the walls of a building. This is particularly important for modern rainscreen construction. Rainwater may cause streaking from the ends of projections, or stains where it has run over metal elements and thence onto the walls. On limestone, the cleanest areas of the façade will be those where rain has been able to wash the black sulphate coating; for sandstone, which reacts with acid rain and then captures soot and other deposits, these will be the darkest areas.

Patterns of streaking and runoff on the exterior walls are a good indicator of a building's exposure, and of how it handles rainwater. Likely areas of strong exposure can then be checked against signs of leakage on the interior.

Here, the unusual pattern of staining on a concrete façade is attributable to a combination of the surface finish of the concrete, and the wind direction down a narrow city street. It is possible to distinguish areas of the façade that are more exposed from those that are more protected (where the discoloured staining has not been washed away).

The condition of the walls must be closely examined to identify possible sources of water penetration. These could include defective pointing, cement mortars, damaged renders or cement renders, or (for modern walling systems) faulty seals and blocked outlets; lost or damaged weather detailing (such as protective drip mouldings) should also be recorded.

BUILDING ENVIRONMENT
ASSESSING THE BUILDING ENVIRONMENT

As buildings age, they will often be altered by their users to suit their current needs. Windows and doors may be blocked, or building materials used in new extensions. Often the alterations and voids are hidden under plaster, where they may pass unnoticed, but may create problems that are therefore very difficult to diagnose.

Right: At Cleeve Abbey in Somerset, early alterations concealed for many centuries below plaster have been revealed for the visitor.

OPENINGS

Openings such as windows are a common location for water penetration. Decay of wood and corrosion of metal frames are typical signs of problems. Painted timber can be tested by pushing the point of a sharp bradawl or similar instrument into the wood; if there is little or no resistance, the wood will require closer examination.

A particular weak point for modern construction will be thermal bridges, which in cold weather can lower the temperature of the building element to the point when condensation begins to form on the interior. The position of potential thermal bridges (exposed metal framework, for example) should be recorded, so this can be checked from the interior.

SURVEYING THE INTERIOR

Once the exterior has been thoroughly examined and recorded, the assessor can move on to the interior. There are two schools of thought as to whether this part of the examination should begin at the top or the bottom of the building, and in fact it rather depends on its condition: if it has been very neglected, the assessor may think it wise to check the condition of floors from the underside before attempting to walk on them.

The fundamental aim is to equate interior deterioration with exterior faults wherever possible, but this is not always easy, since liquid water will travel along the path of least resistance and may appear on the interior at some distance away from the leak where it originated. Measurements are very important, particularly in helping to determine the relative positions of exterior and interior features (such as the relative levels of the exterior ground and the interior floor). The attics, cellars and other hidden areas will need to be checked for signs of water penetration or condensation. Particular attention must be paid to water-sensitive components, especially those in positions where they might be affected by moisture; for example, a sharp bradawl can be used to check the condition of timber joists where they meet an exterior wall.

Although damage such as salt efflorescences and flaking of surface finishes indicate that there have been moisture problems, these may or may not be ongoing. Signs that leaks are still active include recent losses and damage to newly applied surface finishes.

A decorated surface can give a good indication of whether deterioration is active: recent losses will appear bright or even white, since they will not yet have had time to accumulate dust and dirt.

Walls should be examined from the floor upwards, noting any signs of problems. Water rising in exterior masonry walls in localised areas might suggest faulty or blocked gulleys and drains, or problems with rainwater goods. If there is a damp-proof course, the wall itself may be dry, but the floor may be very wet near the wall, and timber skirting boards may be decaying. If the wall is wet at the top, the most likely causes will be blocked downpipes and gutters, poor sealing, or other similar moisture problems at height. Isolated patches of damp could suggest condensation in a poorly maintained chimney, though hygroscopic salts can be another cause. As with the exterior, the patterns of dirt deposition can also be a useful indicator of environmental problems. For example, streaks running down the wall below a window suggest regular condensation on the glass. In modern construction, blocked or faulty internal drains may cause streaking of surfaces below the drain, and localised corrosion or decay.

BUILDING ENVIRONMENT
ASSESSING THE BUILDING ENVIRONMENT

Taking readings of environmental conditions with a hand-held meter

Hand-held electronic meters are now available at little cost; most will measure relative humidity and temperature, and may calculate absolute humidity and dew point. More sophisticated models may have interchangeable probes, allowing the surveyor to take readings of other environmental parameters such as air movement or pollution.

Although hand-held meters will only give spot measurements, and the readings for a single day should never be given too much weight in interpretation, they can still be a handy way to examine the overall behaviour of the building envelope, and can be used to help plan more exact investigations.

Water problems will not always be due to a problem with the building envelope, or to condensation: leaks in plumbing and heating pipes, or even in fire-protection systems, are common sources of problems.

Most assessors find it useful to map superficial decay onto elevations. Relative moisture and salt levels in walls can also be roughly mapped using resistance or capacitance moisture meters, and although the results will not be accurate, the resulting patterns may help to narrow down a hidden source of moisture. It is possible to take spot measurements of temperature and humidity, usually with hand-held meters. Although the information this gives should be approached with caution, it can be a way of making general comparisons, especially when looking at the potential effects of heating: comparisons between different internal spaces, for example; or between the exterior and interior.

Each room will need to be assessed separately, as well as considered in terms of impact on the envelope as a whole. Windows and doors must be checked not only for signs of leaking and other similar problems, but to see whether they are operating correctly.

If the likely source of moisture-related damage is still not clear, it may be necessary to look at the exterior once again, double-checking details that could be causing problems, such as the pointing, the joints between building elements (for example, around windows), and the flashings and seals.

Recent changes to the fabric (for example, the addition of carpets or tiles, or of impermeable paints or wallpapers, or the installation of a new heating system) can be a critical factor, so these must be identified. Changes in the way the building is being used are equally important, as are any alterations that have been made to the environmental management. All evidence of building services, both old and new, will need to be recorded, and the building users questioned to construct a picture of the ways the current services (such as heating) are actually being used.

MAKING DETAILED MEASUREMENTS

Almost every aspect of the building environment has the potential to merit closer investigation and measurement as part of a building performance survey, from the slope of the surrounding ground to the structural soundness of the building elements.

CHARACTERISING THE GROUND SLOPE

If it is suspected that the ground levels are causing runoff problems, or there are subtle issues between interior and exterior ground levels, this can be checked very easily with simple tools (string, a metre rule and a level), though it does require that the surveyor has some assistance. Alternatively, professional surveying equipment can be used.

Determining relative ground levels

Top: Interior floor levels, the difference in the interior and exterior ground levels, and the slope of the ground around the building, can all be determined to sufficient accuracy for most purposes using the simplest of tools: two straight sticks or metre rulers, a tape measure, string and a builder's level, or a line level.

Bottom left: Measurements are taken relative to one point, usually inside the building, with the measurement team working outwards from there; each reading becomes the baseline for the next measurement. The results are marked onto a building plan.

Bottom right: To connect the internal and external measurements, it is usually easiest to note the height of the same window sill on the interior and exterior.

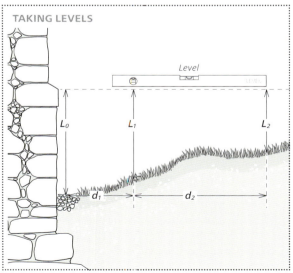

TAKING LEVELS

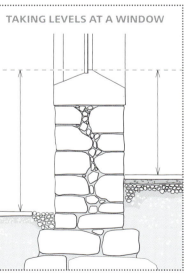

TAKING LEVELS AT A WINDOW

BUILDING ENVIRONMENT
ASSESSING THE BUILDING ENVIRONMENT

240   Determining runoff patterns

Measuring levels is a quick way of plotting the likely pattern of surface runoff, which can prove to be quite complicated. Measurements are made at regular intervals outwards at right angles to the building walls, and plotted onto a plan of the building and its surroundings.

Right: A detail of one such plan.

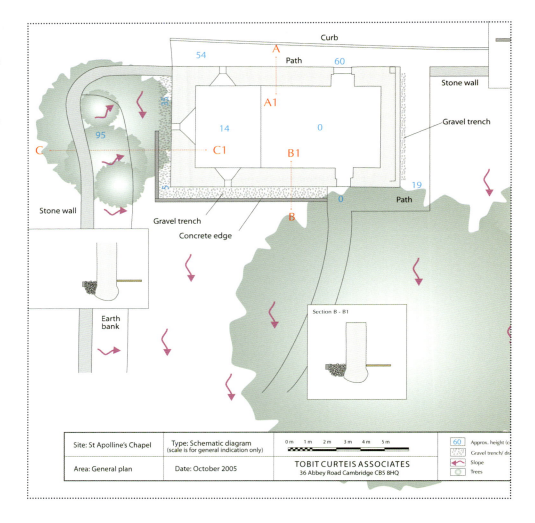

STRUCTURAL PROBLEMS

Many potential signs of structural problems – such as cracks, bulges and displacements – will have occurred during settlement and are not a cause for concern, but recent movement is often a sign of an underlying environmental problem, especially if any major changes have been made to the building or its surroundings in the recent past. Again, old photographs and measurements are a valuable point of comparison.

Signs of ongoing movement include fresh debris, or losses that are not covered with dirt or dust. If the interior or exterior has been recently redecorated but cracks have since appeared, this can be another clue. The assessor will need to examine how the crack faces have come apart, checking whether the break looks fresh and clean (and is therefore likely to be recent), or whether it contains remnants of old paints or fillers.

Cracks and displacements should be measured as accurately as possible, to provide a baseline for future comparison; it can also be helpful to mark the current extremity of the crack in pencil, noting the date and the initials of the assessor. Tell-tales are a useful guide, though none are infallible. Plastic tell-tales allow changes in width to be noted, but require regular checking and recording; it is possible to entirely miss a cyclical change. Plaster test patches over the crack will break the moment the crack moves, forming a permanent record that movement has occurred, but they can give little idea of the magnitude of the change, or of any fluctuations in crack width.

If the problem appears serious, a structural engineer familiar with the behaviour of that type of building structure, and accustomed to conservation work, will need to be called in. They may install more sophisticated electronic monitoring equipment.

Addressing the resulting structural weakness is also a task for the engineer, but it may well be left to the assessor to discover the underlying sources of the problem. Most commonly this proves to be moisture-related deterioration, particularly the decay of timber members. Other possible causes include changed loads (such as aerials added to chimneys, or heavier replacement roof coverings); occasionally the problem will be impacts or other sudden damage.

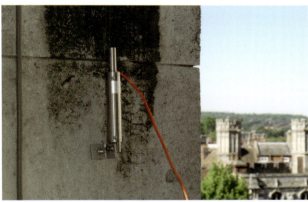

Structural monitoring

Structural engineers can monitor building movements using many different tools, from simple pencil markings and 'tell-tales' that must be read manually (*top right*), to electronic gauges that can be logged to build a picture of the relationship between the movement and the changing environmental conditions.

Parameters that can be monitored electronically include tilt (*top left*), vibration (*bottom left*) and crack displacement (*bottom right*).

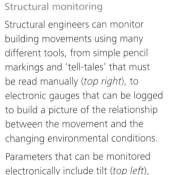

BUILDING ENVIRONMENT
ASSESSING THE BUILDING ENVIRONMENT

INVESTIGATING MOISTURE PROBLEMS

Any survey is more likely than not to encounter problems with the water disposal. This may be as simple as a broken downpipe, or as complex as moisture wicking up between the joints of the flashing, running along the outside of an old pipe, dripping off and soaking into the wall some distance away, and finally appearing on the interior as a patch of salts below a tiled cornice.

The signs of a moisture problem are often very obvious: staining, salt crystallisation, corrosion, growths of algae and mould or even higher plants such as ferns. Timber decay (attack by fungus and insects) is an infallible sign of liquid water.

It can be helpful to remember that (as discussed in **Building Science**) heat and moisture behave in some predictable ways:

- Heat travels from warmer to colder areas
- Liquid water is affected by gravity, and if free to do so will always run down towards the lowest point
- Liquid water will be drawn in to fine capillaries (such as those in permeable materials, or cracks, or fine gaps between two materials), and can then be sucked upwards against gravity
- Liquid water in a permeable material will travel towards areas of lower vapour pressure (from wetter areas into drier areas; and towards surfaces of evaporation)
- If liquid water can form a continuous flow path between a source (say a water table) and an evaporating surface (say an interior wall), then evaporation can carry it very rapidly through even a thick and complex masonry wall
- Liquid water travels very quickly through permeable materials, but the transport of water vapour is extremely slow
- If free to do so, water vapour will travel from areas of higher pressure to lower pressure
- Water vapour will rise (as will warm air)
- Water vapour will condense on surfaces cooler than the dew-point temperature
- Warm air will often be holding more water vapour (so the absolute humidity in an unventilated roof space will tend to increase quite rapidly if the temperature increases)
- Permeable materials will be much more hygroscopic if they are not dry.

With this in mind, the patterns of deterioration will often suggest the likely source of the moisture. However, water can sometimes travel considerable distances before being absorbed into the fabric, and then travel through the fabric some way more before emerging at some evaporating surface, so the leak itself may be far away from the damage.

There may be more than one source of moisture, making it necessary to address the problems identified, and then wait some time to see whether the fabric has begun to dry. If moisture problems remain, further investigation and intervention will be required.

Deterioration of the interior surfaces of external walls is often the most obvious sign of moisture ingress.

Widespread Damage on Interior Wall Faces

Widespread deterioration suggests the problem is either very general, or has been established for a considerable time. General problems could include:

- any weakness that allows rainwater to penetrate
- renders or other treatments that prevent the wall from drying, including cement renders, internal cement tanking that pushes moisture further up walls, AVCLs, and impermeable paints and wallpapers
- water rising from a high water table.

Water rising from the water table ('rising damp') is commonly evoked to explain almost all moisture problems, but in fact is very uncommon: in general, moisture rising from the base of the wall will be found to be due to faulty drains or rainwater goods, or some similar source. Comparing the damage on different walls can be useful: groundwater would rise to more or less the same height in every wall, internal or external (with some allowance for different wall thicknesses, materials and evaporation rates). Localised rising moisture is indicative of a water source nearby: if there is no obvious cause on the exterior, such as a blocked downpipe, the plumbing should be checked.

Certain types of building construction demonstrate characteristic weaknesses that may have caused widespread moisture problems:

- *Masonry construction*
  Thin walls (in older buildings, often internal walls that have become exterior walls because of demolition); deteriorated renders or pointing; and joints, repointing or renders made with cement.

- *Timber-frame construction*
  Faulty infills, allowing water to penetrate between the infill and the frame.

- *Curtain-wall construction*
  Insufficient rain screening, failed seals and blocked internal drainage.

- *Cavity wall construction*
  Cement joints, blocked internal drainage; cavity may be filled with debris or insulation, causing a moisture bridge.

Subterranean Walls

The exterior walls of excavated rooms, or walls that have earth piled against them on the exterior, will invariably be wet, but moisture problems will be worse if there are sources of water and contaminants other than groundwater.

In some cases it may be necessary to call in a specialist to identify the sources of soil moisture; for example, to excavate in search of drain blockages or leaking water services. If the building or its setting is historic, serious excavation works may have to be supervised by an archaeologist. If the source of the water is not clear, an analyst may need to sample and test the groundwater for contaminants.

Localised Damage on Interior Wall Faces

Localised moisture damage is much more common than general moisture ingress, since there are many potential sources: from faulty water disposal or leaking plumbing, to runoff flooding or water penetration through walls in poor condition. For modern construction, problems could arise from condensation associated with thermal bridges, or from rainwater penetration due to faulty seals, or from blocked internal drainage.

When widespread problems do occur, they can often be traced back to a localised issue that has been neglected: as the fabric absorbs more and more moisture, damage spreads further and further. In many cases, attempts to deal with the damp will have addressed not the cause but the symptom, and this will only have made matters worse. For example, applying a waterproof coating to the inside face of a masonry wall with a broken drain at the base will simply push the moisture elsewhere, until it meets a surface through which it can evaporate.

Mass Construction & Masonry

The most likely cause of severe localised moisture-related decay in above-ground masonry or earthen walls is a problem with the water disposal systems, such as a faulty gutter, downpipe or drain, and it is this that should be looked for first. If the moisture is rising from the base of the wall, gulleys and drains should be the first suspect; if the water is leaking down from above, it is most likely to be the rainwater disposal (especially blocked gutters, overflowing hoppers, and blocked or perforated downpipes). Blocked soakaways may lead to moisture backing up through the drainage system.

If all the drainage appears to be in good condition and functioning correctly, then hidden pipes should be suspected. Pipes may have been concealed in boxing, behind wall linings or embedded in the wall. Cellars are often a good starting point for locating hidden pipe runs, because in cellars they are less likely to have been concealed.

If there is no concealed water disposal or plumbing, or if all such potential sources of leaks are in fact in good condition, then attention should turn to more general aspects of the exterior drainage, including the direction and degree of runoff, splash back, and the location of public sewers.

Where there is no obvious source of liquid water, but localised patches of damp have appeared on mass walls that are otherwise dry, it is worth checking for leaks or condensation from chimneys. A less common cause is patches of hygroscopic materials, most commonly salts, wetting as they absorb moisture from the air. The source of these salts varies: deposition of pollutants in chimneys is one, but others include previous moisture problems, and surface deposition from heating systems, from decorating or repair materials, and previous uses of the building. If for some reason it is important to identify the source, it may be necessary to call in a specialist who can determine the types of salt present. ⊖STONE ⊖EARTH & BRICK

Moisture at the foot of a wall may be associated with impermeable flooring, such as a cement screed or an impermeable membrane that does not carry on through the walls.

Timber Construction

Timbered and half-timbered construction can suffer from much the same problems as mass construction and masonry, but the result can be serious decay. Timber cills resting on masonry plinths will not immediately take up water since the grain is laid horizontally, but eventually the wood will begin to decay, especially if water is being trapped at cill level, or the ground level has been allowed to rise above the plinth. ⇒TIMBER ⇒EARTH & BRICK

Modern Construction

Moisture problems in cavity walls can arise from the same sources as for mass construction, especially if the gap between the 'leaves' has been filled; for example, with cavity insulation, or with excess cement and other falling debris. Very localised patches of damp in cavity walls can sometimes be traced to liquid water crossing the gap between the leaves by way of the wall ties. ⇒EARTH & BRICK

Brick walls mortared with cement can develop hairline cracks at the interface between the brick and the cement, through which rainwater can wick. Cement renders or stuccos may also crack, allowing moisture penetration but preventing evaporation. If the wall has a high moisture content, adding vapour-resistant membranes, or even impermeable paints or wallpapers, can easily lead to condensation. ⇒MORTARS

In curtain walls, the materials used to seal the joints between panels have a fairly short lifespan, and rain may begin to penetrate when these start to fail. Drain channels and outlets may also become blocked, especially if sealants are used carelessly. ⇒GLASS

Thermal bridging can be the source of serious condensation problems, and should be suspected wherever parts of the metal frame are exposed to wind-cooling.

Condensation

Condensation events are usually intermittent, and it may only be possible to identify the underlying cause after prolonged monitoring of the microclimate. The most common symptoms are likely to be mould in the coldest areas of the building – where the walls are thickest, or where there are thermal bridges to the exterior (for example, the window reveals) – or in corners or other places where the air circulation is lower.

Moisture appearing on walls episodically is often interpreted as condensation, when in many cases it is due to liquid moisture problems. For example, a wall wetted by a faulty downpipe may transmit water through to the interior during rainstorms.

Condensation in Roof Spaces

It is unlikely that sufficient vapour will be produced in the indoor air to itself cause significant damage in a pitched roof, because typical roof timbers can easily absorb the vapour even from several bathrooms with little rise in the moisture content; the exception will be if quantities of vapour are condensing on the underside of a metal roof, or an impermeable membrane, and dripping back down onto the timber. In most other cases of observable deterioration, there will be an additional source of moisture, such as wet air from wall moisture problems being carried up through the interior of a poorly capped cavity wall by the airflow over the roof. ⇒ROOFING

Opening Up for Inspection

It may not be possible to thoroughly survey some parts of the building without a certain amount of dismantling. This may well be the case for roofs, especially where there is little access to the underside of the roof, for floors and occasionally walls, and for curtain walls and other hollow-wall construction. ➲ROOFING ➲GLASS ➲TIMBER

PREPARING FOR OPENING UP

Good preparation is all-important. Any available information about the construction should be checked to see whether there are any special requirements. In most cases it is wise to call on a specialist to undertake the opening up; this will certainly be necessary for curtain walling, where the construction methods can be particularly complex. ➲GLASS

It is necessary to be aware of the possibility of meeting hazardous substances such as asbestos and lead paint, and every precaution should be taken to reduce risks to the investigator and the building users. For protected buildings, depending on the scale of what is proposed, it may be necessary to obtain listed building consent before any dismantling begins.

CHOOSING SITES

The area chosen for investigation should be inconspicuous, but typical of the building as a whole. Before dismantling begins, it should be photographed both from the inside and the outside, ensuring that good detailed pictures of the interfaces are captured. From this, it will be possible to prepare a drawing of the layout that can be annotated with the findings of the assessment, and with the identification numbers of every dismantled component.

Components will need to be identified and numbered as dismantling proceeds, and detailed records kept of the dismantling method, all the materials found, and their position and condition. Where replacement is necessary, this should also be recorded, as should any other new materials used during reassembly.

SPECIAL CONSIDERATIONS FOR TIMBER FLOORS

Opening timber floors is usually a rather destructive process, which must be approached with particular care. As with all opening up, the first step is to determine the construction; for example, whether the boards are tongue-and-groove, or pegged together in some way. It is also important to locate any concealed services, especially if it will be necessary to cut any timber loose.

If possible, lifting should begin with a short board; it is sometimes necessary to cut a longer board across where it meets a joist, using the finest possible saw. Fine saws or knifes can be used to cut the tongue from a tongue-and-groove board to free it from its neighbour.

Lifted boards should be replaced in exactly the same position, with boards that have been cut short supported on a batten nailed to the side of the joist.

The *Timber* volume in this series has detailed instructions for opening up and refixing wooden floors and panelling. ➲TIMBER

Legal Considerations

In the UK, wildlife is protected by a number of important pieces of legislation, which may affect the investigation of biological problems (especially where these concern bats, and nesting or roosting birds).

The *Conservation Basics* volume in this series discusses the implications of current legislation on building assessment. ⊝BASICS

INVESTIGATING BIOLOGICAL PROBLEMS

Bats

If bats are known or suspected to be roosting in the building, Natural England should be consulted so that the species can be identified and their roosts located (there is some species variation, but generally most droppings will be found around the entrance point to the building and around the roost site). They will also be able to assess other important aspects, such as the size of the colony and how much it uses the various parts of the building.

It is also important to assess the extent of damage, and the risk this poses to the contents and the building use. Droppings and urine marks will need to be recorded over several months, and this can give additional information about the extent and activity of the colony.

With this information, the building managers and Natural England should be able to determine the most appropriate response to the problem.

Birds

The first step when dealing with a bird problem is to identify the species, and determine how the bird is using the building; this will make it easier to investigate possible approaches to control.

Pigeons, for example, should be watched for several days to determine their pattern of activity. If they are on and around the building during the day, especially on the higher parts such as roofs and gutters, but there is little sign of them at night, then they are probably using the building as a perch to look for food (there will probably be a reliable source nearby, such as a park where visitors regularly feed the pigeons). Removing the food source is then the best way of resolving the problem.

If birds appear in the early morning and at dusk, and are rarely visible during the day, then they may well be using the building for roosting or even nesting. To determine the best deterrent strategy, it will be necessary to identify where the roosts are (usually by seeing where guano has collected), what number of birds are involved and whether they are nesting.

BUILDING ENVIRONMENT
ASSESSING THE BUILDING ENVIRONMENT

It can be challenging for the non-expert to distinguish between the remnants of old fungal or insect attack, and ongoing problems.

The dry rot shown here, for instance, is no longer active, but dying back, the underlying moisture issues having been successfully resolved.

Microbiological Growths

Growing algae, mosses and fungi are a sure sign of an excess of moisture: for example, the fungi that can attack timber (such as dry rot, *Serpula lacrymans*) can do so only when the timber involved is very wet. It should, however, be remembered that surface growth and strands may be visible long after the fungus itself has died.

Identifying species may require expert help, but identification may not always be necessary since the effective action in all cases is to remove the source of liquid water.

Insects

Insect activity – especially of pests that feed on rotting timber – can be another sign of possible moisture problems. For example, finding woodlice suggests that there is a source of decaying wood or something similar in the vicinity, but this may have nothing to do with the building.

There are a number of approaches to assessing insect activity, depending on the type of insect involved. The first step in all cases is to look for evidence of dead insects on ledges or in spider webs, and to identify the species if at all possible. The *Timber* book in this series gives a detailed description of insect pests that attack wood, but to give an absolute identification it may be necessary to call in a specialist. ⊙TIMBER

It may be difficult to know from a simple one-off survey of this type whether any infestation is still active, although finding living deathwatch beetle, for example, would certainly suggest an ongoing problem. Monitoring may well be necessary: this can be as simple as cleaning a surface and then checking regularly to see if any significant insect remains have accumulated since the last cleaning.

For insects that attack timber, the condition of the flight holes and the accumulation of 'frass' (the digested remains of the wood) may well give important clues as to whether the infestation is active: clean holes and fresh frass may be indicators. It is also possible to paste thin paper over existing holes before the flight season: if the paper is punched through, then beetles are still escaping from the timber.

Insect traps can be useful, especially for species that are attracted to the traps with pheromones. Where the traps are located is critical to their success, and this may require the services of an experienced entomologist. Traps will need to be checked and replaced regularly, especially since trapped insects can become food for other pests.

INVESTIGATING POLLUTION

In many cases the source of pollutants such as salts will be obvious, and absolute identification is of fairly minor importance. In other cases the nature of the pollutant may give a clue to the source of the moisture problem: for example, the salts travelling into a wall from the water table will be quite different to those arriving from a leak in a sewage pipe.

Water-Borne Pollutants

Pollutants dissolved in liquid water can be analysed in a number of different ways, according to the type of pollutant and the accuracy required. In many cases, simple systems such as salt identification strips will be perfectly sufficient.

Airborne Pollutants

Air pollutants fall into one of two broad types – particulates and gases – and these will need to be assessed in quite different ways:

- Particulates can be sampled passively by exposing sample plates, which can be sent away to an analytical laboratory for identification. The rate of deposition can be determined by checking the samples at regular intervals.
- Gaseous pollutants can be measured with sampling tubes, which may either be active (giving electronic read-outs of concentration) or passive (the tubes must be sent to a laboratory for analysis of cumulative concentration).

In either case it must be remembered that the deposition rate and activity of the pollutant will also depend on the characteristics of the surface that is being affected: its texture, chemistry and exposure.

Wherever possible the underlying source of salts and other pollutants should be identified, and this will help when planning remedial care.

BUILDING ENVIRONMENT
ASSESSING THE BUILDING ENVIRONMENT

ASSESSING OTHER SOURCES OF PROBLEMS

Deterioration arising from other environmental parameters – such as temperature or light, or building occupation – tend to be more complex, and more difficult to completely understand and assess during a building performance survey. As ever, it is best to begin by considering whether any recent changes to the building or its environment and use could have disturbed a previous equilibrium.

The other volumes in this series contain detailed discussions about the impact of various environmental factors on different building materials and systems, and how these should be assessed. ⊃MORTARS ⊃METALS ⊃EARTH & BRICK ⊃ROOFING ⊃GLASS ⊃STONE ⊃TIMBER ⊃CONCRETE

The Painted Chamber, Cleeve Abbey, Somerset

The mechanism underlying the ongoing deterioration of the medieval wall painting in the Painted Chamber at Cleeve Abbey was known to be related to inclusions of dark, porous aggregates in the plaster, but why the damage was limited to the lower part of the painting remained a mystery until time-lapse imaging revealed that for just a few months in winter, direct sunlight hit the wall and heated the surface. The pattern of light exposure was found to correlate exactly with the pattern of damage.

TAKING SPOT READINGS

Spot readings are essentially one-off measurements, which give a single value of critical environmental parameters such as air temperature, humidity or surface temperature at a single time. Spot moisture meters can be useful tools, but only if their essential limitations are understood, and they are not used alone to draw conclusions, in the absence of more reliable data.

Although spot measurements will often be taken as part of a performance survey, they do have considerable limitations as a diagnostic tool; patterns of deterioration, and indications of prolonged problems, are likely to be considerably more informative. For example, it is highly unlikely that the survey will be scheduled at exactly the right moment to capture an episode of condensation; but if this is a regular problem, it should be identifiable from the familiar patterns of deterioration caused by condensation runoff (such as mould growth, staining, decay or corrosion at the bottom of windows).

Spot measurements are most informative if they are used to determine spatial variations (for example, the distribution of moisture across a wall, or of temperatures in different rooms) rather than absolute measurements.

To investigate parameters which change with time, it is better to take readings over time: that is, to monitor. Spot readings tend to be less reliable than monitored readings, where the calibration error can be neglected, and the methods of measurement and the probe positions optimised.

MICROCLIMATE MEASUREMENT

For many years, spot readings of the microclimate were taken with 'whirling hygrometers', instruments designed to give two temperature readings ('wet-bulb' and 'dry-bulb') that could be used in conjunction with a 'psychrometric chart' to calculate a range of thermohygrometric readings, including relative humidity and dew-point temperature. These instruments and charts are now largely obsolete for monitoring purposes, having been replaced by hand-held electronic meters that can give immediate readings of these and other microclimate parameters, and also record measurements. Many hand-held meters can be used with different types of sensors to give spot measurements of other parameters, including air movement, light levels and pollutants.

Spot measurements of the microclimate are often incorporated into preliminary inspections and into analytical investigations, to provide an indication of the ambient environmental conditions at the time of the investigation. There are many hand-held instruments available, most these days using electronic sensors. These are discussed in more detail in the section on **Environmental Monitoring**.

BUILDING ENVIRONMENT
ASSESSING THE BUILDING ENVIRONMENT

MOISTURE CONTENT MEASUREMENT

It would certainly be desirable to be able to easily identify areas of the fabric that have problematic water contents, but it has proved challenging to devise instruments capable of reading moisture contents at a known depth conveniently and reliably and, most importantly, non-destructively. Spot measurements of moisture content are essentially restricted to the surface few millimetres of the wall, and tend to be strongly affected by ambient conditions. A limitation of moisture meters is that they do not actually measure moisture, but rather parameters affected by moisture such as electrical resistance or capacitance, which are also influenced by other factors including the presence of salts. Measurements can therefore be highly inaccurate and misleading.

Tools for Superficial Moisture Measurements

Measurement is considerably easier in timber than in other building materials, but even in timber the method of taking the measurement can greatly affect the results. Too much reliance should not be placed on any instrument; readings should be considered a much more general tool, subservient to the other observations made during the survey.

Most meters are based on the effect of moisture on an electromagnetic signal passed into or through the material. The type of signal, and the wavelength, determine the error and the depth to which the reading refers.

Resistance Meters

The most popular type of hand-held instrument for assessing moisture contents is undoubtedly the resistance meter. This measures the electrical resistance between two metal pins, which are pressed into the surface. This means the method is not entirely non-destructive, but it is less dependent on surface texture than other types of meter. The major weakness of resistance meters is that electrical resistance is greatly affected by salts; it is possible to obtain high readings in salt-contaminated materials that are effectively dry.

Resistance meters were developed for testing fresh wood dried in kilns, and since timber is much less likely than many building materials to contain soluble salts, the results given for this material are comparatively reliable as long as the moisture content is not approaching fibre saturation.

Timber readings are principally affected by where the prongs are inserted: resistance has been found to be 2–8 times higher across the grain than along it; the greatest accuracy is obtained by taking readings parallel to the grain. Other factors must also be considered, not least the calibration (which is preset into the device). Readings will depend on the species, the differentiation between sapwood and heartwood, the equilibrium moisture content, the speed of growth, the way in which the timber was prepared, and even the country of origin. Manufacturers of resistance meters produce calibration tables for different timber species, which show that the error from this source varies from ±1 % moisture content at a moisture-content reading of 12 %, to ±2 % at 20 %. Readings also depend on temperature: the reading error will be +0.15 % per degree below 20°C, and –0.15 % per degree at higher temperatures. Nevertheless, readings can usually show whether timber is dry, damp or wet. A single reading cannot be relied on to predict the risk of decay; multiple readings will need to be taken.

Resistance meters

Resistance meters are reasonably reliable for taking moisture readings for timber, but are not accurate for other materials such as plaster, especially since they will be strongly affected by salts. There is also no reliable way of calibrating to any material other than wood.

Even with wood, the results should be interpreted with caution. For example, readings taken of timber roof beams in good condition during the summer may well indicate that they are quite dry, but readings taken during the winter may suggest they are rather wet; in fact, the beams are simply responding to the changing ambient relative humidity. If a meter indicates that the timber is dry, then this is probably true, but readings suggesting dangerous moisture contents should be viewed with scepticism unless there are other good reasons to suspect that a moisture problem exists.

Taking resistance readings from other materials is much more challenging. Not only are they likely to be inaccurate, but the relationship between moisture and the potential for deterioration is much less established.

Masonry materials are so diverse that, even were salts not an intractable issue, it would be impossible to develop calibrations that were even moderately reliable. Another problem is that it is much more difficult to get good contact between the prongs and the wall (this depends on both the pressure applied and the friability of the surface). It is easy to obtain a wide range of readings simply by pushing the probe a little harder into the wall.

With all materials, resistance meters are most useful not for taking absolute readings of moisture content, but rather as a means of roughly mapping variations. For example, readings of the resistance of the top edge of skirting boards, taken at regular spacings around a room, can indicate that there may be local sources of moisture. Similarly, a regular grid of readings taken on a masonry wall can give a rough pattern of salts and water that may yield unexpected insights, and can help identify the source of problems.

Different instruments will give different readings, so when mapping it is important to use the same instrument to take all readings, and to try as nearly as possible to use the same force when inserting the prongs.

Capacitance Meters

Capacitance meters respond to the dielectric properties of permeable materials, which are very strongly affected by moisture. Hand-held capacitance moisture meters are also slightly affected by contaminants such as salts, but to a considerably lesser degree than resistance meters. They are also less sensitive to temperature, although they will be affected by ice in surface layers under very cold conditions.

Hand-held capacitance meters are completely non-destructive, but because they do not make close contact with the material, they can be very strongly affected by surface roughness and the ambient air conditions. They measure the attenuation of an emitted electrical signal, so the depth of penetration is not predictable, but will vary according to the materials, structure and texture of the wall being tested. In all cases it is likely to be very shallow. Films of moisture on the surface will interfere with the readings.

As with resistance meters, it is impossible to calibrate capacitance meters to allow them to deliver absolute moisture contents, but they can be a quick, convenient and non-destructive way of mapping responses across a surface.

Assessors will sometimes map both capacitance and resistance readings to try to obtain a broader picture. This can be particularly useful if the pattern of moisture and salt deposition is being examined prior to sampling. For example, where the boundaries of areas of salt deposition are not clear, it may be possible to roughly locate them using hand-held meters, optimising the sampling needed to obtain absolute measurements of moisture and salt contents during any subsequent analysis.

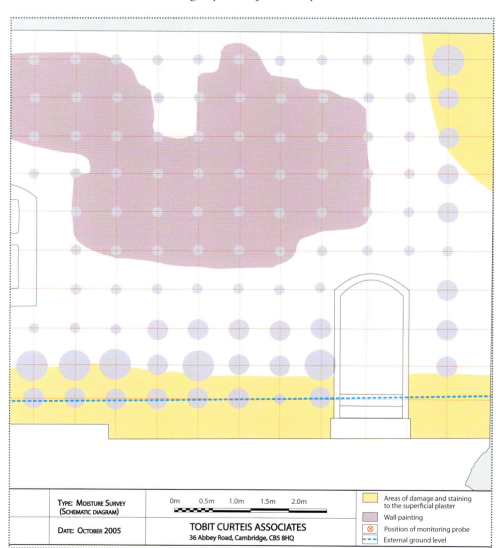

Mapping moisture

Even though moisture meters cannot give accurate readings, and measurement is restricted to the surface, they can be very useful tools for quickly mapping relative response across a surface. This can potentially reveal patterns of moisture content or salt concentrations, which can then be related to building flaws or other sources of moisture.

Right: A detail of a moisture map: here the size of circle represents the strength of the reading.

ASSESSING BUILDING SERVICES & CONTROLS

If deterioration cannot be associated with problems of the building envelope itself, then attention should turn to the building use, and especially the building services.

Again, if the building was stable for a long time, but has now begun to deteriorate, it is easier to narrow down the possible causes. Can the deterioration be dated? What might have been altered in the way the building is being managed that could be causing the decay? Possible avenues for investigation include:

- changes in building use
- changed settings on heating or cooling systems
- the failure of old heating or cooling systems, or changes to an old system
- new heating or cooling systems
- alterations to the way the building is being ventilated.

If, after investigating all the possibilities of this kind, it is still not possible to determine the causes of deterioration or the best means of dealing with them, it may be necessary to make further investigations using specialist equipment or special expertise.

Building services

Although services are recent arrivals in building technology, they have many extremely important impacts on the fabric. Not only do they often alter the indoor temperature, humidity and air movement, they introduce piping and wiring that may run through partitions and external walls, or through hidden conduits. The results are often very complex and poorly recorded, but may have unexpected side-effects.

BUILDING ENVIRONMENT
ASSESSING THE BUILDING ENVIRONMENT

SPECIALIST INVESTIGATIONS

If the causes of an environmental problem or its full ramifications are not immediately clear, more extensive or more detailed investigations may be needed. This often means calling in specialists who can draw on advanced techniques and their own experience.

Many specialist investigations involve assessing materials, or monitoring different aspects of the building environment. Techniques and approaches are continually being refined, and new methods appear regularly. Some transpire to be less than useful, but others will prove to be good additions to the tools that can help to develop an understanding of buildings and their environments.

Specialist investigations do tend to be expensive, so it is important to weigh the time and cost involved against what the analysis might be expected to accomplish. They are most effective when they are focused to test a clear hypothesis about the deterioration. To commission a specialist, the building owner or manager must therefore have given thought to the problem, have formed an initial theory to be investigated, and be in a position to ask clear questions of the specialist and give them the correct background information. If the specialist understands exactly which issues their investigation is meant to address, they will be better able to advise about the appropriate techniques to use, and about how their results could best be integrated into the overall assessment.

In practice, it is often cost-effective to consult a specialist quite early in the assessment programme, so that they can contribute their experience to the structuring of the research. They will be able to explain the benefits and limitations of each of the various techniques, and to suggest other tests that may be desirable, or perhaps necessary.

It is the responsibility of the specialist, once they have assessed all the existing information, to advise the building owner or manager which investigations would provide the necessary information, and how these should be presented to be of maximum utility. Good specialists will be able to present even very complex data and conclusions in a manner that is both understandable and accessible, which will be of prime importance if the results are to have a practical benefit. ⊖BASICS

Reports From Detailed Investigations

The report submitted by a specialist after a detailed investigation or conservation assessment would be expected to include:

- A brief description and history of the building (which may go into detail to cover the area examined most closely during the survey)
- A summary of the reasons for the survey
- An overall summary of the results, identifying key concerns and outstanding issues that may require further investigation
- If the survey concentrated on the condition of specific areas or building components, detailed descriptions accompanied by annotated and dated photographs (together with, where appropriate, decay mapping)
- The results of any additional tests made off-site, such as the results of any analysis
- A description of any suggestions for further investigations, including what these would involve, and what results they might be expected to deliver
- Any additional recommendations
- Reference details for all the documents and other resources consulted.

When to Call in a Specialist

The nature and patterns of deterioration are sometimes less than clear, and it is sometimes advisable to call in a conservation specialist to unravel the problem. Many specialists will be able to advise on more than one aspect of the problem, and will know when to call in further expertise. Most professional organisations have accreditation schemes for their members, but it is also extremely important that the specialist chosen has demonstrable experience with buildings of the type being examined, and of the wider issues of building conservation in general. ➔BASICS

POSSIBLE ADVISERS FOR DIFFERENT TASKS

CASES IN WHICH SPECIALIST ADVICE WOULD PROBABLY BE NECESSARY

1	The building structure is very complex, or building history is confusing
2	The endangered building elements are particularly sensitive and important: very accurate diagnosis and control are essential
3	The deterioration mechanism is complex, or there are several mechanisms involved
4	It is difficult to determine whether the problem is ongoing
5	There are drainage or groundwater problems demanding below-ground investigations

ADVISERS	1	2	3	4	5
ARCHAEOLOGISTS	✓				✓
ARCHITECTURAL HISTORIANS	✓				
BIOLOGISTS (such as entomologists or specialists in fungal decay)		✓	✓	✓	
BUILDING PHYSICISTS		✓	✓		
BUILDING SERVICES EXPERTS (such as an M & E Engineer with experience of historic buildings)		✓	✓		
CONSERVATION ENGINEERS	✓			✓	✓
BUILDING PERFORMANCE SPECIALISTS		✓	✓	✓	
GEOLOGISTS & GEOPHYSICISTS					✓
HYDROGEOLOGISTS					✓
MATERIAL SCIENTISTS	✓	✓	✓		✓
SPECIALIST CONSERVATORS		✓	✓	✓	

BUILDING ENVIRONMENT
ASSESSING THE BUILDING ENVIRONMENT

ASSESSING THE LOCAL ENVIRONMENT

WEATHER STATION DATA

Central weather station data is available for many locations, but the dependence of conditions on the local environment (for example, the impact on windiness of the surrounding topography) makes this type of data of limited use in most cases.

Where the exterior environment needs to be monitored to a high degree of accuracy, it may be possible to install a small weather station to measure parameters such as temperature, barometric pressure, sunlight, humidity, wind direction and speed, and precipitation. This can be done manually, but most modern stations include logging facilities, and measurements are collected hourly using electronic sensors (see **Monitoring Change**). The positioning of the weather station is very important, as this will affect many of the measurements.

Weather is very localised, so weather-bureau data – which is collected only in certain locations, and is moreover expensive to obtain – is likely to be much less informative than logging conditions around the building of interest using a simple electronic weather station.

INVESTIGATING THE GROUNDWATER

Groundwater can have many sources, so investigation must often be wide-ranging, and can rarely be confined to the ground immediately under and around the building; indeed, in most cases the surrounding landscape will be critical, and may alter rainwater runoff or affect buried drainage. Conditions are rarely static, and since problems may be due to factors that occur only periodically, spot measurements can be very misleading.

A proper understanding of every possible source will be needed to determine the best approach to remediation. Any or all of the following may need to be examined:

- local hydrogeology
- runoff
- ground drainage systems, including water supply and sewage pipework, culverts, and other underground water channelling.

Each of these examinations will require separate specialist expertise, and yet the issues they cover may all be interdependent, so it is vital that the overall investigation is coordinated by an assessor able to put all the information together, and to interpret the results in the context of the building and its problems. Even more than in most environmental assessments, investigation of groundwater is likely to be iterative, as tests uncover aspects of the hydrogeology and drainage that were previously unsuspected.

IDENTIFYING THE SOURCE OF WATER PROBLEMS

To determine which of several potential sources of water is causing problems (such as flooding, staining or salt decay), a hydrogeologist may use tracer materials such as dyes, fluorocarbons or radioactive tracers. Although tracer testing is in essence simple and often quite effective, it does require good knowledge of all the possible sources of water, and the correct choice of tracer material. Sampling and analysis of the water at the point of leakage to identify contaminants may sometimes be as effective as using a tracer, and can certainly help to decide whether the principle source is rainwater. or drinking water from the mains, or sewage.

INVESTIGATING THE HYDROGEOLOGY

Investigations of the hydrogeology aim to determine how water flows through the ground under and around the building, and perhaps to assess any contaminants it may be transporting. To do this, the direction of flow must be characterised. This will depend on water temperature and chemical composition, as well as the geological makeup of the ground, and may be affected by buried drainage (even where this is no longer in active use). It will also depend on how rainwater is precipitating into the ground, and thus on the ground cover and the soil. As a result, flow will often be very complex, and may well vary across the site and at depth.

Hydrogeologists will start by reviewing what is already known about the site, such as the location of any suppressed natural watercourses, before beginning *in-situ* investigations. Examination can rarely be limited to areas where the ground is saturated, so soil moisture levels may also need to be taken into account. Investigative techniques include:

- piezometers to measure groundwater pressure and the height of the water table
- infiltrometers to assess rainwater infiltration
- capacitance probes, time-domain reflectometry or tensiometers, to measure soil moisture sampling and analysis of dissolved materials and sediments (sometimes incorporating analysis of microbiological contamination).

BUILDING ENVIRONMENT
ASSESSING THE BUILDING ENVIRONMENT

Soil Assessment

A number of soil parameters are commonly monitored, especially by archaeologists anxious to preserve buried organic remains, including water table height, ground temperature, acidity and alkalinity, levels of dissolved oxygen, reduction-oxidation potential, and electrical conductivity.

Where the water table is sufficiently near the surface, the usual approach is to drill a borehole and insert a 'dipwell' (an open-ended tube, perforated toward the base). The drilled core is usually reserved for soil analysis. To measure the depth of water, a 'dipmeter' attached to a measurement reel is lowered down the hole; this gives a warning signal when it touches water, and depth can be read off the reel. The dipwell can also be used to take samples of water, to be analysed on or off site. Electronic dipwell sensors can log pressure at a specified rate, which is particularly useful when water levels are changing rapidly and need to be correlated with other time-dependent parameters (such as rainfall).

Accurate readings of soil moisture at depths of up to one meter can be made with electrical capacitance probes designed for agricultural science.

Somewhat less invasive methods of monitoring are also available for sites where drilling is not possible, or the water table is too deep for a dipwell. These include moisture cells, time-domain reflectometry [TDR] and neutron-probe measurements. All these have been proposed as well for monitoring moisture contents in building fabric, but accurate readings are generally much easier to obtain in soil, since installation presents far fewer problems (chiefly because it is straightforward to guarantee close contact between the probe and the soil, something that is very difficult to achieve in solid materials).

Calibration does present much the same problems for soil as it does for building materials, and so where possible it is usually better to monitor over time to record change, rather than struggling to obtain absolute measurements.

Assessing soil moisture

It is possible to monitor both the depth of the water table and the chemistry of the groundwater.

Left: Samples being taken by hand from a dipwell; the depth of the groundwater in the borehole will also be measured using a dipmeter. It is also possible to automate these processes and log the results, should the height or chemical make-up of the groundwater be found to be fluctuating rapidly.

Right: Moisture content being measured with a capacitance probe, which can be inserted into the ground, recording moisture content at different depths along its length.

Invasive investigations are expensive as well as damaging (especially if the site includes buried archaeology), but are usually essential if information at depth is needed (for example, to determine geological substrata or groundwater levels). Techniques include taking core samples; the resulting holes can then be used for dipwells to monitor potentially time-dependent aspects of the groundwater, level, contamination and temperature (see **Soil Assessment**), or for long-term or short-term pumping tests to investigate permeability and transmissivity.

Non-invasive investigations commonly include electrical and seismic studies, and more rarely gravity and magnetic mapping. Well-designed non-invasive investigation can cut the amount of invasive investigation that is needed.

INVESTIGATING RUNOFF

Runoff patterns must chiefly be established by observation and plotting of terrain heights, but take into account the nature of the ground surface. As well as the results of the hydrology examinations, this will demand an understanding of surface topography, geology, ground levels and interfaces between different surfaces. General maps will rarely be sufficient; usually detailed mapping will have to be undertaken on site. If the hydrogeology has not already been characterised, it may also be necessary to undertake subsurface investigations to determine rock type, permeability, water content and water quality, using a mixture of invasive and non-invasive investigations.

INVESTIGATING DRAINAGE

Since ground drainage is often a critical cause of building problems, the primary aim of investigation is to map the existing drainage and its condition as completely as possible. In the past this was prohibitively expensive and invasive, but new tools such as drain cameras are making investigation ever easier and more revealing.

Nevertheless, tests of drainage can be very challenging: buried pipework tends to be extremely complex, and very poorly recorded. For buildings of any antiquity, there will probably be many eras of system, and earlier drainage is unlikely to have been completely decommissioned when later systems were installed. It is usual for investigations to reveal forgotten culverts and soakaways, for example, which may be collecting and transporting percolating rainwater or groundwater even if they are no longer otherwise used. Culverts and pipes may also have been added for reasons other than channelling water – as cable ducts, for example – but may still be affecting the ground drainage.

Mapping drainage must always begin with background research, to establish what is known about the drainage history. For buildings with good archives, there may be early drainage plans, or archaeological investigations may have mapped old culverts or early watercourses. Maps of water mains and sewers are available online from local authorities or at a small cost from water utilities, but these are unlikely to include all old routes. It can be difficult to establish who is responsible for each type of drain or sewer, and utility companies may be reluctant to reveal results of leakage tests if they fear these could expose them to liability for damage.

Plans are the starting point for understanding buried drainage

Since water will always have been an important issue, a site of any antiquity is likely to retain vestiges of many periods of disposal and supply. Unknown concealed sources of water can be a great danger to the building fabric, so when problems associated with groundwater occur, it is essential to identify and assess such systems as thoroughly as possible, even where they are apparently redundant.

At Canterbury Cathedral, a myriad of culverts and channels run across the site, with later additions bisecting and sometimes dissecting the monastic supply and drainage systems shown on this map from the Eadwine Psalter, which shows the drainage plan c.1160. Many of the later additions are documented poorly, if at all, and despite its great age, this plan remains the most important record of the placement of the principal water systems across the site.

In 2010, long-standing structural movement endangering the Great South Window was finally traced to a 16th-century extension of the monastic drain shown leading to the site of the well, shown at the top of Eadwine's plan. Excavations revealed this to be a brick-lined culvert that had been reduced in height during Victorian landscaping works, and which was not only leaking, but was being overburdened with water from downpipes and drains added in the 19th and 20th centuries.

Modern maps now supplement Eadwine's plan, and are used to record all aspects of drainage around the Cathedral as they are discovered.

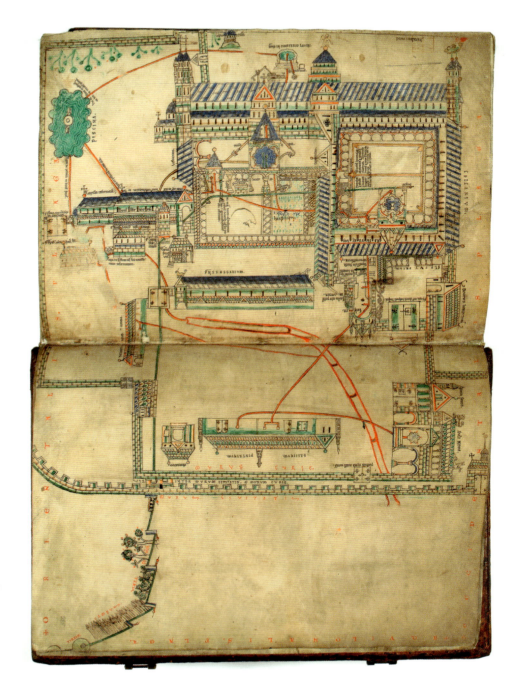

Locating & Examining the Condition of Drainage

Buried drains can be located by digging, but components are usually difficult to find, and extensive excavation may well be needed to find flaws and leakage points. This is not only time-consuming and invasive, but around many historic sites will require archaeological supervision. Investigations that do not require extensive digging are always to be preferred where possible, and fortunately there are many convenient and inexpensive techniques available which can reveal how many parts of the drainage system are behaving separately and as a whole.

Electrical resistance surveys, sonar tracing or ground-penetrating radar [GPR] may all be used to locate components in depth, as well as on a plan. Some GPR systems claim to be able to detect voids and soil erosion around pipework.

The most powerful tool is the simplest: inspection with drain cameras, which can be used to locate buried components, as well as to reveal problems such as root ingress and broken or misaligned pipework. The best choice of camera system will depend on the length of drain being investigated, and the number of bends it has. Push-rod cameras are most effective in 100-mm and 150-mm pipework, but can also be used in drains as wide as 225 mm; and smaller systems are available to examine pipes as narrow as 30 mm in diameter. Self-propelled crawler cameras, which can travel around obstructions, can be used to survey drains from 100 mm–2000 mm in diameter and more than 200 m long. Many systems now incorporate gradient meters as well as sonar or GPS to locate the moving camera on plan and in depth, feeding results back into a dedicated software that can produce a very detailed survey. As ever, successful results will largely depend on the skills and knowledge of the operator.

Flush testing is a simple way of checking whether rainwater or waste water from the building is able to run through those sewers and drains intended to dispose of it safely. One person watches at an open point in the system – a grille over an outlet, perhaps, or an opened gulley, manhole or inspection point – as another pours water from a bucket or hose down the waste pipe, or runs a tap or flushes a toilet. Interpretation demands a good understanding of the drainage system, since there may be multiple outlets; and even if some water runs through successfully, the system may still be leaking.

Bag testing, or testing under pressure, is sometimes used to check for leaks, but this can uncover problems that would never occur under normal operation, and may even initiate leaking in old or fragile systems. It can also be difficult to ensure that all possible inlets and outlets are identified, though this will be necessary if the test is to be correctly interpreted.

Official reports from drain surveys of all kinds will sometimes suggest that although the drain is leaking, the amount of leakage is perfectly acceptable. In terms of the building, however, even a small leak in the wrong place can lead to serious problems; this is one of the principal reasons why testing must be coordinated and interpreted by an assessor with a good understanding of the conservation issues.

Interpreting thermography

Facing page: Thermography is a useful new tool for building assessment, but it must be used with circumspection. As with many sophisticated tools, the equipment is relatively easy to use, but results can be very difficult to interpret correctly. The images on the opposite page demonstrate some of the strengths and weaknesses of this increasingly popular technique.

Revealing hidden details:
1: Where the structure or materials of the building affect the surface temperature, a thermograph can uncover details of construction that may otherwise be hidden.
2–5: A forgotten heating pipe is shown to be the reason for local deterioration previously attributed to other causes.

Limitations and over-interpretation:
6–7: Interpretation requires caution, especially with certain materials such as glass, which – being both highly reflective and strongly radiative – is not well-suited to thermographic measurement. Imaging a hot oven door demonstrates the problem: the thermograph is dominated by reflections, making temperature readings unreliable.

Interpretation rests on how the images are processed:
8–9: Although naturally greyscale, thermal images are often coloured by relating the temperature range to a colour range (most systems give several options for this). This can be helpful, but it is important not to over-interpret the resulting image.

ASSESSING THE ENVELOPE

There are a number of specialist techniques used to examine the building, and to assess the condition of the materials and structure; some of the most common are described here, but new techniques are constantly being developed.

INFRARED THERMOGRAPHY (THERMAL IMAGING)

All objects hotter than absolute zero emit radiation in infrared wavelengths (9000–14,000 nanometres), and the degree of radiation they emit is proportional to their temperature. Thermal imaging uses cameras able to record these wavelengths and present the results as false-coloured images, or 'thermograms'.

With thermal cameras having recently become much cheaper and easier to use, thermal imaging is developing into a standard tool for building investigation. It can be used to examine many different aspects of the building: hidden materials and structure, heat reflection and transmission, and even in some cases patterns of moisture ingress.

The critical aspect of thermography, as with all non-destructive investigations, is interpreting the results. Thermography records only the surface, and so cannot reveal structure at depth unless it strongly effects the surface temperature (as with, for example, timber framing concealed below a plaster skim).

Many factors affect the signal, not least the 'emissivity' of the surface (that is, its ability to emit thermal radiation). The emissivity of glass and metal is much higher than that of masonry or plaster, for example. It is possible to use a thermal camera to measure emissivity, but certain materials – particularly reflective materials such as glass – can be very difficult to image successfully. For this reason, it is important not to over-interpret thermograms (see **Special Topic: Improving Energy & Carbon Performance**).

Another problem with interpretation is the way the data is represented: most processing systems stretch the signal so that the hottest parts of the thermogram are red to white, and the coolest parts blue to black. It is therefore necessary to read the numbers on the temperature scale at the side of the image, which give the temperature range covered by the image; if that range is only a few degrees, there may not be any significant differences in temperature. On the other hand, if the area being studied contains very hot objects (such as central-heating radiators), these may mask more subtle differences. Particular care must be exercised when comparing thermograms: if the scale is not the same, an object that appears white and 'hot' on one image may be cooler than an object that appears blue and 'cold' on the other.

Thermography is very sensitive to weather conditions, but this can be turned to an advantage. For example, it may be helpful to survey buildings with massive walls late at night or very early in the morning after a sunny day, when the walls will be giving up some of the heat they absorbed in the daylight hours.

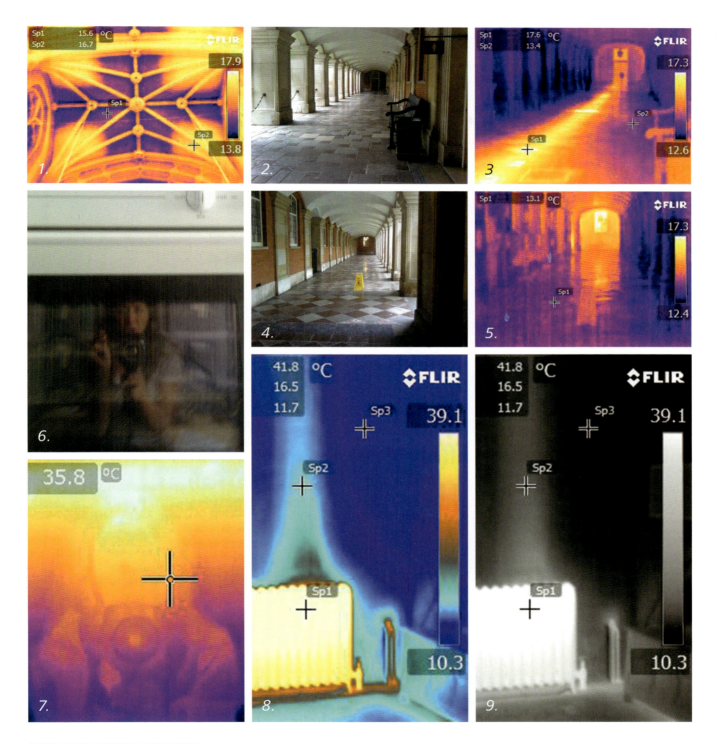

BUILDING ENVIRONMENT
ASSESSING THE BUILDING ENVIRONMENT

IMPULSE RADAR

Impulse radar can be used to locate and measure discontinuities in mass walls and floors (such as voids, failures, internal cracks, old chimney flues and metal cramps). Pulsed radio energy is transmitted into the fabric and the resulting reflected energy is picked up by a detector. Since many things can affect the reflection of radio energy, interpretation is very complex and demands much experience. It may also be necessary to confirm predictions by a certain amount of destructive testing.

ULTRASOUND

Ultrasonics can be used to locate and assess areas of decay and weakness in stone, brick, concrete, metals and timber (it is particularly useful for assessing the integrity of timber joints). It is non-destructive, and can be safely used on very fragile surfaces, including surfaces with decorative painting. For some types of material, it will be necessary to have access to both sides of the element being tested, and it cannot be used where the signal is strongly scattered by a great many interfaces (for example, in a random rubble wall). Where ultrasound can be used it is fast, reliable and inexpensive, but as with all specialist techniques, experience is required to interpret the results.

ENDOSCOPY

Endoscopy can be used to inspect voids, such as underfloor spaces, or the areas behind timber or metal cladding and panelling. If possible the endoscopes are introduced through existing holes, but on occasion it may be necessary to drill to obtain access. The equipment can be as simple as a tube borescope or as complex as a steerable unit with various specialised attachments. Many systems now have the ability to film the inspection; this certainly helps when interpreting the results, as they may well require re-examination later, off site.

The diameter of endoscopes varies, from about 12 mm down to less than 2 mm, but although smaller probes allow penetration into smaller spaces, their focal range, depth of field and strength of light is greatly reduced. It can be very difficult to keep track of the location and orientation of the tip, and a sense of scale, especially since lighting is rarely ideal: indeed, on some occasions, insulation lagging has been identified as dry rot.

NOISE ASSESSMENT

Sound can arrive from so many different sources, and propagate in so many different ways, that assessment is most definitely a specialist task; indeed, Part E of the UK Building Regulations (*Resistance to the Passage of Sound*) requires assessment to be undertaken by specialists registered with the UK Accreditation Service [UKAS].

The primary measurements are the 'weighted sound reduction' index [Rw] (given in decibels), which is modified by a factor [the 'Ctr'] describing the object's ability to dampen low-frequency vibrations. Floors are sometimes described by their ability to mute impact noise, and specifically footfalls.

LOCATING HIDDEN SERVICES

Finding hidden services can be very challenging; fabric is so complex that the results from most non-destructive investigations will usually need to be confirmed by invasive checks. The most commonly used tools used are:

- *Thermography*
  Can be useful for locating hot and cold water pipes.

- *Magnetic Stud Detectors*
  Used to detect ferrous metals, but difficult to set up, and error-prone. The user must interpret the degree of 'pull' on the equipment as it passes over the surface. In some versions, the magnet moves, making an audible click or thud, depending on how greatly it is attracted to the hidden metal; again, the signal strength must be interpreted by the user.

- *Internal Capacitance Detectors*
  Detects hidden materials (including timber) by reading the changes in dielectric constant. Accuracy depends on signal penetration. Cheaper models can detect the edges of hidden components, but models with more sensors and better processors can determine centres.

Buildings are often littered with redundant cabling and piping. Whenever services are located, they should be recorded in the building logbook, and preferably labelled as well for future reference; the label should state whether or not they are still in service.

ASSESSING MICROBIOLOGICAL ACTIVITY

The extent and activity of organic surface growths such as algae can be measured using a hand-held fluorometer containing an infrared diode that emits radiation with a wavelength of 670–700 nm, which causes the growths to fluoresce.

ASSESSING THE BUILDING MATERIALS

IDENTIFICATION & CONDITION ASSESSMENT

Precise identification may be needed to understand what building materials are present, and what treatment materials have been used in the past. It may be necessary to identify pollutant deposits or salt species to understand deterioration.

In most cases absolute identification will involve taking samples of the materials in question, usually for testing in a laboratory. The process of sampling can be very complex: in particular, the selection of locations can have an enormous effect on the interpretation of the results. A specialist will aim to minimise the number of samples, but maximise the information contained in each. If possible, the analyst should also be the person taking the samples. The other volumes in this series contain detailed information about the sampling and assessment of the various different building materials. ⊖MORTARS ⊖METALS ⊖EARTH & BRICK ⊖GLASS ⊖STONE ⊖TIMBER ⊖CONCRETE

ORIGINAL & ADDED BUILDING MATERIALS

Assessing Hidden Wood

Microdrilling can be used to quantitatively assess deterioration in timber, by measuring the speed of penetration of a long, flexible drill-bit about 1–3 mm in diameter. It can give an indication of the severity and extent of decay, the ratio of sound timber to decayed timber, and the precise position of any voids or weaknesses. Softwoods can be difficult to assess with micro-drilling, since the drill has a tendency to track round the softer growth of early wood, giving readings that suggest timber is much weaker than it really is. It can also be difficult to differentiate between narrow and large voids (which therefore need to be cross-checked with another system such as ultrasound). ⊖TIMBER

Assessing Hidden Metal

There are many types of concealed metal, especially iron, that are prone to corrosion, often with very serious consequences for the fabric. These include cramps in masonry, reinforcements in concrete and components of curtain-wall framing. Techniques used to locate and assess hidden metal include eddy-current detectors such as covermeters, half-cell potential testing, impulse radar and ultrasound.

Eddy-Current Detectors

Eddy-current devices are often called simply 'metal detectors'; they work by detecting the changes made by metal in an applied magnetic field. 'Covermeters' are eddy-current detectors using a pulse rather than a continuous signal, and are particularly important for assessing metal reinforcement bars in concrete. By making some assumptions about the nature of the reinforcement, the signal can be processed to determine the thickness of the cover (which is critical to understanding current and future risk from corrosion).

A covermeter survey to locate steel reinforcements in concrete.

Measurement errors chiefly arise from the data processing, and from the particular characteristics of the material: the signal will be affected by the aggregates, and the arrangement of the reinforcement bars. Nearby steel items (such as steel window frames and scaffolding) may also alter the readings. Covermeter surveys are discussed in detail in the *Concrete* and *Stone* volumes of this series.
⊃CONCRETE ⊃STONE

Half-Cell Potential Testing

Half-cell potentials are used to estimate the susceptibility of concealed ferrous metals to corrosion, most typically for steel in reinforced concrete. The metal being tested must be electrically connected, and this must be confirmed through holes drilled down to the metal in at least two places. The material is then wetted, and an electrical connection made between the metal and the surface (the surface electrode is usually embedded in a wet sponge to ensure a good electrical contact, and any surface finish must be removed). The resulting voltages are mapped to show the electrical activity in the area of the metal, and interpreted in terms of 'likelihood of corrosion'. Half-cell testing is discussed in detail in the *Concrete* volume of this series. ⊃CONCRETE

Assessing Moisture Sorption

Glass tubes filled with water (Karsten tubes) can be bonded to the surface of a wall to quantify moisture absorption. This is not a direct analogy for how the wall will handle rain, but it can be a useful way of assessing the impact of (for example) coatings.

Assessing Soils

Which soil properties are important will depend on the questions being asked about the condition of the building, but key properties which can be assessed by an expert include texture, colour, pH, mineralogy, and the percentage and nature of any organic matter (or 'humus'). The soil structure is usually important, since it is more than likely made up of a series of layers, each with different characteristics.

BUILDING ENVIRONMENT
ASSESSING THE BUILDING ENVIRONMENT

Different salts may be involved in one area of deterioration, and occasionally it will be necessary to determine what salts are present: for example, to identify the most likely sources of water.

A simple qualitative analysis can often be made using field tests based on reagent indicator strips.

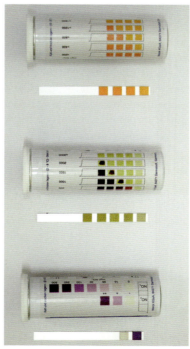

Assessing Salts

Identifying the salts present can occasionally help when trying to find the exact source of water (for instance, some salts are more likely to be found in groundwater than from a blocked gutter). Since salts are themselves a major cause of damage, identification can help when designing remedial treatments including, in some cases, environmental control systems. This does have certain limitations: for example, salt identification is sometimes used to try to determine the range of relative humidities that is most likely to be driving crystallisation cycles, but salts are found in mixtures rather than single species, and these do not have well-established equilibrium relative humidities. Moreover, the crystallisation behaviour in pores (where the worst damage will be occurring) is too complex to be related very easily to the ambient air conditions.

Sampling Salts for Analysis

The most difficult aspect of salt sampling is ensuring that the samples are representative, especially when trying to examine the distribution of salts at depth. The distributions will be those at the time of sampling, so it is important to record the ambient conditions as well.

Salts efflorescing on the surface are the easiest to sample, but they are also most soluble and therefore least worrying of the various types of salt the wall could contain. Surface efflorescences can be sampled by brushing or scraping them away with a scalpel; they are then stored in an airtight container. Another approach is to dissolve the crystals and absorb the solution into a damp poultice material, but this can be risky, since it involves adding more water to an unstable situation. In most cases, poultices will be able to absorb only those salts at or near the surface. To identify salts at depth, it will be necessary to take samples from the wall; salt sampling therefore often forms part of an assessment of moisture content. Quantitative analysis demands laboratory techniques such as ion chromatography (see **Assessing Moisture Content: Sample Assessment** later in this section).

Assessing Paints & Other Coatings

Investigations of paints and other coatings can have many purposes:

- *Historical research*
  Understanding early decoration.

- *Identification of coating type*
  In particular, determining the degree of permeability.

- *Understanding mechanisms of deterioration*
  Identifying previous treatments that may be affecting the moisture transfer characteristics of the underlying material, or causing other conservation problems.

- *Understanding the failure of protective coatings*
  Investigating why and how coatings are failing, and the impact this is having on the underlying material.

- *Preparing for treatment and repair*
  Assessing the suitability of a painted surface for further protective coatings.

All require a different approach, and different specialist advice, but typical investigations include taking small samples to be prepared either for investigation under magnification, or for laboratory analysis of binding media and other components. ⊝MORTARS

To assess the nature and stability of *in-situ* paints on metal, thickness may be measured with magnetic film or eddy-current gauges, and permeability can be examined with chemical marker tests and continuity tests. Paint adhesion to the substrate can be assessed with pull-off tests. ⊝METALS

Painted building features of any antiquity may have undergone repeated redecoration, especially if coating was primarily required for preservation (to protect timber or ferrous metal, for example). The history of painting may well be of great historic interest, and may reveal attempts to deal with persistent deterioration.

Left: Multiple layers of paint revealed at the edge of a loss.

Right A small cross-section, taken from a painted metal railing and examined under magnification, reveals a long history of different colours and types of paint.

BUILDING ENVIRONMENT
ASSESSING THE BUILDING ENVIRONMENT

MEASURING MOISTURE CONTENT

Spot measurements of moisture content can often be very useful, and in some situations may be wise: for example, if an earthen building has been rendered in cement, the moisture content of the underlying earth could be checked to make sure it is dry enough to retain structural stability.

Nevertheless, moisture measurements alone cannot explain most moisture problems. The interpretation of the results must take into account that they are restricted to giving a snapshot of moisture distribution in a system where these are likely to be very dynamic.

There are also many practical problems. For example, moisture content can vary not only because of differences in the exposure of the building fabric to water, but from differences between each of the many materials making up that fabric, and differences within each material.

Moreover, for most building materials and systems there is no reliable way of linking absolute moisture content to deterioration; indeed, there may not be a direct connection between quantity of water and deterioration for materials such as stone, brick and mortar. Damage seems to depend less on the quantity of water than on where it is, whether it is in the form of liquid, vapour or ice, and whether it is stationary or moving. Fluctuations in content drive damage mechanisms such as salt crystallisation, but the actual quantities of moisture involved may be very small and very localised.

In complex situations the answer may be to monitor moisture content rather than measure it, looking for changes that can be equated to changes in the environmental parameters that might be driving problems. However, monitoring also presents a number of practical difficulties (see **Monitoring the Environment** later in this section).

Deterioration is often associated not so much with absolute moisture contents as with changing moisture content or humidity. Timber, for example, will respond to variations in the ambient relative humidity by absorbing or surrendering water until it is at equilibrium with the air. A side-effect of this is that the timber will swell as it takes in moisture and shrink again as it gives it up.

Here, painted decoration has cracked because its response is dissimilar to that of the underlying timber.

NON-DESTRUCTIVE METHODS OF MOISTURE MEASUREMENT

The holy grail of building assessment would be a non-destructive tool that could be used *in situ* to provide a picture of moisture content at depth; in practice, however, any equipment able to measure properties even one centimetre below the surface is likely to be inconvenient in some way, and probably inaccurate. Most are also very difficult to interpret. The following gives a brief description of some of the most important and commonly used techniques.

Thermal Imaging

Since wet materials transfer heat more readily, the patterns of temperature being emitted from the surface can sometimes be used to help identify leaks. Thermography is not a reliable instrument for looking at moisture in every type of wall, and indeed it can be difficult to obtain useful readings from mass construction; the information it gives is qualitative. Interpretation demands a critical eye; it can be tempting to see large differences in image colour as showing large differences in temperature, when in fact the temperature variation is too small to be important, and the colour range is simply an artefact of the signal processing. On the other hand, thermography is a simple and fast way of obtaining patterns that cover large surface areas in a single image.

To optimise the temperature range of the building components, thermography may need to be timed for the very early morning or during suitable weather. Moisture gradients can be inferred from variations in heat radiating from wall surfaces; some researchers are trying to develop ways of making moisture variations more apparent, such as heating or fan-cooling the surface before taking the image.

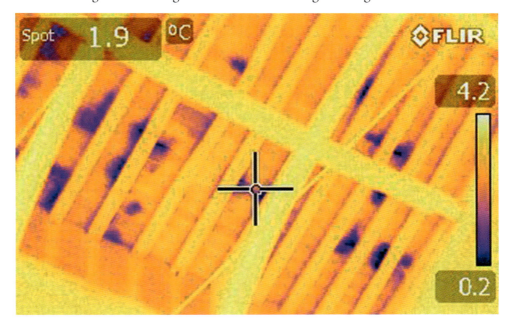

Using infrared thermography for moisture detection

It is sometimes possible to use thermography to help identify water sources, where these affect local surface temperatures. Although it is impossible to predict whether the technique will prove effective in any particular case, it is non-destructive and relatively simple to use, so where the equipment is available it can be a useful adjunct to other investigations.

Here, a thermograph of a church ceiling taken in the early morning reveals patches of condensation. These disappeared later in the day.

BUILDING ENVIRONMENT
ASSESSING THE BUILDING ENVIRONMENT

Signal-Generation Systems

Many different tools for assessing moisture contents are based on sending an electromagnetic wave of some type into the material, and reading either the reflection of the signal or its attenuation as it passes through the material. All these methods tend to be very sensitive to other heterogeneities in the materials and structure. Because the depth of penetration varies, most attenuation systems can give little or no information about variations in the bulk of the wall. Greater accuracy and information could be obtained by reading a transmitted signal, but this requires a receiver to be positioned on the other side of the object, which is not always practically possible. Microwave and X-ray transmission systems have both been tried on mass walls, but many building walls are so thick that the signal is too weak to be useful. Except in sophisticated 'sideways-looking' systems, the picture derived from the readings is two-dimensional, giving the moisture throughout the thickness of the wall, but no information about how it varies with depth.

Techniques include:

- *Microwave attenuation*

    In homogeneous materials, meticulous calibration may sometimes allow a good correlation to be made between attenuation of the microwave signal and the moisture content of the material, but results from inhomogeneous materials (such as bricks and mortar) have so far proved disappointing. Depth of penetration varies considerably, and embedded metal fixings may give false readings.

- *Impulse radar*

    Although it is sometimes possible to record moisture variations with impulse radar systems, without destructive sampling against which to calibrate they cannot be used to determine absolute moisture contents.

- *Ground-Penetrating Radar [GPR]*

    Although ground-penetrating radar can reach depths of up to a metre, in practice it is very difficult to interpret the results.

- *Radiation attenuation*

    Systems that measure the attenuation of X-rays, neutrons or gamma-rays are largely confined to specialist laboratories.

- *Nuclear Magnetic Resonance [NMR]*

    The hydrogen nuclei of the free water molecules in the pores are aligned with a strong magnetic field, and then perturbed with an electromagnetic pulse; the equipment then records their resonating energy and relaxation time. With calibration, NMR can be used for absolute moisture measurement. Powerful equipment is not very transportable; there is a portable system available ('NMR-Mouse'), which measures attenuation rather than field strength, but this gives very little penetration into the wall, and the surface contact must be excellent.

- *Neutron Scattering*

  The fast neutrons emitted by radioactive sources are able to penetrate deeply into materials, by virtue of having no charge. However, they will tend to be scattered by hydrogen, and so will react strongly with water; the amount of scattering will depend on the moisture content of the material. There are two approaches: high-energy neutrons emitted by reactors, which have been used by a number of researchers to investigate moisture distributions in samples of complex building structures; and neutron-moderation gauges using neutrons emitted by passive radioactive sources, which are used in industry. How far the low-power neutrons can penetrate depends on the strength of the source; portable sources are usually not strong enough to examine a massive wall in depth. Testing is expensive, and demands special health-and-safety precautions. Instruments currently under development use X-ray tube excitation, making the instrument much more portable and potentially more powerful, but the health-and-safety risk would be slightly higher.

- *Electrical Resistivity Tomography [ERT]*

  Geophysical technique using an electrical current to measure subsurface electrical resistivity. This records a three-dimensional pattern of electrical resistivity or conductivity.

- *Ultrasound*

  Water transports sound more easily than air (or a dry building material). Ultrasound measurement works by placing a sound generator placed on one side of the wall and a listening device on the opposite side (they must be directly opposite each other). Voids cause interference, and interpretation can be difficult, but the full potential of ultrasound measurement has not yet been exploited.

Systems Using Embedded Sensors

- *Thermal sensors*

  Thermocouples or other electrical thermometers have been used to record the effect of water on the material, and hence to indirectly record the water. The 'dual-probe heat pulse' system uses a probe with two prongs, one of which is heated by an electrical current, while the other measures the resulting temperature change; with care it can be set up to look at the wall in depth.

- *Time-Domain Reflectography [TDR]*

  A TDR probe is very long and two-pronged; the pulse is sent down one prong and read on the other (the signal velocity depends on the dielectric constant). TDR has been used industrially and for reading soil moisture contents, but the practical difficulties of drilling two very accurate and deep parallel holes into a complex wall makes it difficult to apply to most buildings.

- *Near infrared optical fibres*

  This new technique measures the changes in the refractive index of a coating applied to optical fibres as it absorbs moisture from the surrounding material.

DESTRUCTIVE METHODS OF MOISTURE MEASUREMENT

Currently, sampling remains the only effective way of obtaining absolute measurements of moisture content at depth. Solid cores and powder samples drilled from the materials of a wall can be used not only to measure moisture contents, but also to identify the materials and any salts or other contaminants. Both types of sample are usually divided up into segments by depth, so the characteristics of the surface can be compared to those deeper in the wall. Well-designed sampling can therefore produce a picture of the way moisture is distributed in three dimensions (across the wall and within it), and this can give important clues to the sources of moisture problems.

INFORMATION FROM DRILLED SAMPLES

TYPE OF SAMPLE	INFORMATION OBTAINED	COMMENTS
POWDER SAMPLES		
	Can easily be weighed and oven-dried to give readings of the absolute quantity of moisture by weight	Cannot give information about either the state of the water (liquid or vapour), or exactly where it was within the pores All detailed information about the materials (including pore structure) is lost
SOLID CORE SAMPLES		
	Can be very informative about materials (for example, can be used for identification, for studying the pore structure and for pressure testing)	In theory the sample should retain information about the way moisture is distributed in the pores Determining the absolute moisture content is very difficult Samples are much larger than drilled samples, and much more difficult to take: material must be cohesive and compacted Samples can be returned to position after analysis to hide damage

Because it is impossible to repeat a drilled sample – at least not in exactly the same position – this method cannot be used to assess changes in moisture content over time: samples taken at frequent intervals would not only leave the wall full of holes, but would be unreliable because of sample variations.

Non-destructive measurements are repeatable, but usually they will have to be accompanied by some degree of sampling to allow the results to be calibrated.

Taking Samples from a Wall

Sampling is a destructive process, and should be kept to a strict minimum. It will need statutory consent if the building is protected. Since the composition of most mass walls is complex, and impossible to predict (especially on the scale of the samples being taken), it is common to encounter unexpected complexities. For this reason alone, wherever possible the sampling should be undertaken by the person who will be analysing the results.

Samples are spot measurements that reflect the distribution of moisture and contaminants at the time they were taken, so it can be useful to record the environmental conditions before and during sampling – particularly the prevailing weather – and to take this into account when interpreting the results (especially the results of salt sampling). To prevent water evaporating from the sample before it can be read, it must be placed immediately into an airtight container.

Walls are sampled at depth by drilling out material. In most cases a masonry bit is used in a hand drill, and the sample collected as powder, but sometimes a solid core may be drilled out instead. Each method has advantages and disadvantages, and the choice will probably depend on the information being sought.

POWDER SAMPLES

Taking powder samples from a wall is relatively easy, but must be done methodically if the results – particularly of moisture measurement – are not to be compromised. For example, drilling must be slow, and the bit must be cooled regularly, to avoid evaporating the moisture in the sample. Sample size would generally be about 2 g, but this may not always be possible.

The method has been tested and refined over many decades, and has been standardised as Rilem Recommendation MS-D.10.

Collecting a powder sample

Top: Specialists will use various means of collecting drilled samples, including marked-up bits and collectors designed to fit over the bit. The collector shown here is a simple adaptation of a plastic bottle that acts to funnel the drilled powder into a labelled plastic bag.

Bottom: Since samples are divided by depth as well as location, labelling must be meticulous using nomenclature decided in advance.

SAMPLING LINED WALLS

Sampling the wall behind panelling or dry lining can be difficult because the dust tends to fall down the cavity, where it cannot be easily collected. Where the panel cannot be removed, this can be overcome to some extent by using a metal tube to scrape the sides of the drilled hole.

BUILDING ENVIRONMENT
ASSESSING THE BUILDING ENVIRONMENT

SOLID CORE SAMPLES

Removing solid cores from a heterogeneous wall is extremely difficult, especially since using the samples to look at moisture or salt distributions means the bit cannot be water-cooled; a special diamond bit must therefore be used. In most cases the drill will need to be supported on a rig as well. To ensure the core is drilled straight and at right angles to the wall, the rig may need to be fixed to the surface.

Drill speeds will need to vary with the type of material, which can be very difficult indeed in complex rubble-filled walls. Even with very slow drilling, and regular swapping of drill bits, solid cores rapidly become very hot. The precise effect this will have on moisture distribution within the sample will depend on the type of material and its moisture content, amongst other factors, and so is almost impossible to quantify.

REPAIRING SAMPLE HOLES

Holes drilled to take samples are sometimes used for further tests and monitoring, but if this is not the case it is usually better that they be filled. Filling will certainly be a requirement of sampling permission if the building is under statutory protection.

Conservation practice is to use as much as possible of the sample to fill the holes: powdered material can be mixed with lime putty (or other appropriate binder) to make a repair mortar, and a solid core can be returned to place and fixed by grouting with a fine mortar of the appropriate type. ⊖MORTARS ⊖STONE

RILEM Recommendation

MS-D.10: IN-SITU MEASUREMENT OF MOISTURE CONTENT BY DRILLING

Samples are taken with a nonpercussive drill, using a sharp new masonry bit about 9 mm in diameter. Drilling should be at low speed, and the bits should be changed frequently or cooled in methylated spirits between samples.

The drilled material is collected at different depths, usually at increments between 10 mm and 80 mm. Each incremental depth is collected separately, and sealed in its own airtight container to prevent evaporation. This should be labelled with the sample location and depth, and information about the environmental conditions under which it was collected.

In some applications it is common practice to discard the first 10-mm increment because it will have accumulated contaminants such as salts, but for this very reason the surface layer is of particular conservation interest, and so it should always be preserved.

Developing Sampling Strategies

Because it is so destructive, drilled sampling must be kept to an absolute minimum. The number of samples and the locations from which they are being taken need to be based on the hypothesis being tested, but will also depend on the construction of the wall, and on any of the many practical limitations likely to be encountered on site.

Since the aim is usually to answer as many complex questions as possible with the smallest possible number of samples, strategies demand a good deal of background research and pre-planning, as well as close observation. Tools such as hand-held moisture meters can be helpful for narrowing down the many possible locations to those most likely to yield useful information.

The distribution of moisture in a complex wall depends on the materials as well as the moisture source. Whether samples should be taken from the same material in different areas, or from different materials in the same relative position depends on the question being asked of the assessment. To examine the way different materials are affecting the moisture distribution, the specialist would choose locations that make samples as comparable as possible to each other: for example, samples of different walls might be taken at the same height, and samples on the same wall might be taken in a vertical line, at different heights.

Sample distributions

To make samples as useful as possible, it is wise to maximise the comparative information they contain by locating them at similar heights, or in (for example) a vertical straight line.

To investigate moisture problems at the base of a wall, for example, three samples would commonly be taken: one in at the middle of the zone of damage; another around the maximum height of damage; and a third above the zone of damage, all in a vertical line.

In the case shown *right*, a similar set of samples might be taken from an area of the same wall away from the window, so that the effect of the window can be assessed as well.

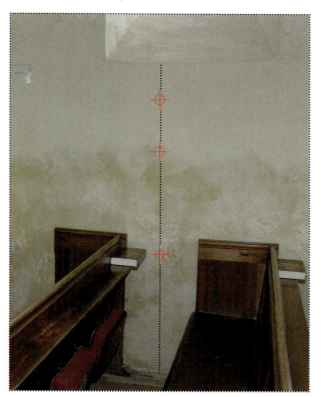

To examine the distribution of water, a minimum of three samples would generally be taken: one where the wall is definitely wet at the surface; one where it is dry; and one where there are signs that the superficial moisture content is changing (for example, around an area of salt damage and efflorescence). Ideally the specialist would attempt to sample the same type of material in each case, but this is not always practical (particularly when the wall is being sampled through plaster, so the underlying fabric is unknown).

BUILDING ENVIRONMENT
ASSESSING THE BUILDING ENVIRONMENT

Health & Safety

CALCIUM CARBIDE

Calcium carbide must be handled with great care, since it reacts violently with water. The acetylene gas given off is a considerable fire and explosion hazard, so appropriate safety precautions must be taken if carbide meters are used on site.

The testing residue and any empty tins of carbide must be disposed of according to local government requirements. These usually require that waste be immersed in a large volume of water for a prolonged period; but the latest recommendations should always be consulted and followed.

Sample Assessment

Powder Samples

The absolute moisture contents of powder samples can be determined either by using a carbide meter on site, or (as is more usual in conservation assessments) placed immediately in sealed containers to send to a laboratory for assessment by gravimetry.

Assessment Using Carbide Meters

Carbide meters were developed for measuring moisture contents of cement, but are useful for any building material that can be reduced to a powder by drilling or pounding; the readings are largely independent of the type of test material.

The weighed sample is placed in a pressure vessel, to which a standardised volume of calcium carbide is then added. The water in the sample will react with the calcium carbide to produce acetylene gas, the volume of which can be directly related to the moisture content of the sample. Readings are taken directly from the pressure gauge at the top of the vessel, which is calibrated to show moisture content.

Carbide meters are accurate, but cannot provide any information about the hygroscopicity of the sample. They are slow to use and require a large sample (six grams), which may be difficult to obtain; they also generate hazardous waste. Nevertheless, they can be useful if the moisture contents of samples must be obtained during a site visit.

Assessment Using Gravimetry

'Gravimetry' is the determination of water content by weight, obtained by comparing the weights of the sample before and after drying.

The sample is removed from its container, placed on a dish and immediately weighed on an accurate balance to find the 'wet weight' [ww]. It is then dried until its weight is no longer changing; this is its 'dry weight' [dw]. The difference between the wet and dry weights is then given as a percentage of the dry weight:

$$\% \, mc = \text{moisture content} = 100 \times \frac{ww-dw}{dw}$$

Samples are usually dried in a ventilated oven, but a desiccator can be used instead (although it may be difficult to reach a true dry weight in this way).

In many laboratories the samples are oven-dried at 103 ± 2°C for about one hour, but although this may be acceptable for uncontaminated brick or mortar, the temperature is so high that it will release the water that is chemically bound in plasters and contaminants. This introduces a large error. It is considerably more accurate to dry samples taken from real walls much more gently: at 20–30°C, drying can usually be completed overnight.

Interpretation of Results

For a number of reasons, caution and experience are needed to safely interpret the moisture-content results from drilled samples:

- Even at equilibrium, the absolute moisture content will depend on the nature of the material being sampled.
- Since samples are most unlikely to be homogeneous, and the measured moisture contents are likely to reflect this, it is difficult to compare samples without considerable error.
- The distribution of moisture in the wall is unlikely to be static, in which case determining the percentage moisture content – a common calculation – is unlikely to be very diagnostic. For example, samples taken to examine moisture distribution at depth in a masonry wall are likely to vary greatly according to the percentage of mortar in the sample. A high reading for one depth increment may therefore reflect hitting a mortar joint, rather than a particularly wet zone in the wall.

Another point to keep in mind is that ideal sampling is usually impossible, obliging specialists to draw conclusions from imperfect or scattered samples. It is then all the more important that the assessor and the specialist both have the best possible understanding of the building fabric, and of the patterns of deterioration, and use these as the principal guides to interpretation.

BUILDING ENVIRONMENT
ASSESSING THE BUILDING ENVIRONMENT

The distribution of moisture in a permeable building element such as a wall will depend on many factors, including its structure and the equilibrium moisture contents of its various materials, as well as on the sources of the water. Therefore, a drilled sample – especially a powder sample, where information about the material is largely lost – must not be interpreted in isolation, but in the light of what else is known about the fabric and its moisture problems.

The examples of powder samples shown here have been simplified to illustrate why moisture distribution alone is unlikely to provide enough information to allow the source of moisture to be determined. Real samples will be even more complex, since many factors will be involved.

The effect of material type:
1, 2: Even if the fabric were saturated, each material would have its own equilibrium moisture content, so drilling in slightly different locations (for example, through stone rather than mortar) can give very different results. This can be difficult when the construction is hidden by a plaster or render.

Very different sources of water can produce very similar patterns of moisture at depth:

3, 4: It can be hard to distinguish between surface moisture from condensation, and moisture building up behind a coating, on the basis of the powder sample alone.

5–8: The pattern produced by capillary rise from a leaking drain could be very similar to that due to water percolating down from a leaking gutter above, or to water penetrating laterally from a leaking downpipe, or to rain wicking through cracks in the pointing and pooling in voids.

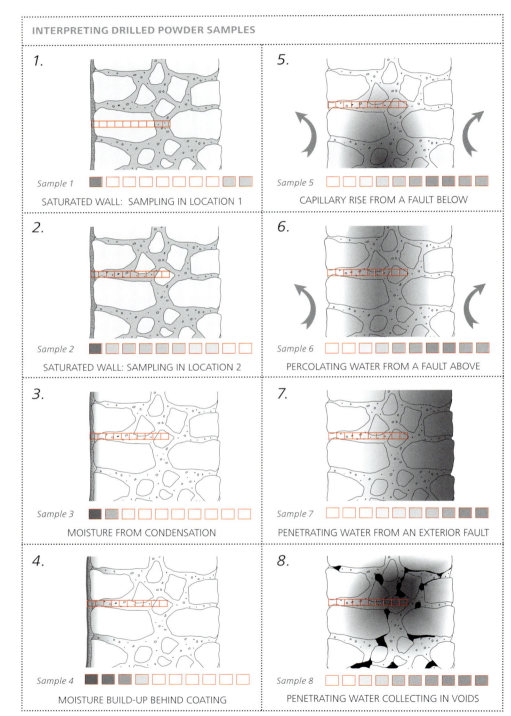

INTERPRETING DRILLED POWDER SAMPLES

1. Sample 1 — SATURATED WALL: SAMPLING IN LOCATION 1

2. Sample 2 — SATURATED WALL: SAMPLING IN LOCATION 2

3. Sample 3 — MOISTURE FROM CONDENSATION

4. Sample 4 — MOISTURE BUILD-UP BEHIND COATING

5. Sample 5 — CAPILLARY RISE FROM A FAULT BELOW

6. Sample 6 — PERCOLATING WATER FROM A FAULT ABOVE

7. Sample 7 — PENETRATING WATER FROM AN EXTERIOR FAULT

8. Sample 8 — PENETRATING WATER COLLECTING IN VOIDS

Solid Core Samples

Solid core samples are difficult to take and difficult to interpret, but they do preserve information that might otherwise be lost: important data about the stratigraphy of the wall, and the pore structure of the materials that make it up.

The basic process for determining the moisture content of a solid core by gravimetry is much the same as for powder samples, but the drying period will necessarily be much longer. The core may have to be subdivided into smaller lengths.

Some specialist laboratories will have equipment (such as gamma-ray attenuation or X-ray tomography) that enables them to examine moisture distributions in solid cores. Measurement processes of this type must take place in a special chamber under controlled environmental conditions, and the process can be difficult and prolonged.

Other Assessments from Samples

Samples taken to assess *in-situ* moisture content can be also used in other ways to better understand the fabric and its condition.

Structure of the Wall

Solid cores, from which it is so hard to obtain good measurements of moisture content, do contain a wealth of information about the materials in the wall. Thin sections can be prepared from them for study under the microscope, to better understand the structure, and permeability can be assessed using standard laboratory tests (with the proviso that all these have limitations, not least that most involve the transfer of inert gases or liquids rather than water, which is anything but inert). The advanced tomography equipment that is now becoming available allows the three-dimensional pore structure of building materials to be studied in great detail, and this has great potential as a tool for understanding behaviour and deterioration.

Since solid samples preserve all the characteristics of the wall, they can also be used to study complex moisture transport processes. For example, the sample could easily be used in a sorption test to look at liquid moisture uptake, or for salt analysis.

Water-Absorption Testing

Water-absorption coefficient tests measure liquid-water uptake in a solid sample. The sample is placed on a support within a dish of water, so that its bottom surface just touches the liquid. The samples can be isolated so that the moisture uptake is due solely to capillary action, or the surface might be exposed to controlled airflow to examine the effect of evaporation.

Moisture uptake is then measured either in terms of the weight gain of the sample, or else the volume of water removed from the dish. The rising water front can sometimes be seen with the naked eye; otherwise, some well-equipped laboratories will be able to track it in various ways.

Hygroscopicity Due to Salts

Powdered samples are often used to assess the contribution of the salts to hygroscopicity. The dried sample is weighed, then placed in an environment with a controlled relative humidity (often set by a salt solution); it will then either lose water or gain water from the environment according to its hygroscopic salt content. It can take three or four days to equilibrate, depending on the size of the sample.

The sample is then weighed again, to obtain a 'hygroscopic moisture content' (the difference between the hygroscopic moisture content and the original liquid moisture content). This is sometimes taken to be the potential moisture uptake of the material, but this wider interpretation neglects the enormous contribution to moisture uptake made by capillary sorption in the original material (since in a powder sample the pore structure will have been destroyed).

Drying Tests

Drying tests have occasionally been attempted to try to assess the activity of water in building materials, but they are much more complicated than wetting tests since it is very hard to establish a clear starting condition (sorption tests can begin the instant the sample touches the water).

Drying itself is a very complex process, greatly affected by hysteresis, which does not make the analysis of drying tests any easier (see **Building Science**).

Using Salt Solutions for Setting Humidity

To test hygroscopicity or other material characteristics affected by relative humidity, and to calibrate equipment for measuring the hygrothermal characteristics of the air [RH], it may will necessary to control the RH in a container. The cheapest way of doing this is with saturated salt solutions: after equilibration, the air in the container will be at that salt's equilibrium relative humidity [RHeq]. Desk-top calibration systems usually use lithium chloride (RHeq ≈ 11.3 % at 25°C), sodium chloride (RHeq ≈ 75.3 %) and potassium sulphate (RHeq ≈ 97.3 %), to provide low, medium and high humidities.

Using salt solutions is not without problems. Contaminants can significantly affect the RHeq, and if the solution is not completely saturated, the air in the container may never reach a steady humidity. To keep the RH stable, the temperature must be kept absolutely steady. The largest possible surface area of solution must be exposed to the air, and the space within the container cannot be too large, so container design can be challenging. Fans are sometimes used to circulate the air, but this can destabilise the equilibrium, and can cause samples placed in the test chamber to dry via evaporation, affecting the assessment of salt hygroscopicity, for example. Finally, salt solutions have sometimes been found to behave in unpredictable ways.

If using salt solutions for calibration, analysis or experimental work, it is important not to just assume the temperature and humidity in the container are those that would be expected, but to monitor for the duration of the work.

Laboratory Salt Analysis

Identifying the salts present in a building material can help to pin down the source of water, since some salts are more likely to be found in groundwater (for example) than in penetrating rainwater. Identification can also help when designing remedial treatments (including, in some cases, environmental control systems).

Solid core samples can show where the salts are in the pore structure, and may reveal the nature of the damage they are causing, but they are not otherwise simple to analyse. Drilled cores lose the information about the nature of the material, but they are easier and less destructive to collect, and much more readily analysed: the salts need only to be dissolved into an aqueous solution.

In the laboratory simple chemical tests can be made to identify different salts in the solution, or quantitative analysis can be undertaken with more sophisticated equipment. ⇒STONE ⇒MORTARS

COMMON METHODS USED FOR ANALYSING SALT SOLUTIONS

NAME	MEASUREMENT	METHOD	COMMENTS
CONDUCTIVITY METERS	Total salt content	Measure electrical conductivity through the solution	Gives reading of overall concentration, but does not identify individual salts Strongly affected by temperature
pH METERS	Acidity or alkalinity, usually of a liquid	Measure pH as the activity of the hydrogen cations surrounding a thin-walled glass bulb at its tip	Must be calibrated regularly, and certainly before each measurement
ATOMIC ABSORPTION SPECTROPHOTOMETRY	Absorption of particular wavelengths of light	Sample is atomised to produce a gas, which is then exposed to a known light source to reveal energy absorption bands	Can detect trace elements
ION CHROMATOGRAPHY	Ions are separated out and detected by conductivity or spectroscopy	A buffered aqueous solution known as the 'mobile phase' carries the aqueous sample through a column containing a 'stationary phase' material (usually a resin or gel matrix) which traps the anions and cations; these are then released by washing the column through with a solution made with ions of the same charge	Can accurately determine type and concentration of ions, but not salt species
INFRARED SPECTROSCOPY	Absorption of infrared wavelengths	Sample is atomised to produce a gas, which is then exposed to a an infrared source to energise the molecules and produce characteristic vibration patterns	Needs only very small samples, and is good with single salts, but interpretation is difficult if multiple salts are present Also possible with crushed samples suspended in oil or even thin sections
X-RAY DIFFRACTION	Identifies salt crystals	Crystalline sample is bombarded with X-rays, and the resulting scattering is analysed	Very accurate way of determining the salts species (rather than the ions), but gives no indication of concentration

MEASURING AIR EXCHANGE & HEAT LOSS

It can be difficult to predict how air will move in a real building because this depends on so many factors, including the temperature and vapour pressure of the interior and exterior air, as well as the local variations in air pressure and air movement. Although an air-exchange rate of (say) 0.5 ach between the interior and the exterior might suggest that all the air in the building will be replaced every two hours, there will be some areas where the air is being cycled much more quickly, and other areas which are staying more or less stagnant. On the other hand, a low air-exchange rate would not preclude a quite vigorous internal air circulation, especially if the room is occupied or has fans, strong heating, or large surfaces of glass.

It is also important to understand where air is coming from and going to. Not all exchange will be between the exterior and interior, and even where it is the difference between interior and exterior conditions that is driving exchange, it may pass through other areas of the building as it moves. This is particularly the case with modern hollow-wall construction, especially when the building also has forced ventilation or an air-conditioning system.

Air movement is usually perceived as a draught if it is higher than 0.25 m per second, but in practice it can be difficult to decide how important a leak is without taking into account how the building is being used.

TESTING AIR EXCHANGE

Investigating air movement

Simple ways of revealing air movement can be particularly helpful, since (unlike specialist techniques) they can easily be repeated under different internal and external conditions.

The smoke from incense sticks or the fluttering of thin strips of tissue paper can be used to locate where the envelope is allowing air exchange, or to reveal the patterns of internal air circulation; it will also be possible to get a good idea of the speed and strength of movement.

SMOKE TESTING

The simplest and most effective test for visualising patterns of air exchange is a smoke test made using a stick of incense, particularly since it can be easily repeated under different internal and external conditions. In this way it is possible to detect air movements driven by particular wind conditions (for example). A very quick test may be all that is needed to determine the main patterns of behaviour, but in complicated cases it can help to test the building once with all the building services disabled, and all the windows and doors closed to give a baseline, and then again as the conditions are altered one by one. The smoking incense should be held near all the likely places where leakage could occur: not only windows and doors, but at the intersections where building elements meet, and around light fittings and other places where holes have been made through the walls or ceiling.

TRACER-GAS TESTS

Tracer-gas testing allows air exchange to be quantified; used together with sampling, it can also give some idea of larger-scale airflow patterns. The method requires a gas with much the same buoyancy as the air, but which can be detected easily, that can be mixed into the room air. Its depletion over time is then monitored. The choice of gas, how it is injected into the air and how it is sampled will all greatly influence results.

For many years the standard gases used for these tests were sulphur hexafluoride and freon, but both are extremely powerful ozone depleters and greenhouse gases, and so have been banned for this use since 2006. The most common choice is now carbon dioxide: although this is rather harder to detect, it does have the advantage that tests can be made with the building in normal occupation.

FAN-PRESSURISATION (BLOWER-DOOR) TESTS

These tests use very high indoor pressures to induce air exchange, and can detect the presence of major air leaks, caused by hidden features such as concealed voids, though they cannot actually locate the voids. Tests cannot show the way the building responds to natural driving forces such as the wind (which will impose a complex pattern of positive and negative pressures on the exterior of the envelope).

To run a blower-door test, all exterior doors and windows except one are closed, and into that remaining opening (usually a door) a large fan is set in place, surrounded by plywood or some other form of sealing. All the interior doors are opened, but the dampers on fireplaces and other operable dampers are closed, and all fans and other exhaust systems are turned off.

The pressure differential between the exterior and interior is measured, and then the blower-door fan is turned on to create a positive or negative pressure differential. The leakier the building, the more air that the fan will need to supply to be able to change the building pressure. Pressurising and depressurising should produce different results, reflecting the envelope's response to directional airflow. To improve accuracy, the results must be corrected for air density.

The result is a measurement of the total air exchange at 50 Pa. This is very high – more than one hundred times the pressure induced by a strong wind – but it is chosen to overwhelm any error from stack-induced or wind-driven airflow, so that the test does not have to be repeated under different conditions. The result is then interpolated mathematically to give an estimate for air exchange at more realistic pressures.

Building Regulations

AIR EXCHANGE REQUIREMENTS

There is no accepted definition for 'adequate' ventilation: this will not only depend on the location of the building and its use, but will change according to the intention behind limiting or increasing air exchange. Regulations may seek to set lower limits to cut pollution from interior sources such as smoking or off-gassing materials, or upper limits to reduce the uptake of pollutants from the exterior, or to decrease the loss of conditioned air from the building (and so reduce energy use).

Different rooms may have special ventilation requirements. In bathrooms and kitchens, for example, ventilation fans may be installed to limit condensation, and to keep moist and possibly odorous air from escaping into the rest of the building.

MEASURING THERMAL PERFORMANCE

ASSESSING THERMAL RESISTANCE

How quickly heat transfers through a building wall is of concern for heating designers, and for efforts to reduce the use of heating and cooling energy in buildings.

The most common parameter used for modelling – the U-value – is often calculated; but calculations often do not agree very well with measurements, so measuring can be a better approach. U-values are measured by attaching a heat-flux metre to the wall, and monitoring surface temperature and air temperatures. The minimum period needed to obtain a good measurement is about two weeks, because in practice steady-state conditions do not occur, and consideration has to be given to the variations in temperatures and heat flows before the U-value can be reliably determined.

CO-HEATING TESTS

Co-heating tests are designed to give a measurement of how an envelope loses heat to both ventilation and the fabric. Like blower-door tests, they cannot be run under ordinary conditions. The unoccupied building is heated with electric resistance point heaters to reach a set temperature for a set period of time (usually 25 °C for between one and three weeks). The electrical energy used to keep the building at this temperature is measured every day during the test, to determine a daily heat input in watts. This is plotted against the daily difference with the exterior temperature; the slope of the graph is taken to be the 'heat-loss coefficient' for the building. This means that the tests must be made in winter, when the difference in temperatures is sufficiently high.

Co-heating testing is quite a new procedure, and the uncertainties – which include overheating and subsequent internal thermal mass effects, and the effect of solar gain – have not yet been studied in great detail or quantified.

Testing Insulating Glazing Units

To determine whether the seals have begun to fail on *in-situ* IGUs in curtain-wall façades, causing moisture to leak into the gap between the glass, one simple test is to cool an area of the glass by applying dry ice, and see whether this causes condensation, as described in the British Standard *BS 1279-2:2002 Glass in building. Insulating glass units. Long term test method and requirements for moisture penetration*. The same test can be used to assess double-glazed windows.

Exhaustive testing of IGUs must be undertaken in a specialist laboratory, and so the window or panel must be dismantled to release the unit. This is difficult and expensive, so it is usually only considered when it is necessary to assess widespread building problems that may have been caused by faulty materials or poor construction. ⊖GLASS

Measuring Thermal Resistance

The base measurement for heat transfer in energy studies of buildings is not in fact the U-value (more correctly called 'U-factors' or the 'overall heat-transfer coefficient'), but its reciprocal: the 'R-value'. This is a measure of thermal resistance: that is, how an object or material impedes the flow of heat through it when there is a difference in temperature on either side. Thermal resistance is not the same as thermal resistivity, which is an intrinsic property of materials; instead, it depends on the object's structure and thickness.

R-VALUES

R-values are expressed as the thickness of the material divided by its thermal conductivity. It is assumed that the degree to which the material transfers heat is linearly related to its thickness, although for complex building elements or composite structures this would not necessarily be the case. The higher the R-value, the more the material resists heat transfer.

R-values are measured experimentally by placing the object of interest between two conducting plates, and determining the energy flux that is needed to maintain a particular temperature gradient. The experiment is usually made under stable conditions, with a steady temperature and all air movement eliminated; such a controlled situation is unlikely to be met with in real conditions. Crucially, the measurements currently consider only conducted heat, and do not take either radiation or convection into account.

U-VALUES

U-values, which were developed to give engineers a simple way of sizing heating equipment, give a figure for the overall heat transfer through a building element, as rate of heat transfer over a given area under set conditions (usually a temperature gradient of 24°C, at 50 % relative humidity, and with no air movement). The units for U-values are watts per square metre kelvin [$W/(m^2K)$], and the smaller the U-value, the better the material at resisting heat conduction.

A U-value based on conduction alone cannot give a complete picture of heat transfer through building fabric, and there is a good deal of controversy and confusion over the use of U-values or 'equivalent U-values' to compare building materials that transmit heat in entirely different manners. Heat will also impinge on the fabric in many different ways, which will vary across the year and even over the course of a day. For example, conductive and convective transfer will be the more important considerations during heating periods, but radiative processes will be the most important consideration in summer, when the intent is to keep the building cool. U-values will also be higher when it is windy.

Another critically important factor is moisture content: for consistency, all laboratory experiments have been made on dry materials, but in buildings the wall materials will never be dry, and water is an excellent conductor of heat. For curtain-walling panels, published U-values are based on centre-of-panel readings, but these can be as much as 33 % lower than readings made at the panel edges. U-value measurements are rarely shown with errors, but it is clear that this is extremely important if they are to be used in any meaningful way.

New definitions and experimental processes are currently being developed that try to incorporate all forms of heat transfer into the measurements of U-value and R-value, but this is far from simple, since it means taking account of many other characteristics including surface temperature and emissivity, and convection in porous materials.

MEASURING U-VALUES

It is possible to measure thermal transmittance with a heat-flow meter, but this is not necessarily straightforward in buildings. One problem is the lack of homogeneity in building elements, and the difficulty of understanding hidden construction materials and detailing. Another is the variance over time of those environmental conditions that affect the thermal transmittance, such as the interior and exterior temperatures, the solar radiation, and wind. One approach is to measure over reasonably long intervals, and then estimate the steady-state transmittance from the mean values of heat flow and temperature, but this is possible only if the thermal properties of the materials are constant over the range of temperatures encountered (and if the change in internal energy in the element is tiny compared to the heat travelling through it).

CALCULATING U-VALUES

In many cases it is simply not possible to meaningfully measure U-values, so they are calculated instead. This is even more controversial, since the results of calculations often differ dramatically from *in-situ* measurements.

Compound systems are particularly susceptible to misleading results from calculation, since they depend on the way the computer model has been set up, which is essentially by layering components. For example, thatch is known from experience to be an extremely good insulator, but this is not always reflected in U-value calculations. This is because thatch is a mixture of straw or reed and air, in approximate proportions of one-to-one; but very different results will result from an oversimplified model that uses only two or three layers (say, 35 cm of straw, 70 cm of air and 35 cm of straw), and a more realistic model that uses myriad thin layers of straw and air.

Thatch is an excellent insulator, keeping buildings warm in winter and cool in summer (as well as thickness and condition, the actual degree of insulation depends upon the type of thatch and how it is fixed, long-straw roofs being more insulating than water reed, for example). Adding insulation to an airtight thatched roof would be counterproductive, since it would mean ventilating the space beneath the thatch and therefore negating the cover's own insulating effect. Where the eaves have been altered, however, and the roofs are no longer airtight, adding insulation could be of great benefit.

MONITORING THE ENVIRONMENT

Sometimes the cause of problems will still not be clear even after a thorough survey and intensive measurement, or it may be suspected that the problems are intermittent or related to wider changes in the building environment. In such cases, environmental monitoring may be the only way to assess relationships between time-varying parameters, such as how the building is buffering the exterior conditions, or whether the size of a structural crack is varying with humidity. It is also possible to use monitoring to understand the way the environment is responding to deliberate changes, such as building renovations or a new heating regime.

Monitoring is the simultaneous recording of one or more environmental parameters, for as long a period as is necessary to capture all the important permutations. In practice, this usually means recording environmental conditions inside and outside the building for at least one year, and preferably two, to cover all the usual seasonal variations, together with various parameters related to the fabric, such as surface temperature.

Some environmental parameters change slowly and steadily, lending themselves to very simple monitoring techniques: deposition of pollutants, for example, requires only occasional sampling. Most other parameters vary so quickly that special recording equipment must be used. The great advantage of this type of recording is that a number of quite different parameters can be recorded simultaneously, revealing relationships between them that might not have been suspected otherwise.

The critical role of environmental monitoring is to determine exactly how the building envelope is modifying the exterior conditions. For this reason, all installations must include a means of monitoring the exterior temperature and humidity, and possibly other weather parameters such as wind and rainfall.

The location of the exterior monitors must be chosen with care, and the equipment protected from conditions that could not only shorten its lifespan, but cause it to give faulty readings. The usual approach is to use 'Stevenson screens', ventilated covers that protect the temperature and humidity sensors from sunlight and wind.

There are two main categories of environmental monitoring:

- *Diagnostic*
  Monitoring to understand building problems or assess alterations.

- *Day-to-day*
  Monitoring for long-term care.

Diagnostic monitoring is best left to specialists with experience recording many types of building and many different environmental parameters, and who have access to specialist equipment; but day-to-day monitoring can usually be managed by the building users once the system has been set up by a specialist.

The following is an introduction to the basic principles that underlie the design of environmental monitoring systems, and the interpretation of their results.

BUILDING ENVIRONMENT
ASSESSING THE BUILDING ENVIRONMENT

DIAGNOSTIC MONITORING

Diagnostic monitoring is often proposed as a standard adjunct to a building survey or a programme of conservation, but it can be time-consuming and expensive, and will only be useful if properly directed. As a general rule, a programme of monitoring should be considered only when the causes of deterioration are not immediately clear, but are thought to be related to time-varying aspects of the building environment.

To be able to design a useful system, the specialist must have some fairly clear idea where the causes of problems might be found: that is, a working hypothesis about the deterioration that can be tested by recording and comparing various aspects of the environment over time. The system must be set up principally to examine this hypothesis, but it must still be kept sufficiently general to be able to capture a wider picture of the building environment since reality is almost always found to be more complex than the hypothesis. Any monitoring will almost certainly uncover aspects of the environment that could not have been revealed by even the most detailed surveys.

In many cases, the monitoring may require a preliminary testing phase to examine the changing environmental conditions more closely before deciding which parameters to measure, and establish the best positions for sensors. Every attempt must be made to test the working hypothesis, even where this may require some lateral thinking about how best to monitor, or some innovative sensors. Since data must not be merely collected, but processed and interpreted as well, it is always important to minimise sensor numbers as much as possible.

DESIGNING A MONITORING SYSTEM

Diagnostic monitoring is likely to incorporate both an electronic logging system able to collect measurements from a series of electronic sensors distributed around the building, and nonelectronic systems to monitor parameters that cannot be recorded electronically.

Choosing the Parameters to Monitor

The choice of parameters for monitoring depends on a clearly defined set of monitoring objectives, which in turn depends on a good understanding of the environmental mechanisms likely to be causing the deterioration that is being investigated.

To be effective, the monitoring programme must acquire all the information needed to understand the problem, but unfortunately – although technology is continually being developed and refined – not every important parameter can be readily monitored. It is easy to concentrate on parameters that are simple to measure (such as relative humidity and temperature), neglecting those that are more difficult (such as light, ultraviolet radiation and airflow). A typical example is the examination of salt deterioration in a masonry wall. The fundamental cause of problems is changing moisture distributions in the wall, due to water transfer within the fabric, and between the fabric and the ambient air; this is due to airflow, relative humidity and temperature, so ideally we would wish to monitor all of these. However, although even very small changes in local air movement will have an important effect on water transfer, airflow is monitored very rarely; usually recording is restricted to the parameters of ambient relative humidity, and ambient and surface temperatures, all of which are much easier to measure. As a result, the picture of behaviour obtained from interpreting the monitoring is significantly distorted.

Computerised environmental monitoring systems have great potential for adaptation to examine complex situations, since many dataloggers can accept signals from almost every form of electronic probe. Here, a surface wetness sensor is being applied to a panel of float glass set into a stained-glass window, as part of a monitoring system to examine the risk of condensation in windows protected with secondary glazing.

Many standard parameters are effectively proxies for measuring what investigators would really like to know. For example, to monitor condensation, current systems either record condensation occurring on a polished mirror, or compare measurements of surface temperature with the ambient dew-point temperature, although in practice there are probably many other factors involved in whether or not condensation actually occurs on a surface (including air movement and surface roughness). The most useful measurements are those that come closest to the true parameter of interest: for example, sensors are currently being developed to measure evaporative water loss from wall surfaces, so that evaporation can be directly observed rather than deduced from temperature and humidity.

Conventional monitoring cannot always provide all the information needed to answer the questions that have been posed. For instance, light sensors can accurately record the exposure at one particular spot, but not the pattern of light falling over the entire surface. If the pattern of deterioration suggests that the distribution of exposure is critical, then environmental monitoring may have to be complemented with techniques such as time-lapse photography or infrared thermography.

The fundamental parameter that investigators invariably wish to monitor is the most elusive: actual deterioration. Recently, several researchers have investigated this using time-lapse video to monitor changes that could only be recorded visually, such as salt crystallisation and material loss, to associate occurrences of damage with changes in environmental conditions. The availability of faster computer processors and cheaper memory should make hybrid systems increasingly accessible.

PARAMETERS FOR ENVIRONMENTAL MONITORING

PARAMETER	COMMENTS
AMBIENT TEMPERATURE	Measured with thermometers of various types
	Care must be taken to ensure that thermometers are not being cooled by moving air
AMBIENT HUMIDITY	Usually measured as relative humidity (as opposed to 'absolute humidity'), by assessing the effect on a moisture-sensitive material (hair hygrometers use the change in the length of the hair; electronic sensors look at changes in the capacitance of a polymer)
	Difficult to interpret without knowledge of the ambient temperature, so these parameters are usually measured together
	Ambient temperature and humidity can be used to calculate other thermohygrometric properties of the air, such as dew-point temperature and absolute humidity
SURFACE TEMPERATURE	Measurement of surface temperature can be remote (measuring the surface emission in the infrared) or direct (attaching a thermometer of some sort to the surface)
	The physical interaction between an attached thermometer and the surface will affect the readings; it is particularly important to prevent them reading air temperature rather than true surface temperature
	The readings of infrared thermometers may need to be corrected for surface emissivity, and dust can also be a problem
RADIANT TEMPERATURE	Mean radiant temperature is commonly monitored with a 'black-globe' bolometer, which contains a temperature sensor inside a hollow sphere coloured matt black to absorb maximum energy; this is a measurement of radiant uptake, not radiant loss
WEATHER	Can incorporate numerous measurements, including wind speed and direction, rainfall, solar radiation, barometric pressure, temperature and humidity
AIR MOVEMENT	Not to be confused with air exchange (which can be measured but not monitored: see Gases)
	Arguably the most difficult microclimate parameter to monitor, since air movement has both speed and direction, and the measurement device will disturb the local air movement; also, the link between damage and, for example, turbulence is poorly understood
	Flow visualisation techniques may be needed to determine the best probe locations, but air movement is very localised and variable, so the ideal location at night may be quite different to the ideal location during the day, and different in summer and winter, in windy conditions and still weather
	Possible alternative may be to monitor the actual parameter of concern instead (such as evaporation)
MOISTURE CONTENT	All useful methods require holes to be drilled in walls
	Dowel methods can indicate wetness or dryness, but not moisture levels
	Most methods are able to monitor moisture levels work by reading the effect of moisture content on the dielectric field
	Except in the rare cases that the field is generated between two capacitance plates, field attenuation must be measured, which reduces accuracy and increases the difficulties of interpretation
SURFACE WETNESS	Measurement of liquid water on the surface, usually by time-of-wetness sensors which record electrical current
	Can be difficult to monitor on permeable materials, where surface water is often immediately absorbed
GROUNDWATER	Typically both depth and chemical content are monitored in specially drilled boreholes
GASES	Range of gases and volatile organic compounds including CO_2
	Used to assess pollutants, or to measure air-exchange rates
POLLUTANTS	Pollutants can reach the building as gases, volatiles or particulates; levels will probably vary seasonally
	May chemically react with the building surfaces, so effective concentration may be rather different to measured concentration
	Two possible approaches: passive (trap to collect pollutant deposits; eventually sent away for analysis), and active (air pumped through a filter or collector solution)

PARAMETERS FOR ENVIRONMENTAL MONITORING

PARAMETER	COMMENTS
LIGHT & RADIATION	Both the intensity of the light and its wavelength will have an impact (infrared, ultraviolet, visible)
	Patterns of light can be very complex and localised
BIOLOGICAL ACTIVITY	Usually necessary to monitor visually; illumination in non-visible wavelengths may help this
STRUCTURAL MOVEMENT	Most variants of local movement can be monitored, including crack width, displacement, tilt and vibration
	Measurements are generally relative to some other part of the structure
BUILDING USE	Monitoring of visitor numbers, opening of doors, vibration from footfalls
MATERIAL CHANGES	In some ways the most difficult parameter to measure, but also the most important
	Can use traps to collect fallen material
	Can look at the deterioration of a standardised material to obtain some idea of possible rates of decay
	Can monitor physical extent of damage (for example, the length of cracks)
	Ideally, records dynamic changes such as surface salt crystallisation, or flaking and loss of deteriorating material

ELECTRONIC MONITORING

Electronic monitoring is based on creating hubs at various points in and around the building with sensors that feed measurements back to some electronic recording system. The first step is to choose the parameters that need to be measured to test the working hypothesis.

Although the process needed to develop a system of electronic environmental monitoring may be complex, the mechanics are for the most part quite straightforward, since almost any sensor with an electronic output can be adapted so that it can be logged, and most can now be made to transmit to centralised computer storage systems ('dataloggers'). This makes installation and data manipulation, interpretation and presentation very much easier. Many dataloggers can now be accessed remotely through a mobile phone or radio signal, which is useful for checking that the system is still continuing to function correctly: environmental monitoring outputs are all too often characterised by critical gaps in the data. On the negative side, remote access means that less time may be spent on site looking at the building.

Deciding the Period & Rate of Monitoring

Both the minimum interval between successive readings and the minimum necessary duration of monitoring will depend essentially on the rates of change of the parameters being examined. However, an efficient monitoring programme must also balance collecting information against the time and cost of the subsequent assessment and interpretation. Higher rates of collection mean larger amounts of data, which means a better chance of recording critical events, but also that more work will be needed for analysis.

Intervals Between Measurements

Dataloggers allow the interval between successive measurements to be set at anything from seconds to hours, or even days; the optimum interval depends mostly on the parameters being measured. To take two extreme examples: changes in groundwater levels and chemistry are likely to be extremely slow, so it is often sufficient to collect a single daily measurement; but to understand the effect of air exchange on condensation, it will be necessary to measure at intervals of no longer than 15 or 20 minutes, to be sure that condensation events are not being missed.

Monitoring Duration

Since the microclimate of a building depends on the exterior climate – which is seasonal – to build up a picture of the interactions between interior and exterior conditions, monitoring will need to continue for at least one full year (or even two years, if the weather proves to be atypical or the situation very complex). On the other hand, conditions in a climate-controlled display case may be almost independent of the exterior weather, and so it may well be possible to characterise the case sufficiently well after no more than a few days or weeks of monitoring.

To understand the effect of changing the building envelope or the controls on the interior, monitoring must be in place both before and after the changes are made, for as long as needed to characterise the environment well enough to confidently assess the effect of the changes.

Planning the Installation

It is rarely necessary – or indeed practical – to try and gather data throughout an entire building. Instead, the specialist will seek to design the system to gain the maximum information from the minimum number of measurement locations and sensors.

Deciding how many data collection points will be needed to understand the environment, and how these will need to be distributed according to the problems being investigated, is the most important part of any environmental monitoring programme. The specialist will need to take account of all the factors that could possibly be contributing to the problems, including the building exposure, the building structure and materials, the way the interior space is partitioned, the vertical stratification of temperature and humidity, and the possibility of intermittent events (such as sunlight entering at one particular time of the year), not to mention building use, and the location of heating, cooling and ventilation systems.

Sensors & Probes

Although terminology is anything but rigorous, it is convenient to use the term 'sensor' specifically to describe the sensitive element which actually measures an environmental parameter, and 'probe' to refer to its housing (a sensor may not work at all without a suitable housing).

Most common sensors are now designed to export a digital signal, and the probe commonly houses the necessary electronics. Even mechanical sensors are now usually fitted into probes that can transform their analogue signal into a digital format.

Most sensors measure the conditions in their immediate vicinity, so when choosing a location for a probe the first step is to decide whether the probe is intended to record the conditions in one specific location (perhaps to examine an unusual pattern of deterioration), or to give readings representative of the building as a whole.

Choosing the Equipment

Choosing monitoring equipment generally means balancing efficiency, accuracy and cost. The decision is best made by a specialist able to understand and assess not only the capabilities of the equipment, but the deterioration mechanisms being investigated.

Dataloggers

Broadly speaking, dataloggers fall into two types:

- *Stand-alone dataloggers*
  A device with integrated sensors, that both measures the parameters and records the results. These are generally battery-powered, and are programmed in advance and then placed in appropriate locations. Some can be remotely interrogated and downloaded, but most must be manually downloaded to a computer.

- *Centralised dataloggers*
  A recording device, to which various external probes can be connected (either by wires or by radio telemetry). This makes downloading and maintenance far simpler and less time-consuming, but must be set up with greater care. In the event of failure or theft, all the data may be lost.

Some stand-alone loggers are supplied with either nonvolatile memory or a backup battery to stop data being lost if the power fails; many rely on volatile memory, which means that the failure of the battery results in complete data loss. For this reason, batteries must always be recharged or replaced before they can fail. Centralised loggers, whether they are hardwired or telemetric, usually run from the mains, but also have system batteries to protect settings and data in a power failure.

Wired systems are relatively robust and provide a constant data signal (radio telemetry probes transmit the data to the logger only at pre-programmed intervals); there is little risk of losing data between the sensor and logger. They are, however, cumbersome and difficult to install.

Radio telemetry systems are becoming common, as technology becomes more reliable and costs drop, but they are vulnerable to problems with signal transmission (especially in large or complex buildings). A more subtle but important difference from wired systems is that in most cases the probes transmit data within a preset period, rather than at a precise moment, and the logger does not record exactly when the data arrives.

To give an example, a sensor programmed to transmit data at 20-minute intervals may send the data at any moment within that interval, so the data from several different sensors may in fact have been collected by the sensors as much as 20 minutes apart. By contrast, hardwired systems effectively receive constant data signals that are then recorded at the instigation of the logger.

Downloading the datalogger

The collected data must be fed into a computer for analysis and interpretation, a process known as 'downloading'. The downloading system depends on the logger, but in general either it is connected directly to the computer (*right*), or else is read remotely through a telephone system or a computer network.

Remote access has a number of advantages aside from convenience. It is easy to check that the system is still collecting data at any time of the day or night; and many loggers can be programmed to transmit a warning message if a predetermined 'alarm' value is breached (for example, in a condensation-sensitive environment, increasing levels of relative humidity could trigger dehumidification equipment).

BUILDING ENVIRONMENT
ASSESSING THE BUILDING ENVIRONMENT

Selecting the Correct Sensors & Probes

Data is only as good as the sensors gathering it, so it is important to understand their accuracy and repeatability. Readings taken for investigating the building environment rarely need to be as accurate as (for example) readings taken for process control in factories. Repeatability of measurements taken by a single sensor, or between different sensors around the building, is much more important than accuracy.

All electronic sensors must be supplied with power, but the way in which this is provided varies. Hardwired probes generally draw their power directly from the datalogger, but radio telemetry probes are generally powered by batteries (like stand-alone loggers, these require periodic renewal; but because battery life can be transmitted along with the data, warnings can be provided to the logger when battery power is low).

Some probes – hot-wire air velocity sensors, for example – require more power than can be provided by batteries. They must therefore be supplied with electricity either directly from the mains, or from solar panels (or some other alternative source).

It is convenient to group probes into 'clusters': this not only makes installation easier, but means that the readings from the sensors are as comparable as possible.

Here, each cluster includes a thermistor reading surface temperature, and a combined relative humidity and temperature [RH&T] probe. All probes are protected from the drying and cooling effects of air movement by screens (a block of green foam in the case of the thermistors, and filters or a Stevenson screen in the case of the RH & T probes). This ensures accurate and repeatable readings.

Most monitoring begins with equipment to measure temperature and relative humidity, often together with surface temperatures. Monitoring exterior and interior microclimates is also standard, as this more than any other comparison reveals how the building envelope is working. The weather station is a particularly useful tool, combining in a single unit the measurement of exterior temperature and relative humidity, rainfall intensity, sunlight, and wind.

Structural monitoring can also be incorporated in a programme of environmental monitoring to check whether or not apparent weaknesses reflect serious problems, and whether or not these are affected by environmental parameters such as temperature or wind. This can mean monitoring ground motion, structural frame response, component response, and creep or settlement.

COMMON ELECTRONIC SENSORS USED TO MONITOR THE ENVIRONMENT

PARAMETER	TYPE OF MEASUREMENT	SENSORS	COMMENTS
AIR TEMPERATURE	Direct	Thermometers Thermocouples Thermistors Resistance sensors	Thermocouples are not reliable when used to measure temperatures close to the ambient air temperature
SURFACE TEMPERATURE	Attached sensors	Thermistors Resistance sensors	Accuracy depends on method of attachment
	Remote sensors	Infrared thermometers Infrared thermography	Readings depend on surface emissivity as well as temperature
AMBIENT HUMIDITY	Direct	Capacitance sensors Dew-point sensors	Need regular recalibration
LIGHT	Direct	Photodetector	Can measure different wavebands
	Indirect	Photodetector	Can measure different wavebands
AIR MOVEMENT	Pattern and speed of flow	Smoke tests Particle velocimetry	Air movement is very variable, so spot measurements can be particularly deceptive
	Speed of flow	Cup anemometers Hot-wire anemometers Ultrasound	The presence of probes can cause turbulence and affect the reading; this is a great problem at low speeds
AIR EXCHANGE	Indirect	Tracer gas	On-off measurement: therefore, conditions under which to monitor must be chosen carefully
	Direct	Door or window opening	Closure of window or door completes circuit May need quite complicated processing to extract both numbers of opening and closing events, and the duration of each separate event
MOISTURE CONTENT	Indirect	Resistance sensors Embedded capacitance sensors Embedded microwave-capacitance sensors	Best systems based on measuring dielectric change, but currently no totally satisfactory method, since sensor must be inserted in a drilled hole, and this changes the characteristics of the material
WATER EVENT	Direct	Strip with a simple printed electronic circuit; presence of liquid water completes circuit	Can be used to detect surface condensation or, for example, blockages in gutters Can be used to trigger an alarm
HEAT LOSS	Indirect	U-value reading with flux meter	U-value is a measurement of conductive heat loss only
AIR POLLUTION	Direct	Air pumped through analytical device	Sensor can be chosen to detect a range of pollutants, or to monitor a single pollutant to a greater accuracy

BUILDING ENVIRONMENT
ASSESSING THE BUILDING ENVIRONMENT

Monitoring Moisture Content

Since water is critical to most decay processes, it would be extremely helpful to be able to monitor moisture content alongside the environmental conditions that should be driving change; this would help develop a better understanding of the underlying processes of deterioration. It would seem more sensible to equate deterioration to changing moisture levels, rather than measurements of absolute moisture content. Monitoring would also be useful for assessing the success of remedial treatments.

For all these reasons, considerable effort has been put into trying to develop monitoring systems, but so far without conclusive success. Nevertheless, there is no doubt that it is much easier to monitor moisture than it is to measure it, since by recording changes over time the problems of calibration and material heterogeneity are avoided.

NON-DESTRUCTIVE SYSTEMS

Most non-destructive measurement systems are limited to looking in from the surface, and so can give little if any idea of moisture distribution with depth. Some attempts have been made to derive three-dimensional readings from capacitance attenuation by varying the frequency of the signal to give different patterns of penetration, but in practice the depth of penetration is too little to give useful results. Higher-powered equipment, such as NMR, has been used with greater success; but for monitoring the problem, the time taken to obtain a single scan can be very long: too long to record transient changes.

Although many systems designed for one-off moisture measurements (microwave attenuation, for example) could theoretically also be used for monitoring, they can be very difficult to operate on site for prolonged periods.

At Howden Minster Chapter House in Yorkshire, soil moisture profile probes have been used to monitor moisture content at several depths in the wall.

Left: Probe being inserted into pre-drilled hole.

Right: Three probes in position to monitor the relationship between moisture content and height. All are connected to a single datalogger.

DESTRUCTIVE SYSTEMS

The fundamental problem with destructive measurements of moisture in walls is that the drilling of the hole and the inserting of the sensor will invariably alter the local conditions within the wall, changing the very thing one is trying to measure.

No absolutely reliable method has yet been developed, but there are a number of basic approaches, and each of these may be found in a number of different variants:

- monitoring the relative humidity [RH] in a drilled hole
- monitoring the moisture content of permeable rods inserted in a drilled hole
- inserting active electronic sensors into the wall.

MONITORING RELATIVE HUMIDITY

Many attempts have been made to monitor moisture content by measuring the relative humidity in cavities drilled in the wall; but in sealed cavities, readings are invariably found to be 100 % unless the wall is effectively dry (it takes very little liquid water to provide the vapour necessary for saturation in a sealed space: see **Building Science**).

MONITORING RODS (TIMBER DOWELS)

A much more successful approach is to insert a rod made from some hygroscopic material such as timber into a drilled hole, and measure its moisture content after it has had time to equilibrate. The rod can either be removed for gravimetric testing, or a resistance meter can be used to measure the change in electrical resistance. To determine a moisture profile through the wall, a rod could be cut into shorter lengths and glued together again with water-resistant materials such as epoxy resin; each length could then be measured independently.

It is common practice to use the holes made when taking drilled powder samples for this purpose, and indeed if holes are drilled deliberately to take rods, the drilled material should always be retained and examined (see **Taking Samples from a Wall**).

The problem is that the rod must equilibrate before measurement, and so cannot be used to track transient changes. For much the same reason that the RH in cavities is almost always 100 %, the readings will be either 'wet' or 'dry'. The system is very useful, however, for assessing broad changes in water content (such as the drying out of walls after severe flooding).

Ideally, the rod would be made from a material that is isotropic, stable in moist conditions and closely correspond to the materials of the wall, and which forms a good seal but remains easy to remove for measurement. Many types of rod have been tried, but the most popular are timber dowels, which are cheap, reasonably consistent (especially when made of softwood), and can be measured fairly accurately with resistance meters. To accommodate swelling they must be a few millimetres narrower than the hole. A 6–10-mm dowel will generally require about 10 days to equilibrate, and should not be left in wet conditions for longer than it takes for timber decay to begin – that is, about six weeks – because decay will alter the moisture-sorption characteristics. As a very general guide, if the rod equilibrates at a moisture content below 17 % the wall can be considered dry; at 18–24 % it is damp; and at 25–29 % it will be wet. Moisture contents higher than this would suggest that the wall is saturated.

The consistency of softwood dowels means that results from one period of monitoring can be compared with those from the next without too much error, even though new dowels are being used.

BUILDING ENVIRONMENT
ASSESSING THE BUILDING ENVIRONMENT

MONITORING WITH ELECTRONIC SENSORS

To date the most successful methods for monitoring moisture contents in building materials are those developed for soil science. There are, however, a number of critical differences between soil and other permeable materials that make effective measurement considerably more complex. In soil, probes can be inserted relatively easily, and the contact between sensor and soil can be very good. To measure moisture in a building material, a hole or holes will need to be drilled, and this is usually very difficult for walls, where the construction is both complex and hidden. The final hole will be larger than the probe, and the contact much less good.

The complexity of building fabric also makes interpretation more difficult than for soil; there is likely to be very much greater variation with depth. This is less serious for monitoring than it would be for measurement, since the aim of monitoring is to record change rather than absolute moisture contents.

Time Domain Reflectometry [TDR]

A time-domain reflectometer has two long waveguides running parallel to each other. An electric pulse is sent down one waveguide, and the signal reflected back through the surrounding medium is collected in the second guide and interpreted graphically through an oscilloscope to give a reading of dielectric constant. Interpretation is usually computerised, but where the material is complex it can result in significant error. More importantly, drilling two long, thin, parallel holes to take the probe can be almost impossible.

Gypsum Moisture Probes

These are electrical-resistance probes developed for soil science; they have a gypsum substrate which acts as a proxy material for the soil; it is assumed that the moisture content of the gypsum will change with that of the surrounding material. As with all electrical-resistance sensors, readings are affected by electrolytes such as salts in the water.

Capacitance Systems

High resolution is sought almost as a matter of course by technical researchers, but in fact for understanding building problems spatial resolution could usually be sacrificed for improvements in temporal resolution. Electrical capacitance can be read very quickly, and is much less affected by salts than electrical-resistance systems.

Soil-Moisture Profile Probes

Developed for monitoring soil moisture contents, these probes generate an electric field and measure the change in capacitance to determine the dielectric of the surrounding material at different depths. The probes can successfully monitor changing moisture, but they cannot give readings for absolute moisture content.

Problems include the difficulties and destruction involved in drilling the sizeable and deep hole required to take the probe, and the influence of the air gap between the probe and the material.

Other Possibilities

Laboratory tests have shown that the changes in moisture content at a series of depths in a sizeable block of stone, held between two capacitance plates, can be read very accurately at high speed. Theoretically, if parallel capacitance plates could be embedded in the fabric, a similar system could be used for *in-situ* monitoring. This is likely to be extremely invasive, and as yet no field trials have been attempted.

Installing the Monitoring System

To make the readings from various probes as comparable as possible, they are grouped together into 'clusters'. For example, a cluster designed to examine the relationship between structural stress and microclimate variation might group together a strain gauge, a probe measuring relative humidity and air temperature, and a surface temperature probe. It is important to position the probes in a cluster as closely together as possible (always ensuring that the presence of the other equipment does not affect the readings).

Probes and other equipment must be protected from conditions that could affect their accuracy. For example, if a humidity sensor is not screened from ambient air movements, such as those caused by draughts or by air rising above heaters, its readings will be unreliable. Both interior and exterior humidity probes may need to be protected with Stevenson screens, and surface temperature probes with covers to prevent air cooling.

Cluster positions in the building are chosen to test the deterioration hypothesis. This usually means measuring the same parameters in different parts of the building, and comparing them with each other and with the same conditions monitored externally. To make the readings as comparable as possible, unnecessary variables must be removed: clusters may be set at the same height from the ground, or (if the intention is to examine stratigraphy) in a vertical line. The fewer the unnecessary differences between the cluster positions, the easier it is to see meaningful differences when readings from different clusters are compared, and to attribute such differences to probable causes.

The choice of sensor positions is critical to the success of a monitoring system

Locations must be chosen to answer the questions posed by the investigation, and to minimise the amount of data being collected whilst maximising the potential information it contains. For example, the clusters shown here have been positioned to examine stratification, and in such a way that they can be easily compared: in vertical lines, and at the same heights, chosen with an eye to the patterns of damage.

It is not always possible to position sensors ideally, especially where the building is being extensively used; some compromise may have to be made between research aims, ease of installation and maintenance, and issues such as health and safety.

This elevation of a monitoring system installed at Westminster Cathedral in London (*right*) shows the location of various clusters (red circles represent surface temperature probes, and green circles relative humidity and temperature probes).

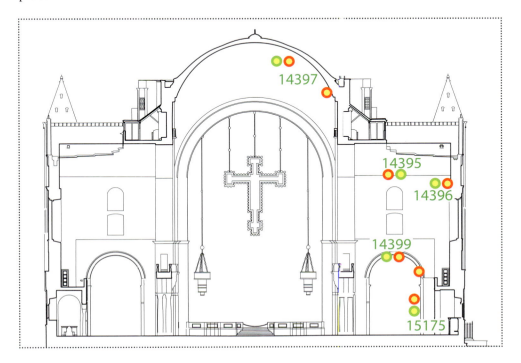

BUILDING ENVIRONMENT
ASSESSING THE BUILDING ENVIRONMENT

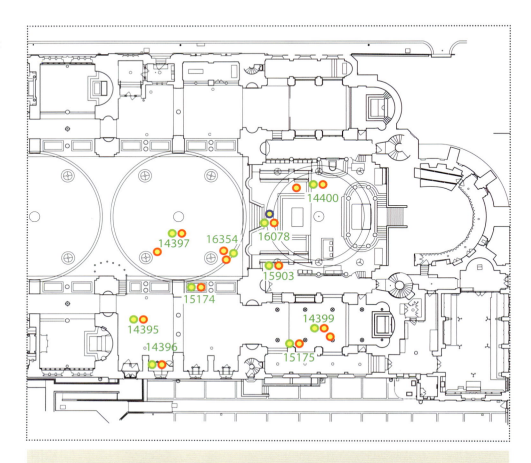

A detail of the plan showing probe positions for a monitoring system at Westminster Cathedral, London.

Sensor Calibration

Calibration defines the relationship between the output of the instrument, and the parameter being measured. For example, an alcohol-glass thermometer is marked with numbers that relate the level of the alcohol to the ambient temperature. To be very accurate, each thermometer would have to be calibrated in a climate-controlled laboratory, to take account of its unique behaviour (the quirks induced by variations in the thickness of the capillary, for example). In many cases, instruments can be mass-produced because the increase in accuracy would not be important enough to justify the extra cost.

Many instruments require regular recalibration; for example, the thin plastic films used to measure humidity will permanently drift if exposed to high humidities for prolonged periods. In most cases they will have to be tested and adjusted yearly, but if conditions are very stable, calibration may only be necessary only every two years or so.

NON-AUTOMATED MONITORING

Although many parameters affecting the building environment (and therefore the interpretation of the monitored data) are recordable with sensors and dataloggers, others will not be, and so will have to be recorded in some other fashion.

The most important parameters of this type are the use of the building, and the external events that may affect the environment. To monitor these it may be necessary to instigate a logbook. As an example, for churches such a logbook might be used to record heating times, services, visitor numbers and the general weather: although monitoring the exterior climate will give readings of wind speed or rain, these will be much easier to interpret alongside a log that records, say, storms. The success of any logbook depends on the diligence of those who have to fill it in, so it is very important that they fully understand the reasons for recording, and that the logbook is designed to make the process as easy as possible. Extra comment should be encouraged, so there should be plenty of space allowed for entering anecdotal information.

Environmental monitoring is often used as a tool for the conservation of important *in-situ* building elements such as wall paintings or mosaics. It is particularly desirable to try to associate deterioration, change and loss with changing environmental conditions, but this is rarely straightforward. To monitor the spread of biological growths, fluorometer readings are sometimes taken at regular intervals. Trays or other collectors can be placed at the base of walls to collect falling debris, which allows the amount of loss to be assessed quantitatively, but the timing of losses will be harder to determine with accuracy. Photographs taken at regular intervals can be used, but this method is not reliable unless the changes are quite significant: very slight variations in illumination or camera angle can produce deceptive results.

For particularly important sites, video recording is sometimes used, but interpretation is tedious and time-consuming, and it is still difficult to be certain exactly when the environmental factor which led to observable deterioration actually occurred: there may be some considerable time delays between environmental change, damage and loss, making cause and effect difficult to establish with certainty.

Another option for monitoring condition is to use proxy materials to assess deterioration rates. Examples of this approach include pollution tests, where a collecting surface or tube is replaced at regular intervals, and sent away to a laboratory for examination. Blue-wool lightfastness tests are an inexpensive and effective way of assessing the deterioration potential of light: samples of specially dyed wool are positioned in the areas of concern, with half the sample shielded from light and the other half exposed. Fading can then be assessed at regular intervals, either by eye, or quantitatively using a colorimeter. Microbiological growth is also sometimes assessed by exposing a test surface which can be tested at regular intervals, but the problem is developing a test surface that is a sufficiently good proxy for the material at risk: for example, if a simple agar-agar plate is used, this is likely to favour quite different growths to those that might occur on an *in-situ* wall surface.

Non-automated monitoring may also be required as a preliminary to the automated monitoring of very complex environmental factors. For example, to understand the impact of sunlight on surfaces, intensity and wavelength may need to be monitored in several locations, but choosing which sensor locations would be the most informative usually demands some degree of time-lapse imaging. Since sunlight will vary greatly over the course of the year, this may have to be repeated several times before the patterns of impact are understood sufficiently well for sensors to be placed with confidence. Similarly, to monitor air movement, some flow visualisation will be required first to build a picture of the basic patterns of airflow and decide where best to place the anemometers.

Environmental monitoring systems, designed to understand problems in a building environment, may sometimes be modified after research has been completed to be suitable for day-to-day monitoring.

DAY-TO-DAY MONITORING

When undertaking background monitoring in a building such as a museum, the methodology behind the positioning of sensors will be very different to that for a diagnostic project looking at building deterioration. In such cases, positioning will depend largely on building use by visitors, and while the number of data points may, in a large building, be relatively high, the concentration of data points within specific areas is likely to be low (generally one or two sensors per room).

INTERPRETING THE RESULTS OF MONITORING

The critical part of diagnostic environmental monitoring is the interpretation. Modern datalogging equipment and graphing software makes the gathering and charting of data quite simple, but interpretation requires an excellent grasp of all aspects of the building structure and environment. It is easy to accumulate a great deal of raw data very quickly, but turning this data into usable and practical information for the building manager can be time-consuming, costly and difficult.

BRINGING TOGETHER INFORMATION FROM DIFFERENT SOURCES

To properly interpret environmental data, it must be correlated with practical issues such as building condition, building use and controls on interior condition. Generally, the first step is to make rough graphs comparing the readings from different clusters, and particularly between the interior and the exterior.

The logged data is then correlated to the information gathered non-electronically, and with anecdotal evidence about when building users feel hot or cold, or find the building draughty. This is important: monitoring takes place over a relatively short period of time in the building's history, and data can only be gathered at a limited number of points. The experiences of those who use the building each day provide a bottom line against which to assess conclusions, and may from time to time provide the key to understanding a building environment of great complexity.

Transforming the mass of data, in many different forms, into usable information is principally a matter of correlating patterns of readings with patterns of events, and interpretation is usually based on comparing trends rather than exact measurements. Without a thorough understanding of the many possible interrelationships between the different environmental parameters it is easy for data to be misinterpreted, and incorrect conclusions to be drawn.

INCORPORATING ERROR

It is also important to take the limitations of the data into account. In most cases there will have been practical constraints on the type of data that could be collected, and many measurements will have been indirect: for example, condensation on a brick wall would be almost impossible to record directly, and so will have to be inferred from measurements of ambient temperature and humidity, and surface temperature. Every measurement will also have some degree of error, incorporating the errors from the equipment and the errors from the way it is being used. Predictable, quantifiable measurement errors are perfectly acceptable, but random errors (for example, inaccurate readings arising from faulty calibration or poor probe positioning) are not.

Most errors can, however, be handled in a fairly broad-brush way: just as problems tend to be fairly obvious in practice, there is rarely such ambiguity in monitored data that the results will be greatly affected by ordinary measurement error.

INTERPRETATION

Environmental monitoring specialists will always refer their findings back to their original hypothesis about the observed patterns of deterioration, even if this ends up being partly or wholly revised as a result of the better understanding of the building environment after monitoring.

In practice, many situations do prove to be remarkably simple to interpret: for example, condensation events can often be related to intermittent heating. At other times, however, variations of microclimate will not equate to any known physical events or material characteristics, and in this case the specialist will need to examine all the possible factors more closely: there may be some aspect of the building fabric or use that has not been sufficiently well characterised. This is why environmental monitoring so often demands special expertise and understanding, not only of the microclimates of buildings, but of all the other aspects that go together to make up the building environment.

Further Reading

Ballard, G. (2007); 'What lies beneath: nondestructive investigation of masonry defects'; in *Historic Churches 2007*; also available at www.buildingconservation.com/articles/nondestructive/nd-masonry.html

Bedford, J., Papworth, H. (eds) (2006); *Measured and Drawn: Techniques and Practice for the Metric Survey of Historic Buildings*; Swindon: English Heritage; also available at www.english-heritage.org.uk/publications/measured-and-drawn/

Booth, S. (2002); 'Measured building surveys'; in *The Building Conservation Directory, 2002*; also available at www.buildingconservation.com/articles/measuredbsurveys/measuredbsurveys.htm

Curteis, T. (2008); 'The survey and identification of environmental deterioration'; in *The Building Conservation Directory, 2008*; also available at www.buildingconservation.com/articles/envdet/environment.html

Demaus, R. (1996); 'Nondestructive investigations'; in *The Building Conservation Directory, 1996*; also available at www.buildingconservation.com/articles/nondestr/nondestr.htm

English Heritage (2006); *Understanding Historic Buildings: A Guide to Good Recording Practice*; London: English Heritage; also available at www.english-heritage.org.uk/publications/understanding-historic-buildings/

Glover, P. V. (2013); *Building Surveys (8th Edition)*; London: Routledge

Howell, J. (2008); *The Rising Damp Myth*; Woodbridge: Nosecone Publications

Lstiburek, J. W. (2009); 'Thermodynamics: it's not rocket science'; in *Building Science Insight 021*; available at www.buildingscience.com/documents/insights/bsi-021-thermodynamics-its-not-rocket-science

MacDonald, L. W. (ed.) (2006); *Digital Heritage: Applying Digital Imaging to Cultural Heritage*; London: Elsevier Butterworth Heinemann

Pinchin, S. E. (2008); 'Techniques for monitoring moisture in walls'; in *Reviews in Conservation*; No.9, pp.33–45

Quarme, G. (1994); 'Quinquennial reports'; in *The Conservation and Repair of Ecclesiastical Buildings, 1994*; also available at www.buildingconservation.com/articles/quinquenn/quinquenn.htm

Ross, K. (2005); *Modern Methods of House Construction: A Surveyor's Guide*; Watford: BRE Trust

Stanbridge, R. (1995); 'Photogrammetry: a practical guide'; in *The Building Conservation Directory, 1995*; also available at www.buildingconservation.com/articles/photogram/photogrammetry.htm

UK Government [CLG, EH, DCMS] (2010); *PPS5 Planning for the Historic Environment: Historic Environment Planning Practice Guide*; available at www.english-heritage.org.uk/publications/pps-practice-guide/pps5practiceguide.pdf

Wingfield, J., Johnston, D., Miles-Shenton, D., Bell, M. (2010); *Co-Heating Test Protocol*; available at www.leedsmet.ac.uk/as/cebe/projects/coheating_test_protocol.pdf

Useful Websites

World Reference Base for Soil Resources: www.fao.org/docrep/W8594E/W8594E00.htm

DIAGNOSIS

This chapter looks at familiar symptoms of environmental deterioration, with a table designed to help the reader move from using the common symptoms-led approach to dealing with environmental problems, to the much more effective approach advocated in this book: that is, identifying and dealing with the underlying causes. It is not a gazetteer of environmental problems, but instead introduces the notion of complexity; how various issues will interact in real buildings, and how a common symptom must be traced back to its roots in failures in the building's design, fabric or use.

Assessment builds a picture of the building envelope, and the way it interacts with its exterior and interior environment, but it is essentially a snapshot of issues at one moment in time; diagnosis puts this information into the long-term context of care and repair. Effective diagnosis demands a robust picture of how the building would behave if it were in good condition, of how it currently is behaving, and of the likely impact of changes that might be made to the fabric or its use.

Most often, a diagnosis of problems in a building's environment is requested because undesirable symptoms have been noticed: leaks, unpleasant interior conditions or deteriorating surface finishes, for example. Diagnosis may also be needed to develop care and maintenance plans, or to confidently design alterations.

Although it is quite common to try to identify the underlying problems from the symptoms they produce, this is rarely possible, because so many different problems will produce damage that looks much the same. 'Damp' at the foot of a cement-rendered exterior wall, caused by a leaking drain at its base, may be indistinguishable from damp caused by water entering the wall from a leaking parapet gutter and travelling down under the force of gravity. Attempting to diagnose from symptoms is also counter-productive when it comes to taking remedial action: if deterioration is to be slowed or prevented, it is the underlying issues that must be addressed, not their symptoms.

REASONS FOR DIAGNOSING

A programme of diagnosis might be initiated for any of a number of different reasons:
- to determine how the building should be managed for the envelope to have the longest possible lifespan with the smallest ongoing input of time and energy
- to ensure that interior conditions are suitable for the intended use of the building
- to decide how to rectify existing problems
- to predict likely future issues, and determine how best to avert them
- to help building alterations to successfully achieve their intentions, without adversely affecting either the operation of the envelope or the interior conditions.

Whatever the aims, effective diagnosis requires a good working understanding of how building environments generally function, coupled with a practical knowledge of the particular building being considered and its environment.

An important dichotomy lies at the heart of diagnosis: on the one hand, every building is unique; on the other, the problems affecting building materials and systems, and the basic ways they behave in response, are very much the same.

In practice, this means that the basic approach to diagnosing differs little, regardless of whether the problem is biodeterioration of the joints in a glass curtain-wall façade (*top right*), moss growth on a medieval ruin (*centre*) or condensation on a 19th-century window (*top left*).

BUILDING ENVIRONMENT
DIAGNOSIS

312 Despite differences in materials, construction and exposure, buildings are more similar than they are dissimilar. Nevertheless, the drivers of environmental problems, such as the transfer of heat and moisture, are so complex that even if it were possible to predict the temperature or moisture content of one particular brick, or one particular wall panel, the same prediction would probably not hold true for its neighbour.

For this reason, *in-situ* observation and measurement will always be the primary tools for diagnosis.

Diagnosis demands a holistic view of the building. The basic design and construction must be considered, together with the materials from which it is made, and the ways those materials interact with each other and the environment. The many complexities introduced by building use will also have to be taken into account: not simply the impact of services, but also the implications of issues such as multiple tenancy, or the use of spaces for activities that may produce moisture or heat or vibration. This wider viewpoint should be considered even when the primary reason for the diagnosis is a small and apparently localised issue, since causes may have their roots elsewhere in the building environment, and remedial action could very well have outcomes that affect other parts of the fabric.

Any diagnosis will have to address some fundamental questions, including:

- What are the principal characteristics of the environment surrounding the building?
- What kind of building is it? What might be expected of this type of construction, or from the building materials that have been used? What would be the likely trouble spots, given the building environment?
- How is it being used? Are there any conflicts between the use of different spaces? Are there any plans to change patterns of use?
- With all this in mind, how should the building be expected to behave? How is it really behaving: does it seem to be functioning correctly, or are there signs of problems?

DIAGNOSING EXISTING PROBLEMS

Often the first indication of environmental issues that is noticed by the building users is damage: the sudden deterioration of internal finishes, signs of 'damp' such as mould or condensation or musty smells, or perhaps unpleasant indoor conditions. Symptoms such as material deterioration are certainly a good warning that something is amiss, but they are of limited help when it comes to diagnosing underlying causes, because so many different problems can lead to much the same patterns of damage. Moreover, an absence of visible damage does not always indicate that all is well with the building or its environment. Attempting to diagnose from effect (rather than cause) also carries the risk that, in the rush to fix the symptoms, the underlying reasons for deterioration will be overlooked, and this can prolong or even exacerbate deterioration.

INTERPRETING SYMPTOMS

The table on the following pages covers some of the symptoms most commonly found in buildings of all types. For each, some typical causes are given, but the list is by no means exhaustive: every situation is unique, and the reasons for observable deterioration may sometimes be very complicated, or related to unusual features of the building or its environment. Often the distribution of deterioration will give the best clues as to its underlying cause or causes. A localised problem is more likely to be traceable to a simple localised fault, whereas generalised deterioration often suggests that there may be more widespread issues. The table's final column gives suggestions for questions that might be asked, or investigations that might be made, to help develop a diagnosis.

The obvious symptoms and signs of deterioration, such as widespread decay and moisture staining at the base of a wall, can be a marker that things are amiss in the building environment, but remedial care demands diagnosis: the identification of causes, which requires the building and its environment to be considered holistically.

BUILDING ENVIRONMENT
DIAGNOSIS

COMMON OBSERVED SYMPTOMS OF ENVIRONMENTAL PROBLEMS

VISIBLE DAMAGE

DESCRIPTION	POSSIBLE CAUSES	ACTIONS TO SUPPORT DIAGNOSIS
TIMBER DECAY (FUNGAL ATTACK) 	Requires prolonged source of liquid water Attack will be confined to wet areas of wood, such as the base of timberwork resting against wet ground	Critical question is whether decay is still active, or evidence of past moisture problems If active, look for source of water (removing this will cause deterioration to stop) Determine whether deterioration is localised or widespread: this may help isolate cause
SALT EFFLORESCENCES 	Liquid water • leaking from above (for example, from blocked gutter, degraded pointing or cement pointing) • penetrating through wall (for example, from blocked downpipe, leaking plumbing) • rising from ground (for example, from blocked drain) May be exacerbated because evaporation is prevented by an impermeable finish or a cement render	Can salts be simply brushed away? Surface crystallisation is not usually very damaging, but less-soluble salts can damage building materials Determine whether deterioration is localised or widespread: this may help isolate cause Source of water may be historic rather than active: salts will continue to effloresce for some time after the source of water has been dealt with and the fabric is beginning to dry
BLISTERING & FLAKING OF SURFACE FINISHES, PLASTER DELAMINATION 	Liquid water • leaking from above (for example, from blocked gutter, degraded pointing or cement pointing) • penetrating through wall (for example, from blocked downpipe, leaking plumbing) • rising from ground (for example, from blocked drain) May be exacerbated because evaporation is prevented by an impermeable finish or a cement render Other causes include poor materials or workmanship	Locate source of water by methodical survey of interior and exterior: • look for leaks and blockages • look for overflows • look for design flaws Determine whether deterioration is localised or widespread: this may help isolate cause Mapping can help to identify relationships between problems and symptoms
STAINING OF SURFACE FINISHES 	Water stains usually suggest a strong source of liquid water, especially from sudden flood; common causes include plumbing leaks Sometimes due to prolonged gradual moisture uptake Staining at height may be associated with condensation or with hygroscopic salts from a chimney flue Rust stains suggest embedded iron, coupled with moisture ingress	Determine whether problem is still ongoing: staining may remain from old moisture problem Determine whether deterioration is localised or widespread: this may help isolate cause Check for possible sources of plumbing leak, such as storage tanks or copper pipes embedded in cement Look for other moisture sources Check for hidden structures and materials, such as blocked chimneys and embedded ironwork

COMMON OBSERVED SYMPTOMS OF ENVIRONMENTAL PROBLEMS

AREAS OF 'DAMP'

DESCRIPTION	POSSIBLE CAUSES	ACTIONS TO SUPPORT DIAGNOSIS
MOULD		
	Most commonly in corners and hidden behind furniture; may be superficial, or may be accompanied by musty smells or other indications of decay Often indicates a liquid moisture problem (usually part of the problem, even where other factors are involved as well) Use of room, especially where ventilation is limited (condensation problems) Impermeable coatings on exterior or interior of wall	Map distribution of decay, and compare to thickness and construction of walls Look for any building flaws leading to liquid moisture ingress, and any signs of condensation, such as runoff under windows. May be necessary to monitor environmental conditions Assess patterns of air movement Look for cold bridges or other cooler surfaces (such as cold pipes) that could attract condensation
MOISTURE AT BASE OF WALLS (SO-CALLED 'RISING DAMP')		
	Source of liquid water; usually from exterior Reservoir may be at the base of the wall, or water may be percolating down through wall from faults in roof, rainwater goods or other higher parts of the building Underlying causes include: • faulty rainwater goods • blocked drains • runoff directed towards building • raised ground level on exterior • rarely: high water table Often exacerbated by impermeable floor finish or exterior wall finish that prevents evaporation	Map distribution of damage: is it localised or general? On interior as well as exterior walls? Localised problems suggest localised sources (that is, not groundwater) Check likely sources of liquid water (such as blockage of exterior drain, impermeable render) If source is unclear, take samples from wall to determine moisture content and distribution Check for wall finishes or other alterations that may be preventing evaporation
MOISTURE UNDER WINDOWS		
	Liquid water penetration around and especially below window: common causes include: • missing or blocked drips under cills • faulty or missing seals around the window • severe condensation on window interior Often exacerbated by impermeable render on exterior preventing evaporation	Check for other sources of water in wall, such as blocked water disposal systems How does rainwater flow around the window? Are the hood mouldings, drips and so on, in good condition? Check for interior conditions causing condensation on the glass and subsequent runoff
GROUND FLOOR MOISTURE		
	Solid ground floor feels cold and damp; may have wet patches, especially near walls, or water beading on impermeable surfaces Most commonly condensation on cold impermeable surface (such as a concrete floor) Liquid water penetration from localised leaks Liquid water penetration from the ground (high water table)	Determine whether deterioration is localised or widespread: this may help isolate cause Map distribution of moisture, and compare to possible building flaws If ground-floor problem is general, excavate to check detailing of floor screed, and so on

BUILDING ENVIRONMENT
DIAGNOSIS

COMMON OBSERVED SYMPTOMS OF ENVIRONMENTAL PROBLEMS

AREAS OF 'DAMP'

DESCRIPTION	POSSIBLE CAUSES	ACTIONS TO SUPPORT DIAGNOSIS
MOIST PATCHES HIGH ON WALL 	Source of liquid water; common causes include: • blocked rainwater goods • chimneys with rainwater penetration • impermeable renders trapping moisture May be hygroscopic salts; sources include: • deposition of combustion products in flue • trapped organic material in flue • building use • internal pollutants (such as sulphate deposits from heating)	Look for decay of embedded timbers (such as joists and lintels) Map distribution of damage, and compare to possible building flaws Look for possible sources of hygroscopic salts If source is unclear, take samples from wall to determine moisture content and distribution, and salt content (look for hygroscopic salts)
CONDENSATION ON IMPERMEABLE SURFACES 	Visible water beading on impermeable surfaces such as glass or metal under certain conditions; wall feels cold and damp to touch; may be damaged finishes or signs of moisture problems (such as decay for timber affected by runoff) May be liquid water problem, with condensation as apparent or real side-effect Unusually thin masonry walls, chilled by wind Liquid moisture problems from other sources, including blocked rainwater goods or drains May well be exacerbated where problems have led to wrong interventions (for example, a cement render)	Under what conditions does water-beading appear? May be necessary to monitor environmental conditions, including surface temperature, and to understand how the heating system is being run Map distribution of damage, and compare to possible building flaws Assess quality of pointing and render, checking especially for fine cracks that could wick in moisture
CONDENSATION INSIDE SECONDARY GLAZING 	Significant condensation on the inside of the glass, occurring regularly; runoff staining below the window; decay of timber cill and horizontal members of windows, or corrosion of horizontal members and joints of metal windows High interior humidity (coupled with cold glass) Insufficient ventilation to exterior, especially where wall has moisture problems	Under what conditions does condensation occur? May be necessary to monitor environmental conditions Look for liquid moisture problems in surrounding wall
CONDENSATION INSIDE INSULATED GLAZING UNIT ('DOUBLE' OR 'TRIPLE' GLAZING) 	Failed seals (these have a limited lifespan) Sometimes cracked glass	Seals can be tested by placing a cup containing dry ice against the glass; if the seals have failed, this will provoke condensation If glass has cracked, look for source: • impact • glazing unit fits too tightly in frame, so that thermal movement causes failure

COMMON OBSERVED SYMPTOMS OF ENVIRONMENTAL PROBLEMS

NON-VISUAL SYMPTOMS

POSSIBLE CAUSES	ACTIONS TO SUPPORT DIAGNOSIS
MUSTY OR DAMP SMELL	
Timber decay Mould growth Most common in areas with limited air circulation	Is the smell present all the time, or only after the room has been shut up? Look for sources of water: most commonly liquid water leaks, but condensation can also be a problem (such as condensation behind impermeable insulation or membranes)
SPACE FEELS 'STUFFY'	
Insufficient air exchange and/or air movement Sources of ventilation such as windows, chimneys sealed up Central air-conditioning system with inadequate filtering or ventilation	Is it a problem at most times, or only in certain conditions or times of the year? Is it a problem in all rooms, or only in certain rooms? Check airflow and air exchange, especially around doors, windows, chimneys
SPACE FEELS DRAUGHTY	
Air leakage through windows, doors or chimneys Open-plan interior: no ability to isolate spaces Poor control systems: heating causing air currents, or pulling in colder air; heating using blowers or localised radiators; air conditioning blowing air too strongly Large areas of glass (thermal bridging)	Is it a problem at most times, or only in certain conditions or times of the day or year? Is it a problem in all rooms, or only in certain rooms? Check condition of windows, doors and so on Check airflow and air exchange, especially around doors, windows, chimneys Check for hidden major air leaks through fabric
SPACE FEELS TOO COLD	
Radiant heat loss to thermal bridges or materials that readily absorb heat from the body, such as: • large areas of glass • thick masonry walls • cold floors Inadequate heating, or heating/cooling system that is badly controlled	Is it a problem at most times, or only in certain conditions or times of the year? What activities are happening in the room? How are occupants dressed? What is the heating system? How is it controlled?
SPACE FEELS TOO HOT	
Solar gain, especially through large areas of glazing Inadequate ventilation Extensive heating system and insulation Inadequate cooling, or heating or cooling that is badly controlled	Is it a problem at most times, or only in certain conditions or times of the year? What activities are happening in the room? How are occupants dressed? Check air temperature, ventilation and air exchange What is the heating/cooling system? How is it controlled? How is the building insulated?
SPACE FEELS HUMID	
Condensation problems Insufficient air exchange and/or air movement Incorrect heating system, or control of heating system Building use involves a great deal of moisture Moisture-resistant materials have been used, such as AVCLs, water-resistant insulation, or impermeable wallpapers or paints	Are there any building flaws letting in liquid moisture? Is it a problem at most times, or only in certain conditions or times of the year? Is it a problem in all rooms, or only in some parts of the building? Check airflow and air exchange, especially around doors, windows, chimneys Monitor to determine vapour content of air, and identify sources of vapour

BUILDING ENVIRONMENT
DIAGNOSIS

DETERMINING CAUSES & RAMIFICATIONS

The fundamental causes of poor building environments can be roughly grouped, with a certain amount of overlap, into issues arising from poor maintenance; from the failure of materials or components with age or exposure; from fundamental flaws in the building envelope such as the design or choice of materials; or from artificial heating or cooling systems that have been poorly designed, operated or maintained.

CAUSES OF ENVIRONMENTAL PROBLEMS

CAUSE	EXAMPLES		
MAINTENANCE ISSUES	BLOCKED OR DAMAGED GUTTERS, DOWNPIPES AND DRAINS Water overflows into fabric	FAILURE OF PROTECTIVE COATING ON TIMBER Water penetrates and is trapped	WINDOW HINGES NOT LUBRICATED Windows will not open or shut correctly
FAILED MATERIALS OR COMPONENTS	GUTTER BRACKETS INSUFFICIENTLY ROBUST OR POORLY FIXED Water overflows into fabric	CRACKED LIME-MORTAR FILLET AROUND CHIMNEY Rainwater penetrates into roof	CASEMENT WINDOW HINGES DISTORTED OR BROKEN Windows will not open or shut correctly
FLAWS IN MATERIALS OR DESIGNS	DOWNPIPES BADLY SPACED OR INADEQUATELY SIZED Water overflows into fabric	CEMENT USED FOR BEDDING RIDGE TILES Brittle material cracks and falls out, increasing risk of wind damage and letting rainwater into roof	NO STAYS ON CASEMENT WINDOW Window can slam open or shut, distorting frame and breaking the glass
CONTROL OF INTERIOR CONDITIONS	POORLY DESIGNED SYSTEM LEADS TO DISCOMFORT Increased heating leads to more damage	INAPPROPRIATE CONTROLS ON HEATING Sporadic use leads to condensation	LEAKING WET HEATING SYSTEM Copper pipes embedded in concrete will corrode

Sometimes a symptom may be traceable back to a single cause, but more often several potential contributory factors will be found, and the primary cause or causes may not be immediately obvious. They may be interdependent, and there may be many knock-on effects and 'vicious circles', where primary damage has led to further deterioration. Water ingress provides the best example of this: the damage that results will often let more water into the fabric, so the problem worsens rapidly. Timber decay can lead to changes in loading that cause structural problems, and these can lead to further water ingress, worsening the problem.

The complexity of environmental deterioration is most clearly shown by a flow chart such as that opposite, which uses a hypothetical example to demonstrate the complications that could potentially arise from a blocked perimeter drain. In this case, the primary symptoms are damage to the interior surface finishes of an external wall and poor interior conditions, but the moisture from the drain is having other less immediately obvious impacts on the envelope. Damage is being exacerbated by poor workmanship and materials: that is, badly specified gutter brackets, and a cement render applied following an earlier misdiagnosis that the damp was due to driving rain penetration.

This example – which is complex but by no means unlikely – makes it clear why diagnosing from symptoms alone is all but impossible. A blocked drain would not be an immediate suspect when trying to understand the decay of a timber window lintel, and yet it is the fundamental cause of this and the other building problems.

The principles of environmental deterioration are straightforward, but to understand the problems of any real building and satisfactorily resolve them, every effort must be made to properly understand the unique characteristics of the case.

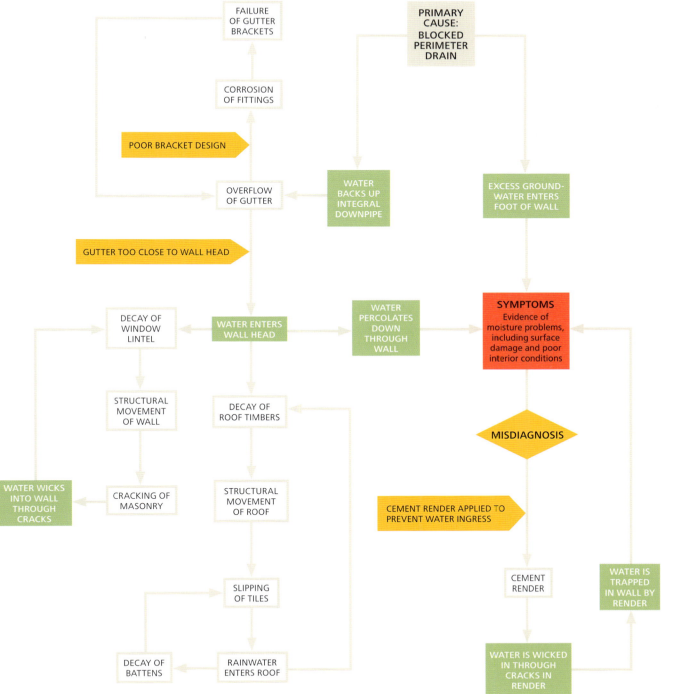

BUILDING ENVIRONMENT
DIAGNOSIS

IDENTIFYING FUNDAMENTAL CAUSES

The first step is to narrow the list of possible causes for the observed symptoms down to those that are likely to be critical, given the type of building and the nature of its environment. There will often be more than one source of problem, especially if deterioration has been continuing for some time.

Looking at the Exterior

In most problems liquid water will be involved, so usually it is best to begin by looking for water sources. All the obvious sources of liquid ingress – including faulty rainwater disposal, drainage and plumbing –- should be removed from contention first, before moving on if necessary to consider more complex and uncommon sources (such as condensation of water vapour). Understanding complex issues may require specialist help, so it is sensible to leave aside complicated potential causes until it is quite clear that they must indeed be critical to the observed problems.

Often this process proves to be quite straightforward, with diagnosis arising naturally out of the environmental survey (see **Assessment**), but sometimes causes will be more obscure, or there may be so many problems that it is difficult to decide which are critical. The best approach is to follow a logical train of reasoning:

1. Is there a pattern to the damage that points towards the source? For example, is there a blocked downpipe on the other side of the wall to a deteriorating interior finish? If the source of water is not immediately visible (missing roof tiles, perhaps), then secondary effects of a high moisture content (such as dark wet patches or algae and moss growth) may well give a clue to its location.

2. If there is no source in immediate proximity to the deterioration, then where might the water be coming from? Water can move considerable distances, so it is important to understand the forces that might be causing it to do so (gravity or capillary pressure, for example; see the **Building Science** chapter). This understanding can be used to look for aspects of the fabric that may be causing water to move: possibilities include a cement render preventing evaporation, or drawing in rainwater through cracks; an internal beam along which water might run, or voids in which it might collect; or a high moisture content that is allowing rain to wick through a wall during storms.

3. Why is the water producing a problem? In most cases leaks will have to be prolonged and substantial to cause serious issues, so if the source of water is intermittent – rainwater, for example – there is likely to be some other aspect of the building envelope that is preventing evaporation, such as a cement render, or the embedding of pipe work (which also inhibits maintenance).

For other environmental problems not associated with water, such as vibration or thermal issues, the same general principle holds true: first eliminate all the obvious and straightforward causes, before considering the complex causes that may need to be studied using special techniques.

Looking at the Interior

If examining the envelope does not reveal the primary causes of problems, then it will be necessary to look more closely at the impact of building use. This may mean studying the effect of services, of activities that produce heat and water vapour, of the distribution of internal partitions and even furniture, and of deliberate environmental controls, from opening and closing windows to heating and cooling (see **Controlling the Indoor Environment**, and **Deterioration & Damage**).

Again, the questions proceed in logical order:

1. How would services, heating and other such interventions be expected to work?
2. Are there any fundamental misconceptions in their design?
3. If the design is reasonable in principle, how could it be failing in practice? For example, copper embedded in cement will sooner or later corrode, so wherever there are both copper pipes and cement it is wise to look for signs of leaking.

DEALING WITH MULTIPLE CAUSES OF DETERIORATION

If several potential causes can be identified for the observed symptoms, remedial action can still proceed. The first step is to deal with the most serious faults, such as blocked drains and rainwater disposal; fixing these must do the building good, even if it does not solve every problem.

When these 'no-regrets' actions have been taken, the building can be reassessed: has action been sufficient to prevent further deterioration? This question can take some time to answer, since symptoms may continue until the building has recovered. Salt efflorescence, for example, will probably worsen as the fabric dries.

If it is clear that necessary repairs have not solved the underlying issues, action will depend on whether they have induced any improvement at all. If not, the fundamental cause has not been identified, and the building will have to be reassessed, perhaps with the help of specialist techniques. In such cases the deterioration will often be found to relate to variations in the environment (seasonal changes, for example), and diagnosis will require monitoring.

If works produce improvement, but problems rapidly recur, there may be underlying difficulties with the building materials or design. For example, a leak may be traceable to a blocked downpipe, but if the pipe is poorly detailed or too small, even the best maintenance may have trouble preventing problems.

OTHER REASONS FOR DIAGNOSIS

AVOIDING POTENTIAL PROBLEMS

Even where symptoms have not yet been noticed, diagnosis can be used to anticipate potential future issues and plan to avoid them. The basis of this is the building's ongoing care and maintenance plan (see **Care & Repair**).

Potential weak spots can be specified in the plan: not only those parts of the envelope that may need slightly more maintenance than others (for example, areas of gutters which tend to block quickly because they are located near trees that shed flowers or leaves); but also those parts that are intrinsically problematic but difficult to alter, which will need to be watched closely (such as embedded downpipes).

Where diagnosis finds flaws that could lead to very serious deterioration, the question arises of how far preventative action should be taken.

The costs of the possible intervention – not only in terms of resources, but also to the building's historic significance – will need to be weighed against the risks of not intervening. If removing a potentially troublesome material or correcting a flawed design is simple, it is usually a wise precaution. If, on the other hand, it is technically difficult or costly, it is usually better to rely on a robust scheme of regular assessment intended to recognise problems as soon as they begin, and deal with them quickly.

The diagnosis should aim to identify all potential weak spots, and categorise them by the possible actions that could be taken:

1. *Weak spots that can easily be remedied*
   For example, inadequate gutter brackets, which can be replaced.

2. *Weak spots that cannot be completely avoided, but where action could be taken to minimise impact*
   For example, hoppers on valley gutters could be given overflow spouts.

3. *Weak spots that cannot be easily remedied or alleviated, which may have to be dealt with in future if problems do occur*
   For example, embedded downpipes are likely to leak at some point, and may need to be lined or even replaced with new downpipes elsewhere.

It should be remembered that even features likely to be troublesome in the long run (such as cement rendering or repointing, or vapour barriers inserted into walls or roofs without due regard for the risks) do not invariably lead to deterioration. Sometimes the best recommendation will be regular monitoring to ensure that issues are caught quickly if they do begin.

ASSESSING PROPOSED ALTERATIONS

Diagnosis is particularly important where the building's owner or manager needs to understand the potential impact of alterations to the building fabric or environmental controls, or the surroundings, or the way the building is being used. In this case, the aim is to determine:

- the likely ramifications of proposed interventions
- which interventions are least likely to have a detrimental effect
- how to minimise undesirable but unavoidable impacts
- how best to monitor the impact of the alterations when they have been completed.

Since the potential impacts will essentially be unknown, it is vital to have the best possible knowledge of what is there at present, and how the system works as a whole; it may well be necessary to bring in specialist advisers.

From a complete picture of the building as it currently is, it will usually be possible to identify those interventions that are likely to cause problems, and also develop some baselines for design. For example, if sensitive furniture and materials have survived intact in a room for many years, the environmental conditions are obviously suitable to their preservation, and should be retained as far as possible through any alterations.

Alterations can risk changing stable environmental conditions for the worse. Where the environment has been benign, it should be altered as little as possible, and never before the current conditions are properly understood.

The 19th-century library held in the Monk's Dormitory at Durham Cathedral provides a perfect example of this approach. Books and timber are both highly sensitive to poor environmental conditions, so the library's good state of preservation after 150 years indicated that there was no need to alter the natural temperature or humidity.

BUILDING ENVIRONMENT
DIAGNOSIS

Further Reading

Glover, P. V. (2013); *Building Surveys (8th Edition)*; London: Routledge

Hetreed, J. (2008); *The Damp House: A Guide to the Causes and Treatment of Dampness*; Ramsbury, Wiltshire: The Crowood Press

Howell, J. (2008); *The Sunday Telegraph Guide to Looking After Your Property: Everything You Need to Know About Maintaining Your Home (2nd Edition)*; London: Ebury Press

Hunt, R., Suhr, M. (2008); *Old House Handbook: A Practical Guide to Care and Repair*; London: Frances Lincoln

Lstiburek, J. W. (2006); 'Investigating and diagnosing moisture problems'; *Building Science Digest 108*; available at www.buildingscience.com/documents/digests/bsd-108-investigating-and-diagnosing-moisture-problems

Park, S. C. (1996); *Holding the Line: Controlling Unwanted Moisture in Historic Buildings*; US National Park Service Preservation Briefs No.39; available at www.nps.gov/tps/how-to-preserve/briefs/39-control-unwanted-moisture.htm

Richardson, C. (1996); 'Structural movement: is it really a problem?'; in *The Building Conservation Directory, 1996*; also available at www.buildingconservation.com/articles/movement/movement.htm

Rose, W. B. (2005); *Water in Buildings: An Architect's Guide to Moisture and Mold*; New York: Wiley

US Department of the Interior (2004); *The Preservation of Historic Architecture: The US Government's Official Guidelines for Preserving Historic Homes*; Guilford CT: Lyons Press

Watt, D. (2007); *Building Pathology: Principles and Practice (2nd Edition)*; Hoboken, NJ: Wiley-Blackwell

CARE
& REPAIR

Caring for the building environment involves both day-to-day maintenance and occasional, more sweeping, interventions. This chapter begins by looking at the regular tasks needed to keep the building envelope in good condition, and then at the scheduling of maintenance. Finally, it considers in some detail the various repairs and treatments that might be considered to deal with more wide-ranging or intractable problems.

Most buildings can absorb considerable stress from their environment without serious damage, but all will require some degree of regular intervention, since exposure and use must always lead sooner or later to some degree of deterioration. For example, roof coverings protect the interior from sun, wind and rain, but weathering will cause their decay and eventual failure. Rainwater will inevitably wash debris into gutters and downpipes, and cause blockages; and doors and opening windows will gradually succumb to wear and tear. Certain building materials need extra management to prolong their lives: for instance, most metals and softwoods require coatings to protect them from corrosion and decay, and these coatings themselves will have to be refreshed regularly.

For the building environment, care and repair follow on closely from assessment: understanding the root causes of a problem usually makes clear what steps must be taken to manage or resolve it. Most often the answer is ordinary maintenance and repair, such as clearing a gutter, unblocking a downpipe, or fixing a broken tile. With good day-to-day care of this kind, more extensive interventions will be required much less often.

DAY-TO-DAY CARE

Everyday care is central to the ownership and management of every type of building; a building cannot survive indefinitely if it is not maintained, no matter how well it has been designed and constructed.

Although even a derelict building can be bought back to life by repair, it is considerably cheaper and more efficient to keep it in good condition in the first place, and this means dealing effectively with problems as soon as they arise. The basic aim of day-to-day maintenance is to keep all those features and systems of a building that protect its fabric, its interior and its contents from the exterior weather in good working order, without changing its character.

Day-to-day maintenance is often seen as a time and cost burden, but the effort necessary to keep a building in good condition is a tiny fraction of that needed to repair the results of neglect.

BUILDING ENVIRONMENT
CARE & REPAIR

The importance of maintenance is so obvious that it must have been recognised from the very earliest periods. Tasks such as limewashing or renewing mud renders are still undertaken yearly in many traditional communities all over the world. Some regular treatments were considered to steadily improve the fabric: for example, limewashing filled hairline cracks and thus limited water penetration; this was sometimes described as 'feeding' the stone. ⇨STONE ⇨MORTARS ⇨EARTH & BRICK

Historians of vernacular architecture have shown how 14th-century landlords were anxious to ensure their tenants maintained the buildings on their holdings, to prevent dilapidation. Good maintenance must have been quite straightforward at this period, because the construction and operation of the buildings were well understood by their occupants as well as by their builders. Most skills and materials were sourced locally, and the buildings were therefore easy to keep in good working condition.

Vernacular cottages and barns were also well able to cope with local weather conditions, simply because those that were not well designed or had been poorly constructed tended to be altered until they worked, or else simply pulled down and replaced with something better. Buildings designed primarily with aesthetics in mind proved more troublesome. Features such as parapets and hidden drains are difficult to maintain, and so are a frequent cause of problems, as evidenced by the terrace houses which began to dominate cities in the 18th century.

Terrace houses and other types of multiple ownership and occupancy also created new problems for planning maintenance. Even where the roof is functionally a single unit (and would therefore best be maintained with a single overall strategy), the owner of each house would often be responsible only for 'their' section of the roof. Who is responsible for a single downpipe that serves two or three houses, each perhaps divided into flats? These aspects of maintenance are rarely built into management plans, if indeed a maintenance plan for the building exists.

Other issues that are currently making care and maintenance difficult include:

- *Different patterns of use*
  The way buildings are used has changed dramatically since the Second World War. Parish churches, for example, were once centres of local life, with twice-daily services being typical, but today they might be used only for a few hours each week.

- *Loss of skills and knowledge*
  Builders were once local, and worked with local materials and systems whose long-term behaviour they understood well. Construction is now more industrialised, often using factory-built components fitted together quickly using an unskilled and itinerant workforce having little or no training, particularly in traditional building techniques and materials. There is little chance to learn from mistakes.

- *Loss of repair materials*
  Many traditional building materials are becoming difficult or impossible to source to the same quality as was previously available. ⇨MORTARS ⇨METALS ⇨EARTH & BRICK ⇨ROOFING ⇨GLASS ⇨STONE ⇨TIMBER ⇨CONCRETE

- *The introduction of services*
  Services such as plumbing and electricity are now central to buildings of all kinds, but they are a recent addition, and their design and installation may not take sufficient account of maintenance needs.

- *Environmental and climate change*
  Environmental conditions may have altered dramatically from those for which the building was designed. For example, rainfall may have become stronger or wind exposure may have changed.

Other issues have arisen from changes in society, and these too have had an enormous impact not only on the way buildings are constructed, but how they are used and cared for. Critical changes include a 'throw-away' culture (where repair is considered less desirable than replacement), increasing expectations of comfort and ease, and the unintended consequences of regulation and legislation.

Owners and occupants increasingly have an expectation that buildings can be made 'maintenance-free'. For example, it has been claimed that many house owners would rather replace their windows every 25 years than repaint them every seven years, even though the cost of replacement is many times greater (and the cost to the environment greater again). Part of the reason for the adoption of modern materials and constructions has been the assumption that they require little or no maintenance. This has led to the inference that a requirement for ongoing care is a drawback peculiar to traditional construction. It has also meant that the maintenance of important modern buildings has often been inadequate.

Another unfortunate change has been the fashion for finishes such as impermeable paints and wallpapers, or waterproof renders, which can hide or even worsen underlying problems. This means that deterioration may only be spotted when it has become very severe, and demanding of radical repair.

Laws and taxes can also have unintended consequences: for example, in England, VAT is charged on maintenance and repair, but not on new construction. Health-and-safety legislation can be interpreted to mean that simple tasks must be done professionally; maintenance that would in the past have been immediately undertaken from a ladder (such as clearing gutters or replacing slipped roof tiles) may be left until a scaffolding can be put in place. Legislation also sets ever-stricter definitions for what constitutes an acceptable environment, especially for work spaces, and building managers may feel obliged to install artificial lighting and climate control, even where these are unlikely to achieve the results expected of them.

Many of these issues will change again over time, and replacement and rebuilding may become less attractive options than they currently appear. Material and energy costs are rising, and with an ever-increasing population, labour costs may begin to fall; there are increasing legislative requirements that buildings be 'sustainable'. Whatever the future may hold, however, the best way of prolonging a building's lifespan and use, and averting problems, is to keep every building under a good regime of ongoing care.

PLANNING CARE PROGRAMMES

Because every building is essentially unique in its construction, environment and use, it should have a specific plan for care and maintenance. This must incorporate a timetable for survey and assessment as well as for regular maintenance tasks, and make provision for more interventive works whenever these are required.

Grant-giving bodies such as English Heritage usually require costed maintenance plans to be submitted as a condition of grants. These documents are usually divided by building element, and for each element a list is compiled of all the necessary tasks and their frequency (occasional, regular or cyclical), the person responsible, and the estimated costs.

In truth, most maintenance falls neatly under the umbrella of 'good common sense': a plan is developed by identifying the sources of potential problems, and then designing a care regime that stops those problems from occurring. What tasks will be needed, and how often, will depend on the type of building, its surroundings and its use. Some (such as sweeping leaves from gulleys) form part of general housekeeping, and should be completed whenever necessary, which in some seasons might even be as often as once every few days. Most other tasks will need to happen seasonally, occasionally, or no more than once every few years.

Where access is easy, maintenance can be less rigorous, simply because it can be more regular. For example, perimeter drains are accessible, and so should be swept clear weekly and after heavy rainfall. By contrast, surveys and maintenance of inaccessible features (such as gutters or flashings that can only be reached with scaffolding or an elevated platform) will need to be much more thorough.

It is not possible, and neither is it wise, to try to generate a perfect maintenance plan in one go. Instead it is best to set up a process of regular revision and refinement. From time to time, this may mean incorporating new information about best practice, or testing innovative methods and materials to deal with intractable problems.

UNDERSTANDING THE BUILDING

Understanding the building is the foundation for good scheduling and budgeting, as well as for quicker and more effective maintenance.

The first step is to bring together all available information about the building's construction and use from surveys and background information, and identify the particular characteristics of the building and its surroundings that will need to be taken into account. Essentially, this means understanding how the envelope behaves under both good and bad conditions. The object is to compile a list of the most likely sources of trouble.

The whole site must be taken into account, including any aspects of the surroundings that could conceivably cause problems (vegetation on or near to the building, or drainage and runoff, or roads running close by, for example). Working methodically around the entire site, all areas of concern should be listed (these will invariably include all parts of the water-disposal systems). Buildings often have features that were designed for convenience or aesthetics rather than maintenance, and which therefore conflict with preservation, and the care programme will need to take into account any intrinsic shortcomings such as these. For example, concealed downpipes will need scheduled regular investigation so that blockages or leaks can be recognised and dealt with as soon as possible.

Areas that have been persistently problematic may often stand out because they have been subjected to repeated interventions. In some cases it will be the interventions themselves that have caused problems. Many of these will be traceable to the changes in building materials and systems since the Industrial Revolution, and particularly since the First World War. This has led to a number of issues pertinent to care and maintenance planning:

- Using materials such as cement, metals, plastics, resins and glass for care and repair can introduce new problems: for example, cement renders and pointing can develop fissures that cause moisture ingress. Some of these problems may not be very well understood, especially those that arise from using modern and traditional systems together.
- Traditional materials such as hand-wrought iron or slow-grown timber can now be very hard to find, making minor repairs much more difficult.
- Building skills may also be difficult to source, particularly those covering traditional methods and materials.

Planning must also take account of the way the building is being used; some patterns of occupation, such as multiple occupancy, can have important implications.

BUILDING ENVIRONMENT
CARE & REPAIR

DEVELOPING AN INSPECTION SCHEDULE

Once a thorough list of potential problems has been compiled, the next step is to determine what will be needed for prevention, or for management where prevention is impossible. ●BASICS

Areas of concern should be rated by the risk they pose to the building, taking into account both the likely severity of any problems that might result, and the significance of any features that might be affected. For example, it is much less dangerous to leave faulty pointing for a year or two than it is to ignore a blocked drain or downpipe, or an area of slipped roof tiles. The resulting schedule can then be used to make:

- a checklist for maintenance surveys
- a list and timetable for routine works.

TIMETABLING MAINTENANCE INSPECTIONS

Three types of inspection will be needed:

- *Periodic inspections*
  Regular scheduled surveys to check the building as a whole, and especially those areas flagged as of particular concern in the survey schedule. These should be undertaken at least twice a year: at the end of spring (when seeds and flowers will need to be removed and biological problems assessed), and at the end of autumn (when leaves will need to be cleared, and the building prepared for winter).

- *Occasional inspections*
  Surveys after potentially damaging events such as storms; these should concentrate on areas known to be sensitive to wind and rain.

- *Scheduled major inspections:*
  Examples include Quinquennial Inspections.

Regular surveys and inspections after damaging events are both best undertaken by the people responsible for the day-to-day operation of the building, who are most likely to be aware of problems. By being obliged to look at the building in a structured way during these surveys, they soon develop a familiarity with the envelope that allows them to inspect quickly and effectively, and also to immediately notice sudden changes.

Those having day-to-day charge of the building should also be part of the major inspections, but these should also include an 'outside eye' (most usually a professional such as a surveyor or architect), who may spot issues that have developed very gradually.

Inspections of all types should include the provision to make minor repairs at the same time (such as clearing downpipes and drains). If the inspection has required special access provisions to be made, it will be sensible to undertake any minor repairs (such as clearing gutters and refixing slipped roof tiles) whilst those provisions are still in place. Similarly, if access is put in place for works, the opportunity for surveying hard-to-reach areas should not be lost.

Repairs that cannot be undertaken immediately should be entered into the maintenance logbook for future action, with an indication of how urgent they are. ●BASICS

Maintenance Logbooks

Regular and routine tasks (such as scheduled surveys, post-storm inspections and clearing of rainwater goods) are entered into a building maintenance logbook, with space to record findings and other works such as minor repairs.

Logbooks act as a reminder to those caring for the building, as well as providing a record of building works which should prove useful in future. There should be space to record the date and details of inspections and works, the weather, and any problems or issues noted at the time, either as notes or drawings (photographs can be an invaluable supplement). Records of actions should include when the work was done and by whom, as well as the materials and methods used.

If, during the inspection, something is noticed that may cause problems in future – such as a critical building element that is nearing the end of its lifespan – this should be clearly flagged in the logbook so that it can be checked in subsequent inspections.

The *Conservation Basics* volume in this series has more information about building maintenance logbooks. ⊝BASICS

British Standards

BUILDING MAINTENANCE

BS 7913: 2013 Guide to the conservation of historic buildings

Defines maintenance as *"the continuous care of a historic building and ... the most common and important activity in their conservation and preservation"*. It notes that: *"The details and methods of managing maintenance are largely determined by the type of historic building strategy. They should specify preventative rather than corrective action with minimum intervention, and repair over replacement."*

BS 7913 also advises that historic buildings should have manuals that describe their maintenance requirements, and log books in which to record checks and maintenance.

BS 8210: 2012 Guide to facilities maintenance management

Standard intended to cover the management of maintenance *"at strategic and technical levels"*, and covering both regular and planned maintenance.

BUILDING ENVIRONMENT
CARE & REPAIR

ROUTINE MAINTENANCE TASKS

Routine care incorporates both the regular maintenance tasks needed to keep the building envelope in good condition, and any tasks identified as necessary during maintenance inspections or required by law (for example, for health and safety).

For each task, it is necessary to determine who has primary responsibility. This will usually be the building owner or manager, but for some building elements it may be a specialist contractor. Where possible it is best not to rely too heavily on external help for day-to-day tasks, since familiarity with the building usually yields the best care, but exceptions include situations where access raises health-and-safety concerns, or where the work itself requires specialist skills (for instance, contractors able to lift metal roof sheets for underside inspection without causing damage).

Even minor interventions will usually involve some loss of original material, and so should not be undertaken without proper consideration (see **Treatment & Repair**). In the end, the urgency of action may depend as much on accessibility as on the severity of the problem. For an accessible element it is usually enough to flag a problem area for regular examination, so that repairs can quickly be instigated if and when the need arises. By contrast, areas of the building that are difficult to inspect should usually be repaired as soon as possible, even if the problem has not yet progressed very far; certainly whilst access is still in place.

Correctly prioritising maintenance tasks demands an understanding of the particular needs of the building. For example, the regular removal of debris (especially dead leaves) is by no means essential for most roof coverings, but it is central to the care of thatch.

Exactly what tasks are required will depend on the building and its surroundings, although there are a number of general tasks that will almost always be required, such as those to prevent common causes of damage before problems can occur, and those to keep important building systems in good working order.

When planning care regimes, it is important to take into account the potential knock-on effects of maintenance issues. For example, much plant growth on walls will have little or no deleterious effect, and can safely be left, but in certain locations even benign plants may trap water and debris, and lead to deterioration. It is important to consider the building holistically.

PREVENTING DAMAGE

Although building owners and advisers may be unable to influence certain fundamental reasons for environmental deterioration (such as the local topography), a number of regular tasks can prevent secondary causes of damage arising.

Some of the dangers of high winds can be reduced if local planting is kept under control. If any tree is close enough to a building to cause damage should it lose branches or be brought down in a storm, it might either need to be cut down or checked yearly by a tree surgeon, who can remove any dead or dying branches and pollard if necessary. Where a Tree Preservation Order is in place, this will require formal planning consent. ⊖BASICS

Tree branches should be pruned back so that they are kept well away from roofs. As well as cutting down on the quantity of leaves, twigs and flowers falling on the roof and gutters, this also allows better air circulation for drying the roof after rain. It is especially important for thatch, where rainwater dripping from overhanging branches can quickly cause decay.

Plant roots should not be allowed to disturb drainage, and should certainly be removed if they have entered drainpipes, or else they will quickly proliferate and block the pipe. The best approach is to keep invasive planting well away from the drainage system, either by replanting or, if the plants are important, by re-routing the drain. This should be coupled with frequent maintenance, so that any blockages can be found and removed quickly, before they can do any serious damage.

If roots have found their way into drains, more extensive intervention will be needed (see **Treatment & Repair**).

BUILDING ENVIRONMENT
CARE & REPAIR

Dealing with Plants Growing on the Building

Non-woody plants are unlikely to do major harm to the fabric, but they should be removed by hand if they are tending to trap debris and water. Any damage should be repaired immediately, to prevent water ingress.

Woody perennial seedlings growing on the building should always be removed, preferably by hand weeding, although larger plants may have to be killed first with a herbicide. For plants that are well established, it may be necessary to first cut back, and then treat the stumps with a herbicide.

Ivy on buildings can sometimes be damaging, but it may also be benign or even in some cases protective: whether removal is necessary or even advisable depends on the particular situation. Ivy produces aerial rootlets that hold its stems onto the surface up which it is growing, but if these remain small they will not be a problem; however, sometimes proper roots are produced, and these may cause damage by growing into the support and thickening. If this has occurred, or if the stem originates from the building rather than from the ground, it is best to remove the plant as soon as possible. Ivy should never be cut at the root and left to die, as this often encourages it to properly root into the support. It has also been found that treating ivy with herbicide before removal actually makes removal more difficult. If removal is necessary, the easiest way is simply to carefully pull stems away from the building in small sections, repairing any damage to the support. The *Conservation Basics* volume includes more details about dealing with vegetation in general and ivy in particular. ⊖BASICS

Bioremediation

Pesticides (including biocides and herbicides) are rarely a long-term option: as well as being dangerous to plants and animals that are not problematic, and possibly to the building fabric, they can be difficult to apply successfully. Even if they do succeed in removing the pest species for a time, the treatment will probably have to be repeated regularly.

One alternative is bioremediation: that is, altering the environmental conditions to make them less suitable for the problematic species. This is very effective for dealing with many of the fungi and insects causing timber decay: these depend on the wood being very wet, so if the source of moisture is removed, the problem will generally resolve itself. In many other cases, however, results are less certain, and there is a real risk that the new conditions may prove ideal for some different pest.

Managing Wildlife Issues

In England most birds and many other animals are protected by law. For example, it is illegal to disturb a bird nest until after the nesting season, and bat roosts must not be disturbed at all except with explicit approval from Natural England.

The best way of treating wildlife damage depends on what the species is, and how it is using the building. If the building is being exploited as a direct source of food, or because it supports some food such as insects, then the primary defence is to remove the food sources wherever possible; but this is something over which the property manager has little control. The best alternative is to protect sensitive areas of the building with nets or something similar. If the building is being used as a shelter, and the law allows the building owner to take action, it may be possible to remove the wildlife, or wait until it has left in the course of the day and then block access; though note that access to bat roosts must never be restricted. For some species, it may be possible to make alternative shelters in less sensitive positions.

Treatment & Repair has more information about approaches to dealing with wildlife issues.

KEEPING SYSTEMS IN GOOD WORKING ORDER

ROOFS & WATER DISPOSAL SYSTEMS

The main focus of building maintenance is invariably the system made up of the roof, the rainwater disposal and the ground drainage systems. Problems with this system should ideally be detected as early as possible, and then dealt with immediately.

Faults in the rainwater disposal will usually be found to be due to blockages, often with associated leaks though joints. Water trapped in cast-iron downpipes by prolonged blockages will eventually lead to the pipe corroding through.

The condition of the roof covering is particularly important if the loft space has been converted or the roof is designed in such a way that penetrating rainwater does not quickly evaporate. It will need to be checked, and repaired if necessary, as soon as possible after any high winds or storms that might have caused damage.

Many traditional roofs incorporated a great deal of natural ventilation, which helped to dry the supporting timbers should any rain penetrate during storms; however, many other roofs with little or no ventilation also survive in good condition.

Elements of the building envelope should be judged in each case by how well they are actually working, and on whether or not there is any sign of deterioration, rather than on theories about 'ideal' design. If a system is functioning well, it does not need to be altered.

BUILDING ENVIRONMENT
CARE & REPAIR

Keeping the Roof Covering in Good Condition

In all roofs, the ridge and hip protection must be kept in good condition, and valleys kept clear of debris. All the weatherings (metal flashings and mortar fillets) should be checked regularly, and repaired or replaced as necessary. Lime mortars should never be replaced with cement, which is brittle, especially to secure ridge cappings: instead, suitable hydraulic lime mixtures should be used, with hair added to fillet mortars to increase tensile strength. The *Mortars, Renders & Plasters* volume of this series gives information about the properties of different mortar mixes. ➔MORTARS ➔METALS

The *Roofing* volume in this series discusses in detail the care and maintenance of the various different roof coverings; the following table gives a synopsis of some of the most important specific maintenance considerations. ➔ROOFING

GENERAL CARE & MAINTENANCE OF ROOF COVERINGS

COVERING	LIKELY ISSUES	ACTIONS
THATCH	Localised and persistent dripping of water can cause thatch to rot	Ensure there are no branches, aerials and so forth overhanging the roof
	Squirrels and birds attacking straw in search of nesting material or insects, or to gain access to roof space	Add netting or wiring; this must be kept clear of debris to prevent trapping water against thatch
SLATES & TILES	Individual tiles or slates have slipped or broken; usually due to wind or foot traffic	Should be straightened or replaced as quickly as possible
	Areas of tiles or slates that have slipped due to failure of battens	Fix source of batten failure (decay due to leak?); replace battens and re-tile
SHEET METAL	Tearing at fixing points, cracking and splitting of sheets due to age, design	Will probably require sheet to be replaced; assess design*
	Perforation due to impact	Patch repair
	Perforation due to underside corrosion	Change underside detailing; replace sheet
	Slippage of sheet due to pitch and detailing	Replace sheet; reconsider detailing to prevent problem recurring*
	Crushed standing seam or hollow roll (usually due to careless foot traffic)	Repair; consider installing duck-boarding or similar protection against damage
ASPHALT	Perforation due to impact	Patch repair

* Although historic designs for roof coverings may be different to modern 'best practice', they usually work very well. On the other hand, various periods of re-roofing may have introduced unsuitable detailing. Existing designs should be retained when the covering is being replaced, unless they are demonstrably causing problems.

Keeping the Water Disposal Systems Functional

Any blockages in the gutters and hoppers or the downpipes should be cleared, and any damage repaired. Gutters do not need to have a fall, but they will not work effectively if their supports are poorly positioned or are failing, allowing the gutter to sag in places. If this is the case, they should be straightened and re-hung, preferably so that any overflow spills out away from the wall. To prevent galvanic corrosion, fittings should be made of metals compatible with that of the gutter. ⊖METALS

Metal gutters and pipes will need regular repainting to prevent corrosion. It is more effective to aim for patch repainting as part of the yearly maintenance, together with very occasional major repaints, rather than to rely on special coatings and linings that promise long maintenance-free lives. If these are to be effective, they require the metal to be cleaned and prepared to a degree almost impossible to achieve on site, and even then they will crack and fail at joints much more quickly. If water is able to enter through cracks, it can cause the deterioration of even very corrosion-resistant metals such as aluminium. ⊖METALS

Blockages in gulleys, drains and soakaways will need to be cleared by rodding or flushing; if this proves ineffective, they will have to be excavated as soon as possible.

Designing for maintenance

When water-handling systems need replacement, it is well worth designing them not only to resist blocking, but to allow easy clearance when blocking does occur.

1–4. It is straightforward to unblock a downpipe that has not been sealed at the joints.

5. Unblocking a well-designed gulley.

BUILDING ENVIRONMENT
CARE & REPAIR

Protecting Gutters from Blocking by Debris

Installing a system to prevent gutters and downpipes from being blocked by debris washing down the roof prevents overflows, and cuts maintenance considerably. Many types of guard are available; as well as systems intended to protect the runs of gutters, there are leaf guards designed specifically to protect the top of the downpipe.

Ideally, protective gutter systems should stop most or all debris, without becoming blocked themselves, or preventing water running into the gutter. Most rely on wind to blow dried debris off from the top of the guard, but some designs are more successful at this than others, and it will also depend on exposure. There is no such thing as a totally maintenance-free system: all will need to be occasionally removed and cleaned, so ease of detachment and cleaning should also be taken into account.

The most suitable system will depend on the type and quantity of debris falling into the gutters, the space available in the gutter, and whether the gutter and the attachment system are compatible. The most effective and longest-lived appear to be brushes and rigid metal meshes.

There are many proprietary systems available which promise to prevent or reduce blockages by leaves, twigs, moss and other debris; one of the most effective appears to be gutter brushes, which do not significantly impair water flow.

Foams & Sponges

Foams and sponges, some rigid and some flexible, are designed to be fixed into the gutter using silicone sealants.

These are not in general a good choice, since they tend to develop a layer of debris on the top that stops water entering. Like gravel-filled drains, they prevent evaporative drying and tend to quickly silt up, encouraging trapped seeds to germinate. Cleaning is difficult and messy.

Reverse Curves

Reverse curves are solid guards with slots to let water through, and shaped to encourage debris to slide off. They are fitted across the top of the gutter.

Reverse curves may be made of plastic or metal; both are quite susceptible to denting and other mechanical damage, and built-up snow and ice can also cause distortion. Surface tension is meant to encourage water to enter through the slots and into the gutter, but this may only happen under light rainfall conditions, and may also be disrupted by wind. The gutter may therefore tend to overflow in storms. Failure is also likely in freezing weather, when the result may be ice dams.

The slots allow finer debris through, and tend to clog very quickly; but systems can be difficult to remove for cleaning. Covered gutters may well attract nesting birds, or insects and rodents seeking shelter.

Meshes

Mesh screens, sometimes curved outwards, are also designed to be fixed across the top of the gutter. Meshes used range from thin and flexible to fairly heavy grilles, in materials ranging from metals to plastics.

Finer meshes tend to block, but coarser meshes may let through certain types of debris, such as pine needles, and so may not be suitable in all locations. Plastic meshes can distort and fail when exposed to sunlight or cold weather, and the finer flexible metal meshes will also tend to curl under the weight of collected debris. Some finer meshes may also be prone to tearing and other damage.

The most robust and effective systems use heavy-duty meshes made of surgical-grade stainless steel. Care needs to be taken to ensure that galvanic corrosion is not caused by the mixture of metals in the gutter, mesh and fixings.

Brushes

Long 'bottle brushes' made of polypropylene filaments, fixed to a core of stainless-steel wire, are designed to simply be laid down in the gutter, and need no extra fixing.

Larger debris tends to be blown off the surface quite easily, and though small pieces of moss or twig may be trapped in the fibres, this does not appear to affect drainage; indeed, these systems do appear to remain effective with very little ongoing maintenance. The brushes may occasionally be visible from the ground, especially if the gutter is shallow. Should this be an issue, they are available in a number of different colours.

Protecting Gutters from Blocking by Ice

To prevent gutters or other parts of the rainwater disposal system from being blocked by ice in high-risk areas, it is possible to install electric trace heating, also known as 'heat tape'. This cannot keep the gutters entirely free of ice or snow, but is intended to keep enough of the system clear to allow meltwater to drain away. The control systems can be very complex, demanding centralised monitoring as well as a supply of power.

CHIMNEYS

Chimney stacks are a common site for moisture penetration, and so must be kept in good condition. Missing pots will need to be replaced, and rain can usually be prevented from running down the flue by capping. Ventilated caps are available both for disused flues, and for flues that are still being used. These can be clay or metal; since they will be very noticeable, it is important to choose materials and designs that will appear in keeping with the building. Suitable lime-based mortars should be used for repairing pointing and mortar fillets. ⊃MORTARS

More serious problems with chimneys may need significant intervention (see **Treatment & Repair**).

WALLS

Leaking through walls of all types can often be traced to problems with the water disposal; finding the moisture source and dealing with it usually resolves the issue, and the walls can then be left to dry without further intervention. If the problem is with the weatherproofing of the wall itself, this should be repaired using appropriate materials.

For traditional and modern walls built with permeable materials, this means repairing the pointing, rendering and weatherings using permeable mortars, so that any water that enters will be able to evaporate again. Earthen walls should be limewashed regularly, even if they are protected with an earthen or lime render. ⊃STONE ⊃EARTH & BRICK ⊃MORTARS

For half-timbered construction, the likeliest point for problems is the joint between the frame and the infill panel, so this should be repaired if it shows signs of cracking or other failure. Most exposed timber is hardwood, which does not require a coating to protect it from the sun and rain. Indeed, water-resistant paints may trap moisture, and lead to decay. A traditional alternative was lime-washing, which was believed to protect the timber against wood borers. ⊃TIMBER

Shingles and other tiled cladding should be checked for breakages and displacements; these should be re-hung or replaced as necessary. ⊃ROOFING

The internal drains of hollow-wall construction will need to be checked and cleared if necessary (this is rarely easy, and unfortunately may sometimes be almost impossible). For curtain walling, the seals will eventually fail and let in water; if so, they will need to be replaced. The fixings on systems such as 'planar' glazing will need to be tightened regularly, especially if the building is very exposed. ⊃EARTH & BRICK ⊃GLASS

OPENINGS

Windows and doors must be kept in good working order: if they are difficult to open or close, users will sooner or later force them into position, and this will cause more damage. Excess overpaint must be cleared away, and hinges and other fittings oiled as necessary.
➔GLASS ➔METALS

All softwood frames will require regular painting or coating; permeable materials should be chosen to minimise the risk of trapping water, which could easily lead to decay. Protective coatings will also be needed for frames made of wrought iron or steel.
➔GLASS ➔METALS ➔TIMBER

INTERIOR MAINTENANCE

The interior should be checked regularly for signs of environmental problems such as staining, blistering or cracking of internal finishes, timber decay, or vermin infestation. Plumbing is a common source of moisture problems, although this is often omitted from standard checklists of potential trouble-spots. All internal pipe work and any storage tanks will need to be inspected regularly and kept well maintained (especially tanks and pipes in roof spaces, where a leak can quickly cause a great deal of damage).

For modern construction, areas which will need regular checking include the seals of IGUs, which have a limited lifespan, and any drainage trays. For planar glazing, the settings on fixing bolts will need to be checked and adjusted as necessary. ➔GLASS

Leaking plumbing is a common source of moisture problems, but one that may pass unrecognised. Here, leaking pipes under a floor have caused serious timber decay.

If mould and condensation cannot be traced back to a problem with the envelope, the heating and ventilation regimes should be assessed, and adjusted as necessary. Any changes will probably need to be monitored closely to make sure they are having the desired effect, and are not introducing new issues.

A detailed checklist of internal maintenance tasks can be found in the *Conservation Basics* volume of this series. ➔BASICS

BUILDING ENVIRONMENT
CARE & REPAIR

General Task Lists for Environmental Building Maintenance

The following tables are adapted from English Heritage guidance, and list the typical tasks needed to care for a building envelope, arranged by when they should be undertaken (weekly, monthly, half-yearly, yearly and less often).

This list is by no means exhaustive, and some tasks listed may not be relevant to every building, but it can serve as a starting point for developing a building-specific maintenance schedule. The other volumes in the *Practical Building Conservation* series will help identify specialist tasks for particular materials, and *Conservation Basics* includes a complete table of all building maintenance tasks. ⊕BASICS ⊕CONCRETE ⊕METALS ⊕EARTH & BRICK ⊕MORTARS ⊕ROOFING ⊕GLASS ⊕STONE ⊕TIMBER

WEEKLY TASKS (OR AFTER STORMY WEATHER)

May be needed much less often, depending on the building type, location, the surroundings, the construction, the time of year and the weather
These checks and maintenance tasks should also be undertaken after storms (it can also be helpful to check operation of envelope during heavy rain)
Roofs, rainwater goods and drainage of curtain-wall façades should be checked after storms
If any temporary repairs are made, a campaign of permanent repairs must be scheduled

ELEMENT	MAIN TASKS	OTHER TASKS (INCLUDING SPECIALIST TASKS)	COMMENTS
GULLEYS & DRAINS	Clear away debris Check function: does water run through correctly?	Clear and repair as necessary	Check after stormy or windy weather
ROOF	Inspect from the ground and accessible high points: look for loss or damage to the ridges, hips and roof coverings Theft of metal has become a serious problem: lead and copper roofs should be checked regularly, particularly if building is not in continual occupation	Repair as necessary For lead or copper roofs at risk of theft, consider installing an alarm or other security system	After stormy or windy weather, chimneys should be checked for damage, and roof spaces for evidence of leaks
GUTTERS & DOWNPIPES	Look for damage and blockages	Repair as necessary	Check after stormy or windy weather

MONTHLY TASKS (SPRING & SUMMER)

May be needed much less often, depending on the building type, location, the surroundings, the construction, the time of year and weather
If any temporary repairs are made, a campaign of permanent repairs must be scheduled

ELEMENT	MAIN TASKS	OTHER TASKS (INCLUDING SPECIALIST TASKS)	COMMENTS
PERIMETER DRAINAGE CHANNELS	Clear away debris Check function: does water run through correctly?	Clear and repair as necessary	Action from May to November: should not be necessary in winter
VENTILATION	ONLY when exterior humidity is low (such as during a prolonged spell of fine, dry weather): open doors and windows to ventilate building		This should never be done early in spring, or in wet weather, since moist air entering may cause condensation

TWICE-YEARLY TASKS

- Tasks to be undertaken in late spring and late autumn (after most blossom and leaf fall), unless otherwise indicated
- May be needed more often, depending on the building type, location, the surroundings, the construction, the time of year and the weather
- Inspect roof and rainwater goods from the ground and accessible high points, or else arrange access equipment
- If any temporary repairs are made, a campaign of permanent repairs must be scheduled
- Decay may not be ongoing; the more familiar the maintenance inspector is with the building, the easier it will be to identify new problems

ELEMENT	MAIN TASKS	OTHER TASKS (INCLUDING SPECIALIST TASKS)	COMMENTS
GUTTERS	Check for cracks and other causes of leaking Check that supports and brackets are working correctly, and that falls are correct (no ponding) Check for blockages, and clear as necessary Check protective guards and netting, and clear as necessary	Repair or replace as necessary If permanent repairs cannot be made immediately, consider temporary repairs using plastic sections; plan for permanent repairs to be carried out	If safe access is an issue, consider installing some means of improved access (such as eye-bolts for tying ladders or protected walkways) Regularly cleaning gutters and/or installing gutter protection will reduce the risk of downpipe blockages
HOPPERS & OVERFLOWS	Check for blockages, and clear as necessary Make sure overflows are clear and functioning Check protective guards and netting, and clear if necessary	Repair or replace as necessary	If safe access is an issue, consider installing some means of improved access (such as eye-bolts for tying ladders or protected walkways) Regularly cleaning hoppers and/or installing protection will reduce the risk of downpipe blockages
RAINWATER DOWNPIPES	Check for blockages, and clear as necessary Check for loss or damage Check that supports and brackets are correctly positioned, and in good repair Check that the water is discharging correctly into drains and gulleys	Repair or replace as necessary	If blockages are a regular problem, consider gutter protection, or redesigning to fix fundamental flaws When replacing downpipes, joints should not be sealed When re-fixing rainwater pipes, consider using spacers to set the pipes away from the wall; this will enable the back to be painted and reduce the rate of corrosion
PERIMETER DRAINAGE	Inspect for cracks and open joints	Repair cracks and open joints with appropriate sealant Repair or replace if necessary	
BELOW-GROUND DRAINAGE	Check that all gulleys and gratings are free from silt and rubbish: clear as necessary Open inspection chambers, to check that water can flow freely into the mains sewerage or the soakaway Check whether plant roots are causing problems Clear and repair as necessary	Use drain rods or high-pressure water jetting to clear blockages Remove tree roots; consider cutting back, or removing trees and shrubs growing close to the line of a drain or divert drainage	Inspect gulleys during heavy rainfall to see whether they back up: this might indicate blockages Lush growth may indicate that roots have entered below-ground pipes
SOAKAWAYS & OTHER WATER DISPOSAL SYSTEMS	Check for blockages	Clear or replace if necessary	Soakaways can be hard to find, so their position should be marked in some permanent way

BUILDING ENVIRONMENT
CARE & REPAIR

TWICE-YEARLY TASKS

ELEMENT	MAIN TASKS	OTHER TASKS (INCLUDING SPECIALIST TASKS)	COMMENTS
EXTERIOR WALLS	Check for signs of structural movement such as cracks and bulging, or displacement of structural members	If movement appears to be active, organise monitoring and investigation by structural engineer	Compare signs of damage with earlier observations: if there is a new problem, to what could it be attributed?
EXTERIOR WALL FINISHES	Check for signs of wear, or problems such as blistering and flaking	Localised repainting, repointing, repair of render If necessary, consider replacement	Are any problems general or localised? If localised, look for source
VENTILATION GRILLES AIR BRICKS WEEP HOLES	Ensure that necessary wall ventilation components are not obstructed (by paint, vegetation or insect nests, for example)	Clear as necessary	Depending on materials and construction and exposure (to flooding, perhaps), it may be wise to consider permanently sealing superfluous wall ventilation
WINDOWS	Check function of opening windows Check glass, frame (timber, metal, putty and so on), lead cames, wire ties and other ferramenta Check any condensation drainage channels and holes, and clear as necessary	Lubricate moving parts as necessary Repair as necessary	Poor function can lead to rough handling, causing more problems
DOORS	Check opening function (hinges and so on) Check function of bolts and locks	Lubricate moving parts as necessary Repair as necessary	Poor function can lead to rough handling, causing more problems
VEGETATION	Ensure climbers are not entering gutters or roof spaces For nearby trees, look for dead branches and signs of ill health Check for root damage to the building or below-ground drainage	Cut back as necessary; remove all invasive species Works may require specialist contractor, or contractor with special access equipment (for example, a tree surgeon may be needed to deal with damaged branches or other signs of weakness) Remove roots near drainage, or divert drainage if necessary	Safe access may be an issue Lush growth may indicate that roots have entered below-ground pipes Avoid cutting back climbing plants, shrubs and trees in late spring or early summer when birds are nesting Algal growth may be a symptom of high levels of moisture: there is little point in removing algae until the source of the water has been addressed
BIRD PROOFING	Check that window ledges, belfry openings, roofs and other sensitive areas are bird-proofed before the spring nesting season In winter (October to February) check for bird nests, and seal access points	Repair and replace protection as necessary	Nesting birds and bats, amongst other animals, are protected by law, and must not be disturbed Consider installing special nesting facilities for protected species
CHIMNEYS & FLUES	Check condition of stack and weathering Check condition of parging or flue liner Where fireplaces or stoves are in use, organise sweeping	Where chimney has spark arrestors, clean away tar and debris from these	Depending on the frequency of use and type of fuel burned, chimneys may need sweeping less or more frequently (if wood fires used year-round, should ideally be swept each quarter)

YEARLY TASKS

May be needed more often, depending on the building type, location, the surroundings, the construction, the time of year and the weather

Roof maintenance should be carried out in late spring, but all other tasks should be scheduled for autumn unless otherwise indicated

Look for defects and signs of problems, but also for any design or materials issues that could lead to problems in the future

If any temporary repairs are made, a campaign of permanent repairs must be scheduled to take place as soon as feasible

ELEMENT	MAIN TASKS	OTHER TASKS (INCLUDING SPECIALIST TASKS)	COMMENTS
ROOF: SLATE OR TILE COVERING	Check bedding and jointing of ridge tiles for cracks and other signs of failure Check for heavy accumulations of moss (holds water, so may increase risk of frost damage)	If there is a moss problem, consider obtaining professional advice Repair as necessary	Most works will require a specialist contractor Where access is difficult, consider ways in which it could be made easier
ROOF: THATCH COVERING	Check fastenings on thatch ridges Check cover for holes, grooves, thinness, bird or animal damage Check for heavy accumulations of moss (holds water, so may increase risk of decay) Check netting for debris; clear as needed	Patch repair as necessary If bird or animal damage is a persistent problem, consider netting If there is a moss problem, consider obtaining professional advice Assess current fire precautions	Most works will require a specialist contractor Where access is difficult, consider ways in which it could be made easier
ROOF: SHEET-METAL COVERING	Check panels for splits or holes, corrosion Check joints and clips	Repair as necessary; if permanent repairs cannot be carried out immediately, make temporary repairs	Most works will require a specialist contractor Where access is difficult, consider ways in which it could be made easier
ROOF: ASPHALT COVERING	Check condition of flat areas and upstands Check for bumps or blistering, and splits, tears or holes in covering Check for evidence of ponding	Repair as necessary; if permanent repairs cannot be carried out immediately, make temporary repairs Bumps and blisters will require immediate attention only if water is penetrating	Most works will require a specialist contractor Where access is difficult, consider ways in which it could be made easier
WEATHERINGS	Check for loss or damage to flashings, flaunching, mortar fillets and other weatherings Renew limewash on mortar fillets and flaunchings as necessary	Repair as necessary; if permanent repairs to lead flashing cannot be carried out immediately, make temporary repairs using adhesive flashing material Splitting of lead flashings may indicate they are oversized or over-fixed: obtain professional advice before renewing	Some repairs may require a specialist contractor Where access is difficult, consider ways in which it could be made easier
VALLEY & PARAPET GUTTERS	Check for blockages and clear as necessary Check for deterioration, damage and any signs of leakage Check for evidence of ponding or overshooting of discharge water	Repair as necessary; if permanent repairs cannot be carried out immediately, make temporary repairs using adhesive flashing Splitting of lead gutter bays may indicate they are oversized or over-fixed: obtain professional advice before renewing	If blockages occur regularly, or the gutter never functions correctly, consider making design improvements
LIGHTNING PROTECTION	Check system is adequate and in good condition (including spikes, tapes, earth rods, and all connections and fastenings)	An approved and experienced engineer should service, repair and upgrade as necessary	Have lightning protection tested every 11 months, so that eventually it has been checked under all conditions

BUILDING ENVIRONMENT
CARE & REPAIR

YEARLY TASKS

ELEMENT	MAIN TASKS	OTHER TASKS (INCLUDING SPECIALIST TASKS)	COMMENTS
ROOF VOIDS	Check for stains and other evidence of roof or gutter leaks Check structural timbers and battens for signs of active decay or insect attack If underside of cover is visible, look for flaws such as defective tile fixings Check for signs of animal damage, or use of the roof by bats or nesting birds	Look for cause of leaks, and repair as necessary Bats and nesting birds should not be disturbed; obtain professional advice If roof is insulated, check insulation for signs of damage or displacement and correct as necessary	Timber decay and insect attack need source of water; this should be located and dealt with to solve problem
COPINGS	Check condition of mortar bedding and joints Remove any vegetation	Repoint and re-bed as required, using appropriate lime-based mortar If guano is a persistent problem, consider installing bird deterrents	If guano is rinsed off, wall below must be protected (runoff can lead to biological growth in previously clean areas)
WALLS: MASONRY	Check for signs of movement (cracking and bulging) Check for surface deterioration, including open joints, and cracked or deeply eroded pointing Check water-shedding features	Arrange for defects to be investigated more closely and remediated	
WALLS: TIMBER-FRAMED	Check for signs of movement and timber decay Check for open joints between timbers and infill panels, or other defects that might let in water Check water-shedding features and flashing Check infill panel for defects	Arrange for defects to be investigated more closely and remediated	
WALLS: EARTHEN	Check for signs of movement such as cracking Check for signs of vermin damage Renew limewash as necessary	Arrange for defects to be investigated more closely and remediated If render is cement, call in specialist to check moisture content of wall	
WALLS: CONCRETE	Check for signs of movement Check for signs of reinforcement corrosion (such as rust stains, cracking and spalling)	Arrange for defects to be investigated more closely and remediated	
WALLS: CURTAIN WALLING	Check gaskets and sealants Check fixings, flashings and protective coatings Check drainage routes, and clear as necessary Planar glazing: adjust bolts according to manufacturer's instructions	Arrange for defects to be investigated more closely and remediated Engage a specialist contractor to carry out minor remedial works, and lubricate moving parts and operating gear	Large areas of modern glazing require inspection, maintenance and repair to be carried out on an annual rolling cycle, with one part of the building thoroughly checked each year
EXTERIOR FINISHES	Check renders for bulging, detachment, cracking, blistering or spalling Check paint finishes for blistering or flaking	Arrange for defects to be investigated more closely and remediated	Problems in exterior finishes may indicate a moisture problem
INTERNAL STRUCTURE & FABRIC	Check for signs of movement in walls Check for signs of moisture problems (for example, staining, damage to surface finishes, mould) and trace cause Check woodwork for signs of infestation	Arrange for defects to be investigated more closely and remediated	Infestations should be checked to see whether they are ongoing; comparison with earlier maintenance inspections is best way of doing this

YEARLY TASKS

ELEMENT	MAIN TASKS	OTHER TASKS (INCLUDING SPECIALIST TASKS)	COMMENTS
FLOOR VOIDS	Check timberwork for signs of fungal growth and timber decay, and trace cause Check for signs of other pests	Arrange for defects to be investigated more closely and dealt with as necessary	
SERVICES	Check that all services are operating correctly Check plumbing for function, and evidence of overflowing and leaks Check water storage tanks; if tank has debris, organise cleaning and improve cover Check that exposed water tanks, water pipes and heating pipes are adequately protected against frost; repair lagging if necessary Check all fire systems and alarm systems	Arrange for defects to be investigated more closely and remediated An approved and experienced engineer should service the fire system and any other alarms	Frost damage could be avoided by installing pressure relief valves (on cold-water piping, the toilets may serve this purpose) It is a legal requirement for landlords to have gas appliances checked annually by an approved engineer
HEATING & BOILER SYSTEMS	Check operation and settings of heating Check chimney pots, flaunchings, mortar joints and fillets, and chimney stacks, for defects Check flues (nests and debris can block in unexpected places, leading to damp, smells, staining and other problems)	An approved and experienced engineer should service the heating system Repair chimney defects as necessary; if stack is cracked or leaning significantly, obtain professional advice Arrange for chimney to be swept; can be the best way to check flues and deal with any problems	It is a legal requirement for landlords to have all gas appliances and flues checked annually by an approved engineer If blockages are a recurrent problem, consider relining or capping the chimney; for disused chimneys, consider ventilated caps to prevent rain penetration

OTHER TASKS

ELEMENT	MAIN TASKS	OTHER TASKS (INCLUDING SPECIALIST TASKS)	COMMENTS
EVERY FOUR TO FIVE YEARS			
ELECTRICAL SERVICES	Inspect all wiring and electrical installations (including portable electrical equipment and church organs)	An approved and experienced engineer should service, repair and upgrade as necessary, in line with Institution of Electrical Engineers regulations	Obligations vary with risk and use of property, and according to statutory requirements: check relevant local government advice
BUILDING & CURTILAGE	Arrange for an accredited conservation architect or building surveyor to carry out a quadrennial or quinquennial inspection		Report should cover building condition, maintenance and repair requirements, timescales and planning
REPAIR & REPAINT	Repaint rainwater goods, timber fascias, doors and window frames (using flexible and permeable coatings to minimise the trapping of water)	Make other redecorations and repairs as necessary	Rainwater goods prone to rusting should be repainted before corrosion can begin, since this makes preparation much easier
OTHER			
DIFFICULT-TO-ACCESS AREAS SUCH AS SPIRES & TOWERS	Whenever other works allow close examination (for example, when scaffolding is erected for other repairs), opportunity should be taken to thoroughly inspect and repair	Arrange for all aspects of area to be investigated more closely, and repairs made as necessary	Specifications for repair should take into account any access difficulties (materials and design should prioritise longevity)

BUILDING ENVIRONMENT
CARE & REPAIR

TREATMENT & REPAIR

To carry out successful interventions, the first step must be to determine exactly what works are intended to achieve. For this it is necessary to think in terms of overall aims, rather than equipment or repairs. For example, if the aim is to prevent walls being wetted by failing gutters, the necessary works might include new gutter supports and repainting, but it will also involve protective systems that prevent the gutters from blocking, and a good regime for ongoing care. In some cases, an improved care regime may mean that extensive repairs are unnecessary.

Interventions will often be to the building controls, rather than to the fabric itself. Here too, caution is needed: ventilation, heating and cooling can all cause the rapid changes in environment that can lead to unexpected problems with the fabric and the contents. This is just as true for interventions perceived to be 'natural', such as opening the window, as it is for 'artificial' interventions such as forced ventilation.

Repairs to deal with persistent environmental issues

Here, long-standing moisture problems have been dealt with by moving the perimeter drains well away from the base of the wall, and installing well-detailed gulleys. The risk of future blockages has been catered for by incorporating easily accessible rodding points.

DEALING WITH PERSISTENT ISSUES

Where recurrent problems cannot be prevented even by the best programme of care, it may be necessary to consider making changes to the fabric or – where possible – the building environment. For example, if the drains block almost every time it rains, it will be wise to consider new and more effective water-disposal systems. This too is a matter of risk assessment: major alterations are most likely to be worth considering where failure will have severe consequences for important parts of the fabric.

Almost always, issues can be traced back to liquid water: a persistent leak, perhaps, or water trapped in the fabric. In the course of maintenance, the sources of any problematic water must be located, and all necessary repairs made to stop penetration and allow the fabric to dry. Often the cause is as simple as a blocked drain, but it is surprisingly common to view the situation as more complex than it really is, and hence to rush into elaborate 'solutions' that may make matters worse. This is as expensive as it is unnecessary: in practice, great improvements often result from very minimal repairs made during day-to-day maintenance.

Sometimes the failure reflects a wider issue: for example, downpipes will block more quickly if they are undersized or badly positioned, or simply too few to handle the area of roof they are expected to drain. In such cases, a different level of intervention will be needed; it may be necessary to rethink the design or materials of critical components of the building envelope.

The keys to effective treatment and repair are a thorough understanding of how the building functions, and a flexible approach to solutions. For instance, it would be unwise to seal windows shut to reduce draughts, if this means that they cannot be opened to increase ventilation if necessary.

Repairs to features that are difficult to access should always be made to the highest possible specification.

It is tempting to try to find perfect solutions that would prevent all future problems, and at the same time not require maintenance. Many proprietary products will claim to deliver this, but in truth perfect answers do not exist: nothing will work on every building under all conditions. Many revolutionary new interventions are quickly found to introduce new and unexpected problems. A safer, and in the long run cheaper, approach is to look for solutions that are 'good enough' to move the building out of danger without incurring additional risk. For example, occasional high relative humidities, leading to condensation in a building where the ambient conditions are usually stable, are best dealt with by installing alarms that notify the building managers when the ambient relative humidity starts to climb, so that they can take action to reduce it, rather than installing a complicated air-conditioning system that attempts to limit the humidity to a narrow band. Intervening only when necessary is not only easier and cheaper, but much better for the fabric and contents.

BUILDING ENVIRONMENT
CARE & REPAIR

Preventing all moisture penetration will be impossible, and 'waterproofing' may simply trap the water, allowing it to do more damage. Every building will eventually suffer some degree of ingress, so the critical task is not to seal the fabric, but rather to ensure that water entering the fabric is able to leave again as quickly as possible.

There is one other type of intervention: major alterations made in response to changes in building design or use. Here flexibility is required too, but for a slightly different reason: because the natural behaviour of the new space is not known, it can be hard to assess the impact of any changes. Again, it is always safest and most cost-effective to proceed quite slowly, step by step, introducing improvements gradually and assessing their impact, rather than immediately locking the building into an elaborate scheme of management that may actually prove unsuitable or unworkable.

Whatever the scale of works being considered, it is necessary to be realistic about the outcomes: some problems really are intractable. Below-ground cellars are a good case in point, since any attempt to dry the wall will simply pull in more water from the ground outside.

Historic repairs may or may not have successfully dealt with the problem they were intended to resolve. They can indicate persistent issues that may still need investigation and thought before a solution is found.

Protected Buildings

Many important historic buildings in England are included in a statutory list of buildings of special architectural or historic interest, compiled by English Heritage for the Secretary of State for Culture, Media and Sport, and some historic structures and sites are designated as scheduled monuments. It is a criminal offence to carry out unauthorised works to a listed building or a scheduled monument. To avoid incurring design and specification costs for work that then proves to be unacceptable, it is wise to discuss proposals with the appropriate authority at an early stage in the project.

LISTED BUILDINGS

At the time of press there were three grades of listing:

- Grade I, covering the top 2.5 % of buildings
- Grade II* ('two-star'), covering the next 5.5 %
- Grade II, covering the remaining 92 % of listed buildings.

Regardless of the grade, when a building is listed the entire building, both inside and out, is protected, as are any fixtures and fittings, and any buildings erected within its grounds (or 'curtilage') before 1st July 1948.

Listing helps to protect buildings from harmful interventions by requiring that a special authorisation, known as 'Listed Building Consent', be obtained from the local planning authority for most alterations, and some repairs. The local planning authority's conservation officer advises on the need for Listed Building Consent. Churches of certain denominations are exempt from the requirement to apply for listed building consent, but must instead apply for permission to the appropriate church authority.

When deciding what works need consent, the relevant authority must consider the effects of the proposed work on the special character of the building. The term 'character' is more extensive than 'appearance', and will also take into account the history of the building, the extent to which the historic fabric might be harmed by the works, and the authenticity of the materials and methods proposed for repair and alteration.

SCHEDULED MONUMENTS

There are over 200 classes of scheduled monument, including historic buildings and structures such as medieval castles, monasteries and farmsteads, and more recent structures such as collieries and Cold War constructions. Scheduling is currently the responsibility of the Secretary of State for Culture, Media and Sport, supported by advice from English Heritage.

Scheduled Monument Consent is required for any work to a scheduled monument, including repairs. Applications for consent are handled by the relevant English Heritage regional office.

BUILDING ENVIRONMENT
CARE & REPAIR

PLANNING INTERVENTIONS

Dealing with problems in the building environment can be as simple as cleaning the gutters, or as complex as redesigning the drainage. By no means all interventions will involve physical works: a simple adjustment of the control regime on the heating system can sometimes deliver enormous benefits. All appropriate options will need to be considered, including the option of not intervening at all.

Interventions in the building environment may be roughly divided into:

- Interventions on the envelope, which may be intended to either improve weather resistance, or to adapt it to meet new requirements for use (for instance, the supply of services such as electricity and water)
- Interventions to the interior environment, which may be intended to either improve conditions for the preservation of the fabric or contents, or to improve conditions for building use.

There may well be conflicts between these various aims and objectives, and there is always the danger that an intervention may cause a hitherto-successful building system to fail. It is therefore vital that any programme of treatment, repair or alteration is planned carefully, and assessed methodically. ⊖BASICS

Interventions to the Envelope

Arguably, the treatment and repair of a building envelope must be planned according to slightly different criteria from those generally governing the conservation of historic objects, where in most cases the priority is to retain as much original material as possible, even where this means that the result will be in a fragile state requiring special ongoing care. Conservation guidelines such as 'minimum intervention' and 'stabilise in the current state', rather than restore to a previous 'better' state, can still be very useful, and should certainly not be lightly discarded, but the priority must be to keep the envelope in good functional condition: failure would endanger the building fabric and its contents, the preservation of which must be the overall conservation priority.

Mostly there will be little or no conflict between preserving the envelope and following the ideals of conservation, but occasionally major interventions or alterations may have to be made, and then wider issues must be considered. For example, rainwater goods may need to be radically altered to correct a poor design or to take account of changed rainfall conditions; or it may prove necessary to reinstate useful features that have been lost over time, such as exterior renders, or rain-shedding hood mouldings and cornices. This might seem radical for very significant buildings, although it should be remembered that buildings of some antiquity will more than likely have seen changes of this scale in their past. ⊖BASICS

The greatest danger is that interventions can have unexpected consequences, sometimes serious enough to cause the envelope to fail. There is a higher risk of this whenever modern materials or methods are used on traditionally constructed buildings.

Many ancient buildings, especially churches, were originally rendered, but have lost their renders over time or as a result of the fashion for revealing underlying masonry. This can lead to persistent moisture problems, and if so one remedy that should be considered is to replace the render.

A lost render was replaced at St Botolph's Hardham (*right*), which contains an extremely important scheme of medieval wall paintings. A major intervention of this kind must be planned and executed to avoid undesirable side-effects; ensuring that the absolute minimum amount of water is introduced into the fabric during works, for example.

Certainly buildings old enough to have proved their basic robustness – and to have had any initial flaws dealt with many years ago – should be altered only with the utmost caution. Even apparently quirky historic alterations should not be removed or replaced lightly: they may be addressing problems that have since been forgotten, or perhaps are no longer well understood.

For modern building envelopes, the understanding of the original construction and of the reasons for later alterations may be considerably more complete, but conservation can be challenging for other reasons. The design and materials used in a listed modern building are likely to have been quite innovative, and therefore at risk of having fundamental problems. Again, it is necessary to proceed with great caution when repairing or altering, since unexpected problems may appear at any time.

When considering interventions to the envelope, there is no 'right' answer: some general issues may need to be weighed case by case.

BUILDING ENVIRONMENT
CARE & REPAIR

ISSUES WHEN PLANNING INTERVENTIONS ON THE BUILDING ENVELOPE

CONSERVATION PRINCIPLE	ARGUMENTS FOR	ARGUMENTS AGAINST
PRESERVATION OF ORIGINAL MATERIALS AND DESIGN	The building is likely to have been designed with local expertise, with a good understanding of the local environmental conditions An older building has proved its success by its longevity	For older buildings, both the local environment and the building use are almost certain to have changed, which may mean the original design is no longer sustainable or even effective
PRESERVATION OF ALL THE CHANGES THE BUILDING HAS UNDERGONE OVER TIME	For older buildings, fundamental problems are likely to have been addressed many years ago, simply to keep the building functional; therefore, alterations may be extremely important practically as well as historically Changes undergone by the building illustrate its history, and preferably should not be reversed or concealed	Useful original features may have been lost over time, or even deliberately removed, to the detriment of the envelope (amongst the many examples: lime-based renders, water-shedding details, exterior shutters)
INTERVENE AS LITTLE AS POSSIBLE (MINIMUM INTERVENTION)	Interventions can have unexpected side-effects (example: diverting water away from one area may move moisture problems elsewhere)	Major interventions may be needed to keep the envelope in functional order (examples include: altering a poor roof design that has caused intractable moisture problems; or applying a lime render to prevent moisture ingress)
CHOOSE WEAK MATERIALS AND SYSTEMS FOR REPAIR	If repairs are too strong, they will make the system, as a whole, weaker and more apt to fail, and the point of failure will usually be in the original material Additions made deliberately weaker can be used to alleviate existing stresses in the system (example: applying a weak lime plaster to a salt-contaminated wall, so that cryptoflorescence occurs within the plaster instead of the wall) Weak materials are easier to remove	Repairs must be fit-for-purpose, so that the envelope remains in good working condition Access is often a serious issue, especially for works on roofs and towers; interventions will need to be longer-lived if the area being repaired is difficult to reach (for example, lacquer coatings may be needed to protect a weathervane on a spire, rather than a wax coating, which is much less invasive but demands regular replacement)
CHOOSE LIKE-FOR-LIKE REPLACEMENT MATERIALS	Traditional materials are reasonably well understood, and relatively easy to repair, giving results that are relatively simple to predict There are many risks involved in introducing new materials into an old system: the less alike two materials are, the greater will be the stresses at the boundary between them (example: if two materials bonded together react differently to changes in temperature and humidity, the resulting movement may break the bond) As yet there will have been little or no chance to see if innovative materials or methods could give problems in the long term: unintended consequences are common, so programmes must always include provision for long-term monitoring and assessment of results	It may be very hard to obtain replacement materials that have the same characteristics as the original (example: modern softwoods, wrought iron) Traditional materials may not always be the best choice: for example, in damp locations, stainless steel is a much better material for fixings than either wrought iron or carbon steel Modern materials such as silicones and stainless steel offer opportunities for safe repair that were not available in the past, and may help solve problems that are otherwise intractable
CHOOSE LIKE-FOR-LIKE REPAIR SYSTEMS	The approaches to traditional building and repair were developed over many centuries, and have proved themselves to be effective A great deal of this knowledge has been lost: when traditional systems are disrupted the information they potentially contain is forfeited	In some cases – particularly modern building systems such as curtain walling – the original materials or designs may be actively causing problems, and long-term preservation might require them to be rethought and perhaps even altered quite considerably

For more information and discussion, see the *Conservation Basics* volume in this series. ⊖BASICS

Interventions to the Indoor Environment

The most common alterations to the indoor environment are those made to adapt it to modern patterns of use and ideas of comfort: the installation of plumbing and central heating, for example. Such changes may be unavoidable: the usability of the building must be given due weight; it is very rare that a building is so historically significant that it can be preserved without having a practical use, and an unused building (no matter how important) is always in danger of neglect.

Nevertheless, altering the indoor conditions can often have unintended consequences, and so should never be approached lightly. It demands a particularly rigorous project-development phase to make sure the problem is well understood, and to understand all the implications of the proposed means of intervention. For sensitive or historically significant buildings, this would usually include monitoring of the existing environmental conditions and a programme of testing. After the chosen alterations have been completed, the project will need to incorporate an explicit phase of post-works monitoring and assessment.

Buildings without a use soon become neglected, or even derelict. Keeping a building in use must therefore always be a priority, but with sensible planning, modifications to the indoor environment can be made that deliver good results with little or no adverse impact on the building fabric.

BUILDING ENVIRONMENT
CARE & REPAIR

DEVELOPING A PROGRAMME OF INTERVENTION

The success or failure of any programme of intervention depends critically on the development stage, and this is especially true for projects that seek to alter the building environment in some way.

So many factors could potentially affect environmental interventions that developing a programme can be a serious challenge, especially where – as is usual – there are constraints on costs and time. Those in charge of a conservation project can find themselves being pulled in many different directions: on the one hand, there may be a worthy desire to keep intervention to a minimum; on the other, ever-greater expectations of performance, and concerns over professional indemnity. These must all be weighed in the light of what the intervention needs to achieve.

Even if intervention is being considered for only a small part of the envelope, it is still important to take the whole building and its surroundings into account, considering not only how the proposed works might affect the building system, but also how the building system might affect the outcome of any works.

Because there are so many possible approaches to resolving environmental problems, the project team (whatever its size) will have to spend some time weighing the benefits, risks and potential collateral impacts of all the proposed interventions, but this really is time well spent. It is invariably more cost-effective to be sure the approach being taken is safe and effective rather than to try to sort out troublesome interventions afterwards (especially if these have not dealt successfully with the problem either). As in all projects, decision-making will be helped enormously by good communication between everyone involved, whether managers, conservators or end users.

Project development involves a number of steps, which will need to be worked through one by one:

1. Ensure that a good understanding of the current building environment is in place (see **Assessing the Building Environment** and **Diagnosis**).

2. Identify the need for the intervention.

3. On the basis of the identified need, determine the exact aim of the programme of intervention (this includes establishing how urgent the problems are, and what would be the consequences if they were left untreated).

4. If there is a real need for intervention, decide exactly what needs to be achieved to solve the problem (that is, develop a scope of works).

5. Identify all interventions that could potentially fulfil the scope of works (these might include changes to process, such as adjustments to the way the building is being used, as well as physical interventions such as treatment, repair or alteration).

6. Discard any interventions that would have an adverse impact on significance of the building, in particular its fabric, or would compromise future care.

7. For each of the remaining interventions, and taking into account the current and future use of the building and the plans for future care and maintenance, decide whether its expected lifespan is acceptable; discard any interventions that are not sufficiently long-lived.

8. Consider the resources needed for each of the remaining interventions: this includes both monetary costs, and staff time and expertise. Assessment should cover the cost of development, implementation and monitoring, as well as the ongoing costs such as running costs and maintenance.

9. From the remaining interventions, choose the most appropriate (this may require obtaining expert advice, and potentially include some preliminary testing).

10. Devise a schedule of works.

It is important that there is no ambiguity about the overall aim of the intervention, which must be decided before any consideration is given to methods or materials. For example, 'to heat the building' is not an aim: rather, the aim might be to achieve comfortable indoor conditions for certain users of the building under certain conditions, or perhaps to provide conditions which slow the deterioration of books or other fragile contents. The underlying issues must be investigated so that the aim can be specified as precisely as possible (in the case of heating, for example, exactly which conditions would be desirable, and which would be contraindicated). This is likely to mean assessing competing claims, and developing workable compromises.

During the project development, which interventions are most suitable will often become quite obvious: for example, discovering that discomfort in a particular case is largely a matter of the occupants radiating body heat into a stone floor would suggest the answer lies not in a new system to heat the air, but rather in simply laying down rugs or carpets.

The schedule of works should include all testing and statutory permissions, and a timetable identifying suitable points for reassessment. It should be written very clearly, and be unequivocal, quantified where possible, and backed up by drawings and photographs; there should be no way in which the intended outcome of the works can be misinterpreted. Variations to the schedule may well be needed as the works proceed and reveal new information, and the assessment process should explicitly allow for this.

The development and management of conservation programmes is covered in detail in the *Conservation Basics* volume of this series. ⊖BASICS

BUILDING ENVIRONMENT
CARE & REPAIR

SELECTING INTERVENTIONS

There are no 'one-size-fits-all' solutions: the best intervention will always depend on the building and its environment, the way it is being used, and the resources available for conservation and ongoing care. A building professional needs to feel comfortable dealing with a wide range of materials and systems, and must be ready to be flexible and think laterally.

It is wise to proceed slowly and methodically, since many hasty interventions intended to deal with problems in the building environment have ended up causing more problems without resolving the underlying issues.

Many unsuccessful interventions are characterised by a kind of wishful thinking that air or water will behave as one would wish them to, rather than according to the laws of nature. For example, it is not uncommon to find drain holes not at the lowest point, but at the point most convenient for the builder, but water will never run uphill simply because that is where the drainhole is to be found; instead it will pool. Another example is provided by the proprietary wall-drying systems that rely on air entering a damp space only when it is dry, somehow knowing to leave again when it has become wet. Often the best way of assessing a complex proposed treatment is to ask: does it make logical sense? Are there any simpler things that could be done instead?

It is surprisingly common to find that drain holes are not positioned at the lowest point of the fall. This leads to water pooling, and may eventually result in leaking.

Selecting Methods & Materials

A physical intervention is always made up of both the materials being used, and the method of working with those materials. There are therefore two aspects to consider when trying to select the best method and materials:

- *Working properties*
  Ease with which the intervention can be made (this includes issues of availability, and of health and safety).

- *Performance*
  The behaviour of the intervention in use over the long term, including effectiveness, durability, and compatibility with surrounding materials and building systems.

In practice, decisions are often made almost entirely on the basis of working properties, but an intervention which does not give the desired result will not be a good choice, no matter how easy it might be to apply, so it is important to give due weight to performance.

Interventions That Hide Deterioration

One consideration that is rarely given sufficient weight when choosing repair materials and systems is the effect these may have on future environmental assessment, or the recognition of problems. To give a simple example, the rapid and effective diagnosis of a wall affected by moisture from a blocked external drainpipe will depend on how the wall has been finished. Lime plasters and limewashes are very porous, so the leak will show on the face of the wall within a short time of moisture entering: staining, tide lines and sometimes salt decay will alert the building users to the fact that there is a problem. By contrast, water-resistant cementitious plasters, plastic paints and vinyl wallpapers are designed to resist staining and deterioration for as long as possible, which means that the leak is likely to remain undetected for a considerable time. Eventually it will be so serious that the resistant coatings will fail, sometimes quite suddenly and dramatically: cracks may appear or paints start to blister and peel. By this stage the prolonged moisture ingress may have led to serious problems such as the decay of embedded timbers.

There are many other examples of this type of issue; it is a fundamental drawback of any system intended to cover intractable underlying failures, including otherwise excellent interventions such as panelling or dry-lining below-ground walls. If such systems are introduced, they will need to be integrated with a programme of regular inspection and assessment, as well as meticulous day-to-day maintenance. For instance, if a subterranean wall is dry-lined, extra vigilance will be needed to ensure that the exterior drains and water-supply pipes always remain in good condition.

Planning for Easy Maintenance

If new elements are introduced to protect the building envelope, it pays to design them for safe failure and easy ongoing care. For example, keeping downpipes straight and well away from the wall not only makes blockages less likely, but makes checking and repainting easy; moreover, any leaks that occur are less likely to do serious harm.

INTERVENTIONS ON THE ENVELOPE

This section gives a brief introduction to the various interventions to the building envelope which might be considered for resolving environmental problems such as water penetration. The other volumes in this series of *Practical Building Conservation* address material-specific interventions.
➔MORTARS ➔METALS ➔EARTH & BRICK ➔ROOFING ➔GLASS ➔STONE ➔TIMBER ➔CONCRETE

DEALING WITH MOISTURE PROBLEMS

The best approach when dealing with moisture problems is to make the basic repairs first (such as correcting faulty rainwater disposal or drainage), and wait for the building to settle; only if problems persist should more complex or risky interventions be considered.

REPAIRS TO THE FABRIC

Roofs

Repair & Replacement of the Covering

Problems with the roof covering are always a concern, since they can lead to a vicious circle: rainwater penetrating through broken tiles, for example, can lead to the decay of the supporting battens, causing more tiles to slip, leading to more decay, and so on. A sure way to destroy a building is to remove its roof covering.

Many roofs can tolerate a fair degree of moisture penetration, however, so long as it is not too concentrated or prolonged. If a problem has been caught in good time, it may be possible to make patch repairs, but eventually every covering will begin to fail on a wider scale, either because of natural ageing (commonly the failure of fixings), or because there are fundamental problems with the design (for example, lead sheets that are too long for the pitch of the roof will eventually slip or split).

Replacing a roof covering demands the most thought and planning, especially where previous repairs have sacrificed traditional details to contemporary practice. For example, staggered eaves may be reduced to achieve a neat line, but at the cost of the protection the overhang provided to the wall below. Important local details such as swept-and-laced valleys may be replaced with a cut and lead-lined valley, which is easier and quicker for the roofer, but does not necessarily afford better protection or longevity. The implications of the changes in roofing design and materials are still not completely understood, but failures of roofs that have not been neglected can often be traced back to alterations.

Changes to ventilation practice are of particular concern, especially because the moisture load in the interior air has increased substantially since the introduction of plumbing and heating. Modern practice during refurbishment is to reduce ventilation through windows, doors and chimneys, but perforations through the ceiling for lights and cabling and access are more common (see **Special Topic: Improving Energy & Carbon Performance**). Adding extra ventilation can be risky, reducing the humidity buffering and drawing up moist air from the interior into the roof. This can lead to condensation problems, especially where there are impermeable materials such as metal or AVCLs.

Converting open attics into living spaces may lead to problems, and even minor treatments such as decorating with impermeable paints can affect the capacity of roof timbers to buffer water vapour.

Traditional and modern treatments for valleys

Over time, tilers developed various ways of handling the transition from one slope to another; these were very effective, and showcased both local designs and the tiler's own skill.

The modern lead-lined mitre valley is less costly to make, but can be more difficult to maintain: leaves and debris can be caught between the slates or tiles, where they are difficult to reach and remove.

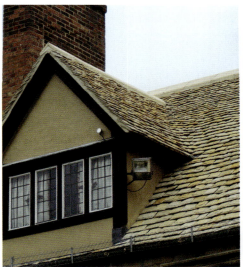

It is of particular concern that building regulations may demand additions such as insulation or AVCLs that have not been tested over the longer term. Many roofs using these materials will not go on to develop moisture problems, but observations to date have found severe roof-space condensation damage only in roofs with vapour barriers, so their use is certainly a risk.

The best general advice for re-roofing is to ensure that the new roof uses the best traditional detailing and workmanship, so that it does not have to rely on additional materials such as AVCLs to make up any deficiencies in design or construction. Where important water-shedding details such as projecting eaves have been lost over time, and there is a chance to reinstate them, this would be a wise measure. If the roof is being insulated, the decision to avoid AVCLs will restrict the choices of insulation material, since some manufacturers require them to protect their material from water.

Detailed information about the repair and replacement of different types of covering can be found in the *Roofing* volume of this series. ➔ROOFING

Correcting Problems in the Original Design

Some roofs will have fundamentally risky features such as horizontal valley gutters, but it is very rare that these can be addressed directly. Instead, the protective detailing (the guttering and flashing, for example) should be of the highest possible specification, and frequent inspection and maintenance should be programmed in to compensate.

If there are clear moisture problems affecting the timbers or the covering, as is sometimes the case when roofing felts or vapour barriers have been used, extra ventilation could be introduced, but if the roof is in good condition and there are no moisture problems, adding ventilation will not be helpful. At best nothing would be gained, and there is always a risk that this could destabilise conditions and lead to undesirable consequences.

BUILDING ENVIRONMENT
CARE & REPAIR

Vapour Barriers in Repair

There is no equivalent to vapour barriers in traditional construction. They were not needed: air will not travel through permeable wall materials such as lime plasters and renders, timber, brick and stone; and any water penetrating is able to evaporate away again. In a traditional roof, humidity was buffered by the mass of supporting timber, and even when the space was poorly ventilated serious moisture problems were unlikely, unless there was a major failure of the covering or localised heavy leaking (from a blocked gutter, perhaps).

Materials such as 'air- and vapour-control layers' [AVCLs] form part of the layered waterproof construction of many modern hollow-wall systems, and are increasingly incorporated into traditional buildings during repair or refurbishment. The usual reason given for this is to protect water-sensitive insulation from condensation, or to prevent air leaks that introduce water vapour and remove heated air from the building or decrease the temperature-buffering capacity of the fabric; but they may also be seen as a way of allowing building works to continue in all weathers, and of preventing moisture problems of all types. Manufacturers maintain that the materials are able to let through water vapour molecules but stop the passage of liquid water, although there is no scientific proof that this is true; and from the point of view of building physics it is difficult to understand. It is also hard to see how any *in-situ* material would not become less vapour-permeable over time, as it accumulates dirt and dust.

AVCLs may be included as a precautionary measure, but in practice in all types of construction, serious localised moisture problems have been found to occur around leaks in AVCLs, either where joints and junctions have not been perfectly sealed, or where the material has been punctured (for example, during electrical works or the installation of light fittings). Installation is challenging, however: it can be almost impossible to detail awkward junctions such as the meeting point of floors and external walls, around windows, or where cables or pipework must pass through. The essential problem is that moisture can enter the fabric from any direction, and an AVCL will slow evaporation.

Problems with Vapour Barriers in Roofs

A particular issue for vapour barriers used in roofs proved to be the tautness of the installation. If the material was stretched tightly into place, thermal expansion and contraction could cause it to tear, and there could also be problems with 'drumming': wind entering the roof space and causing the membrane to vibrate noisily. On the other hand, if it was allowed to hang loosely, moisture from penetrating rainwater or collected condensation collected at the lowest point, and could penetrate through if that touched anything below such as a roof timber (this phenomenon, commonly known as 'tenting', is familiar to all campers: anything touching the underside of a waterproof sheet at the point where water has collected on its upper surface will break the water's surface tension, allowing it to leak through the material).

Problems with Vapour Barriers in Walls

The logic of exactly where a vapour barrier should be located within a hollow wall is very difficult to follow: there are many guidance notes available, giving rules for which will be the 'warm' and the 'cool' side in different climates, exposures, construction types, and internal air conditions. Vapour control is often conflated with air control (as it is explicitly in the use of the term 'AVCL'). Unsurprisingly there have been many failures arising from their use, some of which have proved very serious. Water-resistant surface coatings such as impermeable paints and vinyl wallpapers will act like vapour barriers; their use has also led to unexpected moisture and mould problems, especially in air-conditioned buildings.

SHOULD VAPOUR BARRIERS BE USED?

Because it is safer to have no vapour barrier at all than one that is faulty, AVCLs should not be introduced as a precautionary measure, nor used where permeable materials and systems could give sufficient protection against the movement of air or water vapour. Even a well-considered and well-installed system that evinces no problems when the building is in good condition will quickly fail if water enters from an unexpected direction (for example, from a leak in the gutters or from the plumbing). To reduce the risk, the following rules would need to be followed:

- AVCLs should not be used at all unless they are absolutely necessary
- The most permeable product that still gives reasonable performance should be selected
- They should never be installed on both sides of the component (the roof or wall); that way, if moisture enters, it can at least dry out in one direction
- Great care needs to be taken during installation to avoid tenting, ensure that the membranes are not punctured, and detail all junctions and joints are detailed correctly
- The roof or wall in which they are used will need to be well ventilated (this can be difficult to achieve, especially in a historic building, and it risks introducing other problems).

If the only pressing reason to introduce an AVCL is to protect a particular insulation material that demands their use, it is generally wiser to simply choose an alternative type of insulation that does not have these requirements (see the **Special Topic: Improving Energy & Carbon Performance** for more information about insulation materials).

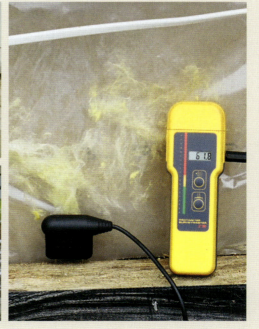

Wall membranes were used in the new timber-framed brick veneer houses shown here, but they trapped such high quantities of moisture that within weeks the floors were stained, and the timber frames sodden. As shown in **Deterioration & Damage: History of Vapour Barriers**, the afflicted buildings were demolished.

BUILDING ENVIRONMENT
CARE & REPAIR

Chimneys

Chimneys are prone to moisture problems both from liquid water penetration and condensation in the flues, which ultimately could lead to structural failure. Ingress of rain and snow can be prevented by keeping the masonry and render in good condition: arguably the major cause of problems has been repointing or re-rendering in cement-based mortars. It can also be helpful to install a vented cap or cowl, but some experimentation may be needed to determine the best way of capping whilst not adversely affecting the draught.

Deteriorated flashings and mortar fillets are a common cause of moisture penetration, but effective repair may prove challenging. For new construction it is often recommended that a lead DPC be inserted in the chimney just above the roof line, but this will rarely be appropriate for conservation work, and the best approach may be rendering with a lime-based mortar, or a programme of more frequent inspection and repair.

If the flue gases have damaged the mortars, moisture penetration through the stack may be a serious problem. Re-parging is likely to be impossible, but repointing or rendering with a lime-based mortar may solve the problem. If not, the stack will need to be dismantled and rebuilt, but rebuilding should be avoided wherever possible because it may be difficult to reconstruct in a way that meets current building regulations.
→ MORTARS → EARTH & BRICK

If the stack is leaning or distorted by salt-jacking, it will be necessary to consult an experienced builder and perhaps a structural engineer. If the chimney breasts in the rooms have been removed without removing the stack, the structural load of the stack will not be correctly supported. Chimney breasts should either be reinstated, or supporting beams bearing onto suitable walls or brackets will be needed.

Care of Flues in Use

A fire or stove using fossil fuels needs ventilation to feed combustion. When the fireplace is being used, it is important to check that draughtproofing and other works have not reduced the air supply, because without insufficient ventilation the chimney may not draw properly, and smoke or carbon monoxide may spill out into the room. Carbon monoxide is dangerous, so alarms are a wise precaution and indeed are now a requirement of the UK building regulations for stoves, but care must be taken to position them correctly, and to keep them properly serviced and maintained.

Where possible, any new chimney pots should resemble the originals, or the chimney may not only appear unbalanced but may fail to operate correctly. Many special pots are available for different types of application: some are intended to improve up-draughts in open fires; others are designed specifically for gas fires. Caps designed for flues in use can be installed if water penetration is a problem. Spark arrestors are also available for thatched buildings, but unless these are scrupulously cleaned and maintained they may add to the fire risk. **→ ROOFING**

Building Control

REGULATIONS FOR WORK ON CHIMNEYS

Any work that affects an existing chimney (including fitting a new stove or a liner) comes under Building Control regulations, which require notice plates to be fixed next to the electricity meter and the stopcock as well as the hearth or flue of concern, indicating the materials and diameter of the flue, and its manufacturer.

Dealing with Condensation Problems

Condensation problems in flues that are being used are often associated with the stack being too cool. The first option is to install a liner; if this is not possible, it may be necessary to manage the problem by lighting fires at intervals during the year to help keep the chimney dry. Combustion water should be kept to a minimum by never burning green wood.

Lining Flues

If the chimney is in poor or uncertain condition, there are problems of contamination, or vertical cracks have developed, flue liners will be essential. Liners are also required by the Building Regulations and the Gas Installation Regulations if the flues are to be used for coal-effect gas fires, or for certain other appliances (such as central heating and domestic hot water boilers).

Although open fires tend to produce lower flue gas temperatures, liners are still advisable to ensure that combustion gases are safely transferred to the exterior. They can also help with condensation problems, although it is important to be aware that re-lining with a wet system will probably add enough moisture to mobilise salts, creating salt stains on the interior walls or making existing stains worse. The space between the original flue and the new flue liner will need to be ventilated top and bottom.

Backfilling around liners with perlite or vermiculite, whilst not strictly necessary, does help in keeping the spacing correct between the liner and the flue. It will also improve the draw of the fire, since the flue gases will stay warm enough to escape quickly, and if the correct loose materials are used it will greatly reduce condensation, leading to a longer lifespan for the liner.

Relining can have unexpected effects: penetrating rain which has previously been absorbed by the old lime parging may run straight down the new flue and drip into the fireplace. All lined chimneys will need either a venting cap or a cowl to stop this.

Not all chimneys are capable of accepting a new flue liner, so an expert should be consulted before deciding on this approach, and before choosing the most appropriate method. There are three basic options: liners that are cast *in situ*, sectional solid liners and metal liners.

Cast ('Pumped') Liners

Casting linings *in situ* involves inserting a toughened inflatable rubber tube into the flue, which is opened up at intervals to ensure the space between the tube and the flue is as even as possible. Into this space is poured a refractory cement mortar containing pumice or vermiculite; when this has set, the tube is deflated and removed. Potential problems are many, including reducing the size of the flue, reducing the strength of the draught through the chimney and the water in the mortar activating salts in the masonry. A cast-in lining is almost impossible to remove. Pumped liners should therefore only be considered where the flue route is so convoluted that any other type of liner would be impossible.

Sectional Solid Liners

Sectional solid liners are composed of blocks of refractory concrete, pumice concrete or terracotta, with male-to-female couplings that allow them to be stacked. They are not bonded to the original flue, and so must be supported at intervals no greater than 2 m apart. Sectional liners are difficult to install, and will only be feasible for unusually large and straight chimneys, or sometimes when the stack is being rebuilt.

Metal Liners

Metal liners are reversible; they reduce the flue area less than solid sectional liners. There are four different types:

- *Rigid sectional liners*

  Stainless-steel sections that are fixed together with special clips, and are usually used to reline large flues for wood-burning stoves.

- *Rigid twin-wall liners*

  Straight lengths and fittings of stainless steel with 25-mm insulation; the external skin is weatherproof and carries the structural load, while the inner liner resists corrosive combustion products, can cope with thermal movement and heats up (which aids the updraught). These can be used internally or externally, and installed with a gap of only 50 mm between it and combustible materials. Like sectional solid liners, they come in sections that must be fitted together and supported at intervals, and so will be difficult to install in a convoluted flue.

- *Flexible double-skin liners*

  Stainless-steel tubes with a smooth inner skin and a corrugated outer skin, that can accommodate bends in the flue, and are suitable for solid fuel, wood or coal-effect fires. The liners come in a single piece, and are pulled into place and then fixed in position; this may not be possible in very convoluted flues. It is common practice to back-fill with perlite or vermiculite. For coal-effect fires the void around the liner is left unfilled, but is sealed at the top and bottom (which may cause condensation problems). In some situations, flexible metal liners may not have a particularly long lifespan, and they will therefore need to be inspected regularly.

- *Gas flex liners*

  Lightweight single-skin liners used for closed gas fires and boilers. Since most of these appliances use their own flue systems, this is a rare application.

Disused Flues

Even when a chimney is no longer used it may well still be a significant feature of the building, and it may also fulfil structural functions, so despite the fact that chimneys can cause problems, it is generally unwise to remove them. In listed buildings, consent will usually be needed even to take away chimney pots. Removing internal chimney breasts is also best avoided if at all possible; such work would need structural engineering advice as well as Building Control approval, and in some cases Listed Building Consent.

Disused flues should be covered with a ventilated cap to stop water ingress. To prevent condensation it is essential to maintain ventilation, although unfortunately the flowing air will cool the inner face of the chimney breast (which is generally made of a single skin of stone or brick).

If the stack above roof level has been dismantled, the flue can be vented by opening the capped flue at the base and at a high level in the upper floor. This approach is less suitable if the stack is still in place, since the upper portion – lacking ventilation – can then become damp. There may also be problems with chimneys on outside walls, as moist indoor air condenses on the cold outer skin. If the flue is sooty, then ventilating it internally can lead to unpleasant smells. There is also a possibility that, in the event of a fire, smoke and flame would be able to pass up through the flue from lower to upper floors, which may not be acceptable if there is fire compartmentation. In either case, it is sensible to fit a smoke detector next to the upper vent.

To stop draughts through chimneys, the flue may need to be partially blocked above the fireplace.

Draughts through fireplaces can be prevented by fitting a register plate, but it is important to be aware that the reduction in ventilation can sometimes lead to moisture problems in the chimney. It is usually wise to ensure that the flue is protected from rainwater ingress by a ventilated cap.

It is possible to install a register plate with ventilation holes, or to block the entire fireplace with a vented panel, but the quickest way to seal a disused flue is with a chimney balloon. This can also be a good option for flues that are used rarely, but it may be less suitable if there is a possibility of using the fireplace in the future: they can be awkward and dirty to remove and reinstall. For flues that are used more often or throughout the winter, it may be better to install a damper, even though this is more expensive and can be quite difficult with some fireplace designs.

BUILDING ENVIRONMENT
CARE & REPAIR

WATER DISPOSAL SYSTEMS

Most well-designed and properly maintained rainwater disposal systems will cope with very stormy weather, although they might occasionally overflow.

What changes and additions are acceptable will depend on the significance of the building, and the severity of the problem. Intractable moisture problems may demand a more invasive approach, with consideration given to interventions such as extending the roof overhangs, adding more hoppers and downpipes, widening downpipes, adding cornices or drip mouldings, or protecting walls with permeable renders. These are all traditional approaches to protection, and indeed there may even be historic evidence that similar systems once existed on the building, and have been lost over time.

Roofing

A roof with eaves drainage should overhang the gutter far enough for the rain to fall into it, but not so far that it overshoots. 'Clipped' eaves (eaves with insufficient overhang) can be a serious problem, especially when combined with roofing felt. Exposure to light breaks down the felt, and wind-blown rain wicks up under the eaves. To repair this, it may be necessary to remove the lowest courses of the covering, and install a lead soaker that runs the full length of the eaves. This should start approximately 30 cm behind the tiles, then run down over the tilting fillet and into the gutter.

BS EN 12056-3: 2000 Gravity drainage systems inside buildings. Roof drainage, layout and calculation states that gutters and downpipes may not be needed on very tall buildings, where rainwater from the roof would be dispersed by wind. Problems can occur, however, if the design concentrates rainwater, which could then stream out with some force. If so, a way may have to be found to prevent the water from collecting.

Rainwater Goods

Repair

Water-handling systems are exposed to very hostile conditions: a 10-cm wide half-round gutter will need to be able to handle as much as 100 litres of rainwater every minute in a torrential downpour. It is therefore critical to keep them in good working condition at all times. If rainwater goods are damaged and cannot be properly repaired at once, short-term temporary repairs should be made. Bituminous or mastic tape can be used to bandage cracked downpipes and sockets, or to line perforated gutters; adhesive flashing strips can be used to seal punctures, cracks and splits in lead valleys and parapet gutters. It must be emphasised that these are never a substitute for proper repairs, and in fact they will probably make permanent repairs more difficult. If it is possible to complete the permanent repairs immediately, that should always be the preferred option.

Where possible, repairs should be made like-for-like, not only to preserve the appearance of the system, but more importantly to preserve function: joints between different materials will always be a point of weakness, especially since they are likely to behave differently when exposed to solar heating and wind cooling.

Facing page: For problematic rainwater goods on historic buildings, innovative solutions may sometimes be needed, such as lining embedded downpipes that are leaking or replacing systems that cannot cope with current levels of rainfall with higher-capacity alternatives.

Here, unusually wide gutters and downpipes have been installed on an important building that was likely to remain unoccupied for some years, and would therefore be at risk from blockages.

There are many options for repair depending on the material. Relining with a waterproof material can be a good option for persistent leaking: for example, timber gutters can be lined with lead or with tar-based paints; and hot-welded plastic sheet has been used to line failing precast concrete gutters. Some relining systems for metal gutters are based on special paint finishes that promise long lifetimes, but since these rely on meticulous preparation of the metal surface to work, they are usually infeasible except for new runs of gutter. ⊖METALS

Some level of augmentation may be needed: for example, if a valley gutter is overshooting, it may be necessary to add a hopper to the outlet. Any permanent new sections should have the same profile as the originals, and be made of the same material.

Replacement

The hostile conditions to which they are exposed will sometimes cause rainwater goods to deteriorate to the point where it becomes necessary to replace, rather than simply repair, them. Partial or complete replacement may also be necessary if the current systems are demonstrably inadequate.

The materials chosen for rainwater goods should always be robust, easy to maintain and of the best possible quality. Metal rainwater goods are prone to galvanic corrosion, so their fixings and fittings must be chosen with particular care. Eaves gutters should be fixed in place using compatible corrosion-resistant brackets, each no more than 1 m apart. They should be positioned with the centre directly under the edge of the roof, and it is wise to incorporate a minimum fall of 1 in 350. The quality of design and installation are equally important.

If the current disposal system cannot cope with the load of water from the roof, more downpipes will have to be installed. These must match the gutter capacity and design, and should have solid brackets under every joint, with these being at intervals no greater than 1.8 m. Many more brackets will be needed for any section of the pipe that is not vertical. In some cases it may be feasible and desirable to install downpipes with wider diameters. Ideally, the downpipes should be set away from the wall to allow for air-drying and maintenance. Where the design does not permit this, extra vigilance will be needed to watch for leaks and repair them immediately, and in extreme cases it may be necessary to line the pipes.

The importance of detailing

Detailing is critical to the performance and longevity of rainwater goods.

Left: Wherever possible, downpipes should be set well away from the wall to allow for easy maintenance, and to prevent leaks from affecting the fabric.

Right: Downpipes will function best if straight. Bends, especially tight bends, reduce flow because of turbulence, and will also tend to block with debris.

Wherever possible, downpipes should be positioned at the centre of a run of gutter, to reduce the maximum load of water and so lessen the chances of overflow.

There are a number of design flaws which should be avoided if possible. Downpipes should not have horizontal sections nor sharp bends, as these may not run freely because of turbulence, even if they are not physically blocked by trapped debris. Nor should downpipes be set to discharge onto an area of roof, especially if the profile of the covering stops the water spreading horizontally over the surface (for example, the standing seams on a metal roof, or the corrugations on a roof covered in pantiles).

Designs that hide failure until it is advanced (gravel filling over drainpipes, for example) should be strictly avoided; it is preferable that any failure should become obvious as soon as possible.

For the same reason, designs must allow for easy inspection and maintenance. Parapet gutters, for example, should be made very easily accessible for inspection, since these must be meticulously maintained. The fall, and the steps and bay design, must all be carefully considered, and the outlets designed to resist blocking for as long as possible.

It is important to build in fail-safe systems. Since even the best-detailed outlets are very likely to block sooner or later, they must be designed to overflow outwards, not towards the wall. If permission can be obtained, it may be worth adding overflow spouts to the hoppers so that blockages are obvious and water is discharged away from the walls. Adding spouts will not only protect the wall in a downpour, but will immediately indicate where an outlet is blocked.

For similar reasons, the joints of downpipes should not be sealed, because blockages will then cause obvious leaking. Moreover, unblocking will then be a simple matter.

Innovative drainage systems such as siphonic downpipes may occasionally be helpful in very intractable situations. Siphonic drainage systems are more complex than simple gravity-fed downpipes, but they can be a good option for large historic buildings where the number of downpipes is restricted for aesthetic reasons, or to improve embedded downpipe systems that are overflowing into the fabric.

Calculations of capacity and behaviour are always approximate, and it is important to test any new disposal system before it is signed off. Testing methods are included in *BS EN 12056-3:2000 Gravity drainage systems inside buildings. Roof drainage, layout and calculation.*

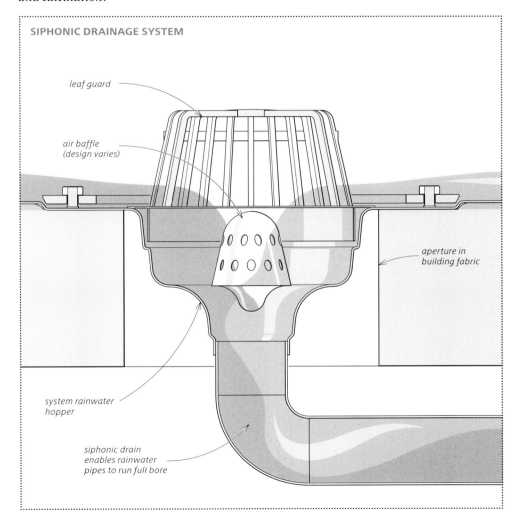

BUILDING ENVIRONMENT
CARE & REPAIR

MATERIALS FOR RAINWATER GOODS

ADVANTAGES	DISADVANTAGES	OTHER COMMENTS
ALUMINIUM		
Light Corrosion-resistant Extruded aluminium can be produced in continuous lengths, minimising joints	Medium life expectancy (up to 30 years for extruded or pressed aluminium, 25–40 years for cast aluminium, but depends on exposure and maintenance) Becomes brittle in extreme cold or with age Tends to corrode at joints	Coatings make recycling difficult Longer life if left unpainted (if coated, needs repainting every 15–25 years or so) Needs more protection in heavily polluted locations or where exposed to sea spray To prevent corrosion, should be protected from contact with or runoff from iron, steel or copper, and mortar or concrete
CAST IRON		
Very long life expectancy if cleaned and painted regularly to prevent corrosion	Brittle: can crack under impact, or because trapped water has frozen Joints must be sealed with oil-based putty to prevent leaks Inside surfaces of joints will need to be painted Heavy: fastenings should be maintained and checked regularly	Painting: rust must be removed, holes filled, insides primed with zinc chromate paint; the finishing coat should be a bituminous paint For new cast iron, the current best option is: • 2 coats zinc-based primer • 1 coat micaceous iron oxide paint • 2 coats gloss paint To prevent galvanic corrosion, repairs or fixings should not be mild steel or other dissimilar metals
COPPER		
Very long life expectancy Light Highly corrosion-resistant Low thermal expansion: can be fitted without expansion joints	Cannot be used on flat bitumen-sealed roofs (ponding can cause high concentrations of acid build up)	Does not need to be painted, but should be protected from contact with (or runoff from) mortar and concrete Resists growths of mosses Compatible with timber, lead and cast iron, but not zinc or aluminium (which will corrode)
GALVANISED STEEL		
Light Strong	Medium life expectancy (up to 30 years, but depends on exposure and maintenance)	To prevent corrosion, should be protected from contact with or runoff from mortar or concrete
GLASS-REINFORCED POLYESTER [GRP]		
Joints can be permanently sealed with fibreglass on interior	Subject to impact damage Can also be damaged by fire and chemical attack Older systems needed repainting every 15–25 years or so (current systems are through-coloured)	Can be repaired Long-term durability is still to be confirmed

MATERIALS FOR RAINWATER GOODS

ADVANTAGES	DISADVANTAGES	OTHER COMMENTS
LEAD		
Extremely corrosion-resistant Can be repaired reasonably easily	Not suitable for eaves gutters Very heavy and soft; susceptible to distortion and damage from impact or rodding Strong thermal expansion and contraction (this must be allowed for in the design) May be attacked by runoff from mortar or concrete, certain stones such as Westmorland slate, or organic materials (such as wooden shingles or moss growths)	Lead downpipes are a prime target for theft Fixings should be copper, brass or stainless steel to prevent galvanic corrosion Where at risk from runoff corrosion, add sacrificial strips of lead as drips The Lead Sheet Association is the best source for the latest advice; the general principle in choosing the correct 'code', or sheet thickness, is that thinner codes will need to be used in smaller pieces (with more joints)
HIGH-DENSITY POLYETHYLENE [HDPE]		
Light Can be produced in continuous lengths, minimising joints Will not corrode	Difficult to paint Long-term durability is unknown	Must be particularly well supported to prevent sagging Requires UV stabilisation
UNPLASTICISED POLYVINYLCHLORIDE [PVCU]		
Very light Can be produced in continuous lengths, minimising joints Will not corrode	Short life expectancy (10–15 years) Strong lateral expansion and contraction: tends to crack or distort at the joints Impact strength reduces with temperature Exposure to UV causes buckling, distortion and discolouration Susceptible to impact damage	If supplied with integral socket, one should be fixed no more than 15 cm from the end Does not require painting, but coloured products will fade on exposure Cannot be recycled, but leaches chemicals when disposed of in landfill
WOOD		
Very long life expectancy if maintained correctly Many different designs, from simple V-shaped gutters made of two planks to complex profiled shapes	Requires good maintenance: blockages must be dealt with promptly to prevent decay New off-the-shelf repair sections may not fit together with original sections Interior should generally be lined with a waterproof material	Correct choice of wood is vital: species include oak, Scots pine, pitch pine, sweet chestnut and elm Performs best when exterior left unpainted (painting increases drying time after rain, and risks trapping water) Durability can be increased by lining the gutter with tar-based paint or lead, or a sheet material such as single-ply roof covering

BUILDING ENVIRONMENT
CARE & REPAIR

Building Regulations

NEW RAINWATER GOODS

Neither the UK Building Regulations, nor other useful publications such as the *BRE Good Building Guide 38* and the British and European Standard covering rainwater goods *BS EN 12056–3: 2000 Gravity drainage systems inside buildings. Roof drainage, layout and calculation*, give directions for best practice in designing rainwater goods, although they do offer good advice on poor practice that should certainly be avoided.

Part H of the 2000 *UK Building Regulations (Drainage and Waste Disposal)* gives practical guidance on sizing and detailing rainwater goods. Exposure is expressed in a very simplified form, using a map of predicted rainfall intensity for England and Wales, as litres per second per square metre for a two-minute rainstorm (for buildings which are unusually exposed or protected, this may be insufficient). The calculations are based on the 'effective area' of roof that is being drained, which depends on the actual area and the roof pitch, as well as on its exposure.

EFFECTIVE AREA OF ROOF BEING DRAINED

PITCH	MULTIPLICATION FACTOR
0°	1.00 × actual area on PLAN
30°	1.29 × actual area on PLAN
45°	1.50 × actual area on PLAN
60°	1.67 × actual area on PLAN
> 70°	0.50 × actual area on ELEVATION

A similar approach is advocated by *BS EN 12056–3*. This advice does not incorporate a correction for exposure to wind-driven rain, although it covers the calculations for including a component of rain flowing onto a roof from vertical walls above, where the weather patterns make this a likely scenario.

Eaves Drainage

When the rainwater is discharged directly from the eaves, precautions must be taken to protect water splashing onto the walls, or through windows and doors, and especially to protect the footings from concentrated discharges (for example, from roof valleys).

Gutters

Gutter sizes depend on the effective roof area and the desired flow capacity. They can theoretically be laid level, but it is better to lay them on a slight gradient, as recommended in *BS EN 12056–3*. The slope should not be so great, however, that one end of the gutter will be set too low to catch all the rainwater coming off the eaves. In either case, they should be laid and detailed so that if they overflow, the excess water will fall away from the building.

BS EN 12056–3 also allows valley and parapet gutters to be laid level, but wherever possible it is wiser for these too to incorporate a fall.

Where incorporating sufficient fall is difficult (as it may well be for valley gutters, parapet gutters or flat roofs), it may well be necessary to take extra precautions to prevent overflowing, such as adding extra outlets.

BS EN 12056–3 also recommends trace heating be installed in gutters that are prone to blocking with ice and snow.

Outlets

The correct size for outlets depends on the effective area being drained, and the size of the gutter.

Downpipes

A downpipe should be at least the same size as the outlet feeding into it or – if it is served by more than one outlet – large enough to take the sum flow of rainwater from all sources. Siphonic downpipe systems (which use hydrostatic pressure rather than gravity) depend on the pipes running full with water when in use, and so must be designed to fill within a minute of the rainstorm beginning; the pipes are therefore considerably narrower than ordinary downpipes, and must be precisely sized and configured; baffle plates must be inserted into the outlets to stop as much air as possible from entering.

If a pipe discharges onto a roof (or a hard surface), it should have a shoe fitted to the end to reduce splashing and divert water away from sensitive parts of the fabric. The roof covering will also need to be reinforced at that point.

Catering for Climate Change

In the UK, the standard roof drainage specifications are based on a rainfall rate of 75 mm/h. According to the BRE, this would probably occur for five minutes once every four years, or 20 minutes once in 50 years (*BRE Digest 188*). For situations where it is critical to avoid all overflowing, the BRE recommend specifying to cope with 150 mm/h, which currently has a probability of occurring for three minutes once every 50 years, or for four minutes once every 100 years.

Projections of future climate in the UK, however, do include an increase in the frequency and severity of storms, and a number of conservation architects and surveyors are reporting that systems which have never before failed are already starting to overflow during rainstorms. It is therefore becoming common to specify a larger capacity when rainwater goods are being replaced.

Since the cost increase will usually be minimal, it is certainly wise to err on the side of caution and specify for greater rainfall, especially if maintenance will be difficult because of the design of the system, or because of access issues.

BUILDING ENVIRONMENT
CARE & REPAIR

Drainage

If drains are intractably blocked, clearance will require excavation. If the problems are due to poor design or workmanship, it may be worth giving thought to a replacement system. Re-excavating is a major intervention, however, requiring work close to the footing of the building, which may have ramifications not only for the stability of the building, but for any buried archaeology. For historic buildings in ancient landscapes, it may well be a requirement to have statutory consent and archaeological supervision for the excavation.

Replacement gulleys and drains will need to use the best design and materials.

Gulleys are never beautiful, and it must be accepted that if they are to be effective then they will probably need to be fairly obtrusive. They should be installed as far away as possible from the footings, so that a failure is less likely to impinge upon the building, and the gratings should never be hidden under gravel or tiles. The trench should be lined with an appropriate geotextile, and the yard gulleys should have silt buckets (plastic bottle traps block very quickly, and are difficult to clear).

The gulley must empty into a land drain: a perforated pipe positioned at the base of the trench, and set on a slope so that water is directed into the disposal system. Some form of impermeable material is generally used to line the trench and protect the pipe from silting up. Pipes can be clay or plastic: clay deforms less, but must be laid on a supporting bed of shingle. The trench is then backfilled with earth, and allowed to grass over. Agricultural drains in fields ('French' drains) are usually filled with coarse loose material such as pea gravel to trap runoff, but this is not necessary for a building drain, and indeed it is ill-advised since the drain would quickly fill with silt.

Like gulleys, drains should ideally be set well away from the footings, so that the inevitable blockages cannot cause moisture problems in the wall. This is also much less structurally invasive than excavating at the foot of the wall, and the drains will be easier to maintain should they fail.

If the drains must be placed close to the building walls, they should be capped with a compacted layer of earth, sloped away from the building to help shed surface water and reduce splashback. Clay is the ideal material for this: it has very fine pores, so it both resists water penetrating from above, and allows water in the ground to rise via capillary action and dry at the surface (see **Building Science**). The clay can be grassed over, but it is unwise to use the area next to the wall for flower beds or for plants with deep root systems that may block the pipe.

Coarse fills such as pea gravel have the opposite effect to clay (allowing easy penetration of rainwater and runoff, but preventing drying), and should therefore never be used. Impermeable paving should also be avoided, whether this is made of cement, tiles or flagstones: it will reduce evaporation, and it is hard to effectively seal the joint between the paving and the wall, which can therefore become a source of moisture ingress. These finishes also make maintenance very difficult. Maintenance of drains at the base of walls is especially critical if the interior floor surfaces are not very permeable: failures would then cause water to rise up the nearest internal walls.

Upgrading rainwater drainage

1. To prevent drains being blocked with debris washed down from the roof, it is better to install gulleys with grilles and traps rather than running downpipes directly into the drains. Because leaks will be a considerable danger to building walls, it is critical that gulleys are designed to allow easy maintenance, and are set well away from the walls. Trenches should be backfilled with fine clay-rich soil, well compacted and grassed over to reduce splashback. If possible the ground should be sloped away from the building.

2. Excavation around sensitive sites may require a preliminary archaeological survey, and a watch to be kept during works.

3. Lining trenches in geotextiles reduces the amount of water and fine soil being washed in, making blockages less likely.

4. The design should avoid tight bends wherever possible.

5. Pipes should be laid on a bed of gravel, and provided with plentiful rodding points (at least one wherever two pipes meet).

6. Modern soakaways often use plastic mesh boxes, which make eventual clearance much easier.

Detailed measured plans should always be made of any drainage, and these should be kept in a safe and accessible place, to make any future investigations or alterations as straightforward and non-invasive as possible.

BUILDING ENVIRONMENT
CARE & REPAIR

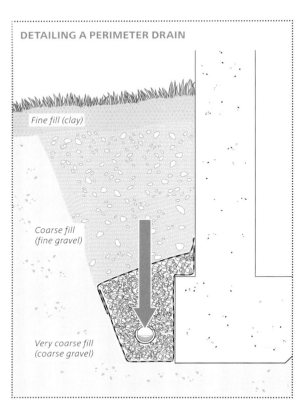

DETAILING A PERIMETER DRAIN

Fine fill (clay)

Coarse fill (fine gravel)

Very coarse fill (coarse gravel)

Since even the best-designed drains will block sooner or later, wherever perimeter drains are positioned they should be laid so that they can be easily cleared with rods. They should be as straight as possible, and have many accessible rodding points, with inspection points at every bend and every joint.

The connections between pipes should not be sealed, since this can hide blockages until they are severe (with potentially very harmful consequences).

Soakaways

Drains may feed directly into the sewers or a nearby watercourse, but more commonly they discharge into a soakaway. Failed soakaways will almost always be found to have silted up, and need excavation or replacement. New soakaways must be positioned and designed with the help of a specialist engineer; the current designs (plastic crates, lined with geotextiles) are currently proving very effective. To prolong their life, soakaways should be given inspection hatches and some means of cleaning.

Correcting Faulty Runoff

If the slope of the ground causes water to run back towards the footings, it is best to re-landscape, but this may not be possible (for example, the surrounding ground may contain important archaeological remains). An alternative would be to install a channel drain placed well back from the walls; where this would be obtrusive, in some cases a well-designed agricultural drain may be used instead.

Wherever possible landscaped slopes and retaining walls must be kept well away from the walls of the building, to permit good maintenance and drainage. The potential for improving the landscaping and drainage will depend on the ground and soil conditions, and so the services of a specialist engineer will almost certainly be required.

Waste Water Disposal

To protect watercourses and the water table from pollution, the disposal of waste water (including rainwater runoff from roofs and paving) is covered by strict regulations.

Sewage

If a toilet or kitchen is being installed for the first time in a remote building where there are no mains sewers for handling foul water (a rural church, for example), some form of disposal system will need to be introduced. This may present a number of challenges, including:

- dealing with intermittent and variable use (most water-treatment systems work best with a steady load)
- long distances to the main sewer
- having to take water delivery and disposal through thick historic walls (delivery pipes are usually 15 mm in diameter, and waste-water pipes around 110 mm; by using a macerator to break up the solids, the latter can be reduced to 22 mm)
- archaeologically sensitive landscape around the building, and poor access for vehicles (many systems require sludge to be removed regularly by tankers).

It may be necessary to think quite carefully about where to site the various components of the system to minimise the impact on the building, the landscape and any buried archaeology, as well as to maximise the efficiency of the system.

The main sewer is always to be preferred if it is available, but if not, systems that discharge to the soil are a good choice provided that the site has good drainage, and the water table is not too high.

The characteristics of the soil can be assessed with a percolation test, as described in *BS 6297:2007 + A1: 2008 Code of practice for the design and installation of drainage fields for use in wastewater treatment*, which also gives methods for calculating the size of sewage components such as tanks and leach fields.

Septic-Tank Systems

In very free-draining soils with low water tables, septic tanks can be discharged into a simple soakaway. In soils less able to accept water, a 'leach field' must be used instead: this is a network of perforated pipes on a gradual incline from the inlet. The water soaks into a clean bed of stone surrounding the pipes, giving sufficient treatment to protect the water table.

Trench-Arch Systems

Although trench arches should ideally be sited in biologically active soil of high porosity, they can work in marginal soils. In very poor soils, a diverter can be installed to alternate between two different trench arches. Macerators can help make trench-arch systems even more effective. Trench arches should be installed with inspection access points at either end.

BUILDING ENVIRONMENT
CARE & REPAIR

Building Regulations

DRAINAGE & WATER DISPOSAL

Part H of the 2000 UK Building Regulations (Drainage and Waste Disposal) gives practical guidance on all aspects of ground drainage, including sizing, detailing and positioning.

DRAINAGE

Upgrading drainage may require permissions from:
- the Local Authority (acting under Part H)
- the water authority
- any neighbouring properties sharing the drains, sewers or manholes.

Planning permission should not be needed unless the property is designated, but detailed advice should be sought from the Local Authority.

Excavation around historic properties will often require special permission, and it may well be necessary to organise archaeological supervision during works. Drainage around a church building will require specific permission from the ecclesiastical authorities.

WASTE WATER DISPOSAL

In England the responsibility for ensuring that waterways and groundwater are not polluted rests with the Environment Agency, and there are similar authorities elsewhere in the UK who act as statutory referees for new planning applications, granting a 'consent to discharge' if waste water is to be run into a stream or river. This consent will be contingent on an agreed level of waste water pre-cleaning being sustained, and inspectors will periodically test to ensure compliance with this requirement.

Sometimes permission can be granted for discharging into a suitable soil, provided that the discharge point is at least 10 m away from any watercourse.

In many areas, however, the law requires large buildings to have a soakaway or some other filtrating system, to prevent the public sewers being overwhelmed in storms; if it is not possible to install a soakaway, excess water can be discharged into a watercourse. Only if neither a soakaway nor a suitable watercourse are available can runoff be sent directly into a sewer.

There are also restrictions governing the location of soakaways. These should never be installed:
- within 5 m of a building or road
- within 2.5 m of a boundary
- wherever the water table could reach the bottom of the soakaway at any time of the year
- wherever contaminants in the runoff could result in pollution.

When choosing the best position for a soakaway, the slope must be taken into account so that the surrounding ground will not become waterlogged.

SYSTEMS FOR DEALING WITH 'BLACK' WATER

OPERATION	ADVANTAGES	DISADVANTAGES
MAIN SEWER		
Waste is discharged directly into the main sewer, which carries it to a central processing plant	Simple and cheap Can cope with intermittent use Does not need maintenance	Sewer may be some considerable distance away from the building There will be a small fee for use
CONSENTED DISCHARGE TO A WATERCOURSE		
Water must be pretreated before it is discharged, to meet the standard set by the Consent to Discharge	Many off-the-shelf pre-processing systems are available	Handling intermittent and varying loads can be difficult Requires deep excavations Treatment systems usually require regular maintenance (including the removal of sludge at intervals), and some a source of power
DISCHARGE TO SOIL: SEPTIC TANK		
Waste water is collected in a tank underground with an outlet slightly below the inlet Heavy matter sinks to form 'sludge', while organic matter forms a floating crust; liquid ('effluent') is discharged into a soakaway or leach field	Familiar system Can cope with intermittent use Does not require power Area over tank can be used	May require deep excavations Requires suitable soil Requires sludge removal at intervals Should not be used where there is a possibility of contaminating groundwater Anaerobic (system must be designed to minimise unpleasant smells)
DISCHARGE TO SOIL: TRENCH ARCH		
Waste is discharged directly into a long, wide and shallow chamber slightly sloping away from the inlet, backfilled with topsoil; the incoming water physically degrades the solid waste, and disperses it down and sideways, and over a wide area Worms in the soil break down the organic matter	Can cope with intermittent use Does not require sludge removal Hard to block Aerobic (no unpleasant smells) Does not require deep excavation, and area over trench can be used as long as traffic is not very heavy	System will be unfamiliar to most building users, and so may be more challenging to maintain Requires suitable soil
CESS POOL		
Waste is discharged into a large holding tank, from which it must be emptied at regular intervals	Can cope with intermittent use	Requires a sizeable excavation Requires regular emptying by a tanker, which will need access Drains must be kept completely watertight to prevent rainwater entering the tank

BUILDING ENVIRONMENT
CARE & REPAIR

WALLS

Dealing with Rainwater Penetration

Pointing & Rendering

If moisture problems persist in a masonry wall after repointing or the repair of the existing render, more invasive works may be needed. For example, it may be necessary to renew a lost render, or sometimes even add a render where the building did not originally have one.

For example, faulty cement joints can be a serious cause of moisture penetration, and can put brick, stone or terracotta buildings at risk, but although it should be helpful to remove the cement and replace it with a more suitable mortar, in practice this would cause too much damage to be feasible. Where moisture problems from this source are intractable, one possible solution is to protect the wall with a permeable render. No other form of coating should be considered, however, particularly not any coatings purporting to be waterproof, as these would simply hinder evaporation.

Where masonry that was originally constructed with lime-based mortars has been repointed with cement, and this is causing problems, the cement can usually be removed safely by using the right tools in the right hands. ⊖MORTARS

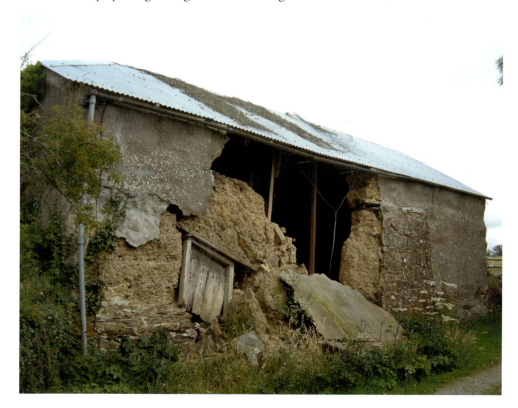

Cement renders

Cement renders are unsuitable for most types of construction, but for earthen buildings they can present such a high risk that, where they have been added, consideration should be given to their removal and replacement with a permeable lime render. Here, penetrating water trapped by the cement has caused structural failure of the walls.

In theory, cement renders should be replaced with lime-based permeable renders, but in practice removing cement without damaging the underlying wall is usually difficult, unless the render is in such poor condition that it is coming away. Moisture issues from this source can be so serious, however, that in some cases consideration may have to be given to removing the render as carefully as possible, and accepting some damage.

If a cement render is left in place, the building will need to be closely monitored to make sure that any problems that could cause water to enter through or behind the render are dealt with immediately. Fissures and cracks should be filled with a flexible and permeable material, such as a lime mortar (a waterproof coating should never be used).

Preventing moisture penetration is of the highest priority for earthen buildings with impermeable renders, since trapped water can cause the decohesion of the clay, threatening the structural integrity of the wall. Expert advice should be sought from a surveyor experienced in dealing with earthen buildings. Removing renders is associated with a risk of collapse, and so must be carried out very carefully; more information can be found in the *Earth, Brick & Terracotta* volume in this series. ⇨EARTH & BRICK

Moisture problems can be very serious for reinforced concrete structures, since water penetration is the most important cause of rebar corrosion. Damaged areas of concrete may need to be cut out so that the steel can be treated, and then patch repaired. In some cases it may be necessary to install cathodic protection. ⇨CONCRETE

If early curtain-walling has severe moisture ingress, it may need to be rebuilt to incorporate some form of rainscreen. ⇨GLASS

Water-shedding details

Water-shedding detailing will eventually degrade as a direct result of its function. If maintenance has been neglected and features such as cornicing have been lost, they should be reconstructed, if possible using the same materials and design as the original features.

Although it may sometimes be possible to slow future deterioration of very exposed elements using lead flashing and drips or other similar detailing, this requires considerable thought, since a poor design can trap water and wick it into the wall.

Post-work inspections should be scheduled to check that the repaired water-shedding details are behaving as they should.

Restoring Water-Shedding Details

Lost detailing should be replicated from contemporary neighbouring buildings if at all possible (providing that their detailing is not faulty). Most detailing of this type will originally have been constructed of stone, or later of brick and stucco. It is of course possible to reconstruct missing stone hood mouldings and cornices in stucco or concrete instead, but the results are not likely to have the same longevity.

However the replacement is made, it must be well anchored, and have no unprotected joints through which rainwater might be able to penetrate.

BUILDING ENVIRONMENT
CARE & REPAIR

Dealing with Moisture from the Ground

In masonry walls that have not been rendered with cement or given some other waterproof finish, groundwater is unlikely to affect more than the first course or two of masonry, but cellars, underfloor voids, and the walls of buildings where the earth has been allowed to build up against the exterior, may be very wet on the interior.

Preventing Lateral Penetration

If there is a problem that cannot be managed by maintenance or repair of the existing drains, or by installing land drains uphill from the building, there are two principal approaches: to add a waterproofing layer on the buried section of the wall, or take back the earth to create a ventilated trench. Both require excavation near the footings, and so will probably need advice from a structural engineer as well as a drainage expert. If the building is listed or the surroundings of historic importance, digging may require statutory consent, and possibly archaeological supervision.

Excavation

Historically, the ground outside basements or cellars in use was sometimes dug away to match the interior ground level, forming well areas or perimeter passageways. This approach allows the walls to dry out and stay dry, but excavation around an existing building is a costly and invasive exercise that may have both structural and archaeological implications, and could change the character of the building. It is only possible where excavation would not endanger the structure, and where it does not impinge on building or landscape significance. Excavations should generally incorporate a land drain as a fail-safe.

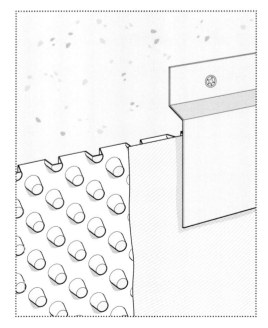

To separate an exterior wall from the ground abutting it, and thereby prevent lateral penetration of water, one approach is to use a geodrain. This must be capped at the top to ensure that water flowing down the walls travels over the geodrain, rather than behind it.

Waterproofing

Waterproofing coatings and metal flashings are not likely to have long lifespans when buried and exposed to quantities of water and salts from the ground, and so a modern geodrain (a plastic barrier with integral drainage channels) may be a better choice. This will need to connect at the bottom to the drain, and be flashed at the top to prevent water washing down the walls from entering. It will need to be replaced when it begins to fail.

Barriers such as geodrains do entail some risk. There is likely to be some leaking through and especially under the barrier, and if water does get in to the wall, it will be able to dry only towards the interior.

Damp Proofing

Damp proofing, which was first introduced in the second half of the 19th century to prevent damage from faulty sewers, is now an automatic inclusion in new construction. A damp-proof course [DPC] is a layer of some waterproof material such as sheet lead, slate, bituminous felt or plastic carried through the entire thickness of the wall just above the ground, to cut off water rising from the footings. This may be bedded into the joint between two courses of masonry, or set on the top of the plinth supporting a timber frame or an earthen wall, or some other moisture-sensitive form of construction. A damp-proof membrane [DPM] is usually a thick sheet of polythene, which may be used in various ways: for example, to protect church monuments positioned against exterior walls, or to isolate a concrete floor slab.

Injected 'damp-proofing' systems are not recommended for building conservation: not only is there no evidence that they work, but the risk from the associated cement renders and the damage from drilling multiple holes into the wall through which large quantities of liquid are introduced make them unacceptable (see **Deterioration & Damage: Problems Due to Alterations & Interventions**).

It is very rare that a DPC or DPM will be found to be a desirable option for controlling water: it risks moving the moisture problem elsewhere. To protect a building with its footing immersed in water, the damp proofing would need to form an unbroken barrier across the floor and through the walls, and an internal perimeter drain would need to be installed together with a pump to take the water it collects back to the exterior. Retrofitting damp-proof coursing into a building which was never designed to incorporate one is extremely invasive: to protect timber cill beams resting on damp masonry plinths from decay the frame would have to be jacked up section by section to insert the DPC; masonry walls would need to be cut through section-by-section using special saws, or long drills and chisels. It is difficult to imagine any situations where such invasive works would be justifiable.

Drying Wet Fabric

It is rarely necessary to install any special systems to dry walls recovering from moisture problems, except perhaps where the source of the water was widespread and prolonged: a flood or fire, for example (see the **Special Topic: Dealing with Disasters**).

Drying proceeds in two stages, and it is only the first – Stage I, where there are liquid flow paths from the centre of the material to the surface – that is able to remove substantial quantities of moisture from bulk material (see **Building Science**). Where possible, it is desirable to prolong Stage I drying so that more moisture is removed from the walls, so it is usually best not to accelerate the process to any great degree: slight airflow and good air exchange can often be helpful, but strong heating and too-powerful fans can easily dry the surface pores, moving the process into Stage II drying (which is very slow). Rapid drying also increases the risk of material damage.

Certainly drying should not be accelerated until all leaks have been dealt with: if the moisture sources have not been removed, drying will never be effective, whatever the mechanism. Trying to dry fabric wetted continually by a high water table, for example, would simply pull more water through the wall, exacerbating deterioration and raising the humidity within the room.

Proprietary treatments for drying 'damp walls', such as electro-osmosis, are generally unnecessary, and may prove counter-productive.

BUILDING ENVIRONMENT
CARE & REPAIR

Patent Systems for Drying Wet Walls

Moisture problems are such a concern for building managers that there is a thriving industry in systems for drying 'damp' walls, or reversing 'rising damp'. One of the greatest concerns raised by these types of systems is that they divert resources of time and money that would be far better spent in dealing with the sources of the moisture problem. To properly assess the effectiveness of a proprietary system for drying walls, it would be necessary to make no other changes to the building before or during the testing period (for example, not to fix faults in the water disposal systems). In practice this would be a very risky decision, since moisture ingress should always be halted as soon as possible.

Many proprietary systems (such as wall injection) are unsuitable for conservation use because of the impact they have on the building (see **Deterioration & Damage**), but other systems are relatively innocuous. One that is commonly proposed is 'electro-osmotic damp-proofing', which derives from systems used in analytical laboratories.

ELECTRO-OSMOTIC SYSTEMS

Liquids can be induced to migrate through a porous material by applying an electrical potential difference across them; this is used for analytical processes such as capillary electrophoresis.

Although early attempts to use electro-osmosis to dry walls used a circuit to set up a voltage drop between the wall and the ground ('active' electro-osmosis), this was found to move quantities of salts to the electrodes, which were then rapidly destroyed.

As an alternative the manufacturers turned to 'passive electro-osmosis', where the potential difference was supplied by the natural potential differences found within walls, and between the walls and the ground. It was claimed that since damp walls contained an electrical potential, the earthing of this would cause the water to move back down towards the ground. In fact, as the Building Research Establishment [BRE] pointed out in its 2004 book *Understanding Dampness*, these potential differences actually arise from the capillary movement of water and salts, so earthing them (if that should be possible) might be expected to increase upward flow rather than drive the moisture downwards. Although between 1961 and 1968 one company had installed 20,000 passive systems in the UK, there was no evidence that they had worked, and the industry returned to active systems, this time using electrodes that resisted corrosion.

These too proved disappointing, and experiments revealed a number of complications that would make it very difficult to dry real walls *in situ*:

- the forced water movement stopped once the pores were no longer completely saturated
- if there was a significant concentration of salts, the flow through clay bricks dropped to zero
- although in a saturated wall an applied current could drive water from the anode to the cathode, in uncarbonated mortar joints the water moved in the opposite direction, which significantly inhibited the overall flow.

In fact, the potential difference needed to reverse the enormous forces driving capillary rise in a wall would have be so large as to be impractical and even dangerous, so it is little surprise that neither the active nor passive systems have been shown to be effective in tests. Indeed, experiments by the BRE found that any drying they produced could actually be attributed to the rendering and plastering which was part of the systems being tested.

Damp-proof membranes

DPMs are often considered as a means of protecting church monuments from deterioration due to salt decay or corrosion of the supporting metalwork.

Where an important monument is at risk from persistent moisture problems in the wall or floor (whether because of intractable environmental problems, or because resources are insufficient to guarantee good maintenance), a DPM may be a possible solution. In practice it can prove challenging, particularly for wall monuments, since it is almost impossible to fix monuments back in place without piercing the membrane.

It must also be recognised and considered acceptable that, with a DPM in place, the water which no longer evaporates through the monument will travel elsewhere in the fabric.

If at all possible, it is much more effective, and much safer, to control the water at its source. This, fortunately, is extremely unlikely to be the water table; problems are almost always traceable to problems with the rainwater goods or drainage, usually compounded by high ground levels or cement pointing, or renders that prevent evaporation (see **Deterioration & Damage**).

Occasionally a DPC or DPM may be proposed as a way of providing extra protection to fragile and moisture-sensitive building elements, which might be at particular risk from future moisture ingress (for example, an important monument in an isolated church that may not always be maintained to a high standard). The damp proofing will cause the moisture to move elsewhere to evaporate, so it must be certain that protecting the important element is worth the increased risk to the rest of the fabric.

To function, the protection must form a continuous layer, unpunctured by fixings, and this can be extremely difficult to achieve (especially on walls). The lifespan of the intervention depends on the chosen material, and the conditions within the wall. The more invasive the installation, the more robust should be the material; and even lead may eventually corrode and need to be replaced.

Floor Replacement

If there is no continuous damp-proof course running under the ground floor and through the walls, covering the floor with an impermeable material such as concrete (or even with a floor finish such as vinyl) will greatly reduce the evaporation of any groundwater, which will therefore be driven up the internal and external walls. If such a problem exists and is severe, it may be necessary to replace the floor with a permeable material. A floor made from a permeable mortar such as 'limecrete' (hydraulic lime mixed with a low-density aggregate such as expanded clay) will also be better at buffering humidity, helping to reduce condensation problems.

The *Mortars, Renders & Plasters* volume of this series describes the construction of limecrete floors in detail. ⊖MORTARS

BUILDING ENVIRONMENT
CARE & REPAIR

Treatment of Below-Ground Interior Walls

If it is not possible to entirely prevent lateral penetration into a cellar, crypt or other space that is partly or completely below ground level, approaches to dealing with the interior space depend on the use to which it is being put.

If the space does not need to be made habitable, it is easiest and safest to simply accept a certain amount of dampness, and use the space as it was originally intended (that is, as cool storage for moisture-resistant materials, and to help stabilise the conditions in the habitable rooms above). To limit salt decay of the wall, heating and ventilating should be avoided unless the walls have been protected with a sacrificial lime plaster that could be replaced at intervals. ⊜MORTARS

Wall Finishes

For most subterranean walls, the best approach to dealing with damp is often to simply mask the deterioration by plastering, or with panelling or dry lining.

The traditional approach was to use limewash or a lime plaster with hydraulic additives, which could be replaced should patches of discolouration and decay become too disfiguring. Replacement also served to remove the accumulated salts. If permeable plasters and renders are introduced, these should be based on lime and should never contain gypsum (which will remain slightly soluble, and will introduce more salts). It is wise to make sure that any paint finish or other decoration is also permeable, so that penetrating water can evaporate. Soluble salts will then crystallise on the surface, where they can be brushed away, rather than lifting the finish. ⊜MORTARS

Timber panelling or modern dry lining hung on battens fixed to the wall can be very effective, and will usually have a longer lifespan than sacrificial plasters and renders. It will also greatly improve occupant comfort in cold conditions, since it cuts the radiant loss of heat from the body into the walls (see **Special Topic: Improving Energy & Carbon Performance**). To deliver an acceptably long lifespan, the fixings will need to be able to resist water and salts, but it should not be necessary to ventilate the panelling in any way (see the box on **Cavity Ventilation**). It should, however, be designed to open with relative ease, to allow the state of the wall to be checked every now and again, and catch any leaks or other avoidable moisture problems before they become serious.

Other popular solutions include waterproof finishes such as tanking (see **Making Attics & Cellars Habitable**). This can be effective if the entire wall is treated, but if the walls are not entirely below ground level, it is not advisable to waterproof only that part of the wall that lies below the ground, since this will simply push penetrating water higher up the wall until it reaches a point where it can evaporate.

Making Attics & Cellars Habitable

Pressure from the property market, and changes in living habits, have led to the widespread conversion of previously uninhabitable spaces such as attics and cellars. Most were originally designed to help the building buffer the exterior environment, and were used only for storage. Making them into living space requires limiting the penetration of water so that it can neither spoil the surface finishes, nor cause problems for the contents or the occupants by encouraging mould growth or decay; the impact on the building envelope will also need to be taken into account.

With space at a premium, especially in cities, converting cellars into living and working spaces is an increasingly common intervention, but one that requires good planning if moisture problems are not to prove an issue.

BUILDING ENVIRONMENT
CARE & REPAIR

ATTIC CONVERSIONS

The effect that converting an attic may have on the envelope depends on how the new space is expected to be used, as well as on the design and materials of the roof.

Attics used purely for storage can be kept separate from the rest of the house: the floor can be made as airtight as possible (and insulated if necessary), and the whole attic space can be kept ventilated. Even if some water gets in during rainstorms, it will be able to dry again. In cool conditions, ventilation removes any vapour rising from the building, and in locations with substantial snowfall it keeps the roof cold enough to prevent ice dams created by melting snow. In hot weather, the ventilation helps remove not only hot air rising through the building, but the solar-heated air in the attic.

If the intention is to use the loft for bedrooms or living space, it will need to be coupled with the interior, so any insulation or air barriers will need to be placed at roof rather than ceiling level. This can create challenges for keeping the roof structure in good condition. Good ventilation is always difficult to achieve with complex roofs, but it is immeasurably harder when it must be applied to the small space between the lining and the covering. To avoid condensation and moisture accumulation, it is very important to ensure that humid air from within the building is not allowed to penetrate. In cool climates, the most effective way of doing this is to use an insulation material with low air permeability, and to provide an airtightness layer in the form of a wet-applied plaster ceiling. This will also reduce draughtiness, which is a common complaint in attic conversions. In areas prone to snow, there will also need to be a vented airspace between the insulation and the covering.

All conversions will make accessing the underside of the roof difficult, so moisture problems will be harder to spot and harder to fix. Other technical issues include structural stability, fire resistance, noise and access.

CELLAR CONVERSIONS

Transforming subterranean spaces into usable space is often very complex. The chief problem is stopping water penetrating laterally from the ground into the walls and floors, spoiling the finishes and producing an unpleasantly dank environment. The first step in every case is to ensure that there are no avoidable sources of such water; for instance, leaking drains or water mains. Sources such as these may be making the crypts and cellars in many older buildings much wetter than they would have been in the past, when the water table was the principal source of groundwater. It is sensible to ensure that all treatable water sources are identified and dealt with before any other works begin, since tanking very wet cellars has been known to drive water elsewhere in the fabric.

For external walls that are partly or totally below ground level, the most effective way of dealing with lateral penetration is to move the earth back from the exterior wall, add a drain, and then either line the wall with some damp-proofing material before backfilling once more, or better still leave an open and well-ventilated trench (see **Treatment of Below-Ground Interior Walls**). This approach was taken in the past when many large houses and terraces were built; the 'basement' rooms were deliberately cut off from the ground by drained areas, wells, or even passageways. Removing the earth around foundations after construction is a risky process, however, and it may well prove impossible.

Alternative solutions must take into account not only the importance of the building and the intended usage and expected lifespan of the conversion, but the amount of moisture which needs to be handled. Converting a cellar that routinely floods will require a very different approach to converting a basement where no more than a small amount of groundwater is seeping through the walls.

In cases where the degree of moisture ingress is small, dry lining or panelling to hide some of the deterioration of surface finishes can be sufficient to make the space usable for most purposes. Where ingress is serious and intractable, the floor and walls may need to be waterproofed; it is important not to seal only the floor, as this may drive the water further up the walls. It may be necessary to incorporate perimeter drains to collect any water entering and take it well away from the fabric, and possibly pumps as well. If none of these approaches are feasible because of the significance of the walls or of the floor covering, or because of archaeological remains, it may not be possible to successfully convert the cellar.

Converting completely subterranean spaces such as coal stores under footpaths is even more difficult than converting cellars, since it is almost impossible to prevent moisture seeping down from above. Tanking, cavity membranes or other systems that completely line the vault with waterproof material – the most successful approach – are susceptible to tearing, cracking and leaking as a result of vibrations from traffic above, or from digging or drilling nearby. It is also difficult to successfully detail lighting and other services: wires must be run across the surface, and fixings that might puncture the lining or tanking must be strictly avoided.

British Standards

BS 8102:2009 Code of practice for protection of below ground structures from water from the ground

BS 8102 does not consider the damage that may be inflicted by the installation of structural waterproofing systems, nor does it differentiate between the types of buildings to which it may be applied. It is therefore important to bear in mind that most waterproofing systems will severely damage the walls and floor, and so will rarely be acceptable for use in historic buildings.

BUILDING ENVIRONMENT
CARE & REPAIR

METHODS FOR CONVERTING BELOW-GROUND ROOMS

	DESIGN CRITERIA	COMMENTS
EXTERNAL WORKS		
EXCAVATION	Base of trench should be beneath internal floor level and drain to a central point, preferably away from the walls of the building Retaining walls should be far enough from the building walls to permit maintenance	Expensive Invasive: may have structural implications Can change character of building
EXTERIOR TANKING	Moisture barrier and drain installed, and the surrounding ground returned to its original level	Invasive Increased water pressure towards the internal floor, especially where it joins the walls
INTERNAL WORKS		
DRY LINING	Panelling installed that leaves the walls untouched behind a finished internal surface Panelling must not be in direct contact with the wall, but fixed to battens instead	Traditional approach (lath-and-plaster linings) Use water-resistant materials for battens Success depends on the severity of the moisture problem: most successful if problems are quite mild Use permeable paints and wallpapers
SACRIFICIAL PLASTER	Permeable plaster (usually based on lime) allowed to absorb moisture and salts Replaced when deteriorated	Finish will visibly degrade, and will need regular refurbishment or replacement Allows salts to be removed at regular intervals Good evaporative surface Use permeable paints and wallpapers
CAVITY MEMBRANE SYSTEMS	Lining with special waterproof sheeting fixed directly to wall; this can then be decorated Lining must include the floor Usually drained with a sump and pump, even when this is not strictly necessary	Must be very carefully detailed and maintained to prevent the lining being breached (for example, there can be no fixings to the surface that might penetrate the sheet) Junctions are the weakest points Will leak if lining is torn or punctured
INTERIOR TANKING	Impervious coating (usually based on cement) to prevent water penetration Tanking must include the floor	Must be very carefully detailed and maintained to prevent the tanking being breached (for example, there can be no fixings to the surface that might penetrate the tanking) Junctions are the weakest points Will leak if tanking is cracked or punctured Cracking is a great risk, since cement is brittle

DEALING WITH TEMPERATURE PROBLEMS

DIFFERENTIAL HEATING & COOLING

Cracks and tears in materials such as metal, glass, terracotta and concrete, due to thermal expansion and contraction coupled with incorrect detailing, will usually appear quickly. For new building elements, the only solution is to reconstruct the damaged area so that it includes more (or more effective) expansion joints. ⊖METALS ⊖CONCRETE ⊖EARTH & BRICK ⊖GLASS

If older building elements suddenly begin to deteriorate, the deterioration will need to be traced to its source: something will have happened to either change the element's exposure to heating or cooling, or to prevent the movement that results. For example, metal roof sheets can quickly fail if they have been re-laid over boards coated with bitumen: the bitumen will soften in the sun and then glue the underside of the sheets to the boards, which will then be at risk of tearing from thermal movement.

Even sound materials that have been correctly detailed will eventually begin to fail from wear and tear.

FREEZE-THAW DAMAGE

Freeze-thaw damage in porous materials will only occur if the material is saturated, so the first step is to deal with the source of water. Often the damage will also be associated with poor materials, such as badly fired bricks or inferior stone.

In thin masonry walls that have moisture problems, internal wall insulation can lead to freeze-thaw damage because the wall is no longer being warmed by the indoor air, especially if the insulation (or any associated AVCLs) is causing condensation. In this case, removing the insulation should be seriously considered.

ICE & SNOW ON ROOFS

In areas with heavy snowfall, pitched roofs should be equipped with snow guards or hooks to prevent the snow sliding down the roof and causing damage below. It will be necessary to deal with the underlying cause, whether this is poor insulation or heat rising into the roof space through gaps in the ceiling, or between the ceiling and the wall.

Persistent issues with water freezing in gutters may need to be dealt with by installing heating tapes.

BUILDING ENVIRONMENT
CARE & REPAIR

DEALING WITH LIGHT-INDUCED PROBLEMS

Discolouration and degradation of wood can be prevented by surface coatings that absorb or reflect ultraviolet light and limit moisture uptake, although these will need to be maintained; preference should be given to stains and linseed-oil paints, and other permeable coatings that do not trap moisture. Since the rate of surface loss from light degradation is generally around one millimetre per century, it may be best to forego surface coatings in any situation where the discolouration is acceptable.

Acceptable light levels have never been conclusively established for all materials, especially with regard to the ancillary effect of radiant heating, but materials sensitive to ultraviolet radiation will certainly be protected if the sunlight is filtered so that it contains no more than 75 microwatts per lumen (equalling an incandescent lamp). Direct light causes far more damage than diffuse, so for sensitive contents it may be sufficient just to move them out of the sunlight. It must be remembered that in winter, when the sun is low, direct sunlight may enter into rooms that are exposed only to diffuse light over most of the year.

Any desire to set limits for incoming sunlight through windows must be balanced against the wish to see the objects and, of course, to look outside. The choice of method will be restricted by the significance of the windows and of the glass they contain. For windows glazed with hand-made or early machine-made glass, solutions may need to be quite innovative. For example, where the window itself cannot be treated, it may be possible to add filters to existing or new secondary glazing. ⊖GLASS

Filtering sunlight

Filters may limit solar heating and the ingress of damaging wavelengths of sunlight, but they will also affect colour rendition and illumination.

Films are available that can be applied to *in-situ* glass, but it should be remembered that these have short lifespans, and can prove very difficult to remove when they have begun to fail. They should never be applied to early hand-made or machine-made glass.

In some cases, it may be possible to install laminated glass made with integral filters into secondary glazing.

OPTIONS FOR LIMITING SUN DAMAGE THROUGH WINDOWS

INTERVENTION	COMMENTS
ADHESIVE SOLAR FILMS	Fitted to one side of the glass, to reduce the transmission of ultraviolet radiation, visible light or solar heat (or a combination of these)
	Relatively cheap and easy to apply
	Do not require replacement of existing glazing
	Can damage glass (so not appropriate for hand-made or early machine-made glass)
	Easily scratched
	Not durable if applied externally
COLOURLESS UV FILTERS	Prevent the passage of all radiation below 400 nm, but transmit all visible radiation
YELLOW-TINTED FILTERS	Absorb all ultraviolet and short wavelength visible radiation
	Alter colour rendition
VARNISHES CONTAINING UV ABSORBERS	Must be painted onto the inside of window glass
	On windows exposed to extreme temperatures, cause cracking and condensation (and so damage to glass and destruction of varnish)
	Easily abraded during cleaning
SELF-SUPPORTING ACRYLIC SHEETING CONTAINING UV ABSORBERS	Yellowish tint
	Easily scratched, which can cause problems with glare
	Existing glazing must be replaced, or acrylic used to make secondary glazing
LAMINATED GLASS	The layer of plastic (polyvinyl-butyral) contains ultraviolet absorbers
	Expensive
	Existing glazing must be replaced, or the laminated glass used to make secondary glazing
BLINDS	Usually made of a white or cream-coloured fabric which gives a diffuse light whilst inhibiting the passage of direct sunlight
	Must be either left closed, or opened and closed in response to sunlight (there are automatic systems for this, though commonly it is done by hand)
	Must be well fitted
CURTAINS	Usually made of thick fabric which prevents the passage of all, or most, light
	Must be either left closed, or opened and closed in response to sunlight (there are automatic systems for this, though commonly it is done by hand)
	Must be well fitted
SHUTTERS	Made of wood or similar materials; sometimes have holes, but otherwise prevent all light ingress
	Must be either left closed, or opened and closed in response to sunlight
	Must be adjusted manually

BUILDING ENVIRONMENT
CARE & REPAIR

DEALING WITH POLLUTION

Pollution is rather a difficult problem to deal with, since many of the major sources are outside the control of the building managers, and may vary according to the weather or the building use. The seriousness of the problem will also depend on the type of pollutant, and the way it reacts with the building fabric. For example, sulphates are a serious problem for limestones, since they react with the calcium carbonate to form soluble calcium sulphates.

The fundamental steps to limiting pollution damage are:
1. Cut the amount of pollutant as much as possible.
2. Prevent the pollutant meeting sensitive surfaces.
3. Take steps to reduce the interaction with sensitive surfaces.

It is far easier to deal with the sources of interior pollution (such as smoke or cooking fats) than with exterior sources, but there are some ways in which it might be possible to alleviate environmental pollution, such as planting trees and bushes to collect gases and particulates. Deposits such as bird droppings can be avoided by preventing birds roosting on sensitive surfaces (see **Dealing with Biological Problems**).

Most pollution damage requires that certain catalysts be present as well, notably water and heat. By eliminating these, it may be possible to protect particularly fragile parts of the building. Deterioration can also be reduced by a cleaning regime; although cleaning has its own risks, it is usually better to clean lightly and often, rather than wait for the pollutant to accumulate and react with the surface of the material.

Where the exterior environment would be hostile to the building contents, it will usually be necessary to limit air exchange with the interior; this might be as simple as keeping the windows closed when the pollution is at its worst, or as complicated as installing filter systems. Positive pressure systems (where the internal air is kept at a higher pressure than the exterior, so that the exchange is always outwards) are used in buildings where clean air is critical (for example, in research laboratories or certain hospital wards), but these are rare in other types of building.

Pollution will be automatically absorbed by many permeable materials: whether this is good or bad depends on the significance of the materials, and the impact the pollution would have on them. It may be possible to intentionally absorb some gaseous air pollutants onto neutralising materials such as activated charcoal or silica gel. Usually neutralising systems are passive, but it is possible to design active systems that pump the air through the absorbent.

House plants have been shown to absorb carbon dioxide, as well as indoor pollutants such as benzene, formaldehyde and other gases from building materials such as fibreboards, carpets and paints (see **Special Topic: Buildings & Human Health**).

DEALING WITH BIOLOGICAL PROBLEMS

There are many products and technologies devoted to bioremediation. Biocides (pesticides and herbicides) are rarely a long-term option: as well as being dangerous, they can be very difficult to apply successfully. Even if they do succeed in removing the pest for a time, the treatment will probably have to be repeated every few years, so it is much more cost effective – as well as safer – to solve the underlying environmental problems that are producing conditions in which the pests thrive. There is a risk, though, that the new conditions may be ideal for some other problem creature or plant.

DECAY ORGANISMS

In practice, most decay problems will solve themselves if the underlying source of moisture is removed, though this may take some time. ⊙TIMBER

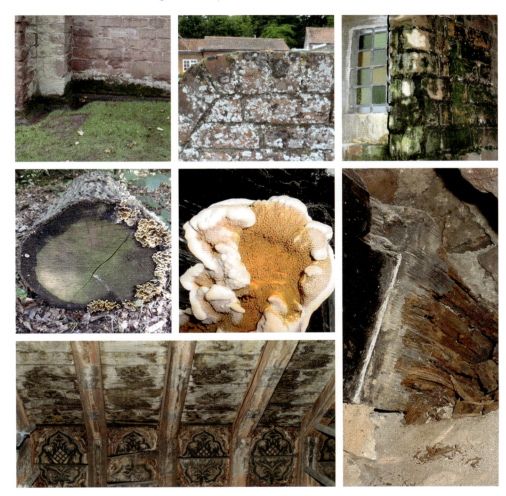

Microorganisms will grow wherever there is water and a source of nutrients

Top left, centre and right: Most micro-organic growths are innocuous, or at worst disfiguring.

A few growths, such as the fungi that cause timber rot (*middle left and centre*), can cause serious damage (*bottom left and right*).

In all cases, the remedy is to remove the source of moisture.

BUILDING ENVIRONMENT
CARE & REPAIR

Algae & Moss

Algae and moss growing on buildings are often indicative of damp conditions. If the source of water is removed they will die, and remains can then be brushed away. Stubborn traces should be removed with wooden or plastic spatulas, which are less likely to damage the substrate than metal tools. ➔CONCRETE ➔MORTARS ➔STONE

Where removing all sources of moisture is difficult, algae can be killed by ultraviolet irradiation. Periodic irradiation can form part of routine maintenance, and permanent installations are also possible. ➔MORTARS

Dealing with Fungi

For every case that requires substantial intervention, there are dozens of fungal attacks that require little more than the removal of the moisture source. It is also important to be quite sure that the problem is ongoing before major interventions are undertaken; often the fungus that has been found is in fact dead, the original outbreak having been caused by problems long since resolved.

If there is a major outbreak that is still active, it is important to consult an experienced and independent specialist to advise on minimum intervention. Stripping back and irrigation with fungicides is common, but it is both extremely damaging and completely unnecessary. Once the source of water has been removed, fungicides are rarely needed, and even then are usually used only in small quantities to prevent the fungus fruiting as it dies.

Insects

Wherever possible, insect pests should not be controlled with pesticides, not only because of the health risks, but also because frequent retreatment will be needed. It is better to make the building less desirable to the pest species.

For example, if mason bees have been attacking mortar joints, chemical control would mean injecting the bee holes with an insecticide, and spraying the walls every autumn. One successful means of control for mason bees, however, has been to rake out the joints squarely to a depth of at least 15 mm, before repointing using an appropriate mortar that is just hard enough to discourage the bees. This should be done in late summer. Other options include hanging fine mesh over the wall to prevent entry. ➔MORTARS

The *Timber* volume in this series has extensive information about the treatment of biodeterioration and insect pests. ➔TIMBER

Health & Safety

PESTICIDES

A pesticide is any product designed to prevent, repel or kill a pest. In the context of historic buildings, the pesticides most likely to be used are insecticides, fungicides, rodenticides and herbicides. Since these are toxic to certain organisms, they may also pose a risk to other plant or animal species (some of which might be protected by law) as well as to humans; for this reason their use, storage and disposal are strictly controlled. ➔BASICS

Pesticides should be used only where they are strictly necessary. An essential preliminary is an expert diagnosis that has unambiguously identified the pest and confirmed that the attack is ongoing.

Root barriers cannot stop root growth, but only deflect it: plant roots are strongly attracted to water and nutrients in soils, and will often find ways under, through or around even the best barriers.

These photographs of a section of the medieval moat wall at the Tower of London, which collapsed suddenly as a result of the root growth of a neighbouring plane tree, show how the wall has deflected the roots, but structural damage has nonetheless occurred as the deflected roots have thickened.

PLANTS

If tree roots have found their way into drains, the most satisfactory solution will usually be to replace the damaged pipe, preferably re-routing it further away.

There has been some research into chemicals that might kill off some parts of a root system whilst not killing the plant, but so far without notable success. It may be better to install a 'root barrier' – a geotextile or membrane sometimes impregnated with copper compounds or other chemicals that repel growing root tips – which is embedded in the ground between the plant and the drain (or other sensitive part of the building). Root barriers have also been used to isolate soil contaminated with knotweed or other highly invasive species, but no barrier can ever be completely effective, since roots can always grow under them or around them, if not through them.

WILDLIFE

Wire mesh and netting are the most common and effective ways of restricting access to areas that are providing a direct food source for birds and other animals. For example, birds can be prevented from stripping freshly-puttied windows by a temporary cover of monofilament net designed to protect fruit, and thatchers occasionally advise that roofs of long straw must be protected from birds and squirrels with wire netting (squirrels will chew through plastic). This has drawbacks, and should not be considered unless absolutely necessary.

If possible, it may be better to deal with the source of food instead. For example, cutting insect infestations in shingle roofs can reduce woodpecker damage; this could perhaps be achieved by installing metal sheeting under the shingles, or (if re-roofing) by laying the shingles onto boards that are spaced more widely apart. ROOFING

BUILDING ENVIRONMENT
CARE & REPAIR

Managing Birds

Whether birds cause serious problems depends both on the habits of the species, and on where the perches, nests or roosts are located on the building. Since many different birds depend on buildings for nest sites, it may be necessary to balance nature conservation and building conservation. Information about the conservation status and the control of different bird species can be obtained from the Royal Society for the Protection of Birds.

Many different approaches to bird deterrence have been tried, including flying hawks, scarers and audible repellents, but these do have certain drawbacks, not least that their action is not species-specific. Culling is often proposed for controlling pigeon populations, but it is never effective unless the population is very small and isolated; otherwise, birds in neighbouring areas will simply move in.

All bird nests are protected by law: it is illegal to intentionally disturb or destroy the active nest of any wild bird. Nestlings must be allowed to fledge before any action is taken to block access or remove nests. If nests are found during roofing works, eggs and nestlings should not be disturbed, and Natural England should be consulted.

Endangered species should be allowed to nest wherever there is no direct conflict. If the roof must be sealed off to prevent damage, nest boxes can be positioned under the eaves for threatened birds such as starlings, sparrows and swifts; these can be cleaned after the breeding season to limit the number of parasites. Shelves can also be fitted below the nests to catch droppings.

If nests must be removed, it will be necessary to ensure that they are no longer in use (for larger buildings and commercial properties, it is wise to seek advice from an independent specialist organisation such as the Pigeon Control Advisory Service).

Laws Protecting Birds

All wild birds, together with their nests and eggs, are protected by the Wildlife & Countryside Act 1981. It is an offence to damage or destroy an active nest, or to prevent the parent birds having access to it. In the case of birds that are listed on Schedule 1 of the Act, such as the barn owl, it is an offence even to disturb the birds when they are near or at the nest.

In England, General Licences are issued by the Government to allow 'authorised persons' (the owner or tenant of the land or property, or someone acting with the owner's permission) to kill or capture certain species of birds, including feral pigeons. General Licenses allow people to carry out activities that affect protected species without the need to apply for a personal licence. They are only used for activities that carry a low risk for the conservation or welfare of the protected species, and where a personal licence would be routinely issued. If a building manager plans to act under the authority of a General Licence, they must be satisfied that they are eligible to do so and must act within the provisions of the relevant General Licence: the conditions of the licence must be checked carefully to ensure that the situation is covered, and to comply with these conditions. If the planned work cannot be carried out under the provisions of a General Licence, a specific or individual licence must be sought from Defra. Details of general licences can be found at *www.naturalengland.org.uk/ourwork/regulation/wildlife/licences/generallicences.aspx#a*

Legislation can change rapidly according to the conservation status of the bird, so it is important that the latest advice is sought from the relevant government department before any action is taken. The website of the Royal Society for the Protection of Birds (RSPB) also has excellent and detailed advice (*www.rspb.org.uk*).

Preventing Perching

Feral pigeons and other troublesome birds will perch on buildings to overlook regular food sources. If perching is a problem, the most important step is to try to remove the source of food (for example, preventing people feeding pigeons in the area).

Preventing Roosting & Nesting

Birds such as pigeons need to be prevented from entering areas where they may roost or nest in numbers, such as courtyards, balconies and windows, or around statuary or pipe work. Roosting sites may also be popular with other more desirable birds; but fortunately pigeons are large, so it is often possible to exclude them and not the smaller songbirds.

The problem will have to be dealt with in the winter, ideally between October and February when birds should have finished nesting. Any holes or gaps giving access to the roof or some other sensitive area of the building will need to be cleaned out and sealed, which should be done mid-morning to minimise the risk of trapping any roosting birds. If there is any doubt as to whether all birds have left, a fine wire mesh can be fixed over the entrance, and checked at intervals to ensure that no birds are trapped; permanent repairs can be made when it is certain that no birds remain.

The access to the site will then need to be repaired, or blocked off with netting or the correct wire or nylon mesh. Monofilament mesh, for example, comes in a range of sizes: 19 mm for birds as small as sparrows, 28 mm for starlings and larger birds, 50 mm for pigeons, and 75 mm for gulls. If well installed, netting can be relatively inconspicuous, and does not noticeably reduce light levels in the building. However, it does tend to trap windblown leaves and rubbish, so maintenance is an important issue.

Netting and mesh
Netting can provide some protection from birds for elaborate features on the building façade, but it is not necessarily unobtrusive.

BUILDING ENVIRONMENT
CARE & REPAIR

DEALING WITH PIGEON PROBLEMS

NETTING, MESH & CHIMNEY COWLS

Monofilament netting is a good choice for blocking off areas likely to attract roosting or nesting birds. Chimneys may need to be protected with a cover of 'aviary mesh', a fine mesh made from galvanised steel. Steel mesh can also be used for protecting gutters and hoppers.

If jackdaws are a problem in a large chimney, the chimney should of course not be used until the nestlings have fledged. Once the nest is empty, it should be removed, and the chimney should be capped or protected with a wire cowl. The chimney should be cleaned before autumn each year by a qualified sweep.

SPIKES

Birds like to sit on the leading edges of ledges and cills to look for food, which can be prevented by anti-roosting spikes of steel or plastic fixed to the surface (usually using a silicone-based glue that does not penetrate the building material, and can be removed at a later date). Spike systems are available for many types of building element, from roof ridges to chimney pots and gutters, and are considered the most reliable and cost-effective method for managing feral pigeons.

Spikes can look odd on some building elements, but on the whole they are surprisingly discreet. However, they will trap debris on the ledge, and in some locations will need to be cleaned regularly. The lifespan of the silicone adhesive will be limited by its exposure, but it will certainly need to be replaced at intervals.

SPRUNG WIRES

Nylon-coated stainless-steel wire (with a diameter too small for pigeons or gulls to grip) is attached by tension springs to either horizontal or vertical posts, so that the wire will bounce about if a bird tries to land on it; this appears to disorientate them and make them avoid that perch.

Post-and-wire systems are relatively discreet and effective, and can effectively deter birds looking from perching, but they should not be used to protect sites used for roosting or nesting. Because the wire must be kept in tension, they are difficult to install on some surfaces, and are best suited to long flat elements such as windowsills, roof ridges and cornices. Where possible, posts should be slotted into drilled holes, but for many historic buildings this would be too invasive; in this case it is possible to use special posts with wide plastic bases, which can be glued in place with a silicone-based glue. The problem is that the glue must be allowed to cure before the system can be put under tension, and this can take several days.

DEALING WITH PIGEON PROBLEMS

REPELLENT GELS

Perching points are coated with a non-setting polybutylene gel that sticks to the feet of birds. Although it is nontoxic, it is unpleasant and discourages them not only from using that perch, but any other surfaces that appear to be gel-coated. There is a considerable risk that birds may transfer the sticky product to their wings or eyes; and again gels are not species-specific; the property owner may face legal action if a protected bird is injured or killed. To prevent the worst risk – roosting birds being 'glued' in place – in the UK the gel must always be coated with a special sealant.

There are problems for the building as well: the gel is hard to remove, can trap moisture and dirt and debris, and over time will tend to soak into porous materials such as stone and mortar, causing staining and other problems. Gels are also expensive, particularly since they have a short lifespan and must be reapplied yearly, if not more often.

SLOPING CAPS FOR PERCHES

A common roosting or nesting area is on ledges or the building façade, particularly where these are protected by projecting features such as eave overhangs. This can be prevented by capping the ledges with an angled cover. Proprietary anti-pigeon slopes are available, and generally use slippery PVC sheeting, but bespoke slopes can be made of other materials including plywood, as long as the angle of the slope is increased to make up for the decreased slipperiness.

Similar cappings could be used upside-down to prevent swallows building nests under overhanging eaves.

Care needs to be taken with detailing, especially with regards to water-shedding. The slope installation should not increase the risk of water penetration into what is already a fairly weak area of the envelope.

DECOYS

Static models in the form of a bird of prey (most commonly an owl) can be mounted high up on, or above, the building to deter roosting and nesting, but research commissioned by the UK's Department for Environment, Food and Rural Affairs [Defra] suggest that this is ineffective at best, and in some cases may even attract rather than deter pest species which flock to mob the decoy.

Kites in the form of birds of prey can be tethered to the building, to give a convincing imitation of a live raptor to deter pest species. Defra's research suggest that pigeons and other pest species quickly become habituated to moving decoys, just as they do to still ones.

BUILDING ENVIRONMENT
CARE & REPAIR

DEALING WITH PIGEON PROBLEMS

BIO-ACOUSTIC, SONIC & ULTRASONIC DEVICES

The hunting calls of birds of prey can be broadcast at intervals to deter the pest species; it is also possible to broadcast loud noises such as cannonfire, but this is less desirable for the occupants of the building.

Electronic repellents using similar equipment to emit ultrasound rather than audible signals are also available, but there is little evidence to suggest these are effective. They should not be used in locations known to have bats.

To prevent rapid habituation, the frequency and timing of broadcasts must be varied continually.

BIRDS OF PREY

Both wild and trained birds of prey have been used to try to deter pigeon roosting and nesting.

Considerable reductions in pigeon numbers have been reported when peregrine falcons have taken up residence, and tall buildings such as cathedrals may add peregrine nest boxes to encourage this.

Another approach is to fly a trained raptor near the roosting sites: a series of closely spaced visits are made to cause the pigeons to move from the site, after which control is maintained by routine visits. Success depends on whether or not the pigeons become habituated to the visits, and this in turn depends on the species of raptor used – hawks are much less effective than falcons, for which the pigeon is natural prey – and also on whether or not the raptor is allowed to kill.

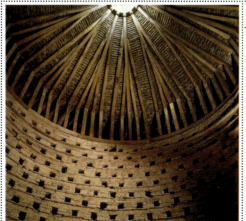

ARTIFICIAL BREEDING SITES

Some good results have been reported from dovecotes installed on or near the building, and routinely replacing any newly laid eggs with artificial eggs (simply removing the eggs encourages the birds to lay again). This steadily reduces the population, but does not encourage new flocks to enter the area.

Working Around Bats

All bats are protected, together with their roost sites (even if they are not always present). If bats are roosting in the roof of a building, their access must not be impeded, so if roof repair work is needed, advice will have to be sought from the relevant statutory nature conservation agency, or the Bat Conservation Trust. ⊖BASICS

Dealing with Rat Runs

Rats will burrow holes and long runs into earth walls, especially if they are damp. In all cases of suspected rat damage, an expert in cob construction will need to be consulted to establish the extent of the runs and the most suitable method of repair. If the wall has not been structurally compromised, the voids can be grouted with a thin earthen mortar, but it is usually better to cut out the burrows and insert new blocks. ⊖EARTH & BRICK

BUILDING ENVIRONMENT
CARE & REPAIR

MODIFYING THE INTERIOR ENVIRONMENT

Adjusting the interior climate is perhaps the most difficult aspect of building conservation, and it certainly requires the best understanding of how the envelope operates as a whole. Alterations can be dangerous, and without proper planning they may also fail to achieve expectations.

PLANNING INTERVENTIONS

COLLECTING SUPPORTING INFORMATION

Since the outcome of any intervention of this kind depends not only on the exact nature of the building and its surroundings, but on the precise way it is being used, every situation will be unique. There have been many attempts to develop standard approaches to conditioning indoor air, but in practice these never prove successful: the complex behaviour of the individual building must be understood, or else it is too easy to introduce problems rather than solutions.

In most cases – certainly if the building is very significant, or has very complex environmental problems, or contents and fabric that could be damaged by unsuitable interior temperatures or humidities (wall paintings or fine woodwork, for example) – it will not be possible to develop a programme of modifications without first reaching a practical understanding of the current environment. This may well demand environmental monitoring, and it is usually safest to begin to collect at least a year of data before works are proposed to begin. The collected information will also provide a baseline against which the post-intervention environment can be compared.

DETERMINING THE AIM OF INTERIOR MODIFICATIONS

Defining the precise aim of the modifications is fundamental to success, but surprisingly rare. To give a typical example, it is common to launch a programme to 'improve the heating of the building'; in fact, the underlying aim is not heating *per se*, but rather providing the building users with a better degree of comfort. If the stated aim is user comfort, it becomes clear that the first step must be to discover why and when the various users feel uncomfortable, and to use this information to find ways of ameliorating the causes of discomfort. If the building has multiple uses or many different types of user, each will have to be considered and understood.

By taking the time to closely analyse the needs of the building and its users before beginning to think about solutions, the best approaches to intervening will often become obvious. In most cases the best solution will not be a single piece of equipment, but a hybrid approach combining conditioning systems with behavioural change, and very simple interventions such as folding draught screens or carpets on the floor.

The first step is to narrow down the needs of the project. Essentially, modifications to the interior environment have one of two purposes: to provide safe conditions for fragile fabric or contents, or to provide better conditions for the building use (a greater degree of user comfort, or perhaps particular temperatures and humidities for process control). These aims can be in conflict, so understanding the exact needs of the situation is vital.

NARROWING DOWN THE NECESSARY OUTCOMES

WHAT IS NEEDED?	ISSUES TO CONSIDER
Very stable air temperature and humidity (usually for the protection of sensitive contents; most common in museums)	How much range and speed of variation is permitted? Rapid small changes may be more damaging than slow changes of greater magnitude
	Can conditions be allowed to vary at all at different times of the day, or at different seasons?
	Close control of temperature and humidity is very difficult to achieve, and requires air to be flowed through the conditioned space: this is usually possible only in sealed cases
	Spaces that have changes in patterns of use or location of contents cannot be closely controlled (for example, presence of users will increase temperature and humidity, and movement of furniture will affect airflow)
	Are there any associated issues, such as security?
Increased thermal or humidity buffering to reduce the response of the interior to the exterior conditions	Humidity buffering can be increased in two different ways: • by decreasing air exchange • by increasing materials in the indoor space that will temporarily absorb water vapour
Improved environmental conditions for users	How, when and why do the various users feel uncomfortable?
	Desirable conditions will depend on exactly what the users are doing in the space, and how they are dressed
	There may be conflicts between the needs of different groups of users
Ease and reliability	Since different users will have different ideas of comfort, flexibility is critical to success
	Controls will need to be transparently simple to use
Sustainability	Sustainable systems demand limiting the amount of energy used not only for running the system, but also for installation and ongoing care and maintenance

Since the effects any intervention might have on either the interior environment or the fabric of the building are almost impossible to predict, it is important to proceed slowly, assessing the impact of each alteration or addition before beginning on the next step. Flexibility is key to success: it should be possible to adjust the modifications in response to the way the real building environment is found to be behaving. It is safest to begin with those elements of the proposed solution that are likely to give the greatest improvement for the least risk; as well as being more likely to produce the desired indoor environment, this methodical approach almost invariably proves to be better for the building fabric.

Most modifications will fall into one of two categories:

- *Interventions that are intended to modify the building envelope*

   Permanent or temporary interventions, generally intended to increase the envelope's buffering capacity. In general, this means eliminating moisture problems and dealing with thermal bridges, or taking action to limit the air exchange between the interior and exterior.

- *Interventions that are intended to modify the air conditions*

   Systems designed to heat or cool the air, or control air movement.

In terms of the fabric, the best interventions will be those that are not only the least invasive, but also the least likely to have damaging side-effects.

ALTERATIONS TO THE ENVELOPE

COLD WALLS

Where exterior walls are cold enough to impair the use of the internal space, the first step is to identify the reason for the discomfort. This could be because the wall is very thin, is being cooled by air leakage or has a moisture problem (wet materials transfer heat much more easily), or because there are significant thermal bridges. These distinctions are lost when the wall is assessed in terms of heat transfer alone (that is, U-values), but they are very important when it comes to making a building comfortable with the minimum use of energy (see **Special Topic: Improving Energy & Carbon Performance**).

Any moisture ingress issues should be dealt with as a priority, but if ensuring that the wall is dry does not solve the problem, then more radical solutions will be needed.

Dealing with Radiant Heat Loss

For buildings with massive walls or floors, or with walls composed of materials with a low thermal inertia such as glass and metal, the problem is most often the occupant losing body heat to the fabric.

To deal with this, the walls or floors can be covered with a material that blocks the radiant heat exchange, such as wood or textiles. For masonry walls, tapestries sometimes performed this role in the past. These were taken down and stored in the summer months, when they were not necessary for this practical function, and would be at risk from condensation.

Increasing the Thermal Buffering

Since wet materials readily transfer heat, the first step to optimising the thermal buffering of a building – especially one that is traditionally constructed – is to eliminate all sources of liquid water and allow the fabric to dry.

Dealing with Thermal Bridges

Thermal bridges tend to be a greater problem for modern construction, where metal and concrete are used extensively.

Common weak points include balconies and overhangs, windows, and the framework of curtain walling. The interior and exterior elements must be thermally isolated from each other, so that heat will not transfer through in either direction. This can involve works as simple as installing curtains, or as challenging as severing components to install thermal breaks.

Heat transfer through windows depends on both the glass and the frame; metal frames in particular are effective thermal bridges. The most effective means of dealing with this is to install a second, less thermally conductive, screen to entirely cover the window: for example, shutters, heavy curtains or secondary glazing.

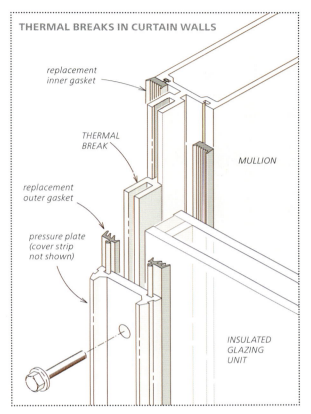

THERMAL BREAKS IN CURTAIN WALLS

Where the thermal bridges are major structural elements of the building (for example, where the metal framework of a building has been extended to support verandas or balconies), effective improvement may be almost impossible; special advice will need to be taken from a structural engineer. Thermal paints exist, but there is no evidence that they are effective, and cladding with a material such as timber may be the only way to minimise the problem. ➔GLASS

Insulation

For decreasing thermal exchange through walls, insulation is often proposed as a solution, but this must be approached with care. The first step should be to ensure the wall is perfectly dry, and there is no likelihood of future water ingress: insulating a wet wall will not work, and it will put the fabric in danger.

The best insulator is still air; materials with high U-values function by trapping air in pores. For cavity walls, it may prove just as effective – and considerably safer – to locate and repair any flaws that are allowing air to circulate in the cavity than to install cavity-wall insulation.

For solid walls, internal insulation cannot be too thick, because that would prevent the wall from being warmed by the interior air, putting it at risk of developing condensation and frost damage. Tests suggest it is safe to insulate with thin sheets of permeable material such as timber or fibreboard, battened off the wall to create a small space behind. This is reminiscent of traditional panelling, and has the additional benefit of reducing radiant heat loss. Impermeable insulation materials such as expanded polystyrene should be strictly avoided, as should impermeable finishes such as modern paints and wallpapers.

BUILDING ENVIRONMENT
CARE & REPAIR

Timber panelling is an excellent way of improving indoor air conditions for users in cold climates: it not only has some insulating effect (increasing the thermal buffering of the envelope), but, more importantly, it dramatically cuts the loss of body heat into the walls, greatly improving user comfort (see **Special Topic: Improving Energy & Carbon Performance**).

Exterior insulation does not have these problems, since the most heavily insulated wall can still be warmed by the indoor air. Although the insulation can be much thicker, this can make it very difficult to detail without introducing points through which rainwater can leak (around windows, for example). For buildings with historic façades, external insulation may be unacceptable for aesthetic reasons.

Since the insulation will prevent evaporation to the exterior, rigorous monitoring will be needed to ensure that hidden leaks or other sources of moisture can never develop. It may be safest to treat the insulation as a form of rainscreen, introducing drainage between it and the wall to remove any moisture that is able to penetrate.

For more information on insulation, see **Special Topic: Improving Energy & Carbon Performance.**

MOISTURE BUFFERING

Since permeable materials are excellent moisture buffers, increasing moisture-buffering capacity is usually very simple: increase the surface area of materials such as timber and lime plasters, and decrease the areas of impermeable surface (glazed tiles or vinyl wall and floor coverings, for example). ⊖TIMBER ⊖MORTARS

It is useful to remember that perfectly dry materials will resist moisture uptake, so moisture-buffering capacity should improve over time, as new materials equilibrate to the natural environment.

ALTERING AIR EXCHANGE

There is much conflicting advice available about desirable rates of ventilation, partly because controlling ventilation has so many potential effects, good and bad: increasing air movement, removing internal moisture or pollutants, preventing exterior pollutants from entering, reducing loss of heating or cooling energy, or allowing the safe use of combustion heating, for example (the **Special Topic: Buildings & Human Health** discusses some of the health implications of limiting ventilation). These different needs may well be in conflict, but if the time is taken to understand the real requirements of the situation, it may well be possible to find approaches that satisfy most or all.

Often the air-exchange requirements will vary across the building: for example, bathrooms and kitchens will need more ventilation to the exterior than other rooms, not only to reduce moisture build-up, but to prevent unpleasant smells drifting through to the rest of the building. Requirements will also change with the weather, and indeed with the seasons.

Cutting Air Exchange (Draughtproofing)

Air exchange is one of the most important ways by which the interior climate is influenced by the exterior. Leakage through the fabric allows conditioned air to escape the building, and lets non-conditioned air in. To minimise the energy used to heat or cool indoor air, cutting air exchange to a minimum is now strongly encouraged (see **Modifying the Interior**, and the **Special Topic: Improving Energy & Carbon Performance**), but 'draughtproofing' is not an entirely benign intervention – especially when carried to extremes – since it will also cut air movement and could lead to condensation problems.

Even very simple draughtstripping can dramatically reduce air exchange around doors and windows.

In some buildings there could be major hidden voids through which air is escaping; smoke tests or blower-door tests may have revealed these. If at all possible these should be repaired, or else air barriers (such as a lime-based plaster) added to prevent air transfer through the surface.

Draughts Through Doors & Windows

Air leakage around openings can be dealt with by temporary or permanent draughtproofing, though the first and most important step is to make any repairs needed to bring the door or window back into good working condition. ⊝GLASS ⊝TIMBER

Doors and windows of most types can be draught-proofed with brushes or rubber stripping (where they are closely fitted into the frame, strips may need to be set into routed grooves). The effect can usually be tested with temporary stripping before major draughtproofing improvements are made.

BUILDING ENVIRONMENT
CARE & REPAIR

Heavy lined curtains will dramatically cut draughts of all kinds: for example, they can be used to prevent air coming through letter boxes set into doors, which are tricky to draughtproof in other ways. Another advantage of curtains is that they can be removed and stored during those seasons when the indoor air is not being heated, and draughts are acceptable or even desirable. ⇨GLASS

For windows, curtains are commonplace, but more permanent options include shutters or secondary glazing, which will also help with the radiant heat exchange that can cause occupants to feel considerable discomfort. If secondary glazing is being considered, it is usually better not to fully draughtproof the window, since this would limit drying should there be a source of moisture either from the wall or the interior causing condensation on the inside face of the window. ⇨GLASS

Permanent options for cutting air exchange through doors are more complex. If the door is opened frequently, or left open for long periods, it may be necessary to consider some form of draught lobby. Commercial buildings may need to consider installing manual rotating doors. Air curtains are another common measure: these are created by installing a strong fan above the doorway to blow air across the opening; sometimes the air is heated as well. Air curtains are most effective if the exterior winds are not too strong, and they must produce a sheet of moving air wide enough to cover the entire doorway. Like all electronic systems, they can be complex and require quite sophisticated controls, as well as a considerable input of electrical energy.

Draughts Through Chimneys

A chimney for an open fireplace will be a cause of significant draughts whenever it is not in use. A good remedy is to fit a damper in the throat of the chimney or the flue, or at the top of the chimney. These should not prevent all air exchange, since a small flow will be needed to ventilate the flue and prevent moisture problems. The best dampers are those that can be easily opened and closed using a handle that indicates the position of the flap.

Disused fireplaces can be fitted with register plates to cut air movement in the chimney. To prevent moisture problems, it is best to use plates with small holes to allow some ventilation: even disused chimneys should never be entirely blocked, since they are always prone to being rain-wetted, and ventilation will help drying.

'Positive Pressure' Buildings

Some specialist buildings (such as laboratories or industrial clean rooms) must be set up so that all air exchange is from the interior towards the exterior. For this, filtered fans are installed to bring air into the interior faster than it can be lost to the exterior (thus keeping the interior at a higher pressure). It can be very difficult to maintain positive pressures throughout a complex building under all weather conditions, so clean rooms are often very simple in form, and positioned in the centre of the building so that they have no walls abutting the exterior.

Increasing Air Exchange (Ventilating)

Ventilation should only be introduced or increased where there is a demonstrable need for it: that is, high timber moisture contents coupled with high ambient humidities and mould growth, or the need to provide fresh air for occupants. It is also important to have a clear understanding of exactly how the ventilation might operate, and the many effects it could have on the fabric (causing condensation on cold floors, for example).

There are many ways in which building users attempt to increase ventilation, some more successful than others.

BUILDING ENVIRONMENT
CARE & REPAIR

Ventilation is often intended to help dry wet building elements, or improve an interior climate that is unacceptably humid, but this tends to address the symptom rather than the cause of moisture problems. There are certainly cases where increased air exchange and air movement may help to prevent moisture problems, but in the long term this will only be successful if the source of water has been identified and removed (otherwise ventilation will simply pull even more moisture through the fabric).

It is also necessary to keep in mind the differences between exchange rates and flow: ventilation by opening doors or windows may or may not cause air to move through those areas where the fabric is wettest (for instance, at the base of the wall, or in corners).

If air exchange is intended to bring in less humid air, it is necessary to know whether the relative air conditions in the two spaces are suitable. The relative humidity in the exterior may be lower, but if the temperature is higher, the absolute humidity may be higher too, so more moisture will be brought in. This may happen, for example, when the windows of an historic building are thrown open in spring: warm, moist air floods into the cold building, increasing the absolute humidity, forcing the dew point lower, and causing condensation. In buildings with a high level of thermal inertia, this behaviour can occur throughout the year, and indeed the large variations in the exterior environment may mean that what is good practice on one day is bad on the next.

There are certainly many situations in which some ventilation is essential (particularly in modern structures), but it is generally poorly understood. Ventilation does not automatically improve whenever a few holes are drilled, and a little air movement is not necessarily better than no air movement at all.

What is almost certain is that any form of ventilation should be controllable: uncontrolled ventilation will cause more unstable internal conditions, reducing the internal–external buffering and microclimatic stability provided by the building envelope. Even if the absolute humidity is indeed marginally reduced, materials and structures sensitive to fluctuations in microclimate may begin to deteriorate. Ventilation can be a useful tool as part of wider intervention, but used in isolation it is at best a temporary solution and, at worst, an additional source of deterioration.

Using Chimneys for Ventilation

If a disused flue is vented from inside to outside, it can provide useful 'trickle' ventilation: for example, in rooms with well-fitting windows that allow only limited air exchange. If a suitable flue runs past, extra vents can even be provided for rooms that did not originally have fireplaces.

Disused flues can also house ducts from extractor fans (for example, from kitchens and bathrooms, running, say, to a discreet air brick on the back of a disused flue). This can often provide a less intrusive solution than a cowl projecting through a roof line or a vent through a façade.

When venting extractors into a chimney, the air duct must run the full distance along the flue and be sealed around the point of discharge, or moist air venting into the flue could condense, causing damp and staining.

Understanding Ventilation in Cavities

The place of ventilation in the building environment is currently characterised by extreme views: on the one hand some architects and other building practitioners firmly believe that ventilation is invariably good for the building fabric; on the other, some building services engineers believe in the almost complete suppression of natural ventilation, not least to reduce the loss of energy used to condition building interiors (see **Modifying the Interior Environment**). What is the best advice?

Ventilation of subfloor cavities using underfloor ventilation grilles began in the late 19th century with the intention of preventing dry rot, which was then believed to be dependent not on water, but on still air. Over the next century the use of such ventilation grilles conflated with the provision of weep holes intended to let liquid water out from cavity-wall voids, until ventilation grilles and air bricks came to be seen as a way of guaranteeing the drying of all types of building cavity.

The Edwardians were very keen on ventilation, and bequeathed a number of beliefs in its efficacy that still heavily influence building regulations. The most contentious is perhaps the desire to ventilate cavities by equipping cavity walls and underfloor spaces with vents and grilles. The argument advanced for this is that they allow air exchange between the exterior and the cavity, and that this encourages drying. As a result, all types of building cavity can be found vented, often retrospectively: holes are drilled into dry linings and the plinths of church pews, and gaps are made around beam bearings. Passive ventilation is used in rainscreen wall systems, and in secondary glazing systems designed to protect stained glass from moisture damage and vandalism. Some of these systems are very effective, but others are not. To understand why this is the case, it is necessary to look at how ventilation of small cavities actually operates, and how it might be expected to affect moisture contents. **◉EARTH & BRICK ◉TIMBER ◉GLASS**

In heated Victorian and Edwardian houses, which allowed considerable air exchange between the interior and exterior, the air rising up and exiting through the roof seems to have been sufficient to draw air in from through the underfloor spaces upwards through the timber floorboards, keeping them in good condition.

Ventilation of cavities has two aims: air movement to drive evaporation from any wet materials; and air exchange to remove moist air from cavity and replace it with drier air from elsewhere. But does cavity ventilation always work, and is it always desirable? There are a number of known advantages and disadvantages:

POSSIBLE OUTCOMES OF CAVITY VENTILATION	
POTENTIAL ADVANTAGES	**POTENTIAL DISADVANTAGES**
Air movement is the major driver of evaporative drying	There is some experimental evidence that very slight airflow may encourage the growth of decay fungi like dry rot
If the exterior air is drier, air exchange will reduce the moisture content of the air in the cavity	If the exterior air is wetter, air exchange will increase the moisture content of the air in the cavity
	Ventilation holes can act as conduit for liquid water, as well as for insects and other pests
	Making holes in the fabric is destructive

BUILDING ENVIRONMENT
CARE & REPAIR

How well can passive ventilation of small cavities be expected to work? The demands on it are very complex.

To effectively dry a cavity, the source of moisture in the cavity must be finite (ventilation would never be able to dry a floor cavity that is humid because it is in contact with a water source). Apart from this fundamental requirement, the ventilation itself must also meet certain criteria:

- the incoming air must have a greater capacity for evaporation than the air in the cavity, either because the flow rate is higher or because its absolute humidity is lower, or preferably both
- moist air must be drawn out from the cavity by the airflow as the drying air is drawn in
- the airflow must wash the entire cavity well, leaving no dead (stagnant) spaces
- for cavities vented to the exterior, significant ventilation must occur successfully under most weather conditions
- for cavities vented to the interior, significant flow must occur under ordinary room conditions, or must be able to be induced by some simple means such as heating.

Until recently, little research of any kind had been made into how cavity ventilation operates in practice, and none of this had been experimental. Models of air velocity within a range of underfloor cavities, ventilated with 225-mm × 150-mm air bricks set at 1-m intervals suggest that, once friction is taken into account, a fifth of the cavity would see airflows of only 0.005 ms^{-1} at most (that is, they would be effectively stagnant).

Vertical cavities such as walls or the spaces behind dry lining are typically ventilated by making openings at the top and the bottom, with the idea that flow will be driven from bottom to top by the stack effect. It is by no means clear that this would be strong enough to overcome the resistance to flow in a real cavity, which will contain rough surfaces, battens, fixings, and a great deal of dirt and debris.

Building cavities are complex, with rough internal surfaces (such as the reverse side of a wall made from plaster and reed matting, as shown here), as well as studs and other supporting members that will disrupt air movement.

Doubts about the efficacy of cavity ventilation have led to considerable dispute: for example, many practitioners suggest that all underfloor vents should be closed up, whereas others insist that they are critical to keeping floor timbers in good condition. English Heritage is currently involved in a number of research projects looking at the actual behaviour of different types of cavity ventilation, and the information given here summarises the outcomes to date.

RESEARCH INTO VENTILATION OF SMALL CAVITIES

STUDY I: VENTILATION IN THE CAVITIES OF DRY-LINED BRICK WALLS

Research sponsored by English Heritage and the Office of Public Works Dublin, and undertaken by the University of Manchester.

A rig was constructed to allow the visualisation of flow patterns arising from different arrangements of openings in a vertical cavity. Experimental results were compared to the predictions generated by modelling using Computational Fluid Dynamics [CFD].

QUESTIONS EXAMINED DURING THE RESEARCH

Does passive ventilation by drilling holes at the top and bottom of dry lining actually work, and if so, under what conditions?

What are the optimum number of holes, and the optimum arrangement?

If passive ventilation is not sufficient, can simple methods such as heater placement drive effective exchange and flow?

GENERAL OBSERVATIONS	COMMENTS
Significant airflow will not occur in a small cavity unless the incoming airspeed exceeds 5 m/s (18 km per hour)	Relatively high air speeds are needed to drive air into a cavity; these are unlikely to be achieved with an opening that is not well exposed to winds blowing directly onto the wall
When the cavity was vented to the exterior, effective airflow was only possible if the opening was very exposed, and then only if the air movement (wind) was in the right direction	Since friction limits the airflow at ground level, the incident air velocity is likely to be very low even if the vent is well exposed Exterior floor vents (especially those venting ground floors) are rarely well exposed, and indeed are often obscured or even blocked by plants and paint
Air movement within the cavity is very turbulent, with many areas of stagnation	The cavity used in the experiment was in fact relatively smooth and uncluttered, so in real buildings turbulence will be greater again
Larger openings do not necessarily equate to better airflow A battery of smaller openings (as found in an air brick, for example) is better for ventilation than a few large openings	Larger openings have less turbulence and friction around the inlet, but the air travelling in through a smaller opening has a better 'jet' effect that helps to reduce vortices and dead spaces within the cavity
Given a sufficient airflow, spacing vents horizontally about a metre apart greatly reduced the number and size of stagnant air pockets, although it did not completely eliminate them	The way openings are distributed is much more important than the size of each opening
Flows in wall cavities with openings at the top and bottom are from top-to-bottom, not bottom-to-top as it would be if driven by buoyancy (the stack effect)	Because the induced wind pressure is affected by ground friction, air pressure will be smaller at the bottom of the cavity than at the top, and this overwhelms any stack effect
Significant air movement could not be generated by temperature gradients across the wall	Typical temperature gradients in masonry wall constructions would not be sufficiently great to drive effective drying

BUILDING ENVIRONMENT
CARE & REPAIR

STUDY 2: VENTILATION IN PROTECTIVE SECONDARY GLAZING SYSTEMS

Research sponsored by English Heritage, and undertaken by Tobit Curteis Associates.

The aim of the study was to develop best-practice recommendations for protective glazing systems by drawing together the existing research from the UK, and by both measuring and modelling how airflow rates are affected by the design of the glazing.

QUESTIONS EXAMINED DURING THE RESEARCH

To what extent do the depth and surface topography of the 'interspace' gap between the internal and external glass layers, and the size and design of the vents, affect the airflow, and thus how effectively does the system provide thermal buffering and reduce condensation events?

How do historic protective glazing systems compare with current systems?

How good does the passive ventilation have to be to reduce condensation events sufficiently well to ensure the survival of the original glass?

GENERAL OBSERVATIONS	COMMENTS
The movement of the air in the cavity is driven mostly by buoyancy, and depends on the temperature difference between the cavity and the space towards which it is vented	Hot air rises, so when the interspace is heated by sunlight falling on the secondary glazing, there will be an upwards flow that draws room air in through the vents at the base of the window
	If the temperature of the glass drops because the sun has set, or because a cooling breeze has picked up, the interspace air will lose heat and begin to fall, drawing in more warm air from the room through the vents at the top
	In northern Europe the interior is often warmer than the exterior, so on average the interspace air will be cooler; therefore, most commonly there will be a down draught
Where airflow is disrupted (for example, by small and uneven vents, or because the interspace is small and cluttered with ferramenta), it is weaker and more turbulent, and so less able to efficiently draw in air or effectively dry the cavity space	The exact patterns of air movement will depend on the shape and size of the window

Monitoring the surface temperatures and environmental conditions in the intra-glazing spaces of a protective glazing system.

RESULTS

From these experiments (together with observations of *in-situ* cavities), a number of useful conclusions can be drawn:

- It is not possible to create a 'wash' of air through a cavity simply by making openings at the top and at the bottom; flow through the space must be driven by some quite sizeable force.
- In a vertical cavity, the stack effect is not strong enough to compete with all the other forces acting on the air, such as friction, airflow hitting the openings, or localised heating or cooling.
- One possible driving force is the heating and cooling of the exterior wall by the sun and wind; this is significant for materials of low thermal inertia such as glass and metal, but very much weaker for materials with high thermal inertias such as brick, stone or timber.
- Patterns of airflow will depend on the shape and position of the openings, the shape and size of the space being ventilated, and the difference between the relative humidity of the ventilated space and of the space with which it is exchanging air.

Taken together, the experiments allow the comparison of ventilation in a complex cavity where the walls are constructed from materials with high thermal inertias, with ventilation in a simpler cavity where friction and flow disturbance are much smaller, but the walls are made of materials with very low thermal inertias.

BEHAVIOUR OF AIR IN VERTICAL CAVITIES

THERMAL INERTIA OF MATERIALS MAKING UP THE CAVITY WALLS

HIGH THERMAL INERTIA	LOW THERMAL INERTIA
Flow driven by air blowing directly into cavity	Flow driven by buoyancy (driven by wall temperature) and by air blowing directly into the cavity
Heating – for example, by radiators at the base of a wall – is insufficient to drive flow	Considerable airflow can be induced by heating or cooling a wall
If there is any airflow, it is likely to be from top-to-bottom, due to ground effects on the moving air in the exterior	The direction of airflow will depend on the relative temperatures of the interior and exterior walls

One other outcome of the experiments into cavity ventilation is that to discover the precise behaviour of air in any real cavity, there is little alternative to measurement: air movement is very complex, and comparison with current modelling tools such as Computerised Fluid Dynamics [CFD] demonstrated that these are not sufficiently sophisticated to be able to predict air movement under such conditions (a fundamental weakness in flow modelling remains quantifying the impact of wall temperature and moisture content in small cavities).

On the other hand, developing good building practice does not require precise models of air movement, and the experiments have confirmed site observations that suggest there is little to be gained from most cavity ventilation where the walls of the cavity are composed of materials with low thermal inertias.

BUILDING ENVIRONMENT
CARE & REPAIR

RECOMMENDATIONS FOR CAVITY VENTILATION

If there is no building issue requiring ventilation, it would be unwise to introduce it; and many moisture problems will be better dealt with by identifying the source of the water and removing it. If, however, a problem exists that can be managed in no other way, it is important to approach the introduction of ventilation slowly and methodically, testing its effects with care.

To successfully ventilate small vertical cavities (such as the spaces behind panelling or dry-lining), these would have be kept clear of all debris, and ventilation provided by a series of grilles at top and bottom, no more than one metre apart, and preferably in the interior wall. Openings would need to be positioned to take account of any internal timberwork or other structures that could impede flow. The results should be monitored to make sure that a flow is indeed being generated, and that there are no unexpected problems as a result.

It is unwise to rely on cavity ventilation to deal with a major moisture problem: although with sufficient movement, even quite humid air can cause evaporation, in a compact and complex space good airflow will be virtually impossible to achieve.

Cavities should not be ventilated in such a way that the openings could be a conduit for liquid water (including rainwater) to enter the wall.

If a cavity must be vented to the exterior, it should be positioned where it is most likely to benefit from direct air impact.

If the thermal resistance of the wall is important for energy-saving reasons, cavity walls should not be ventilated as this will reduce the insulating effect of the cavity (see **Special Topic: Improving Energy & Carbon Performance**).

Horizontal Cavities

Horizontal cavities such as subfloor voids were not explicitly studied in the experiments reported here, but it is possible to make some logical observations:

- It is not immediately clear what underfloor ventilation would be expected to achieve.
- Flow will be impeded by structural components of the void, and by dirt and debris in the space; even if there are many vents to the exterior, it is more than likely that there will be many areas in which flow is slight or non-existent.
- Vents under ground floors will be prone to water ingress, and ground effects will greatly reduce airflow through them.

FUTURE RESEARCH

Many questions do still remain, particularly with regards to the behaviour of suspended ground floors. Because of the much greater surface area and the drawing power of airflow through the building, the stack effect is likely to be considerably more important, and may indeed draw air through a suspended timber floor, or indeed a timber ceiling, keeping the materials in good condition. With building regulations increasingly frowning on high rates of air exchange between the interior and exterior, however, and floors and ceilings increasingly being made airtight, what may happen to timber floors suspended over damp ground spaces is unclear. It may be that under these conditions the underfloor vents become a much greater liability, with moisture able to enter but not easily escape. Several research groups are currently looking at this and similar questions.

DEALING WITH NOISE PROBLEMS

The aim of acoustical engineering is to reduce unwanted direct sound, and any reverberations and other indirect noise. The envelope must be able to mute external sources (including road and rail traffic, aircraft, and factories), and the internal partitions must not transmit so much sound that occupants of one room are disturbed by those in another. There are many different ways of achieving these goals, including placing noise barriers or buffer zones between the source of the noise and the listener, installing sound absorbers and dampers, or using active 'anti-noise' sound generators. Noise control is always easiest when the noise is made up of a narrow band of frequencies.

In single-occupancy buildings, soundproofing often focuses on preventing exterior noise from entering, often by increasing the soundproofing of windows by curtains, shutters or secondary glazing. Insulated Glazing Units (double- and triple-glazing) can also be effective, as long as the window frame is not also transmitting vibrations.

Small alterations to limit the transmission of air (such as draughtproofing, fitting baffles into redundant chimneys or sealing the holes through which services enter the building) can give major improvements, though it may be necessary to reconcile conflicts between the need to reduce airborne noise and the need for natural ventilation. If the noise is coming from one direction, it may be sufficient to concentrate soundproofing in that direction only, rather than trying to deal with the entire envelope.

In multi-occupancy buildings, the emphasis is more commonly on soundproofing between the spaces within the building.

The transfer of noise through buildings is related to the ways the various materials and structures react to acoustic waves. This can be very complex, especially where the structure is not simple, making the exact source of problematic noise difficult to trace.

BUILDING ENVIRONMENT
CARE & REPAIR

The transmission of noise through the fabric is often difficult to deal with, and it will always be more effective to identify and deal with the causes of reverberation and resonance rather than trying to address the symptoms.

One common treatment is damping with materials that are able to absorb and dissipate the incoming energy (often by transforming it into heat), or which can reflect or refract noise from the listener. The material must correspond with the frequency of the sound. Porous open-cell foams are very good at suppressing medium-high frequencies, but are less effective for low frequencies and transmitted vibrations; resonant dampers – which function primarily by reflecting energy – are most effective for low to medium frequencies (and must be closely matched to the noise).

To reduce footfall and other impact noise, either the source of the noise must be eliminated, or its outcome must be muted (for example, by soft flooring). Traditionally, suspended floors were often filled with soundproofing materials such as sawdust, sand or lime pugging. Modern options include rock wool or silicate cotton (glass wool), either as a loose fibre or a mat. This is often installed from above to protect early ceilings, but it is important to be aware that lifting original timber floors is not always easy. Again, it is important to consider the effect any changes may have on other aspects of the building environment, such as ventilation and evaporation. ➔TIMBER

In severe cases acoustic engineers may consider isolating sections of the fabric (installing a floating floor, for example), or increasing the structural mass, but the effectiveness of such major works would depend on the materials and structure of the building, and of any proposed alterations.

For some types of building (large churches or performance venues, for example), specialist acoustic engineers may also be called in to design amplification systems. These must successfully transmit sound without causing distracting reverberations or feedback.

Building Regulations

PART E: RESISTANCE TO THE PASSAGE OF SOUND

Part E of the Building Regulations requires that partitions in new houses, and properties undergoing a *"material change of use"*, must meet a minimum standard for sound insulation, as tested by a UKAS-accredited laboratory or a European equivalent. Short-term surveys usually measure over a day or a week, but in some cases it may be necessary to monitor vibration or noise for months or even years. It is often wise to test both before and after any changes are made to the fabric.

Part E recognises the difficulties associated with adapting historic buildings, but requires the exclusion of noise to have been properly assessed, and possible approaches to mitigation considered methodically.

CONDITIONING THE INDOOR AIR

The indoor air is usually conditioned – heated or cooled, and sometimes humidified or dehumidified – to improve the comfort of the building users, but many conditioning systems fail because they do not address the real reasons for discomfort. When improvements to indoor conditions are being considered, it is always tempting to rush immediately into 'solutions', but this is likely to lead to expensive interventions that do not solve the underlying issues. For example, the usual approach to dealing with discomfort in buildings in cold climates is to decide that heating is necessary, choose a new heating system and then concentrate all the effort of the project on its installation. Common problems from this approach include deterioration of the fabric and contents (cracking of timber, for example), the introduction of unexpectedly unpleasant conditions (such as intermittent condensation), high energy bills, and in many cases continued or even increased discomfort due to unsuitable temperatures and humidities, or greater air convection and draughtiness.

The first and most important step to a successful intervention is to determine exactly how the building is being used, and exactly how and why the different users feel uncomfortable. If sufficient time is taken to properly assess need, the best ways of improving comfort will often become obvious.

Users generally feel unsuitable temperatures more strongly than unsuitable humidities, though both can cause discomfort. Air movement is an important but neglected issue: users may feel cold in a draught, even if the air temperature is very warm. Similarly, radiant heat loss will be a strong source of discomfort near certain materials. On the other hand, solar gain can make users uncomfortably hot even in cool conditions. Not every user will have the same idea of comfort, and indeed conditions that feel fine to users sitting still may be uncomfortably hot to users who are active. For this reason alone, flexible systems that allow individual occupants some control invariably prove more successful than centrally controlled systems that have been designed to provide certain fixed conditions, which are increasingly common in large buildings. Such systems can also put unacceptable burdens on the fabric, since they require extensive ducting and piping, and may well demand the removal of internal partitions.

It is good practice to consider conditioning different areas of the building in different ways, taking into account the behaviour of the structure and the materials as well as the building use. For example, kitchens and bathrooms should retain the potential to ventilate to the exterior (so any windows should be easy to open and close). Rooms that require cooling in summer and heating in winter, but have massive floors or walls, could use rugs and timber screens to prevent radiant heat loss in winter; in summer, when the radiant loss is an advantage, these could be stored away. The control of any system is also important. If controls are inflexible the system will not deliver comfort, but if they are too complex than they may be used incorrectly.

Finally, there is the important issue of affordability to consider: with energy prices rising steadily, many energy-intensive systems may become prohibitively expensive to run, and there are environmental impacts to be considered as well (see **Special Topic: Improving Energy & Carbon Performance**). It is essential that both the building manager and the professional advisers take into account the whole-life costs of any proposed system (that is, the material costs of the installation, its predicted lifespan and its running costs), to ensure that the system is sustainable.

BUILDING ENVIRONMENT
CARE & REPAIR

CONTROLLING TEMPERATURE

If interventions to control radiant heat loss and draughts are not sufficient to make conditions comfortable for occupants (or suitable for the use of the space), systems that heat or cool the air will have to be considered. These are not simple interventions: it is easy to produce conditions that are hostile to the fabric, and which do not deliver good conditions for occupants either. The planning stage is therefore of great importance, and plenty of time and care should be spent on determining the true needs of the occupants, and the real constraints presented by the building fabric, before beginning to design any heating or cooling system.

Heating

Heating is by far the most common control on indoor conditions in northern Europe, and the temperatures expected of building interiors have become steadily higher as central heating has become more common (see **Special Topic: Improving Energy & Carbon Performance**).

Comfort heating can be achieved by convection or radiant heating (or a mixture of both). The following table lists the characteristics of each system, but in practice whether a particular characteristic is an advantage or a disadvantage often depends on how the space is being used. For example, radiant heating is a good means of heating a person seated in a known position, or for combining heated areas with cooler areas in spaces with multiple purposes. Convective heating is more suitable if the entire space must be conditioned to a single temperature. In many cases, combined systems may be the most effective, especially if separate controls can be provided for each of the components.

TYPES OF HEATING

	ACTION	ADVANTAGES	DISADVANTAGES
CONVECTIVE HEATING	Heating the air in the space, which means users lose less body heat to the air	Once conditions have stabilised, a user moving through the space will meet more or less constant air temperatures	Less efficient than radiant heating, both in terms of heating and the energy costs; Difficult to locally heat; Relatively slow to reach final operating temperature; Convection can produce uncomfortable currents of air
RADIANT HEATING	Radiators* to directly heat building users	Uses relatively little energy, but provides good comfort as long as radiators can be correctly positioned; Allows localised heating; Quick to reach operating temperature	Heats the users directly: people moving out of range of the radiators will be cold; Very high surface temperatures can be a fire risk

* The water-filled heat storage units that are a common part of central heating systems are called 'radiators', but this is something of a misnomer: in fact, they transfer more heat to the air by convection rather than by radiation

Design Criteria for Heating Systems

To design a good heating system, it is important to understand the reason heating is felt to be required: there will be great differences between systems intended to provide occupant comfort, and systems intended to heat the room air to a certain temperature or to warm particular parts of the fabric.

For occupant comfort, the considerations are particularly complex, and include more than a little psychology as well as physiology: bar heaters are felt to be more effective if they glow red rather than white, for example. The aim is to deliver a sensation of comfort, but this will depend on the person, and on the activities they are undertaking in the space: a kitchen or a gym will need to be much cooler than a lounge room. People will often feel warmer when the air is drier. Draughts and radiant heat loss (through large areas of glass, for example) can make users feel cold even in a room where the air temperature is high.

There are many factors (other than the type of heating) which could affect the outcome, including the shape and contents of the rooms being heated, the nature of their surfaces, and where the heating elements are placed. The siting of radiators, for example, has been vigorously debated. In Scandinavia and other very cold countries they are almost always positioned under windows, and until recently this was also standard practice in England; the reasons given include the increase in room air circulation, better comfort levels (the radiant heat loss into the window is balanced by the radiant heat gain from the radiator) and a reduction in condensation on the glass. The problems of siting radiators in this way include a greater temperature differential on either side of the window (which will drive heat flow outwards) and the possibility that long curtains may cover the radiator as well as the window, greatly reducing efficiency. It is now more usual to position radiators on internal walls.

This diagram depicts the results of one of a series of BRE flow-visualisation tests undertaken during the 1960s. In a glass-walled room with no windows, air circulation is driven by a heating pipe in the bottom right corner. The air rises to the ceiling and eventually falls on the other side of the room, losing buoyancy as it is cooled by contact with the surfaces.

A 'radiator' connected to a wet central-heating system emits 55 % of its heat as convection (driving rising warm air), 40 % as radiation and 5 % as conduction back into the wall.

BUILDING ENVIRONMENT
CARE & REPAIR

Radiant heaters are not renowned for beauty, but they can be an excellent solution where the aim is to heat people without heating the fabric or the air. Since there is no point in running this type of heating when building users are not present, they can also be very efficient.

Traditional coal and wood fires were very effective radiant heaters, but produced considerable ventilation and low air temperatures; thus the interior relative humidity stayed fairly constant over the course of a year. Electric radiant heaters are based on resistance elements through which a current is passed, causing them to heat and emit energy, mostly in near-infrared wavelengths; in 'quartz' heaters, the element is enclosed in a quartz tube that protects the element and cuts the loss of energy through convection. These types of heaters are very effective at heating users, without heating the air.

Most modern heating systems aim to raise air temperatures, and so will cause relative humidity to fluctuate. In situations where this could have a critical effect on the fabric of the building or its contents, heating is usually controlled by humidistats (which keep the indoor conditions within a desirable range of relative humidities) rather than thermostats (which switch the heating system on or off according to the temperature).

One problem with control by thermostats or humidistats is that there is always a lag between the time taken to measure the change and the time taken to respond to it. This can cause rapid fluctuations (which is particularly undesirable if the intention is to stabilise conditions so that the impact of the heating on the fabric and contents is minimised). To minimise fluctuations, the sensors must be installed so that they can quickly read significant changes, but are not affected by other factors. For example, they should not be installed directly above heaters, where the rising hot air may produce unexpected results.

Many new heating systems will require new flues (it is quite rare to be able to use the existing flues, though some ways of doing this are discussed below). The choice of system may be constrained by the type of flue needed, and the ramifications of punching this through the envelope, especially where the building has statutory protection. In many cases it may be a matter of choosing the 'least worst' option, rather than finding an ideal system.

Just as important as installing the correct heating system is making sure that it can be serviced easily, and that the building users understand the way it is intended to be run and can control it properly. The best-designed heating system will fail if it is not managed correctly: for example, localised radiant heaters will not have any significant heating effect on the air, so it would prove wasteful and unsatisfactory to attempt to use them for this purpose. Another common mistake is to install overly complex controls; a simple system is much more likely to be operated effectively and efficiently.

Types of Heating Regime

Localised Heating

Localised heating can take many forms, including electric radiators and radiant heaters ('electric fires'). These can be portable or fixed in place, and may form part of a more complex centralised heating system.

Localised heating has energy-use and cost benefits, but its greatest advantage is that although the users are kept comfortable, there should be little effect on the wider building environment. This means that the damaging fluctuations in temperature and humidity caused by heating can be minimised. The most common disadvantage is user comfort: outside the heated areas, the temperature may be uncomfortably low. On the other hand, local heating gives the most comfortable conditions for occupants in buildings that are heated only spasmodically.

Part of the trick to successful local heating is to understand how the space is being used; this way the heaters can be positioned in the optimum positions to keep the occupants comfortable. A little psychology will not go amiss, either: users have found white quartz radiant heaters much more effective after they have been covered with a reddish filter.

Background Heating

An increasingly common approach is to try to maintain a low level of background heating in the building at all times, even when it is unoccupied, increasing temperatures to comfort level when it is in use. This limits the extent of the temperature change, and therefore in a dry building with little or no exchange of air with the exterior, it also limits the resulting changes in relative humidity.

Background heating is less effective in buildings with a great deal of air exchange, or with sinks of moisture such as wet walls, where the effects of the top-up heating on humidity can still be very strong.

Conservation Heating

The system generally known as 'conservation heating', developed by the National Trust and others, is based on humidistat rather than thermostat controls, and is intended to stabilise relative humidity in historic buildings for the benefit of the fabric and contents. When the relative humidity changes, this initiates an increase or decrease in temperature that is intended to keep the relative humidity within preset margins.

This means that the temperature may drop well below comfort level, particularly during winter when the absolute humidities tend to be low. While this is entirely appropriate for museums that can close during the winter, it is not suitable for most occupied buildings. Humidistat controls are sometimes combined with thermostatic control for buildings where comfort heating may be required only periodically.

As with all control systems relying on the effect of air temperature on the building fabric, conservation heating systems will usually need to provide substantial convection, which may cause other problems.

BUILDING ENVIRONMENT
CARE & REPAIR

Early radiators are often beautiful, and will represent a considerable investment in materials and infrastructure. Most can be brought back into service with quite minimal adjustment, even when the new heating is designed to run at different pressures to the old. Advice should be sought from a heating engineer with experience in dealing with older systems.

It is better not to leave radiators unpainted or give them a metallic finish (*right*), as this reduces their emissivity and thus their heat output; the effect is, however, quite small, except in the case of chrome finishes, which can reduce output by as much as 20 %. It is not necessary to remove a metallic finish: overcoating with a non-metallic paint will be enough to restore lost efficiency.

Reinstating Early Heating Systems

Owners of older properties that have been altered as the fashions changed over time would often like to reinstate one of the earlier means of heating, but this is rarely straightforward. Even exposing an early fireplace blocked in the 20th century can be difficult: it is very easy to accidently damage historic decoration (decorative carpenter's marks or painting, for example) on and around what would have been an important focus of the building.

The historical value of any later insertions or alterations must be assessed before deciding whether they can be removed; for protected buildings this will mean consulting the Local Authority Conservation Officer, and probably applying for consent.

If there are any doubts at all about the structural integrity or water-tightness of a flue or chimney stack, it will need to be investigated by an experienced structural engineer, surveyor or architect, since inserting a flue liner and the stresses from heating and cooling cycles will exacerbate any existing problems.

A survey is particularly important if the chimney is to be reused for an open fire without a lining: in this case the stack will be subjected to large heating and cooling cycles, as well as chemical damage from compounds in the smoke. It may be an interesting challenge to get an open fire to draw correctly and not smoke; it is often the height rather than the width of the opening that proves critical. At Arundel Castle, for example, draught problems were eventually cured by fitting glass quarries in a metal framework under the lintels of the fireplaces to reduce the height of the opening with minimal visual impact. It may be necessary to determine the direction of the prevailing winds, and adjust the stack accordingly.

Thatch & Wood-Burning Stoves

A fire in any type of roof is extremely dangerous, but the quantities of combustible materials in a thatch covering mean that once a fire takes hold, it is likely to spread rapidly and be difficult to extinguish. Open fires and solid-fuel stoves are a recognised danger, and indeed some insurers will not provide cover for a thatched building with a solid-fuel stove.

The cause of some thatch fires is not fully understood. Most thatch fires start in or around the chimney, and there is a close relationship with the use of wood-burning stoves. Some fires are thought to be the result of defective chimney masonry that allows hot flue gases to come into direct contact with thatch, but in other cases it appears that burning brands, ejected from the chimney and coming to rest on the surface of the thatch, may be the cause of ignition. Fires may also be caused by bonfires, poor positioning of security lights, hot works within the roof space and chimney fires.

To reduce the danger, chimneys must be kept in good repair, and swept and checked regularly. It may be wise to consider fitting an appropriate flue liner. To limit burning brands rising up the chimney, it is important to burn only well-seasoned hardwood (waste paper should not be discarded on the fire). If the chimney is very short, it may be necessary to consider increasing its height as this may reduce the risk of burning brands landing on the thatch surface. Spark arrestors at the top of chimneys had been thought to provide some extra protection, but there is evidence that if they are not kept scrupulously clean they may actually increase the risk, and most advisers no longer recommend them.

The *Roofing* volume of this series includes more information about the causes and prevention of fire in thatch. ROOFING

BUILDING ENVIRONMENT
CARE & REPAIR

Devices & Mechanisms for Heating

OPEN FIREPLACES

Open solid-fuel fires are the traditional method of heating old buildings, and although they are much less efficient than solid-fuel stoves, opening up an old fireplace is often desirable, particularly if it has an inglenook.

Open fires can use wood, coal, smokeless fuels or gas. Most wood is in the form of logs, which must be dry and seasoned for at least one year to prevent harmful deposits of creosote or resinous material that prevent the chimney drawing correctly, and can seep through the chimney walls to cause staining. Wood and most types of coal are illegal in areas where smoke-control regulations are in place. Smokeless fuels can be burned in any location, and burn more efficiently than either coal or wood. Gas fires are usually designed to give the effect of a wood or coal fire, but they need a supply of gas and a suitable flue, in which the combustion gases are converted and then vented safely away. If the fireplace has a damper, this will need to be left open.

ROOM HEATERS & STOVES

Room heaters and stoves – enclosed appliances for burning fuels such as wood, coal, wood pellets and gas – are available in a wide range of designs, and are much more efficient and less draughty than open fires. Some can burn wood and coal without creating smoke, allowing them to be used with these fuels even in smoke-control areas.

Some room heaters have glass doors, through which the fire can be seen as well as felt. Heat also radiates through the rest of the stove casing, and is transferred through the room by convection. Some are freestanding, but many are partly or fully recessed into a wall or an existing fireplace, and some recessed models have back boilers that can supply hot water into a wet central heating system, or into an insulated storage tank for domestic use.

The temperatures of flue gases can be significantly higher than those from open fires, so there is a greater risk of heat damage or fire; room heaters must always be installed by a registered heating engineer who is qualified in the type of fuel being used. The flue will always need to be lined, and if a flexible metal liner is chosen it will need to be double-skinned. If a chimney cannot accommodate an adequate liner, it will not be able to be used with a room heater or stove.

UK Legislation

SMOKE CONTROL LEGISLATION

The *Clean Air Act* of 1956 gave local authorities the ability to declare smoke-control areas, in which it is an offence to emit any smoke from a domestic chimney (except for the very small amounts from burning authorised 'smokeless' fuels). There is an exemption for appliances that can burn bituminous coal or wood without creating smoke.

For further information about smoke-control legislation, authorised fuels and exempted appliances, or to check whether a particular building is within a smoke-control area, building managers will need to contact their local authority or visit www.uksmokecontrolareas.co.uk.

SIZING FLUES

Details of correct size of flue for different fuels are given in the *Building Regulations Approved Document J*.

WET CENTRAL HEATING

In wet central-heating systems, water heated in a boiler is sent through a sealed loop of pipes and radiators positioned throughout the building. The earliest boilers were 'pot boilers': sealed containers under which a fire was lit. These were very inefficient, and improvements were soon made, such as in sectional boilers, where hollow cast-iron units connected together with coupling pipes are used to surround the heat source. The most important types of boiler are:

- *Fire tube*
  Fire-tube boilers are similar to the types of boiler used for steam locomotives, and have been used to heat large industrial buildings. The heat source is a 'firebox' surrounded by a jacket of water; the combustion gases are directed through a series of flues running through the boiler, and heating the water within it to make steam: the steam is collected at the top in a 'steam dome', which houses a regulator with valves to control the exit of steam, and thus the pressure. Modern fire-tube boilers include fans to increase the draught of gases through the system.

- *Water tube*
  In water-tube boilers, the pipes are used to send water through the heated combustion gases, rather than the gases through the water. There are various arrangements of piping, including coils and finned pipes to increase heat exchange, and the heated water rises to a regulating 'steam drum'. Water-tube boilers can run at much higher pressures than fire-tube boilers, and are less likely to suffer major failures.

- *Condensing*
  Condensing boilers are much more complicated than other types. They are designed to take the fullest advantage of the heat energy in the combustion gases: heat rising through the primary heat exchanger is rerouted over a secondary heat exchanger by means of a fan. The water in the gases condenses, and is collected at the base of the flue manifold, from which it is discharged. To make this work, there must be a significant temperature difference between the gases (at 200–250°C) and the water, as this drives convection. When the boiler is in 'condensing mode', it is very efficient (87 % efficiency or more, as opposed to around 75 % efficiency for other types of boiler), but for this the return water temperature must be less than 55°C, which will depend on the system of pipes and radiators being fed by the boiler.

The ability to site the required flue sensitively is often critical to the choice of heating system.

Here the existing chimney and a roof vent have both been ignored, but in fact an old chimney is often a good place to run the flue from a new boiler fired by solid fuel, oil or gas. This change of use would usually require the flue to be lined.

Boilers can run on various types of fuel, and it is often this that governs the choice of system. The other critical factor is the way the exhausting of combustion gases must be handled. The exhaust gases of some modern boilers are quite cool, and so may condense before reaching the top of a tall chimney. Boilers of this type can now be fitted with flues that vent the exhaust gases through the wall of the building instead (sometimes they run a short distance up the chimney first, until they can be diverted to a convenient and inconspicuous position on the exterior).

BUILDING ENVIRONMENT
CARE & REPAIR

TYPES OF FUEL USED FOR BOILERS

Solid Fuels

Solid fuels include wood and wood-based materials such as pellets; coals such as anthracite, dry-steam coal and strong-to-weak caking coals; and coke. These require storage, and produce ashes and other solid waste products that must also be stored before being discarded. Their energy output is lower than gas or oil, and emissions requirements may restrict their use in some areas.

Oils

Oil comes in various classes, each of which have different advantages and disadvantages. Kerosene (Class C2 oils) are used in domestic boilers; Class D gas oils are heavy, but are cheaper than kerosenes and work well in larger boilers. Fuel oils (Classes E, F, G and H) are by far the cheapest option, but require more complicated storage and equipment since they must be preheated to burn correctly. The exhaust gases are high in sulphurs and other pollutants, so they are generally only suitable for use with systems incorporating tall chimneys.

Gases

Coal gas (or 'town gas') is now rarely used, but natural gas delivered through the gas mains is common, and requires no storage. If not completely burnt, natural gas will give off carbon monoxide, so systems must have the correct burner stack or flue. Liquid Petroleum Gas [LPG] is propane and butane, products of oil refining; it must be stored in tanks with a free flow of air around them.

CHOOSING A BOILER

CONSIDERATIONS TO BE TAKEN INTO ACCOUNT

FUEL CONSTRAINTS	INSTALLATION REQUIREMENTS	VENTING & FLUES
AVAILABILITY For example, gas boilers are unlikely to be feasible in rural areas with no reliable central supply	**SIZE** How big is the boiler itself? Can it be installed without major alterations to the building?	**SYSTEM REQUIREMENTS** What type of venting and flues are part of the manufacturer's specifications?
DELIVERY Will access be needed for large trucks?	**MAINTENANCE** How accessible will the boiler be for servicing, and eventual removal and replacement?	**EMISSION REQUIREMENTS** The Building Regulations and Building Control measures will specify the minimum requirements for venting; there may also be specific local requirements (such as those under the *Clean Air Act*)
STORAGE How much fuel will need to be stored on site? How close must storage be to the boiler?	**PROXIMITY TO FUEL** How close do the boiler and the fuel store have to be?	**CONSTRAINTS OF ENVELOPE** Is the façade very important? How will the envelope be punctured with the least possible damage to the fabric?
COST What are the current and projected future costs of the fuel?	**VENTING** How does the installation position constrain the location of the vents and flues?	**POTENTIAL DAMAGE** Would the gases emitted by the flue pose any danger to the fabric? If so, can this be relieved by re-routing or alternative designs?
WASTE Are there any solid by-products such as ash? If so, how will these be stored and disposed of?	**OTHER REQUIREMENTS** How do special requirements (such as the need for drains to dispose of the collected condensates from condenser boilers) constrain siting?	

UNDERFLOOR HEATING

Although at 80–90 W/m² underfloor heating is not strong enough to heat the air to 'comfort level', systems tend to prove very popular with users, especially in large buildings, because they warm the feet and also prevent the discomfort caused by radiant heat loss from the body into the floor. This is a reminder that the current emphasis on air temperature may not be the best way of approaching comfort heating.

There are two main systems:

- *Electric systems*
  The floor is heated by running a current through resistance elements (cables, pre-formed cable mats, bronze mesh and carbon films) embedded into the floor.
- *Hydronic systems*
  The floor is heated by running hot water (or a mixture of water and anti-freeze) through embedded pipes in a closed loop from a boiler; the same system can also be used for cooling, by using cold instead of hot water. Early systems were prone to leaking, since the pipes were usually copper and the screed concrete, a combination that tended to induce corrosion. Early plastic pipes were also liable to fail, especially at joints, but modern systems based on extruded plastic seem to have overcome many of these problems.

Temperatures are limited by user comfort: the floor will feel uncomfortable if it is hotter than 29°C, and for most rooms 21°C is the preferred choice. The effect on furniture and other contents resting on the floor must also be considered.

The choice of floor covering is important. Carpeted floors, for example, will need to operate at higher internal temperatures than tiled floors. The emissivity, reflectivity and absorptivity of the surface must be taken into account: the most effective radiators are unpolished floors with very high emissivities. If the system is designed to cool in summer, it is desirable to have a high absorbance and emissivity, and a low reflectivity.

Efficiency demands reducing heat losses into the ground as much as possible. These depend largely on the thermal conductivity of the soil, which in turn depends on moisture content (a soil with a moisture content higher than 20 % can transfer as much as 15 times more heat than the same soil with a moisture content of less than 4 %). Heat may also be lost into neighbouring building cavities.

There is little point in installing underfloor heating without a layer of insulation underneath, and in most cases excavating the floor to sufficient depth is the greatest part of the cost. In buildings with sensitive archaeology, underfloor heating may prove difficult or impossible.

Another design consideration is the danger of 'parasitic heat transfer', which occurs if the heating pipes or cables are too close to other heating or cooling devices such as refrigerators, cold water lines, or ducts for air conditioning or ventilation. To prevent problems, pipes and cables must be well insulated.

Systems are commonly set into a concrete screed, but this can make repair and replacement extremely expensive. Weaker hydraulic-lime mortars are a better choice for this purpose, and they will also allow drying should an hydronic system develop leaks. ⊃MORTARS

Finally, the floor movement must be taken into account, especially since the heating itself will cause episodes of thermal expansion and contraction. All floors will need to incorporate expansion joints.

BUILDING ENVIRONMENT
CARE & REPAIR

The required flues and vents are often necessarily obtrusive, and whether these can be sited sensitively may prove to be a deciding factor when choosing between different heating systems.

Installing New Heating Systems

When considering heating for sensitive historic buildings, it is important to have a thorough idea of how the microclimate is functioning in the absence of heating, preferably including at least a year of monitoring. This gives a good background against which to assess the impact of the heating on the fabric, and whether it is behaving as intended.

Because of the different ways in which heating can be provided, it is essential that the heating type be well matched to the building and the way it is being used. For example, a common mistake is to try to heat the whole airspace with radiant heating units that were in fact designed to heat nearby bodies.

The heating system must certainly work effectively, but it should also be easy for the users to understand the underlying principles. Mistakes, such as managers thinking they can save money when a building is empty by turning off a system set for background heating with top-up heating during use, can be costly to the fabric as well as the budget.

Using Existing Chimneys for New Systems

The essential first step is to ensure that the chimney is in good condition, and safe to use. If the flue is to be lined, any necessary repairs to the stack should be made first. The chimney should then be tested according to the type of fuel that is to be used; what will be needed to make the chimney suitable will be covered by the Building Regulations and British or European Standards for various types of heating appliance.

The appropriate cross-sectional area of the flue will depend on the type of heater, and the size of the fire opening. For example, a large open fire will need a flue with a cross-section at least 15 % of the size of the opening. For an open-flue solid-fuel fire, the flue must be at least 5 % of the opening, but this may have to be increased if the chimney is less than 5 m high, or if there are bends in the flue.

Many early fireplaces have chimneys that are too large for modern heating equipment. If necessary, the size of the opening at the base of the flue can be reduced with a register plate (usually a horizontal, fireproof metal plate with a central opening to allow the fire to be used, to which the flue liner can be connected). If the fire is very large, a hood can be attached to the underside of the register plate to guide smoke into the flue. Register plates above open fires will need to be provided with dampers.

Cooling

Cooling is becoming a more serious issue for buildings in England as a result of not only changes in climate and land use, but also because buildings host more and more appliances that produce heat as a by-product of operation. The increased use of large areas of glazing and materials with a low thermal inertia such as metals means that solar heating can be a serious issue in summer.

The first step in reducing heat is to identify sources of heat that can be dealt with passively, perhaps by landscaping with shade trees, or adding awnings or blinds. Appliances can be used less often, changed for models that output less heat, or perhaps vented or moved to areas where the natural ventilation can remove the heat from the building. Other behavioural changes can be enormously helpful: for example, before the sun rises, drawing any blinds, shutters and curtains, and closing the windows on the side of the building that receives the morning sunlight.

Aside from shading, natural ventilation is the primary means of cooling buildings, though its performance depends on the outdoor conditions. Cross-ventilation by opening doors and windows can be extremely effective, especially in climates where there are good natural breezes and the night air is relatively cool. It works in two ways: not only replacing hot interior air with cooler air from the exterior, but also by cooling the occupants (the 'wind-chill' effect: moving air cools by convection and evaporation).

A detail from a 19th-century advertisement for awnings

Victorian awning systems were designed not only to shade, but also to funnel air through the building.

To determine the best way of cross-ventilating, some experimentation is required: the trick is to force the air to take a path that ventilates as much of the room as possible; opening windows on opposite sides of the room will generally cool only the space between. It is usually best to leave some windows closed, so that the air through them does not interfere with the desired flow.

The air should come in from the coolest location: the shady side of the building, for example. Air speed (and thus the sensation of cooling) can be increased by making sure that the opening through which the air enters is smaller than the one through which it exits. If possible, it is helpful to include an exit vent in the attic, into which the warm interior air will be rising. A clear path should be kept both outside and inside the windows, to let the air flow without obstruction.

BUILDING ENVIRONMENT
CARE & REPAIR

In very hot weather, or for certain designs of building, natural ventilation may not be enough to achieve sufficient cooling, and users will need to introduce mechanical cooling systems. These fall into three categories:

- fans
- evaporative coolers
- refrigerative air conditioners.

Fans

Fans do not cool the air, but rather the occupants (by wind-chill). They are by far the cheapest and most effective means of mechanical cooling, and are very useful even where air-conditioning systems are installed.

Fans can be run with the windows and doors open, and indeed are most effective when used to enhance the natural airflow through the buildings. They should be positioned so that the moving air will wash over the occupants. Many different types are available, including models that oscillate to move the air over a wider area. They vary widely, particularly in noisiness; a large fan running at low speed generally makes less noise than a small fan running at high speed.

Where they can be installed without damage, the most effective are ceiling fans, which can be very large (larger blades can move at much less speed and still produce the same cooling effect). These will be most effective when positioned 2.1–2.7 m above the floor and 25–30 cm below the ceiling. They should be kept at least 45 cm away from the walls.

'Whole-house' fans pull air in through open windows, exhausting it through vents in the attic and roof, and can provide as much as 60 ach if the building design allows. Cooling is regulated by closing windows in unoccupied parts of the building, and opening them in rooms with occupants. Vents can be covered in winter.

Evaporative Coolers

Evaporative coolers work by passing hot dry air through a wet filter; the evaporation from this cools and humidifies the air. They work best in relatively dry climates, and require a high rate of airflow: windows must be kept open so that air can pass freely though the building. Portable units, wall- or window-mounted and ducted systems are available; all require good maintenance, including regular draining and cleaning.

Refrigerative Air Conditioners

Refrigerative air conditioners use the same technologies as refrigerators to remove heat and moisture from the air, and are very energy-hungry. Cooling the smallest possible area of the building is usually more efficient than cooling multiple rooms or a whole building. Efficiency can be greatly improved by using fans as well: with moving air, occupants will generally be able to set the control thermostats much higher.

CONTROLLING HUMIDITY

Humidification

Humidification may occasionally be considered for conservation reasons: either to prevent damage to materials sensitive to low relative humidities, or to prevent salt crystallisation. The underlying reason for very low relative humidities is generally heating: in winter the incoming air will have a very low absolute humidity, so heating will reduce the relative humidity to levels that are uncomfortable for users and detrimental to moisture-sensitive materials such as glues (lifting of veneers is a common problem for antique furniture placed in buildings with central heating).

The interior relative humidity can be increased either passively or by using mechanical humidifiers: the latter must be used with care, as they can raise the relative humidity to high levels, and some types may introduce pollutants into the air (including chalk dust in areas with hard water).

Passive Humidification

Any source of water will help supply the air with moisture, which will help the air to settle at a 'natural' relative humidity. Sources could include pot plants, as well as water reservoirs (these are often hung from the central-heating radiators, where the extra heat helps the water to evaporate into the air). The reservoirs will need to be kept full.

Mechanical Humidification

There are a number of devices available for mechanical humidification, including:

- *Evaporative Humidifiers*
  Consists of a reservoir, a 'wick' (a filter that absorbs water from the reservoir and provides a larger surface area for evaporation) and a fan to move the humidified air around the room. Tanks need to be kept filled with water, and wicks (which tend to become mouldy) will need to be replaced regularly.

- *Vapourisers*
  These devices boil the water in the reservoir, so that it is released into the air as steam. The heat source in poorly designed humidifiers can be prone to overheating.

- *Impellers*
  A rotating disc flings the water at a diffuser that breaks it into fine droplets. Unlike the moist air from evaporators or the steam from vapourisers, this water can contain impurities, such as pathogens, so tanks should be cleaned regularly.

- *Ultrasonic humidifiers*
  A metal diaphragm creates water droplets by vibrating at an ultrasonic frequency. Like impellers, ultrasonic humidifiers must be cleaned regularly to prevent contamination.

BUILDING ENVIRONMENT
CARE & REPAIR

Environmental Control of Salt Decay

Theoretically, salt cycling could be minimised by maintaining an environment so that the humidity remains above or below the RHeq of the salts concerned. In reality, establishing the extent of the 'critical envelope' of destructive relative humidities is rarely feasible, for a number of reasons:

- The RHeqs are calculated in free air, and are very unlikely to pertain to the air within the pores, where solubility and relative humidity alike will be affected by factors such as surface reactivity and pore size.
- Salt mixtures have different RHeqs to those of single salts, and these will not be stable. For example, at 20°C, the equilibrium relative humidity for a mixture of sodium nitrate and sodium chloride (which each have RHeqs of around 75 %) has been measured, and found to range between 67.9 % and 73.9 %. The solubility of calcium sulphate, which in isolation is so low that it will dissolve only in liquid water, increases if it is combined with sodium chloride; it may then go in and out of solution as relative humidities fluctuating around 75 %.

Since the mixtures of salts in building materials are almost always very complex, calculating the equilibrium relative humidity of salts may therefore not be very useful. The safest approach for preventing salt damage is usually to keep the environment stable, whether that means it is constantly humid or constantly dry. There are rarely any perfect solutions, and often the best that can be hoped for is to minimise the rate of deterioration.

Dehumidification

Although the relative humidity of air can be reduced by increasing its temperature, this will not decrease its absolute humidity (the actual amount of water in the air). Indeed, in historic buildings, raising the temperature can often actually raise the absolute humidity, by increasing the amount of water evaporating from the fabric. To reduce moisture contents, air of a lower absolute humidity will need to be introduced, or else water vapour must be removed from the existing air by mechanical means: that is, by using dehumidifiers (see **Controlling the Interior Environment** and **Modifying the Interior Environment**).

The first step is to decide whether or not the area can really be dried. Dehumidifying a damp cellar, for example, will not normally be beneficial if there is a continuing source of moisture available through the walls or floor; indeed, it may well exacerbate moisture problems.

A fundamental problem with dehumidifiers is that they are often installed when the source of moisture is still active: in other words, they are used to try to treat the symptoms of the moisture problem rather than its cause. Using dehumidifiers in this way will simply accelerate the transport of water through the affected fabric, with all the consequent deleterious effects that may have. They are also often used in spaces too large for the capacity of the machine: the system must be designed to be adequate for the purpose if it is not to fail.

It also important to ensure that the space is suitably enclosed, so that the system is not trying to dry out the entire building or, worse still, the outside air. When local dehumidification is being undertaken on an active building site, this may mean restricting entry to some areas, or perhaps constructing temporary polythene doors with the type of rapid fastenings found on tent flaps.

Dehumidifiers require meticulous care and maintenance; in winter they have a tendency to ice up. The accumulated water in refrigerant systems must either be manually removed very regularly, or there must be some system of piping it away. There may also be an issue with the temperature increase in the conditioned air, which may affect other aspects of the building environment.

Dehumidification by Air Conditioning

The fundamental issue with using air-conditioning systems – which combine dehumidifying with cooling and heating – to provide suitable environmental conditions for sensitive fabric or contents is that they are designed to deliver to a different definition of 'stability'. An air-control plant is designed to keep the temperature and humidity within a very tight chosen range, and it does this by rapidly cycling conditions within that band. For conservation, the priority is instead for slow change: that is, the permissible degree of variation in humidity and temperature can usually be quite high, as long as the changes occur slowly and steadily.

For traditional buildings in England, air conditioning should not be necessary, but for modern buildings with large floor plates and non-opening windows, or large areas of glazing or cladding with low thermal inertias, it may be required to make the building comfortable even in winter. Air conditioning may also be considered where the contents of the building must be kept cooler than normal (in computer rooms, for example).

Air-conditioning systems developed alongside buildings dependent on ducting and forced ventilation for the provision of fresh air, and centred on providing a single set of conditions throughout the building. This is not only inefficient, but almost impossible to do successfully. It is best not to try to achieve all the necessary conditions for the indoor air with a single system, but rather to break up the system to reflect the different conditions that must be achieved. For example, 'comfort' temperatures and humidities will be different for different users, and will also depend on what they are wearing and doing: areas for intense physical activity will need to be cooler than areas in which people are sitting, and areas where refrigeration or massed computer equipment are pumping out heat will need to be managed differently to, say, a library.

The building envelope is also critical to the operation of the system: the materials, design and exposure will affect local heating and cooling; and the internal divisions of the building (together with the furniture) will affect the operation of the distribution systems and the feedback controls. Another issue is the quality of the air being circulated through the system, which depends not only on the filtering systems which process the air drawn in from the exterior, but also on the cleanliness and efficiency of the ducting systems. The effective and efficient approach is not to use ducts to move centrally conditioned air around a building, but instead to condition it where it is needed.

AUTOMATIC CONTROL SYSTEMS

Use of devices that can be controlled electronically, from motors to open and close awnings and blinds, to electric lighting and HVAC [heating, ventilation and air-conditioning] systems, has allowed the development of centralised controls for adjusting building systems. Early systems were based on potentiometers and other solid-state controls, but most current systems use microprocessors.

Centralised building management depends very much on the design of the sensor system. This can be challenging, especially in complex spaces, or spaces that have multiple uses. Response time is a particular concern: attempting to restrict temperature or humidity to a narrow band may induce rapid fluctuations, especially for systems where the source of heating or cooling has little thermal inertia. Some of these problems can be reduced by the choice of conditioning system; for example, systems based on oil-filled heaters are more stable than those based on air blowers. Yearly recalibration is a necessity.

Integrated Building Management Systems [BMS] have become increasingly common as a result of the drive towards decreasing energy use in buildings, although in practice centralised systems can prove more energy-hungry than systems under local control (for example, centralised lighting in office buildings can prove extremely wasteful in comparison to desk lamps). Part of the reason for this is that they are asked to do many different things at once – providing fresh air and thermal comfort, and energy efficiency, for example – and some of these aims may be in conflict. Malfunctions can be serious, since they could quickly lead to environmental problems such as damagingly high or low interior temperatures and humidities, or uncontrolled airflows.

Building Services Engineering

Building services engineering covers all aspects of the engineering of the internal environment of a building to make it usable, including the design, installation, commissioning and monitoring, and the ongoing care and maintenance of any mechanical, electrical or health-and-safety systems. This covers all electrical lighting and communications, plumbing, and heating and air conditioning, as well as other systems for security, fire prevention and detection, and so forth, and additional engineered installations such as escalators and lifts. There is an increasing emphasis on sustainable and low-carbon design.

In the UK, the professional body for building services engineers is the Chartered Institution of Building Services Engineers [CIBSE].

BMS systems can prove rather unpopular with occupants, since they remove control over local environments from individual users. Goals are set for large areas, and for 'standard' users, and they often take little or no account of the various activities being undertaken in the space, for which temperature and lighting requirements may be very different. Settings may take little account of the weather or of how occupants are dressed: a year-round temperature and humidity may be sought, regardless of the season.

The improvement and optimisation of control systems are currently subjects of considerable research; in particular, into making better use of occupant feedback, and allowing a measure of local control. Wireless control systems may permit sensors to be placed in positions that better reflect the needs of users, and also produce more stable conditions.

ASSESSING INTERVENTIONS

It is most unlikely that treatment or repair will completely resolve every issue with a building environment. Not only can deterioration never be entirely eliminated, but even the best treatment will not last forever. Indeed, some materials – putties and sealants are obvious examples – have quite short lifespans. Changes in the environment will continue after treatment or repair, and this too will affect long-term outcomes.

The results of treatments and repairs will therefore need to be reassessed regularly to ensure that they are still functional. Major alterations should be assessed against the original criteria for intervention: that is, are they successfully fulfilling the aims expected of them?

Where possible, it is best to set up a formal monitoring process, with resources set aside specifically for this purpose. It should be possible to integrate this into the building's care and maintenance plan. Environmental monitoring can also be a very useful tool for judging the outcome of certain interventions, especially adjustments to the interior environment. It is extremely important to begin monitoring well before any works begin, to ensure that there is a baseline of data against which to assess outcomes. Where the works are part of more wide-ranging alterations to the building, determining a baseline against which to judge an intervention can be very challenging. Usually a second complete year of data will need to be collected after the works are completed, to give the best chance of isolating the impact of the intervention from all the ordinary variations in exterior conditions and building use.

Ongoing assessment has an important side-benefit: it is the best way for architects, surveyors and other building specialists to find out how added materials and systems behave in real environments over longer periods of time. This information is vital to the development of future practice, so results should be disseminated as widely as possible.

The intrinsic complexity of the building environment means it is unlikely there will ever come a time when all the answers will be known. Building systems always reveal new surprises to the alert specialist, and moreover there will always be new materials and systems that need to be understood. On the other hand, the basic principles underlying behaviour (as set out in this book) are surely constant, and will always provide a sound basis for understanding and conserving the building and its environment.

BUILDING ENVIRONMENT
CARE & REPAIR

Further Reading

Bishop, J., McKay, H., Parrott, D., Allan, J. (2003); *Review of International Research Literature Regarding the Effectiveness of Auditory Bird Scaring Techniques and Potential Alternatives*; Report by Central Research Laboratory for Defra; available at *archive.defra.gov.uk/environment/quality/noise/research/birdscaring/birdscaring.pdf*

Brand, S. (1994); *How Buildings Learn: What Happens After They're Built*; London: Viking

British Standards Institution (2000); *BS EN 12056–3: 2000 Gravity drainage systems inside buildings. Roof drainage, layout and calculation*; London: BSI

Building Research Establishment (2000); *Disposing of Rainwater*; *BRE Good Building Guide 38*; Watford: BRE Press

English Heritage (2004); *Grants for Historic Buildings, Monuments and Designed Landscapes: Maintenance Plans*; available at *www.english-heritage.org.uk/publications/historic-buildings-monuments-and-designed-landscapes-maintenance/*

HM Government (2010); *Building Regulations Approved Document E – Resistance to the Passage of Sound*; available at *www.planningportal.gov.uk/buildingregulations/approveddocuments/parte/approved*

Howell, J. (2008); *The Sunday Telegraph Guide to Looking After Your Property (2nd Edition)*; London: Ebury Press

Hunt, R., Suhr, M. (2008); *Old House Handbook: A Practical Guide to Care and Repair*; London: Frances Lincoln

Moodie, M. (2001); *Waste Water from Churches*; available at *www.gloucester.anglican.org/downloads/913.doc*

National Renewable Energy Laboratory, U. S. Department of Energy (2001); *Cooling Your Home with Fans and Ventilation*; available at *www.nrel.gov/docs/fy01osti/29513.pdf*

The National Trust (2006); *Manual of Housekeeping: The Care of Collections in Historic Houses Open to the Public*; Oxford: Butterworth-Heinemann

Office of the Deputy Prime Minister (2002): *Approved Document of the Building Regulations 2000; Part H: Drainage and Waste Disposal: H3: Rainwater Drainage*; available at *www.planningportal.gov.uk/uploads/br/BR_PDF_ADH_2002.pdf*

Park, S. C. (1996); *Holding the Line: Controlling Unwanted Moisture in Historic Buildings*; U. S. National Park Service Preservation Briefs No.39; available at *www.nps.gov/tps/how-to-preserve/briefs/39-control-unwanted-moisture.htm*

Pike, C. (2011); 'Sound insulation in historic buildings'; in *The Building Conservation Directory 2011*; also available at *www.buildingconservation.com/articles/soundinsulation/soundinsulation.htm*

Rock, I. (2012); *Period Property Manual: Care and Repair of Old Houses*; London: Frances Lincoln

Saunders, D., Mapp, P., Sacre, P., Templeton, D. (1998); *Acoustics in the Built Environment: Advice for the Design Team (2nd Edition)*; Oxford: Architectural Press

Taylor, R. (1999); 'Chimneys and flues'; in *The Building Conservation Directory 1999*; also available at *www.buildingconservation.com/articles/services/chimney.htm*

Trotman, P., Sanders, C., Harrison, H. (2004): *Understanding Dampness: Effects, Causes, Diagnosis and Remedies (BRE Report 466)*; Watford: BRE Press

Useful Websites

The Bat Conservation Trust: *www.bats.org.uk/*

Building Science Corporation: *www.buildingscience.com*

Church of England's resource website: *www.churchcare.co.uk*

CIBSE Heritage Group: *www.hevac-heritage.org*

The Pigeon Control Resource Centre: *www.pigeoncontrolresourcecentre.org*

SPECIAL TOPICS

CONTENTS:

Buildings & Human Health

Dealing With Disasters

Improving Energy & Carbon Performance

BUILDINGS
& HUMAN
HEALTH

THE MODEL LODGING-HOUSE.

THE CELLAR.

HEALTH & BUILDING ENVIRONMENT

Buildings are intended to protect their occupants, but they are not always comfortable, and in certain conditions they can actually be a source of illness and even death.

Although some problems arise from dangerous materials incorporated in the fabric (such as asbestos), most stem from the environment in and around the building either supporting damaging gases or particulates, or creating conditions suitable for disease-causing microbes to thrive. The term used to describe these problems is 'indoor air quality' [IAQ], although certain pathogens living in building systems can affect people living some distance away. The IAQ will be decreased by anything able to induce poor health: smoke and other particulates, chemicals such as formaldehydes, gases such as carbon monoxide and radon, and microorganisms such as dust mites and moulds.

Although other aspects of the building, such as glare or excessive noise, can make occupants uncomfortable and even ill, IAQ is becoming ever more important as the principal health-and-safety issue, particularly as more and more buildings have been equipped with centralised air-control systems, and air exchange with the exterior has been reduced. In developed countries, most people now spend almost their entire day in buildings, working, eating and sleeping. The health problems they may acquire as a result range from the merely bothersome to the extremely serious:

- *Multiple chemical sensitivities* [MCS]
  Poor health in some occupants, which appears to be related to the length of time they have spent in a particular building. A proposed cause is hypersensitivity to certain chemicals or other contaminants, but this diagnosis is by no means certain.

- *Sick building syndrome* [SBS]
  Poor health in most or all occupants (including headaches, sore throat, tiredness, repeated colds and flu) that can be linked to the amount of time they have spent in a particular building, although it is not possible to identify either a specific illness or an underlying cause. Linking cause and effect is often extremely difficult, since occupants will be exposed simultaneously to a wide range of air contaminants.

- *Building-related illness* [BRI]
  Poor health with a common set of symptoms in most or all occupants, which can be unambiguously related to the length of time spent in a particular building; investigation reveals a clear cause (for example, Legionnaires' Disease linked to the growth of the *Legionella* bacteria in the building's air-conditioning system).

In 1984, the World Health Organisation [WHO] published the findings of research into sick building syndrome, noting that in some air-conditioned buildings it was causing a drop in productivity estimated at up to 40 %, and an increase in absenteeism of as much as 30 %. However, IAQ concerns are not limited to developed societies nor to modern buildings: in a more recent report, the WHO attributed around two million premature deaths worldwide every year to illnesses arising from the burning of solid fuel for heating and cooking.

Two cartoons from an 1850 copy of *Punch* magazine contrast the grim and unhealthy conditions in a poor dwelling with the excellent conditions in a 'model' lodging.

BUILDING ENVIRONMENT
SPECIAL TOPIC: Buildings & Human Health

COMMON INDOOR AIR CONTAMINANTS

PRINCIPAL SOURCE		CONTAMINANTS
BUILDING & FURNISHING MATERIALS	Fabric Underlying ground	Dust, glass fibres, asbestos fibres, radon
	Paints and glues, including those in laminated wood Cleansers, disinfectants and solvents	Volatile organic compounds [VOCs] such as formaldehyde Heavy metals such as lead
	Off-gassing (such as the softeners and solvents released by many industrial plastics)	Toxins of various types and degrees of seriousness (such as cyanide from some types of rubber-based sealants)
	Treatments such as biocides	Biotoxins
MICRO-ORGANISMS	Furniture	Dust mites
	Damp materials Stagnant water	Fungi spores, mould spores, bacteria
BUILDING USE	Heaters burning carbon-based fuels Diesel-powered generators Combustion engines (for example, cars)	Carbon monoxide; particulates
	Furniture Occupants	Carbon dioxide; dust
	Photocopiers Electric motors Electrostatic air cleaners	Ozone

The storage tanks of air-conditioning systems, which are often found on the rooftops of commercial buildings, can support the growth of microorganisms such as *Legionella* bacteria.

HEALTH HAZARDS IN BUILDINGS

An assessment of health hazards in a building may be desired for one of two basic reasons:

- works are being proposed that could expose the workers or other building users to hazardous materials (such as asbestos, lead or bird droppings)
- building users are reporting health problems that could be associated with the building or its contents (such as respiratory problems).

Although health problems reported by occupants can arise from any combination of contaminants, the underlying causes are often linked to environmental issues such as inappropriate temperatures and humidities, or insufficient intake of outdoor air.

In cities particularly, commercial buildings are often airtight and use central air plants deliberately designed to limit air exchange with the exterior. This makes it easier and cheaper to condition the building air, and reduces the need to precondition incoming air to bring it to the right temperature or to filter it to remove pollutants, but its unfortunate side-effects cannot be denied. In poor air-conditioning systems, the building air is run through the ceiling and underfloor spaces, which are usually very dirty; even ducts and filters may only rarely be cleaned.

ASSESSING HEALTH HAZARDS

Assessments of hazards during building works in the UK are covered by the Health and Safety Executive. The latest regulations and practice recommendations should always be consulted and followed (*www.hse.gov.uk*).

It is harder to assess health problems associated with use of the building, because potential causes are many, and active factors are challenging to isolate. Not only all information about symptoms, but the nature of the building itself, will need to be taken into account. For example, if the building was constructed in the 20th century, or has major 20th-century renovations, asbestos may be a risk.

An assessment survey should be made to investigate all possible causes of discomfort, including the lighting and heating, the fabric and furnishings, and the air plant. Forced ventilation should be checked to determine the mix of outdoor and indoor air, the air distribution, and the nature and state of the ducting and the filtration systems. All possible issues, from mould growth to ozone-generating equipment or sources of standing water, will need to be mapped and compared to patterns of occupancy and illness.

In some cases it will prove necessary to call in experts to analyse samples of the air and from building surfaces, or to monitor pollutants, or to study airflow. Further information about general environmental monitoring can be found in **Assessing the Environment: Specialist Investigations**.

BUILDING ENVIRONMENT
SPECIAL TOPIC: Buildings & Human Health

HAZARDS & ACTIONS

TOXIC MATERIALS

Asbestos Fibres

Asbestos, a naturally occurring fibrous silicate mineral able to strongly resist heat and chemical damage, became very popular with builders and manufacturers of building products in the 19th century as a flame retardant or an insulator, and to add tensile strength and flexibility. It was used widely: as a compound for dry walls and jointing, in sheeting and tiles, in cladding, roofing felts and shingles, as an additive for plasters, cements and textured coatings, and as lagging for pipes and for general heat and sound insulation. Unfortunately, asbestos proved to be extremely dangerous, with inhalation of dust causing malignant lung cancer, mesothelioma and asbestosis. Health concerns began to be raised in the early 1900s, but restrictions on production or use did not become common until very much later. In the UK, building products containing asbestos were extensively used throughout the 1960s and 1970s, and importation, supply and use of all forms of asbestos was not finally prohibited until 1999.

Asbestos removal

Asbestos dust is not only extremely toxic, but very fine. During removal, working areas must be kept sealed and at a lower pressure to prevent dust being drawn out. This can be seen in the bowing inwards of the plastic sheeting installed for asbestos removal at an historic swimming bath in Swindon.

This sealing is the primary practical problem facing specialist removal companies; swathing the area in airtight sheeting can take several days. It also raises important conservation issues if the building surfaces are fragile or significant: great care will need to be taken to develop and put into practice a technical approach to attaching the sheeting that does not cause damage, and is easily reversed.

Asbestos is therefore likely to be found somewhere in any building constructed or refurbished at any time in the 20th century. The incidence of asbestos-related death will certainly continue to increase as diseases develop, as asbestos-containing products begin to break down, and as people become exposed to hidden asbestos during building works: by 2013, 4000 workers in the UK were dying each year from asbestos-related diseases, and this figure is expected to reach 10,000 by 2020.

The Health and Safety Executive (which names asbestos as the single greatest cause of work-related deaths in the UK) publishes detailed guidance on the responsibilities of managers of non-domestic premises to manage any asbestos risk; the latest regulations and guidelines can be found on their website (*www.hse.gov.uk*).

Lead

Lead is toxic to many organs and tissues, and interferes with the development of the nervous system, making poisoning particularly serious in young children. The main cause – common in many older buildings – is the dust from deteriorating lead paint (small children may also eat paint flakes). Stripping lead paints without adequate care to protect against dust or fumes can cause serious poisoning. Another common household source is drinking water fed through lead pipes, or pipes that have been soldered in lead. Strict regulations now govern the use and disposal of lead-containing paints, and other similar materials.

Guano & Other Animal Deposits

Bird droppings can cause several diseases, including Psittacosis (a flu-like illness that can lead to pneumonia). Problems are most common in workers cleaning or working in areas heavily soiled with guano, and must be avoided by wearing protective clothing, such as face masks and gloves, and taking care not to touch the eyes or mouth with unwashed hands.

MICROORGANISMS

Anthrax

Anthrax is an acute disease caused by *Bacillus anthracis* bacteria, which can be fatal without correct treatment. In the 1990s there was a brief period of concern that animal hair used as reinforcement in historic plasters could preserve anthrax spores. The English Heritage guidance published at the time still holds true: "*No cases of occupationally-acquired infection among construction workers who may have handled historic plaster have been recorded.*" ⊖MORTARS

Moulds

Moulds, the most common sign of poor IAQ, grow rapidly: given suitable temperatures and humidities, and a source of nutrients, colonies will start to appear in only one or two days. In buildings, the limiting factor to growth is usually humidity: moulds will not appear until the relative humidity starts to exceed 75 %, and most species require a relative humidity of at least 85 % to flourish. A source of liquid water is also essential, whether this is a leak or condensation, or both. Some species also need a stimulant to break dormancy, such as thermal shock or a chemical activator (sometimes a detergent used to clean the surface).

Health Risks from Moulds

Moulds produce spores in enormous quantities; these are often black or some shade of green, which gives mould its characteristic appearance. Inhaling spores is the primary health hazard, and the smaller the spore, the further it will penetrate into the respiratory system.

In the USA, *Stachybotrys* (a black mould with sticky spores, which is usually found on substrates rich in cellulose such as wallpaper) has been subjectively linked to a range of clinical symptoms, and thus the subject of huge compensation claims. Buildings in which *Stachybotrys* has been found – particularly schools – have been closed, and even demolished. *Stachybotrys* requires a low sugar and nitrogen content, and therefore tends to colonise in the wake of other moulds such as *Penicillium* and *Cladosporium*. It also needs a relative humidity higher than about 93 %, and most studies have found that *Stachybotrys* typically makes up less than 3 % of the fungi found in buildings.

A few species (popularly called 'toxic moulds') produce mycotoxins, which can be dangerous if ingested or absorbed through the skin. *Aspergillus flavus* produces aflatoxin, a potent carcinogen, and *Stachybotrys chartarum* notoriously produces a group of mycotoxins called trichothecenes, which have been used in biological weapons; dry mould is considered more hazardous than wet mould, as it is easier to inhale the spores. In truth, however, a link between toxic moulds and health problems in humans has never been decisively proven.

British Standards

BS 5250:2011 Code of practice for control of condensation in buildings

BS 5250 describes the causes and effects of surface and interstitial condensation, and gives recommendations for their control, as well as for remedial works. This standard covers:

- methods for calculating the risk of surface and interstitial condensation
- typical quantities of humidity generated by various building uses and occupation levels
- figures for the thermal conductivity and vapour resistivity of common building materials
- guidance for builders and owners
- design to avoid moisture-related problems
- remedial works.

There are several reasons for this, which serve to illustrate why the health risks may actually be much less than popularly supposed:

- *Stachybotrys* is generally found with other moulds, many of which will be producing mycotoxins of various kinds; if the environment is wet enough to support the mould, then there will be a wide range of other potential allergens present
- mycotoxins are produced in very small amounts
- toxin production depends on the environmental conditions as well as the strain of mould, so the presence of the mould does not necessarily mean the toxin is present
- the depth of penetration into the respiratory system is inversely proportional to particle size, and *Stachybotrys chartarum* spores are rather large (greater than five microns, and often much larger).

Although the toxic mould risk has undoubtedly been inflated by the media and by damage litigation, health problems certainly do exist. Many people may be largely unaffected (at least in the short term), but others can have very serious allergic reactions. Prolonged exposure to high concentrations of spores may cause sensitisation, producing symptoms such as breathlessness, coughing and fever, and may permanently damage the lungs.

Again, it is usually difficult to attribute an allergic reaction to spores alone, because typically there are other potential causes present, such as pollen or tobacco smoke.

One common group of moulds (*Aspergillus*) can induce a condition known as 'aspergillosis', the symptoms of which range from acute to chronic, and may even include a ball of fungus forming in the lungs of victims with suppressed immune systems ('aspergilloma').

SPORES CAUSING ALLERGIC REACTIONS		
SPORE SIZE (MICRONS)	SITE OF ALLERGY	POSSIBLE CONSEQUENCES
>10	Nose	Rhinitis
4–10	Bronchi or bronchioles	Asthma
<4	Lung alveoli	Alveolitis

Treatment

Mould growth can be countered by correcting the environmental problems that have allowed it to flourish. Removing the source of liquid water is the primary treatment, and this will often lower the relative humidity at the same time. Increasing ventilation and insulation will also help. Paints and other decorating materials containing 'anti-mould' ingredients are widely available, but these should not be seen as a viable alternative to improving the environment.

Dust Mites

Dust mites live in fragments of shed human skin, and an old pillow, for example, can contain thousands of living and dead mites. The most common mite (*Dermatophagoides pteronyssinus*) measures less than 0.2 mm, and its faecal pellets 10–24 µm; a single gram of dust can contain as many as 250,000 pellets.

Dust mites thrive in warm and humid conditions; ideal habitats include carpets, soft furnishings and mattresses. Their favoured temperature is about 20°C, and although they require the air around them to have a moisture content of about seven grams of water per kilogram of dry air, they can tolerate drier room air conditions if they are living in (for example) warm, sweat-moistened bedding.

Health Risks from Dust Mites

Pellets and disintegrated dead mites both contain a protein called 'Der p 1', which is able to cause allergic rhinitis, sinusitis and asthma in about a fifth of the population.

Treatment

The old approach of airing bedding, and keeping bedrooms cool, served to make conditions less suitable for dust mites. Washing bedding at temperatures above 58°C will kill the mites and destroy allergens, and regular vacuuming of carpets and mattresses helps to contain the mite numbers.

Bacteria

A number of bacteria can flourish in buildings, but the most notoriously dangerous is *Legionella pneumonophila*, the aquatic organism that causes legionellosis, commonly known as 'Legionnaires' Disease' after its identification as the cause of an outbreak of illness in Philadelphia in 1976, which killed 34 people. *Legionella* thrives in stagnant water at 25–45°C (the optimum temperature is around 35°C); ingesting or inhaling contaminated water can lead to infection. Potential sources include industrial cooling towers, the water coolers of large air-conditioning systems, humidifiers and nebulisers, hot tubs, and hot water systems. In most cases the water is inhaled as an aerosol. Outbreaks are most common in buildings with complex water and cooling systems, but can spread more widely: an outbreak caused by a contaminated industrial cooling tower in Pas-de-Calais, France, infected people living more than 6 km away.

Treatment

The UK Government's Health and Safety Executive recommends weekly monitoring and quarterly routine testing of all wet cooling systems.

Thermal sterilisation is difficult, so in hospitals and other buildings where the occupants may be particularly susceptible to infection, sterilisers combining UV irradiation and ultrasonic cavitation are commonly used to treat hot-water systems. Copper-silver ionisation is used to eradicate *Legionella* from industrial water distribution systems and cooling towers, and this tool is now being adopted by hospitals.

GASES

Carbon Monoxide

Carbon monoxide is undoubtedly the greatest health hazard in buildings. It can be produced by any equipment burning hydrocarbons – including heaters, generators, gas rings and stoves, and cars – and results from incomplete combustion. The 'town' gas used during the late 19th century and throughout much of the 20th century was produced from coal, and released substantial quantities of carbon monoxide when burnt; but the gas used now is mostly methane, which happily gives out much less carbon monoxide.

Health Risks from Carbon Monoxide

Exposure to carbon monoxide at concentrations of more than 100 ppm is dangerous. When inhaled, it enters the bloodstream where it preferentially combines with haemoglobin, preventing the uptake of oxygen (amongst other adverse effects on respiration). The resulting oxygen starvation can damage the central nervous system and heart, and continued exposure will eventually result in death. Unfortunately the gas is colourless, odourless and tasteless, and so is very difficult for people to detect, not least since the effects of poisoning include light-headedness and confusion. Chronic exposure to low levels of carbon monoxide may not prove fatal, but can lead to depression, confusion and memory loss.

Treatment

The best treatment is prevention. Any equipment generating carbon monoxide in a confined space must be inspected regularly, and used only if the space is well-ventilated (or has vents to channel the exhaust gases directly out of the building). By law, any rooms heated with wood-burning stoves must also be fitted with carbon-monoxide detector alarms.

BUILDING ENVIRONMENT
SPECIAL TOPIC: Buildings & Human Health

Radon

Radon is formed from the disintegration of radium, which is itself a breakdown product of uranium, and it is highly radioactive. It is found in low concentrations in most soils, particularly over granite, and is drawn into buildings from the ground.

Health Risks from Radon

Accumulated radon will decay to form radioactive products such as polonium, which attach to dust. If this is ingested, it will lead to an increased risk of lung cancer (it has been estimated that about 5 % of lung-cancer deaths in England are associated with radon exposure).

Concentration is measured in becquerels per cubic metre (Bq/m^3); an average indoor concentration is about 20 Bq/m^3, but far higher levels may be found in some parts of the country (maps are produced by the Health Protection Agency). Where there is a risk of high exposure, it is sensible to monitor concentrations. Part C of the Building Regulations sets the level for remedial action at 200 Bq/m^3, and under the 1999 *Ionising Radiation Regulations*, action must be taken in any school, public building or work place if the level has reached 400 Bq/m^3. ⊖BASICS

Radon is discussed in detail in the *Mortars, Renders & Plasters* volume of this series. ⊖MORTARS

Treatment

Radon can be excluded from living areas by sealing gaps and cracks in floors and walls, which may be sufficient for concentrations below about 500 Bq/m^3. Improved underfloor ventilation is sometimes recommended, but this can be hard to achieve.

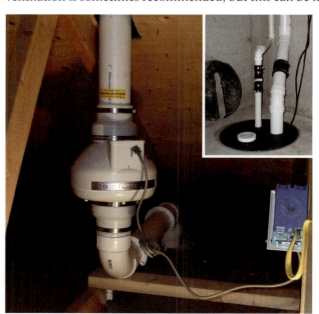

Effective remediation involves removing the radon gas, usually by installing a sump beneath the floor to one side of the building. The radon is sucked into this by an induced negative pressure, and discharged away from the building through an external pipe that terminates above the eaves. Most systems will require an extractor fan in the pipe, which is kept running continuously.

Other Gases

- *Carbon dioxide*

  Carbon dioxide is generated by the respiration of the building occupants, and the indoor concentration of the gas is used often to assess air-exchange rates. Unlike carbon monoxide, carbon dioxide is not dangerous except at extremely high concentrations, but it can cause drowsiness and headaches. Concentrations should be less than 600 ppm above the concentration in the exterior air, and the UK standards for schools say that carbon dioxide levels at seated head-height should not exceed 1500 ppm when averaged over the school day.

- *Nitrogen dioxide, nitric oxide*

  Combustion processes (gas stoves and paraffin heaters, for example) can produce nitrogen dioxide and nitric oxide, both toxic gases; nitrogen dioxide is also very reactive. At fairly low levels – the ASHRAE standards give beyond 0.053 ppm for nitrogen dioxide – they irritate the mucous membranes, causing coughing, shortness of breath and nausea.

- *Ozone*

  Ozone is produced by certain electric devices (such as photocopiers and printers), and as a by-product of other types of pollution. It can irritate lung tissue, and will also react with many materials (including skin oils) to produce toxic and irritating chemicals, and very fine particulates.

- *Volatile Organic Compounds [VOCs]*

  VOCs are organic chemicals of various types, which can cause various health problems (some are known or suspected to cause cancers). Symptoms associated with exposure include irritation of the eyes, nose and throat, headaches and dizziness, and allergic skin reactions. VOCs are emitted by a wide range of materials commonly found in and around buildings, including fuels, paints and paint strippers, cleaning agents, adhesives, pesticides, and office equipment such as copiers and printers.

SUMMARY OF TREATMENTS FOR DANGEROUS GASES

The basic remedy for gases and other airborne contaminants is to improve ventilation, especially in areas with open-flue appliances. This will also decrease concentrations of water vapour. One technique to improve air quality without increasing energy use is 'demand-controlled' ventilation: instead of setting a fixed rate of air replacement, carbon-dioxide sensors are used to control the ventilation dynamically.

Air filters can also be used to trap some pollutants. Some success has also been claimed from introducing house plants to absorb VOCs and other contaminants.

Further Reading

Bluyssen, P. M. (2014); *The Healthy Indoor Environment: How to Assess Occupants' Wellbeing in Buildings*; London: Routledge, Taylor & Francis Group

Bornehag, C.-G., Blomquist, G. *et al.* (2001); 'Dampness in buildings and health'; in *Indoor Air*; Vol. 11; pp.72–86; also available at *www.myc-tech.com/myndigheter/socialstyrelsen/norddamp.pdf*

Clancy, E. (2011); *Indoor Air Quality and Ventilation*; Chartered Institution of Building Services Engineers Knowledge Series, KS 17; London: CIBSE

Committee on the Effect of Climate Change on Indoor Air Quality and Public Health, Institute of Medicine (2011); *Climate Change, the Indoor Environment, and Health*; Washington DC: National Academies Press

Dimitriloupolou, C., Crump, D., *et al.* (2005); Ventilation, *Air Tightness and Indoor Air Quality in New Homes*; Building Research Establishment Report BR 477; Garston: BRE Bookshop

Dudzinska, M. R. (ed.) (2011); *Management of Indoor Air Quality*; Boca Raton, Florida: CRC Press

English Heritage (1999); *Anthrax and Historic Plaster: Managing Minor Risks in Historic Building Refurbishment*; available at *www.helm.org.uk/guidance-library/anthrax-and-historic-plaster/*

GreenFacts (2008); *Indoor Air Quality*; Report for the DG Health and Consumers of the European Commission; available at *ec.europa.eu/health/opinions/indoor-air-pollution-l1_en.pdf*

Hess-Kosa, K. (2011); *Indoor Air Quality: The Latest Sampling and Analytical Methods (2nd Edition)*; Boca Raton, Florida: CRC Press

US Environmental Protection Agency (2013); *The Inside Story: A Guide to Indoor Air Quality*; Washington DC: EPA; also available at *www.epa.gov/iaq/pubs/insidestory.html*

World Health Organisation (2011); *Indoor Air Pollution and Health*; WHO Fact sheet No.292; available at *www.who.int/mediacentre/factsheets/fs292/en/index.html*

Useful Websites

Health & Safety Executive: *www.hse.gov.uk*

DEALING WITH DISASTERS

CATASTROPHIC DAMAGE

All buildings are potentially subject to catastrophic events, although the type and extent of the risk depends on location, materials and structure, and use. Disasters are not only the result of natural occurrences such as storms, but also of accident or even deliberate vandalism. The resulting damage can take many forms.

COMMON CAUSES

It is rather difficult to divide causes of disaster into neat categories, because in many cases there is a great deal of overlap: fires lead to flood damage from firefighting, for example, and a storm which brings a tree down onto a roof, or a car which crashes into a wall, may also break plumbing pipes and cause interior flooding. Indeed, whatever the primary cause, the worst deterioration usually arises from water entering the building as a result and, sadly, from the subsequent attempts to dry the fabric.

FIRE

Arguably the greatest cause of catastrophic damage to buildings, fire may occur as a result of other emergencies such as earthquakes, lightning, or vandalism, but most often can be traced back to building use. Common causes include faulty electrical wiring, unswept chimneys, and candles or hot lamps burning near flammable materials.

The damage caused directly by the fire itself is usually not as severe as that attributable to the water used to extinguish it. Stone and brick heated by fire may crack when suddenly doused with cold water, and over the longer term the great quantities of water added to the fabric may lead to timber decay and salt damage. Since the heat from an ordinary fire will not be high enough to kill fungi, decay may break out again in areas where there had been outbreaks in the past, which had been brought under control. Environmental problems of many kinds may continue for decades after the fire itself.

STORMS

Most storm damage is caused by high winds. These have both direct impacts (lifting or distorting roof covers or cladding, for example), and indirect impacts (lifting and throwing other objects onto the building, such as trees and tree branches). Taller buildings and buildings surrounded by tall objects are at greatest risk, as are exposed building elements such as roof ridges and chimneys. The initial damage is often less severe than the rain penetrating the damaged building, especially if holding repairs are not made immediately. Tall or very exposed buildings will also be at risk from lightning, which can damage the envelope directly, but it is most dangerous if it leads to a fire.

Flash flooding is another likely result of storms, especially in cities where there are so many hard surfaces that ground drainage is easily overwhelmed in heavy rainfall.

Fire is perhaps the most devastating disaster that can befall a building in England, since the direct damage from the heat and flames may be equalled or even exceeded by the water damage from fighting the fire.

BUILDING ENVIRONMENT
SPECIAL TOPIC: Dealing with Disasters

FLOODS

Floods can be caused by many agents inside as well as outside. For individual buildings, flash flooding is usually the most damaging manifestation, since by definition it arrives with little or no warning.

CAUSES OF FLOODING

TYPE	CAUSES	COMMENTS
COASTAL FLOODS	Building location Storm surge Sea-level rise	Largely unavoidable Usually arrives with reasonable warning Introduces salt-laden water
RIVERINE FLOODS	Building location Storminess	Largely unavoidable Usually arrives with reasonable warning Duration varies: can result in long-term exposure to standing water Water is often polluted
RUNOFF FLOODS	Drainage problems Main supply bursts	Events can be sudden and unexpected Increasingly common in both rural and urban locations, due mostly to changes in ground cover Water may be polluted Exposure to water is usually brief
INTERIOR FLOODS	Plumbing leaks Overflows Firefighting	May be sudden, or a sudden escalation of a long-term problem that has passed unnoticed Water is usually contaminated

IMPACTS

After objects thrown onto a building by high winds, the most common cause of impact damage is motor vehicles colliding with the building. Less common events include explosions, where the damage is caused both by the pressure wave and by thrown debris.

DELIBERATE DAMAGE

The most common example of deliberate damage to historic buildings is the intentional breaking of glass, but vandalism can affect many other parts of the fabric as well.
➔EARTH & BRICK ➔GLASS ➔STONE ➔METALS

Currently, one of the most worrying forms of deliberate damage is the theft of metal components, particularly roof coverings. In many cases the targeted building is quite remote and sporadically used (a parish church, for example), which means the theft may not be noticed until after there has been significant rain damage. This is an increasingly serious issue, and a number of initiatives have been introduced to address it. ➔ROOFING

EARTH MOVEMENTS

SUBSIDENCE

Subsidence can arise from a number of different sources: geological movement and flooding, but also changes in local soil moisture content, groundwater levels or mining.

EARTH TREMORS

In some countries, earthquakes and tremors are a major risk to buildings, and the local vernacular architecture is able to cope either because it was designed to stay standing, or because it was built lightly and designed both to collapse with little danger and to be easily reconstructable.

For more recent building, research over the past few decades has had considerable success in developing designs that can cope with even very severe earthquakes. The buildings that are most at risk are therefore those constructed stiffly with brittle and heavy materials such as concrete to mid-20th-century building codes, or older buildings that have been repaired with these materials.

Earthquakes are often associated with subsequent damage from fires and flooding (especially indoor flooding from broken plumbing).

Even in relatively benign geological areas such as England, tremors and earthquakes are surprisingly common, and can cause major damage to tall building elements such as chimneys, towers and spires.

Here at St Mary Magdelene, Waltham on the Wolds in Leicestershire (*right*), a photograph of the inside of the spire after an earthquake in 2008 (*left*) shows how the masonry was extensively dislodged.

BUILDING ENVIRONMENT
SPECIAL TOPIC: Dealing with Disasters

PREVENTION

It is not surprising that the most practical way of dealing with environmental building disasters such as fires and floods is to prevent them happening in the first place, or if they do occur to minimise their severity as much as possible.

Although the building managers will have no control over the causes of coastal or riverine flooding, or of earthquake, for most other sources of environmental disaster (including flash flooding), there are many ways to reduce the likelihood of damage. The role of emergency planning in disaster mitigation is beyond the scope of this book, but some of the practical interventions that can be made to the building envelope to prevent damage are discussed below.

The *Conservation Basics* volume of this series covers disaster management and emergency planning in detail. ⊃BASICS

Training of emergency teams allows the damage from a disastrous event to be minimised. Both the emergency services and any building staff or volunteers should be well-drilled in all the actions that may be needed: here, the removal of endangered building contents using a human chain is being practised during a training day.

Disaster Management

The best way of dealing with building disasters is good planning well in advance: planning to prevent problems happening in the first place, so far as that is possible; and planning to minimise damage if the worst does occur.

The organised thinking that must go into developing emergency plans is always useful, and indeed there are many cases where a plan developed for one type of emergency (such as a fire) has proved very helpful in an emergency of a very different kind (such as a major security alert).

RISK ASSESSMENT

The first step is a thorough risk assessment. The complexity of such a plan depends on the size and significance of the building and its contents, but even the most modest cottage will benefit from an assessment of likely problems, repeated every few years, or whenever major changes are made to the building or the building use.

For some buildings, a particular risk may be so high that it will have affected the way the building was originally constructed or used: for example, a house in a riverside village that has been flooded regularly since the Middle Ages is almost certain to have been constructed with materials able to dry out quickly, and important rooms such as the kitchen may have been located on upper floors rather than the ground floor or basement. Any unusual layouts or construction details may be worth investigating in this light.

RISK MANAGEMENT

Determining where the building is most susceptible to catastrophic damage should automatically lead to a certain amount of risk management. For example, noting that the building is at risk from falling branches can initiate a programme of surgery on nearby trees. Vehicle impact damage can often be prevented by adding protective bollards and height indicators.

Some interventions to prevent risk, such as protecting stained-glass windows with exterior protective wiring or glazing, have significant environmental implications, and will need to be assessed in that light. ➔GLASS

EMERGENCY PLANNING

A well-designed and up-to-date emergency plan is important for any building, and will greatly reduce loss and damage. The plan identifies the people who will need to be contacted immediately should an emergency occur, the actions they will need to take, and the materials and equipment they will need to have available to stabilise the building and its contents.

For large buildings, regular scheduled consultations and drills with the local emergency services – especially the fire brigade – will ensure that they are familiar with the building and its contents, and understand any special actions that would need to be taken when tackling the emergency and have full access for all the necessary equipment.

The key is to prevent as many as possible of the other problems that might arise in the train of the initial disaster. For example, having a fully developed emergency plan in the event of a fire will limit the degree of water damage from firefighting, prevent subsequent exposure damage, and avoid later damage from poor drying and repair.

Emergency planning is discussed in greater detail in the *Conservation Basics* volume of this series. ➔BASICS

BUILDING ENVIRONMENT
SPECIAL TOPIC: Dealing with Disasters

ALTERATIONS TO THE BUILDING ENVELOPE

Aside from the many passive and managerial actions that can be taken to reduce the risk of disaster, there are a number of interventions on the building envelope that prevent or reduce damage from flood and fire, and less common disasters such as lightning strikes and earthquakes.

FLOOD-PROTECTION ALTERATIONS

Floodproofing can take many forms, including meticulous maintenance of plumbing and other internal sources of water. For ground floods, where the sources are coastal flooding, riverine flooding or flash flooding, the options are trying to divert the water away from the building, or to stop it at or preferably before it reached the envelope. For buildings prone to repeated ground flooding, it may also be wise to limit damage by internal rearrangements.

IMPROVING RESISTANCE TO GROUND FLOODS

Measures to prevent or limit the damage from ground floods vary widely in cost, effectiveness and invasiveness; no single solution is right for every building, and indeed most would only be considered for buildings at significant risk. Modifications fall into three groups:

- works to the surroundings to make flooding less likely
- works to the building to stop floodwaters entering
- works to the building to restrict the amount of damage if floodwaters do enter.

Factors to be considered when weighing up the cost of intervention against the likely benefit include the types of flooding that are likely to be encountered (both sources and duration), how often such floods may occur, how much warning is likely to be received, and of course the exposure of the building. For example, a basement flat in a city may be at sufficient risk from flash runoff floods, water-main bursts or blocked sewers to make it worthwhile to install some form of permanent low barrier at the base of the door.

Making Flooding Less Likely

Most district flood prevention work is the province of the Environment Agency and associated government organisations, but there are a number of actions that can be taken if the building owners have access to the surrounding ground, and there are no insurmountable issues related to historic landscapes or gardens, or buried archaeology. The most important are:

- to ensure that any existing land and building drainage is in good condition, or install improved drainage systems
- to re-landscape to redirect surface water away from the building, and to replace impermeable surfaces with materials that allow the water to soak into the ground.

Preventing Water Entering the Building

Floodwater can enter the building through:

- floors and exterior walls (especially through cracks and joints)
- windows and doors
- other apertures in the envelope, such as vents, air bricks, pipe ducts, and gaps around piping and cabling
- partition walls from neighbouring properties
- back-flowing plumbing systems and sewers.

The first step is therefore to find some way of permanently or temporarily sealing any flaws or apertures. Permanent actions include repairing faulty pointing, replacing cracked cement renders, and sealing gaps around piping and cabling that passes through the exterior walls. For apertures that have important uses, such as doors and drainage holes, sealing methods will need to be demountable. This stops them acting if the flood arrives without warning, so it may be necessary to consider hybrid systems if the risk of flash flooding is very high.

Buildings may have little protection against runoff floods, which can result from burst water mains and sewers, as well as from heavy rainfall.

There are a number of systems designed to be applied to the building perimeter to stop floodwaters entering. Most will only hold the water back for a short time, but this may be long enough to prevent damage from flash floods, or (for floods of longer duration) to allow the building contents to be moved or otherwise made safe. Structural engineers do generally advise, however, that no more than one metre or so of floodwater should be held back at the building envelope, since the pressure exerted on the exterior walls by more water than this could cause structural damage.

BUILDING ENVIRONMENT
SPECIAL TOPIC: Dealing with Disasters

SYSTEMS TO PREVENT GROUNDWATER ENTERING

SYSTEM	ACTION	EFFECTIVENESS	COMMENTS
Impervious 'skins' or sealants	Attempts to add a waterproof layer to the surface of the building walls	No evidence that these hold water back for any time, though they will slow post-flood drying	Damaging as well as ineffective: SHOULD NOT BE USED
Permanent door guards and window guards	Permanent physical barrier (such as a built-up front doorstep)	Will hold back low levels of water for several hours	Cannot be made very high, because of limitations on access Can have a significant impact on the appearance, character and performance of the building Useful in areas subjected to sudden and brief flash flooding
Partial tanking of lower-ground-floor elevation	Waterproofing layer applied to base of walls; must be used in conjunction with barge boards, or some other means of sealing doors and low windows	Will hold back water for several hours	Can have a significant impact on the appearance, character and performance of the building Tanking can make post-flood drying more difficult Dependence on barge boards means system cannot prevent unexpected floods
Temporary door guards and window guards	Physical barrier put in place when flood warning received	Will hold back water for several hours	Will not prevent an unexpected flood Air bricks and vents should be sealed only during flood, and then removed to improve drainage and drying
Air brick and vent covers	Snap-on covers for air bricks and vents, to put in place when flood warning received	Will hold back water for several hours	Will not prevent an unexpected flood Air bricks and vents should be sealed only during flood, and then removed to improve drainage and drying
Sandbags	Physical barrier put in place when flood warning received	Will hold back water for several hours	Difficult to lay effectively Pick up contamination Storage problems Will not prevent an unexpected flood
'Skirt systems' designed to isolate the entire building	A flexible waterproof membrane installed in a duct around the perimeter of the building, which can be pulled up onto supporting posts when a flood threatens	Will hold back water for 20–60 minutes	May be difficult to install on sensitive or complex sites If water table is prone to rising, system will also need sumps and pumps Will not prevent an unexpected flood
Permanent barriers (bunding walls, gates and additional drainage around the site)	Prevent water reaching any building on the site Can be separate, or incorporated into boundary walls and fences, or made part of landscaping	Protection will depend on design	May be difficult to install on sensitive or complex sites Permanent, so give protection against unexpected floods

Property-level flood protection

In flood-prone locations, it can be worth installing measures that will hold floodwaters back for a short time at least, such as temporary door guards (*left*), or air brick and vent covers (*right*).

LIMITING DAMAGE FROM GROUND FLOODING

Properties with a history of repeated flooding – where it is clear what types of flood will occur, and what form it will take when it does – may be well-advised to consider certain alterations that could limit damage to the fabric and contents (such as making sure that services at risk are raised above flood level), or that will help the building dry out more quickly and safely after a flood.

ACTIONS TO PREVENT DAMAGE OR HELP DRYING	
BUILDING ELEMENT	**ACTION**
Electrical wiring	Position cabling and switches well above the likely flood level
	Run cables down from the ceiling rather than up from the floor
Kitchens	Position on upper floors rather than ground floors or basements
Basements and cellars	Install a sump and a submersible emergency power supply to help drainage after flooding
Room partitions	Position partitions so that good through ventilation is possible for post-flood drying
Plumbing	Fit with backflow valves
Concrete floors	Replace with lime-based mortar to help post-flood drying
Cement renders, gypsum plasters, plasterboard panels	Replace with lime-based plaster to help drying and avoid the need to replace materials after floods

Any additions or alterations to the building should always be designed and constructed with floodproofing in mind.

BUILDING ENVIRONMENT
SPECIAL TOPIC: Dealing with Disasters

FIRE-PROTECTION ALTERATIONS

Like flood proofing, fire protection must combine preventative measures with measures to limit damage should a fire occur. There is no ideal approach; the best system will take account of the building, and the way it is being used. Where the ideal protection system would harm the building or its use, it may be possible to compromise by concentrating effort on the least-damaging options: for example, improving alarm systems in preference to altering exit doors.

Owners and managers of historic buildings concerned about fire are strongly advised to consult a Fire Safety Engineer, who will be able to advise on all aspects of prevention, protection and damage limitation. ⊃BASICS

FIRES IN BUILDINGS

A fire has three requirements: some source of heat for ignition; combustible materials (that is, fuel); and oxygen (most of which will come from the air, but some may also be found in certain types of fuel).

Fire Safety Engineering

Fire Safety Engineering [FSE] is the discipline studying and developing methods for protecting people and their environments from fire and smoke, by:

- understanding how fires develop (fire dynamics and modelling fires of all kinds)
- building design, layout and space planning to reduce the occurrence of fires, and limit their impact
- risk analysis
- developing fire prevention programmes
- designing active fire protection (alarms, and systems to suppress fires)
- designing passive fire protection (fire and smoke barriers, and compartmentalisation)
- designing systems for smoke control and management
- assessing human behaviour during fires, and using this knowledge to develop escape facilities.

FS engineers deal with all types of fires, including wildfires, and can help building owners and managers identify risks, and design safeguards to prevent, control and reduce the effect of building fires.

Once a fire begins in a typical room, it may proceed through several stages:

1. Most of the heat from the fire rises to the ceiling in a plume of hot smoke and gas, setting up convection currents and entraining the surrounding air, which increases the bulk of the plume and cools it slightly. At this stage, only 20 % or so of the fire's heat radiates outwards, which in most cases is not enough to cause the fire to spread.

2. As the fire gets larger and produces more heat, the percentage of entrained cooler air decreases, and the smoke layer at the ceiling becomes thicker and hotter, until it begins to radiate heat downwards. Heated materials may begin to emit flammable gases, which will rise and join the hot smoke at the ceiling, which becomes increasingly flammable.

3. If there is enough oxygen in the room, the flammable gases at the ceiling may build up to the point of 'flashover': the smoke and gas mixture ignites, together with all the remaining combustible materials in the room.

4. The fire either spreads to adjoining spaces in the building, or else it consumes all the fuel in the room, and then decays and finally burns out.

In a small room with very little ventilation, a fire may quickly consume much of the oxygen, after which it will burn slowly, creating quantities of smoke and eventually self-extinguishing. However, an oxygen-starved fire may explosively re-ignite if more oxygen is introduced: if a door is opened, for example, or a window breaks in the heat.

PROTECTION

Risk Assessment

Fire-risk assessments are the key to balancing the conflicting requirements for protecting life, protecting property and retaining the character of a historic building. These look at the potential damage a fire could cause, as this determines what work, if any, would be required to ensure the building would survive. The assessment must consider:

- *The location of the building*
  This would cover exposure to lightning or to wildfires, for example, as well as the potential for fire to spread from nearby buildings.

- *The nature of the building*
  This includes the materials, the construction, and the location and state of repair of the internal partitions, as well as the size and shape of the rooms themselves.

- *The contents of the building*
  The materials and location of furniture and other contents, which could provide fuel in the event of a fire and will also affect the way the fire develops.

- *The building use*
  This will provide most potential sources of ignition, and also will affect firefighting.

- *Access for firefighting*
  This must take into account the proximity of the building to firefighting services, potential problems such as roads too narrow for fire appliances, and the general shape and size of the building (particularly its height).

Design of the Internal Spaces

Ceiling height has a dramatic effect on the spread of smoke and flames. A fire in a room with a high ceiling will grow more slowly not only because the entrained air can cool the rising smoke plume more effectively, but because the hot smoke layer will need to grow much thicker before it is able to heat the combustible materials below.

The design and condition of the internal ceilings, floors and walls will have an enormous bearing on how a fire might spread. For example, if the tops of the windows are higher than the tops of the doors, the heat from the fire may break the glass; this may allow the smoke to escape. On the other hand, full-height timber panelling can give flames an easy path to travel from the floor to the ceiling; and hidden voids may form paths for fire to spread unnoticed, as well as making firefighting much more difficult.

Combustible Materials

How readily a material will burn depends not only on the type of material, but its shape and size: for example, although timber is in general sensitive to fire, it is extremely difficult to ignite large-section oak beams, but very easy to set fire to lightweight wooden panelling or floor pugging made with wood shavings and sawdust.

BUILDING ENVIRONMENT
SPECIAL TOPIC: Dealing with Disasters

Studies of fire-damaged buildings have shown that lath-and-plaster walls are many times more fire-resistant than generally assumed.

Fire resistance of building components is unpredictable, and therefore difficult to characterise. For example, although lath-and-plaster walls are often considered to fail in under eight minutes, tests carried out in the late 1960s (and confirmed by studies of fires in historic buildings) have shown that they can in fact last for as long as 45 minutes. Fire-resistance will vary, because it depends on many factors, including the size and spacing of the laths, the way they are fixed (and whether any metal fixings are corroded), and the quality and thickness of the plaster.

The contents of the room are also critically important when it comes to the spread of fire: not only their combustibility, but their quantity and their location.

Assessing the Risk to Life

If a building can be evacuated quickly, this will allow the fire brigade – whose primary role is to save lives – to quickly focus their attention on bringing the fire under control and saving the fabric. There are a number of simple ways to increase occupant safety, including properly thought-through evacuation plans, signage and emergency lighting. Voice alarms, for example, have been shown to cut total evacuation time, which eases some of the pressure on other fire-safety provisions.

The Regulatory Reform (Fire Safety) Order 2005, which came into effect in October 2006, requires assessments of fire risk to be made for all buildings except single-occupied dwellings. Since it is intended to ensure the safety of building users, the FSO does not specifically encourage property protection, but some of its requirements will also help preserve the building from fire. Guides to the FSO are available online at *www.communities.gov.uk/fire/firesafety/firesafetylaw/*

Access for Fire Services

In some locations, it may take considerable time for fire services to arrive. If this is the case, then the building protection will have to be improved to compensate.

The larger or taller a building is, the more of the perimeter the fire services will need to be able to reach to effectively fight a fire. This can be a serious issue in historic town centres, where buildings may have very narrow frontages, and little or no access to the side or rear.

Access may change over time, with local building works or changes to street furniture or planting. The firefighting appliances will also change, affecting access requirements. *Approved Document B* of the Building Regulations gives recommended road and gate widths, and weight-bearing capacity for roads and bridges, but it is a wise precaution to ask the local fire service to visit regularly to discuss their particular requirements and those of the building in the event of a fire.

FIRE PREVENTION

Controlling Sources of Ignition

To prevent fires occurring, the primary requirement is to identify – and as far as possible eliminate – all potential sources of ignition.

Of the 350,000 or so fires dealt with each year by the UK's fire and rescue services, only a few are due to building failures such as chimney fires, electrical faults or faulty appliances, or to natural causes such as lightning strikes. By far the majority of fires can be traced back to human error: cooking, cigarettes and candles; overloaded electrical circuits; mishandled lighting and heating; careless use of fireplaces and barbecues, or of working equipment such as soldering irons, welding equipment and blowlamps; and in some cases, arson. This makes prevention by far the most important means of reducing fire damage.

Prevention, and the legislation covering fire protection of buildings, is dealt with at length in the *Conservation Basics* volume of this series, but the following gives a synopsis of those aspects of prevention of particular relevance to the building envelope. ➔BASICS

Open Flames

Many appliances using open flames, such as kerosene lamps and gas heaters, present additional risks associated with the storage of fuel. Fireplaces (including gas fires) should always have fire guards.

Cooking

Kitchens are the most common location for fires to begin; they often involve burning fats and oils, so any attempt to use water to extinguish them is likely to do more harm than good. For this reason, fire blankets and appropriate extinguishers should be provided near the exit route, where they can be reached quickly.

Electrical Equipment (Overloading, Faulty Appliances, Faulty Wiring)

Although faulty appliances and wiring can start fires, a much more common cause is human error or neglect: for example, unskilled modifications of circuitry, overloaded power points, worn insulation on wiring. Insulation can also be destroyed by rodents, especially in roof spaces and other hidden areas. The insulation on flexes can be damaged if they are left too near hot surfaces, or where they will be prone to mechanical damage.

Heating

Quartz infrared heaters reach surface temperatures of up to 900°C, depending on wattage, and radiant bar heaters ('electric fires') can reach temperatures as high as 1000°C: these and other portable heaters have been known to ignite furniture and drapery. Since heaters of this kind work by heating people, not the air, they can and should be turned off whenever there is no-one present.

Fan heaters can quickly overheat if they are accidently or deliberately obstructed; if, for example, they are knocked over, or clothes are draped over them to air. Boiler rooms become a fire risk if they are used to store combustible materials.

BUILDING ENVIRONMENT
SPECIAL TOPIC: Dealing with Disasters

Lights

Lighting is a common source of fires, especially where a lack of ventilation impedes air cooling (perhaps because the lamp is covered in some way). The glass of an exposed incandescent lamp can reach anything from 100°C to 300°C (depending on wattage), but if fabric or paper is allowed to rest on it, the heat being emitted by the burning filament will be trapped and the temperature will quickly rise (and cotton, for example, can ignite at 200°C). Tests allowing different materials to rest on a torchière fitted with a 300-W halogen lamp and no protective grill showed that it took just 24 seconds to set a polyester-cotton t-shirt alight, and 77 seconds to ignite cardboard. An advantage of light-emitting diodes [LEDs], which run at low temperatures, is a much-reduced fire risk, although associated transformers should be sited to avoid overheating.

Downlights recessed into ceilings are one of the most troublesome types of fitting, being a fire risk if dust is allowed to collect on the upper surface or on the transformer, or if the fitting is surrounded or covered by insulation materials (particularly loose-fill insulation). Fire hoods can protect surrounding materials for up to an hour should a recessed fitting catch alight.

Lamp surface temperature depends not only on the type of lamp, but its wattage and design. There is a great deal of variation, but the following table gives an idea of the temperatures involved.

SURFACE TEMPERATURES FOR DIFFERENT TYPES OF LAMP

LAMP TYPE	SURFACE TEMPERATURE	COMMENTS
Tungsten halogen	~500–900°C	Some display lights must be kept level to within 5° to prevent halide migration (which has been the cause of several fires in shop windows)
Quartz-halogen (50 W)	~120–135°C (rear lens 150–210°C)	—
Metal halide	~100–130°C	Great deal of variation according to lamp type
Incandescent (60 W)	~130°C	Temperatures can become much higher if glass is covered
Incandescent (25 W)	~45°C	Temperatures can become much higher if glass is covered
Fluorescent	~60°C (near cathodes 80°C)	Greatest risk is overheating of choke
Compact fluorescent	~60–80°C	Greatest risk with older lamps is overheating of condenser
LED	35–44°C	Transformers may present a fire hazard

Lightning Protection

The risk from lightning-induced fires has substantially increased since buildings began to incorporate electrical services, but the enormous discharge of energy in a lightning strike can have other effects, including physically destroying the fabric. It will readily travel through open and weathered joints, dislodging the masonry. For tall or exposed buildings, good lightning protection is essential.

The areas of a building that will be most vulnerable to lightning strike will be those closest to the lightning leader as it reaches striking distance, and this is not necessarily the highest point. Streamers may even develop from the sides of a building if it is very tall or very exposed. For this reason alone the design of lightning protection systems is an expert task. Lightning protection is covered by the National Federation of Master Steeplejacks and Lightning Conductor Engineers, and should conform to the principles laid out in the standard, *BS EN 62305: 2011 Protection against lightning*; English Heritage has also produced several guidance leaflets for protection of historic buildings. This section introduces the basic components of a lightning protection system, and discusses how protection must be designed to be reliable and effective.

Lightning protection systems incorporate an external system to direct the current to earth, and an internal system to prevent sparking inside the building. The external protection has three components: the air termination, the down conduction and the earth termination.

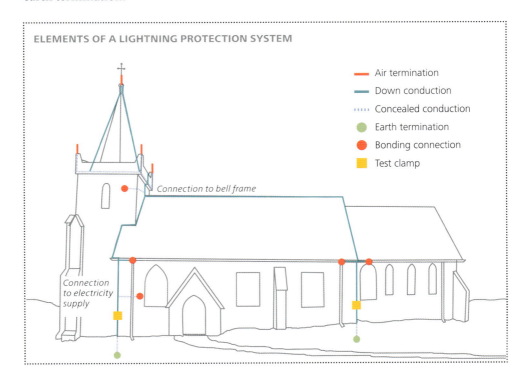

ELEMENTS OF A LIGHTNING PROTECTION SYSTEM

— Air termination
— Down conduction
····· Concealed conduction
● Earth termination
● Bonding connection
■ Test clamp

Connection to bell frame

Connection to electricity supply

BUILDING ENVIRONMENT
SPECIAL TOPIC: Dealing with Disasters

Lightning

To understand how lightning protection works, and therefore how it must be designed, installed and maintained to be effective, it is useful to have a basic understanding of how the lightning actually occurs. Although the precise details of the process are still disputed, the basic mechanisms are well understood.

Thunderclouds build up static charges, inducing an equal and opposite charge on the ground below. The strength of the induced electric field is proportional to the distance between cloud and ground, and the induced charge will be strongest on those parts of the ground closest to the base of the cloud: typically, tall features such as trees or towers.

Lightning is the sudden discharge of this electric field. A charged region in the thundercloud sends out a channel of ionised air, called a 'leader', which jumps towards the ground in a series of steps, each anywhere from 45 m to 100 m long. As the leader approaches the ground, it causes one or more 'streamers' of ionised air to rise towards it from the ground, wherever the induced charge is greatest. When a leader meets a streamer, the static energy in the cloud will be able to discharge through it, causing a 'return stroke'.

Although the ionised channel may be only a centimetre or so wide, and the stroke may last for only a few millionths of a second, an enormous amount of energy is released: the current is on average around 30,000 A and the peak power is about a terawatt; where the stroke hits the ground it can produce temperatures as high as 30,000°C, which is easily hot enough to fuse silica in the soil. What is more, most lightning strikes are made up of multiple individual strokes (typically three or four, although there may be more).

If the charge is induced in the top of the cloud rather than in the ground, a leader may form within the cloud itself, and may travel more or less horizontally for several kilometres before finally heading down towards the ground. This 'positive' lightning is particularly dangerous because it is much stronger, having travelled much further before discharging; the current will be around 10 times greater. It will also be harder to predict, since it may strike well away from the centre of the storm ('a bolt from the blue'). Fortunately, positive lightning makes up less than 5 % of all lightning strikes.

Lightning striking St Andrew's Church in Ramsbottom, Lancashire, blew off a pinnacle, which fell through the roof of the church below and caused severe damage to the interior (*top*).

Examining the area of the lost pinnacle, it is possible to see where the energy has travelled through the masonry joints, splitting and dislodging the stone (*bottom*).

Air Termination

The air termination directs the lightning so that it strikes safely by producing streamers that attract the leaders within striking distance. The system is made up of conductors or 'air terminals' (such as lightning rods, spanned wires and cables, and intermeshed conductors) placed on or above the building. Special attention must be paid to the building's corners and edges, and other prominent features from which streamers might begin, such as spires and pinnacles. The air terminals must be connected together, and then to 'down conductors' spaced around the outside of the building.

Three basic methods are used to determine the numbers and locations of the components of the air-termination system:

- *Mesh method*
  Creates a Faraday cage around the building, distributing the electrical charge over the surface so that the charge inside is zero. To do this with minimum expense, the mesh usually incorporates any metal components on the building exterior, such as gutters and downpipes. The size of the mesh depends on the level of protection required, and it must incorporate all the edges and protruding components of the structure.

- *Rolling sphere method*
  Creates a protected zone thicker than the striking distance over the building, by positioning air terminals to protect any point which could be touched by the surface of a sphere with a radius equal to the minimum striking distance (in the UK, it is usual to assume a striking distance of 60 m). This can be done on a computer model, but it is usually easier to make a scale model, and literally roll over this with a scaled ball (this is certainly the easiest way of envisaging how the system works). The smaller the sphere, the greater the level of protection, but the system will be much more complicated and expensive.

- *Protective angle method*
  Uses the same principle as the rolling sphere, but adapted to allow simple theoretical calculations. The protective angle is determined by the striking distance (which depends, amongst other things, on the height of the air terminals). The zone of protection must include every part of the building, but can be cone- or tent-shaped.

British Standards

BS EN 62305:2011 Protection against lightning

BS EN 62305 is divided into four parts:

- *Part 1: General principles*
  Gives an introduction to the other parts of the standard.

- *Part 2: Risk management*
  Covers how to determine the required level of protection. A series of National Annexes allows countries like the UK to use their own interpretation and perception of risk to compile some of the underlying parameters.

- *Part 3: Physical damage to structures and life hazards*
  Defines four protection levels, based on likely minimum and maximum currents; these relate directly to classes of protection systems.

- *Part 4: Electrical and electronic systems within structures*
  Structural lightning protection must be integrated with transient overvoltage or surge protection; this means that as well as a structural protection system, the building must have overvoltage protection or a fully coordinated set of surge protection devices.

Every lightning protection system will need to be tested annually by a qualified engineer. It should also be tested after any lightning strike, to make sure it has not been damaged.

BUILDING ENVIRONMENT
SPECIAL TOPIC: Dealing with Disasters

Down Conduction

The down conductors are the most obvious parts of the lightning protection system: the system that connects the air termination to the earth termination, allowing the lightning to be safely discharged.

To allow for failure, all buildings at risk, no matter how small, must have at least two down conductors. Towers and spires will need conductors running down diagonally opposite corners, and connected together every 20 metres with horizontal conductors ('coronas'). The down conductors should be as straight as possible, and incorporate some means of testing the earth electrode at a convenient height: low enough to be reached when necessary, but not so low that it can be easily tampered with.

The down-conduction system must connect all major metallic elements of the building together, including rainwater goods, service wiring, flues and bell frames. Although this is often neglected, it is absolutely essential since it prevents dangerous potential differences occurring during a lightning strike.

Earth Termination

The earth termination is composed of a series of electrodes – rods, plates or mats made from copper – designed to safely disperse the lightning current into the ground. This will probably require careful planning, and quite possibly consultations with specialists. Buried services must be avoided, and (for example) if the underlying strata is rock, a bore hole will be needed, and special systems may have to be developed to overlay conductor tapes. Around older buildings, digging may need to be supervised by an archaeologist.

Fire Risk During Building Works

Building works will introduce a number of additional fire hazards, which will need to be explicitly assessed and mitigated as far as possible. These include changes that:

- increase the risk of ignition (such as site lighting and hot works)
- increase the amount of fuel (such as stored building materials and packaging)
- affect the fire-warning systems (such as the isolation of fire detectors to stop false alarms caused by dust)
- increase the risk of fires spreading (such as the removal of doors and other partitions)
- make firefighting difficult (including the absence of water supplies, poor access because of storage, hoardings or site huts, and untested fire drills).

In practice, it is often the smaller works such as decorating or plumbing that lead to fires, so it is important that the site manager makes all workers aware of their responsibilities whilst on site.

Controlling Sources of Fuel

It is almost impossible to completely eliminate all sources of ignition, but by keeping combustible materials to a minimum (the rate at which a fire grows is closely linked to the ratio of fuel to room volume), and ensuring they are kept well away from potential ignition points, if a fire does occur it will be more likely to be slow-growing.

Poor housekeeping can lead to fires, and also help them to spread rapidly. As well as avoiding the careless storage of flammable liquids or the accumulation of flammable materials such as paper, extractor fans should be kept free of dust and grease, and electrical equipment and heaters should be kept well maintained.

FIRE PROTECTION

Choosing the most appropriate level of fire protection can be challenging, with the legal obligation to ensure the safety of occupants needing to be balanced against the need to protect the building itself, and – in the case of significant buildings – to do the least possible harm to the historic fabric and character of the building. The following questions will help to narrow down the many possible approaches to protection:

- What would be the biggest threats to the building if a fire occurred?
- Can these threats be reduced to an acceptable level without making alterations to the building?
- If alterations are necessary, which would involve the least intervention, and be the most sympathetic to the building's fabric and its significance?
- Will the alterations be as effective as hoped? For instance, an unmonitored fire alarm system will not provide any protection when the building is unoccupied.
- Will the alterations be affordable and sustainable? Is there a more cost-effective alternative?
- Is the level of proposed alterations commensurate with the risk to the fabric? A working seven-storey wooden windmill located three miles from the nearest road will need much more protection than a brick-built railway arch in a town centre.

Detection & Alarm Systems

Some form of fire or smoke alarm is a necessity for most buildings. Automatic fire alarm systems vary greatly in complexity. They may detect temperature rises, convected or radiant thermal energy; smoke, gases or other combustion products, or flames or any combination of these. In the UK, systems are categorised by their principal function (which may be protecting building users, or the building itself).

The design of alarm systems must take account of the structure of the building, and the places where fires will be most likely to begin. The emphasis must always be on fires that would not be quickly detected by the building occupants (perhaps because the location is hidden, or not in common use). Systems will always require some degree of duplication as a fail-safe.

How much building damage can actually be prevented by the alarm depends on the time taken to detect the fire, the time it takes for the emergency services to respond and the fire's growth rate.

Some fire and rescue services will not respond to automatic alarms unless there is confirmation that there is a real fire. A Call Receiving Centre will telephone the property and ask the occupier if there is a fire before passing the call onto the fire service, but if the building is unoccupied at the time of the call some services will send one fire engine to investigate, and others will simply ignore the alarm. Where the local fire service has this policy, it may be necessary to consider a multi-sensor or 'double-knock' alarm system.

TYPES OF DETECTOR

OPERATION	SITING	COMMENTS
POINT DETECTORS		
Individual heat or smoke detectors, usually connected to form a fire detection system by wires or radio linking	Ideally as close to the centre of the ceiling as possible (may be difficult with ornate ceilings) In practice, often placed close to the wall above the door, so that detector cannot be seen when entering the room	In early stages, natural air currents influence movement of smoke as much as convection currents from the fire; currents through doorways and windows can keep the smoke away from nearby detectors, rendering them ineffective Recessed detectors, or detectors placed above holes in the ceilings or hidden behind beams and lights, may prove ineffective
BEAMS		
Transmitter sends beam to receiver; activates if beam is interrupted by smoke	Beam not very wide, so detector should be located as near to the ceiling as possible (where smoke spreads out)	The lower the detector is located the longer it will take for the smoke layer to fill down and reach it
ASPIRATING (AIR-SAMPLING) SYSTEMS		
A small sampling tube is inserted through the ceiling, which is connected to a sampling chamber; this draws the air through a glass tube and detects smoke when it scatters light or an infrared beam	Can either have a central sampling point (air from all the rooms covered is drawn along tubes), or several local sampling points connected to fewer sampling tubes Must be enough space for the sampling chamber Long pipe runs should be avoided	Size of tubes may make it difficult to fit without lifting floorboards above The noise of the fan may be obtrusive Running costs (including replacement filters and power to the fan) must be taken into account
VIDEO		
Fixed video cameras linked to a computer programmed to recognise the movement of smoke to raise the alarm If building is smoke-filled, the firefighters can study the tape to find exact location of the fire	Smoke must contrast with the background or the cameras will not recognise it Lighting must be kept on overnight, with a high level of emergency lighting so that smoke can be detected	Ideal for very large spaces such as churches or halls, where the smoke would cool and stop rising before it reached conventional ceiling detectors Expense can be offset by the fact that fewer cameras are needed than conventional detectors; the system can incorporate other security features
INFRARED POINT SMOKE DETECTION		
Smoke scatters an infrared beam	Fitted flush with the ceiling, so less visible than other point detectors	100 mm in diameter; requires a 75-mm hole in the ceiling Each detector needs a 24-V power supply, as well as the alarm cable

PREVENTING FIRES SPREADING

Around half of all of fires do not spread beyond the item that was first ignited, and 80 % do not spread to adjoining spaces. The critical factors governing the spread of fire inside a building are:

- the shape and size of the room
- the availability of oxygen
- the type and availability of fuel
- the amount of fuel in the item originally ignited
- how close the resulting fire is to other combustible materials
- how close the fire is to the walls of the room, since this governs how well entrained air will cool the smoke plume.

Compartmentation

Dividing the interior with fire-resisting partitions will limit the size of any fire and reduce the risk of it spreading. Current fire-safety standards rely heavily on measures to stop fires spreading (such as enclosing staircases and corridors, installing fire doors across passageways, and upgrading existing doors).

Meeting these regulations can put great demands on historic buildings; and buildings that have been over-compartmented can be difficult to use; there must be sufficient escape routes from every area, and these must be kept well maintained.

Fires can spread rapidly through terraced houses if the roof spaces have not been compartmentalised.

BUILDING ENVIRONMENT
SPECIAL TOPIC: Dealing with Disasters

UPGRADING PARTITIONS

	POSSIBLE UPGRADES	COMMENTS
FLOORS & CEILINGS	The floor and ceiling below contribute to the horizontal fire compartmentation If the ceiling is made of lime plaster at least 25-mm thick and is in good condition, it will give good fire protection	If there are any doubts about the fire resistance of a ceiling or floor, a fire barrier can be installed between the joists If sound insulation is required between floors, this can incorporate a degree of fire resistance
DOORS	Panelled timber doors are built to withstand environmental changes, which gives them a degree of stability during a fire The thinnest parts (such as the fielding around panels) may allow burn-through	The thinnest parts of the doors can be upgraded by applying intumescent paint, paper or veneers (according to the original finish) Fitting intumescent strips around the door edges and top can help prevent the door leaf distorting
VOIDS	Blocking ventilation Sealing around pipes and cables	Altering ventilation can have an adverse impact on the environment (this will need to be monitored) Sealing and insulation can cause overheating
ROOF SPACES	Barriers are very important upgrades The barrier must line up with other compartment lines, and must be built to withstand falling debris (note that many materials become weaker when hot)	Structural engineering advice will be needed to design fire barriers in roof spaces If the structure below can support the extra weight, the best approach is to use masonry infills (concrete block or brick) The installation should be planned to make use of existing structures such as chimney stacks, so only the triangular spaces on each side need to be filled

If compartmentation is to achieve its aim of limiting fire spread, it will need to be designed to take account of any hidden voids in the fabric. Any holes cut to allow cables or pipes to pass though the partition must be sealed with mineral wool, lime plaster, or some other fire-resisting material.

Fire-Suppression Systems

Fire-suppression systems aim to fight fires at a very early stage, before they have the chance to become well established.

Environmental issues have restricted the use of halon gases, so the most common systems are based on water, halon replacements or oxygen reduction. Water systems are probably the most efficient at extinguishing fires in a building which is not particularly airtight, because unlike gaseous and oxygen-reduction systems they do not rely on being contained, although they may require a degree of over-engineering to compensate for potential leaks. Sprinklers and water mists have one important advantage over most gas systems: they are not limited to a 'one-off' discharge, but can continue to work for as long as necessary.

Sprinklers & Water Mist Systems

Although introducing quantities of liquid water into a building is always risky, by acting early, and directly onto the fire, sprinklers and mist systems use much less water than fire hoses. Since such systems can prevent flashover, if they are in place the doors and glass will not be exposed to high temperatures, and so will provide fire protection for longer. A well-positioned sprinkler head may indeed remove the need to upgrade these components to compartmentation standards, or to provide a fire lobby.

The sprinkler or mist system must be designed to be able to deal with the likely fire loads in the rooms it is protecting. Systems for historic buildings do not need to be as complicated as those for industrial applications: for example, a bedroom in a country house can usually be protected with a single sprinkler head. The most challenging problem is finding space for the piping, particularly the risers, which can be up to 150 mm in diameter; this aspect will need to be considered at an early stage. Where possible, advantage should be taken of building voids, but this does increase the risk from unseen leaks. In sensitive buildings it may be necessary to use far smaller pipe sizes, which means a water mist system will probably need to be selected. These use less water than sprinklers and can therefore have smaller pipes, but they do operate at higher pressures.

Systems are designed to prevent accidental triggering, but there will always be some chance of leakage from the piping. CPVC piping is especially prone to catastrophic failures, with causes ranging from poor installation through to impact damage, or deterioration from contact with PVC cabling or exposure to aerosols or sunlight. The materials of the pipe work must also be chosen so that the water is kept as clean as possible.

Positioning of outlets is critical: the fire must not be too far developed by the time its heat reaches and triggers a sprinkler head. Concealed heads are available; these have covers held in place by a solder having a lower melting point than the sprinkler head, so they drop away quickly when heat reaches them.

Other Firefighting Equipment

Having appropriate fire extinguishers to hand can be an excellent way of protecting property, but since encouraging occupants to fight fires can have health-and-safety implications, those expected to use extinguishers should receive proper training: a trained person can extinguish a fire four times larger than an untrained person can handle. Most importantly, users will need to be able to distinguish between a fire that can be fought with water, and a fire where this would be dangerous or disastrous.

Extinguishers should be provided on the exit routes from each area, so the operator can move back towards safety.

PREVENTING OTHER COMMON TYPES OF DISASTER

IMPACT

Any tall object which could damage the building if it fell should be inspected regularly, and repaired as necessary. Tall trees in particular must be kept under control, to ensure there is no danger from falling branches nor from the tree itself.

Structures at regular risk from traffic damage (such as buildings on busy corners, bridges and gateways through which vehicles pass) should use warning signs, coupled with speed bumps and other traffic-calming measures to reduce the speed of impact. In serious cases, height markers and bollards can be installed to completely prevent the passage of oversized traffic.

It is common to see ancient archways and bridges over roads or driveways with severe damage where they have been hit by passing trucks or buses; total demolition by such impacts is sadly not unknown.

This problem has become worse since the introduction of satellite navigation systems, which may lead large vehicles to take unsuitable roads. The best means of prevention is to install warning signs well back from the structure, together with bollards or height markers that are sturdy enough to physically stop oversized vehicles.

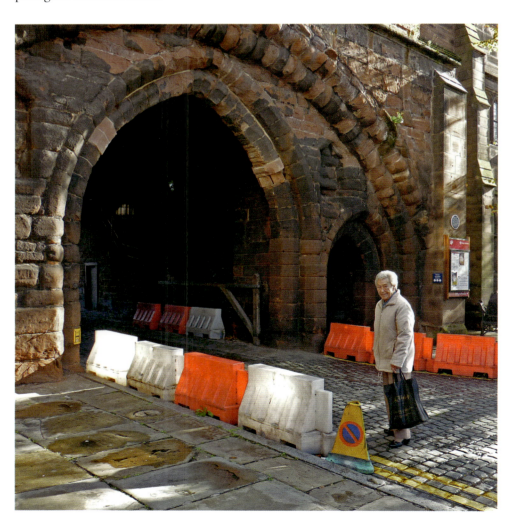

METAL THEFT & OTHER VANDALISM

487

The primary strategy is to make theft as difficult as possible, though it is important to do this without compromising maintenance or emergency access. Actions include:

- increasing security around the perimeter of a building, including lockable gates and other physical boundaries that prevent unauthorised vehicles gaining access
- removing any easy means of access onto roofs:
  - taking away water butts, waste bins and trees
  - hiding ladders away, and taking care to secure any scaffolding
  - painting the upper sections of downpipes, guttering and scaffolding with anti-climb paint (this is governed by regulation: paint must not be applied to the lowest two metres of downpipe, and a warning notice must be prominently displayed)
  - covering the lower sections of lightning conductor ribbons using metal cages or sheaths securely fixed to the building
- anchoring metal objects such as railings with steel armatures (this may require the advice of a specialist conservator, and perhaps listed building consent)
- marking the metal so that it can be identified if it is stolen (this may already be required by many insurance policies)
- installing an alarm system.

Careful mothballing of empty buildings can limit the decay that invariably attends disuse.

Replacement roofs can be either fitted in a more secure manner (for example, by using hollow rolled lead which is harder to remove than wood-core sheet lead), or with less valuable materials such as tern-coated stainless steel. On a listed building, these changes will require consent. It is also possible to install alarms, or use special fixings that lock the metal to the roof whilst still allowing thermal movement. ➔ROOFING

Metal roofs should be checked as often as possible: because of the weight of the metal (lead in particular), thieves may be able to remove only a small amount at a time, and will count on being able to make a number of visits over a period of days.

The main discouragement to vandalism is also increased security. Buildings are very much more likely to be vandalised if they appear to be neglected, so if a building must be left empty for a prolonged period, it should be properly 'mothballed': in particular, windows should be protected with boards or screens.

BUILDING ENVIRONMENT
SPECIAL TOPIC: Dealing with Disasters

ACTING AFTER A DISASTER

REDUCING COLLATERAL DAMAGE

SECURING & STABILISING

If a disastrous event has damaged a building, the first step should be stabilisation. The Emergency Plan should have ensured that trained personnel were immediately available, together with any materials needed for immediate protection (such as tarpaulins). The plan should also include the emergency contact details for any specialists that might need to be called in (such as structural engineers, builders, conservators and archaeologists). ⬤BASICS

The first actions are structural shoring-up, and the support of any delicate building elements at risk of collapse. Another major priority is to ensure that no further water enters the site. In particular, damaged roofs must be covered as soon as possible, which may mean installing a temporary cover. Sadly, if the building is so badly damaged that its future is uncertain, months or even years can sometimes elapse before such protection is finally provided, but this approach is far from cost-effective.

TYPES OF TEMPORARY ROOF COVER		
	ADVANTAGES	**DISADVANTAGES**
Tarpaulins and polythene sheet	Inexpensive	Repeated removal and reinstatement would be needed to allow works
		Only really suitable for temporary protection, or for restricted areas of damage
Scaffolded roof, open at the sides	Gives reasonable protection	Rain may blow in at the sides
	Maximises ventilation and therefore drying	Risk of failure during gales
Scaffolded roof with sides enclosed	Good weather protection	Minimal ventilation, so allows little or no natural drying
	Likely to be secure even in gales	

Any protection is better than none, but it is worth choosing the best option available. In practice, the choice is likely to be based on cost, time of year and building location: for example, in an exposed area, a light open scaffolding that would favour drying might be unsuitable.

Stabilising to limit loss

Here, scaffolding is being erected to shore up the façade of the Cupola Building in Bury St Edmunds, in the immediate aftermath of a devastating fire.

BUILDING ENVIRONMENT
SPECIAL TOPIC: Dealing with Disasters

PRELIMINARY ACTIONS AFTER FLOODING

Before entering a building after a flood, it will need to be made safe: in particular, the electricity supply must be turned off at the mains; all other supplies should be disconnected as well. It is necessary to wear protective clothing, particularly stout boots, since there may be hidden hazards. The doors and windows should be opened to increase the air exchange, reducing the interior humidity and allowing drying to begin. If the masonry of a chimney has become wet, fires should not be lit until it is dry again: the heat could turn the moisture to steam, causing structural damage to the stack.

Depending on the nature and extent of the flood, it may be necessary to call in specialist advice from architects, surveyors or conservators experienced in the remediation of the type of building, and the building materials that have been affected.

PUMPING

Pumping before the floodwater has receded is pointless: as long as the groundwater table remains higher than the basement, water will continue to seep in through the walls until the groundwater level finds equilibrium. Floodwaters must be allowed to recede naturally, though this process can be helped by creating drainage holes.

Pumping water from a flooded basement or cellar does entail some risk: if the surrounding groundwater level is high, pumping could increase the external force on foundation walls to the point where fragile or thin-walled structures could collapse inwards. Before considering pumps, the local drainage conditions outside and around the building must therefore be assessed.

IMMEDIATE CLEANING & DECONTAMINATION

Masonry flooded by seawater should be thoroughly rinsed down with clean salt-free water as soon as possible, and then allowed to dry slowly to minimise chloride-salt damage to soft masonry.

Mud, dirt and debris should be removed as soon as possible after the floodwater has receded. Cavities – including electrical outlets, ducts and chases, and from drains, gulleys and inspection chambers – will need to be opened up to allow draining, cleaning and drying. It is best to clean as soon as possible, since it is safer and easier to remove the mud while it is still wet. Most of the debris should be removed mechanically, using brooms and brushes, or plastic and wooden scrapers, and shovels rather than metal (since saturated surfaces are usually very delicate). The final cleanse will probably require rinsing with clean water, but pressure washing should be avoided. Opened areas should be allowed to dry thoroughly before they are closed up again.

Attempting to clean decorative features and damaged or loosened elements can be risky, and indeed it is probably wise to leave tasks of this sort to experienced specialists.

Recording

491

The disaster and its aftermath should be recorded as thoroughly as possible, preferably with photographs and even videos.

After the building has been made safe, detailed photographs and notes should be taken of all damage, and of any areas that must be opened up for inspection or drying. Damage will also need to be recorded with a condition survey.

When St Ethelburga's Church in the City of London was all but destroyed by a bomb in 1993, archaeological teams moved in quickly to record the placement of all fallen pieces of glass and masonry. This type of recording is vital should any attempt be made later to reconstruct the building.

BUILDING ENVIRONMENT
SPECIAL TOPIC: Dealing with Disasters

ASSESSING DAMAGE AFTER DISASTER

Once the building has been secured, the damage can be assessed. As in all conservation projects, assessment should be based on a survey informed by the available background information. For historic buildings, architects, conservators and archaeologists will probably be needed to map the location of fallen elements, and to determine condition. This will allow the maximum amount of material to be saved; and original material should always be preserved wherever possible. ⊝MORTARS ⊝TIMBER ⊝GLASS

Because disastrous events often damage the building envelope, the outcomes can be divided into:

- *Primary damage*
  Damage that is evident immediately or within a very short time after the disaster.

- *Secondary damage*
  Problems that appear later as a long-term result of the original building damage, or because of incorrect remediation.

In the long term, it is usually water that causes the most damage, even if the original problem was not a flood. Great quantities of water are used to fight fires, and of course a lost or damaged roof will let in rain. Even parts of the building that were not actually burning may still have been 'damped down' to contain the fire. Sometimes (especially if the walls are of stone masonry), much of the water will run down through the fabric, leaving the upper walls relatively dry. On the other hand, basement walls that are dry after a fire or other disaster in the upper parts of the building may become wet over the subsequent months as the water migrates down.

Ground floods that do not rise above floor level are unlikely to cause significant damage in most properties, although there may be problems with water entering cellars, basements and the voids beneath suspended ground floors, especially if this cannot be extracted fairly quickly.

Primary damage from flooding includes staining, timber distortion (wood may expand as it absorbs water and then shrink again). Secondary damage is common, and usually traceable to moisture being trapped in hidden areas of the fabric, or travelling through the fabric from the original site of ingress. Wet materials may suffer freeze-thaw damage if the temperature drops below 4°C. Moreover, many forms of remedial intervention – such as removing plaster or timberwork – can finish by being considerably more damaging than the original flood.

Water will often be trapped by materials laid as an intermediate layer between floorboards and ceilings (often called 'pugging'). It is often wise to remove a few floorboards in the vicinity of beam and joist ends, and also at intervals across the room, if this can be done without too much added damage. This will allow the underfloor area to be inspected, and it will also help drying.

STRUCTURAL DAMAGE

AFTER FIRE

A structural engineer is likely to be very cautious about removing any timbers that have been damaged in a fire, since these might still be providing support. The charring of the surface will tend to have protected the bulk of the timber from the fire, and despite appearances it may be in good condition (though this will depend on the type of wood, the size of the timber and its exposure to the fire).

AFTER FLOODING

Unless there has been significant washing-away of the supporting ground, or the building has been struck by waves or heavy flotsam, flooding is unlikely to lead to serious structural instability. Floods can, however, exacerbate existing structural weaknesses. Signs of damage include:

- bulging or dislodged masonry (especially at the corners of the building)
- cracks wider than 6 mm above doors and windows, and at the ends of façades
- significant leaning, tilting or subsidence that was either not evident or not as pronounced before the flood.

If any of these signs are found, it will be necessary to seek the opinion of an experienced structural engineer. It will facilitate the assessment if the engineer can be provided with some evidence of how the area looked before the disaster, such as recent photographs and reports.

ASSESSING DAMAGE TO FUNCTION

Aside from structural instability, other issues (such as post-flood moisture and mould growth) may prevent building use.

DAMAGE TO SERVICES

Services are especially vulnerable to flood damage, and indeed may consume much of the cost of remedial action. Electrical systems, gas supplies and pipework will need to be opened up, and cleaned if necessary: seawater and other contaminated floodwater can corrode metal fittings, including conduits and switch boxes, and meters will almost certainly need to be replaced. All cabling and piping will need to be tested and re-commissioned by qualified service engineers, and some sections may need to be removed and replaced; if this means major works to the fabric, it will probably be necessary to consult with the Local Authority Conservation Officer.

Major floods will often cause the mains drainage to block; if this is the case, the rainwater handling and waste drainage from the building will both need to be closely monitored until the central system has been repaired by the water authority (unblocking private drains is the responsibility of the building owner). Repeatedly flushing sinks and toilets will help rinse the sewer system clean.

ASSESSING MATERIAL DAMAGE

A one-off flood should not cause serious damage to timber so long as it is allowed to dry afterwards: conditions will need to be poor for quite some time before decay mechanisms become destructive. Problems occur when liquid water is trapped: for example, in wall cavities, cill plates, under floors, behind panelling or under impermeable finishes. ⊝TIMBER

Corrosion of embedded steel or iron components such as concrete reinforcements can lead to serious structural problems, particularly in seawater floods. Cracks, deformations and rust stains in critical components such as reinforced-concrete lintels or beams should be inspected by a structural engineer. ⊝METALS ⊝CONCRETE

Modern gypsum-based plasters are water-sensitive and hygroscopic. The calcium sulphate in the plaster is partially soluble in cold water, so they will deteriorate in a flood, and may well need remedial treatment or even replacement. ⊝MORTARS

The Progression of Timber Decay

Moulds will usually begin to appear within a week or two after a flood or fire. The first are usually *Pyronema* species, which have salmon-pink globular fruits. They may also produce massive – even alarming – amounts of white surface growth, which is often mistaken for dry rot. After a while these species will be overtaken by other moulds. During the six months following a flood, the most obvious colonising fungi will be the 'plaster moulds' (the jelly fungi *Peziza*), which will usually be found growing vigorously on subfloor debris.

None of these microorganisms have any significant ability to degrade wood or other cellulose-based building material. The first damaging fungus is usually *Chaetomium globosum*, which is often found on wallpaper and produces a mass of white hyphae containing black speck-like fruits.

Fungi able to degrade timber do not begin to take hold until eight or nine months after the disaster (although this will depend on the time of year, and of course on a continued high moisture content in the fabric). The first to appear is usually the ink-cap fungus (*Coprinus*), which can damage hardwood ceiling laths and is frequently a problem in subfloor voids.

Serious decay fungi, such as cellar rot, dry rot and *Asterostroma,* do not normally become prominent until about two years after a flood or fire; and if debris has been cleared away and there are no enclosed and stagnant cavities, spore germination should not occur at all. However, since strand-producing fungi can spread rapidly from an existing source if the conditions are right, extra care must be taken if the building already has a pre-flood history of this type of decay.

Checking Hidden Areas

To check moisture levels and condition, to clean, and to allow any trapped moisture to evaporate, it may be necessary to investigate hidden parts of the fabric, such as voids under floors and behind panelling, box shutters and linings to door and window reveals, under stairs and inside cupboards, and in service conduits.

Fibre-optic borescopes are made with diameters as small as 6 mm, and can easily be inserted into voids through natural gaps or holes, made by drilling or by temporarily removing small sections of material, although interpretation of the results does demand considerable experience and skill. Techniques such as infrared thermography can also be useful, especially for locating hidden sinks of water.

OPENING UP

Opening up gives much better access, but to limit damage as much as possible it will need to be approached with great caution and careful planning. For example, if a floor is made of high-quality timber connected together by tongues or pegs, it may be hard to lift boards safely, and in some cases it may be better to consider removing part or all of the ceiling below instead. If the building has statutory protection, it will probably be necessary to obtain Listed Building Consent beforehand.

In no case should opening-up be allowed to develop into 'stripping out', which will invariably prove more damaging than the flood itself.

A good visual record should be made first of the area to be opened up (photographs, for example). As elements such as floorboards are dismantled, they should be labelled on the reverse side so that they can be put back in the same place and orientation after they have dried. ⊖TIMBER

Stripping Out

Some of the post-flood actions encouraged by insurance companies and loss adjusters – and even by contractors inexperienced in dealing with historic buildings – may be extremely damaging to the fabric, and may indeed contravene listed-building protection. The local planning authority's Conservation Officer should be consulted first if any stripping out or accelerated drying is being considered.

Typical examples of treatments that can cause severe damage without producing significant benefit include stripping of lime plaster from walls, and discarding wet timber floors and panelling.

Although some water-sensitive materials (modern gypsum panel board, for example) may be destroyed by prolonged exposure to floodwater, most stripping out is quite unnecessary, and may even be counter-productive. Permeable lime-based plasters generally help drying by providing an extensive surface for evaporation, and will also collect any transported salts. Even if eventually they may incur so much salt damage that they do require replacement, they should be left in place for as long as possible, and certainly until the building has dried.

Most dirty and damaged building elements can be revived by cleaning and careful drying, and the worst affected should still be retained long enough to be used as a model for a replica.

BUILDING ENVIRONMENT
SPECIAL TOPIC: Dealing with Disasters

REMEDIAL ACTIONS

After stabilisation and assessment, the next priority is to remove debris, separating out salvageable materials for safe storage. In historic buildings, salvage will need to be accompanied by conservation assessment and archaeological recording. ➔BASICS

Brickwork and stonemasonry may take years to completely dry after a flood or fire, and there are few measures that can accelerate this with any success. What is more, there will often be a conflict between the natural ventilation needed for evaporation and the various interventions that restrict air movement and air exchange, such as shoring up, scaffolding cover to protect the damaged building from rainwater, and security envelopes designed to protect it from intruders.

If the flooding has been significant or prolonged, then professional help and equipment will probably be needed to plan effective drying.

DRYING A FLOODED BUILDING

Good post-flood drying essentially means finding a workable compromise between conflicting needs: the need to remove the maximum amount of water from the fabric, and the need to make the building habitable quickly.

There is always pressure for buildings to be occupied again as soon as possible after a flood, but it is important not to try to dry too quickly (for example, by using industrial dehumidifiers producing very low ambient humidities): this can cause salts to migrate through old stone and plasterwork (causing blistering, powdering and exfoliation), and painted surfaces may peel and flake. Delicate contents made of materials such as wood veneer may also suffer. Turning on the central heating at full blast is also not to be recommended; maintaining temperatures above 18°C in a very humid environment may encourage mould growth.

Rapid drying may also move the system too quickly into Stage II drying (see **Building Science**). The surface will dry out, but the bulk of the wall will be left wet, and the overall rate of water removal will slow dramatically; then, after a short time, the surface will be become wet again as liquid flow paths to the surface re-establish themselves. In this case, secondary damage such as mould growth will often begin to appear just as repair works are finished, so that the building users must move out again and the surfaces must be redecorated, multiplying the disruption and expense.

The best general advice is to dry the building out reasonably slowly, as much as possible through natural means, but aided by mechanical fans where scaffolding or other protective covers are limiting natural ventilation and air movement. If the fabric is massive and the flooding was prolonged, this slow and gentle drying can sometimes take months, but it is effective and will not destroy irreplaceable building fabric. Drying time depends on factors such as the exterior and interior conditions (for example, the time of year), the construction and materials of the building, the nature and duration of the flood, and the height of the water table.

To dry the building out effectively, the rate at which evaporation can extract water from the fabric must match the rate at which it can be removed from the building (whether by air exchange or dehumidification); otherwise, the relative humidity will increase and drying will slow down, or humid air will move into other drier parts of the building, causing problems elsewhere.

Although loss adjusters and contractors may strive for a 'drying-out certificate', it is rarely clear what the previous pre-flood condition of the building actually was. Some parts (such as below-ground cellars) may well not have been 'dry' before the flood, and it would clearly be unrealistic to try to take these back to a state drier than their natural condition. Essentially, the building will be 'dry enough' when there is no longer any risk to the fabric or to the users. One guide is that fabric moisture levels are no longer changing; another is that the building is dry enough to successfully repair and redecorate. In both cases, some simple monitoring will probably be needed.

It may be possible for building users to return even if the walls are not yet absolutely 'dry', as long as there is sufficient air circulation to allow steady ongoing drying and there are no health issues; but this may mean limiting the amount of furniture in the building for the first year or two.

PREPARING THE BUILDING FOR DRYING

Before beginning works on a flooded building, it may be necessary to seek the help of a conservation professional experienced in dealing with the type of building and building materials; the Local Authority Conservation Officer may also be a good source of advice. If the building is protected by law, many of the works suggested here will require statutory consent before they can begin.

Exterior

Mud and silt must be cleared away from the bases of external walls, to return the surrounding ground to its original level. If the building has air bricks, and there is no immediate risk of more flooding, any blockages or protective covers should be removed.

Interior

Furniture should be moved out of the building or, where this is not possible, pulled away from the walls, and preferably jacked up from the floor (it will need to be shifted regularly during the drying process). The aim is to make sure that moving air can reach all corners of the room, and that there is plenty of air exchange with the exterior (in this case, the exterior air will almost always be drier than the interior air, so ventilation can be trusted to be helpful). Fans are often useful.

Where possible, all windows, roof lights and doors (including the doors of flooded cupboards) should be opened wide. Windows and doors that have been saturated may need temporary support framing to preserve their shape as they dry. If stairs have flooded, the under-stair space will need to be kept open so that they are exposed to ventilation from below as well as from above; this will help reduce mould growth.

Cavities

If any water is trapped in the fabric (for example, within cavity walls) this may need to be drained or pumped dry, but care should be taken to do the least damage possible to the fabric. Where possible, wet underfloor spaces should be helped to dry by lifting a number of floorboards (usually every sixth one), even if the boards themselves are dry. Butt-jointed boards are relatively easy to lift, as are boards that have already been cut to accommodate services such as radiator pipes, but floorboards that are tongue-and-grooved, or very old and tightly fitting, will need to be lifted by an experienced carpenter. ⊖TIMBER

Insulation that does not tend to absorb water may have to be removed temporarily from flooded spaces to allow drying; any insulation that has been saturated should be discarded (it will no longer be effective, even after drying). Special precautions will need to be taken if there is any risk that the insulation might contain asbestos.

Joinery

Timberwork should be left in place wherever possible, although it will probably be necessary to remove some sections to allow for expansion and contraction. Although seasoned timber will distort when wet, it will regain its shape when dry; for this reason floorboards and panelling should be stacked flat to dry (see **Storage**).

Green timber, on the other hand, may distort as it dries. For timber of any importance, it is wise to seek the advice of a specialist. ⊖TIMBER

Surface Finishes

As long as they have no historic significance, cement renders, wallpapers and plastic paints (all of which trap moisture) should be removed. Lime-based plasters, which are very permeable and may actually help the fabric to dry, should not.

Gypsum-based plasters will almost certainly fail when exposed to moisture, and will be slow to dry. Areas of plain gypsum plaster can often be removed except in very significant buildings, but dealing with decorative stucco and other important plasterwork will need the advice of a specialist conservator. ⊖MORTARS

Softwood will dry more slowly if it has been coated with an impermeable paint or varnish, but it is not always possible to remove these safely from wet timber, and if they have historic significance, retention should be preferred. ⊖TIMBER

Carpets and underlay, vinyl, linoleum and other impermeable surface coverings should all be removed, together with any sheets of hardboard or fibreboard (which are of no historic importance or intrinsic material value, but can absorb considerable quantities of moisture).

Storage

Salvaged items must be recorded, labelled and safely stored. Items should be sorted by size and type, and stored in such a way as to allow them to dry as quickly as possible. Timber, for example, should be laid flat and built into stacks, padded if necessary to protect decorative detailing. Everything should be inspected at regular intervals so problems can be detected and acted upon quickly.

The environment within the store should be dry and well ventilated, or if controlled, the controls should be set to a temperature of 18–20°C and a relative humidity between 45 % and 60 %. If a suitable store cannot be found then it is often safer to leave the salvaged items *in situ*.

If absolutely necessary, most moulds and minor fungi can be controlled by surface application of a fungicide, but expert advice should be sought.

Monitoring Drying

Flooded buildings must be regularly surveyed as they dry, to watch for any signs of deterioration.

The interior and exterior temperatures and humidities should be monitored to help estimate the speed with which water is being removed.

Moisture levels in the fabric can be established approximately using (for example) drilled samples. The initial readings form a baseline measurement, against which regular readings can be compared as the fabric dries. Wooden dowels can be inserted into the drilled holes, and monitoring the moisture content of these is a straightforward way of checking whether the fabric is drying out (see **Assessing the Building Environment**).

The building is generally considered 'dry' when:

- the internal conditions have stabilised
- the moisture content of the fabric has stabilised
- the amount of moisture remaining is not enough to support active growth of mould, mildew or fungi, or to support an insect infestation.

As the building (and in the case of widespread flooding, the surrounding land) dry out, the walls, floors and mortar joints may begin to fail. Cracks from foundation erosion will worsen as the building settles, whereas cracks that shrink or stop expanding when the water content of the soil returns to normal will probably be due to temporary hydration and expansion of clay. Cracks appearing in foundation walls or around openings should be investigated by a structural engineer.

Underfloor timbers should be inspected for signs of decay six months after flooding; after this, annual inspections should be sufficient.

ACCELERATED DRYING

If natural conditions are not enough to allow effective drying after a flood (for example, if the building is under scaffolding or boarded up against unauthorised entry), some means of improving conditions artificially will need to be found. Drying with the aid of equipment such as fans and heaters can be risky, and so demands a good deal of care and management: for example, the rapid increase in absolute humidity caused by pulling moisture out from the fabric can cause moisture problems elsewhere in the building if air exchange is not properly controlled. Nevertheless, moderate accelerated drying can be helpful in many circumstances if some simple guidelines are followed.

REDUCING THE RISKS OF ACCELERATED DRYING

SYSTEM	ACTION	REDUCING RISK
MECHANICAL VENTILATION WITH FANS	Controlled air movement with fans to accelerate evaporation	Make more efficient by tenting. Ensure good air exchange with drier spaces to keep the absolute humidity as low as possible
INJECTION DRYING	Increased air movement through cavities by hoses fed through small holes into the cavity. Can be set up to drive air in at one end of the cavity and suck it out from another	Should have relatively little impact on the rest of the building. Can be difficult to ensure good flow in very small or complex cavities; results can be unpredictable, especially if spaces are complex or interlinked
BACKGROUND HEATING	Heating to around 18–20°C to raise the evaporative capacity of the air	Control by humidistats (not thermostats). Use mechanical ventilation as well, and ensure sufficient air exchange
DEHUMIDIFICATION	Removes water vapour from the air as it passes through the machine	Controls (humidistats) must be very carefully positioned. Reduce impact on other parts of the room or building by tenting

It can be challenging to increase drying rates without damaging sensitive building materials or contents. Here, the risk from drying with a blower has been reduced by isolating the area being dried with plastic sheeting.

Dehumidifiers or heaters should not be used if the interiors contain wall paintings or other very sensitive surface decoration (whether on plaster or timber). In this case, specialist conservators should be called in to advise on the safest method of drying, with the least risk of causing adverse outcomes such as salt damage, paint flaking or mould growth.

LONGER-TERM ACTIONS AFTER FLOODING

Salt efflorescences should be brushed off and removed as they appear. If a wall is badly affected by salts, it may be useful to consider sacrificial pointing or plastering. Very permeable lime-based mortars can give a preferential surface for drying, and safely collect salt contamination so that it causes less damage in the stone or brick. Lime-based mortars should also be used in reinstatement works rather than cement or gypsum; this will afford greater resistance in any future flooding. ⊃MORTARS ⊃EARTH & BRICK ⊃STONE

Surfaces should not be finished with materials that make them less permeable (for example, sealants or impermeable paints), since this will slow drying. If it is imperative to redecorate before the fabric has dried, permeable coatings such as limewash or distemper (which are also able to adhere to a damp surface) should be used instead. ⊃MORTARS

Flooding and drying can loosen or weaken the structural joints in staircases. Once the building is dry, loose treads should be stabilised with additional underside blocks and fixings. ⊃TIMBER

Areas that have previously suffered from serious decay (dry rot, for example) should be closely checked at regular intervals after flooding, since the water may cause the problem to recur. In some cases, it may be necessary to dismantle the joinery in such areas as a precaution. ⊃TIMBER

If the condition of any building element or material affected by the flood gives cause for concern at any point, a specialist conservation professional should be consulted for assessment and advice. ⊃MORTARS ⊃METALS ⊃EARTH & BRICK ⊃ROOFING ⊃GLASS ⊃TIMBER ⊃STONE ⊃CONCRETE

Further Reading

Cassar, M., Hawkings, C. (2007); *Engineering Historic Futures*; University College London: London; also available at eprints.ucl.ac.uk/2612/1/2612.pdf

Donlon, T. (1997); 'Lightning Protection for Historic Buildings'; in *The Building Conservation Directory, 1997*; also available at www.buildingconservation.com/articles/lightning/lightn.htm

English Heritage (2000); *Technical Advice Note: Lightning Protection for Churches: A Guide to Design and Installation*; English Heritage: London; also available at www.english-heritage.org.uk/professional/advice/advice-by-topic/buildings/services/lightning/

English Heritage (2006); *Technical Advice Note: Protection Against Lightning and the New Standard's Key Requirement*; English Heritage: London; also available at www.english-heritage.org.uk/publications/protection-against-lightning/

English Heritage (2006); *Technical Advice Note: Surge Protection Equipment: A Guide to Selection and Installation in Historic Buildings*; English Heritage: London; also available at www.english-heritage.org.uk/publications/surge-protection-equipment/

English Heritage (2010); *Technical Advice Note: Flooding and Historic Buildings (2nd Edition)*; English Heritage: London; also available at www.english-heritage.org.uk/publications/flooding-and-historic-buildings/

English Heritage (2011); *Theft Of Metal From Church Buildings*; London: English Heritage; also available at www.english-heritage.org.uk/publications/theft-metal-church-buildings/

English Heritage (2011); *Vacant Historic Buildings: An Owner's Guide to Temporary Uses, Maintenance and Mothballing*; London: English Heritage; also available at www.english-heritage.org.uk/professional/advice/advice-by-topic/buildings/maintenance-and-repair/vacant-historic-buildings/

Forrest, R. (1996); 'Strategic fire protection in historic buildings'; in *The Building Conservation Directory, 1996*; also available at www.buildingconservation.com/articles/fire/fire_protection.htm

Gibbon, D., Forbes, I. (2001); 'Fire suppression in historic buildings'; in *The Building Conservation Directory, 2001*; also available at www.buildingconservation.com/articles/firesup/fire_suppression.htm

Jackman, P. E., Passey, H. (1998); 'The sleeping policeman: the role of compartmentation in fire protection'; in *The Building Conservation Directory, 1998*; also available at www.buildingconservation.com/articles/compart/sleeping.htm

Maxwell, I., Ross, N., Dakin, A. (eds) (1998); *Fire Protection and the Built Heritage (Conference Proceedings)*; Edinburgh: Historic Scotland; also available at conservation.historic-scotland.gov.uk/publication-detail.htm?pubid=8599

McDonald, R. (2003); *Introduction to Natural and Man-Made Disasters and Their Effects on Buildings: Recovery and Prevention*; London: Architectural Press

National Fire Protection Association (2010); *NFPA 909: Code for the Protection of Cultural Resource Properties – Museums, Libraries, and Places of Worship (2013 Edition)*; Quincy, Massachusetts: NFPA

IMPROVING ENERGY & CARBON PERFORMANCE

INTRODUCTION

The drive to reduce energy use and carbon emissions is one of the greatest pressures for change in the historic built environment today. The impetus comes from government policies and initiatives to mitigate climate change, maintain energy security, reduce domestic energy costs and tackle fuel poverty.

A fundamental challenge is to preserve and enhance the character and significance of the historic environment, at the same time as reducing its energy use and the contribution it makes to carbon emissions. Existing buildings represent a substantial investment of embodied energy, so provided their energy use in operation is not excessive, retention is not only good heritage conservation, but intrinsically sustainable.

Unfortunately, poorly considered solutions will not only threaten the building and the well-being of its occupants, but may also fail to deliver the expected benefits. When working with an existing building, it is vital to understand and work with – rather than against – its physical characteristics, technical qualities, heritage significance, and the way it is being used.

Technology and approaches are changing rapidly, so this **Special Topic** does not aim to present the latest information at time of press, but rather to help readers gain a sufficient understanding and perspective to be able to critically assess plans for reducing energy use and carbon emissions, and to ask the right questions of advisers.

Sources for up-to-date information are given in the reference boxes at the end of the chapter, and throughout readers are referred back to the main text, where some of the underlying issues are discussed in detail.

Improving Energy & Carbon Performance is divided into three sections:

- *Background*
  Why energy use and carbon emissions must be reduced, where they originate from in the built environment, and where improvements might be made.

- *Energy planning*
  Understanding energy use within buildings, determining improvements, identifying appropriate energy-saving measures, combining them into well-integrated packages, and finally implementing them in the correct order.

- *Practicalities*
  Information to assist the development of an Energy Plan, including checklists for many common measures that might be considered, listing strengths, weaknesses and other issues.

Facing page: Across the globe, the city has come to be defined by its use of energy, and increasingly of electricity.

Climate Change

The surface of the earth is warmed by the presence of heat-trapping 'greenhouse' gases [GHGs] in its atmosphere, such as water vapour, carbon dioxide, methane, nitrous oxide and ozone. Both climate modelling and measured climate data strongly suggest that the planet is currently warming steadily, and this is worrying since information about natural climate cycles taken from ice-core data and the patterns of natural agents that affect climate (such as solar cycles) indicate that instead we should currently be passing through a relatively cold phase. The observable temperature rise correlates closely with the industrial-scale exploitation of fossil fuels, so the consensus is that it must be attributable to 'anthropogenic forcing' (the blanket term for the many man-made pressures on the climate, such as rapidly increasing levels of GHGs – especially carbon dioxide – in the atmosphere, the accumulation of other pollutants and the dramatic changes in land use).

It is extremely hard to predict the exact effect of global warming on local weather patterns and regional climates. To use the example of the British Isles, although it seems likely to become hotter – especially in the cities – if the warming of the oceans should disrupt the Gulf Stream it would become very much colder. What is almost certain is that rapid change coupled with more heat and moisture in the atmosphere will destabilise climates, producing more severe storms and spells of extreme weather. Indeed, there are indications that this might already be happening: over the past few years in the UK, for example, there has been an increase in episodes of strong rains and flooding interspersed with very dry spells, and in winter cold snaps interspersed with periods that are much warmer than usual for the time of year. Observations of plant growth and animal behaviour suggest that the winter season is becoming shorter.

This is of great concern; but on the positive side, if human activities are causing the observable climate change, then by changing behaviour we have the potential to limit the extent of changes, and thus avert catastrophe. Action to tackle climate change takes two forms: 'mitigation' (actions intended to reduce the causes of the change, such as carbon emissions); and 'adaptation' (actions intended to prepare for a changed climate).

A Frost Fair on the Thames during the winter of 1683–4

Since the Industrial Revolution began, and fossil fuels began to be used more and more extensively, there has been a steady rise in average global temperatures. Very cold winters are becoming increasingly rare.

Large cities such as London are always several degrees warmer than the surrounding countryside, because of the many hard, heat-retaining surfaces with low heat reflectance, which absorb heat by day and release it at night. Heat is produced by industry, buildings and traffic, and there is less greenery to cool by shading and transpiration. Together this is known as the 'urban heat-island' effect. Frost fairs are now a thing of the past.

BACKGROUND

The world is facing the consequences of two centuries of relatively cheap energy, including rising levels of greenhouse gases [GHGs] in the atmosphere, particularly the carbon dioxide [CO_2] released when fossil fuels are burnt. It is forecast that this will cause global average temperatures to rise, and although exactly how the resulting change in climate will affect local weather patterns is very difficult to predict, it is almost certain that more heat and moisture in the atmosphere will create more extreme weather. Environmental problems have also arisen from the inefficient use of resources and from poor waste management.

Many countries are now seeking to radically reduce their GHG emissions (the UK is legally committed to an 80 % cut on 1990 levels by 2050), and also to protect the environment from other sources of harm. The building stock is inevitably coming under the spotlight, being the largest single user of energy and of many other resources.

Buildings are thought to offer better prospects for reductions than other sectors, particularly manufacturing and transport. In 2010, 44 % of CO_2 emissions generated in the UK came from energy use for day-to-day building operation; particularly conditioning the interior environment, and powering electrical equipment. Another 10 % were associated with building work: collecting, processing and transporting raw materials; making building products and taking them to site; construction; and maintaining the building over time.

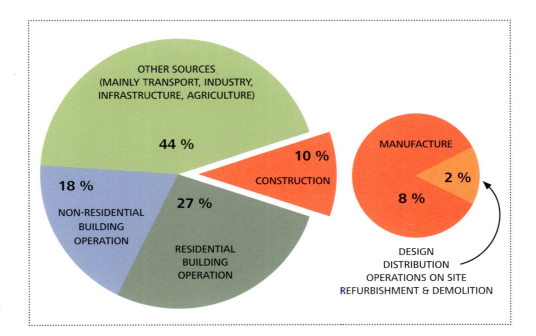

Pie chart constructed from the UK Department of Business, Innovation and Skills *2010 Innovation and Growth Team Report, Low Carbon Construction*, showing the proportions of UK carbon emissions attributed to the built environment.

BUILDING ENVIRONMENT
SPECIAL TOPIC: Improving Energy & Carbon Performance

Over the past two centuries, the amount of energy consumed to make and operate buildings has increased tremendously. The Industrial Revolution relied upon the exploitation of fossil fuels, starting with coal. Lower energy costs made energy-intensive materials like glass and steel easier and cheaper to make, and as a result new architectural systems began to replace traditional forms of construction. At the same time, developments in mechanised transport made centralised processing and production feasible, and soon led to larger and more sprawling cities. Habits and expectations of individuals and organisations also changed, while building operation became more energy-dependent (see **Controlling the Interior Environment**, in the main text of this volume).

Energy Use & Carbon Emissions

To reduce emissions, the options are to save energy, reduce electricity use and switch to low-carbon energy supplies.

When burnt, the carbon and hydrogen in fossil fuels combine with oxygen to produce heat, carbon dioxide and water. The quantity of carbon dioxide released in relation to the amount of energy produced (expressed as kilograms of CO_2 per kilowatt-hour [$kgCO_2/kWh$]) depends on the fuel source, and the efficiency of the system used to convert it to heat or electricity. The percentage of emissions attributable to using electricity is very high, because on average UK thermal power stations deliver roughly a third of the energy contained in the fuel as electricity at the point of use. In the UK between 2005 and 2010, a typical carbon factor (the emission rate per unit of energy at the point of use) for electricity was 0.53 $kgCO_2/kWh$, while that for gas was 0.185 $kgCO_2/kWh$. UK government policy is to reduce the carbon content of national electricity generation, but this will take time to happen.

Regardless of its carbon content, saving electricity is important because of its relatively high energy cost. After accounting for generation and distribution losses, thermal power stations in the UK deliver only about a third of the energy contained in the fuel as electricity at the point of use (as a comparison, the efficiency of an 'A-rated' gas, LPG or oil-fired boiler is around 90 %).

THE IMPACT OF THE ENERGY SUPPLY

The choice of energy supply for a building will have many effects at the national level:

- *Avoided requirements*
  Power from local renewable generation (solar, wind or water power) may be intermittent, which means that central supplies may be called upon from time to time. This has implications for the national supply in terms of capacity, management and efficiency, as well as on carbon factors.

- *Reduced requirements*
  The benefits of improved efficiency at the local or community level (for example, using electricity in heat pumps, or fossil fuels in Combined Heat and Power [CHP] systems) may not be entirely straightforward. Energy use can increase if a CHP is not available, or a heat pump is inefficient at the time the electricity grid is under stress because of a cold winter spell.

- *Lower-carbon fuels*
  Burning gas produces less carbon per kWh than burning either oil or coal, but the associated methane leaks from production and distribution need to be properly taken into account.

- *Biofuels*
  Biofuels must be sustainably produced, so a high proportion of the carbon released when they are burnt can be sequestered by the growth of new crops. Unfortunately, some biofuels require high inputs of fossil fuels to produce, and others may be provided unsustainably.

ENERGY & CARBON IN THE BUILT ENVIRONMENT

Given a particular site and context, the three most important influences on a building's energy use in operation are:

Fabric
The principal factor to be considered is how effective the building envelope is in providing a suitable indoor environment passively (including buffering of heat, humidity, and solar gain; providing natural ventilation and lighting via daylight).

Equipment
The equipment is the actual user of energy. This includes both the fixed building services (principally heating, cooling, ventilation, hot water, and lighting), and the other energy-consuming equipment (for example, the computers and appliances used for business, cooking, or entertainment).

People
Factors to consider include how the occupants maintain their buildings; the standards they consider appropriate for the internal environment; the technical services and equipment they bring in; and how they occupy the spaces.

These factors are highly interdependent: for example, the effectiveness of a building envelope will critically depend on how well it is maintained, and the control, maintenance and operation of the technical systems will affect fabric, people and the amount of energy used. The complex system of fabric, equipment and people must be looked at holistically if the use of energy in the building is to be understood and reduced.

BUILDING ENVIRONMENT
SPECIAL TOPIC: Improving Energy & Carbon Performance

WHERE THE ENERGY & CARBON GOES

Energy is used in constructing (and demolishing) a building, in maintaining it and in operating it.

CONSTRUCTION ENERGY ('EMBODIED ENERGY')

Construction is an investment of energy, the return on which increases the longer the building remains in use. This was once intended to be decades, if not centuries; and indeed vernacular buildings can be seen as models of sustainability, being constructed with local skills and knowledge, using locally sourced materials. This also made them straightforward to repair and maintain. That so many survive is a testament to their inherent robustness and adaptability. Traditional building materials such as timber, earth, stone, brick and lime mortar not only had long lifespans in relation to the energy used to produce them, but could also be reused or recycled; some, like timber and thatch, were renewable.

Today, about 10 % of carbon emissions in the UK are attributable to the manufacture and transport of building materials (particularly metal products, glass, cement and plaster, and structural clay products such as bricks and tiles) and to the construction process itself. The choice of material and design for modern construction often takes little account of long-term durability or minimum embodied energy. There is also a trend towards replacement or major refurbishment rather than repair or alteration; some commercial buildings stand only a decade or two before being demolished. Construction materials account for 90 % of mineral extraction in the UK and some 60 % of the total waste generated.

MAINTENANCE ENERGY

All buildings require a certain amount of regular care and repair to ensure longevity, and to support acceptable interior conditions. The materials and energy needed for maintenance can be minimised by good design, careful choice of materials, and skilled construction. Since excess moisture tends to be the fundamental agent of deterioration, a principal requirement is to keep all the systems designed to handle water in good working condition (see **Environmental Deterioration**, in the main text of this volume).

Traditional construction systems often emphasised longevity, and were based on durable materials such as stone and brick. Water-sensitive materials such as timber and earth were protected by good design coupled with protective coatings such as paints and renders that could extend their lifespan (see **Care & Repair**, also in the main text). Maintenance of these buildings was not energy-hungry, since it relied on handwork, and materials were often sourced locally. By contrast, many modern building components have shorter lifespans and very different maintenance regimes, often including regular replacement of items (from mastic seals to entire cladding systems).

The other volumes in this series include detailed discussions of the maintenance needs of many common materials and buildings systems of all periods. ⊖MORTARS ⊖METALS ⊖STONE ⊖EARTH & BRICK ⊖ROOFING ⊖GLASS ⊖TIMBER ⊖CONCRETE

Replace, Repair, Retain, Reuse or Recycle?

The 1987 *Brundtland Report* defined a 'sustainable society' as one that could meet the needs of the present without compromising the ability of future generations to meet their own needs; if it did not, society would be unsustainable. What does this mean for the built environment, where so much use of energy and materials is concentrated?

MATERIALS

Many construction materials are 'non-renewable', derived from raw materials in finite supply that, once used, cannot be replaced within a human timescale. These include familiar traditional materials like stone, clay, lead and iron. The UK Government's 2000 Performance and Innovation Unit report, **Resource Productivity**, noted that:
"Over 90 % of non-energy minerals extracted in Great Britain are used to supply the construction industry… Some of these are common, and over-exploitation is unlikely, but others (e.g. certain metals) are rare [and] difficult to exploit without making sacrifices such as the loss of agricultural land …"

Renewable construction materials are largely made from plant-derived substances that could potentially be replaced indefinitely; these include wood, straw used in thatching and earthen walling, and certain modern polymers from plant feedstocks. If not properly managed, however, renewable resources can become exhausted. For example, although timber is essentially renewable, longer-lived hardwood trees can take hundreds of years to replace, and current softwood supplies do not have the durability of the slow-grown timber widely used in traditional joinery. ⊃TIMBER

WASTES

Since considerable amounts of time and energy must be invested into producing building materials, recycling and reuse was normal for many centuries. Even simple materials such as old earthen and lime mortars were broken up and added to new mixes, while timber and high-energy components such as stone blocks, bricks and glass and metals were reused repeatedly. ⊃STONE ⊃EARTH & BRICK ⊃GLASS ⊃TIMBER ⊃METALS

Some recent building materials, such as cement and plastics, are more difficult to recover and recycle, especially when part of composite units such as PVCu windows or reinforced concrete. Government statistics for 2008 identified 101 million tonnes of construction waste yearly (35 % of total UK wastes), and to this should be added much of the 86 million tonnes of spoils from mining and quarrying (another 30 % of the UK total). Efforts over the past decade have significantly increased the proportion of construction waste being recycled or reused, but by tonnage this mostly goes towards aggregate and 'beneficial landfill', rather than reuse in the traditional sense.

Top: Older buildings often incorporate materials from earlier structures.

Bottom: Modern construction based on energy-expensive materials such as cement, steel and aluminium represents a substantial source of worldwide carbon emissions, especially since the lifespan of many of the resulting buildings is very short.

BUILDING ENVIRONMENT
SPECIAL TOPIC: Improving Energy & Carbon Performance

OPERATIONAL ENERGY

When individual businesses and households had to provide their own energy for heating, cooking and lighting, it took time and effort: for example, wood for burning needed to be grown, harvested, transported and prepared. As a natural result, fuel was used sparingly; and buildings incorporated fixtures such as window shutters and wainscoting, and furnishings such as draught screens, to retain warmth and reduce the demand for heating.

As fossil fuels began to be exploited on an industrial scale, energy grew cheaper. First gas, and then electricity, began to be supplied centrally, making it easy to use – and waste – large amounts of fuel without noticing. At the same time, developments in engineering services encouraged building designs and layouts to become more energy-dependent.

Expectations and habits also changed: it became common to heat the whole house, rather than just the one or two rooms in which the family gathered in the evenings. Warmer internal environments and heated transport accustomed people to wearing lighter clothing. In commercial buildings, systems have been increasingly designed to maintain a 'standard' environment throughout the year; currently overheating in winter and overcooling in summer are common in office environments. Despite concerns about energy security and climate change, new buildings frequently waste energy: for example, by having glass walls but making poor use of daylight. Meanwhile, electrical appliances have increased in numbers, and are often left running or on standby even when not in use.

Before the advent of cheap energy, buildings were designed and used to derive maximum benefit from natural resources such as daylight.

Where Does the Operational Energy & Carbon Go?

The quality of data available for energy use and carbon emissions is variable, and can be inconsistent; but the most important issues for buildings in the UK include:

- *General Issues*

    Building services – heating and cooling systems – can waste large amounts of energy, particularly where they are complex, not properly commissioned, or where occupants are unable to control them effectively. Meanwhile, the energy used to power other electrical equipment and appliances such as computers, audio-visual equipment, and cooking equipment – the 'unregulated loads' – may be as great or greater than that consumed by the fixed building services.

- *Domestic Buildings*

    The UK Government's Department of Energy and Climate Change [DECC] publishes a Housing Energy Fact File. In 2013 this estimated that, of the total energy consumed by the average UK dwelling, 60 % was used for heating, 21 % for hot water, 14 % for electrical appliances, 3 % for lighting and 3 % for cooking. At the same time, almost 50 % of carbon emissions were associated with heating.

- *Non-Domestic Buildings*

    In the UK, the non-domestic building stock outputs much the same proportion of carbon for heating as the domestic stock, but much less for hot water. Considerably more energy is used in the non-domestic sector for lighting, mechanical ventilation and cooling, and catering (which are all predominantly electrical end-uses). Electronic appliances, server rooms and catering kitchens all offer considerable scope for making energy savings, both by adjusting operations and by selecting more efficient equipment.

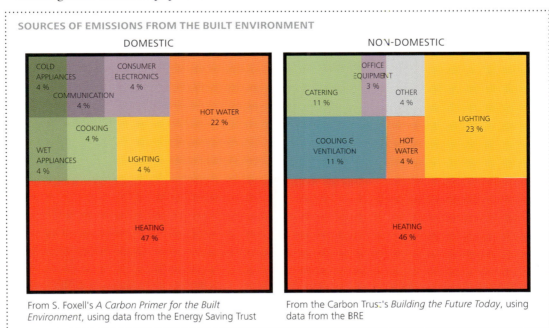

SOURCES OF EMISSIONS FROM THE BUILT ENVIRONMENT

From S. Foxell's *A Carbon Primer for the Built Environment*, using data from the Energy Saving Trust

From the Carbon Trust's *Building the Future Today*, using data from the BRE

REDUCING ENERGY USE & CARBON EMISSIONS

Initially, UK government initiatives to control fuel consumption were aimed at reducing energy use for heating, mostly by introducing and progressively increasing insulation standards for new buildings. Building regulations were then extended to take more account of airtightness, the efficiency of engineering and control systems, and carbon emissions. Currently more attention is being given to upgrading existing buildings, but with a bias towards insulating the fabric and changing to renewable energy supplies.

Government policy and industry measures have tended not to follow through from construction into operation, rarely reviewing actual outcomes in operation to inform future actions. Consequently, gaps between design and actual performance are being widely reported, with new buildings and refurbishments often using much more energy than had been predicted. There are many reasons for this, including inaccuracies in the data and models used to predict energy performance, and incorrect assumptions about the thermal behaviour of existing buildings. Inadequate specification of measures and inappropriate procurement processes may be coupled with poor installation, integration and commissioning. In addition, there is often a poor understanding of how occupants and management use their buildings, and engineering and control systems may be over-complicated and difficult for occupants to use effectively. Finally, energy use by unregulated loads does not fall within the scope of energy-related building regulations, and so is rarely taken into account in design calculations.

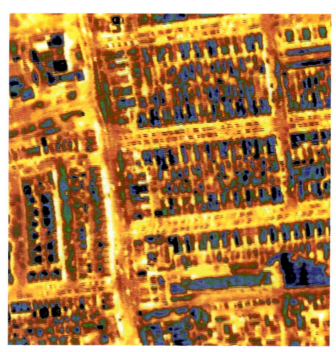

An aerial infrared image of terraced buildings in London shows that very similar buildings can lose very different amounts of heat.

The wide range of heat outputs shown here will arise from many factors, including the presence or absence of loft insulation, and the reflectivity and solar heating of different roofing materials, and the different ways in which the occupants live.

Concerns have also been raised about other unintended consequences of energy-saving measures, such as increased airtightness leading to poor indoor-air quality. Climate-change projections suggest there will be a rise in health problems related to overheating, particularly in cities (due to the 'urban heat-island' effect). Issues have often been approached piecemeal, and not always with a balanced perspective, which has led to a good deal of conflicting advice.

IMPROVEMENTS FOR EXISTING BUILDINGS

There is a widespread view that existing buildings are by definition higher consumers of energy, and that to substantially reduce energy use and emissions demands radical actions, particularly alterations to the fabric. The true situation is more complicated, but it also offers more opportunities.

The opportunities for saving energy used for services other than heating are often very similar in both existing and new buildings. In new construction, however, cutting energy use and carbon emissions would generally start by optimising the location, orientation and design of the building to minimise the load on energy-consuming building services. Existing buildings must be approached in a different way, since the fixed elements of the fabric will be difficult to change (especially if no major building alterations are planned).

When planning improvements to any existing building, it is vital to stop and think carefully about which measures are likely to be appropriate in that particular case, as opportunities and constraints will vary. The most appropriate measures will differ substantially from one building to the next, no matter how similar they may initially appear. A balance must be struck between the requirements and the aspirations of the occupants, the energy and carbon savings being sought, and all the wider environmental and technical issues (not least the building's heritage significance). With care and forethought, and by considering the building holistically, it is possible to devise packages of measures that not only offer lasting improvements in terms of lower energy use, but better occupant satisfaction, whilst still respecting the technical and cultural integrity of the building.

Energy-saving measures for existing buildings carry both risks and benefits.

Technically, many measures can improve the internal environment (for example, by making spaces warmer and less draughty); however, some may adversely affect the performance and longevity of the fabric or its use (particularly measures that lead to moisture problems or poor indoor air quality: see the **Special Topic: Buildings & Human Health**). If the systems designed to control indoor conditions and save energy become too complicated, they will be susceptible to shortcomings in design, installation, commissioning and operation, and hence to disappointing energy performance, and unaffordable running and maintenance costs; *"keep it simple and do it well"* is always a helpful guideline.

Culturally, improving energy and carbon performance may give a welcome opportunity to protect and enhance a historic building, and ensure that it remains viable into the future. On the other hand, ill-considered alterations can easily undermine its heritage values and wider significance. The *Conservation Basics* volume in this series gives more information about understanding the significance of buildings in their surroundings, and the statutory processes intended to protect these values. ⊖BASICS

Performance of Traditional Construction

It is often presumed that the energy use of traditionally constructed buildings is necessarily high, with some arguing that energy savings alone could justify demolition and replacement with new construction. This belief appears to have derived principally from modelling: in 2007, English Heritage looked at records of actual energy use in a number of traditional houses, and found consumption up to 40 % lower than predicted by the RdSAP modelling tool used to prepare Energy Performance Certificates [EPCs]. Similarly, monitoring solid walls indicates that the U-values in the standard tables typically used for assessment calculations tend to be high (see the following box on **Heat Transfer Rates & U-Values**).

In fact, measurements have revealed much less correlation between building age and energy use than had been anticipated. Solid walls are usually rather better insulators than standard calculations would suggest, and wet-applied plaster finishes can make some traditionally constructed buildings more airtight than many modern structures made of prefabricated elements dry-lined with plasterboard. For example, results obtained in a series of air pressurisation tests carried out in different parts of a large medieval building indicated average air permeability levels between 5.8–9.3 $m^3/hr.m^2$@50Pa (under the Building Regulations, 10$m^3/hr.m^2$ is the limiting value for air permeability in new buildings).

Other features may further reduce the energy demands of traditional buildings, including high thermal inertia, greater subdivision into rooms, and elements such as shutters, blinds and awnings on windows. Many older buildings also enjoy better daylighting, as well as easier-to-operate artificial lighting systems. In addition, shallow floor plans and opening windows allows them to operate with fewer energy-hungry engineering services than newer buildings which must rely more on artificial lighting, air conditioning, and complicated control systems that too often operate services too liberally and limit user intervention. As such, traditional construction incorporates many sustainable and low-energy features that could be adopted to benefit modern construction practice.

Some older buildings are also occupied less intensively, with occupants putting more modest demands on the services. Indeed, research from bodies such as the Sustainable Traditional Buildings Alliance [STBA] and *in-situ* measurement of buildings of all types indicate that many older buildings use less energy to produce the same level of occupant satisfaction.

Not all traditional buildings perform well, however. Many have been compromised by poor maintenance, and the loss of original energy-saving features such as shutters, heavy curtains, wall panelling and carpets. Thoughtful retrofitting can repair such losses, and introduce new elements such as loft insulation, secondary glazing and more efficient equipment that will reduce energy requirements further, as well as improving conditions for occupants.

It is important to set about improvements in ways which will engage the building's users, and which will work with – rather than against – the building's character.

Opportunities and constraints will vary. As the performance triangle of people, equipment and fabric suggests, saving energy is an enterprise that is as much social and cultural as it is technical, and the building's occupants must be thoroughly engaged in the process. The optimum approach is likely to be quite different for any two buildings, even if they are superficially very similar in terms of fabric. By considering the building holistically, it should be possible to devise approaches that can deliver both lasting reductions in energy use and carbon emission, as well as greater occupant satisfaction, whilst still respecting the integrity and significance of the historic structure.

The best results will come where the occupants are willing to reconsider wasteful habits, and to take enough time and effort to identify which improvements will be the most effective and least risky. Follow-through is very important. Community-scale projects can help engage and motivate, and collective action may also allow energy to be purchased, managed and generated more efficiently, or perhaps allow the supply to be decarbonised. Community schemes may be backed by environmental not-for-profit organisations and local authorities, but in the end every successful project can be traced back to enthusiastic individuals.

There are great opportunities for cutting energy use in the built environment simply by reducing wasteful practices, such as trying to heat glass conservatories so that they can be used as living space year-round. Understanding where the energy is going is the first step.

BUILDING ENVIRONMENT
SPECIAL TOPIC: Improving Energy & Carbon Performance

BASIC PRINCIPLES OF ACTION

Given the wide range of influencing factors, there can be no 'one-size-size-fits-all' solution to making energy and carbon savings. Nevertheless, there are some general principles that can and should be applied across the board:

- *Understand the context*

    Understand the impact of such factors as location (local environment; and the building's exposure to wind, sun and rain); design and condition of the building and its systems; and the occupancy (function and use). It is also important to take into account all the opportunities and resources available for making changes.

- *Engage the people*

    Success cannot be achieved solely by technical means; the owners, managers and occupiers of the building must be fully involved in the plans for saving energy.

- *Reduce the demand that will fall upon energy-using systems*

    Prevention is better than cure! This is not just a matter of improving the envelope (for example, by dealing with flaws in its thermal performance, or perhaps undertaking landscaping and planting to provide shading or windbreaks), but of questioning current expectations, habits and standards to decide what is really necessary. For example, comfort standards can range from very flexible to highly prescriptive (see the **Box: Comfort & Discomfort**).

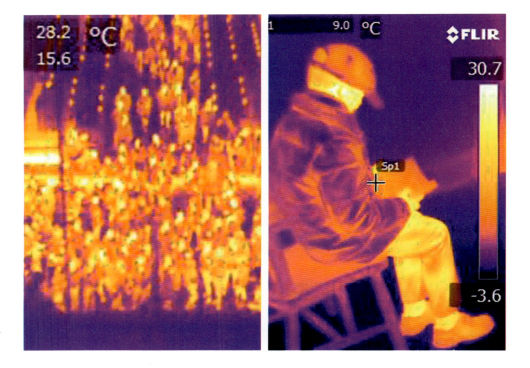

In cold climates, comfort is about not losing heat to the surroundings, rather than gaining heat from heated air. By appreciating this, it is possible to increase comfort at the same time as decreasing energy use. Here, thermography of a cathedral service shows how much heat is lost from the human body (*left*). That loss is greatly reduced by appropriate clothing (*right*).

- *Increase efficiency*
  Building services (such as heating and lighting) and other energy-using equipment (such as computers or appliances) should be designed, selected and run to use as little energy as possible.

- *Improve controls*
  Making control systems as efficient as possible demands careful attention to detail; many systems are far from being as effective, manageable and responsive to the real needs of the users as they might be.

- *Avoid waste*
  It is essential to commission and control energy-using systems properly, and to switch all energy-using equipment off or down when not really needed. Too much of the equipment in buildings today operates wastefully, or is left on unnecessarily.

- *Use lower-carbon energy supplies*
  Sources with lower emissions may mean using on- or off-site renewable energy (such as solar, wind or water power), selecting lower-carbon energy supplies (such as gas or wood instead of coal), or in some cases Combined Heat and Power [CHP] systems.

- *Avoid unmanageable complication*
  Complication invariably is the enemy of good performance.

- *Review*
  Measures of all kinds should be assessed carefully as they develop from initial ideas through design, selection, installation and commissioning, and on into use. The aims should be both to understand how the measure performs as part of the overall system, and to minimise unintended consequences (for example, increasing insulation and airtightness can lead to overheating, moisture problems, and poor indoor air quality).

In new buildings, it is sensible to start with location, orientation, form and fabric, so the loads falling on energy-consuming building services can be minimised. Existing buildings must have different priorities, as the fixed elements of the fabric tend to be the most difficult to change, unless major alterations are planned.

The Multiplier Effect

Measures used in combination can have a powerful 'multiplier effect', and make radical savings: for example, halving the demand, halving the carbon in the energy supply and doubling the efficiency of equipment will cut carbon emissions by seven-eighths.

Measures should ideally exploit this multiplier effect, but too often it is neutralised. For example, an emphasis on renewable energy supplies has meant some buildings fitted with biomass boilers have a much larger heating demand than necessary, because using a 'low-carbon' fuel has counteracted efforts to reduce demand and improve efficiency.

Comfort & Discomfort

'Thermal comfort' is not an absolute: it depends not only on the building fabric, the physiology of the occupants, what they are doing and what they are wearing, but also on a wide and subtle range of social and cultural expectations. Undue attention is often given to air temperature, although that is only one contributory factor. For example, where the air temperature in a room is at nominal comfort level, a person will feel uncomfortably cold if they are losing radiant heat to a large cold surface like a window or a stone wall; conversely, they will be comfortable at a lower air temperature if they are close to a radiant heat source such as an open fire, or underfloor heating that reduces heat loss into what would otherwise be a large sink of radiant energy and helps to keep their feet warm. Technical studies often use 'operative temperature' instead of air temperature; this is a weighted average of the air temperature and the 'mean radiant temperature' (a simplified measure of the amount of radiant heat a human body will exchange with the surrounding surfaces), and also allows for the effect of air movement.

Many traditional buildings had thick walls of high thermal capacity that helped to buffer external temperature changes, and were partitioned internally. Occupants relied more on influencing their own microclimate, and less on conditioning the environment itself. Screens were used to cut draughts in winter and were folded away in summer; windows, shutters, blinds and awnings were adjusted according to the time of day and year, fires were lit in some rooms but not in others, and heavier clothing was worn when necessary.

Achieving thermal comfort

Essentially, comfort is defined by its absence: users will be satisfied with their environment when they do not feel uncomfortable.

Discomfort can be caused not only by the temperature of the air, but by the way the air is moving, the humidity, the solar gain, and the emissivity and temperature of the various surfaces. Clothing and levels of physical activity will have a very strong impact.

Given the opportunity, occupants will adjust themselves and the room conditions until they feel comfortable: and indeed, having some control over the thermal environment has been shown to be necessary to the sense of comfort. Traditional houses included numerous ways in which the occupants could adapt their environment, and reduce discomfort from heat and cold (*right*).

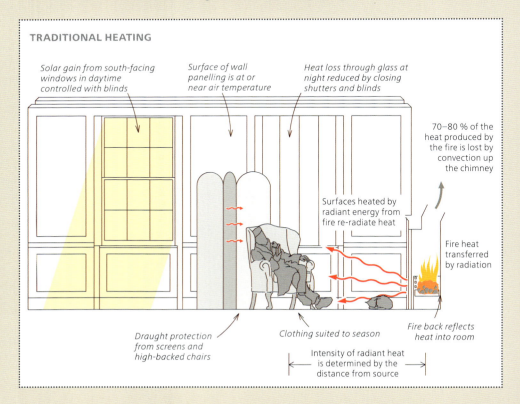

People's expectations of comfort and convenience increased during the 20th century. Although local radiant heating, task lighting and personal ventilation systems were available, these were steadily replaced by centralised heating and cooling, and as open-plan spaces became popular, it became more difficult to condition different parts of a building to suit local use. A new industry supplying heating and air conditioning was able to turn comfort into a commodity, stressing uniformity over adaptability and variety, and pushing solutions away from the production of environments that need little in the way of services towards increasingly complicated technical systems that consume a great deal of energy, and are often hard for occupants to control.

This trend has also helped to shape attitudes – not least of policymakers – towards internal environments. As the editors of *'Comfort in a Lower Carbon Society'* (a 2008 special edition of *Building Research and Information*) observed, the UK's lower-carbon policy agenda presents the 'problem' of comfort in a very particular way: for example, putting forward the notion that an adequately heated house requires an air temperature of about 21°C in the main living areas and 18°C elsewhere; despite the fact that repeated surveys have shown that occupants can be happy over a much wider range of temperatures.

Comfort strategies and control settings have an enormous impact on energy use. For example, in southern England, turning down the thermostat by just 1°C in a fully centrally heated dwelling may reduce its annual heating energy consumption by 10 % or more. Greater savings again can be made by not heating to a constant temperature all the time, but instead being responsive to the actual needs of the occupants. Surveys have shown that, as long as they have some control over conditions, building users tend to be happier in what might be regarded by service engineers as 'non-optimal' environments than they are under tightly controlled environments that offer no latitude for adjustment.

A fundamental reason for this is that when an individual has a 'crisis of discomfort' (that is, when they find conditions unacceptably uncomfortable: hot, or cold, or stuffy, or draughty, for example), they will wish to make changes: the so-called 'adaptive principle'. This does not necessarily mean altering the temperature; they might instead shut a window, put on a jersey or go to a warmer place. Occupants can also be quickly annoyed by fully automated controls that do not do what they want: for example, if they close blinds at a time when they would have liked to enjoy the sunlight; or open windows when it is noisy outside.

Understanding and dealing with crises of discomfort, and allowing for adaptive control, are the pathways towards simpler, lower-energy solutions to comfort heating and cooling that also provide greater occupant satisfaction.

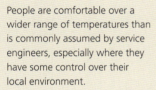

People are comfortable over a wider range of temperatures than is commonly assumed by service engineers, especially where they have some control over their local environment.

Studies by Hui Zhang and fellow researchers at Berkeley have shown that there is little benefit from controlling the air to keep it in the range 21–24°C: 80 % of occupants were happy as long as the temperature was 19.5–25.5°C. Simply by adding radiant panels and ceiling fans, this could be extended to 18–28°C, and systems that allowed occupants to adjust their own local environment themselves increased this to 16–30°C.

The researchers believe that the lower end of the range might be extendable further with different types of local heating, citing experiments which showed that people could be comfortable in vehicles with air temperatures of 12°C if the seats were heated. There may be some potential to transfer this finding to buildings where air heating is difficult, such as churches.

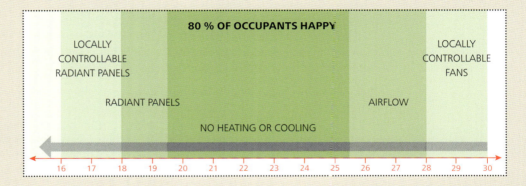

BUILDING ENVIRONMENT
SPECIAL TOPIC: Improving Energy & Carbon Performance

ENERGY PLANS

Before beginning to consider improvement measures, it is vital to prepare an Energy Plan for the building. A good plan will protect and enhance the historic environment, identify the energy and carbon-saving measures that best suit the individual building and its users, and ensure that the measures chosen are sensible, proportionate, cost-effective and low-risk, as well as sympathetic to the context. It will structure and coordinate all the many activities that may have to be undertaken, help to ensure that the most appropriate measures have been identified and all their risks properly considered, and finally that the selected actions are implemented in the right order.

When considering improvements to an existing building, it is currently common for the building fabric to appear at the top of the action list, an approach that is often encouraged by legislation. While 'fabric first' is a good principle for new construction, priorities in existing buildings will be different: the potential for fabric interventions will be constrained by cost, space and technical risk, not to mention potential impacts on the character and significance of the building and its surroundings. On the other hand, measures focused on equipment, appliances, controls, operations and waste avoidance should prove very rewarding.

The current models of the thermal envelope used to predict improvements from fabric alterations are often based on incomplete theories and inappropriate assumptions. Energy savings may therefore fall short of predictions, sometimes by large margins. Some measures may end up using more materials and energy than they will actually save over their lifetimes.

Interventions can also have unwelcome consequences, of the kind that the main section of this volume discusses at length. The harm may be direct or indirect; for example, direct harm would be caused by measures that require the loss of building features (such as hood mouldings, string courses and cornices) that not only contribute to the building's character and significance, but perform important technical functions. Indirect harm would occur if the interventions led to poor air quality, or encouraged the growth of moulds and fungi that might seriously affect the condition of the building and the health of its occupants.

To ensure that interventions are as safe and effective as possible, the building and its environment need to be well understood. As well as minimising technical risks, this will also increase confidence that any harm to significance will be outweighed by demonstrable benefits. From this, some simple guidelines follow:

- Do not undertake any actions that might cause the building envelope to deteriorate in whole or in part, particularly those that run the risk of trapping moisture from external or internal sources.
- Do not undertake any actions that would compromise the building's use: for example, by reducing air exchange to the extent that there might be risks to the health of the occupants.

Another compelling argument for developing a proper understanding of the fabric before making any changes is that historic buildings are repositories of both good as well as bad practice. For example, original features such as shutters, vestibules and wall panelling helped to make interior conditions more comfortable with limited amounts of fuel. If these have fallen into disuse, it may be relatively easy to restore them: if lost, it may be possible to replace them. Often there will be opportunities to introduce new features of this type to a building, even where they were not fitted originally.

PREPARING AN ENERGY PLAN

The Energy Plan must aim to save energy and carbon; provide satisfactory conditions for users; and preserve and where possible enhance the significance of the building. It should consider the building holistically, looking at its occupancy and use, its fabric, its services and appliances, and of course its use of energy, and from this, identifying the energy- and carbon-saving measures that best suit the structure and its users. For an existing building, it should also aim to both protect and enhance the historic fabric.

With the present state of knowledge it is not always easy to do all of this with confidence – particularly where alterations to the fabric are concerned – so a clear plan of action is an absolute necessity. Energy planning is a logical process that takes into account all the factors that are influencing demand in the building. It can be divided into six stages:

1. Understand the context and objectives
Where are we? Where would we like to be?

2. Review the current situation on site
What have we got? What does it mean?

3. Make a Preliminary Energy Plan
Identify problems and opportunities.

4. Make a Detailed Energy Plan
What can we do? Devising integrated strategies for improvement.

In practice, one or more of Stages 1–4 may well overlap; particularly for less complicated buildings, or individual dwellings, or cases where there are fewer heritage constraints on what can be done.

In due course these first four stages would be followed by:

5. Design and implement the preferred strategy
How do we go about doing it?

6. Record the process and review the outcomes
Where did we get to?

Implementation needs to be carefully timetabled and controlled because measures can be closely interrelated, not just physically, but in the effect they might have on the internal environment; for example, cutting unwanted air infiltration will reduce heat loss and draughts, but the indoor air will also become more humid, and this could lead to condensation, mould and decay. Where implementation is phased, the outcomes of earlier phases should be reviewed so subsequent work can be amended as required.

BUILDING ENVIRONMENT
SPECIAL TOPIC: Improving Energy & Carbon Performance

The range and depth of investigation and documentation involved in making the Energy Plan needs to be in proportion to the size and sensitivity of the building, and the scale and complexity of the proposed work.

For a simple building, a short but comprehensive report and checklist will usually be sufficient. It may take no more than a day to reach Stage 3, with a second day to discuss the Preliminary Energy Plan and agree a Stage 4 Detailed Energy Plan. For more complex buildings or situations, a formal comprehensive Energy Plan will be needed. In this case the skills of a specialist consultant may be welcome, but it must be remembered that most energy assessors and building-services engineers will be more familiar with technical systems than with how buildings behave – particularly historic buildings – so it is important to select the right adviser, and weigh their recommendations carefully.

Rebound & Prebound Effects

There is growing evidence that measures installed to reduce energy use in new and existing buildings often fail to achieve the savings predicted: this is known as the 'design-performance gap'.

Technical reasons are numerous – including a tendency of designers to report only the energy consumption by those end-uses covered in the building regulations; inaccuracies in the data and models used to predict energy performance; incorrect assumptions about the thermal performance of existing buildings; inadequate specification; poor installation, integration and commissioning of measures; and ineffective electronic control systems – but a very important cause is the way people occupy, use and operate buildings. Poor operational management, and incomprehensible or unusable control systems, can all reduce savings.

'Rebound' and 'prebound' effects are more subtle, but extremely important.

The rebound effect (also known as 'Jevons' Paradox') occurs when improvements in efficiency allow energy-consuming services to become more affordable to run, and so to be used more liberally. For example, once a building with poor thermal buffering has been improved with insulation, occupants may feel able to afford turning up the thermostat, or heating more rooms, or leaving doors open between rooms. Where buildings use renewable energy, or combined heat and power systems, the energy provided may be regarded as 'free' and therefore used more liberally (for example, not bothering to turn lights off).

More recently described is the prebound effect, a closely related situation where buildings are using much less energy than predicted by calculation prior to upgrading (reducing the actual savings achieved). For example, one study found measured energy use for heating traditional houses was about 30 % lower than that calculated. The essential cause is the adapability of occupants: if fuel is felt to be expensive or the building hard to heat, many will adapt their expectations accordingly, and not attempt to achieve what might be regarded by calculators as a 'normal' comfort standard. The prebound effect is particularly important for traditional buildings, where problems with calculations are compounded by flaws in the assumptions made about thermal behaviour.

The existence of such effects makes it doubly important to review existing levels of energy use before embarking upon upgrading measures; trying to understand the habits and attitudes of all the occupants, and if possible gaining their commitment to using the Energy Plan to really reduce energy and carbon.

STAGE I:
UNDERSTAND THE CONTEXT & OBJECTIVES

The context will be unique to the specific building and will be a major influence on what measures are appropriate. One size does not fit all. Seven principal aspects need to be considered:

- *The objectives of the exercise, including the primary motivation, and the likely scope of and budget for any implementation work*

    The initial brief may range from a short exploratory survey to identify opportunities to reduce energy bills, or save carbon or increase comfort, through to a comprehensive exercise in preparation for some intended major work of repair, alteration, extension or reuse.

- *The character and significance of the building and its setting*

    This may be statutory: if a heritage asset is designated, this will affect what alterations may (or may not) be acceptable. An important historic building should have a Conservation Management Plan, of which the Energy Plan should form a critical part, since it will affect both day-to-day maintenance and future work plans.

- *Local climate, orientation and exposure*

    Many factors of the building's setting will affect energy use and constrain options, the most important being wind and rain exposure; for example, if the building is subjected to regular driving rain, options for wall insulation will be significantly reduced. It is also important to consider solar gain and wind effects (the main text of this book includes detailed discussions of the impact of the building's setting on its environment).

- *The state of repair of the building*

    The fabric will need to be put into good condition before making any changes affecting insulation and finishes, both internally and externally. Moisture-related problems are a particular risk, since problems may be hidden by energy-saving work, and only be recognised after major damage has occurred. For the same reason, the likely quality of future maintenance must be assessed, because this will need to be taken into account when weighing options.

- *The current level of energy use*

    Energy use might be high or low for the type of building under consideration, depending on the intensity of its use, the standards to which it is operated, the efficiency of its systems, or the diligence of its occupiers and management.

- *The building occupation*

    The effect of the occupier is enormous, so there is a risk that calculations based on standard assumptions about occupation may under- or over-estimate consumption or potential savings. For example, the annual energy use of two seemingly identical dwellings, with similar households, on similar incomes, in the same area, can vary by a factor of three or more; interventions requiring significant capital investment might be cost-effective for a high energy user, but not for a low energy user.

- *The level of commitment of the occupiers and management*

    Motivation and understanding will be critical to the success of the improved building. Occupiers and managers could be anything from highly engaged environmentally conscious owner-occupiers, to corporate landlords who need solutions able to cope with tenants doing the wrong things. A high energy user might operate new measures wastefully, and therefore not capture the savings; a low-energy user might make good use of measures that might not normally be regarded as cost-effective. The greater the commitment, the more solutions can be tailored to habits and preferences, though measures also need to be robust to allow for possible future changes in occupation.

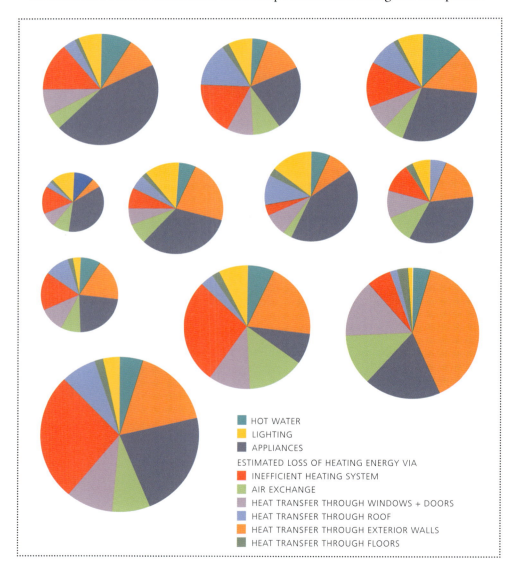

These pie charts, based on energy assessments, show how wide the variations can be in the energy used by different households, even on a single estate of similar dwellings.

The area of each pie chart represents the proportion of the energy that was recorded as being consumed by one household (in comparison to the overall consumption of the estate); the slices indicate how that energy was being used.

Differences will have a myriad of underlying reasons, including building fabric; type of dwelling (for example house or flat, and if the latter, what position the flat occupies in the building); type, age, and condition of services; and the personal requirements and tastes of the occupants.

- HOT WATER
- LIGHTING
- APPLIANCES

ESTIMATED LOSS OF HEATING ENERGY VIA
- INEFFICIENT HEATING SYSTEM
- AIR EXCHANGE
- HEAT TRANSFER THROUGH WINDOWS + DOORS
- HEAT TRANSFER THROUGH ROOF
- HEAT TRANSFER THROUGH EXTERIOR WALLS
- HEAT TRANSFER THROUGH FLOORS

STAGE 2: REVIEW THE CURRENT SITUATION

Very often the on-site investigation can be made at the same time as Stage 1, particularly in smaller and less-complex buildings.

Site investigation consists of assessing the building and how energy is likely to be being used within it, reviewing energy use and equipment, and determining opportunities and constraints that may affect the Energy Plan.

REVIEWING THE BUILDING & HOW IT IS WORKING

The review of the fabric should follow the principles set out in the main text of this volume (see **Assessing the Building Environment**), taking into account anything that might influence its present and future energy use. Points to record include:

- the size, shape, dimensions and physical characteristics of the building concerned; the location, orientation, shelter and exposure; and any related factors that might affect energy demand
- the design, materials and construction, including natural advantages and disadvantages (for example, the availability of natural ventilation, or daylight, or the likelihood of solar overheating)
- the building condition, especially factors likely to affect performance (for example, signs of water leaks, condensation, mould, or whether windows are poorly maintained and draughty)
- how the building and the spaces, and facilities around and within it, are being used
- any particular aspects of the fabric that might adversely affect comfort or energy performance
- all the arrangements for ventilating moisture-generating areas such as kitchens, bathrooms and laundries
- the nature of the internal environment in the principal spaces: how well the fabric is buffering the exterior conditions, and the cause of any poor buffering (for example, draughts or large areas of glazing)
- any existing energy-saving features, including insulation, draught sealing, shutters, double or secondary glazing; their type, location, condition, how well they appear to be performing, and how occupants use them
- any particular aspects of the fabric that might adversely affect comfort or energy performance, make improvements difficult, or provide future potential
- a summary of any opportunities for making improvements, and of possible risks and constraints.

The review should include comments from the occupants, if only informal ones, seeking views on what works, what needs improving and any sources of discomfort (including problems that may only occur intermittently, perhaps in particular spaces under certain operational or weather conditions). This input is vital, because the review will normally take place at one point in time, and possibly outside the heating season. It may only be possible to deduce some aspects of performance by approaching them from several different angles.

Measuring Thermal Performance

To fully understand how the building envelope is performing, measurement will sometimes be needed. A variety of techniques and equipment can be used; few are technically challenging, though all demand some expert interpretation. Expertise may also be needed to judge which factors are critical: for example, draughts can be a major source of discomfort, and therefore put greater occupant demands on the conditioning systems, but they do not necessarily originate from air leaks; many are triggered or exacerbated by local heating or cooling (cold air returning over the floor to replenish the hot air rising from a radiator or convector, or downdraughts from tall, cold window surfaces).

Measurements can be made at three levels: basic (typically spot checks made with relatively easy-to-use equipment); intermediate (requiring more time or preparation, or more elaborate equipment); or advanced (often needing specialist equipment and expertise, and possibly disruptive and time-consuming). Only rarely will the answer to the questions being asked be so critical as to require advanced assessment.

The table below summarises some of the main methods used to measure air infiltration, heat transfer and radiant heat exchange when assessing the thermal performance of the envelope for an energy assessment; more details of measurement and monitoring can be found in the main text (**Assessing the Building Environment**).

MEASUREMENT TECHNIQUES

GENERAL COMMENTS	BASIC	INTERMEDIATE	ADVANCED
AIR INFILTRATION			
Occurs not just through doors and windows, but via holes and cracks, where window and door frames meet the walls, between floorboards and often behind skirtings	Hand-held smoke sticks or chemical smoke puffers; note that there may be constraints on using these in some historic interiors Dry ice	Fan pressure testing can quantify the infiltration rate and allow targets for improvement to be set; specialists can usually make tests within a few hours, even on large buildings Pressure testing is also valuable in the course of alteration work, to establish quality standards and to identify any remaining sources of leakage	Tracer gases or smoke tests to find rates and routes of air circulation (latter will require smoke detectors to be switched off, and neighbours and fire authorities to be alerted) All smoke generators leave deposits on surfaces, and so smoke tests may not be possible in sensitive historic interiors
HEAT TRANSFER THROUGH THE FABRIC			
Tests here can be useful, but are only practicable in cold weather, typically November to February U-values are not constant, but will vary with moisture, wind and solar radiation	Checks of the thermal envelope can be made with an infrared camera, which can draw attention to areas of excessive heat loss Interpretation is challenging and needs care, especially when looking at glass and metal	Heat-flux sensors attached to the surface of the fabric at typical points, to monitor heat movement; to calculate U-values, exterior and interior temperatures must also be measured Will usually take several weeks for readings to become steady enough for an assessment of thermal transfer	Co-heating tests, which measure the energy used to keep a building at typically 25°C, are best suited for research, as the process takes several weeks (during which the building cannot be occupied) Cannot be used if the building fabric or contents are sensitive
RADIANT HEAT EXCHANGE			
The loss or gain of radiant energy from occupants can be difficult to measure accurately, because not all the surfaces in a room will be at the same temperature	Empirical (sensation of heat loss)	Infrared cameras	Black-globe thermometer to measure the 'mean radiant temperature' at a particular point, and readings used to determine the 'operative temperature' (weighted average of air temperature and mean radiant temperature, with allowance for air movement)

REVIEWING ENERGY USE & ENERGY-CONSUMING SYSTEMS

The review of the energy use and equipment should include:

- annual energy consumption, by fuel and preferably by end-use
- a summary of how the building is managed and maintained, and of how the services and equipment are operated and controlled (both centrally and locally)
- an assessment of each item of energy-consuming equipment: what is there, its size and condition, its appropriateness to the building and the building's uses, and how it is being operated
- a summary of how committed the building occupants and managers are to reducing energy use
- a summary of any opportunities for making improvements, and of possible risks and constraints.

Determining how and where energy is being used will not only make it clear what actions would be likely to reduce consumption most effectively, but could also draw the attention of occupants to wasteful practices and habits, obtain their detailed feedback, and trigger simple and effective behavioural improvements.

Limitations on thermal imaging

Imaging glass is particularly difficult: glass is opaque to infrared, and it is also highly reflective. It is perilously easy to over-interpret thermal images of façades: here, the same windows imaged twice in quick succession on the same camera show a wide variation in 'surface temperature' readings, due almost entirely to reflectivity.

Inaccuracies must be minimised as far as possible by controlling how and when the image is taken, by processing the images with care, and finally by interpreting the results in the light of a good understanding of how building systems behave.

BUILDING ENVIRONMENT
SPECIAL TOPIC: Improving Energy & Carbon Performance

Obtaining Data on Energy Use

ENERGY SURVEYS

An Energy Survey should aim to quantify how much energy is being used to operate the building, for what purposes and to what standards. This will allow energy use to be benchmarked against comparable buildings and provide a baseline against which improvements can be measured. As with other aspects of building evaluation it can be undertaken at three levels:

- *Basic survey*s: simple data on annual energy use collected by source, from fuel bills and other records; this gives an initial view of how much energy is used, and the information can often be collected and reviewed by people without any special technical knowledge
- *Intermediate survey*s: these take account of how energy use varies with season (and sometimes time of day), and identify any unusual activities or energy end-uses that may need to be taken into account (for example, restaurants, swimming pools, pottery kilns, server rooms and outdoor lighting)
- *Advanced surveys*: these look in detail at each end use, particularly those with high usage or uncertain usage.

In Stages 2 and 3, the aim should be to collect just enough information to be able to formulate the Preliminary Energy Plan: this normally requires only a basic survey. Intermediate and advanced surveys would usually only be undertaken in Stage 4, and then only if necessary.

For the more complex buildings, techniques such as the CIBSE TM 22 Energy Assessment and Reporting Method (with its associated software) are designed to help the surveyor organise data in a proportionate manner, drilling down from one level to the next only when and where necessary, and returning to add more detail if and when required.

Energy monitors of various kinds are becoming more widely available and easier to use.

The base unit clips on to the main power supply cable (*right*) and sends information to a hand-held device that gives readings in both kWh and the cost equivalent (*left*).

INFORMATION FROM ENERGY CERTIFICATES

Some public buildings are required to have Display Energy Certificates [DECs] based on annual energy use. DECs for buildings over 1000 m² must be updated annually, and can be a useful source of data, benchmark comparisons and historic trends. Energy Performance Certificates [EPCs] are based on theoretical calculations rather than measurements.

DECs and EPCs are also accompanied by reports suggesting measures to improve energy and carbon performance. These are prepared using a standardised, low-cost approach: they may provide some useful input to an Energy Plan, but should on no account be relied upon as a principal source of information.

DETAILED MEASUREMENTS OF ENERGY USE

Utility Meters

'Half-hourly' meters are mandatory for the larger buildings and sites that have peak electricity loads of 100 kW or more. As the name suggests, these monitor consumption every half hour and transmit the readings to the electricity supplier. If requested, suppliers will provide this information to customers, and it can be invaluable: revealing, for example, how much electricity is used at weekends, whether equipment comes on too early in the morning or stays on too late at night, and how patterns of use vary with season.

Government policy in the UK is for all gas and electricity supplies to have 'smart meters' by 2020, and these are already in place in some sites. These not only transmit the recorded pattern of energy use back to the supplier, but can help to integrate on-site renewable energy supplies, and switch on and off customer-selected non-essential loads (such as tumble driers) in response to the availability and price of electricity. Local display units, usually wirelessly connected to the meter, allow customers to review their own energy use, and investigate trends.

Energy Monitors

Energy monitors can help energy surveys to obtain more information on patterns of electricity use, both at the main supply where utility information is not available, and more locally. They include simple plug-through kWh meters for power sockets, monitors that clip to incoming mains supply cables, or to outgoing ways from consumer units and distribution boards, and more sophisticated professional equipment. The simpler monitors record totals only, but many can now also log patterns of demand over time, typically accumulated over 15- or 30-minute intervals; though more frequent logging is sometimes desirable.

Energy monitors can be used not only to monitor what normally happens, but investigate the results of switching off and on different equipment, or operating it in different ways. It should be noted, however, that many of the widely available monitors able to clip onto incoming mains cables measure apparent power [kVA], not true power [kW], and so can give inaccurate results (particularly at low loads, and when assessing electronic equipment and electric motors).

REVIEWING OPPORTUNITIES & CONSTRAINTS

Opportunities and constraints that may affect the Energy Plan will be many, and may include:

- any items identified during the reviews of the building and the energy use
- any statutory designations affecting the building or its setting
- a summary of the local planning policy framework derived from local-authority guidance documents (including Supplementary Planning Documents and Conservation Area appraisals)
- an assessment of the resources necessary for action; this may include plans for change, occupancy constraints, budgets, and any opportunities to combine energy-related measures with other planned maintenance, repairs, alteration and extension work
- tenancy arrangements and management issues that could make it difficult to undertake some measures, and to integrate the operation of a building well with the activities of its occupiers
- other constraints (for example, statutory protection of nesting birds or roosting bats in a roof).

Even where an historic building is protected by law, there may be considerable scope for sensitive energy-saving improvements on the exterior. For example, neighbouring houses may retain early energy-saving features such as shutters and awnings, giving a model for potential improvements.

STAGE 3: THE PRELIMINARY ENERGY PLAN

The Preliminary Energy Plan brings together the findings from the initial review, with an assessment of how the building is performing at present and where energy is being used, and identification of any problem areas. It can also be the point at which the energy use of the building is compared to benchmarks or other similar buildings, where these are available.

The Preliminary Energy Plan should consider the scope for savings in four main areas:

- *Operations*

  Savings made by adjusting the way the building and its systems are being used, controlled and managed to minimise energy demands, and to avoid waste. The simplest way of saving energy is to use less of it: turning things down, switching things off, and reviewing operating settings and schedules.

- *Equipment*

  Savings made by reducing the demand on building services and other equipment, and increasing its efficiency.

- *Fabric*

  Typically savings will involve draughtproofing, insulation and window improvements. The scope for fabric alterations is likely to be limited by technical risks (particularly in relation to moisture), impacts on historic significance and logistics (cost, disruption and loss of space).

- *Energy supply*

  It may be possible to reduce carbon emissions by changing fuels, or using renewable or community systems.

Simple operational adjustments such as turning down radiator thermostats will save significant amounts of energy.

BUILDING ENVIRONMENT
SPECIAL TOPIC: Improving Energy & Carbon Performance

The weak points of the building – and by extension, many of the necessary and desirable improvements – will have been identified during Stage 1 and Stage 2. If there are several possible interventions to deal with the same issue, these should be prioritised by considering the risk each entails, the resources it would use, the benefits it might offer, and any issues related to its integration with other measures and the timing of implementation.

A triage process is a useful way to separate possible measures into those that involve little or no risk (green), those that are uncertain but might merit further investigation (amber), and those that are best avoided (red). The aim should be to develop well-integrated packages of work that minimise knock-on effects.

Context is critical; as shown in the diagram on the facing page, it is not possible to see interventions in isolation, nor to come up with generic recommendations.

The Preliminary Energy Plan should be discussed with the building's owners or managers at an early stage, to obtain initial feedback on the problems identified and the measures proposed. At the same time, it is desirable to agree on the scope of Stage 4 (the Detailed Energy Plan).

CONSIDERING EARLY ACTIONS

A Preliminary Energy Plan will often identify opportunities for simple, cost-effective improvements that could be undertaken quickly. The most obvious of these is tackling neglected maintenance, but reducing energy waste should also be a priority. This can mean identifying and dealing with:

- *Poor operational practices*
  The availability of advice and guidance is critical; this is best provided face-to-face.

- *Poorly adjusted, faulty or inappropriate controls*
  This is a common problem, not just in terms of use; it may also be a result of inadequate design, installation, commissioning, ergonomics, and feedback to users and management.

- *Poorly-maintained or malfunctioning systems and equipment*
  Uninsulated or poorly insulated hot water cylinders and pipes, for example.

- *Straightforward low-cost fabric-related measures*
  Typical such measures include draughtproofing, repairing or upgrading insulation in accessible roof void spaces, reinstating shutters or draught lobbies, or adding blinds, awnings or external shade planting.

If the building is to continue in much the same use – and provided the items affected are not scheduled for early replacement anyway – doing the low-cost measures rapidly should be considered. This early work will not only save energy, but can help build confidence and allow revised baselines to be set, against which further improvements can be reviewed.

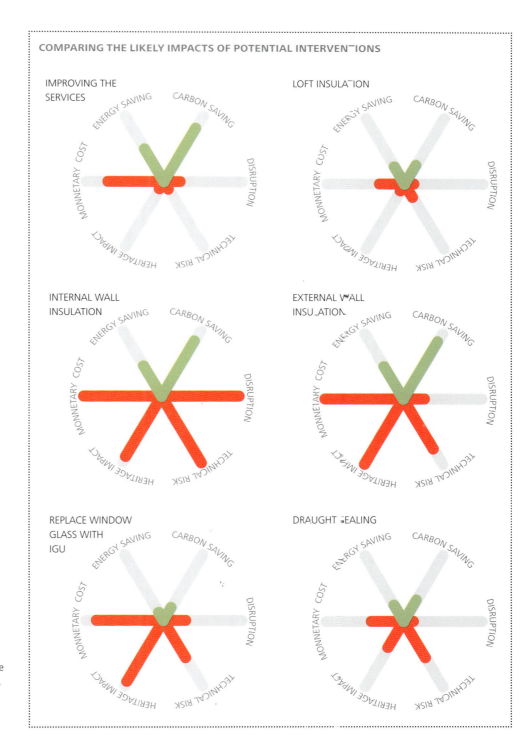

These diagrams illustrate a simple graphical method for comparing the relative costs and benefits of proposed improvements, helping to select those that will deliver the greatest benefits for the lowest possible risks and costs.

No numbers are shown, because ratings will entirely depend on the context. For example, if external wall insulation is being considered for a rear façade, the heritage impact may be quite small; but if the same wall is exposed to driving rain, the technical risk may be very high. Similarly, benefits may well depend on current energy use.

BUILDING ENVIRONMENT
SPECIAL TOPIC: Improving Energy & Carbon Performance

The Risks of Energy-Saving Measures

Measures to reduce energy use in buildings may not always perform as anticipated. They may fail to produce the savings predicted, or cause problems for occupants (including summer overheating or reduced indoor air quality). They may even have a counterproductive effect: for example, extra insulation could lead to condensation, create thermal bridges or trap moisture from leaks. This would not only lead to deterioration of the building fabric: wet materials will conduct heat very effectively, so the intervention could end up increasing rather than decreasing heat loss. Ill-considered retrofits can also damage or destroy the very features that make a historic building significant.

Costs of remediation after misguided measures can be very high, so it is vital to properly assess the risks and benefits of any potential measure, and not to undertake any action for which the risks cannot be minimised or removed. No energy-saving measure should be chosen without reasonable confidence that it will work effectively in combination with other measures and give demonstrable benefits over its lifespan.

Good design, specification and installation can solve many problems, but the paucity of good data from existing buildings (whether old or new) can make it difficult to predict the true impact of proposed measures. The more risky the action – or the more effort it requires – the more detailed the assessment will need to be to reach the level of confidence necessary to incorporate it in an Energy Plan. It is always wise to be pessimistic about potential gain as well as potential risk.

UNDERSTANDING TECHNICAL RISKS

The technical risks of retrofitting are often not fully appreciated. For instance, with solid-wall insulation, although the risks of condensation are much discussed, the much more acute risk of trapping liquid water ingress from building flaws or poor maintenance is often overlooked.

While many aspects of the interaction of heat, moisture and buildings are reasonably well understood, what actually happens will depend on the exact nature of the fabric, and the many external and internal inputs. This makes it impossible to predict with confidence what exactly will happen in every location; surveying is therefore a critical tool (see **Deterioration & Damage** and **Diagnosis**, both in the main text).

Nonetheless, modelling is widely used to predict behaviour. Many common models are over-simplified or even erroneous: for example, the 'Glaser Method', used in the British Standard **BS 5250:2011 *Code of practice for the control of condensation***, can give very misleading results. More sophisticated and effective models (such as those discussed in **BS EN 15026:2007 *Hygrothermal performance of building components and building elements***) incorporate many more variables (including specific material properties, internal environment, local climate and some aspects of liquid water movement), but remain incapable of modelling a real building, with its many joints and interfaces, and its complex moisture history. The main use for modelling is not as a replacement for observation, but as a way of comparing possible outcomes from different energy-saving measures. If used for this purpose, however, it is important to be sure that the assumptions made by the model are appropriate to the situation being considered, and that the model has been calibrated by comparing predictions to measurement.

THE RISK OF NOT PAYING BACK ENERGY COSTS

Many energy-saving measures will pay for themselves rapidly in energy terms, but for others there is a real risk that they may use more energy and other resources than they save over the long term. Account should therefore be taken of:

- the total energy and carbon costs of the measure, including its production, transportation, installation and wastage
- the measure's lifespan, including the energy and carbon costs of operation and maintenance over the entire period
- the energy and carbon costs of removing and replacing the measure at the end of its useful life, including the feasibility of cost-effective recycling or reuse
- any potential impacts on the building envelope, especially over the long term.

Data can be hard to find, and complex supply chains often make exact figures impossible to obtain. Fortunately, a broad-brush triage approach will usually be sufficient for decision-making, grouping measures together as 'red' (high-energy in relation to savings), 'green' (giving rapid overall reductions) or 'amber' (uncertain, requiring more investigation).

Payback periods

If interventions only needed to be made once, and did not require refurbishment or replacement, payback periods would be comparatively straightforward to calculate and compare. In practice, however, almost all interventions have limited lifespans, and will need a regular input of energy over and above running costs. As these graphs show, this can make some interventions unsustainable over the longer term, even if they dramatically cut yearly running costs.

Top: A graph showing the payback periods for interventions that never need replacement or refurbishment.

Bottom: A graph showing the much longer delay before an intervention with a finite lifespan is able to recoup the energy costs of its production and installation. Intervention B will never reach this point, but will always cost more energy than it saves.

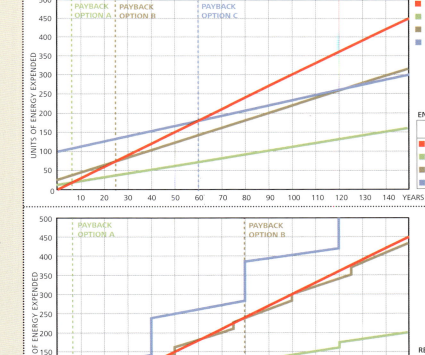

BUILDING ENVIRONMENT
SPECIAL TOPIC: Improving Energy & Carbon Performance

The outcomes may also unearth new issues and unintended consequences. For example, adopting less generous time and temperature schedules for heating might suit most spaces, but may trigger complaints about underheating in some rooms. This may in turn expose the reasons why the settings had been more liberal (perhaps because of poor heat distribution, undersized heat emitters or excessive local heat loss). New or amended recommendations for local improvements to heat distribution, heat output, insulation or airtightness can then be made.

The measures suggested may be classified by the type of intervention, and the level of cost or difficulty. This is shown in the table below, which includes examples of the type of measures that might be considered under each category, and shows how a triage assessment might be imposed.

CLASSIFYING POTENTIAL MEASURES

TYPE OF ACTION	TYPE OF INTERVENTION		
	PEOPLE IMPROVING HABITS & MANAGEMENT PRACTICES	**EQUIPMENT** CHANGES TO BUILDING SERVICES & OTHER ENERGY-USING EQUIPMENT	**FABRIC** MEASURES AFFECTING THE BUILDING ENVELOPE
SIMPLE LOW RISK AND LOW COST	Better monitoring and control of energy use Make building users more aware of energy and carbon performance, and provide information they can act upon Switch off lights and equipment when not required Adjust thermostats slightly to reduce winter heating and summer cooling Wear clothing suitable to the seasons Make better use of existing energy-saving measures such as shutters and heavy curtains	Is all the equipment in the building necessary? Replace equipment at the end of its life with more efficient models Replace electric lamps with more efficient types Simple improvements to controls, such as better (or better-located) switches, timers and programmers, room or zone thermostats, and thermostatic radiator valves Simple supplementary heating (for example, local electric panel heaters) to avoid whole building systems running unnecessarily	Make simple low-cost repairs and improvements to tackle sources of moisture leakage Identify and tackle sources of unwanted air infiltration, including windows, doors, holes and cracks. Refurbish original energy-saving features such as shutters Reduce radiant heat loss with blinds, carpets, wall coverings Reduce draughts with heavy curtains over doors and windows Simple roof insulation (at ceiling level in loft spaces)
INTERMEDIATE SOME RISK AND/OR MEDIUM COST	Technology to assist management or user interaction (for example, real time displays)	Replace inefficient equipment before the end of its natural service life Install new heating or cooling plant to replace or upgrade existing items Modify heating, cooling and ventilation systems to provide better local or zone control More comprehensive control upgrades	More extensive draughtproofing Add energy-saving reversible features, such as shutters or secondary glazing, where these did not exist before Insulate walls internally using thin permeable board or permeable plaster Render exterior with permeable mortar Insulate pitched roof at rafter level Replace lost internal partitions or draught lobbies
CHALLENGING HIGHER RISK AND/OR HIGHER COST	N/A	Completely new heating, cooling and ventilation systems Some renewable energy systems	Reconstruct roofs Insulate flat roofs Insulate walls thickly

STAGE 4:
THE DETAILED ENERGY PLAN

Stage 4 involves devising strategies for improvement. It is important not to rush to solutions until the strengths, difficulties and consequences of all proposed measures have been considered carefully (both individually, and in combination). The Detailed Energy Plan should aim to identify exactly where energy savings could and should be sought.

To do this the situation must be examined holistically: measures must be considered as integrated well-balanced packages that respect the integrity of the building, taking account of interactions, identifying combinations that offer the most gain for the least risk and cost, and finally reviewing how they might actually perform in everyday use.

The process will include:

- devising measures that respond to real needs, and are suited to the specific building and locality
- evaluating the measure's effectiveness, benefits, cost and suitability for occupants and management
- assessing the impact on the building's character and significance
- assessing the technical risks (for example, moisture accumulating in the fabric)
- reviewing the risks of other unintended consequences
- ensuring the measures finally selected still form an integrated package.

Any faults identified in the building envelope should be dealt with first. Basic maintenance is often regarded as outside the energy agenda, but it is essential to saving energy, as well as improving comfort and reducing risks. Priority should be given to tackling any water ingress (for example, from cracks and defective rainwater systems) to avoid damage and increased heat transfer.

Most measures will require energy and materials to manufacture, and more again for installation and maintenance. Some will also require diligence from occupiers: the question to ask is whether this will be forthcoming and cost-effective. Projected energy benefits will have to be weighed against these energy inputs to determine whether the result is likely to be an overall reduction in energy use or emissions over the lifespan of the proposed measure and the building.

The more complex the measure is to design, implement, operate and maintain, the greater the risk of unintended consequences. Therefore, a good rule is to give preference to the simplest measures practicable, and implement them as well as possible. The best solutions will tend to be robust, with minimal need for ongoing monitoring, management or maintenance, and capable of bringing year-round benefits. For example, window shutters can both cut heat loss in winter and reduce solar gain in summer, if the occupants understand their functions and use them appropriately.

CONSIDERATIONS FOR A DETAILED ENERGY PLAN

Dealing with Uncertainties

Some measures identified in the Preliminary Energy Plan may be attractive in principle, but their effectiveness, and their risks and benefits in practice, may be uncertain. More investigation will then be needed to develop the Detailed Energy Plan, to decide whether or not to include those measures. This might entail:

- detailed condition assessments
- monitoring of the internal environment, the building fabric or the energy use
- installing mock-ups: for example, to decide whether draught screens will reduce uncomfortable draughts, a screen of plywood or even cardboard could be put into place for a short time; or samples of more efficient lighting or new room controls could be installed on a trial basis (this often proves rewarding, revealing hidden aspects and drawbacks before full implementation)
- undertaking pilot studies: for more extensive or challenging projects, a package of measures could be tested in one area of the building, and then rolled out more widely only if the results prove positive.

Ideally, any necessary investigations of this kind would be completed as part of Stage 4, but the need to obtain approvals, funding, support or materials may mean that some will need to be postponed until the early part of Stage 5.

Integrating Measures into Packages

Measures are likely to interact with each other, and with the building. When developing a package, these interactions will need to be assessed; in particular, how the combination of building use, heating, ventilation, insulation and moisture might affect the internal environment and the fabric. This will mean taking account of:

- the physical integrity of the building envelope, particularly against rainwater ingress
- the thermal integrity
- air infiltration and ventilation
- the risk of insulation causing condensation
- any building work associated with the measures proposed
- the integrity, usability and manageability of building services, and their control systems
- the context.

Physical Integrity of the Envelope

The most severe problems will tend to occur where different elements come together. For example, externally insulated walls will have potential weak spots at junctions with the roof, the ground, windows, adjacent properties, rainwater pipes and other services. Eaves and window cills can be a particular problem, funnelling water in behind the insulation; root penetration can occur from the ground; and rainwater pipes or other building services can create a wide range of problems for design and workmanship.

Thermal Integrity of the Envelope

If one part of a building is insulated much more than another, or if the insulation stops in places, the uninsulated parts may become thermal bridges that – being both relatively and sometimes absolutely colder – will be more susceptible to condensation, mould and rot. The most common location of problems is at or near junctions (where it can be difficult to ensure continuity of insulation).

Roof insulation is sometimes omitted towards the eaves, for example, and as a result, mould is found in upper corners of upstairs rooms. Similarly, wall insulation may be omitted around the windows, which may give problems in the window reveals.

Air Infiltration & Ventilation

High levels of air exchange with the exterior will inevitably cause considerable loss of conditioned air, so reducing this is often a priority. More than three-quarters of the total heat lost through unrestored sash and casement windows tested for English Heritage escaped through gaps in and around the frame. Some buildings are relatively airtight, however; and sufficient ventilation must be retained to maintain indoor air quality, and remove excess moisture for the good of the fabric and the occupants. Combustion air will also have to be provided for any open-flued appliances. Moisture from bathrooms, kitchens, laundries and other wet areas is best ventilated away at source, which also stops it circulating to other parts of a building.

Insulation & Condensation

Many human activities – metabolism, but also washing and cooking – generate moisture. Mostly this leaves via ventilation and air leakage, but a smaller amount travels into the fabric and furnishings. The permeable materials and systems that characterise traditional construction are able to buffer humidity, absorbing and releasing moisture as conditions change. For evaporation some ventilation will be needed; otherwise, moisture will continue to build up and problems such as mould may occur.

Walls made of permeable building materials act like sponges, and will not readily absorb water through their surfaces unless they are already wet. Once wetting begins, however, the wall will absorb water more and more quickly, increasing its thermal conductivity. This also means that the wall may cool enough to allow condensation, adding more water to the system. Insulating with impermeable materials inhibits evaporation, and may cause condensation, increasing the moisture load; permeable insulation materials are therefore to be preferred. Even so, if the internal environment is too humid, or if too-thick internal insulation makes the wall too cold, condensed moisture could still accumulate; modest amounts of insulation are normally safest.

If a wall has a chronic moisture problem from this or some other source, any increase in its temperature will also increase the rate of moisture released into the interior, and thus the requirement for ventilation.

Building Work

The proposed measures may have a physical and visual impact on the building's character and integrity. The most obvious example is building services, which require distribution systems: the pipes, cables, ducts and flues. It is of concern that many services have very short lifespans; major works which may have only a very short lifespan should therefore be avoided. It is wise to reuse existing conduits wherever possible.

Building Services & Control Systems

Building services have become increasingly difficult to understand and to use, as technology has become more sophisticated and systems more complex (often in the name of energy saving). While complexity can increase the potential efficacy of services, it also increases the potential for error. It is best to avoid systems that are too complicated or hard to operate. To be effective in use, the system needs to have a strong narrative developed connecting the design intent, the user experience, and the management and maintenance requirements. The service engineers should discuss this in detail with the occupants before the Energy Plan is approved, so the narrative can be used by both parties not only during the design and specification stages, but during installation, commissioning, handover and into use. Too often the technology can come to be seen as an end in itself, while the design intent and the user experiences are forgotten.

Dealing with Heritage Assets

The historic character and significance of the building (whether or not it is designated) will affect what measures may be acceptable. Before any energy or other interventions are considered, an assessment should be carried out to determine the significance of the building, and how it might be harmed by interventions. The range and depth of the investigation and its accompanying documentation should be kept in proportion to the scale and complexity of the proposed works, and the sensitivity of the building. In some cases, it may be necessary to prepare a formal 'conservation plan'; in others, a less detailed (but still comprehensive) 'conservation statement' may suffice. If works are proposed to a listed building or other designated asset, then a written statement of justification will usually be required to support the application for consent. ⊖BASICS

The planning department of the local authority should be consulted at an early stage, and will be able to offer useful guidance on whether the proposed work will require Listed Building Consent or planning permission. They may also be able to comment on which measures are likely to prove most effective, and least risky or damaging for that type of building.

Measures to improve energy performance should follow the same guiding principles as any other type of conservation repair or intervention (see **Care & Repair**, in the main text); that is:

- consider only techniques and materials that have been demonstrated to be appropriate for the fabric of the building and its use
- interventions should be reversible, and not prejudice future interventions
- interventions should contribute to the sustainability of future management and maintenance.

Context

The appropriateness of any package of measures will vary tremendously with the context of use and operation, and its relationship to the fabric. For example, external insulation and slow-responding heating systems such as underfloor heating would be unlikely to suit a building that is intermittently occupied.

Phasing Measures

Once the most appropriate measures have been identified and formed into coherent packages, the next step is to consider how best to phase the work.

Even where every possible measure could theoretically be completed at once, a phased programme will often be preferable, because it can incorporate continuing assessment and review. This allows the Energy Plan to be adjusted in response to the gains made, and very importantly it gives time to uncover unanticipated problems. It may be possible to begin with the low- and medium-cost measures, or with a complete pilot installation in a single room. The more expensive or intrusive measures may be best left until natural opportunity points arise (when equipment has come to the end of its life, for example; or disruptive works might be timed to coincide with major repairs or alterations).

The appropriateness of a measure will also be affected by the order in which it is implemented. For example, if a new heating system is installed before the demand for heating has been reduced (by tackling sources of discomfort, behaviour and heat loss through the fabric), the chosen system will inevitably be oversized and possibly over-complicated. This may also lead to problems of efficiency and control when the demand is eventually reduced. Another example of the dangers of undertaking measures in the wrong order is leaving window improvements until after wall insulation has been introduced. This could lead to thermal bridging at reveals, and thus to problems of condensation and mould.

KEEPING THE ENERGY PLAN UNDER REVIEW

The Energy Plan must not be seen as a static entity: it should be reviewed and adjusted if necessary as work is completed, and whenever the use of the building changes or fabric alterations are being considered.

The STBA Retrofit Guidance Wheel

In 2012, a number of heritage organisations (including English Heritage, Historic Scotland, the National Trust and the Society for the Protection of Ancient Buildings [SPAB]) became concerned about the potential technical risks of energy-saving retrofits to traditionally constructed buildings, and the possible dangers to their significance and their long-term survival. They supported the formation of the Sustainable Traditional Buildings Alliance [STBA], to help coordinate research into the energy performance of standing buildings (especially those of traditional construction), their long-term behaviour post-retrofitting, and to promote a technically informed, responsible approach to energy-saving interventions in buildings.

Amongst other initiatives, the STBA has developed their Responsible Retrofit Guidance Wheel: an interactive web-based tool to help users explore measures that minimise potential risks to a dwelling's technical performance, energy performance and heritage value; identify interactions between measures; and combine measures into sensible, economic, low risk packages. It also points users to related guidance and publications. Users are asked to fill in basic contextual information (a multiple-choice version of Stage 1 of the Energy Plan). They are then presented with an interactive wheel showing measures in three groups around its circumference:

- Fabric: windows, doors, walls, roof, floors, and chimney
- Services: heat generation, heat distribution, hot water, electricity generation, lighting and ventilation
- People: documentation, user interfaces, involvement and maintenance.

When a particular sub-heading is selected, a range of measures is displayed, together with the estimated level of risk in three areas: technical performance, energy and carbon saving, and heritage. For each particular measure, the risk levels are shown on three concentric rings round the perimeter in a scale from green (minor concern), through amber (medium concern) and light red (high concern), to dark red (major concern); these colours change with context.

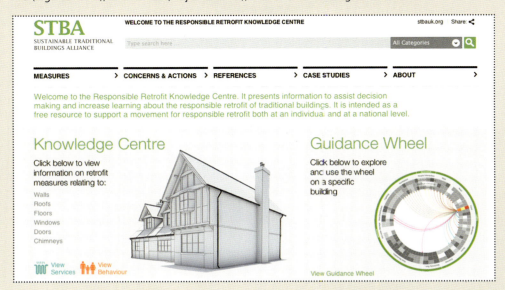

BUILDING ENVIRONMENT
SPECIAL TOPIC: Improving Energy & Carbon Performance

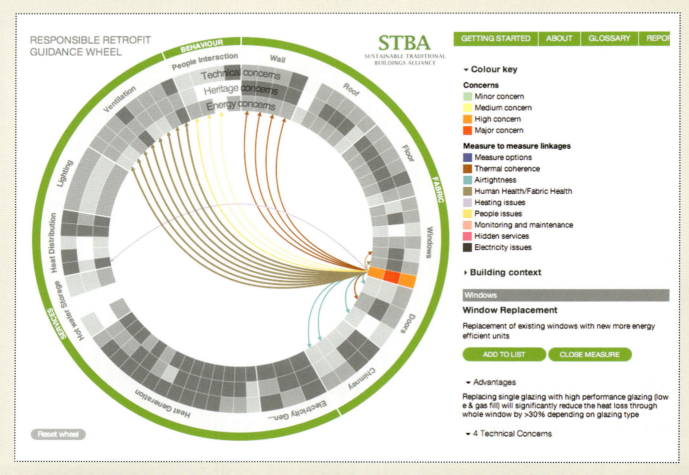

The STBA Guidance Wheel

In the example shown here, the guidance wheel is being used to look at the implications of window replacement. In this case the building of concern is historically significant, so 'replacing the windows' shows dark red (major concern); for a building of little architectural character this would change to amber. In both types of building, energy risks will show light red, because replacement often has a long payback time. Technical risk is also light red, because background ventilation might be insufficient unless appropriate arrangements are made.

The colour-coded arrows running across the centre of the wheel show how window replacement links to other issues, including ventilation and controls. These would need to be carefully considered during the process of devising a properly integrated solution.

STAGE 5: DESIGN & IMPLEMENTATION

The fifth stage of Energy Planning is to convert the Detailed Energy Plan into a coherent project for implementation. This step covers not only final selection, detailed design, specification and procurement, but also arrangements for commissioning, handover, and effective ongoing support and assessment. Detailed design and implementation is outside the scope of this **Special Topic**, but it is possible to highlight some of the issues that will need to be taken into account.

For a scheme to be successful, in the first place there will need to be adequate funding, as well as access to appropriate professional expertise and practical skills; and also sufficient time to prepare the project, obtain any necessary consents and carry out the work. Improvements that have been hastily designed, inadequately specified or badly installed and commissioned seldom perform satisfactorily, and in the worst cases can be harmful both to occupant health and the building fabric.

The more risky the action, the more its success will depend on high standards of design, detailing and workmanship. Design development must therefore pay close attention to exactly how the work will be carried out (for example, when installing insulation, exactly how the joints will be sealed and how items penetrating the insulation will be handled). The need for technical rigour may not be properly appreciated by many builders, so it is vital both to prepare very detailed specifications and – once the project begins – to ensure that all work is closely supervised. Communication is often the key: when installers appreciate the design intent, and the principles and issues critical to a good installation, they will often take pride in doing things well.

Any technical systems will need user-friendly controls that can be clearly explained to users and operators. Ideally, the function of a controller and how to use it should be readily apparent from its design and location, and explained both on paper and verbally. Since this seldom happens automatically, it must be stressed by those commissioning the works at all stages of implementation.

Achieving good results is not just about getting the design and technology right: the procurement system must carry the design intent right through to practical reality. Unfortunately designers, builders and their clients usually regard a project as complete the day it is handed over, and so do not routinely follow through into use: passing on their knowledge, learning from the occupants and discovering how the building actually performs in operation. This has been a major contributor to performance gaps. Adopting elements of handover management processes such as Soft Landings can help to improve the focus on outcomes during design and implementation, and prepare the way for effective follow-through, aftercare and feedback during Stage 6.

Managing Handover

Designers and builders are usually commissioned and paid to design and build, not to follow through beyond completion and into use. As a result, many have limited experience or understanding of how buildings actually perform in operation. This exacerbates performance gaps, not least for energy.

POST-OCCUPANCY EVALUATION

Post-Occupancy Evaluation [POE] is the process of evaluating how an occupied building is working for the first few years after construction or alteration (it is a subset of Building Performance Evaluation, which can be done at any time in the building's life). The lessons learned during the POE are used to not only improve the performance of the building itself, but also to develop better practices for future work.

A stepwise approach is normally preferable, undertaking advanced investigations only if and when necessary:

1. *Basic evaluation*
   Indicative evaluation by means of walk-through surveys, informal discussions and brief examination of records. For example, users may report parts of a building as feeling cold or draughty.
2. *Intermediate evaluation*
   Diagnostic evaluation using structured surveys, questionnaires and instrumentation. For example, infra-red photography and smoke tests might reveal excessive heat loss in places.
3. *Advanced evaluation*
   Investigative evaluation, usually concentrating on very specific issues. For example, the air infiltration rate in one area might be measured using pressurisation or tracer-gas tests.

All three levels are action-oriented, and should aim to address issues of interest to designers and specifiers rather than researchers. That said, advanced evaluations may sometimes require equipment and skills available only from research institutes or specialist consultants.

When POE first emerged in the 1960s, evaluations were generally undertaken by independent investigators having little or no connection to the companies that had worked on the building; the focus was usually on occupant satisfaction. Today the approach is more broad-based, and ideally undertaken by investigators that are in close touch with, but not dominated by, the organisations that carried out the work being evaluated. Most POEs assess technical and environmental performance as well as surveying occupants. Attempts are also being made to incorporate follow-through and feedback into the work of designers and builders, using techniques such as 'Soft Landings'.

SOFT LANDINGS

Soft Landings is a formal means of integrating outcomes into the procurement process for building work, providing a natural progression into POE and feedback. Like POE, it was initially developed for large buildings with complex engineering systems, but the basic approach can be usefully applied to the smallest and simplest retrofit project. The aim is to discover any problems with the commissioning of the new services and systems, and to help occupants find the best ways of using them.

Instead of focusing only on the weeks or months immediately before and after handover, Soft Landings is incorporated into the project from the beginning. It has five steps:

1. Briefing: the aims of the project should include a clear focus on in-use outcomes (on the part of the client as well as all members of the project team)
2. Design and implementation: management of expectations will help to ensure the project does not drift off course, and that the focus on outcomes is maintained
3. Handover: ensuring better operational readiness in the period leading up to handover
4. Initial aftercare: the first few weeks or months after handover should be used to fine tune the building and its systems, deal with snags, and enable users and operators to understand the new systems
5. Longer-term aftercare and review: assessment and adjustment should continue for the first two or three years after handover, and should ideally involve not just team members but independent BPE advisers, who will be able to provide objectivity and a wider perspective.

Studies of Soft Landings in practice have stressed the importance of client commitment from the start: only this can really bind teams together. Leadership can be provided by 'Soft Landings Champions' (members of the client, design and building team who undertake to maintain the focus on outcomes); without at least one of these, as everyone concentrates on getting the job done they can easily forget the original purpose of the project.

Up to the point of handover, there need be no additional cost, as any extra effort is rewarded by improvements in the efficiency and effectiveness of the design and construction process. Initial aftercare can also be done efficiently if well planned. The greatest difficulty is usually getting support from contractors. Longer-term aftercare and POE will need to be funded separately from the construction budget, but it can nevertheless prove very cost-effective since it helps avoid pitfalls, deliver a successful outcome, and minimise operating costs. As long as time and cost pressures are not allowed to impinge on commissioning, Soft Landings can deliver better energy performance and happier occupants.

CLOSING THE LOOP

Sharing useful information about lessons learned and outcomes (both good and bad) – not just within the project team, but to the wider building sector and beyond – is the only way to determine best practice, and fill the current gap in practical knowledge.

BUILDING ENVIRONMENT
SPECIAL TOPIC: Improving Energy & Carbon Performance

STAGE 6: RECORDING & REVIEWING

Since performance in use is never completely predictable, once part or all of an Energy Plan has been implemented, the outcomes of the measures adopted should be evaluated and the Plan reviewed accordingly.

This often-neglected stage allows adjustments to be made to improve performance, efficiency and occupant satisfaction. Even the best-intentioned interventions can have unintended consequences. The requirements and opinions of occupants will also change with time, and with experience of using the altered building and its systems. Any emerging problems can also be detected before they become serious. Participants will learn from the experience, to the benefit of the project, of future phases, and of practice generally.

Performance too may change with time: for example, as the building and the equipment ages and as its use evolves. Clear, useful feedback on performance also tends to reinforce energy-conscious behaviour amongst occupants and management.

For these reasons, some permanent means should be found for gathering and interpreting the necessary data. This could be as simple as making arrangements for monthly recording of by-fuel energy use. Routine recording of utility consumption will become easier with the arrival of smart meters. Sometimes it may be useful to install monitoring equipment: for example, to check where the energy is going, or to record the internal environment or the moisture content of the fabric.

PRACTICALITIES

This final section reviews some of the issues that commonly arise when considering energy- and carbon-saving opportunities of different types, including the problems that might be encountered, the measures for improvement and the possible downsides. It starts by considering simple opportunities for improving the fabric, including reinstating and enhancing existing features. It then provides more details (including an introductory discussion and a series of checklists) for reducing the energy used by services (heating, ventilation, air conditioning and hot water systems) and other equipment, for interventions to improve the thermal performance of the envelope, and finally looks at some issues regarding lower-carbon energy supplies.

Technology and best practice are evolving rapidly, so only general guidelines are given here. When preparing an Energy Plan, it is important to check the latest advice. Sources of up-to-date information are given in the **Useful Websites** and **Further Reading** boxes at the end of this **Special Topic**.

There are many proprietary products designed to cope with difficult situations, such as draughtproofing metal-framed windows. These can be extremely helpful, but technical details and the long-term behaviour of the product under similar contexts should always be examined with care before final decisions are made.

SIMPLE FABRIC IMPROVEMENTS

REPAIRING & ENHANCING EXISTING FEATURES

The energy performance of buildings can usually be improved simply by making repairs. It may also be possible to reinstate or upgrade original energy-saving features that have fallen into disuse. Sometimes such features might be added where they did not originally exist; measures of this kind will tend to work with the building rather than against it.

CONTROLLING INFILTRATION & AIR MOVEMENT

Air infiltration can account for as much as half a building's loss of conditioned air. Traditional measures for controlling infiltration and air movement include draught lobbies, heavy curtains, shutters, screens, or simply closing doors between rooms. All also help to control noise and dust.

Infiltration through windows may be largely resolvable by repair: this can halve the building's loss of heat.

Doors and windows can be draughtproofed using any of a broad range of products, from simple do-it-yourself strip systems to more elaborate but highly effective draughtproofing that demands professional installation.

Other gaps in the envelope may also need attention, including cracks between the reveals and the frames of windows and doors, and holes made for pipes, ducts and cables. Air leaks can often be found in hidden corners, such as cupboards, ducts and plenums, where the finish may be of poor standard. Permeable lime-based renders and plasters make an excellent air barrier.

➔ **MORTARS**

Disused flues can be another source of unnecessary ventilation and heat loss. If this is the case, a 'chimney balloon' can be inserted for the winter and removed if necessary in summer, when ventilation may be desirable. Alternatively, a register plate fitted with openable vents can be installed within the flue above the fireplace, as was common in Victorian and Edwardian fireplaces. Chimney-pot caps can help to reduce air infiltration as well as rain penetration; these should be ventilated to prevent condensation problems (see **Care & Repair**, in the main text).

If external doors are opened frequently, draught lobbies may be a solution, but they do require considerable space. In public buildings where automatic doors are required, the lobbies would ideally need to be carefully designed or at least 6 m deep, to avoid the inner and outer doors being opened at once.

Air curtains (a high velocity jet of air from ceiling to floor provides a barrier while the door is open) are expensive to do well, and may not function under all wind conditions. Most installations found in shops and offices are not true air curtains at all, but door heaters; these may improve comfort, but will add to the amount of heating required and thus to the energy use.

Heating does not necessarily increase comfort. Warmed air will rise, creating currents that pull cold air from elsewhere. The natural response to discomfort from draughts is usually to turn the heating up, which may well exacerbate the problem.

Tall spaces are particularly prone to issues of this type. For example, at Peterborough Cathedral one element of the heating was Victorian gurney stoves, converted to gas in the 20th century. This thermal image of the stoves in action shows that they were reaching surface temperatures in excess of 160°C, but were having little warming effect except in the immediate vicinity (note that the heating of the 1.5-m thick wall can be detected on the exterior).

As the heating of the vault suggests, this system led to severe draughts through the Cathedral.

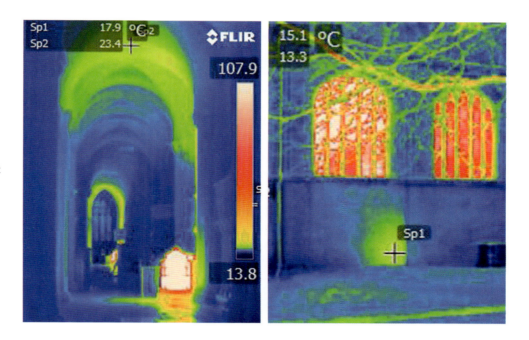

ISOLATING CONDITIONED AREAS

To reduce the energy used to condition spaces, interiors were traditionally subdivided with permanent or movable partitions. The modern fashion for removing doors, walls and even floors undermines this. Larger volume spaces are also more prone to draughts, which will often be exacerbated by heating-related convection currents.

Great improvements can be made by simply replacing doors, or by subdividing open interiors into conditioned and unconditioned areas. It may sometimes be worth taking isolation further: for example, partitioning off an occupied area, or insulating the internal walls, floors and ceilings surrounding it (this may only be possible if other major work is being done at the same time). For suspended timber floors and stud partitions, cellulose fibre insulation can sometimes be blown in through small holes. The material has the added advantage of being permeable and moisture-absorbing, so will help to avoid any condensation problems. It is important to keep maintenance and care to a high standard, however, since if it gets wet this material will permanently collapse.

The unconditioned areas may need a certain amount of ventilation and perhaps heating to keep them dry.

Conditioned areas may also be isolated with buffer zones such as draught lobbies and corridors, or even conservatories. The best approach in cold weather is to keep the heating off in the buffer spaces and the doors shut, though sometimes a small amount of background heat may be required to reduce contrasts and avoid condensation. Heating conservatories, even if they are double-glazed, greatly increases heat losses.

BUILDING ENVIRONMENT
SPECIAL TOPIC: Improving Energy & Carbon Performance

REDUCING RADIANT HEAT LOSSES

Radiant heat losses can be reduced – making occupants more comfortable with less heating – by interposing lightweight, fast-responding materials between the people, and the cold surfaces of walls, windows and floors. Traditionally this was done either with materials that could be put away in summer (curtains, shutters, movable screens, tapestries and painted cloths, and carpets), or with permanent elements such as wooden wainscotting or panelling. This is still a very effective approach.

The thermal performance of panelling can sometimes be improved by insulating behind it, but permeable materials should be used to prevent trapping water in the wall.

Radiant heating panels are also sometimes a good choice for improving local comfort. For example, low-power panels can be placed under desks, and controlled by push-button timers that give perhaps an hour of heat before needing to be reset.

PROVIDING PROTECTION FROM SOLAR GAIN

Solar shading is most effective if it is external: once the radiation has got through the window, it can be intercepted by a blind, but most of the heat will stay in the room. Awnings, blinds and shutters can be used to reduce unwanted heat gains; deciduous plants can shade in summer, but in winter will let sunlight reach the building, reducing the requirement for artificial heating.

IMPROVING USAGE & CONTROL

Occupants can often save considerable amounts of energy by using the building a bit differently: the need for heating, cooling and lighting will depend on what they are doing, what they are wearing, and the equipment they use. The effectiveness or otherwise of the building services will play a strong part, as will their ability to control other factors such as the windows, the lighting and the water taps. Physiology and psychology are also important: it is well known that people can tolerate much colder air temperatures if their feet feel warm, for example; and radiant heaters are often felt to be more effective if they glow red.

It is worth thoroughly exploring behaviours. Some building users will be very willing to change habits or experiment with new options, and although others will point out the many factors that are stopping them making improvements (for example, dress codes, management practices, or problems with the controls on building services), this too will be helpful since it will give strong pointers to where action might be taken.

Furniture can also be used to help keep people comfortable: traditionally, for example, settles and wing chairs not only added to the insulation provided by clothing, but collected and reflected the radiant heat from the fireplace. Heated seats, carpets and local radiant panels can be an alternative to strongly heating the air, especially in spaces such as churches where trying to heat the air is likely to prove difficult and expensive, and encourage draughts.

IMPROVING BUILDING SERVICES

Heating, ventilation, air conditioning [HVAC] and hot water systems are the largest energy users in most buildings. These services and their associated controls are composed of three elements: the main plant (for example, the boiler), the units at the point of delivery (such as the radiators) and the distribution systems (the pipes, ducts and valves). They affect the fabric (both because of the physical interventions needed to make them work, and because of the interior environment they help to create), and in turn are influenced by its requirements.

By their nature, the HVAC systems can have subtle but important effects on comfort, and hence on energy demand. For example, poorly designed systems may cause local airflows that will be interpreted as draughts, while well-designed systems can counteract the discomfort caused by radiant heat loss or gain (see **Care & Repair: Conditioning the Indoor Air**, in the main text).

To work efficiently, services need to be well matched to the characteristics of the building and the needs of its users. It is therefore important to try to reduce the energy demands placed upon the systems as much as possible before beginning to alter the systems themselves. Good maintenance is also vital, to ensure that the systems are always operating to their maximum efficiency and that manufacturers' recommendations are being followed.

Building services – heating, air-conditioning and artificial ventilation – are critically linked to the building occupancy. In both design and operation, systems will need to respond closely to the patterns of use and the needs of the occupants.

BUILDING ENVIRONMENT
SPECIAL TOPIC: Improving Energy & Carbon Performance

HEATING & COOLING

The modern expectation has been that central systems can and should provide near-uniform year-round conditions throughout a building, but this is increasingly being questioned. Many other options are available.

Even where the system is centralised, it is seldom that all spaces in the building would need to be heated or cooled to the same level. Individual room controls should therefore be considered. These can range from simple thermostatic radiator valves [TRVs] that reduce the flow of water as the temperature rises toward the chosen setting, to more sophisticated electronic devices. It is important to provide the right amount of local control, making it easy to use, but limiting the opportunities for wastage or inappropriate settings: this needs careful thought. Temperature controls will need to be intelligently positioned; certainly well away from any direct sources of heat or cold.

Where heating boilers are used, it must be made impossible for them to operate unnecessarily (for example, firing up or circulating hot water when there is no demand). Suitable indoor and outdoor thermostatic controls can allow for this. 'Temperature compensation' can also be considered: the temperature of the circulating water is lowered as it becomes warmer outside, which gives the double benefit of reducing the chance of overheating and increasing the efficiency of modern condensing boilers.

Conservation Heating

In important historic buildings, the priority may not be occupant comfort, but rather the preservation of the fabric and the contents. In this case, heating might be used to control the relative humidity rather than the temperature.

This is the principle of the 'conservation heating' method used by the National Trust and others to protect their historic houses, and it is feasible because most of these are shut to the public in winter: with conservation heating the building will be cold in winter and warm in summer (although always kept in the range of 5–22°C). Winter temperatures will commonly be only 5°C or so warmer than the exterior, so supplementary heating may need to be provided for staff in some areas.

There is little argument for trying to heat the air to more than 18–20°C, or to cool it to less than 25°C, and in summer this temperature range can be extended if local fans are used. The cooling effect of fans comes from air moving over the body – the fan itself in fact adds a small amount of heat – so they can and should always be turned off when nobody is present.

Supplementary local heating is very flexible, and (for example) fast-responding radiant heaters in spaces used only occasionally, or in occupied parts of larger spaces, can give substantial savings in the energy used for heating. On the other hand, electricity is relatively expensive and carbon-intensive, so fast-responding radiant heaters will need to be operated economically. A good approach is to use runback timers, which will switch on at the press of a button and off after a pre-set period. The timer should, however, incorporate a manual 'off' switch.

Where thermally massive buildings are in intermittent use, radiant heat losses to the cold surfaces will considerably reduce thermal comfort, even if the heating is fast-responding and the air temperature nominally satisfactory.

In warm weather, many buildings become too hot in the afternoon because of the heat trapped in the fabric the previous night. The remedy is to arrange night ventilation, and ensure that it is used. This may require some discussion with insurance companies, and the ventilation will need to be secured against entry.

HOT WATER

Most buildings in England use their central-heating boilers to generate hot tap water as well, either in a storage cylinder or on demand with a 'combi' boiler. Alternatives are electric-storage or instantaneous water heaters (these are sometimes also used in addition to a central-heating boiler); although gas would be a cheaper and less carbon-intensive alternative, electric water heaters can be efficient, particularly for remote outlets that a central system could not serve economically.

The simplest and cheapest way of saving energy used to heat water is simply to use less, either by behavioural change or by removing the supply from outlets where hot water is not necessary. Other low-cost measures include changing to low-output shower heads and putting flow restrictors on taps for which the supplies are too generous. Storage vessels and distribution pipework should be well insulated. Good controls are also important, including linkages to ensure that boilers switch off when hot water is not required.

Thermostats should be adjusted thoughtfully, to maintain water at the temperature required for use but no more (though this must be hot enough to prevent *Legionella* problems: see the **Special Topic: Buildings & Human Health**).

Higher-cost measures include solar heating: appropriately sized panels can typically meet over half a building's hot water demand across a year. Solar heating is particularly effective outside the heating season (when heating boilers have nothing else to do, and so run inefficiently). In some instances it may be possible to install a supplementary heat exchanger that uses the heat in the boiler-flue gases – which would otherwise be wasted – to preheat the incoming cold water.

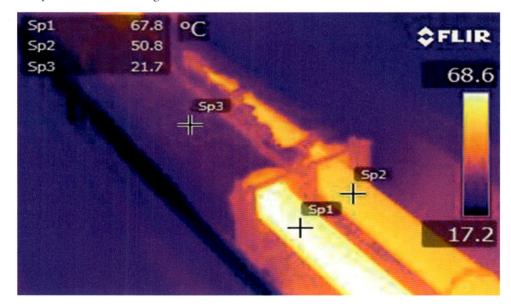

Insulating ('lagging') of hot-water pipes – whether these are used for water supply or heating – is critical to conserving energy, as shown by this thermal image of the heat lost through damaged lagging. Insulation also reduces the risk of heat damage to fragile building fabric and fittings.

BUILDING ENVIRONMENT
SPECIAL TOPIC: Improving Energy & Carbon Performance

VENTILATION

One of the simplest ways to ventilate a building is to open a window; of itself this uses no energy, though heating or cooling energy may be lost. The development of the counterbalanced sash provided sophisticated control: the window was in a single plane that permitted any design of curtain, blind or shutter to be used; everything was possible from a very slight flow to a full open pane; the air could be directed over the body or above the head; and if the window was open both at the top and bottom, natural buoyancy effects could be exploited. They had a propensity to leak air when closed, but this can now be addressed by modern draught seals. Sash windows must always be kept in good working condition if the occupants are to take full advantage of these helpful characteristics. Casements – old or new – are less flexible, but stays can be used to give some measure of control. ⮕GLASS

Where buildings that have been retrofitted to achieve high standards of insulation and airtightness, or where indoor conditions are set by central control and management systems, windows will usually be kept shut, so mechanical ventilation will be needed to remove the excess moisture generated by activities within the building and maintain acceptable indoor air quality.

Many modern building-service systems are specifically designed not to allow local control of ventilation, but the ability to open and close windows may allow occupants to be more comfortable with less expenditure of heating and cooling energy.

Mechanical ventilation with heat recovery [MVHR] systems can reduce the associated energy losses by using the warm air extracted from the building to pre-heat the fresh air drawn in from the exterior. These range from through-the-wall room units to components of more elaborate HVAC system.

A typical domestic MVHR system comprises an electrically powered fan to draw air ducted in from kitchens and bathrooms and exhaust it outside via a heat exchanger. A second fan draws air in via a filter and the heat exchanger, to be ducted to outlets in living areas and bedrooms. MVHR units can be quite bulky, and if they are poorly selected or not ideally located, noise may sometimes be a problem; they are then at risk of being switched off by occupants. Whether or not an MVHR system saves energy depends largely on its efficiency and operation and how airtight the building is: tests have shown that the benefit of heat recovery is not significant except under high standards of airtightness (an air permeability of not more than 3 m^3/m^2 per hour at a pressure of 50 pascals, and ideally less than 1 m^3/m^2 per hour).

CONTROL SYSTEMS

Building services can be theoretically made very efficient with centralised, automated control, but this demands good design, installation, commissioning, documentation and user interfaces as well as informed and responsive management. This sadly is rare; and even where conditions are ideal, centralised systems can still waste energy and cause dissatisfaction if they have not taken sufficient account of the occupants.

If centralised systems are to be made to work, there are a number of important questions to ask. Do all occupants get the services they need? What happens if they find themselves uncomfortable and would like it to be hotter, cooler, fresher, brighter, darker or less glary? If needs are not properly accommodated, services may be provided efficiently but too liberally, or occupants may take actions that undermine the design intent (such as leaving blinds down when good-quality glare-free daylight is available). Buildings with simpler, more responsive, controls often prove to use less energy in the long run.

Even where an appropriate control strategy has been devised, the system will need to be clearly explained to the building users. In public and commercial buildings, the management must also be willing and able to respond quickly to problems and complaints. A good approach is to follow a Soft Landings strategy: that is, have a clearly developed design intent, an effective handover, and a period of aftercare and post-occupancy evaluation, to fine-tune the system and take proper account of occupant feedback.

The table on the following page presents some of the critical issues that will need to be considered about the building services when preparing an Energy Plan, organised by the three elements that together make up every building-service system: main plant, point of delivery, and distribution system.

CHECKLIST: REDUCING THE ENERGY USED BY THE BUILDING SERVICES

MAIN PLANT (& GENERAL ISSUES)	POINT OF DELIVERY	DISTRIBUTION SYSTEMS
ORIGINAL HEATING & COOLING SYSTEMS		
What were the original arrangements (for example, boilers or warm air furnaces)? Are they still present? What is their use and condition? Are they of historic interest?	What were the original arrangements (such as fireplaces, radiators and warm air outlets)? Are they still present? What is their use and condition, including any chimneys and flues? Is there any natural ventilation? Is it appropriate? How good is it at controlling air quality, moisture and overheating?	What were the original arrangements (that is, pipes, ducts, plenums)? Are they still present? What is their use and condition? Are they of historic interest?
HVAC SYSTEMS		
What are the current sources of heating, cooling and mechanical ventilation? What is their age, condition and capacity, and efficiency? Are they appropriate for current and future requirements? If not, what would be? Is humidification or dehumidification used anywhere? If so, review its need, function and appropriateness. If curators request conditions for objects that would threaten the building, consider alternatives such as buffered display cases.	How is heating (and, where appropriate, cooling and mechanical ventilation) provided? To what standards? Is it effective? Are outlets appropriately located, sized and in good condition? Is supplementary heating used (woodstoves or electric heaters)? Are there opportunities for more localised systems in some places (such as radiant panels)?	How is air, heat and cooling distributed? Where appropriate, the arrangements of pumps, pipes and ducts should be outlined. Are any items of ventilation plant installed? If so, what do they do, what condition are they in, and how are they controlled? Is this appropriate and effective? Are pipes and ducts adequately insulated? What is the state of the filters? How often are they changed?
HVAC CONTROLS & OPERATIONS		
What are the normal operating schedules and settings for each system and item of plant? How do they relate to building occupancy? What changes are made to suit weekly, seasonal and out-of-hours uses? Who does this, where and how? How easy is it? Is the control regime appropriate to the use of the building and the potential of the plant? Can users understand the controls? Is the main plant efficiently controlled? Who operates the controls? Could this be improved?	How are conditions in the rooms controlled, and to what levels? Who makes the adjustments? Are the settings and times of operation appropriate? Are there any problems in relation to service, comfort, efficiency, moisture and condensation? Can people understand the controls? How could systems and settings be improved? Is there scope for using local heaters or fans to improve personal comfort, and reduce the energy used by central systems?	What is the pattern of use of the building? Is the system 'zoned' to suit patterns of use? If so, is it operated accordingly? Could it be? Would local systems be more efficient than central systems, including for out-of-hours use?
HOT-WATER SYSTEMS		
Is hot water provided by the main heating plant, a separate central hot water system or point-of-use systems like electric instantaneous or storage? If by central heating boilers, is the system efficient in summer? Older systems can be very wasteful. What is the system's age, condition and capacity and efficiency? How well is it insulated? What are the temperature and time settings? Are they appropriate? Do they comply with requirements for bacteriological control? Is the system appropriate? How could it be improved? Is there scope for solar heating?	Are the taps and other hot water outlets in satisfactory condition, without evidence of drips? Are all the hot water outlets necessary, or could some be cold water only? Is the time taken to get hot water and its temperature satisfactory? Are flow rates from taps, shower heads and so on sufficient or excessive? If excessive, consider installing low-flow outlets or flow limiters. Do any outlets require an elevated water temperature (for example, in catering kitchens)? Might these be better served by an independent or a booster system?	What is the configuration and condition of the hot-water pipework system? Are there any local supplementary or point-of-use water heaters? Is the layout compact, or are there long lengths of pipe to some outlets? If so, consider local point-of-use heaters, particularly for remote outlets with only occasional use. Are the pipes of an appropriate size (too big may increase warm-up times and heat losses) and properly insulated?

OTHER ENERGY-USING EQUIPMENT

Most other energy-using equipment is electrical, and much of it can be considered by unit and by room, rather than as integrated systems. Its consumption can often be estimated by multiplying the load in kilowatts by the hours it will be in use over a year, but this calculation must be applied with circumspection, because:

- the actual load is seldom that quoted in the documentation provided by the manufacturer (particularly for electronic equipment, where the numbers quoted are often much higher than the actual requirements in practice)
- much equipment has variable power requirements, so a figure for average usage must be determined over a typical week or operating cycle; fortunately, useful information is becoming available on the internet, and appliance loads can also be monitored using low-cost plug-through meters
- an increasing amount of equipment (for example, communications equipment, lighting control systems and computer equipment) stays connected continually; therefore, annual energy use can be high, even when the item uses only a small amount of power.

When estimating rather than measuring, it helps to split the estimate into three time periods: heavy use, light use, and nights and weekends. Some buildings and end-uses may require more time periods (for example, holiday times in schools and seasonal times for lighting).

If replacement of services or appliances with more efficient models is being considered, the whole-life cost of the proposed changes must be taken into account. Lower-energy equipment must still be manufactured and maintained, and the equipment it replaces must be disposed of. Sometimes the best approach is to delay replacement until the existing equipment comes to the end of its life, and then choose the most efficient replacement.

LIGHTING

The European Union is phasing out tungsten and tungsten-halogen lamps. Choosing replacements for these lamps – or indeed any lamps – can be challenging, given the variety of products on offer and how quickly new products are arriving. Some simple rules established by lighting engineers can be a helpful guide:

- Use fluorescent or LED light fittings for all ceiling, wall-mounted and portable lights that need to be on for more than two hours every day.
- Replace incandescent lamps with fluorescent or LED equivalents, but only where the fitting can accommodate the new lamp, and give acceptable levels of light output, light distribution and colour rendering. For example, when replacing reflector lamps in recessed downlights, too much light from a globe lamp may be absorbed; while some LED reflector lights may be too weak, too harsh or have too high a colour temperature, making their light seem too blue.
- Replace any fluorescent fittings over 15 years old with efficient units with electronic control gear.

Colour temperature will have an impact on efficiency: brighter white LEDs will illuminate a space more effectively than warmer-coloured lamps. It is also important to be aware that redundancy is becoming a serious issue, as the rapid changes in technology quickly render some types of lamp (and even their associated fittings and cabling) obsolete. This greatly increases whole-life energy costs, so it is best to choose systems that are simple and flexible: for example, using standard patterns of lamp.

CHECKLIST: REDUCING THE ENERGY USED BY LIGHTING

QUESTIONS TO ASK	POSSIBLE MEASURES	COMMENTS
DAYLIGHT		
How well daylit are the spaces? Is the daylight used effectively, or do the electric lights stay on? Are issues such as glare and solar gain restricting use of daylight? Are furnishings and so forth well arranged in relation to the daylight available, and to minimise glare?	Can occupants and management be encouraged to make better use of daylight? Can daylight be improved: for example, by making sure blinds are open in the morning, by providing better blinds, or by redirecting daylight with mirrors or white-painted surfaces?	Is the lighting well-located in relation to the way the space is being used? Try to operate lights in relation to use, availability of daylight and other restrictions. Blinds and window films can be used to reduce glare from the upper parts of windows, and redirect light to the ceiling
INTERIOR LIGHTING		
What types and numbers of light fittings are there? What are the types and ratings of the lamps? How long are the lights operated, and under what conditions? Are illuminance levels satisfactory, poor or excessive?	Lamp replacement can be a good low-cost measure. Replacement of fittings may not be cost-effective, unless the fitting needs replacing or is used a lot: it is important to be sure that replacement is really necessary	Take care: new installations can often be over-lit. Take care when considering replacement lamps and fittings; some have shortcomings in extended warm-up times, illuminance, light distribution, colour temperature, glare or service life. Where possible try out samples first; mock-ups will soon reveal potential problems
LIGHTING CONTROL		
Is the lighting controlled at the point of use (task lighting) locally by room, or more centrally? Does room control allow for a variety of settings? Are lighting controls well-located and appropriately labelled? Are automatic controls of any kind provided?	Consider local lighting, rather than lighting whole spaces, particularly where occupancy is light or patchy. Manual light switching related to room use and daylight availability will suit many spaces where occupants can be in control. Presence detection can be useful in situations where people would not normally be able or expected to switch the lights on and off	A good general rule is to have a manual ON switch, and both an automatic and manual OFF switch
EXTERIOR LIGHTING		
What types and numbers of light fittings are there? What are the types and ratings of the lamps? How generous is the lighting? How is it controlled?	Review efficiency of lamps, times of operation and illuminance levels. Can the lit area be reduced, or switched using presence-detectors?	Some low-cost fittings (such as tungsten halogen) are high users of energy. Neighbours may dislike switching by presence detectors

APPLIANCES & OTHER EQUIPMENT

Electrical equipment in buildings is proliferating. Much is selected and specified with little regard to its energy use; questions are often dismissed with phrases such as *"it uses less than a 100-W light bulb"* (in fact, a 100-W lamp left on will use 876 kWh over a year, which is a quarter the annual electricity use of a typical UK household). It is important to keep asking awkward questions, seeking information on projected energy use or monitoring items of equipment (perhaps with simple, low-cost 13-A plug-through meters).

Many specialists share the lack of focus on energy: the assumptions made by building-services engineers, and the advice given by catering and information-technology suppliers and specialists, may be inaccurate and misleading. It may therefore be necessary to obtain independent advice, particularly when considering large installations such as catering kitchens, server rooms, and information-and-communications systems.

CHECKLIST: REDUCING THE ENERGY USED BY APPLIANCES & OTHER EQUIPMENT

QUESTIONS TO ASK	POSSIBLE MEASURES	COMMENTS
SECURITY, IT & COMMUNICATION SYSTEMS		
What control, security, communications and alarm systems are there? Does lighting have to be kept for security purposes or to use cameras?	Consider higher-sensitivity security systems, and low-energy security lighting with presence detection	All these systems tend to operate around-the-clock; some need not (for example, non-emergency telephone and wifi systems when the building is unoccupied)
KITCHEN APPLIANCES		
What equipment is there? Is it appropriate and efficient? How is it operated? Is it switched on, or does it stay on unnecessarily? Do vending machines stay on when the building is unoccupied?	Replace inefficient items, and improve controls and operating practices. Hot-water boilers may be fitted with timers, but are they used? For vending machines, consider special purpose timers based on occupancy	Commercial catering equipment is frequently inefficient and operated too liberally, with everything being turned on first thing. Ventilation systems can be inefficient. Catering specialists can often over-specify requirements; seek an adviser who understands both catering and energy saving
OTHER ELECTRICAL EQUIPMENT		
Electrically powered devices are proliferating, many of which are left on all the time, if only in standby mode. Is the equipment necessary? Is it efficient? Is it left on unnecessarily?	Review the energy impacts when purchasing or being supplied with equipment. Make sure equipment is switched off when it is not required	Energy-use information is available from EU energy-labelling schemes and on comparison websites
SPECIAL AREAS & END-USES		
	Some buildings contain special items with very high-energy uses; for example, computer server rooms: these offer substantial opportunities for improvement in equipment selection, operation and with the associated building services such as air conditioning	Do not rely on suppliers, building professionals, or even technology consultants, for advice on the efficient specification and operation of the technology itself; specialist expertise is required which understands both the technology and its energy performance

BUILDING ENVIRONMENT
SPECIAL TOPIC: Improving Energy & Carbon Performance

IMPROVING THE BUILDING ENVELOPE

If heat from the interior is being lost into or through the fabric, more energy may have to be expended to keep the interior conditions acceptably warm. There are four principal factors that affect the performance of the building envelope:

- *Air leakage*

  In severe cases air leakage can account for half the heat loss from a building. Draughtproofing will often offer the simplest and most immediate potential for improvement, provided that the required amount of ventilation is maintained.

- *Thermal resistance*

  Low thermal resistance allows heat to travel quickly between the interior and exterior; for this reason, insulation is probably the most widely advocated retrofit measure.

- *Thermal inertia*

  Massive structures stabilise temperatures and can be relatively good insulators.

- *Radiant heat exchange*

  Materials able to easily absorb radiant heat can make occupants uncomfortable.

All of these factors may come into play. Looking at a problem such as overheating, causes could include low thermal inertia, insufficient ventilation, and high solar or internal heat gains (for example, if safety, security or noise has restricted window opening, and consequently ventilation).

To reduce energy loss, it is vital to understand the underlying causes. For example, if the problem is heat being absorbed into the fabric, options include lining the walls and floor with materials that resist heat transfer (that is, act as an insulator between the air and the surface), such as wood and fabric, or a proprietary insulating material.

Discomfort from draughts and loss of conditioned indoor air via leaks through the envelope were traditionally dealt with in various ways, not least fabric repairs.

Left: *Portières* (door curtains) were popular in Victorian and earlier periods, and can still be a very effective solution, blocking leaks through (for example) the letterbox, as well as through the frame.

Right: Draught lobbies are an excellent way of preventing the loss of both heating and cooling energy. As energy became cheaper, many were converted to living space and heated, but great benefits can be obtained by returning them to their original purpose.

INCREASING THE THERMAL RESISTANCE

The envelope's thermal inertia can either help or hinder temperature control. Massive structures will stabilise interior conditions, and thick solid walls can be good insulators; but to bring the air in such a structure up to a higher temperature than the building achieves naturally may demand continuous heating.

Overheating is a potential problem that is often forgotten, despite the risk of increased temperatures due to climate change. It can sometimes be a problem for buildings with thick solid walls if internal insulation has been installed to allow heating to higher air temperatures when the building is occupied only intermittently. This can increase the risk of summer overheating, but may be moderated in buildings with brick internal walls or solid floors, or even thick layers of lime plaster on stud walls.

INSULATION

Insulation to increase the thermal resistance of the envelope is probably the most widely advocated retrofit measure, and can mean many things, from low-risk insulation of roof spaces at ceiling level to risky internal and external solid-wall insulation.

In many cases, a better understanding of how the envelope is behaving, and of the causes of occupant discomfort, may point to alternative approaches to minimising energy use for conditioning the building interior.

To make feasible the riskier forms of insulation (such as wall insulation, or insulation applied directly under roof coverings), the insulation materials must be installed in such a way as to avoid creating thermal bridges or condensation problems, or trapping water from other sources. Ventilation will need to be able to quickly remove moist air from kitchens, bathrooms, laundries and other wet areas to stop it moving into other areas of the building, and heating must generally be provided in all rooms to prevent condensation problems if water vapour does migrate.

It can be very difficult to meet these criteria in existing buildings. Although modern construction makes use of the damp-proof membranes and air- and vapour-control layers recommended for insulation installations, these can have variable results, and they integrate very poorly with traditional construction (this is discussed extensively in the main text). Adding such elements without sufficient thought may lead to trouble in all types of building, including modern hollow-wall construction: they can trap or concentrate moisture that previously evaporated harmlessly, introduce new routes for water ingress, or create opportunities for condensation within the fabric or on surfaces that are less well insulated, and therefore colder. The insulation itself can conceal moisture problems until they are well advanced.

Before deciding to retrofit more challenging insulation measures, it is important to be absolutely sure that they are not only required and cost-effective, but that all their risks are well understood and well managed. Any existing problems (such as rain penetration or defective drainage) must be resolved first, and excellent future maintenance must be guaranteed. In critical locations, it is worth considering installing time-of-wetness sensors attached to an alarm, or perhaps to monitor the moisture within the wall, to give an early warning if problems do occur.

Simple Monitoring of Moisture in Walls

Retrofitting insulation to walls, especially solid walls, can lead to moisture accumulation from condensation, or make it more difficult for water entering the wall from other sources such as leaks to disperse. It may also conceal the evidence of the problem, preventing it being dealt with. Where such risks have been identified, it is worth considering installing moisture sensors, so non-intrusive checks can be made. The results will be most valuable if moisture levels have also been determined before improvements were carried out.

One simple, low-cost method of monitoring how the wall is behaving is to log the electrical resistance of any structural timbers on the cold (outdoor) side of internal insulation; for instance, wall plates or the ends of built-in floor joists. Pairs of stainless-steel screws are driven into the wood, parallel with the grain and 20–25 mm apart. If there are no accessible structural members, simple moisture sensors can be made from small blocks of pine (typically 25 × 45 × 5 mm-thick) installed on the wall surface, behind the insulation.

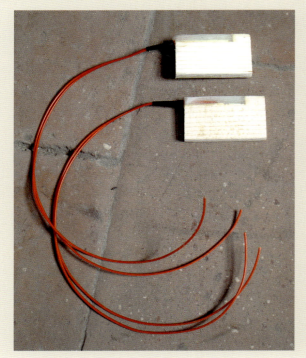

Each pair of screws (or pins) is wired to a terminal block in a convenient location. There, resistance readings can either be checked from time to time with a moisture meter, or recorded by a datalogger. The absolute readings are less important than the pattern of readings over time, which should reveal if moisture contents have started to rise. A long-term and continuing upward trend would suggest that water is accumulating, giving early warning of the need for investigation (**Assessing the Building Environment**, in the main text, gives more information on monitoring moisture contents).

Moisture sensors made from small pine blocks. Each block contains a pair of embedded electrodes which are connected to a data logger, or to a terminal block where moisture can be monitored with a resistance moisture meter.

Heat Transfer Rates & U-Values

The heat transfer coefficient through building elements, commonly called the 'U-value', is expressed in W/m^{2}K. U-values are calculated by adding the thermal resistances of all the components that make up the element, and taking the reciprocal to provide a measure of heat transmission. The higher the U-value the poorer will be the thermal performance of the building envelope. Calculation procedures and typical reference values can be found in sources such as *CIBSE Guide A*, but as *in-situ* measurements are beginning to reveal, published values do not necessarily correspond well with the behaviour of the materials and construction actually present. More often than not, walls in traditionally constructed buildings perform better than initially calculated. The reasons for this include:

- *Differences in materials properties*
  For example, the thermal conductivity of bricks from different buildings have been found to vary by a factor of three; published values tend to be conservative.
- *Details of the construction*
  Lime mortars and plasters in particular may account for more of the wall than commonly assumed. Real walls contain hidden materials and voids, which may even be acting as insulating airspaces.
- *Variation of thermal conductivity with moisture levels*
  The thermal conductivity of permeable materials increases as they become wetter (water is an excellent conductor of heat). In some buildings monitored, very dry walls have been found to have U-values as low as 0.6.
- *U-values depend on the environmental conditions*
  Values are not constant, but will change with different exterior and interior temperatures. For this reason, tables may give values for different levels of exposure.

PUBLISHED & MEASURED U-VALUES

	PUBLISHED*	MEASURED	REGULATIONS
PITCHED ROOF (NO INSULATION)	2.3		0.18 (0.25)
PITCHED ROOF (COLD ROOF; 50 mm INSULATION)	0.71		0.18 (0.25)
PITCHED ROOF (COLD ROOF; 200 mm INSULATION)	0.21	0.16 ± 0.30	0.18 (0.25)
FLAT ROOF (NO INSULATION)	2.3		0.18 (0.25)
FLAT ROOF (50 mm INSULATION)	0.71		0.18 (0.25)
FLAT ROOF (WARM ROOF)	0.23		0.18 (0.25)
DRY BRICK WALL (DENSE BRICK + PLASTER)	2.1	2.1 ± 0.2	0.26 (0.35)
DRY BRICK WALL (POROUS BRICK + PLASTER)	2.1	1.3 ± 0.3	0.26 (0.35)
SUSPENDED TIMBER FLOOR (100-mm INSULATION)		0.32 ± 0.30	0.22 (0.25)
WINDOW (SINGLE GLAZED)	4.8	4.40 ± 0.30	1.4 (2.0)
WINDOW + SHUTTERS		2.0 ± 0.3	1.4 (2.0)
WINDOW + LOW-E SECONDARY GLAZING		2.0 ± 0.3	1.4 (2.0)
WINDOW + LOW-E SECONDARY GLAZING + SHUTTERS		1.4 ± 0.3	1.4 (2.0)
WINDOW + VACUUM SECONDARY GLAZING		1.0 ± 0.3	1.4 (2.0)

* Values taken from *CIBSE Guide A*

The table gives some typical values for existing, upgraded and new construction under normal exposure (published values also include sheltered and severe exposures). Published figures are often taken to two decimal places, and unfortunately do not include error values; this is highly misleading since U-values are so variable.

The Building Regulations give notational and limiting U-values (shown in brackets) for new dwellings. It is possible for existing buildings to approach these values for windows and pitched roofs by using quite straightforward, reversible measures, but there is still a dearth of measured data.

BUILDING ENVIRONMENT
SPECIAL TOPIC: Improving Energy & Carbon Performance

Types of Insulation Material

Still air has a low thermal conductivity, and therefore has the potential to be an excellent insulator; but if there are convection currents these will transfer heat. For this reason, most insulation materials trap air in pores or voids to prevent convection. There are four main types:

- *Permeable plasters and renders*
  Traditional materials like lime plasters and renders are permeable and long-lived; they also make effective air barriers. Additives such as hemp fibre can significantly increase the insulating effect.

- *Natural fibrous materials*
  Natural products like sheepswool or wood fibre (which is available as loose-fill or made into boards) can absorb considerable quantities of moisture without becoming saturated, releasing it as conditions change. These are organic materials, and so can also support natural decay processes – including insects and rot – particularly if they are wet.

- *Manufactured fibres and foams*
  Most manufactured fibres are mineral, and most foams are plastic; most allow water vapour to pass through them relatively easily but not be absorbed. If this encounters a cold surface (such as the surface of a wall that has been insulated internally), it may condense and cause problems. These materials are therefore often used together with vapour-control layers such as aluminium-foil facings.

- *Hi-tech materials*
  More advanced products such as aerogels and vacuum panels have extremely low thermal conductivities, and so are effective at lesser thicknesses (typically 10–25 mm). This can be very useful where space is tight – for example, in window reveals – but these materials are expensive.

Making an informed choice can be difficult: manufacturers are continually releasing new products, and it can be hard to compare published data since commercial tests are conducted in different ways and reported using a wide range of units. It is rarely made clear how the thermal characteristics have been measured, nor what the error in that measurement might be. Some products (for example, multilayer foils) have been subject to major uncertainties, and argument continues.

For traditionally constructed buildings, it is normally safest to choose insulation materials that are permeable and hygroscopic, do not prevent water in the wall from evaporating, and retain the fabric's ability to buffer moisture.

Technical Issues

Insulation will present different issues and have different requirements according to the building element, and where in the building element the insulation is being positioned.

Warm Side or Cold Side?

When insulating, it is often recommended that a vapour barrier be installed on the 'warm' side to prevent problems of condensation. Usually the warm side is assumed to be the heated room, but the exterior can be warmer than the interior, especially if the building is artificially cooled. Even in buildings without air cooling, 'summer condensation' can sometimes occur when strong sunshine drives moisture deeper into the fabric.

Avoiding Thermal Bridges

Thermal bridging can be a problem at the joints and edges of insulation material, or wherever building components or fittings penetrate it (cold-water pipes are an extreme example). There will inevitably be gaps and discontinuities in retrofitted insulation, particularly at window reveals, and between the external walls and the floors and partitions. It can take great attention to detail (and no little ingenuity) to ensure that every awkward junction is well insulated and air-sealed.

Ensuring the integrity of the insulation layer, avoiding thermal bridges and controlling air leakage are important design considerations when retrofitting insulation. For example, when insulation is installed in a roof between rafters, it can be difficult to deal with awkward junctions, and there will be gaps and discontinuities unless very high standards of workmanship are obtained. Therefore, 'buildability' is an important factor that should be carefully thought out at the design stage.

BUILDING ENVIRONMENT
SPECIAL TOPIC: Improving Energy & Carbon Performance

The impact of thermal bridges increases with the amount of insulation. Heat loss at the bridge will work against the benefits of the insulation, but more importantly there is a real risk that water vapour will condense on the cold surfaces beside or behind the insulation. Studies of existing buildings suggest that upgraded wall insulation may begin to deliver increasing risks and diminishing returns as U-values fall towards 0.3 W/m²K, a point that is typically reached as the thickness of insulation reaches about 100 mm (depending on the material and the wall being upgraded); after that, thermal bridging becomes a limiting factor, and the risk of moisture problems escalates. Under these circumstances, there is little benefit in applying more than about 100 mm of ordinary insulation; indeed, it may be preferable to use less and allow more heat to reach the wall and warm it.

Superinsulation

Superinsulation – adding 200–300 mm or more of insulation to building envelopes – was developed for new construction, but has recently been promoted for retrofitting existing buildings (so-called 'deep retrofits' or 'extreme refurbishments'). The emphasis this places on taking care over construction detailing to avoid air infiltration and thermal bridges is useful, but actual and potential moisture problems in the original fabric will need consideration as well. If the insulation is internal, there are risks of trapping moisture, and of overheating due to the thermal mass of the original structure being isolated.

It can be difficult and expensive to achieve the standards demanded of superinsulation systems, which come with a high embodied-energy cost. As an approach, superinsulation also rests on the assumption that an ideal heating system should keep an entire building warm year-round, which in most cases would not be necessary, and may indeed be undesirable. Many occupants prefer bedrooms to be cooler, for example, and will therefore open the windows slightly, although this inevitably compromises efficiency.

The dependence of superinsulation on mechanical ventilation systems also carries inherent risks related to design, installation, commissioning, operation, and of course maintenance. Those familiar with the long-term performance of buildings also express concern about the longevity of the air barriers, sealants and insulation products essential to superinsulation, and what may happen to the fabric once these begin to age and fail.

Superinsulation

The 1970s oil crisis led to research into 'superinsulated' buildings: structures that would require very little heating, because the loss of heated air would be prevented by installing heavy insulation, triple glazing and air barriers; minimising thermal bridging; and making use of solar heat gains. Air exchange would be strictly controlled to prevent heat loss through air leakage, Mechanical Ventilation Heat Recovery [MVHR] systems being used to reduce ventilation heat losses, and to help redistribute heat from warmer to cooler areas.

Work in the USA led to an influential publication, Nisson and Dutt's 1985 *The Superinsulated Home Book*. This then influenced work in Canada, and in Germany and Austria, where the 'PassivHaus' standard and software were developed. More recently, the government programmes in Canada have stopped, but PassivHaus has become the best known approach to low-energy buildings, with a growing band of enthusiastic supporters in the UK. It has both a 'standard' system for new build, and a system known as 'EnerPHit' intended for retrofit work.

PassivHaus is not precisely 'passive', since it requires mechanical ventilation and a small amount of heating. Systems include the following requirements:

- *Heating demand*
  New build: a maximum of 15 kWh per square metre of treated floor area [m² TFA] per year
  EnerPHit: a maximum of 25 kWh/m² TFA per year

- *Primary energy use for all purposes*
  New build: no greater than 120 kWh/m² TFA per year
  EnerPHit: no greater than 120 kWh/m² TFA per year; augmented if necessary, but only to the extent that the actual heating demand prediction exceeds 15 kWh/m²

- *Maximum air infiltration rate*
  New build: 0.6 air changes per hour at a pressure of 50 pascals
  EnerPHit: 1.0 air changes per hour at a pressure of 50 pascals.

To meet this standard, U-values must be in the region of 0.1 W/m²K, which means that large amounts of insulation must be incorporated (typically a thickness of 200–300 mm). EnerPHit recognises the problems that may arise with internal wall insulation of this thickness, and so allows the U-value requirement to be relaxed to 0.3 W/m²K where internal insulation is being retrofitted. This may make it difficult to achieve the 25 kWh/m² heating standard unless the external wall area is relatively small (for example, in terraced houses and flats).

The PassivHaus standard uses energy use per area as a guide to savings; this unfortunately favours larger buildings over smaller, especially in houses, since households will tend to have the same number of energy-using appliances whatever the floor area.

While fixed standards like these have advantages for new build, they are more questionable for existing buildings, where the most appropriate retrofit solutions will be those that take proper account of context. Solutions that were developed in and for continental climates may not be entirely appropriate for the milder and damper English climate, particularly towards the west of the country.

INCREASING THE THERMAL RESISTANCE OF WINDOWS

Daylight and natural ventilation through windows can provide energy benefits if properly controlled, but glass has a high thermal conductivity, so glazing – windows and glass walling – will act as thermal bridges, transferring heat between the exterior and the interior. Indeed, single-layer glazing loses heat from the interior much faster than any other building element, particularly when the effect of air leakage is also included.

Glass will also draw radiant energy from occupants in cold weather, or let through solar radiation which causes them to feel hot, and so glazing can be a major source of the discomfort that leads to an overuse of heating or air cooling. Depending on orientation and time of day, the heat loss through glass may be more than offset by solar heat gains, which often provide a beneficial contribution to heating; on the other hand, poorly ventilated spaces with large areas of glass may overheat even in winter.

Exactly how much the glazing contributes to the overall heat loss of a building will depend on the area given over to glass, and the nature of the rest of the envelope.

The relative area of glazing in a façade can differ greatly

The extent of glazing is critical when weighing the cost and benefit of measures to reduce heat loss though the building envelope.

If windows form only a small proportion of the envelope – as is commonly the case with earlier buildings – there may be little point in more costly or disruptive measures such as secondary glazing (unless these deliver other benefits as well). On the other hand, if glazing dominates the façade (as it does with many important post-war buildings), finding ways of reducing heat transfer though the glass may be a priority.

Glazing is a system comprising both the glass and the frame, and both must be taken into account when trying to understand energy loss and make improvements.

Modern windows tend to use sealed Insulated Glazing Units [IGUs] in double- and triple-glazed configurations; low-emissivity coatings, insulating spacers and inert gas fills are often used to further reduce thermal conductivity. Even so, conditioned air can be lost through gaps in the frame, or between the frame and the surrounding wall. The materials of the frame will also act as thermal bridges. This is not a problem with timber, but metal frames will be excellent conductors of heat unless they incorporate thermal breaks.

Thermal bridging can sometimes lead to condensation on and around window frames, particularly where metal-framed windows are re-glazed with IGUs, or there are cast-iron window surrounds, mullions, cills, lintels or balconies. If the condensation is only occasional and the cause of the thermal bridging is not decorative, a layer of timber or plaster can sometimes be added on the interior to cut the bridge; this will also absorb much of the transient moisture. Thermal and moisture-absorbing paints are sometimes proposed for metal components, but they tend to have little effect. In potentially damp areas, extra room ventilation may be needed to lower the moisture content of the interior air, preferably by extraction at source.

For upgrading glazing, the traditional approach of shutters or secondary glazing provides good and often reversible opportunities. These will reduce heat transfer through the frame as well as the glass, and cut air infiltration as well.

Timber shutters are very effective at preventing heat transfer, but can only be used when it is desirable or possible to stop the light coming in, or the occupants seeing out (they can perform a useful security function). Installing secondary glazing – a second window or sheet of glazing, usually on the interior side – overcomes these issues. If secondary glazing is being contemplated, care must be taken to avoid condensation problems in the interspace: this is most easily done by not draughtproofing the original windows. The design should not impede the other functions of the window, particularly ventilation. The performance of secondary glazing can be enhanced by low-emissivity coatings, and if the secondary unit is glazed with twin glazing, IGUs or vacuum glazing, the combination can match the highest-performing modern windows.

IGUs can have quite short lifespans, failing when the seals give way and let in water vapour that then condenses on the interior of the glass; and they are difficult to repair or recycle, so whole-life costs must be taken into account. Vacuum glazing is a thinner and lighter alternative, but although accelerated tests indicate it may have a longer life, this has not yet been fully verified in practice.

Measures can also be combined with great success; for example, installing external shutters, secondary glazing and curtains. This can prove very effective indeed, since it reduces all forms of heat transfer, including draughts and radiation discomfort. Historic buildings often used this approach; on the windows of some of its houses, the National Trust has found remains of multiple layers (including awnings, internal and external shutters, and blinds).

Choosing Appropriate Measures

When selecting the best measures for a particular window in a particular building (there is no reason why all windows should be treated the same way, and indeed this is unlikely to be the case), all other functions of the glazing must be reviewed to ensure that all those needed are retained (especially letting in light; controlling ventilation, glare and heat gains; and sometimes providing a means of escape). For example, will secondary glazing inhibit summer ventilation, maintenance of the original window or access to blinds? Can both windows be cleaned easily?

The glazing provides much of the character of a building, so for historic buildings in particular, alterations need special care. Hand-made and early machine-made glass must always be retained: it is irreplaceable, and gives subtler reflections than flat glass. If glazing has to be replaced, the frame sizes and profiles should be preserved wherever possible. ➲GLASS

Standard designs of shutters and secondary glazing may be difficult to fit to non-standard windows. Their details may also be inappropriate, though the product range is improving. History reveals a wide range of approaches that could easily be adapted by a joiner. The *Glass & Glazing* volume in this series shows many examples of these, including panels that slide into pockets below or beside the window, folding systems that are asymmetrical or fold back along the wall rather than into architraves like the familiar Georgian and Victorian shutters, and shutters for bay windows. It is worth being creative: for example, if wall panelling is being added or restored, shutters and secondary glazing might slide back behind it.

Wooden shutters can reduce heat loss at night and solar gain during the day, and can improve security at the same time.

Left: The clever design of sash windows allowed them to be used to let air into a room in windy conditions (when casements would risk slamming shut and breaking), and even when the shutters or curtains had been closed for privacy or security, or to reduce radiant heat loss.

Right: Shutters can be installed in place of heavy curtains; as well as folding, panels may slide into boxes below or to either side of the window, and can be integrated with panelling, providing thermal benefits to the wall.

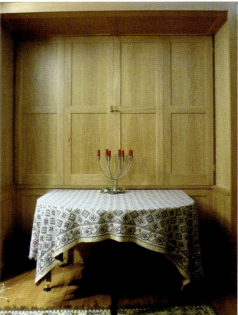

Taking the season of benefit into account

The design of a retrofit should take into account the fact that it may not offer year-round benefits. For example, secondary glazing will often be wanted only in winter (the exception is when it also acts as soundproofing).

Early secondary glazing – as seen here in Carlisle – was usually made in the form of casement windows that could be opened when the weather was warm. Another approach is to design the secondary window to slide back into pockets below or to the sides of the window when it is not being used. Demountable secondary glazing is also available, but this can present storage problems.

The optimum distance between primary and secondary glazing is typically 50–60 mm. Wider gaps are better acoustically if the window reveals are lined, but worse thermally, owing to convection currents up the inner pane and down the outer.

To reduce condensation risks on the original window, the interspace gap should be ventilated by a small amount of air, usually outside air: the best approach is to simply not draught-seal the original window. More elaborate vents are used when stained-glass windows are equipped with external protective glazing. It is also important to deal with all moisture problems in the surrounding wall. ⊝GLASS

BUILDING ENVIRONMENT
SPECIAL TOPIC: Improving Energy & Carbon Performance

Buildings constructed at a time when energy was cheap often have envelopes with little thermal mass, as well as serious problems with thermal bridging.

In significant contemporary buildings such as the Grade II* Nottingham Playhouse, great sensitivity will be needed to undertake the thermal upgrading necessary without compromising the appearance.

In single-glazed curtain walling installed before the 1980s, it may be possible to replace the glass with IGUs. In a continuously heated building with large areas of glazing, IGUs have been demonstrated to repay their embodied energy in less than a year, but by no means all buildings are heated this much or have such extensive areas of glass.

If IGUs are installed in metal frames, the frames may attract condensation, so advice should be sought from a specialist façade engineer. Sometimes thermal breaks can be introduced (for example, between the outer pressure plate, and the inner mullion and transom profiles), but often secondary glazing may be a more robust solution (see **Care & Repair**, in the main text). ⊖GLASS

Technically, the optimum spacing between the panes of an IGU is 16 mm, which gives a robust and effective unit. Thinner IGUs are often preferred for windows in historic buildings, because they are simpler to fit into the original frames, but as the gap drops below 10 mm, performance deteriorates rapidly.

| U-VALUES OF A LOW-E, ARGON-FILLED IGU ||
GAP BETWEEN PANES	APPROXIMATE U-VALUE
16 mm	1.2 W/m²K
9 mm	1.6 W/m²K
6 mm	2.1 W/m²K

The checklist on the facing page summarises a range of improvements for windows, with increasing levels of cost and difficulty.

CHECKLIST: IMPROVING THE THERMAL PERFORMANCE OF WINDOWS

ACTION	GENERAL COMMENTS	OTHER CONSIDERATIONS
SIMPLE ACTIONS		
ADD CURTAINS & BLINDS	Can reduce both heating loads in winter, and cooling loads in summer	Traditionally, windows may have had different curtains for summer and winter
REFURBISH OR REPLACE LOST SHUTTERS	External shutters protect against both solar gain and heat loss, and provide security and weather protection Internal shutters are good at reducing heat loss, but are less effective against heat gain	Shutters can be of many types, designs and sizes Some traditional windows had both internal and external shutters Consider incorporating draughtproofing in new and refurbished shutters, to enhance performance
INTERMEDIATE ACTIONS		
ADD SHUTTERS	Shutters were made to suit almost every type of window	Consider designing bespoke shutters
ADD SECONDARY GLAZING	Cuts draughts and reduces heat losses through the existing window frames, not just the glass Traditionally, widely used in cold climates, and for noise control (often with open-in casements) Traditional designs used wood-framed secondary sliding sash windows and casements Many commercial models use sliding, fixed or hinged panels in metal frames, but the frames are a thermal bridge Wooden-framed systems can be designed to fold or slide away like shutters	Primary and secondary windows must open and shut with ease where natural ventilation is required Poor heat conductors make better frame materials (for example, wood rather than metal) Do not draughtproof the primary glazing, so the interspace has some ventilation by external air, reducing the condensation risk For best thermal performance, secondary glazing can use hard-coated low-emissivity glass, or an IGU, which will last longer than normal since it is protected from the weather
ADD AWNINGS OR OTHER SHADING & WEATHER PROTECTION	Can protect windows from solar gain, or let them stay open for ventilation when raining Some Victorian models were specifically designed to assist ventilation through the window	Solar films and varnishes can be used to reduce solar gain, but they have short lifespans and are difficult to remove; they would not be suitable for use on handmade or early machine-made glass
CHALLENGING ACTIONS		
REPLACE GLASS	Single glazing can be replaced with IGUs, but unlike secondary glazing, this will not directly reduce draughts or heat transfer through the frames; it can, however, be combined with draughtproofing Vacuum glazing is relatively expensive, and where safety glass is required, a protective film will need to be applied	Hand-made and early machine-made glass are important assets, and should be retained IGUs are energy-intensive to manufacture, and have a short lifespan; the thin IGUs often fitted into older window frames may be even more energy-intensive, owing to both the low thermal-transfer gases they contain and their shorter lifespan Metal frames are cold bridges and are especially likely to attract condensation if reglazed with IGUs
REPLACE WINDOWS	For buildings with statutory protection, replacement of original windows is unlikely to be permitted Where windows are not original and are ineffective, it can be wise to consider replacing them with better designs Replacement should be of the highest quality, and take into account whole-life costs: with maintenance a timber window can last for hundreds of years; by contrast, a PVCu double-glazed window will need to be replaced after 10–30 years, depending on quality	Early materials (such as forest-grown hardwoods and softwoods, and hand-wrought iron) were of a quality and durability that it would now be difficult or impossible to match, and should always be retained Rarely windows will be in such a poor state that complete replacement is less expensive than repair and upgrading, but usually even very neglected windows can be brought back into condition relatively easily, and upgraded with systems such as secondary glazing

INCREASING THE THERMAL RESISTANCE OF ROOFS

Many traditional roof coverings were poor insulators, with the obvious exception of thatch. Roofs can therefore offer good opportunities for adding insulation, particularly in accessible, unoccupied void spaces, where insulation can be cheaply and simply laid between and above ceilings joists.

Ease and suitability depends on access, the configuration of the roof and whether the roof space is used for accommodation. Insulation at ceiling level (loft insulation) is the easiest and least risky option, but if there is habitable accommodation in a roof space, insulation will have to be positioned in line with the roof slope at rafter level, creating a 'warm' roof. In this case, design and installation is more challenging, and is likely to involve more disruption.

Insulation at rafter level may be installed in one or more of three positions, each presenting different risks and benefits:

- beneath the rafters
- between the rafters
- above the rafters (that is, directly beneath the roof covering).

Flat & Low-Pitched Roofs

Improving the performance of flat and low-pitched roofs has many similarities to insulation at rafter level, but with some important differences:

- the roof covering is impervious (either a membrane, an asphalt, or a metal), so ventilation can only occur around the edges or through special-purpose arrangements
- the natural buoyancy of air in a pitched roof assists its natural ventilation and the dispersal of moisture; a flat roof does not have this benefit, so moisture is more likely to accumulate.

In spite of this, a number of metal-clad flat roofs with limited amounts of ventilation have been found to perform well, but they can be vulnerable to changes associated with adding ventilation or insulation.

In addition, lead, zinc and aluminium roofing can be affected by underside corrosion from intermittent evaporation and condensation. This can greatly reduce their lifespan, even under conditions where the effect of the moisture on the rest of the roof structure is minimal. Organic acids from timber decking exacerbate the effect, with oak and manufactured boards (such as plywood) being particularly corrosive. Separating membranes do not necessarily solve this problem, and may exacerbate it. ⊖ROOFING

The checklists on the following pages summarise a range of improvements for pitched roofs, and for the more difficult case of flat and low-pitched roofs.

CHECKLIST: INCREASING THE THERMAL RESISTANCE OF PITCHED ROOFS

ACTION	GENERAL COMMENTS	OTHER CONSIDERATIONS
SIMPLE ACTIONS		
INSULATING AT CEILING LEVEL (LOFT INSULATION)	Will usually be the simplest, cheapest and most straightforward approach Creates a 'cold roof': roof space must be ventilated by outside air to remove water vapour generated by the activities in the building Traditionally, air infiltration between slates and tiles usually provided enough ventilation; when sarking felts and membranes are included, specific arrangements need to be made Over-ventilation will reduce the effectiveness of the insulation	Any joints and junctions where the insulation meets the walls, and where the ceiling is punctured (by lights and roof hatches), must be well sealed Take care when placing insulation over electric cables, particularly if carrying high currents; ideally, cables should run in the cold space above the insulation Insulation should not be pierced by light fittings or any other fixtures, but covering the fittings and services with insulation can be a serious fire risk; the appropriate types of fitting must be selected and properly installed (see the **Special Topic: Dealing with Disasters**)
INTERMEDIATE ACTIONS		
INSULATING AT RAFTER LEVEL	Ventilation may need to be introduced between the insulation and the roof covering to reduce the risk of condensation	
	INSULATING BENEATH THE RAFTERS	
	Can be installed without stripping the roof covering or changing the height of the roof Leaves the maximum room for natural air circulation under the roof covering May reduce the amount of usable floor space	Installation must be airtight: even small gaps can lead to cold bridging and condensation, especially if the roof has an impermeable underlay Care will need to be taken with detailing at junctions and around openings
	INSULATING BETWEEN THE RAFTERS	
	Does not increase the visible height of the roof or reduce the usable floor area of the accommodation Effective ventilation should be provided above to remove excess moisture and water vapour Thickness of insulation will be limited by the depth of the rafters which, in addition, may form a potential thermal bridge	A high level of workmanship is required to minimise gaps between the rafters and the insulation; for this reason soft pliable insulation materials are preferable to rigid boards Insulation should never be fastened to or sprayed on the underside of slates or tiles, as this makes it impossible to maintain or reuse the roof coverings Infiltration of moist air from within interior must be minimised: cracks in ceilings and around service penetrations should be sealed, and recessed lighting fittings should not be used
	INSULATING ABOVE THE RAFTERS	
	Becomes an option when the roof is being re-covered Raises the level of the roof coverings, which may often be unacceptable or impractical Roof structure is on the warm side of the insulation, reducing the risk of moisture accumulation Decreases solar gain through the roof	Insulation can sometimes be fitted as an unbroken layer, avoiding thermal bridging Undulations in roof slopes, which often make an important contribution to the visual character of old roofs, can make installation difficult; high standards of workmanship are required The additional weight of insulation can sometimes make it necessary to strengthen the roof Spray foams on the underside of roof finishes should not be used, as they may trap moisture; the roof covering also becomes difficult to reuse

BUILDING ENVIRONMENT
SPECIAL TOPIC: Improving Energy & Carbon Performance

CHECKLIST: INCREASING THE THERMAL RESISTANCE OF FLAT & LOW-PITCHED ROOFS

ACTION	GENERAL COMMENTS	OTHER CONSIDERATIONS
SIMPLE ACTIONS		
INSULATING AT CEILING LEVEL (FOR ROOFS WITH ACCESSIBLE VOIDS)	Relatively straightforward and economic Creates a 'cold roof': roof space must be ventilated by outside air to remove water vapour generated by the activities in the building Can be difficult to provide adequate ventilation	Must take into account the same issues and considerations as pitched roofs (see **Checklist**) Not regarded as robust, particularly above spaces producing moist air (such as kitchens, bathrooms, densely occupied spaces) If chosen, the roof void will need to be inspected regularly
INTERMEDIATE ACTIONS		
INSULATING BELOW THE CEILING	Sometimes insulation and a new ceiling can be installed beneath the original ceiling; more rarely the original ceiling is not significant, and can be replaced The installation should be airtight and vapour-resistant, otherwise too much moist air may enter the void space	Care should be taken with detailing at junctions and around openings: even small gaps, holes or cracks can lead to condensation One instance in which vapour-control layers may be necessary to stop rising moist air; but this is not a preferred option, since water can enter from other sources and other directions (including roof leaks)
CHALLENGING ACTIONS		
INSULATING IN THE JOIST ZONE (ROOFS WHERE VOIDS ARE NOT ACCESSIBLE)	Not recommended, owing to various risks, but may sometimes be possible to combine with insulation under the joists	Where this approach is chosen, a good ventilation space (ideally 150 mm or more) should be retained between the upper side of the insulation and the underside of the roof deck
INSULATING ABOVE THE DECK WEATHERPROOFING DIRECTLY ABOVE INSULATION	Creates a 'warm roof' Commonly used in modern construction, especially in the form of proprietary systems, but heavily reliant on the integrity of the weatherproofing layer above the insulation, the vapour barrier beneath and any ventilation of the interspace	The height of the roof will need to be raised Not normally recommended: if chosen, consider obtaining a package from a reputable supplier, with appropriate warranties
INSULATING ABOVE THE DECK VENTILATED LAYER BETWEEN INSULATION & WEATHERPROOFING	Creates a 'ventilated warm roof' Recommended for metal roofs, particularly lead and zinc Allows a very good air, water and vapour seal to be applied between the insulation and the roof structure; sometimes the original roofing membrane may be used for this purpose The ventilated airspace should be: • 150–200 mm deep for a pitch up to 3° • 100 mm for a pitch from 3° to 20° • 50 mm for a pitch greater than 20°	The height of the roof will need to be raised, and the structure may need reinforcing Flat-roof inlets and outlets should be equivalent to a 25-mm continuous slot (as the pitch increases, the size can be reduced); insect screens may be needed, but ensure they do not block with debris (slots are better than meshes) Ventilation needs to be provided around (or above and below) obstructions such as rooflights, and complex geometries such as hips will need arrangements for ventilation towards the apex
INSULATING ABOVE WEATHERPROOFING	Creates an 'inverted roof' Waterproof insulation (such as extruded polystyrene) is placed above the weatherproofing layer, and weighted down with ballast or paving slabs On small roof areas not subject to heavy foot traffic, lighter-weight pre-screeded interlocking insulation slabs can be used Weatherproofing layer must be of good quality and properly tested (for example, by adding water with rainwater outlets blocked)	The height of the roof will need to be raised, and the structure will often need reinforcing Can be very durable, because the roofing membrane is protected from temperature fluctuations and ultraviolet light damage Requires special drainage outlets that admit water from both the surface and the waterproof membrane levels Flowing water during rainstorms will degrade insulation performance

Green Roofs

Vegetation was often used for small vernacular buildings in some cold climates. For example, sod roofs were widespread in rural Scandinavia until the beginning of the 18th century. Occasional uses in the UK include the 1830s' Temple Mill at Holbeck in Leeds, where the roof was covered with grass to help keep the interior humidity of the mill high enough to spin flax.

The current interest in green roofs has a number of motivations, including increasing biodiversity, adding green space in cities, cooling by cutting solar gain and increasing evaporation, protecting interiors from temperature extremes, slowing down rainwater runoff, and providing places for people to grow food.

Green roofs are an attractive idea, though there are cheaper and easier ways to insulate. Since storing water in the roof covering is a risk, they must be planned and designed thoughtfully, and require meticulous attention to detail to avoid accelerated decay of the roof structure, particularly around the edges.

The traditional approach began with a layer of birch bark waterproofing, protected by about 75 mm of sand, to encourage rain to drain to the eaves, and covered by two layers of turf from local meadows. The first layer of turf was laid grass-side down and the second grass-side up. They eventually rooted together to form a single system thick enough to survive a dry summer. The turf was initially held in place along the eaves by stones, later replaced by 'verge boards': logs or wooden beams of a shape and size set by local tradition, fixed to the rafters by wooden hooks protected with birch bark.

Traditional green roofs

These houses in Tórshavn, on Streymoy in the Færoe Islands, have traditional sod roofs laid on birch bark (which can be seen at the eaves).

The turf and sand physically protect the bark from sunlight and extreme temperatures, as well as from mechanical damage, giving it a much longer lifespan. The same mechanism extends the life of the waterproof membranes and cavity-drainage membranes used in modern green roofs.

BUILDING ENVIRONMENT
SPECIAL TOPIC: Improving Energy & Carbon Performance

A modern green roof

The extensive green roof on the headquarters of Transport for London (above St James underground station) consists of native wildflowers seeded and planted into the substrate. The planting and design followed guidelines published by the Buglife conservation charity, and is intended to encourage rare invertebrates.

More recent Scandinavian-style roofs used sarking boards covered with bituminous roofing felt, and a cavity-drainage membrane laid dimpled-side down. Sometimes a layer of insulation was placed over this, followed by another layer of cavity-drainage membrane, and finally the turf. The membranes help protect the insulation from waterlogging, but the roof slope must be at least 1 in 50.

Today, green roofs are often constructed on a concrete or plywood deck with a waterproofing layer placed on top of the insulation (or sometimes below waterproof insulation to form an 'inverted roof'). Root protection may be integrated into the waterproofing, or provided by a capping sheet. The green covering usually includes a protection layer, a drainage layer, a filter sheet, the substrate (or growing medium), and finally the plants.

On large roofs, drainage layers are important since they let rainwater move laterally to the drainage outlets, but a degree of waterlogging can sometimes be desirable: there are examples of wet meadow roofs covered with orchids (such as the St Galen Hospital in Switzerland). How much moisture a green roof can hold will be determined by the depth of the substrate, and the strength of the roof structure. Thin substrates are lighter, but cannot store much water, so tend to be vegetated by drought-tolerant sedums and wild flowers; deeper substrates can support a wider range of plants, including shrubs, but are much heavier. Ultra-lightweight variants using less than 80 mm of substrate are too vulnerable to drought, and should normally be avoided.

Substrates are specially blended to be free draining and absorbent, typically using pumice or crushed brick mixed with 20 % or less of organic matter. The choice of planting is also critical, and is best informed by what naturally flourishes locally, but bearing in mind that the roof environment will almost certainly be much drier. Research into 'soft capping' for protecting ruined walls has shown that drought- and wind-tolerant local wildflowers and sedum are much more likely to thrive than commercial grassy turf, and these are also likely to be the best choices for roofs in very dry areas, on shallow substrates or on very sloped roofs. ⊖ROOFING ⊖STONE

INCREASING THE THERMAL RESISTANCE OF WALLS

Wall insulation is one of the most difficult and expensive retrofit measures, requiring careful investigation and assessment before it can be safely considered. Not only does it dramatically affect the building's appearance, but it is complicated and risky, and offers less certain benefits than most other measures. To plan improvement to reduce heat loss without threatening the fabric requires a good understanding of the current level of thermal performance, how the moisture is distributed, and how water and heat is likely to travel through the materials and systems of the wall.

There are essentially three ways to add insulation: on the outside, on the inside and by filling cavities where these exist (particularly in framed and cavity-wall construction). Each poses different risks and costs, and must be managed in different ways. As with all forms of insulation, the most important technical risk is that of trapping moisture – whether from leaks or condensation – and hence increasing heat loss and the risks of fabric decay.

Rendering & Plastering

The thermal performance of solid walls and cavity walls can often be improved by externally rendering or internally plastering with permeable lime-based plasters, which will also help them resist moisture penetration and allow any moisture that does enter to evaporate away. Wet-applied materials of this kind have the added advantage of avoiding joints and being easy to detail at junctions; they also make a very effective air barrier. Good results have been achieved by adding hemp fibre to the mix to increase its insulating properties.

A traditional approach to making interiors comfortable with a minimal use of heating is revealed by the presence of both wall paintings or decorative plasterwork and hooks, for hanging painted cloths or tapestries, as here at Elcho Castle in Perth. As confirmed by household records, the textiles were hung up in the cold seasons (when they would dramatically reduce radiant heat loss into walls), and taken down and stored in the summer, when the humidities would be high enough to risk condensation and mould, and radiant heat loss would not be a problem.

Another successful treatment, which provided year-round benefits, was to install wooden panelling or wainscotting. As well as a remedy for discomfort due to radiant heat loss, timber attached to battens on the walls also provided a reasonable degree of insulation without increasing the risk of condensation or other moisture problems.

BUILDING ENVIRONMENT
SPECIAL TOPIC: Improving Energy & Carbon Performance

Many buildings that now have walls with a tendency to damp originally had external rendering. Historic records may provide arguments for replacement, especially where the exposed masonry is in need of protection.

All other types of wall insulation carry particular risks, which must be well understood and correctly mitigated if the intervention is to be successful.

Interior Wall Insulation

The major risk of internal wall insulation is an increased risk of condensation, since the insulation itself reduces the amount the wall is warmed by the heating system. A robust approach is to use a permeable material, and limit its thickness. Tests in Germany have suggested that permeable insulating board up to about 15 mm thick, battened off the wall by 20 mm or so to create an airspace, can provide useful improvements with minimum risk. This is, effectively, wooden panelling. Although it does not dramatically increase the thermal resistance of the wall, it improves thermal responsiveness and reduces radiant heat loss, and hence the demand for heating.

In some buildings, greater improvements may be sought, but as the thickness of insulation increases, so do the risks. Very thick interior insulation can also significantly reduce the space within a small room.

Exterior Wall Insulation

In principle, a better solution is to insulate on the exterior. External wall insulation helps to protect from condensation since it keeps the whole wall warm and allows it to act as a thermal buffer, increasing temperature stability and reducing the tendency to overheating that can be the result of internal insulation.

The major technical difficulty with this approach is that the insulation will be exposed to the weather. Most materials will need to be protected; the most common practice is to render over the insulation, but alternatives such as timber cladding and slate and tile hanging are also possible, and may prove more robust since they can provide a rainscreen and introduce a ventilated external layer.

It is also important to consider water-shedding details to protect the insulation at weak points such as at the top of the wall, and around the windows and doors. Unfortunately, exterior insulation will partly or wholly cover any existing protective features such as roof overhangs, cornices and hood mouldings, or make them less effective, so redetailing will have to be very carefully considered. If water is able to get into the wall by travelling through or around the insulation – perhaps via a gutter overflow – it will be trapped, and because the exterior insulation is preventing evaporation, it will move into the interior.

The loss of original features is also a serious problem for historic buildings; exterior insulation will have a dramatic impact on the building's appearance. Even if it is already rendered or stuccoed, the building will look very different not just because the detailing has altered, but because the dimensions and proportions have been changed. This is unlikely to be permitted on an important façade.

Cavity-Wall Insulation

Cavity-wall insulation is not visible, but it presents some serious technical issues. To be injected into the cavity, the insulation material must be loose-fill or foam, but the latter is not recommended since it is irreversible (even loose fill will be impossible to remove completely, which is problematic when it begins to degrade). To successfully fill the cavity, it must be free of obstructions, but this is rarely the case.

The tops of cavities may sometimes be open into the roof space. They should be closed, not only to prevent water ingress, but to prevent the internal circulation of air. This may be enough to achieve significant thermal benefits.

Whatever material is used, there is a real risk that moisture will find its way across the cavity to the inner leaf. Before contemplating any work, borescope investigations should be made to hunt for possible moisture sources, and thermal and moisture bridges; these must be dealt with before work begins. Cavity-wall insulation is not suited to early designs of cavity walls that used bricks to bond the leaves together rather than metal ties.

Insulation of Framed Walls

It may sometimes be possible to insulate a framed wall when either the exterior cladding or the interior finishes are being removed for maintenance or refurbishment. The options are similar to those for insulating roofs at rafter level: that is, insulation can be placed on the inside of the framing, between the framing or on the outside.

If insulation is entirely within the framing, the frames will act as thermal bridges: this will be a particularly serious concern if they are made of metal (as, for example, in modern curtain-walling). It is therefore best to couple insulation between the framing with interior or preferably exterior insulation.

Dealing with Below-Ground Walls

Because the walls of basements and cellars are insulated by the ground outside, heat loss is already very much lower than it would be through walls exposed on the exterior to the air, so the benefits to be gained by wall insulation are unclear. Basement walls are also likely to contain a fair amount of moisture, so insulation is technically difficult.

The demand for insulation may be in response to occupant discomfort, and may perhaps be alleviated by dealing with radiant heat loss by installing panelling or dry-lining. This will also conceal salt stains and other signs of moisture; while this may help make the room feel more comfortable, it should be possible to easily open up the panelling regularly to check that moisture problems are not worsening (below-ground rooms are susceptible to leaks from drains and water mains, for example). Internal insulation is normally inappropriate, as it may create or exacerbate moisture problems.

The checklist on the following pages summarises a range of improvements for walls.

CHECKLIST: INCREASING THE THERMAL RESISTANCE OF WALLS

ACTION	GENERAL COMMENTS	OTHER CONSIDERATIONS
SIMPLE ACTIONS		
REPAIR (INCLUDING REPOINTING & REPAIRS TO PERMEABLE RENDERS)	Appropriate repairs will improve airtightness and water penetration (a dry wall will transfer much less heat); the materials volumes in this series give information about the repair of walls of various types	The correct intervention depends on the materials and construction of the wall; but permeable materials such as lime mortars and renders should always be used Consider replacement of impermeable renders and mortars where practicable
INTERMEDIATE ACTIONS		
RENDERING	Applying a permeable render can benefit both solid and cavity walls Renders will cut air infiltration and water penetration Dry walls have much more thermal resistance	Use only permeable materials such as lime-based mortars; additives such as hemp can increase insulating capacity Rendering will alter the appearance of the building Many older buildings were rendered in the past, so there may be a precedent in historic records
PLASTERING	Applying a permeable plaster can benefit both solid and cavity walls	Use only permeable materials such as lime-based mortars Additives such as hemp can increase insulating capacity
INTERIOR HANGINGS OR PANELLING	Lining the interior with thinnish sheets of permeable material, battened off the wall, will improve thermal response and reduce radiant heat loss	There will be an impact on appearance, and some reduction in the usable area of the room; panelling may be difficult to detail around original features such as decorative cornices It is wise to design panelling to be easily openable to check the condition of the wall behind

External wall insulation will have a serious impact on a building's appearance, though if a façade is in poor condition it may sometimes be possible to incorporate the measure into a sensitive programme of improvement or restoration.

External insulation carries a high technical risk, and so must be meticulously well designed and installed. The loss of water-shedding details such as drip mouldings can lead to water ingress, and leaks may occur at eaves and cills, and around pipework (note the water stain at the corner of the window here). This is of great concern since the insulation will also reduce evaporation from the wall, and may hide signs of water problems until they are very well established.

CHECKLIST: INCREASING THE THERMAL RESISTANCE OF WALLS

ACTION	GENERAL COMMENTS	OTHER CONSIDERATIONS
CHALLENGING ACTIONS		
INSULATION	Demands careful design, correct choice of materials, good detailing and extremely high standards of workmanship	
	Methods and materials will vary according to type of wall, and whether it is being insulated externally, internally or by filling a cavity	
	Great care must be taken to eliminate all possible moisture sources from the wall before works begin	
	Internal and external wall insulation will hide the condition of the wall beneath, so it is wise to consider installing time-of-wetness sensors or other moisture monitoring to reveal problems should they occur	
	INTERNAL WALL INSULATION	
	Permeable, hygroscopic insulation would normally be preferable	To limit thermal bridging, partial insulation may be necessary to upper floors, partitions and party walls where these meet the insulated wall
	Thickness may need to be limited to reduce condensation risk	
	Significantly reduces interior floor space, which can be problematic in small rooms	Internal services, including electrical wiring and heating pipework, may need to be rerouted
	Installation requires the occupants to vacate the building	
	Tends to cause problems of thermal bridging	
	EXTERNAL WALL INSULATION	
	Where space is available, exterior wall insulation can safely be made much thicker than interior wall insulation	Carries a significant risk of inducing or exacerbating liquid-moisture problems
	Advantage can be taken of the thermal mass of the wall to help buffer temperature fluctuations and reduce risks of summer overheating if night ventilation is adequate	External pipes, gutters and other services will usually need to be removed and altered before replacement
	Can be installed while the building remains in occupation	Detailing (especially around openings, and at cornices and eaves) must be meticulous, since any water entering from leaks or condensation will be trapped behind the insulation; problems may go unnoticed until they become very serious
	Presents fewer problems with thermal bridges than internal wall insulation	
	Insulation must be protected from the weather by a render, or some other protection such as cladding, or hanging tiles or slates	
	CAVITY WALL INSULATION	
	Increases the thermal resistance of the wall, but does not affect its appearance	Carries a significant risk of inducing liquid-moisture problems
	Least risky in dry, sheltered areas; caution is needed in sites prone to driving rain	If the cavities open into the roof space, they must be closed
	Loose fill materials should be used rather than foam to give some potential for extraction (which is still extremely difficult)	Borescope investigations should be made to locate moisture sources, and thermal and moisture bridges; these must be dealt with before insulation
	Cavity walls can also be insulated internally or externally	Not suitable for cavity walls bonded with bricks
		Always use reputable contractors, and obtain appropriate insurance-backed warranties
	INSULATION OF FRAMED CONSTRUCTION	
	Sometimes possible when cladding or interior finishes are removed for maintenance	If insulation is entirely within the framing, the frames will act as thermal bridges; it is therefore best to combine insulation between the framing with a complete skin of render or insulation (preferably on the exterior)
	Options are similar to those for insulating roofs at rafter level	

IMPROVING THE THERMAL RESISTANCE OF GROUND FLOORS

The temperature difference between a room and the ground underneath is typically small in comparison with that between the room and outside air. Heat loss will be significantly greater through areas of the floor near external walls than through the centre of the floor, and total heat loss will depend on construction of the floor, the amount of exposed perimeter in relation to its overall area, the composition and thickness of the walls, and the amount of underfloor ventilation (if any).

Care must be taken to ensure that the potential benefits of thermal mass are taken into account when insulation and other improvements to existing floors are being considered, otherwise the presumed advantages of added insulation may not live up to expectations. Solid ground floors have a high thermal capacity, and so can help to maintain a steady temperature in the internal environment. As well as buffering fluctuations in interior air temperatures, a solid ground floor behind south-facing windows can absorb a great deal of solar gain during the day (helping to avoid room overheating), releasing the warmth slowly at night.

The principal causes of occupant discomfort on ground floors are radiant heat loss, and draughts through gaps between the boards of suspended timber floors. Floor coverings, rugs and draught sealing can be very effective in improving comfort levels, particularly if they prevent people from getting cold feet.

The benefit of insulating solid ground floors is usually outweighed by the cost, the disruption to occupants and the impact on heritage significance. If, however, a solid floor has to be replaced for other reasons and it is possible to accommodate the additional depth of excavation required, adding insulation will probably be worthwhile. A good option is to use insulated limecrete, which is robust and permeable. ⊖MORTARS

Insulation is essential if underfloor heating is being installed, to prevent heat being lost into the ground. In this case, if the screed is thick enough to serve as a heat sink, the insulation can be laid over the supporting concrete slab; if the screed is thin, however, the slab itself will have to form part of heat sink, and the insulation will need to be laid underneath it.

Suspended floors can be also be insulated. Ideally, insulation should be added from below, but buildings in England rarely have sufficient underfloor space to allow this. Where access cannot be gained from below, floorboards will have to be lifted, and this will inevitably damage historic floors. ⊖TIMBER

The appearance of the floor can be a very distinctive feature of a building, and patterns of wear or unevenness will contribute to its character and significance. These will be very difficult to recreate when a floor is lifted and relaid. ⊖MORTARS ⊖EARTH & BRICK

The checklists on the facing page summarise a range of improvements for suspended and solid ground floors.

CHECKLIST: INCREASING THE THERMAL RESISTANCE OF SUSPENDED TIMBER FLOORS

ACTION	GENERAL COMMENTS	OTHER CONSIDERATIONS
SIMPLE ACTIONS		
ADD RUGS OR CARPETS	Reduces radiant heat loss and draughts through floorboards Close (fitted) carpeting will reduce air leakage through gaps in floorboards	Floor coverings and underlays must be permeable to avoid trapping moisture
INTERMEDIATE ACTIONS		
DRAUGHT-SEALING	Reduces air leakage between skirting boards and floor, and through gaps between floorboards Moisture problems must be eliminated before work begins, and a good monitoring and maintenance regime set into place	Reducing air movement in the floor void may affect the moisture equilibrium
CHALLENGING ACTIONS		
ADD INSULATION FROM ABOVE OR BELOW	Method of installation depends on whether floorboards can be lifted without undue damage (or are being lifted for other work to be carried out), or whether access can be gained from below Moisture problems must be eliminated before work begins, and a good monitoring and maintenance regime set into place	Reducing air movement in the floor void may affect the moisture equilibrium Any electrical services will need to be repositioned above the insulation, or preferably in the ventilated void space beneath the insulation to avoid overheating

CHECKLIST: INCREASING THE THERMAL RESISTANCE OF SOLID GROUND FLOORS

ACTION	GENERAL COMMENTS	OTHER CONSIDERATIONS
SIMPLE ACTIONS		
ADD RUGS OR CARPETS	Reduces radiant heat loss	Floor coverings and underlays should be permeable
INTERMEDIATE ACTIONS		
ADD INSULATION OVER EXISTING FLOOR	Thin, high-performance insulation board can be installed with minimal disturbance to the original floor Moisture problems must be tackled before work begins, and a good monitoring and maintenance regime set into place	Floor level will be raised, so skirting boards may need to be removed and reinstated, doors will have to be shortened, and junctions with staircases resolved
CHALLENGING ACTIONS		
REPLACE EXISTING FLOOR WITH NEW INSULATED FLOOR	Insulation used will be impermeable, so work can affect moisture distribution in walls and other adjacent fabric Moisture problems must be tackled before work begins, and a good monitoring and maintenance regime set into place	Often carried out in conjunction with underfloor heating It may be possible to lift and reinstate some historic floor finishes, but the pattern of settlement and wear will be lost Excavation risks undermining wall foundations
	CONCRETE SLAB Usual approach; insulation may be laid above or below the slab	
	LIME-CONCRETE SLAB Insulation material is either mixed within the lime concrete, or laid as a layer beneath the slab For same strength, will need to be thicker than concrete slab, and so may require deeper excavation	

BUILDING ENVIRONMENT
SPECIAL TOPIC: Improving Energy & Carbon Performance

INSTALLING LOWER-CARBON ENERGY SUPPLIES

Carbon (through not necessarily energy) can also be saved by reducing the carbon content of energy supplies. This could be done centrally, by altering the way electricity is generated, or locally by using low-carbon or zero-carbon technologies (termed 'LZC' in the UK Building Regulations). LZC technologies can be applied at building level, or shared at community or district level.

The main renewable energy sources are wind, solar, hydro and geothermal. Other supplies do emit carbon, but less than would be generated by conventional sources, at least for well designed and well-operated systems. They include those powered by the combustion of renewable fuels such as wood; combined heat-and-power [CHP] systems that capture heat that normally goes to waste in power stations; and heat pumps, which use less electricity to provide heat than direct resistance heating.

A solar array on the aisle roof of Bradford Cathedral

The installation of a solar array at Bradford Cathedral was made relatively straightforward by the fact that the roof of choice was steel, and hidden behind a parapet. With a carefully designed fixing system, the installation thus had minimal effect on the fabric or the significance of the building.

The installation was the culmination of an extensive programme of energy saving at the Cathedral that ensured energy use has been minimised, allowing the solar array to provide a much greater percentage of the building's needs. Schemes of this kind are currently popular because excess energy can be sold back to the Grid; however, the potential revenue is rarely as good as hoped.

Unusually, at Bradford the costs and potential gains were assessed pessimistically rather than optimistically, and the result has therefore been a marked success.

Heat Pumps

Heat pumps are not renewable energy, but instead are a more efficient way to use electricity than direct electric heating. They operate like a refrigerator in reverse: heat is abstracted from a low-temperature source (the external environment) by boiling a refrigerant at a reduced pressure in an evaporator; the refrigerant gas is then compressed and fed into a condenser, where it liquefies, giving out heat to air or water which is then used to heat the building, before being returned to the evaporator. Some are reversible, and so can provide cooling and dehumidification in warm weather.

There are three principal types of heat pumps:

- *Air source*
  These extract heat from the outdoor air using a fanned heat exchanger, much like a car radiator.
- *Ground source*
  A few metres down, the ground is at a steady temperature. Ground-source heat pumps work by extracting this heat into water – usually containing salt or antifreeze – in closed loops of pipework, which pass through the evaporator. The pipes are run either vertically through drilled boreholes, or horizontally in trenches.
- *Water source*
  These extract heat from a large body of water, such as a lake, river or groundwater. Systems may be either closed-loop (as with ground-source heat pumps) or open-loop, where the water is abstracted from the body of water, pumped to the evaporator and returned to the source.

The ratio of heat output to energy input is called the Coefficient of Performance [CoP]. Data from manufacturers tends to quote the heat pump's CoP under standard conditions, but actual efficiencies tend to be lower because conditions may not be optimal. Electricity use by the associated fans, water pumps and controls also needs to be taken into account. It is not unusual for a system including a heat pump with a quoted CoP of 4 to have a year-round average CoP of 3 or less: that is, it is providing three times as much heat as the electricity it uses. At current prices, this typically makes heat pumps economically competitive with oil, but not with natural gas.

The efficiency of heat pumps decreases as the temperature difference between the exterior and the interior increases, and so they are most effective at supplying low-temperature heating systems such as underfloor heating. They can also be used to supply hot-water radiators, but since the practical limit for water temperature is in the region of 50°C, radiators will need to be considerably larger than they would for a traditional central-heating system running at 80°C.

The outdoor heat-transfer surface needs to be properly sized, or else the heat source may be depleted. This would not only reduce capacity: for air-source and water-source pumps, it could lead to freezing problems with the air and water coils.

The most important issue for closed-loop ground- and water-source heat pumps is that leakages can be more expensive to remedy. The antifreeze chemicals in the closed circuits also have the potential to pollute water supplies, including groundwater.

BUILDING ENVIRONMENT
SPECIAL TOPIC: Improving Energy & Carbon Performance

Restoration of Linton Falls Hydroelectric Power Station

The best choice of microgeneration system will depend first and foremost on the possibilities provided by the building's location. Hydroelectric schemes, for example, will need access to a source of fast-moving or flowing water.

The 1909 hydroelectric power station at Linton Falls in the Yorkshire Dales drew power from a 2.7-m weir on the River Wharfe, which had originally supplied a mill.

When the National Grid arrived in 1948 the station was decommissioned and fell derelict, but in 2011 it was restored by local engineering company J. N. Bentley, who added two 2.4-m diameter, 19-m long Archimedean-screw turbines. These can generate enough power for 90 houses, saving some 500,000 kWh of electricity per year, saving over 250 tonnes of carbon emissions in relation to the typical production of UK mains electricity.

Top left: The derelict power station.

Top right: One of the two screws being lowered into place in its housing.

Bottom: The restored power station in operation.

The benefits of any technology depend on how appropriate, cheap and efficient it is, and on how much energy, carbon and money it really saves. This is often not easy to determine. Critical questions to ask of a proposed system include:

- Does it really suit the particular building and use? Will the potential savings outstrip the whole-life energy and environmental costs? What if it runs at less than full efficiency? Ideal situations are rarely found in practice, and efficiency will drop as equipment ages.
- Can the system be fitted safely with no adverse impact on the fabric, particularly for systems placed on roofs?
- Are there any other restrictions, such as planning, environment, archaeology, noise or visual intrusion?
- For biomass, how renewable is it in truth? This will depend on the source of the fuel, and how it is cultivated, processed and transported.

LZC systems will often require some backup. Many wood burners have trouble coping with low loads; and renewable electricity production tends to fluctuate with the source, so will need to be balanced by exchanging energy with the electricity grid, importing or exporting as required. This will have implications for mains electricity costs, and also for carbon factors, which will need to be taken properly into account. LZC heating often benefits from added heat storage, to help increase inertia and integrate the backup.

There are more costs to LZC systems than the initial set-up: operation and maintenance expenses are often higher. Some systems also have relatively short lifespans, which has implications for life-cycle value (including issues surrounding embodied energy).

The Energy Plan should consider the long-term implications of lower-carbon energy supplies, examining how equipment needs to be maintained, the requirement for good and safe access, and how the system might eventually be removed at the end of its life without harming the building.

The checklist on the following pages lists some critical considerations for various LZC options, including characteristics, capacity, installation, operation and maintenance of the system.

CHECKLIST: CONSIDERATIONS FOR LZC SYSTEMS

SYSTEM CHARACTERISTICS	ENERGY SUPPLY & USE	CONSIDERATIONS FOR INSTALLATION
SOLAR WATER HEATING		
Comprises collector (which uses the sun's radiant energy to heat water), pipework, hot-water tank Collectors can be evacuated-tube or flat-plate Existing water-storage tank must usually be replaced with much larger tank fitted with heat-transfer coils (from the solar heater and from the conventional boiler) Effective control is needed of the pump that transfers the heat from panels to cylinder and the operation of the supplementary heating; controls must also have good user interfaces and their operation made clear to the user, or else much of the available solar energy can easily be wasted	In England, sunlight can heat water for a typical home during summer, and for about 50 % of hot water used during winter Evacuated-tube collectors about 40 % efficient; flat-plate collectors about 30 % efficient A south-facing 30° pitch is considered optimal, but this is not critical: collectors can still be effective on east and west faces or at reduced inclines, although the yield will be lower	Not very sensitive to partial shading Collector size needed for typical household = 2–4 m^2 Normally fixed on roof, but it can also be away from the building If roof-mounted, weight and wind-loading must be taken by the rafters: will need to be assessed by an experienced conservation engineer Must not compromise watertightness or maintenance of the roof Pipework and control cables running from collector into building may conflict with structure and finishes if roof-mounted If mounted externally, there may be conflicts with buried archaeology, drainage and other services Pipework will need insulation
PHOTOVOLTAICS		
Photovoltaic [PV] cells convert radiant energy from the sun into direct current electricity; this may be used directly to charge batteries and run DC equipment, but is usually converted to alternating current by an inverter to displace mains electricity System composed of array with DC cables to the inverter(s), which is then connected to the building's mains electrical distribution system Requires isolation switch so array can be disconnected for maintenance or repair; in grid-linked systems, the inverter must disconnect the array automatically if the mains fails or is isolated	In the UK, a well-orientated installation will provide in the region of 800 kWh per year per kW of installed peak capacity [kWp] A typical UK household (no electric heating) uses about 3300 kWh of electricity per year, so would need 4 or 5 kW; many roofs are too small (2 or 3 kW is more common) At the time of writing, efficiencies of cells available on the market were in the range of 12–20 %; but performance is improving rapidly Combined PV and Thermal [PV-T] cells are also available, providing both electricity and hot water	Very sensitive to partial shading (for example, by vegetation or neighbouring buildings); where some shadowing is unavoidable, modular inverters can increase efficiency (one per panel or pair of panels) South-facing 30–50° pitch considered optimal for most of the UK Area needed to generate 1 kW: 6–10 m^2, depending on panel efficiency Normally fixed on roof, but it can also be away from the building Usually fixed to roof on a frame above the roof covering, but can also be combined with covering (such as solar slates) If roof-mounted, weight and wind-loading must be taken by the rafters: will need to be assessed by an experienced conservation engineer Must not compromise watertightness or maintenance of roof
BIOMASS BOILERS		
Similar to conventional boilers, but use logs, chips or pellets as the fuel source	Size of boiler depends on the heating load Wood-fired stoves can also be fitted with a back boiler to provide hot water	Larger than conventional boilers; may need dedicated plant rooms Requires sizeable storage area for fuel (which must be kept dry to burn properly and prevent growth of toxic mould) Ash storage will also be needed Automatic models also require feedscrews with straight-line connections to fuel stores Needs good access for delivery of fuel, removal of ash and maintenance, including flue and chimney cleaning Care must be taken to minimise fire and explosion hazards from flues, chimneys, feedscrews and fuel stores

MAINTENANCE	FAILURE	DESIGN LIFE	PERMISSIONS
Every year: • Clean the glass • Check glazing seals, insulation, fixings and pipework; look for signs of leaks, corrosion or persistent condensation • Check pressure, and pressure relief valve • Ensure there is no air in the system, and that automatic air vents are not leaking Every five years: antifreeze should be tested Every 20 years: drain and check thoroughly	Causes include frost damage because antifreeze has degraded, pump failure, leaking (especially through the air vent) Poor performance may be due to wrongly set differential temperature controller (so pump operates too little or too much), incorrect pump speed, air in the pipes, poorly positioned temperature sensors, missing or damaged pipe insulation, or auxiliary heater (such as a boiler or immersion heater) being on too much and usurping the load	20–25 years	Fixing to building with statutory protection would require consent
Remove dirt and debris regularly with warm water and a brush, or a high-pressure hose Cut back trees and other vegetation to prevent overshadowing Keep records of output to establish normal monthly outputs, and allow detection of under-performance	Faults with the inverter may mean no electricity is provided Inverter is likely to fail well before lifespan of panels is reached Sometimes wiring problems, failed panels	Lifespan of cells: monocrystalline 25–30 years polycrystalline 20–25 years hybrid 20–25 years Life of inverters used to convert the generated DC to usable AC: 5–15 years	Fixing to building with statutory protection would require consent
Ash pan or bin must be cleared frequently Chimney and flue pipe must be regularly swept to remove ashes and soot (quarterly or half-yearly, depending on use and fuel) Yearly or more frequent servicing by qualified engineer	Automatic boilers tend to be the most troublesome element Fuel quality can affect combustion or the fuel feed for automatic boilers Wood chips may be too damp, or contain debris that fouls fuel or ash feeds If stored carefully pellets are more consistent in quality than chips, but they can sometimes be damaged during pneumatic transfer and become too dusty	8–20 years or more, depending on maintenance	Flue must meet regulations for wood-burning appliances (insulated stainless-steel flue or appropriate lining), with appropriate isolation from combustible parts of the fabric New flues and chimneys will probably need planning permission

BUILDING ENVIRONMENT
SPECIAL TOPIC: Improving Energy & Carbon Performance

CHECKLIST: CONSIDERATIONS FOR LZC SYSTEMS

SYSTEM CHARACTERISTICS	ENERGY SUPPLY & USE	CONSIDERATIONS FOR INSTALLATION
GROUND-SOURCE HEAT PUMPS		
Pump extracts thermal energy from ground using embedded closed loop Loop can be in a vertical borehole or a horizontal trench Loop may need to be filled with brine or antifreeze to stop freezing in winter	The higher the circulation temperature required, the less efficient the heat pump Most efficient supplying low-temperature heating systems, especially underfloor heating	Type of system and possible depth of the loop depends on geology, topography and archaeology of ground, and location of existing services Trenches commonly use spiral 'Slinky' plastic pipe in excavations 1.2–2.5 m deep; extensive and disruptive, and likely to conflict with buried services and archaeology Boreholes usually 10–15 cm in diameter and 15–120 m deep; damage is localised so may be feasible for small sites or sites with significant archaeology Boring demands specialist equipment and knowledge
WATER-SOURCE HEAT PUMPS		
Pump extracts thermal energy from a body of water (such as a lake, stream or aquifer) May be closed-loop or open-loop CLOSED LOOP: requires less pipework than ground-source systems because heat transfer is more efficient	The higher the circulation temperature required the less efficient the heat pump, so most efficient supplying low-temperature heating systems (such as underfloor heating)	Requires proximity to suitable body of water OPEN LOOP: In areas of rising water table, it may sometimes be permissible to extract groundwater and discharge it to the surface
AIR-SOURCE HEAT PUMPS		
Uses a heat pump to extract thermal energy from the exterior air	Can supply low-temperature heating systems, preferably underfloor or warm air; though radiator systems at about 50°C are common, these are less efficient	Units can be installed internally or externally Care must be taken to avoid exhaust air recirculating to the intake, or else efficiency will drop as the air gets colder Noise can be an issue, both internally and particularly externally If the whole unit is internal, sizeable holes will need to be made through the building envelope for intake and exhaust air Some heat pumps are 'split', with internal and external units requiring only water or refrigerant pipes and electric cables between them Tend to run out of capacity in cold weather when they are most needed, in which case supplementary heating may be required
WIND TURBINES		
Convert kinetic energy of wind into electrical energy Horizontal-axis turbines with three blades are most common Vertical-axis turbines also available, but tend to be less efficient and require higher wind speeds	Most will only work at wind speeds above about 4 m/s; may not be viable where typical wind speed is below 4.5 m/s For optimum yield, should face towards the prevailing wind	Local topography (particularly surrounding buildings) can greatly reduce energy production It is normally inadvisable to fit a turbine to a building, owing to the forces and vibrations generated Turbine must be high enough for blades to escape turbulence; can make turbines unsuitable for urban and suburban areas Buried cabling running from the turbine into the building may conflict with buried archaeology, drainage and other services

MAINTENANCE	FAILURE	DESIGN LIFE	PERMISSIONS
Check regularly for leaks Yearly before start of heating season check water pump, external pipework and antifreeze (if used) Periodic checks by a qualified service engineer to manufacturer's recommendations; for small systems this may be every three years, for large systems annually	Must be correctly specified and designed: if pipework extracts more heat from the ground than can be naturally replaced, efficiency will drop dramatically, and some heat pumps will bring on supplementary electric resistance heating	15–35 years for heat pump, and associated pumps and pipework Heat pumps typically warrantied for 2–3 years, but with good maintenance should work for 20 years	Will need consent if archaeology might be disturbed
Yearly before start of heating season check water pump and external pipework Periodic checks by a qualified service engineer to manufacturer's recommendations. For small systems this may be every three years, for large systems annually	OPEN LOOP: • prone to corrosion and fouling of equipment • aquifer systems may transfer silts to the discharge borehole, risking blockage • frost risk, particularly where circulating volumes are small or water pumps do not operate continuously	15–35 years for heat pump and associated pumps and pipework Heat pumps typically warrantied for 2–3 years, but with good maintenance should work for 20 years	OPEN LOOP: Will require permission from the Environment Agency (often both an 'abstraction licence' and a 'permit to discharge') Systems extracting more than 20 m³ per day (such as a heat pump of more than about 3 kW output capacity) will also require an extraction and discharge licence
Filters should be changed often, and fans and coils kept clean; air-inlet grills should be checked every few weeks and cleaned if necessary Yearly before start of heating season: check heat pump and associated fans, pumps and controls, clean evaporator, remove any vegetation near inlet Every three years – or to manufacturer's recommendations – heat pumps and any refrigerant pipes should be checked by a qualified service engineer	Ambient air temperatures fluctuate considerably, so can be unreliable Must be correctly specified and designed: if exchanger is undersized, water vapour can freeze around heat exchanger, forcing pump into a 'defrost' cycle Undersized or poorly constructed systems can be noisy If poorly positioned, may recycle own cooled air, decreasing efficiency	10 years Heat pumps typically warrantied for 2–3 years, but with good maintenance should work for 20 years	External installations may require planning permission
Yearly or two-yearly checks; may need more frequent repair as the turbine ages	Batteries in off-grid systems will need to be replaced every 6–10 years Inverter is likely to fail before lifespan of turbine is reached Moving parts and exposed parts are likely to fail first; the most common failures are the gearbox (where present) and rotor blades	Up to 20 years The inverters used to convert the generated DC to usable AC have a life of 5–15 years	Will probably need planning permission: local planning authority will look for issues concerning visual impact and proximity to land boundaries

BUILDING ENVIRONMENT
SPECIAL TOPIC: Improving Energy & Carbon Performance

CHECKLIST: CONSIDERATIONS FOR LZC SYSTEMS

SYSTEM CHARACTERISTICS	ENERGY SUPPLY & USE	CONSIDERATIONS FOR INSTALLATION
SMALL-SCALE HYDROELECTRIC POWER		
Converts kinetic and potential energy of running water into electrical energy Driven by water either flowing down a watercourse, or falling from a height	Energy output depends on the product of volume flow rate and height through which water falls (the 'head') High-head systems much more cost-effective, but many UK sites are low-head (3 m or less)	Requires proximity to a good source of running water, or to water at two different levels (for example, between a storage pond and a stream) Permission required from the Environment Agency: can be difficult to obtain
COMBINED HEAT & POWER [CHP] SYSTEMS		
Captures waste heat from electricity generation Most systems use internal combustion engines; gas turbines seldom used in building applications Sterling engines can be used, but proportion of electricity generated is small Fuel cells have potential, but are currently expensive Biomass systems (such as wood gasification) are available, but maintenance-intensive, can be unreliable and unsuited to intermittent use	Most units supply hot water at 70–80°C maximum Must run for 3500 hours a year or more to be economical (in general the longer the operation, the greater the savings) Generation overnight will sometimes be uneconomic, depending on electricity tariffs Most cost-effective system will be sized to cover the baseload only Generated heat is not 'free', but obtained at some loss of electricity in relation to a gas-fired power station; to be cost-effective and save carbon, a good use must be found for the generated heat	Selection is difficult: must have a very good picture of building electricity and heating use Electricity contracts and tariffs must be reviewed carefully; there can be major advantages depending on the schedules of operation and the levels of reliability Will need more frequent and complex servicing than conventional boilers, so good maintenance access is important Care must be taken to minimise noise and vibration Internal combustion engines have relatively high nitrogen-oxide emissions in relation to boilers Sometimes unwanted heat in summer can be used in an absorption chiller to make chilled water for cooling, but suitable applications are rare, and efficiency is relatively low

MAINTENANCE	FAILURE	DESIGN LIFE	PERMISSIONS
Regular overhaul of parts exposed to water; check bearings, packing box and shaft sleeves, servomotors, cooling systems for bearings and generator coils, seal rings, wicket-gate linkage elements, and all surfaces Screens require regular checking and clearing of debris	Moving parts and parts exposed to water are likely to fail first The most common failures include blades being abraded or pitted by cavitation, and fatigue cracking	Depends on system and maintenance, ancient water wheels may be successfully restored and run with modern electronic controls	Environment Agency conditions can be onerous, and will normally require an 'abstraction licence' An environmental impact assessment will usually be a condition of any planning consent
Pumps and filters must be kept clear Systems using electric fans and radiators must be maintained to minimise noise and vibration Treat water in evaporative coolers to prevent corrosion and bacterial growth Regularly check gas detection and ventilation Dampers controlling flow of exhaust gases in bypass ductwork must be checked regularly	Failure of the gas compressor, cooling systems, gas detection systems or the ventilation can lead to the CHP shutting down	PEMFC fuel cells: around 10 years	Domestic systems can be installed in place of standard domestic boilers, so planning permission may not be required unless there are changes to the flue openings

BUILDING ENVIRONMENT
SPECIAL TOPIC: Improving Energy & Carbon Performance

598

Communal power generation is by no means a new idea: before the National Grid, windmills and watermills provided the power for communities to undertake energy-intensive tasks such as grinding corn or pumping water out of fields; in the Industrial Revolution steam-powered engines were also worked locally.

This approach to LZC energy production offers strong cost-benefits. It allows installation, running and maintenance costs to be shared, and power use to be spread (making it easier to balance generation and load).

The historic environment offers many lessons for sustainable living, and is a resource of information and experience that could be much more widely exploited.

Useful Websites

ENGLISH HERITAGE

www.english-heritage.org.uk/energy-efficiency/

Guidance on microgeneration includes: *Small-Scale Solar Thermal Energy and Traditional Buildings* (2008); *Micro Wind Generation and Traditional Buildings* (2010); ; *Small Scale Solar Electric* (2010); *Energy Efficiency and Historic Buildings* (2012); *Heat Pumps* (2013): *www.english-heritage.org.uk/publications/*

OTHERS

There are many useful websites with extensive links to up-to-date practical information. These include:

Building Science Corporation: *www.buildingscience.com*

Carbon Buzz: *www.carbonbuzz.org*

Carbon Trust: *www.carbontrust.com*

Energy Saving Trust: *www.energysavingtrust.org.uk*

Green Building Adviser: *www.greenbuildingadvisor.com/*

Historic Scotland: *www.historic-scotland.gov.uk/index/learning.htm*

National Park Service, US Department of the Interior: *www.nps.gov/tps/sustainability.htm*

Society for the Protection of Ancient Buildings: *www.spab.org.uk/advice/energy-efficiency*

Sustainable Traditional Buildings Alliance: *www.stbauk.org*

Usable Buildings Trust: *www.usablebuildings.co.uk*

Information and advice about community projects is available from *www.gov.uk/community-energy*
and *www.energysavingtrust.org.uk/Communities/Support-and-guidance/*

Information about Soft Landings can be found on the website of the Building Services Research and Information Association [BSRIA]: *www.bsria.co.uk/services/design/soft-landings/free-guidance*

Energy details about domestic electrical equipment can be found at *www.sust-it.net*

BUILDING ENVIRONMENT
SPECIAL TOPIC: Improving Energy & Carbon Performance

Further Reading

Asif, M., Davidson, A., Muneer, T. (2002); *Life Cycle of Windows Materials – A Comparative Assessment*; Napier University, School of Engineering: Edinburgh; available at ohp.parks.ca.gov/pages/1054/files/uk%20window%20frame%20lca.pdf

Borowy, I. (2014); *Defining Sustainable Development for Our Common Future: A History of the World Commission on Environment and Development (Brundtland Commission)*; London & New York: Routledge

Cabinet Office, Performance and Innovation Unit (2001); *Resource Productivity: Making More With Less*; Performance and Innovation Unit report; London: The Cabinet Office

Carbon Trust (2009); *Building the Future Today*; available at www.carbontrust.com/media/77252/ctc765_building_the_future__today.pdf

Chartered Institution of Building Services Engineers (2002); *Guide to Building Services for Historic Buildings*; London: CIBSE

Dunnett, N., Gedge, D., Little, J. (2011); *Small Green Roofs: Low-Tech Options for Homeowners*; Portland, Oregon: Timber Press

Foxell, S. (2014); *A Carbon Primer for the Built Environment*; London: Routledge

Gedge, D., Dunnet, N., Grant, G., Jones, R. (2007); *Living Roofs*; Sheffield: Natural England; also available at livingroofs.org/images/stories/pdfs/living%20roofs.pdf

Heath, N., Baker, P., Menzies, G. (2010); *Slim Profile Double-Glazing: Thermal Performance and Embodied Energy*; Historic Scotland Conservation Group Technical Paper 9; Edinburgh: Historic Scotland; also available at www.historic-scotland.gov.uk/slim-profile_double_glazing_2010.pdf

McCloud, K., Hunt, R., Suhr, M. (2013); *Old House Eco Handbook: A Practical Guide to Retrofitting for Energy-Efficiency and Sustainability*; London: Frances Lincoln

Dengel, A., Swainson, M., (2012); *Overheating in New Homes, A Review of the Evidence*; NHBC Foundation Research Review NF 46; Milton Keynes: IHS BRE Press on behalf of the NHBC Foundation; available at www.nhbcfoundation.org/Publications/Research-Review/Overheating-in-new-homes-NF46

Nicol, F., Stevenson, F. (2013); 'Adaptive comfort in an unpredictable world'; in *Building Research & Information*; Vol.41, No.3; pp.255–258

Palmer, J., Cooper, I. (2013); United Kingdom Housing Energy Fact File; Report for the Department of Energy and Climate Change; available at www.gov.uk/government/publications/united-kingdom-housing-energy-fact-file-2013

Pinno, F., Möllmann, K-P., Vollmer, M. (2008); 'Thermography of window panes – problems, possibilities and troubleshooting'; in *Inframation 2008*, Proceedings Vol.9; pp.477–492; also available at opus4.kobv.de/opus4-fhbrb/frontdoor/index/index/docId/525

Saunders, H. D. (2011); 'Six misconceptions about rebound and backfire'; on *The Breakthrough Online*, 24 January; available at thebreakthrough.org/archive/six_misconceptions_about_rebou

Shove, E. (2005); 'Changing human behaviour and lifestyle: a challenge for sustainable consumption?'; in Ropke, I., Reisch, L. (eds): *Consumption – Perspectives from Ecological Economics*; Cheltenham: Elgar; pp. 111–132; also available at www.psi.org.uk/ehb/docs/shove-changinghumanbehaviourandlifestyle-200308.pdf

Shove, E., Chappells, H., Lutzenhiser, L., Hackett, B. (2008); 'Comfort in a lower carbon society'; in *Building Research and Information*; Vol.36, No.4; pp.307–311

Smil, V. (2008); *Energy in Nature and Society: General Energetics of Complex Systems*; Princeton: MIT Press

Zhang, H., Arens, E., Pasut, W. (2011); 'Air temperature thresholds for indoor comfort and perceived air quality'; in *Building Research & Information*; Vol.39, No.2; pp.134–144

GLOSSARY

A-rated
The maximum rating for a domestic boiler under the SEDBUK [Seasonal Efficiency of Domestic Boilers in the UK] rating scheme. A-rated boilers are rated at 90 % efficient or higher in terms of average annual efficiency in typical domestic conditions.

Absolute humidity [AH]
The actual number of water molecules in air at a given time, expressed in terms of the ratio of the mass of water vapour to the volume of air (grams of water per cubic metre of air, g/m^3).

Absorption
The physical take-up of molecules or ions into a permeable material, as when water vapour is absorbed by capillarity into stone or brick.

Ach
Air changes per hour: a way of expressing the air-exchange rate.
See also Air-exchange rate

Acoustic energy
A form of mechanical energy produced by vibrations in air molecules travelling through matter as a compression wave. Used to describe all vibrational energy, even when the frequency is well outside the human range of hearing (ultrasound).

Adaptation
Initiatives and measures to reduce the vulnerability, or increase the resilience, of natural and human systems to actual or expected climate change impacts.

Adsorption
The chemical bonding of molecules or ions to molecules on the surface of a material, as when polar water molecules are adsorbed on the walls of pores within a permeable material, or when pollutant gases and particulates are adsorbed on the surface of a building stone during soiling.

Aerogel
Low-density, nano-porous, ultra-lightweight material typically made from a silica gel, from which the liquid component has been extracted and replaced by air.

Air conditioning
The artificial treatment of air to adjust its temperature, humidity, cleanliness, quality and circulation. It typically uses the evaporation of liquefied gas to both chill the air and remove water vapour by condensation.

Air curtain
Insulation by means of a high-velocity jet of air between floor and ceiling.

Air-exchange rate
The rate at which a given quantity of air is exchanged between two locations (for example, the replacement of interior air by exterior air through open doors or windows due to air pressure differences). The air-exchange rate is expressed either in litres per second, or as 'air changes per hour' [ach].

Air movement
The flow of air from one place to another: for example, as a result of air exchange, building use, natural or forced ventilation, or convection from hot and cold surfaces (especially heaters and windows).

Air-source heat pump
A heat pump that transfers heat from outside to inside using an external heat exchanger to extract heat from the air, or vice versa, using an internal heat exchanger.

Air terminal
Lightning rod or conductor such as spanned wires and cables or intermeshed conductors, placed on or above a building.

Air- and vapour-control layer [AVCL]
A vapour barrier intended also to retard the migration of air.

Ambient air
The air present at a particular time and place; any unconfined portion of the atmosphere.

Ambient temperature
The temperature in the atmosphere surrounding the volume or parcel of air being considered.

Amplitude
The distance from the centre line of a transverse wave to its crest or trough; in electromagnetic energy, it expresses the strength of the electromagnetic wave.

Anemometer
An instrument for measuring air speed.

Anion
A negatively charged ion.

Anthropogenic forcing
The forcing, or exacerbation, of climate change by human activities (notably the combustion of fossil fuels, agricultural processes or deforestation practices).

Aquifer
Underground geological formation or layer from which groundwater can be extracted.

Aspirating smoke detector
Smoke detector consisting of a small sampling tube which draws in the air to a sampling chamber, where any smoke in the air will scatter a beam of visible or infrared light.

Atomic absorption spectrophotometry
Quantitative analytical technique for determining chemical elements in a sample by the absorption of radiant energy by free atoms in the gaseous state.

Attenuation
Reduction in amplitude, density or energy as a result of effects such as friction, scattering or absorption. Attenuation methods in materials analysis – such as microwave attenuation and ultrasound – measure the decrease in strength of an electromagnetic signal as it travels through a material.

Autoxidation
Oxidation that occurs in the presence of both oxygen and ultraviolet radiation.

Aviary mesh
Fine bird mesh made from galvanised welded wire.

Back boiler
Boiler supplying hot water for heating, which is built in behind a fireplace or is an integral part of a gas fire.

Biofilms
Colonies of microorganisms and extra-cellular slime forming films of varying thickness on surfaces.

Biofuel
Any liquid, gaseous or solid fuel produced from biomass: for example, soybean oil, alcohol from fermented sugar, black liquor from the paper manufacturing process or wood as fuel. Traditional biofuels include wood, dung, grass and agricultural residues.

Biomass boiler
Boiler that uses logs, chips or pellets as the fuel source.

Bioremediation
Control of plant or animal pests by altering the environmental conditions to make them less suitable for the problematic species. An effective way of dealing with many of the fungi and insects causing timber decay.

Black globe thermometer
Instrument for measuring radiant temperature, that consists of a hollow sphere – coloured matt black to absorb maximum energy – with a temperature sensor at its centre.

Blower-door test
See Fan pressurisation testing

Bressumer beam
A horizontal, supporting beam set above a fireplace opening, an opening in an external wall or (in timber-framed construction) set forward from the lower part of a building to support a jetty.

Brittleness
The tendency to fracture without appreciable deformation and under low stress.

Buffering
The attenuating effect of building materials on the atmospheric fluctuations (for example, in temperature, relative humidity, air pressure or radiation) originating either outside the building (due to the external microclimate) or inside the building (due to heating, lighting, air conditioning, and use or occupancy). The use of permeable materials and mass construction in traditional construction make it particularly effective at buffering.

Building envelope
The weathertight skin separating the interior environment of a building from its external environment; it is made up of the roof, walls, windows, doors, floors and foundations, and systems for controlling and disposing of water (including rainwater goods, roof coverings, damp-proof courses and drains).

Building management system [BMS]
An integrated system for controlling building engineering services.

Building-related illness [BRI]
Poor health involving common symptoms in most or all the users of a particular building, with a demonstrable link to the length of time spent in the building and evidence pointing to a specific cause.

Building services
Services and systems used to manage the interior environment, utilities and comfort of a building. They supply heating, lighting, ventilation, electrical power and water, as well as communications and fire security.

Buoyancy
An upward force on an object immersed in a gas or fluid that opposes the force of gravity. In air, any object that is less dense than an equal volume of air will rise. As air is heated it expands and becomes less dense, so hot air will rise.

Calibration
The process of determining absolute values corresponding to the graduations on an instrumental scale, setting the relationship between the output of the instrument and the absolute values of the parameter being measured.

Capacitance meter
Electronic device for measuring capacitance (the ability of a material or system to store an electric charge). In environmental monitoring, capacitance sensors are used to record the dielectric properties of permeable materials such as earth, mortar, brick and stone, and thus indirectly the moisture content. Hand-held devices obtain a shallow moisture-content reading from the attenuation of an electric field applied at the surface.

Capillarity
The spontaneous flow of a liquid in a confined space, such as a narrow tube or between two flat surfaces laid close together. Essentially, it is a consequence of the intermolecular forces that occur within the liquid, and between the liquid and the walls of the space. Can cause liquids such as water to rise against gravity; the narrower the space, the higher the rise. Also known as capillary action or wicking.

Capillary
Any tube or vessel narrow enough to cause liquid flow by capillarity.

Capillary action
See Capillarity

Carbide meter
Device for measuring free moisture content of drilled masonry or soil samples. The powder sample is weighed, then placed in a sealed flask with a measured amount of calcium carbide powder. The flask is shaken vigorously, and the moisture in the sample reacts with the calcium carbide to produce acetylene gas, which exerts a pressure on the flask that can be read on an external gauge.

Carbon emissions
Release of carbon dioxide into the atmosphere from the burning of fossil fuels for activities such as industrial production, transportation and power generation.

Carbon factor
The rate of carbon emission per unit of energy in a given activity, expressed as $KgCO_2/kWh$.

Castrol stove
Cooking stove developed in France in 1735, constructed of masonry with fire-holes covered by perforated iron plates. The design, a precursor to modern coal-fired metal heating stoves, was the first to enclose the fire in a sealed combustion chamber vented to a flue via a stovepipe. This allowed the airflow to be regulated, increasing the combustion temperature and virtually eliminating the loss of heat by convection.

Cation
A positively charged ion.

Cavity membrane system
A modern form of dry lining using a special plastic sheet, fixed directly to the wall with waterproof fixing plugs and integrated floor drainage, and then covered with plaster or some other finish.

Cavity wall
A wall consisting of an inner and outer leaf of brick or blockwork, separated by a cavity and tied together with wall ties.

Cement
In the general sense, any binder, but more specifically, any composite material that relies for its initial set on the hydration reaction of water with dicalcium and tricalcium silicates.
See also Roman cement

Chemical energy
Energy associated with the atomic, molecular or aggregate structure of a material. In chemistry, it refers to the potential of a material to be altered by a chemical reaction, or to alter other materials.

Chimney balloon
Inflatable bag to prevent heat loss through an open flue. The device can be installed in a flue during the heating season and then removed for the summer months.

Clay
In soil science, a fine-grained soil containing particles finer than 2 μm in diameter, chiefly composed of silica, alumina and water.

Climate
Average atmospheric conditions that prevail for a given location over time.

Clipped eaves
Eaves with insufficient overhang.

Coefficient of performance
The ratio of heating or cooling provided by a system in relation to its energy consumption.

Cogeneration
See Combined heat and power [CHP]

Co-heating test
Thermal-performance test to measure heat loss in buildings. The unoccupied building is heated to a set temperature for a set period of time (usually 25°C for between one and three weeks). The energy in watts used to keep the building at this temperature is measured daily to determine heat input. This is plotted against the daily difference in exterior temperature, to project a heat-loss coefficient curve for the building.

'Cold' roof
A roof system comprising insulation below or between the joists above the ceiling, and a 'cold' airspace between the insulation layer and the roof deck. The air space must be ventilated to prevent interstitial condensation affecting the roof structure or covering.

Colorimetry
The science of measuring the physical and spectral characteristics of colours. In environmental science, the main reference is the Munsell Scale, which defines colours using a number and letter system based on three colour dimensions: hue (red, blue, green and so forth), value (lightness or darkness) and chroma (intensity or saturation).

'Combi' (or combination) boiler
Boiler capable of heating domestic water direct from the mains without requiring a hot-water storage cylinder.

Combined heat and power [CHP]
Energy supply system in which waste heat is captured for use in water or space heating as a by-product of electric power generation in a power plant; also known as cogeneration. 'Micro CHP' refers to the use of conventional generators such as internal combustion engines, Sterling engines and fuel cells to generate electric power and heat simultaneously on a small scale for individual power needs.

Compact fluorescent lamp [CFL]
Energy-saving fluorescent lamp, consisting of a gas filled tube or coil and an electronic ballast, now widely used in place of incandescent lamps.

Compression
Pressure on an object caused by a compaction (crushing) force.

Compression wave
Wave propagated by compression of the fluid in which the wave travels; acoustic energy travels as a compression wave.

Computational fluid dynamics [CFD]
Branch of fluid mechanics that uses numerical methods and algorithms to analyse problems involving flows of fluids and gases such as air.

Conchoidal fracture
Smooth, curved fracture, as in glass and other amorphous materials.

Condensation
The process of forming a liquid from its vapour. When moist air is cooled below its dew point, water vapour condenses, forming a film of liquid water or a cloud of mist. Water vapour can condense on surfaces (superficial condensation) or inside pores, or on the internal interfaces between materials (interstitial condensation).

Condensing boiler
Boiler in which the water vapour in the flue gases is condensed and discharged, so that latent heat generated by the combustion process can be recovered and used to increase boiler efficiency.

Conduction
The transfer of thermal energy by direct contact between molecules, from one part of a substance to another and to another substance in physical contact with it.

Conservation heating
Heating of interior spaces using controls based on humidistats rather than thermostats; used to try to stabilise relative humidity in historic buildings for the benefit of the fabric and contents.

Conservation Plan
A written statement, of varying complexity, that sets out the way in which significance has been understood, the issues identified and the strategies proposed for management of a heritage asset. It includes a careful analysis of fabric and its significance, and serves as both a record of the way judgements were reached, and an operational decision-making tool to guide maintenance, repair, alteration, use and development.

Conservation Statement
A synthetic overview of a given heritage asset, which includes an appraisal of its heritage values, a summary of its significance and an initial assessment of the issues likely to affect its future management.

Convection
The transfer of thermal energy in a liquid or gas by a combination of fluid circulation (a form of kinetic energy) and conduction. The driving force for natural air convection is buoyancy: as those packets of air in contact with a source of heat become hotter and rise, their place will be taken up by packets of the surrounding colder air, which are heated and rise in turn, perhaps losing heat and falling again as they meet cooler surfaces. This process produces a 'convection current'.
See also Buoyancy

Convective heating
A heating system that warms the air by convection. The category includes hot-water central heating, electric convective heaters (both passive and fan-assisted), under-pew convective heaters, hot-air blower systems and portable fan heaters.

Core sampling
Removing a sample of material, most commonly from a wall, for determining chemistry, petrography or moisture content at depth. Samples can be drilled powder or solid cores.
See also Powder samples, Solid core samples

Corrosion
Decay of metal caused by an electrochemical reaction between the anode and cathode of a corrosion cell in the presence of water and oxygen. At the anodic site, the metal loses electrons and forms soluble metal salts; these electrons combine with the water and oxygen to form hydroxyl ions (OH−), which in turn react with the cations and dissolved oxygen at the associated cathodic site to form a corrosion product (for example, rust, in the case of iron).

Crisis of discomfort
A sensation of discomfort – for example, finding a room hot, cold, stuffy or draughty – sufficient to impel a person to take some action (such as opening a window or turning on a heater).

Cryptoflorescence
See Subflorescence

Curtain wall
In modern parlence, a construction system where the exterior walls are clad with lightweight metal framing members and infill sections, which carry no building loads other than their own weight.
See also Face-sealed, Rainscreen

Damp-proof course [DPC]
A layer or course of waterproof material (such as sheet lead, slate, bituminous felt or DPM) carried through the entire thickness of the wall just above the ground. First introduced in the middle of the 19th century in the form of interlocking tiles intended to combat the rise of contaminated water from faulty early sewers, and subsequently included in the building codes to prevent groundwater rising in walls.

Damp-proof membrane [DPM]
A sheet of polythene or other hydrophobic material used to prevent the transfer of moisture from wet areas (such as the ground or areas of damp masonry) into internal walls, floors and finishes, or into sensitive fixtures such as monuments.

Datalogger
A portable electronic device for recording data over time in relation to place. It may be a stand-alone device with integrated sensors, or a centralised device with remote sensors connected by wires or radio telemetry. In either case the sensors relay data electronically to a microprocessor and internal memory within the datalogger, from which it can be periodically downloaded onto a computer for synthesis and analysis.

Dead load
The weight of a structure and any permanent loads fixed to it. Also referred to as 'fixed load' or 'static load'.

'Deep' retrofit
Whole-building approach to retrofitting using high-performance materials and techniques, such as high R-value insulation systems, triple glazing and energy-efficient HVAC systems, to avoid air infiltration and thermal bridges. Aside from the comfort aspects, the objective can be a difficult one to achieve within historic structures. Also referred to as 'extreme' refurbishment.

Dehumidification
The process of reducing the moisture content of air, achieved either by desiccation (exposing the moist air to a special material able to effectively absorb water vapour) or by refrigeration (passing moist air over a cold surface – usually a refrigerating coil – so that the water vapour condenses).

Deliquescence
The absorption of water from the atmosphere by a hygroscopic solid to the extent that the solid dissolves to form a concentrated solution; some deliquescent materials such as certain salts and salt mixtures absorb atmospheric moisture so readily that they will never crystallise under normal conditions. Salt crystals may expand considerably as they absorb moisture before deliquescence.

Der p 1
A digestive enzyme produced by the dust mite, associated with allergies and other health symptoms in humans.

Detailed Energy Plan
Energy Plan that develops findings from a Preliminary Energy Plan to establish a holistic strategy for reducing energy consumption, considering a range of packages or measures in relation to user needs, costs, technical suitability, heritage impacts and projected benefits.

Dew-point temperature
The temperature at which moist air is cooled sufficiently for condensation to take place. Since warmer air can hold more moisture, the dew-point temperature increases as the amount of moisture in the air increases. If the temperature of a surface falls below the dew point of the air, the air coming into contact with that surface will be cooled enough to deposit the water molecules it no longer has enough energy to support.

Diagnostic monitoring
A type of environmental monitoring used for the specific purpose of obtaining a diagnosis of building defects or conditions and their consequences. Diagnostic monitoring is necessarily critical and selective, focusing on specific hypotheses and parameters tailored to given situations. It differs from day-to-day or routine environmental monitoring for on-going environmental control in building or collections management.

Dielectric
A substance – solid, liquid or gas – of very low electrical conductivity, which can sustain a static electric field.

Dipwell
An open-ended tube, perforated toward the base and sunk into the ground, used for monitoring groundwater. A 'dipmeter' attached to a measurement reel is lowered down the tube to record the depth of the water table.

Display Energy Certificate [DEC]
A certificate (similar to the Energy Performance Certificate), required in England and Wales under the EU Energy Performance of Buildings Directive [EPB Directive] for all larger buildings that are occupied by a public authority, and which are frequently visited by the public.

Double-knock alarm system
Fire detection system in which two sensors in the same detection zone must be activated in order to trigger the alarm. Also known as 'coincident detection'.

Down conduction
The conduction path of a lightning protection system linking the air termination and the ground termination. It must connect together all major metallic elements of the building, including the rainwater goods.

Draught
1. A current of air, particularly one that is intruding into an enclosed space.
2. The draw of a chimney; that is, the degree to which (by virtue of its height and the airflow across the top) a chimney sets up a pressure gradient which keeps air moving in a stack effect.

Dry lining
A traditional palliative for dealing with damp walls. Includes timber panels fixed to battens on the wet wall, sometimes incorporating isolating membranes or vapour retarders, and cavity-membrane systems.
See also Cavity membrane system

Dry weight
The measured weight of a material or sample of material after it has been exposed to a controlled temperature (generally 105°C) until its weight is no longer decreasing.

Dual probe heat pulse
Thermal sensing technique for measuring water content and thermal properties of soils. It uses a probe with two prongs; the first is heated by an electrical current, while the second measures the resulting temperature change.

Ductile
Adjective referring to a material that can be readily deformed (drawn or stretched) under tensile stress.

Ductile fracture
Type of cracking produced when a ductile or elastic material is stretched beyond its yield point.
See also Ductile, Elastic, Yield point

Dynamic load
A load changing over short periods of time, caused by (for example) wind, vibration or impact.

Earth terminal
Copper rods, plates or mats at the earth termination of a lightning-protection system, intended to safely conduct a lightning current to the ground.

Eddy current
An electrical phenomenon in which circulating currents generated by varying electromotive forces are produced by changes in a magnetic field. When an electromagnetic field is induced in a stationary conductor (such as concrete or masonry), eddy currents are produced and these can be picked up using a sensor. This is the basis of analytical techniques such as potential mapping and metal detection.

Efflorescence
Crystalline deposits (ranging from loose and powdery to hard and compact) resulting from the evaporation of water from a salt solution, which can form on the surface of a porous material exposed to air.

Elastic
Describing a material that can easily resume its original shape after being distorted by a stress, once that stress is removed.
See also Stress

Elastic limit
The limiting value of the deforming force beyond which an elastic body cannot return to its original shape or dimensions when the stress is removed. In engineering, it corresponds to the highest stress that can be applied without producing a measurable amount of plastic deformation.

Electrical resistivity tomography
Geophysical technique for imaging of subsurface hydrology using an electrical current to measure electrical resistivity.
See also Tomography

Electrolyte
Any liquid or solid substance, or its solution in water, which can conduct electric current through ionisation: aqueous solutions of acids or metal salts (including rainwater or runoff) are electrolytes.

Electromagnetic energy
The energy emitted and absorbed by charged particles; it travels as a transverse wave, with various amplitudes and frequencies.

Electromagnetic radiation
The emission and propagation of electromagnetic energy; often thought of in the form of waves of different amplitudes and frequencies.

Electro-osmosis
The motion of liquid in porous materials brought about by applying an electrical potential difference across the material. By inducing 'electro-osmotic flow', electro-osmotic damp-proof treatments supposedly cause water to travel back towards the ground, though there is no evidence of long-term practical success.

Embodied energy
The sum of energy required (measured in megajoules per kilogram, MJ/kg) for any building material or full product life cycle, from growth or extraction to manufacture or processing, and including packaging, transport, installation, de-installation and disposal. Mass concrete and concrete blocks tend to have a low embodied-energy rating; plastics, and highly refined metals such as copper and aluminium, a high rating.

Emissivity
The ratio of emissive power of a surface at a given temperature to that of a black body at the same temperature: in other words, the ability of the surface to emit radiation (governed by the type of material and especially by its surface texture and reflectivity).

Endoscopy
Non-destructive technique for localised visual examination of small hollows or cavities using an 'endoscope', consisting of a flexible tube with optics and a lighting system attached to a viewing system (a video monitor or eyepiece), to which images are transmitted via fibre-optic cables.

Energy
The property of matter and radiation which is manifest as a capacity to perform work (such as causing motion or the interaction of molecules).
See also Acoustic energy, Kinetic energy, Potential energy, Radiant energy, Work

Energy monitor
Basic monitoring device consisting of a sensor attached to a power cable at the consumer unit to measure the electrical current passing through, connected wirelessly to a hand-held monitor that can display electricity usage in units of energy used, cost or carbon emissions. Energy monitors can be used to investigate real-time consumption rates while modifying usage patterns for electrical appliances, thereby optimising energy use. They do not transmit data to the energy supplier.

Energy Performance Certificate [EPC]
A certificate first introduced in England and Wales in 2007 as part of the EU Energy Performance of Buildings Directive [EPB Directive], which documents the energy performance of a building. Under the legislation in force at the time of press, it must be issued by an accredited energy assessor for any domestic and commercial property when built, sold, modified or let.
See also Display Energy Certificate

Energy Plan
Plan for managing energy consumption in a building with the aim of reducing carbon emissions, providing satisfactory conditions for building users, and maintaining or enhancing the significance of a building. A Preliminary Energy Plan is a tool for identifying problems and opportunities, and a Detailed Energy Plan establishes energy conservation strategies for the building.

Energy security
The goal of a given country, or the global community as a whole, to maintain an adequate energy supply. Measures encompass safeguarding access to energy resources; enabling development and deployment of technologies; building sufficient infrastructure to generate, store and transmit energy; and ensuring appropriate delivery and access to energy at affordable prices.

Energy survey
Systematic collection and analysis of data, in order to determine how much energy is being used to operate a building, for what purposes and to what standards. A simple survey may analyse basic data such as heating costs over time, and is used to develop a Preliminary Energy Plan. Intermediate surveys will process this information in relation to seasonal consumption patterns, peak energy demands and so on. Advanced surveys look in detail at consumption related to particular end-usage.

Envelope
All the elements of a building, such as walls, glazing, cladding, roofs and floors, that separate the interior from the exterior environment.

Environmental monitoring
The simultaneous recording and processing of data from selective environmental parameters, usually with the aid of specialist equipment such as dataloggers, from carefully selected sites and for as long a period as is necessary to capture all the important cycles, trends or permutations of a building environment.
See also Diagnostic monitoring

Equilibrium moisture content [EMC]
The percentage moisture content of a hygroscopic material at a particular ambient relative humidity. It may take several weeks for materials to reach equilibrium with the surrounding environment. At a given relative humidity, different materials will exhibit different EMCs (that is, they will be holding different amounts of water).

Equilibrium relative humidity [ERH, RHeq]
The relative humidity of air when in equilibrium with an adjacent hygroscopic material. In soluble salts, it is the relative humidity needed for a given species of salt crystal to deliquesce.

Ettringite
A mineral composed of hydrated calcium aluminium sulphate that is a normal hydration product in wet concrete or cement, but also an important contributory factor in sulphate attack.

Evaporation
The conversion of a liquid into a vapour. The rate of evaporation increases with a rise in temperature, since it depends on the saturated vapour pressure of the liquid. It also depends on air movement: moving air has a very much greater capacity for evaporation than still air of the same absolute humidity and temperature.

Evaporative cooling
Cooling caused by passing warm, dry air – by natural ventilation or by artificial means – over a body of water so that water molecules evaporate. It is the basis of passive cooling using water in hot, dry climates.

Evaporative drying
The release of water molecules in the form of vapour by a hygroscopic material, especially under the effects of air movement.

Evaporative humidifier
A simple humidifier consisting of a water reservoir, a wick (a filter that absorbs water from the reservoir and provides a larger surface area for evaporation), and a fan to move the humidified air around the room.

Exothermic
In thermodynamics, an interaction or reaction that produces energy in the form of heat.

External wall insulation [EWI]
Insulation on the exterior (sometimes called the 'cool') side of an external wall.

Face-sealed system
Type of curtain-wall façade system: a fully water-resistant single-skin exterior cladding with watertight joints designed to repel water; contrast with rainscreen.
See also Curtain wall, Rainscreen

Fall
The gradient of a slope, measured as a percentage, ratio or angle.

Fan heater
See Convective heating

Fan pressurisation testing
Airtightness or air exchange test using a 'blower-door' fan to create a positive or negative pressure differential in a sealed space. Used to detect major air leaks caused by hidden features such as concealed voids.

Fatigue
Weakening of materials subjected to continuous stress.
See also Stress

Fillet
A band of mortar used to weatherproof a joint between two building elements: for example, a roof and an abutment.

Fire-tube boiler
Large boiler consisting of a 'firebox' surrounded by a jacket of water; the combustion gases are directed through a series of flues running through the boiler, heating the water within it to make steam, which is collected at the top in a 'steam dome' housing a regulator with pressure-control valves.

Flaunching
A mortar fillet used to attach a chimney pot in place.

Flashing
Sheet lead or some other impervious material used to cover joints in the building envelope to prevent rainwater ingress, used, for example, at abutments, parapets, valleys and around openings.

Flow
The property of a fluid that allows it to continually deform under applied shear stress, the molecules gliding over one another without resistance. As one molecule moves, it entrains (or pulls along with it) the neighbouring molecules.

Flue
A void or duct through which combustion gases are removed from a fire or boiler.

Flue liner
Liner made of metal or some refractory material, designed to protect the chimney from flue gases. Refractory liners are either composed of blocks of refractory concrete, pumice concrete or terracotta with male-to-female couplings that allow them to be assembled, or cast in place by inserting an inflatable rubber tube into the flue and pumping a refractory cement mortar into the space between tube and flue (a 'pumped' liner).

Fluid
A substance that continually deforms, or flows, under a shear stress, and will take on the shape of the container into which they are put. Most familiar fluids are liquids, but they can include gases, plasmas and even some plastic solids.

Fluorescence
The emission of light by substances that have absorbed light or electromagnetic radiation.

Fluorometer
Device for measuring fluorescence; used to detect biological molecules by stimulating fluorescent emission at a specific frequency with an infrared light-emitting diode.

Force
Any physical influence or agency that could potentially cause a body to move or change shape.
See also Stress

Forced ventilation
Ventilation achieved intentionally by driving the movement of air in a particular direction: for example, using a mechanical fan or the drawing power of a fire.

Fossil fuels
Naturally occurring fuels, especially coal, oil and natural gas, derived from organic matter and formed millions of years ago in the earth's crust.

French drain
Trench, typically 50–60 cm deep, and usually having a perforated agricultural pipe at its base to collect and control large volumes of water. Invented by American farmer and engineer Henry French to drain agricultural land (and for this reason also known as a 'land drain'), but often used around building foundations to protect walls from penetrating groundwater. In England, gravel is sometimes used as backfill, but this should be avoided.

Gas mantle
Device for improving gas lighting, invented in 1885 by Carl Auer von Welsbach. Consists of a bag of fabric mesh impregnated with rare earth metallic salts which burn with an incandescent flame that emits relatively low levels of infrared energy.

Geodrain
Waterproofing membrane for protecting below-ground walls, composed of high-density polyethylene sheet welded to a non-woven geotextile.

Geotextile
Non-biodegradable, woven or non-woven sheet, usually of polypropylene or polyester fibres. Their properties vary: some are water-resistant and others water-absorbent. Suitability should be confirmed before use.

Glaser Method
A method of hygrothermal simulation, originally developed in the 1950s, which uses software to calculate interstitial condensation risk based on temperature and vapour pressure over time, and commonly used in British and European Standards to assess hygrothermal performance. The method excludes some important factors (notably hygroscopic sorption and liquid water movement in masonry walls), and is therefore potentially misleading.

Glass-transition temperature [Tg]
The temperature at which a viscous liquid, on cooling, becomes an amorphous or glassy solid.
See also Viscosity

Gravimetry
Chemical analysis of a material by separating the constituents and measuring their relative weights. Used for determining particle-size distributions, or calculating percentage moisture contents by weight of the various components of a sample of soil or mortar.

Green roof
Any vegetated roof, especially a modern roof sown with vegetation in a growing medium over a waterproof membrane. It may contribute to local biodiversity, provide thermal and sound insulation, reduce solar gain, and slow down rainwater runoff.

Greenhouse gases [GHGs]
Gaseous constituents of the atmosphere, both natural and anthropogenic, that absorb and emit radiation at specific wavelengths within the spectrum of thermal infrared radiation emitted by the earth's surface, the atmosphere and clouds. The primary greenhouse gases in the earth's atmosphere are water vapour [H_2O], carbon dioxide [CO_2], nitrous oxide [N_2O], methane [CH_4] and ozone [O_3]; others include halocarbons, and other chlorine- and bromine-containing substances, sulphur hexafluoride [SF_6], hydrofluorocarbons [HFCs], and perfluorocarbons [PFCs].

Ground-penetrating radar
Non-destructive analytical technique, using pulsed radio energy transmitted from an antenna held against the wall surface and reflected back to another antenna. Different materials absorb and reflect differently, so impulse radar can be useful for locating cracks, voids and embedded materials.

Ground-source heat pump
A heat pump that transfers heat to or from the ground by means of a heat exchanger, using the earth as a heat source in winter or heat sink in summer.

Groundwater
Water located beneath the earth's surface in soil pore spaces or rock formations.

Gully
An inlet to transfer surface water and waste-water from downpipes into the drainage system.

Gurney stove
Early coke-fired heating system developed by British inventor Sir Goldsworth Gurney in the 1850s, comprising a heavy circular iron stove with projecting ribs to maximise heat output, and a water basin to increase humidity.

Gutter
Channel for disposal of rainwater from a roof. Eaves gutters are often laid with a fall towards the outlet, but are narrow and essentially work by building up a head of water pressure along their length. Parapet gutters, which are wider, need to be laid with a slope of at least 1 in 80.

Gypsum moisture probe
Electrical-resistance probe developed for soil-science applications, with a gypsum substrate which acts as a proxy material for the soil.

Half-cell potential testing
An analytical technique used in combination with other techniques (notably resistivity testing) for investigating corrosion in concrete. The potential difference between the reinforcement steel and a stable reference electrode can be measured on the concrete surface using an electrode linked to a high-impedance voltmeter (known as a 'half cell'). A steep potential gradient would normally signal an area of appreciable corrosion. Corrosion potential can be mapped to indicate 'likelihood of corrosion' in different areas.

Halogen light
Incandescent light that uses a halogen gas (bromine or iodine) combined with a tungsten element in a bulb of fused quartz or high-silica glass. Halogen lamps have a higher light output than other incandescent lights, but operate at high temperatures, and are regarded as a greater fire hazard than compact fluorescent or LED lights.

Harling
A roughcast finish, chiefly used in Scotland and the north of England, using a wet, gravelly mix that is thrown ('harled') on to a masonry wall using a curved harling trowel.

Header tank
A water tank, typically located in an attic or roof space, used to maintain a constant water pressure in an indirect water supply (in a hot water supply, also known as a feed-and-expansion cistern).

Heat exchanger
A device for transferring heat from one fluid to another without allowing them to mix. In heating systems, heat exchange involves passing the warmer fluid through a series of coils or fins to maximise the contact surface area with the cooler fluid. In air-conditioning systems, heat exchange is via condensers (which remove heat of compression from the refrigerant) and evaporators (which enable the refrigerant to draw heat from the surrounding air).

Heat-flux meter
Instrument used to measure the heat transferring through a building element.

Heat of vaporisation
The amount of heat needed at boiling point to convert a liquid to a gas or vapour.

Heat pump
A device that supplies heat energy extracted from a heat source (ground, water or air) to a heat sink, usually by means of a vapour-compression cycle similar to that used in refrigeration.

Heat sink
Any medium or environment that absorbs heat.

Heat tape
A heating element in the form of an insulated tape, maintained in contact with the various parts of a rainwater-disposal system to prevent blockage by ice in high-risk areas.

'Hollow wall'
Any wall construction system that uses an external 'leaf' of water-resistant material to inhibit the transfer of liquid water from the exterior, and at least one internal leaf from which it is separated by a cavity; contrast to a traditional solid-wall system. Includes cavity walls and modern curtain-wall systems; commonly incorporates internal drainage and/or ventilation, and layers of vapour barrier or insulation.

Hopper
In rainwater disposal, a top-loading collector at the head of a downpipe to collect rainwater from a gutter.

HTHW [High-temperature hot water]
Hot-water heating system, with water piped under pressure at a flow temperature greater than 120°C. Commonly used wherever there is a continual demand for steam or hot water.

Humidifier
A device for increasing the ambient absolute humidity.

Humidistat
Electronic instrument for measuring and controlling humidity rather than temperature.

HVAC [Heating, ventilation and air conditioning]
Branch of building-services engineering that deals with interior environmental comfort in large buildings, and the plant and systems that regulate it.

Hydraulic pressure
The air pressure ahead of a water front set in motion by the forces (including capillarity and gravitational flow) that drive the uptake of liquid water in permeable materials. Can be great enough to cause fracturing and spalling of building materials, and the failure of coatings.

Hydrogeology
The study of the distribution and flow of groundwater.

Hydronic heating
Any system of heating that uses water as a heat-transfer medium, such as heated steam or hot-water radiators, or hot-water underfloor loops.

Hydrophilic
Having an affinity with water: will readily form a solution in water or absorb water both as a vapour and as a liquid.

Hygric mass
Property of permeable building materials that enables them to absorb, hold and release water molecules as temperatures and air pressures change.

Hygroscopic
Able to take up moisture from the atmosphere. Permeable materials tend to be hygroscopic because of the reduction in vapour pressure in the pores that occurs as a result of condensation, capillarity and salt action.

Hygroscopic moisture content
The amount of moisture a material would normally take up from the air when in a state of equilibrium (so excluding any moisture taken up from other sources such as the capillary uptake of liquid water).

Hypocaust
A Roman heating system that used furnaces to channel heat through open spaces under floors.

Hysteresis
In broad terms, the retardation, or time lag, between a cause and its effect; for example, the hysteresis effect between the wetting and drying of masonry is influenced by the surrounding environmental conditions (such as temperature, air movement, relative humidity) and also by the physical properties of the masonry (such as pore structure, chemistry).

Ice dam
Ice formed as meltwater hits the exposed cold areas of a roof or rainwater-disposal system, causing damage or defects at the eaves in prolonged cold weather.

Impeller humidifier
Humidifier with a diffuser that uses a spinning disk to turn water from a reservoir into a fine mist.

Impulse radar
Highly specialised, non-destructive analytical technique using pulsed radio energy, transmitted from an antenna held against the wall surface and reflected back to another antenna. Different materials absorb and reflect differently, so impulse radar can be useful for locating voids, embedded wood, metal and plastic.
See also Ground-penetrating radar

Incandescent lamp
Lamp that produces light by passing an electric current through a tungsten-wire filament, enclosed in a glass globe filled with inert gas. Incandescent lamps are poorly efficient and are being superseded by more energy-efficient types such as compact fluorescent lamps.

Indoor air quality [IAQ]
The quality and characteristics of the air in buildings (notably in terms of gases, dust and particulates, moulds, spores, VOCs, and radiation present), especially insofar as they affect the health of building users.

Infrared radiation
Radiation in wavelengths longer than that of visible light (between 760 nm and 1 mm).

Infrared thermography
Specialised non-destructive analytical technique using cameras fitted with infrared detectors and filters to record variations in the infrared radiation emitted by building materials and features. Can be used to detect voids, concealed or embedded materials, moisture penetration, and to measure thermal performance.

Insulated glazing unit [IGU]
Factory-made double- or triple-glazed panel, with two glass panes enclosing a hermetically sealed space; in the UK, often known as 'double glazing' or a 'double-glazed unit', especially when used in windows. Modern IGUs are built from float glass, and the cavity is either evacuated of air, or filled with an inert gas such as argon, krypton or xenon. IGUs are commonly used in curtain-wall construction, and increasingly for windows.

Internal wall insulation [IWI]
Insulation (such as thermal laminate board) placed on the interior (sometimes called the 'warm') side of an external wall.

Interior microclimate
The measurable environmental conditions, and their patterns and trends at the interface of interior space and building fabric. Includes a range of parameters such as temperature, relative humidity, air movement and air quality.

Interstitial condensation
See Condensation

Inverted roof
An inverted form of 'warm' roof system, in which closed-cell, water-resistant insulation is laid on top of a continuous waterproof membrane (roofing felt, asphalt or polymer) placed over the deck. A protective layer, such as gravel or slabs, is laid on top. Also known as an 'upside-down' roof.

Ion
An atom or group of atoms that has either lost one or more electrons (and become positively charged), or gained one or more electrons (and become negatively charged).
See also Anion, Cation

Ion chromatography
An analytical technique in chemistry using ion-exchange resins to separate ions from a sample. Sample solutions pass through a pressurised chromatographic column where ions are separated by an ion extraction liquid (or 'eluant'), allowing the different species to be quantified.

Isotropy
Property of materials that are uniform in all directions.

Jevons' Paradox
The concept that improvements in efficiency allow energy-consuming services to become more affordable to run, and so to be used more liberally. Named after British economist W. Stanley Jevons.

Kinetic energy
The energy inherent in the motion of a body; the ability of an object in motion to do work.

Knapen tube
Low-fired clay tube or 'siphon' inserted at an upward angle into masonry as a treatment for humidity in walls. According to its inventor, Achille Knapen, moist air within the wall would percolate into the siphons, where it would be swapped with dry air from the exterior. Such systems are no longer thought to have a drying effect.

Leach field
Network of perforated pipes on a gradual incline, used for disposal of organic waste from a septic tank in soils less suited to a soakaway. The water soaks into a clean bed of gravel surrounding the pipes, which protect the water table from contamination. Also known as a 'septic drain field'.

Leaching
The solid-liquid transfer (that is, the dissolution and transport) of soluble compounds such as lime and clays, salts, organic acids and metal ions, via the percolation, evaporation or capillary movement of a liquid.

Leader
Column of ionised air through which static energy from a thundercloud travels downward towards the earth.

Legionnaire's disease
Form of pneumonia caused by inhaling aerosols containing certain species of the *Legionella* bacterium, which thrive in warm stagnant water.

Light-emitting diode [LED]
Solid-state lamp that emits light from a semiconductor by means of electroluminescence (rather than by thermal radiation of an electrically charged filament).

'Limecrete'
A neologism adopted for modern lime concrete based on hydraulic lime, especially materials incorporating lightweight or expanded clay aggregate; commonly used for making insulated permeable floors.

Limelight
Early form of lighting used in theatres; produced by heating a cylinder of calcium oxide in an oxyhydrogen flame, which then emits an extremely hot white light.

Limewash
Paint made from pure putty lime, diluted with water and sometimes coloured with added pigments. Various materials may be added to provide waterproofing (for example, tallow, which is mixed in during slaking) or to help binding (for example, casein or linseed oil).

Liquid flow path
A route, such as that formed by micropores and capillaries in a permeable material, that permits liquid water to be drawn from an area of high vapour pressure to an area of lower vapour pressure and towards surfaces of evaporation.

Live load
The changing load in a building produced as a result of use and occupancy, and excluding wind loads and seismic loads.

Load, Loading
A mechanical force applied to a structure or component.
See also Dynamic load, Live load, Static load

Local geography
All the various elements characterising the area around a building, from the underlying geology to the surrounding buildings and the way they are used, trees and vegetation, drainage and runoff, and including above- and below-ground services, and the vibration or other impact they may have on the building.

Low or zero-carbon [LZC] technologies
Technologies for the production of heating, cooling and power that yield low-carbon emissions, and which are typically derived from renewable energy sources either in whole or in part.

Malleability
The property of metals and alloys that allows them to be readily shaped and formed (for example, by hammering or rolling).

Mason bee
Name given to several bees of the genus *Osmia*: solitary insects that may nest in buildings in soft mortars, earths and even stone, either by exploiting existing holes (especially on sun-warmed south-facing walls), or by excavating systems of galleries or tunnels.

Mean Radiant temperature [MRT]
The average temperature effect on a human body produced by a radiant heat source within an enclosed space (calculated from surface temperature values using a mathematical formula).

Mechanical energy
The sum of all the potential and kinetic energies in a mechanical system, which depends on the motion and position of all its parts.

Mechanical ventilation heat recovery [MVHR]
Energy-efficient ventilation system that uses a 'counter-flow' heat exchanger between air leaving the building and the air coming in. In heated buildings, this extracts most of the heat from the outgoing air.

Meniscus
The curvature of the surface of a liquid; caused by surface tension within the liquid.

Micropore
Pores and capillaries with diameters smaller than 2 nm in diameter.

Microwave attenuation
Highly specialised analytical techniques that measure the absorption of electromagnetic energy by water molecules in a sample exposed to microwave radiation.

Mist
A suspension of water droplets formed when water vapour condenses on the surfaces of airborne particles or ions.

Mitigation
Technological change and changes in activities that reduce resource inputs and emissions per unit of output. With respect to climate change, mitigation means implementing policies to reduce greenhouse-gas emissions and enhance sinks.

Monofilament netting
Bird netting made from 'monofilament' polymer fibre.

Mortar fillet
Mortar used to waterproof joints in the building envelope.

Multilayer foil
Thermal insulation product made of multiple layers of reflective foil and thermal foam, marketed as a thinner, high-efficiency alternative to conventional insulation.

Multiple chemical sensitivities [MCS]
Poor health in some building occupants that appears to be related to the length of time they have spent in a particular building. A proposed cause is hypersensitivity to certain chemicals or other contaminants, but this diagnosis is by no means certain.

Neutral Pressure Point [NPP]
In a moving body of air driven by the stack effect, the point in the column at which air pressures are equalised: below this point, negative pressure causes air to be drawn in from the exterior; above, positive pressure causes air to be drawn out from the interior.

Neutron scattering [NS]
Specialised instrumental technique that uses different experimental methods to observe the scattering of 'fast neutrons' emitted by a radioactive source as they pass through matter; since they tend to be slowed by light elements such as hydrogen, the presence of water can be indirectly ascertained. How far the neutrons can penetrate depends on the strength of the radioactive source.

Nuclear magnetic resonance spectroscopy [NMR]
Instrumental technique that determines the structure of chemical compounds by measuring the resonating energy of the nuclei of particular isotopes – especially those of carbon and hydrogen – when stimulated by an electromagnetic pulse. With calibration it can be used to measure moisture content.

Off-gassing
The emission of volatile gases (such as VOCs) by construction materials under normal conditions of temperature and pressure.

Operative temperature
A weighted average of the mean radiant and ambient air temperatures at a given place in a room, including an allowance for air movement.

BUILDING ENVIRONMENT
GLOSSARY

Ozone
An allotrope of oxygen consisting of three oxygen atoms [O_3], formed by the disassociation of oxygen [O_2] molecules in the stratosphere in the presence of ultraviolet light from the sun.

Parasitic heat transfer
Transfer of heat between poorly insulated heating pipes or cables, and other heating or cooling devices such as refrigerators, cold water pipes, or ducts for air conditioning or ventilation.

Parging
Lime-hair plaster used for flue and chimney linings.

Particle (image) velocimetry [PIV]
Technique for measuring the flow of a fluid or gas, in which tracer particles are seeded into the host material, illuminated with the aid of a laser, and recorded so that their velocity can be measured.

Passive design
A building-design approach that aims to maintain thermal comfort and reduce operational energy costs using natural energy sources without electrical or mechanical assistance. The approach will consider climate, layout and orientation, as well as systems for heat-energy capture and storage, natural lighting, and natural ventilation.

Passive humidification
Adding moisture to the air in a room by introducing a source of water into the room (such as a water reservoir hung from a central-heating radiator).

Passive ventilation
Natural ventilation using wind pressure and natural convection, together with openings in the building envelope such as windows and doors, vents, or air-bricks. 'Passive stack ventilation' relies on the stack effect to achieve air movement. In small voids and cavities, passive ventilation is often constrained by the resistance to airflow of rough surfaces, the geometry of ventilation grilles, and features within cavities such as studding or beams walls.

PassivHaus standard
Energy-efficient design approach developed in Germany in the early 1990s, which aims to achieve thermal comfort solely by 'post-heating' or 'post-cooling' of the fresh air mass (that is, by using MVHR to extract heat from incoming air) without the need for additional air recirculation.
See also Superinsulation

Percentage moisture content
The amount of moisture held by a hygroscopic material at a given time under certain conditions, as determined by gravimetry or other methods; can be used in conjunction with knowledge about the material and its behaviour, to evaluate moisture levels and risks to materials and components.

Permeability
The ability of a material to transmit fluids (especially water or gases), notably through its pores.

Photon
Subatomic particle of light and other forms of electromagnetic radiation.

Photovoltaic cell [PV]
A semiconductor that converts radiant energy from the sun into electrical energy.

Pitch
The gradient of a roof slope, normally given as a percentage or an angle.

Planar glazing
Frameless glazing system in which glass panels are attached to a slender internal armature by bolts, connectors or vacuum pads; pioneered by Pilkington in the 1980s.

Plastic
An adjective referring to a material that, once deformed by a stress, more or less permanently retains that deformation even when the stress is removed.

Point detector
Individual heat or smoke detector usually connected to a fire-detection system by wires or radio link.

Polarity
Describes the behaviour of a molecule that has an asymmetrical distribution of the electron cloud, and thus a permanent 'dipole moment', being positively charged at one end and negatively charged at the other. This creates strong electrical attraction between molecules. Water molecules are polar: the oxygen atom has a slight negative charge, and the two hydrogen atoms a slight positive charge, producing strong intermolecular bonds ('hydrogen bonds') between water molecules.

Pollutant
Any waste material that contaminates air, soil, or water. A 'primary' pollutant is emitted directly from a source; a 'secondary' pollutant is formed as a result of chemical or photochemical reactions involving primary pollutants (examples include ozone, 'acid rain' and nitrogen dioxide).

Porosity
The ratio of voids to solid matter in a material, expressed as a percentage of total bulk volume. Transfer of liquid water and water vapour in porous materials – permeability – depends not so much on pore ratios (or 'absolute porosity') as on how the pores connect to one another and to the exterior, and on their shape, size and chemical characteristics (that is, the 'effective porosity').

Portière
Heavy curtain hung across the inside of a doorway to reduce heat loss.

Post-occupancy evaluation [POE]
A building-performance evaluation that establishes how an occupied building is working (in terms of thermal performance) over the first few years after construction or alteration.

Potential energy
Stored energy, or the ability of an object to do work because of its position (for example, an object at height which releases that energy when dropped) or its structure (for example, a gas under pressure).

Powder samples
Core samples taken using an ordinary drill bit, with drillings separated by depth. Commonly used to determine moisture content, material chemistry (especially salt content) and that element of the hygroscopicity due to the material chemistry.
See also Core sampling

Prebound effect
A situation where upgraded buildings are found to use much less energy than those predicted by calculation prior to upgrading. An essential cause is the adaptability of building occupants, who may respond to constraints (such as high fuel costs) by adaptation rather than by looking to attain 'normal' comfort standards.

Precipitation
Any product of atmospheric condensation, including rain, snow and fog.

Preliminary Energy Plan
An Energy Plan that brings together data from an Energy Survey in order to consider how energy savings may be implemented in four main areas: altering operational practices; upgrading equipment; making interventions to building fabric; or considering alternative energy supply sources.

Preliminary survey
A form of survey aimed at providing an initial, broad overview of the construction and condition of a building, structure or site (in particular the way it handles water). It is usually preliminary to a wider programme of quantified or detailed survey and analysis. Normally carried out with no special access.

Pressure-moderated rainscreen
A type of rainscreen having a vented cavity behind the outer skin to try to equalise pressures across the system, and so prevent rainwater being drawn in through joints or defects (compare to face-sealed systems). Also known as 'pressure-equalisation rainscreen systems'.
See also Curtain wall, Face-sealed system

Probe
See Sensor

Psychrometric chart
A graph of the thermodynamic parameters of moist air at constant pressure, showing the correlations between dry-bulb temperature, wet-bulb temperature, dew point, relative humidity, moisture content, humidity ratio, specific enthalpy and specific volume. From a measurement taken of any two parameters, the chart can be used to find values for the other parameters.

Pugging boards
Boards laid in the spaces between floor joists in traditional timber floors, the cavities being filled with 'pugging' (ash, sand, or commonly mortar) to provide sound insulation.

Push-rod camera
Compact digital video camera mounted at the end on a flexible cable, used for pipe inspections.

Quantified survey
A form of survey aiming to quantitatively assess and map those aspects or trends that appear to be critical to a building's performance, such as the physical relationship between moisture-related problems and sources of water.

Quartz heater
Type of infrared heater in which a tungsten-wire filament is enclosed in a quartz-glass tube that protects the element and cuts the loss of energy through convection. These heaters are very effective at heating users without heating the air.

Quinquennial inspection
Periodic condition survey undertaken on a five-year cycle; primarily used for maintenance planning and management.

R-value
A measure of thermal resistance: that is, how an object or material impedes the flow of heat through it when there is a difference in temperature on either side. It is expressed as the thickness of the material divided by its thermal conductivity. Thermal resistance depends on the object's structure and thickness.
See also Thermal conductivity, Thermal resistivity

Radiant bar heater
See Radiant heating

Radiant energy
The term commonly used in radiometry, solar energy, heating and lighting to refer to all types of electromagnetic radiation.

Radiant heat barrier
A single layer of a heat-reflecting sheet material such as aluminium foil; useful in hot climates for reducing peak and seasonal heat gain. Provides only modest reductions in heat loss.

Radiant heating
A heating system that transmits energy directly to the surface of a person or object without noticeably heating the air in between. This category of heating includes open fires, electric pew-back heaters, wall-mounted panel heaters, overhead electrical radiant units (including infrared and electric-bar heaters) and underfloor heating.

Radiant heat transfer
Transfer of thermal energy from a source of heat by means of electromagnetic radiation.

Radiant temperature
See Mean radiant temperature

Radiation
See Electromagnetic radiation, Radiant energy, Acoustic energy

Radiative transfer
See Radiant heat transfer

Radon
A radioactive gas occurring naturally in low concentrations in most soils, particularly over granite, and drawn into buildings from the ground.

Rainscreen
A common type of double-skin protective outer envelope in cladding or curtain-walling systems. It is designed to protect an airtight inner skin from moisture by venting the gap between the outer and inner leaves in such a way as to inhibit moisture penetration across the seal, and protect against driving rain with sealed joints supported by drainage and ventilation. The main types are the pressure-moderated rainscreen and the drained-and-ventilated rainscreen.

Rebound effect
A situation where energy demand increases after implementing efficiency measures, due to the perception that overall energy costs have diminished and energy-saving actions can therefore be relaxed.

Reflection
The bouncing-back of some or all of an electromagnetic pulse at a boundary between two materials. In signal-generation systems for non-destructive analysis (such as impulse radar), the bouncing back of electromagnetic pulses coming into contact with remote objects (as opposed to the attenuation of the signal, as measured in microwave attenuation and ultrasound techniques).

Refrigerative air conditioner
Air conditioner that removes heat and moisture from the air using vapour compression (much like a domestic refrigerator).

Relative humidity [RH]
The ratio of vapour pressure of water in the air to the vapour pressure of water in saturated air at the same temperature; in other words, the percentage of saturation at a given temperature. Air at 50 % RH is holding half of the number of water molecules it potentially could hold at that temperature. As the temperature increases, the air can support more water vapour, so air with an RH of 50 % at 25 °C will be holding a great deal more moisture than air of 50 % RH at 15 °C (that is, it will have a much higher absolute humidity).

Relieving arch
Blind arch built into a masonry wall to relieve the load on a lintel below.

Resistance meter
An electronic device for determining electrical resistance by measuring the flow of an electric current between electrodes inserted into the sample. In porous materials, electrical resistance changes with moisture content, and proprietary meters may convert resistance (in ohms, Ω) into a percentage moisture reading, but resistance meters cannot measure absolute moisture content, and they are strongly affected by salts.

Resistivity
A property of a material that makes it oppose the flow of electrical current. Resistivity of a conductor is determined by the length and cross-sectional area of the conductor, and is measured in 'ohm-meters' [Ωm]. By extension, 'thermal resistivity' is the ability of a material to prevent the flow of heat through it.

Resonance
The tendency of a system to oscillate in response to energy waves received at its own natural frequency.

Retrofitting
Improving one or more aspects of an existing building's performance by introducing new products or systems such as thermal insulation, low-carbon energy supply systems, or seismic stabilisation features.

Rising damp
Poorly defined in the building literature, and often loosely used to describe water entering walls from all sources, including those at height. For the purposes of this series, strictly defined as water from the water table that is drawn up into the permeable building fabric by capillary action.

Roman cement
Originally a strong natural cement produced by calcining calcareous stone nodules containing around 11 % iron oxide (giving the cement a rich brown colour); developed and patented in 1796 by James Parker.

Root barrier
A geotextile or membrane, sometimes impregnated with copper compounds or other chemicals to repel growing root tips, embedded in the ground to control the spread of tree roots.

Run-back timer
Mechanical timer that can be manually activated by a switch and will then switch off automatically at the end of a preset period.

Sacrificial finish
A finish, such as a plaster or limewash, designed specifically to protect the substrate (for example, by absorbing salts and contaminants) and to be replaced whenever its condition deteriorates to the point of being unacceptable.

Safe lintel
Inner lintel, often concealed by interior wall finishes, supporting the wall above.

Salt
A compound resulting from the reaction of an acid and a base, in which a hydrogen atom in the acid is replaced by a positively charged atom such as a metal ion. Salts are typically neutral, ionic (electrically charged) and crystalline at ordinary temperatures.

Salt solution
Solution of salt dissolved in water, forming an electrolyte.

Sand
Loose material, consisting of rock or mineral grains (especially quartz grains) with a particle size in the range of 62.5 µm–2 mm.

Sarking boards
Layer of wooden boards or underlay laid onto rafters to provide a wind-and-rain barrier for roof coverings.

Saturation
The point at which a volume of air at a given temperature is holding the maximum possible amount of water vapour (that is, 100 % relative humidity).
See also Dew-point temperature, Relative humidity

Scupper
A drain from a roof or gutter, running through a parapet.

Sensor
The sensitive, detecting element which actually measures an environmental parameter (as distinct from the probe, which houses the sensor).

Settlement
Conventionally, downward movement of a structure or part of a structure, a pile or group of piles, during, immediately after or some time after construction. The term may be extended to include the establishment of balanced relations between a building and its environment.

Shoe
An angled pipe at the foot of a rainwater pipe to divert the discharge away from sensitive parts of the fabric.

Sick Building Syndrome [SBS]
Poor health involving a variety of symptoms that is linked with an individual's occupancy of a specific building, but where it is not possible to identify a specific underlying cause.

Sink
See Heat sink

Siphonic drainage
Drainage system for large roof and gutter areas which uses hydrostatic pressure rather than gravity alone; depends on the downpipes running full with water when in use, so that a negative pressure forms at the top. Siphonic downpipes are considerably narrower than ordinary downpipes, and must be carefully sized and configured, with baffle plates to restrict air entering the pipe.

Smart meter
Electricity or gas meter that transmits energy-use patterns by mobile telephone signal to the energy supplier (meaning that readings do not need to be taken by the supplier). Most devices also employ wireless technologies to send information to an in-home display [IHD], allowing customers to monitor real-time energy use and cost.

Smoke hood
Early chimney consisting of a timber frame above the mantel of a hearth, typically plastered with wattle and daub, directing smoke to an opening in the roof.

Smoke test
Simple test performed using (for example) a stick of incense to observe some of the characteristics of airflow patterns over a short period, notably the direction and speed of flow.

Soakaway
A deep hole or trench excavated on the downhill side and well away from the building, and usually filled with rubble, hardcore and the like. Fed by a surface drain, a soakaway can hold sudden overflows of water, allowing them to percolate slowly into the surrounding ground.

Soaker
Section of sheet metal or other impermeable material inserted under slates or tiles at valleys, abutments and ridges to form a watertight junction.

Sod roof
Natural vegetal roof covering, widespread in rural Scandinavia until the beginning of the 18th century, consisting of sods laid on layers of birch bark on sloping wooden boards.

Soft capping
The technique of using soil, turf and vegetation (principally grasses) to protect exposed wall tops. Known to protect the covered masonry from deterioration by freeze-thaw weathering, and to reduce the potential damage to underlying stone from the thermal expansion and contraction of the exposed wall tops.

Soft Landings
A procurement framework that integrates building-performance evaluation into the building project before tender, so that designers and builders remain involved in the project after handover to review building performance and work with occupiers to optimise building services. Though developed for large buildings with complex engineering systems, the Soft Landings approach can be applied to retrofit projects of all kinds.
See also Post-occupancy evaluation

Soil
Freely divided material derived from rock and organic matter, and composed of particles in a range of sizes. Soil type is determined in relation to particle sizes: broadly speaking, the coarsest grains (diameter 0.0625–2 mm) are known as 'sand', medium grains (0.0039–0.0625 mm) as 'silt', and the finest grains (<2 μm) as 'clay'.

Soil-moisture profile probe
Probe developed for monitoring soil moisture content. By generating an electric field, the instrument measures the change in capacitance to determine dielectric properties of the material at different depths. The probe can monitor changing moisture, but not absolute moisture content.

Solid core samples
Samples taken using a hollow diamond drill bit, to investigate material or moisture content at depth, or bulk properties of the materials such as porosity or strength. Samples are much larger than drilled powder samples, and much more difficult to take.
See also Core sampling, Powder samples

Sorption
A general term for the take-up of fluids such as water into a permeable material; incorporates both absorption and adsorption.

Splashback
Phenomenon by which water or runoff strikes a more or less level surface abutting a wall so that water droplets bounce up against the wall, posing a risk of moisture ingress.

Spot readings
In environmental assessment, one-off measurements that give a single value at a single time. Most useful for determining spatial variations in a given parameter: for example, the distribution of moisture across a wall at a given time. Spot readings are always less accurate than monitored readings, which are repeated over time, and where the methods of measurement and the probe positions can be optimised.

Stack effect
Ventilation caused by the difference in pressure between the bottom and top of a column of air. In a building, this causes air exchange and convective movement, with warm air being lost through apertures higher up in the building, such as chimneys, upstairs windows and the roof, and being replaced at the bottom of the building with cooler air drawn in from the exterior through windows and other apertures near the ground.
See also Convection

Static load
A steady or unvarying load on a building, such as that produced by the weight of the fabric, and the fixtures and fittings. Also known as the 'fixed load' or 'dead load'.

Statics
The branch of applied mathematics concerned with describing the way forces combine to establish equilibrium. In a 'statically determinate' building there is only one possible way the internal and external forces could be balanced, so at equilibrium the structure could be described by a single solution to a more-or-less simple equation; but all real structures are more or less 'statically indeterminate' (that is, the equation is complex and could have many possible solutions).

Stevenson screen
An enclosure to shield meteorological instruments against precipitation and direct heat radiation, whilst allowing air to circulate freely around them.

Storm sewer, Storm drain
Surface water drainage designed to carry away runoff from roofs, roads, paved areas and seepage from soakaways, usually discharging into streams, rivers or watercourses.

Strain
Deformation or change in the dimensions of a body in response to an applied stress.

Stress
An external force acting on a body, and tending to cause deformation or change in its dimensions. 'Tensile stress' exerts a pulling force, and a 'compression stress' a crushing force.

'Structural glazing'
Poorly defined term commonly used to designate late 20th- and 21st-century curtain-wall systems with a minimum of fixings visible externally. The glass panels are not supported by a frame, but instead are fitted in a way that allows live loads to be transferred directly through the glass to a supporting substructure.

Stucco
An imprecise term, derived from the Italian word for 'plaster', with no specific material connotations: it may refer equally to exterior render or interior plaster based on lime or another binder. In England, historically, it has meant different things at different times, but it is generally associated with Regency and early Victorian exteriors.

Structural sealant glazing [SSG]
Glazing and curtain-walling system that uses silicone adhesive to attach glass or other panels directly to the supporting frame, without mechanical fixings.

Subflorescence
Crystallisation of soluble salts below the surface or within the pores of a porous material rather than at the surface. Also known as 'cryptoflorescence' or 'interstitial crystallisation'.

Sun burner
A ceiling-mounted gas lamp favoured for large public buildings in the late 19th century, consisting of a cluster of burners connected through the ceiling to a flue vented to the exterior so that the fitting also provided room ventilation.

Superinsulation
An approach to building design pioneered in the USA and Canada that uses various techniques to maximise energy efficiency (airtight envelopes, high levels of wall, floor and ceiling insulation, elimination of cold bridges, triple glazing, and mechanical ventilation heat recovery).
See also PassivHaus standard

Surface tension
The property of a liquid that makes it behave as though its surface is enclosed in an elastic skin, resulting from intermolecular forces. In the bulk of a liquid the molecules are attracted to other molecules equally on all sides, but at the surface the attraction is unequal, so the molecules are pulled back towards the body of liquid. In water, surface tension is a product of the hydrogen bonding between different water molecules.
See also Polarity

Swellability
A material characteristic that describes the material's capacity to increase in size or volume as a result of internal pressure, most commonly as a result of absorbing water.

Tanking
The use of impervious materials or finishes on the outer or inner sides of walls or floors below ground level, to prevent moisture from the ground appearing on the surface of the interior wall.

Temperature compensation
Reduction in energy consumption of a hot-water boiler by means of a valve that modulates the water flow temperature in response to changing exterior air temperatures.

Tensile strength
The resistance of a material to tensile stress, given as the maximum tensile load a material can tolerate before failing.

Tensile stress
A force tending to pull apart or stretch a material.

Tension
The strain on an object caused by a tensile stress.

Terrain
The physical character of an area of land, including features such as elevation, slope, and orientation.

Thermal break
Materials or elements of low thermal conductivity, introduced to impede heat transfer between building elements having high thermal conductivity and thus reduce thermal bridging. Examples include air cavities between glazing, rigid insulation around steel members, and polyurethane strips built into metal window and door frames.

Thermal bridge
Heat loss or transfer through a building envelope from warm to cold areas by way of building elements made of materials with low thermal inertias (typically very conductive materials such as metal or glass), or through relatively less well-insulated areas of the envelope. Also known as 'cold bridging'.

Thermal comfort
The condition of mind which expresses satisfaction with the thermal environment, a variable governed by humidity, temperature, materials and colours of surrounding surfaces and air movement, as well as clothing, activities and so on.

Thermal conductance
The quantity of heat that passes through a material of a particular area and thickness in a given period of time when the temperatures of its two faces differ by 1 K.

Thermal conductivity
The ability of a material or system to conduct heat: depends on the material's properties and moisture content, and the temperatures involved. Mostly measured as energy transfer per thickness of material per degree of temperature difference [W/(mK)].

Thermal energy
1. In engineering, the energy present in a system by virtue of its temperature.
2. In thermodynamics, the kinetic and potential energy associated with the random motion of atoms and molecules in a body in a state of thermodynamic equilibrium.

Thermal inertia
The ability to absorb, store and release heat energy. Thick-walled traditional buildings, for example, can absorb and store heat effectively, and transmit it slowly, because of the mass, density, specific heat capacity and conductivity of stone, brick, lime mortar, and earth.

Thermal mass
See Thermal inertia

Thermal resistance
See R-value

Thermal resistivity
The reciprocal of thermal conductivity.

Thermal transmittance
See U-value

Thermistor
A type of resistor where the resistance varies with temperature; widely used as a temperature sensor.

Thermocouple
A thermoelectric device used as a temperature sensor. Consists of two conductors of different materials – usually metal alloys – joined together; the potential difference generated between the points of contact gives a measure of the temperature difference between them.

Thermogram
An image, usually false-coloured, generated by infrared thermography, and revealing the pattern of emissivities.

Thermostatic radiator valve [TRV]
A valve used in hot-water radiators, which reduces the flow of water to the radiator as the room temperature rises.

Tiltmeter
Instrument for measuring small changes in the horizontal, sometimes used in assessing structures.

Time-domain reflectometry [TDR]
Highly specialised technique for measuring the electrical conductivity of permeable materials, especially soils, by measuring the velocity of electrical pulses passed through the material via electrical cables to an embedded probe.

BUILDING ENVIRONMENT
GLOSSARY

Tomography
Digital imaging technique using any kind of penetrating wave to record a single plane or section through a solid object. Sectional data from different projections can be processed by computer to generate a three-dimensional image. Magnetic resonance, neutron scattering and electrical resistivity are among the many different kinds of energy source used in computer tomography applications.

Topography
All aspects of the physical geography of a place: not only shape, relief and geological features, but also the vegetation and any man-made structures.

Total heat-loss coefficient
Constant intended to describe the sum of all the heat losses through a building envelope due to conduction, ventilation and air infiltration, expressed as work per temperature difference per area [$(W/K)/m^2$].
See also U-value, Co-heating test

'Toxic moulds'
Moulds known to produce mycotoxins (notably some species of the genus *Stachybotrys*), which can be harmful if ingested or absorbed through the skin.

Tracer-gas testing
Method for testing air exchange through a building envelope, in which a known quantity of 'tracer gas' is injected into the indoor air, and its depletion over time is monitored. Suitable gases have much the same buoyancy as air, but which can be detected easily; carbon dioxide has been the usual choice since restrictions were imposed on the use of ozone-depleting gases such as sulphur hexafluoride.

Transmission
The passage of an electromagnetic pulse through a material.

Trench-arch system
An aerobic sewage management system, useful where access to public sewers may be limited and only intermittent use is expected. Waste is discharged directly into a long, wide and shallow chamber slightly sloping away from the inlet, which is backfilled with topsoil and capped with slabs; incoming water physically degrades the solid waste and disperses it so it can be broken down by worms in the soil.

Trickle ventilation
Air exchange provided by small vents in a window, designed to allow minimum background ventilation to reduce condensation, mould growth and other indoor air problems.

Troposphere
The lowest zone of the atmosphere, where the air can interact with the earth's surface; this interaction produces the local variations in air temperature and humidity from which the weather largely derives.

Turbulence
Movement of fluids in irregular eddying or vortex motions. Turbulence in and around buildings is caused by different air velocities, temperatures and pressures.

U-value
A measure of the rate of heat loss or heat transfer through a given area of material or structure under the impetus of a temperature difference between the two faces of the material or structure. Expressed as a number, and commonly used as an absolute measure of heat transfer through building envelopes, although, in fact, it is a variable strongly affected by interior and exterior conditions.

Ultrasonic humidifier
A 'cool mist' humidifier with a metal diaphragm that vibrates silently at ultrasonic frequency, releasing a very fine mist of droplets from a water reservoir.

Ultrasound pulse velocimetry
Highly specialised non-destructive analytical technique for revealing cracks, voids, fracture planes and variations in density by measuring the speed of high-frequency sound waves transmitted through a material.

Ultraviolet radiation
Radiation in wavelengths shorter than that of visible light, in the range 10–400 nm.

Unregulated loads
In domestic energy consumption, the energy usage not derived from building services and not assessed for the Energy Performance Certificate (for example, the consumption of energy for IT and telephones, domestic appliances and white goods).

Urban heat island effect
The effect of heat generation in urban areas arising from industry, buildings, traffic and other human activity, as well as surface heat reflection and absorption, which produces a significantly warmer climate than that of surrounding non-urban areas.

Vacuum glazing
Double glazing with an evacuated cavity and thin supports separating the glass. The technology allows for very thin glazing units with improvement in thermal insulation compared to gas-filled units.

Vaporiser humidifier
'Warm mist' humidifier that boils the water in a reservoir so that it is released into the air as steam.

Vapour barrier
Any sheet material or membrane (including roofing felt and bitumen) intended to restrict or prevent water vapour transfer. Referred to by many names, including 'vapour-control membrane', 'vapour retarder', 'vapour-control layer' [VCL].
See also Air- and vapour-control layer [AVCL]

Vapour pressure
The pressure exerted by a vapour; also the pressure exerted by the vapour of a material in equilibrium with its liquid or its solid form. In building-environment terms, usually the amount of water vapour in air, expressed in terms of pressure [N/m^3, or Pa]. Increasing the number of water molecules in the same volume of air increases the vapour pressure until the air finally reaches saturation.

Ventilated warm roof
Modern system for metal roofing in which sheet metal is separated from the roof deck by a vapour control layer, insulation, breather membrane and ventilated airspace, with ventilators being installed both at the eaves and the apexes to ensure continuous airflow. The design is intended to minimise thermal pumping (the suction of liquid water into the roof) and minimise corrosion of susceptible metals.

Ventilation
The management of air exchange and air movement in buildings by natural or mechanical means, ostensibly to reduce humidity, replace stale air, and dilute or evacuate gases, dust and particulates.

Viscosity
The property of a fluid that describes its resistance to deformation by shear stress or tensile stress (and informally corresponding to 'thickness'); caused by friction between neighbouring parcels of the fluid moving at different velocities.

Volatile organic compounds [VOCs]
A group of organic chemicals that easily form vapours at normal temperatures, including a number of solvents used in modern paints, adhesives, sealants and coatings, such as benzene, styrene, xylene, toluene, formaldehyde. Known to be air pollutants and hazardous to human health; use is now restricted in the EU.

Vulcanised rubber insulation [VIR]
Type of insulated electrical wiring, often braided with fibres and run within steel conduits, or protected by a lead sheath. Introduced in 1908, and used widely until replaced by materials such as PVC in the 1960s.

'Warm' roof
A roof system with insulation material placed immediately below the roof covering. A vapour control layer [VCL] is placed between the insulation and the roof deck, so that joists and everything below the VCL are on the 'warm' side.

Waterproof roof covering
A roof cover composed of waterproof sheet materials with sealed joints (including sheet metals and asphalts), so that rainwater runs down the surface towards the eaves or gutters. The roof will fail if the cover is perforated.
See also Water-resistant roof covering

Water-resistant roof covering
A roof cover composed of small discrete units (such as thatch, tiles, slates and shingles), assembled in layers to divert rainwater towards the eaves or gutters. The roof will fail if the pitch is not sufficiently steep.
See also Waterproof roof coverings

Water-source heat pump
A heat pump that transfers heat to or from a sizeable body of water by means of a heat exchanger, using the water as a heat source in winter or a heat sink in summer. They can be either open- or closed-loop.

Water table
The highest point or level of water in an aquifer, below which the ground is completely saturated with water.

Water tube boiler
Boiler consisting of pipes that convey water through heated combustion gases rather than the other way around. Piping may be finned to increase heat exchange, and the heated water rises to a 'steam drum' equipped with a regulator. Water-tube boilers can run at much higher pressures than fire-tube boilers.

Weathering
1. The physical disintegration and chemical decomposition of materials on exposure to atmospheric agents.
2. Building details such as flashings or mortar fillets that are designed to direct water away from vulnerable construction features such as joints or openings.

Weep hole
Detail sometimes employed in hollow-wall construction, made by omitting mortar from some of the vertical joints in a course at the base of the wall to allow water to drain, and sometimes to promote air drying.

Weighted sound reduction index [Rw]
An index of sound insulation (or rather, of noise reduction), expressed in decibels and calculated by means of an adjustment factor [Ctr] used to measure an object or material's ability to dampen low-frequency vibrations. The higher the Rw, the more effective the sound insulation.

Whirling hygrometer (or psychrometer)
Instrument for measuring moisture content in the atmosphere. The 'whirling' or 'sling' type (which is spun in the air on a handle or cord) has two thermometers – 'wet-bulb' and 'dry-bulb' – that may be used in conjunction with a 'psychrometric chart' to calculate a range of thermohygrometric readings, including relative humidity and dew-point temperature. The instrument has now largely been superseded by hand-held electronic devices.

Wicking
See Capillarity

Wind catcher
Tall, capped tower with one face open to the prevailing wind, used in hot climates to channel air into the building to cool down the interior.

Wind chill
The cooling effect, due to evaporative and convective heat loss, on a warm surface exposed to a current of moving air.

Wind washing
Cool exterior air flowing into and through a roof space or hollow wall cavity, reducing the effect of any insulation.

Work
The transfer of energy from one physical system to another, especially the transfer of energy to an object by the application of a force that moves the object in the direction of the force. It is calculated as the product of the force and the distance through which the object moves, and is expressed as newton-metres [Nm] or joules [J].

X-ray diffraction [XRD]
Laboratory technique for identifying crystalline materials, useful for identifying the mineral composition of binders, pozzolans, aggregates and salts.

Yield point
Point at which plastic deformation takes place in a material placed under a constant load.
See also Ductile fracture

Young's modulus
The ratio of tensile stress to tensile strain in an elastic solid; also known as modulus of elasticity.
See also Strain, Stress

INDEX

Note: page numbers in italics refer to illustrations; page numbers in bold refer to tables

A

absolute humidity [AH] 39, 107, 416, 440
  see also humidity buffering; relative humidity [RH]
accelerated drying 500–1, **500**
access for fire services 474
access for inspection and repair 226–7
acoustic energy in materials 31, *31*
Actane 201
adhesives
  breakdown by sunlight 169
  moisture damage 153
aerogels 566
air-and-vapour control layers [AVCLs] 184, 186, 363, 364–5
air barriers 184, 566
air bricks 101, *101*, **346**, 417, 418, **470**
air conditioning 425, 438, 441
  early examples 129
  health hazards 449, **450**, 451
  problems with 207
  temperature and humidity fluctuations *111*, 207, 441
  see also heating, ventilation, air-conditioning [HVAC] systems
air cooling see cooling
air curtains 414, 550
air exchange 117
  increasing 203, 415–16
  measuring 286–7, **528**
  monitoring **299**
  reducing 413–14
  requirements 287
  see also airtightness; ventilation
air flow see air movement
air infiltration see airtightness
air movement 117
  monitoring **294**, **299**, 305
  and ventilation 416
  visualisation *427*
air quality see indoor air quality [IAQ]
air re-circulation 129
air-source heat pumps 589, **594–5**
air temperature
  monitoring **299**
  and thermal comfort 520, *521*
  see also ambient temperature and humidity

airborne pollutants see atmospheric pollutants
airtightness 104
  energy-saving measures 541, 550
  leading to condensation 192, 203
  testing 286–7, **528**
  traditional construction systems 516
  windows and doors 192
algae 248, 400
alterations to buildings see building alterations
aluminium
  rainwater goods 374
  roofing 576
American Society of Heating, Refrigerating and Air-Conditioning Engineers [ASHRAE] 42
ammonium salts **158**
animal deposits 176, *176*, 453
animal-related damage 175–6, 336
  see also bats; bird problems; rodents causing damage
annual inspection and maintenance **347–9**
anthrax hazard 453
Argand burner 134, *136*
artificial lighting 133–8
  see also electric lighting
asbestos
  health and safety 225, 452–3
  removal 452
ASHRAE [American Society of Heating, Refrigerating and Air-Conditioning Engineers] 42
Aspergillus 454, *455*
asphalt roof coverings 61, 178, **338**
asphalt, temperature damage *155*
atmospheric pollutants 5, 171, 249, 398
atomic absorption spectrophotometry 285
attics 102
  conversion to living space 197, 362, 391, *392*
  see also roof space
audible sound 31
auto-oxidation 154
automatic control systems see control systems
AVCL [air and vapour control layers] 184, 186, 363, 364–5
awnings 132, 192, 437

B

back boilers 127
backfilling drains 198, *198*

background heating 429
accelerated drying **500**, 501
background research 215, 218–20
bacteria 456
barn owls 402
basements see cellars; subterranean spaces
Bath stone 43, *43*
bats 176, *176*, 247, 407
Bazalgette, Joseph *139*
below-ground drainage see drains
below-ground walls see subterranean walls
biocides 336, 400
biological problems 160, 172–6, 247–8, 399–407
  see also animal-related damage; bird problems; microbiological growths; plant growth
biomass boilers **592–3**
bioremediation 336
bird nests 402, *403*
bird problems 175, *175*, 176, 247, 401–3
  deterrence **346**, 401–3, *402*, **404–6**
bituminous-felt roof coverings 61, 178, **338**
blinds 192, **397**
blistering, of surface finishes **314**
blower-door tests 287
blue-wool lightfastness tests 305
BMS [building management systems] 442
boilers 433–4, **434**
  controls 554
  inspection and maintenance **349**
  using existing chimneys 206
borescopes 495
box gutters 68, 69, *72*
breaking strength 27
bressumer beams 85, *85*, 172
BRI [building-related illness] 449
brick walls see masonry; walls
British Standards
  BS 1279-2:2002 *Glass in building. Insulating glass units. Long term test method and requirements for moisture penetration* 288
  BS 1339-1: *Humidity. Terms, definitions and formulae* 42
  BS 5250:2011 *Code of practice for control of condensation in buildings* 186, 454, 536

British Standards (cont.)
   BS 6297:2007 + A1:2008 Code of practice for the design and installation of drainage fields for use in wastewater treatment 381
   BS 7913:2013 Guide to the conservation of historic buildings 333
   BS 8102:2009 Code of practice for protection of below ground structures from water from the ground 393
   BS 8210:2012 Guide to facilities maintenance management 333
   BS EN 12056-3:2000 Gravity drainage systems inside buildings. Roof drainage, layout and calculation 370, 373, 376–7
   BS EN 15026:2007 Hygrothermal performance of building components and building elements 536
   BS EN 62305:2011 Protection against lightning 477, 479
brittle fracture 26, 27
brittleness **28**, 91
buffering 103, 104
   see also humidity buffering; thermal buffering
building alterations 195
   assessment to prepare for 214, 323
   building services 255
   flood protection 468–71
   surveying 236
building contents *see* furnishings
building handover 546–7
building history
   investigating 218–19
building location and setting 233, 546–7
building management systems [BMS] 442
building materials
   air contaminants **450**
   assessment 268–71
   biological attack 160
   chemical attack 156–8
   combustibility 473–4
   components made of several 167
   embodied energy 510
   light damage 154, *169*
   mechanical breakdown 151, *151*
   moisture damage 152, *153*
   rainwater goods 67, **374–5**
   recycling and reuse 511, *511*
   renewable 511
   for repairs 328
   selecting 361
   temperature damage 155
   toxicity 225, 452–3
   see also headings for specific materials

building occupation *see* occupation of building
building performance surveys 221–55
   exterior 234–6
   health and safety 225–7
   interior 237–55
   making detailed measurements 239–54
   on-site work 231–2
   recording 228
   surveying the setting 233
   tools and equipment 230
   undertaking 229–32
Building Regulations
   air-exchange requirements 287
   chimneys 126, 366, 368
   drainage and water disposal 382
   fire protection in tall buildings 140
   rainwater goods 376
   sound insulation 424
   U-values 565
building-related illness [BRI] 449
building services 139–43
   assessment 255
   control systems 442, 541, 545, 557, **558**
   damage to 493
   energy-saving measures **538**, 541, 553–7, **558**
   energy usage 513
   inspection and maintenance **349**
   locating hidden services 267
   maintenance 329
building-services engineering 442
building use 202–8, 328
   monitoring **295**, 305
   see also occupation of building
burning brands 431

C

calcium carbide 280
calcium salts 157, **158**
calibration of instruments 304
calor-gas heaters 121, 204
Cambridge Timberproofing Laboratories 201
candles 135
capacitance meters 253, 260, 300, 302
capillarity 45
capillary absorption 47
capillary rise 88–9, *88*, 164, 195, 283
carbide meters 280, *280*
carbon dioxide [CO_2]
   emissions 507, *507*, 513
   reducing 514–19

carbon dioxide [CO_2] (cont.)
   indoor pollutants 459
carbon monoxide alarms 366, 457
carbon monoxide health risks 122, 366, 457
carbonates **158**
Carlton House Gardens 136
cast-iron rainwater goods 67, **374**
Castrol stove 127
catalytic converters 127
Cauchy, Augustin-Louis 24
cavities *see* voids
cavity membranes 393, **394**
cavity ventilation 417–22
cavity walls 78, *78*
   insulation 197, 411, 583, **585**
   moisture problems 183, 243, 245, 498
   ventilation 78, 183, 417, 422
ceiling fans 128, 438
ceilings 55, 102
   converted attics 392
   fire resistance 476, **484**
   perforations 195, *197*, 476
   removal 195, *196*
   soundproofing ('pugging') 424, 492
cellars
   conversion to living space 391, *391*, 393, **394**
   see also subterranean spaces
cement-based plasters 190
cement-based renders 89, *89*, 187, *187*, 188
   cracking 245, 385
   with damp-proofing 201
   earthen walls 385
   removal 385
cement mortars 183
   cracking 63, 245
   removing 384
central heating
   effect on relative humidity 204
   historical perspective 122, 125
   temperature control 521
   wet systems 433–4
   see also hot-water central heating
cess pools **383**
Chabannes, Marquis de 119
change of ownership, assessment at 214
change of use
   assessment for 215
   monitoring **295**
   sound insulation 424

charcoal fuel 124
Chartered Institution of Building Services Engineers [CIBSE] 530, 565
chemical attack 156
chemical energy in materials **21**, 30
chemical reactions 30
chemical sensitivities 120, 449, 459
chemical testing 285
cherry pickers 226
chimney balloons 369, 550
chimney pots 123, 342, 366
chimneys
   bird problems **404**
   early examples 122–3, *123*
   fire risk 124
   heat loss *520*
   inspection and maintenance 342, **346**
   moisture problems 191, 366
   multiple flues *124*, 125
   repairs 342, 366–9
   salt decay 191, *191*, 234, 366
   structural problems 191
   surveying 234
   sweeping 124, *124*
   use for new heating systems 436
   see also flues
chloride salts 157, **158**
CHP [combined heat and power] systems **596–7**
CIBSE [Chartered Institution of Building Services Engineers] 530, 565
cladding systems 77, 78, 79–80
   inspection 266, 342
   maintenance 342
   problems 183, 188
   protecting external insulation 582, 583
   ventilation and drainage 183
   see also rainscreen walls; tile-hanging; weatherboarding
clay-rich soils 8, 165
Clean Air Act 1956 125, 432
climate and cooling **130**
climate change 329, 377, 506
co-heating tests 288, **528**
CO_2 *see* carbon dioxide [CO_2]
coal-burning stoves 127, 204, 432
coal fires 124, 126, 428, 432
coal gas 434, 457
coal stores under footpaths 393

coatings
   assessing 271
   doors and windows 343
   and hydraulic pressure 47
   and hygric buffering 107
   inspection and maintenance **348**
   moisture ingress 189
   preventing light damage 396
   for rainwater goods 339, **374**
   water-resistant 186, 198, 361, 364, 386
   window glass 396
   see also paints
coefficient of performance [CoP] 589
cold roofs 197, **565**, 576, **577**, **578**
colour fading 169
combination boilers 140
combined drainage systems 87
combined heat-and-power [CHP] systems **596–7**
combustion gases 432, 433
   sulphate pollution 121, 204, *204*
comfort heating 426, 435
comfort, thermal *see* thermal comfort
communal power generation **598**
community energy-saving schemes 517
compartmentation 483–4
compressive strength 25, **28**
concrete
   expansion joints 167
   floors 101, 195, 389
   precast gutters 179
   walls 348
   see also steel-reinforced concrete
condensation 40, *40*, 42, 46
   caused by airtightness 192, 203
   caused by heating 121, 204, 205–6, *206*, 232
   caused by impermeable insulation 541
   caused by thermal bridges 236, 245, 540, 571, 574
   in chimneys and flues 191, 206, 367
   code of practice for control 186, 454, 536
   damage from heating 205
   diagnosis 316
   on glass 155, 205, *205*, **316**, 414, 571
   and insulation 197, 411, 540–1, 567, 582
   investigation 237, 245, 251, 273
   and moisture damage 155
   monitoring 293, *293*, 295, **299**
   parapet gutters blocked by ice and snow 178
   roof spaces 65, 197, 245, 362, 363
   secondary glazing **316**, 414, 571, 573
   and solar gain 223
   solid floors 100, 204, *205*, **315**, 416

condensation (cont.)
   'summer condensation' 567
   and vapour barriers 183–6
   and ventilation 65, 110, 183, 203, 362, 416
   in voids and wall spaces *41*, 182, 563
   on walls 182, 203, *203*, **316**, 541, 582
   wind-chilled surfaces 76, 166
condensing boilers 433, 554
condition mapping 224, 229, 238
   moisture measurement 253, *254*
condition surveys 215
conduction 29, 105
conductivity meters 285
conservation heating 429, 554
conservation principles 354, **356**
conservatories *517*, 551
construction energy 510
construction materials *see* building materials
construction waste, recycling and reuse 511, *511*
control systems 442, 541, 545, 557, **558**
convection 29, 105
convective heating systems 121, 426, **426**, *551*
cooling 128–9, 437–8
   options for different climates **130**
   physical effect on materials 35
cooling fans 438, 554
cooling systems
   assessment 255
   energy-saving measures 554, **558**
CoP [coefficient of performance] 589
copings, inspection and maintenance **348**
copper rainwater goods **374**
corrosion 156
   cast-iron downpipes 194
   metal-clad flat roofs 576
   metal window frames 189
   organic salts 173
   parapet gutters 178
   steel reinforced concrete 147
corrugated metal roof coverings 61
cost-benefit assessment 216
covermeters 268–9, *269*
cracking 26–7
   cement renders 187, *187*
   coatings 189
   monitoring 241, *241*
   mortar joints 183
   surveying 240–1
   temperature induced 155, *155*

critical crack length 27
cross-ventilation 128, 437
Crossness Pumping Station 139
cryptoflorescences 157
culverts 87
curtain walls 79, 79
   inspection and maintenance **348**
   maintenance 342
   moisture problems 188, 243, 245
   opening up for inspection 246
   rebuilding 385
   reducing heat losses 574, *574*
   surveying hazards 225
   thermal breaks in 411
   see also insulated glazing units [IGUs]
curtains
   limiting draughts 414, *562*
   limiting sun damage **397**
Cuvilliés, François 127

D

damage assessment 492–4
damage, deliberate 464
damp-proof courses [DPC] 89, 389
   injected 201, 389
   retrofitting 387
damp-proof membranes 183–6, 195, 389
   see also geotextile linings
damp-proofing
   below-ground walls 90, 190
   concrete floors 101, 195
   injected 201
   proprietary systems 199–201, 388
   see also vapour barriers
damp smells **317**
dataloggers 297, *297*
Davy, Humphrey 138
day-to-day care 327–44
day-to-day monitoring 306
daylight 132, **560**
   see also solar gain
de-icing salts 157, 171
De la Rue, Warren 138
deathwatch beetle 160, 248
DEC [Display Energy Certificates] 531
dehumidification 130, 207, 440–1
   accelerated drying **500**, *501*
   air conditioning 441
desiccant dehumidifiers 130, 157

design faults 177–92
   avoiding potential problems 322
   chimneys 191
   walls 182–90
   water-handling features 178–81
   windows and doors 192
deterioration processes 14, 147–8, 151–60
   avoiding potential problems 322
   biological 160, 172–6, 247–8
   causes and ramifications 318–21, **318**
   chemical attack 156–8
   dealing with multiple causes 321
   interpreting symptoms 313, **314–17**
   light damage 154, 169, *250*
   mechanical breakdown 151
   moisture-related damage 152, *153*, 155, *155*
   temperature damage 155
dew-point temperature [DPT] 40, *206*
   see also condensation
diagnosis 311–23
   avoiding potential problems 322
   dealing with multiple causes 321
   determining causes and ramifications 318–21, **318**
   interpreting symptoms 313, **314–17**
diagnostic monitoring 292–305
   equipment 296–8, **299**
   installation 296, 303
   moisture-content monitoring 300–2
   non-automated monitoring 305
   parameters to monitor 292–3, **294–5**
   period and rate of monitoring 295–6
   positioning sensors 296, 303, *303*, *304*
   sensor calibration 304
dielectric properties of water 38
differential thermal movement 34, 155, 167
   roof coverings 63, *167*, 178
   treatment 395
   windows and glass 167, 178
dimensional change 155, 167
   thermal inertia 91
   wet materials 94
   see also differential thermal movement
dipwells 260, *260*
disaster management 467
disastrous events 209
   action after a disaster 489–91
   common causes 463–5
   damage assessment 492–4
   prevention 466–87
   recording 491
   remedial actions 496–501
   salvage storage 499

dismantling *see* opening up for inspection
Display Energy Certificates [DECs] 531
door curtains 414, *562*
doors
   design faults 192
   draught-proofing 413–14, *413*, 549, 550, *562*
   fire resistant **484**
   inspection and maintenance **346**
   maintenance 343
   surveying 236
double glazing *see* insulated glazing units [IGUs]
downpipes 69, 70, 72
   blocked 193, 194, 373
   concealed 177, 180
   discharging onto roofs 57, 377
   faulty 180, 372
   historical perspective 66, *66*, 67, *67*
   inspection and maintenance 344, **345**
   positioning 361, 372, *372*
   protecting from blocking by debris 340
   replacements 371–3, *371*, *372*
   siphonic 373, 377
   sizing 377
DPC *see* damp-proof courses [DPC]
DPT [dew-point temperature] 40
drain cameras 263
drainpipes 73, 378, *379*
drains 73
   blockages 339
   Building Regulations 382
   capping and backfilling 198, *198*, 378, *379*
   inspection and maintenance 194, **345**
   leakage 263
   locating and examining 264
   plant roots affecting 335
   repair and upgrading 378–80, *379*
   testing 263
   trench linings 378, *379*
draught lobbies 550, *562*
draughtproofing 192, 413–14, *413*, 549, *562*
draughts
   diagnosis **317**
   disused flues 369, 414, 550
   heating-related 551
   perception of 286
   ventilating open fires 123, 124, 366, 430
drilled samples 276–9, 282
drips, window cills 84, 192
Driver, Charles Henry 139
'dry' 152, 499

dry lining 390, 393, **394**
   inspection and sampling behind 277, 361
   ventilation 418, 419, 422
dry rot 248
drying of permeable materials 47–8
drying tests 284
drying wet fabric 387, 388, 496–501
ducted heated-air systems 125, 126
ductile fracture 26–7, *27*
ductility **28**
dust mites 456

E

earth movements 165, 170, 465
earthen floors 100, 107
earthen walls
   inspection and maintenance **348**
   limewash 75, 342
   moisture problems 244
   renders 75, 187, 385
earthquakes 165
eaves gutters 68, 69, 72, 376
   brackets 179, 371
   faulty 179
   interventions 370, *371*
eddy-current detectors 268–9
Edison, Thomas 138
efflorescence 156, 157
   assessment *237*
   diagnosis *314*
   sampling *270*
   silicone damp-proofing 201
elasticity 24–5, **28**
electric fans *see* fans
electric lighting 138, *138*
   energy-saving measures 559–60, **560**
   fire risk 476, **476**
electric radiant heaters 428, 554
electric trace heating, protecting gutters from blocking by snow and ice 342, 377
electric underfloor heating 435
electrical appliances 142, 561, **561**
electrical conduits 143
electrical equipment 561, **561**
electrical fires 475
electrical resistivity tomography 275
electrical services, inspection and maintenance **349**

electrical wiring 143, *143*
electricity consumption 508
   energy-saving measures 559–60, **560**
   monitoring 531
electricity supply 142, 508
Electricity (Supply) Act 142
electro-osmosis 201
electro-osmotic systems 388
electrolytes 156
electromagnetic spectrum 22, *22*
electronic meters, hand-held 238, *251*, 252–4, *253*
electronic monitoring 295–9
electronic sensors and probes 296, 298, *298*, **299**, 302, 564
Ellis, Peter 79
embedded downpipes 177, 180
embedded sensors 275
embodied energy 510
emergency planning 466, *467*
emissivity 29, 105
endoscopy 266
energy
   exchange of energy 23
   forms of 20, **21**
   interaction with materials 24–31
   law of conservation of energy 19–20
energy monitors 531
energy performance 516, 520
Energy Performance Certificates [EPCs] 531
Energy Plans 522–48
energy-saving measures 515–19
   appliances 561, **561**
   building services **538**, 541, 553–7, **558**
   classifying interventions **538**
   comparing the relative costs and benefits 535
   cost effectiveness 537, *537*
   design-performance gap 514, 522, 524
   insulation 563–9
   lighting 559–60, **560**
   listed buildings 542
   modelling tools 536
   risks 536–8
   simple fabric improvements 550–2
energy supply and carbon emissions 508
energy surveys 530–1
energy usage 510–13
   households compared 525–6, *526*
   reviewing 529–32

English Heritage
   energy-performance investigations 516
   grants for repairs 330
   lightning protection guidance 477
   listed buildings 353
   research into cavity ventilation 418–21
environmental assessment 213–307
   background research 218–20
   energy performance 527
   iterative approach 216, *217*
   planning 214–17
   specialist investigations 256–307
   see also building performance surveys
environmental deterioration *see* deterioration processes
environmental monitoring 291–307
   electronic monitoring 293, 295–9, **299**
   interpreting the results 306–7
   after interventions 408, 443
   locating equipment 291, 296
   monitoring moisture content **294**, *299*, 300–2, 564
   non-automated monitoring 305
   parameters to monitor **294–5**
   post-flood drying 499
EPC [Energy Performance Certificates] 531
equilibrium relative humidity [RHeq] 107, 157, *159*
escape from fire 474
ettringite 234
Euler, Leonhard 24
evacuation of building 474
evaporation 40, 41–2, 47–8, 205–6
   driving moisture movement 14, 46, 47, 48, 88–9, *88*
   measuring 293
   moisture-resistant materials inhibiting 164
      AVCL [air and vapour control layers] 364
      damp-proofing 185, 190, 198, 389
      exterior insulation 412, 582, *584*
      impermeable finishes 107, 110, 189
   see also drying
evaporative coolers 129, 438
evaporative cooling 128, 166
evaporative humidifiers 439
Evelyn, John 125
excavation
   around basements 101, 386, **394**
   close to building 378, *379*, 382
exterior environment 5–9, 163–76
   see also atmospheric pollutants

exterior lighting 560
exterior surveys 234–6
exterior temperatures 167–8
exterior walls
    inspection and maintenance 346
    insulation 197, 412, 582, *584*, **585**
external alterations 195, 582
extractor fans 416, 480
extreme weather events 506

F

Faber, Oscar 126
fabrics, light damage 154
failure mechanisms 26–7, 32–48
    failure under load 32–4
    moisture in building materials 37–48
    thermal behaviour 35–6
    see also deterioration processes
fan heaters, fire risk 475
fan-pressurisation tests 287
fans
    accelerated drying 500, **500**
    cooling 438, 554
    extractor fans 416, 480
    incorporated into heaters 126
    thermal comfort *521*
    ventilation 128
fatigue strength **28**
fillets *see* mortar fillets
fire compartments 483–4
fire damage 463, 493
fire detection and alarm systems 481, **482**
fire grates 124, 127
fire prevention 475–80
fire protection 481–5
fire risk
    assessment 473–4
    during building works 480
    sources of ignition 475–6
fire safety engineering [FSE] 472
fire spread 473–4, 483–5
fire suppression systems 484–5
fire-tube boilers 433
firebacks 123
firefighting equipment 485
fireplaces 123–5, *123*, 126
    disused 369, 414

fires in buildings 472
flaking, of surface finishes 237, **314**
flashing 63, 164, 338, **347**
flat roofs 178, *576*, **578**
flexible metal flue liners 432
flood damage 464, 492, 493, 494
flood protection 468–71
    actions to prevent damage or help drying **471**
    systems to prevent ground water entering **470**
flooding events
    longer-term actions after 501
    post-flood drying 496–501
    preliminary actions after 490
floor coverings *100*
    impermeable 190
    for underfloor heating 435
    water damaged 498
floor finishes 100–1, *102*
floor joists *102*
floorboards 101
    lifting 495, 498
floors
    fire-resistant **484**
    see also solid ground floors; timber floors
flue-gas temperatures 432, 433
flue liners 191, 367–8, 432
flues
    bringing back into use 430, 436
    condensation problems 191, 206, 367
    dampers 124, 414
    disused 368–9, 414
        draughtproofing 550
        venting extractors into 416
    draught 123, 124, 366, 369
    historical perspective 122, *123*
    inspection and maintenance **346**
    for new heating systems 428, 436
    positioning 433, *433*
    traditional linings 123, 126, 191
    use for new heating systems 436
fluorometers 267
flush testing 263
foam-plastic insulation 566
footfall 424
force, definition 20
forces acting on buildings 33–4
foul-water systems 381
fracture mechanisms 26–7
fracture strength **27**

framed walls
    insulation 583, **585**
    see also timber-framed buildings
Franklin, Benjamin 127
freeze-thaw damage 94, *94*, *155*, 168, *168*
    preventing 395
freezing weather 95
French drains 88, 198, 378
Frost Fairs *506*
FSE [fire safety engineering] 472
fuel oils 434
fuel types 434
fungi 243, *248*, *399*
    timber decay 160, 399, 494
    treatments 400
    see also moulds (organic)
fungicides 399
furnishings
    air contaminants 450
    dust mites 456
    effect on internal environment 109–10
    inhibiting air flow 195
    see also curtains; wall hangings

G

galvanised-steel rainwater goods **374**
gargoyles 68, 69
gas boilers using existing chimneys 206
gas fires 432
gas fittings and fixtures 137, *137*
gas flex liners 368
gas fuel 434, 457
gas heaters 121
Gas Installation Regulations 367
gas lamps *135*
Gas Light and Coke Company 136
gas lighting 136–7, *137*
gas mantle 137
gas pipes used as electrical conduits 143
Gas Regulation Act 1920 141
gas supply 141
gaseous pollutants 398, 457–9
    sampling 249
    treatments 459
    see also atmospheric pollutants; indoor pollutants
geodrains 90, 386, *386*

geology 8
geotextile linings 88, 378, *379*
GHG [greenhouse gases] 506, 507
glass-reinforced polyester [GRP] rainwater goods 374
glass roof coverings 61, 128, 178
glass walling 79
   see also curtain walls
glazing 81
   condensation problems **316**
   dimensional change 155, *155*, 178
   heat losses 570
      reducing 91–2, 570–4, **575**
   historical perspective 132, *570*
   solar films 192, **397**
   structural 79, 80
   U-values **565**
   see also curtain walls; insulated glazing units [IGUs]
glossary 602–8
glues
   break down by sunlight 169
   moisture damage 153
grants for repairs 330
grates, fire 124, 127
gravimetry 280–3, *281*
green roofs 579–80, *579*, *580*
greenhouse gases [GHGs] 506, 507
Griffiths, A. A. 27
ground drainage 87–8
   blocked or faulty 181
   investigating 261–3
ground floors 100–1
   improving flood resistance 468–71
   insulation 586, **587**
   see also solid ground floors; suspended floors
ground levels
   drainage problems 181, *190*
   measuring 239–40, *239*
ground movement 165, 170, *170*, 465
ground-penetrating radar [GPR] 263, 274
ground-source heat pumps 126, 589, **594–5**
groundwater 9, 165
   investigation 259–63
   monitoring **294**
GRP [glass-reinforced polyester] rainwater goods 374
guano 176, 453
   see also bird problems

gulleys 70, 73
   blockages 339
   drainage problems 181
   inspection and maintenance **344**
   upgrading 378, *379*
   water pooling 360
Gurney stoves *116*
gutter brushes *340*, 341
gutter guards 341
gutters 68, 72
   faulty 179
   historical perspective 67
   ice dams 95–6, *96*
   inspection and maintenance 193, 339, **344**, **345**, **347**
   maintenance 370
   precast concrete 179
   protecting from blocking
      by debris 340–1, *340*
      by ice 342, 377, 395
   relining 370–1
   sizing 376
gypsum-based plasters 390
   water damaged 494, 498
gypsum crusts *156*, 157, 171
gypsum moisture probes 302
gypsum plasters 390

H

habitats for animals 175–6
half-cell potential testing 269
half-timbered construction
   infill panels 183
   maintenance 342
   moisture problems 245
hand-held electronic meters 238, *251*, 252–4, *253*
handover of building 546–7
harling 77
hazardous materials 225, 452–3
HDPE [high-density polyethylene] rainwater goods 375
header tanks 140
health and safety
   asbestos 225, 452–3
   calcium carbide 280
   gaseous pollutants 457–9
   guano and other animal deposits 453
   indoor air quality [IAQ] 449
   lead 453

health and safety (cont.)
   legislation 329
   micro-organisms 453–6
   pesticides 400
   poor ventilation 120
   protective clothing and equipment 230
   surveying hazards 225–7
hearths 123
heat convection 29, 105, *551*
heat exchange through the envelope 91–2, 105–6, *514*
   measuring **528**
   see also heat transfer; thermal resistance
heat losses *see* energy-saving measures; radiant heat losses
heat pumps 589, **594–5**
heat radiation *see* radiant heat exchange
heat recovery 557
heat tape 342
heat transfer 29, 36
   see also thermal resistance
heat-transfer coefficient *see* U-values
heating regimes 429
heating stoves 432
   creating draughts 551
   historical perspective *116*, 125, 127
   sulphate pollutants from 204, *204*
heating systems 121, 204–6, 426–36
   assessment 255
   controls *111*, 126, 206, 521, 554
   design criteria 427
   energy-saving measures 554, **558**
   historical perspective 122–7
   humidistat controls 428, 429
   inspection and maintenance **349**
   installing new systems 436
   localised heating 429, 554
   physical effect on materials 35
   reinstating early systems 430
   and relative humidity [RH] 204, 205
   temperature and humidity fluctuations *111*
   see also boilers; central heating; heating stoves; radiant heating systems
heating, ventilation, and air-conditioning [HVAC] systems
   control systems 442, 557
   energy-saving measures 553–7, **558**
heave 165
herbicides 336
Hereford Cathedral *136*
herring gulls 176

hidden areas *see* voids
hidden metal 268–9
hidden services 267
hidden wood 268
high-density polyethylene [HDPE] rainwater goods 375
historic repairs and alterations 352, 355
historical perspectives
    rainwater drainage 66–7, *66*
    roof coverings 60, *61*
    roof structure 58–9
    wall construction 74–5
historical research 218–19, 261, 262
hollow-wall construction 183
    maintenance 342
    moisture problems 194
    vapour barriers 364–5
    waterproofing 192
    see also cavity walls; cladding systems; rainscreen walls
Hooke, Robert 24
hoppers (rainwater) 69, *69*, 72
    faulty 193
    inspection and maintenance **345**
hot-water central heating 433–4
    early examples 125–6
    leakage 207
    underfloor heating 435
hot-water pipes, insulation 555
hot-water systems 555, **558**, **592–3**
House of Commons 136
House-to-House Electric Light Supply Co 142
humidification 439
humidistats 428, 429
humidity buffering 107–8, *108*, **409**, 412
humidity control 439–40
    see also humidistats
humidity measurement 238, 251
humidity problems **317**
Hurst, Dr H. 201
HVAC *see* heating, ventilation, and air-conditioning [HVAC] systems
hydraulic platforms 226
hydraulic pressure 47
hydroelectric power 590, **596–7**
hydrogeology, investigations 259, 260
hydrology 9
hydronic underfloor heating 435

hydrophilic surfaces *45*
hydrophobic surfaces 45, *45*
hygric mass 107
hygrometers *251*
hygroscopic moisture content 284
hygroscopicity 46, 107, 284
hysteresis 48

I

IAQ *see* indoor air quality [IAQ]
ice dams 96, *96*, 168
ice, protecting gutters from 342, 395
ignition sources 475–6
IGU *see* insulated glazing units [IGUs]
impact damage 209, *209*, 464
    preventing 486
impact noise 424
impact strength **28**
impellers (humidifiers) 439
impermeable finishes 186, 198, 329
    condensation **316**
    floor coverings 110, 190
    inhibiting evaporation 107, 189, 190
    see also water-resistant coatings
impulse radar 266, 274
inappropriate materials 331
inappropriate treatments 187–9, 190, 198
indoor air quality [IAQ] 449
    air conditioning 441
    airtightness affecting 514, 541
    diagnosing problems **317**
indoor environment *see* interior environment
indoor pollutants **450**
    from combustion heaters 121, 204, *204*
    gaseous pollutants 457–9
    micro-organisms 453–6
    reducing 398
infill panels 183
infrared radiation 29
infrared spectroscopy 285
infrared thermography 264, *265*, 267
    moisture detection 273, *273*
inglenook fireplaces 123, *124*
injected damp-proofing 201
injection drying **500**
insect pests 160, 248, 400
insect traps 248

inspection hatches (rainwater drainage) 71
inspection schedules 332, **344–9**
insulated glazing units [IGUs] 92, 571, 574
    condensation problems **316**
    inspection and maintenance 343
    sound insulation 423
    testing 288
    thermal breaks 411
    U-values **574**
insulation 411, 563–9
    avoiding thermal bridges 567–8
    causing freeze-thaw damage 395
    energy-saving measures 540, *541*
    ground floors 190, 586, **587**
    hot-water pipes 555
    materials 566
    risks 563–4
    roofs 197, 363, 576, **577**, **578**
    superinsulation 568–9
    and vapour barriers 185
    walls 106, 197, 581–3, **584–5**
        cavity construction 197, 411, 583, **585**
    warm side or cold side? 567
    water-damaged 498
interior environment 10
    air temperature 520, *521*
    alterations 195
    buffering by the building envelope 103–8
    controlling 111, 202, 442
    diagnosing problems **321**
    effect of building occupation 109–11
    historical changes 115–16
    interventions 357, 408–9, 425
    see also indoor air quality [IAQ]; indoor pollutants
interior lighting *see* lighting
interior wall insulation 411, 582, **585**
intermittent heating, causing condensation 205–6, *206*
internal capacitance detectors 267
internal structure and fabric 100–2
    alterations 195
    inspection and maintenance 343, **348**
    isolating conditioned areas 551
internal walls 102
interventions
    planning 354–61
    reviewing results 443
    selecting 360–1
    see also treatment and repair
ion chromatography 285
ivy on buildings 336

J

jackdaws 176, **404**
John Rylands Library *143*

K

Karsten tubes 269
kerosene lamps *134*, 135
kitchen appliances 561, **561**
kitchen fires 475
Knapen tube 199–200
knowledge and skills 328

L

laboratory salt analysis 285
ladders 227
lamp types and fire risk **476**
land drains 198, *198*, 378
land use 7
laser theodolites *223*
lath-and-plaster ceilings 102
lath-and-plaster walls 418, 474
lead, discolouration by pollutants 171, *171*
lead flashing 63, 164, 338, **347**
lead paints
    health and safety 225, 453
    permeability 189
lead pipes, health risks 453
lead rainwater goods 67, **375**
lead soakers 63
lead-tetraoxide discolouration 7
leaf guards 340
leakage (of air) *see* airtightness
leakage (of water)
    monitoring **299**
    wet heating systems 207
Legionella 456
legislation
    smoke control areas 432
    wildlife protection 247, 402
    work spaces 329
light damage 132, 154, 169, *250*
    monitoring 305
    preventing 396
    protective coatings 396
light monitoring **295**, **299**
light sensors 293

light switches *138*
lightfastness tests 305
lighting 131–8
    artificial 133–8
    natural 132, **560**
    see also electric lighting
lightning protection **347**, 477–80
lime-ash floors 100
lime mortars
    carbonation cycle 30, *31*
    elasticity and plasticity *170*
    fillets 63, 338
    permeability 57, 74, 184
    pointing 88
    reinstatement works 501
lime-plaster floors 100, 107
lime plasters
    moisture absorption 107
    porosity 361
    post-flood drying 498
    sacrificial 390, 501
lime renders 75, 77
limecrete 389
limelight 135
limestone
    permeability 43, *43*
    rainwater damage 171, *171*
limewash 75, 328, 342
    below-ground walls 390
    porosity 361
Lincoln's Inn Fields *141*
Lindsay, James Bowman 138
linings *see* dry lining; flue liners
lintels 85, *85*, 192
listed buildings 353, 542
local environment, assessment 233, 258–63
local land use 7
local materials 328
localised heating 429, 432
loft insulation 197, 576, **577**
logbooks 305, 333
London Argand *136*
low-energy lamps 559
low- or zero-carbon [LZC] technologies 588–91, **592–7**

M

macerators 381

magnesium salts 157, **158**
magnetic stud detectors 267
maintenance 193
    avoiding potential problems 322
    chimneys 342
    day-to-day care 327–44
    doors 343
    energy consumption 510
    half-timbered construction 342
    inspection schedules 332
    of interior 343
    logbooks 333
    planning care programmes 330–3
    preventing damage 335–6
    rainwater disposal systems 339–42
    roof coverings 337–8
    routine 334–44
    schedules **344–9**
    walls 342
    windows 329, 343
malleability **28**
mason bees 400
masonry
    freeze-thaw damage 168
    inspection and maintenance **348**
    moisture measurement 253
    moisture problems 243, 244, 245
    relieving arches 85
    sampling from 277–9, *277*, *278*, *282*, *283*
    thermal buffering 106
    U-values 565, **565**
    see also chimneys; mortar joints; stonework; walls
masonry roofs 59
material change of use *see* change of use
material properties 24–7, **28**
materials *see* building materials
materials sampling *see* sampling of materials
mechanical humidification 439
mechanical ventilation with heat recovery [MVHR] 557, **558**
membranes, vapour barriers 183–6, *185*, 364–5
mesh screens for gutters 341
metal-clad flat roofs 576
metal flashing 63, 164, 338, **347**
metal-framed windows 410, *549*
metal gutters and pipes **374**, **375**
    repainting 339, 371
    replacement 371
metal roof coverings 61
    care and maintenance **338**

metal roof coverings (cont.)
   inspection and maintenance 347
metal roof sheets, dimensional change *155, 167, 395*
metals
   assessing hidden metal 268–9
   corrosion *see* corrosion
   theft 464, 487
microbiological growths 248, 399–400, *399*
   anthrax hazard 453
   assessing 267
   sources of contamination **450**
   testing 305
   see also moulds (organic)
microclimate measurement 251
microdrilling 268
micropores 43, *46*
microwave attenuation 274, 300
mineral-wool insulation 185–6, 566
mitre valleys 363
mobile elevated platforms 226
modelling tools
   energy performance 516
   energy-saving measures 536, 543–4, *543–4*
modern construction systems 34
   air conditioning 441
   airtightness 104, 182
   decay processes 148
   interventions 355
   maintenance inspections 343
   moisture problems 245
   thermal bridges 93, 236
   walls 78–80, 235
   windows 84, 92, *192*
   see also curtain walls; hollow-wall construction
modern materials 34, 106
moisture absorption 47, 107
   testing 269, 283
moisture buffering *see* humidity buffering
moisture content 37–48, 152
   affecting thermal conductivity 565
   effect of temperature 94
   measurement 252–4, 272–85
      destructive methods 276–85
      non-destructive methods 273–5
   monitoring **294, 299**, 300–2, 564
   in relation to deterioration 152, 272, *272*
   and salt crystallisation 152
   sudden or varying *153*
   and thermal conductivity 36

moisture entrainment 44, 76
moisture meters **294, 299**, 302, 564
moisture resistance *see* rain resistance
moisture-resistant coatings *see* impermeable finishes; water-resistant coatings
moisture sensors 564, *564*
monitoring *see* environmental monitoring
monitoring rods (timber dowels) 301, 499
monthly inspection and maintenance **344**
mortar fillets 63, 338
mortar joints 63, 183
   inspection and maintenance 338, **347**
   moisture transfer through 47
   repointing 183, 384
mosaics 305
moss 248, 400
moulds (organic) 453–5
   behind vinyl wallpapers 207
   in corners of walls 182
   diagnosis **315**
   health risks 454–5
   investigating 245
   spores causing allergic reactions **455**
   treatment 455
movement *see* differential thermal movement; ground movement; structural movement
multiple causes of deterioration 321
multiple chemical sensitivities [MCS] 449
multiple ownership and occupancy 328, 423
Murdoch, William 136
musty smells **317**
MVHR [mechanical ventilation with heat recovery] 557, **558**
mycotoxins 454, 455

N

National Grid 142, *142*
National Trust 429, 543, 554, 571
natural fibrous insulation 566
natural gas 434
natural lighting 132, **560**
natural ventilation 128, *129*, 437
near-infrared optical fibres 275
nest boxes 402
nesting sites 402–3
neutral pressure point [NPP] 97
neutron scattering 275

night ventilation 554
nitrate salts 157, **158**
nitric oxide 459
nitrogen dioxide 459
NMR [nuclear magnetic resonance] 274, 300
noise
   assessment 267
   problems 208
   suppression 423–4
   transmission *423*, 424
nuclear magnetic resonance [NMR] 274, 300

O

occupant behaviour, energy usage and control 525–6, *526* **538**, 552, 557
occupant comfort *see* thermal comfort
occupation of building
   effecting internal environment 109–11
   handover of building 546–7
   post-occupancy evaluation [POE] 546
odour problems **317**
oil fuels 434
oil lamps 134–5, *134, 135*
oil paints *see* paints
on-site work 231–2
open fires 432
   flues 367, 430, 436
   historical perspective 122, *122, 123*, 126
opening up for inspection 246, 495
operational energy 512–13
operative temperature 520
optical fibres 275
organic growths 399–400, *399*
   see also microbiological growths; plant growth
overflow spouts 69, 72, 193, 372
overflows, inspection and maintenance **345**
overheating 562, 563
owls 402
oxalates 158
ozone 459

P

paint analysis 271
paint finishes
   cracking 272
   inspection and maintenance **348**

paint finishes (cont.)
   light damage 154
   on plaster 107
   see also coatings; lead paints
painting
   below-ground walls 390
   doors and windows 343
   inspection and maintenance **349**
   metal gutters and pipes 339
paints 189
   anti-mould 455
   assessing 271
   water-resistant 186
panelling *see* timber panelling
paraffin heaters 121
paraffin lamps *134*, 135
parapet gutters 67, 68, 69, 180
   blockage by ice and snow 178
   gradient 377
   inspection and maintenance **347**, 372
   moisture problems 178
   repair 370
parasitic heat transfer 435
parging 123, 126
particulates (pollutants) 171, 249
partition walls 99, 102
passive cooling 128, 554
passive humidification 439
PassivHaus 569
patents
   hot-water boiler systems 125
   oil lamps 134
perimeter drains 350, *379*, 380
   blocked 318, *319*
   capping and backfilling 88, 198
   inspection and maintenance **344**, **345**
periodic inspections and surveys 222, 332, **344–9**
Perkins, Angier Marsh 125
permeability measurement 43
permeable materials 43
   capillary absorption 47
   capillary rise 88–9, *88*
   dimensional change 94
   drying of 48
   hydraulic pressure in 47
   hygroscopicity 46, 107
   moisture content 94
   moisture damage 152, *153*
   rain penetration 74
   salt contamination 156, 157

permeable materials (cont.)
   water-vapour movement 46–7, *46*
   wetting 45–7
pesticides 336, 400
pH meters 285
photography 228, 305, 491
photovoltaics [PV] **592–3**
physical properties 24–7, 28
pigeons *175*, 247
   deterrence 402, 403, **404–6**
planar glazing 80, 342, 343
plant growth
   causing damage 173–4, *173*, 335–6, *335*, *401*
   inspection and maintenance **346**
plaster ceilings 102
plaster delamination **314**
plasterboard 102
plasters
   animal hair in 453
   below-ground walls 390
   cement-based 190
   insulating effect 566, 581, **584**
   water-resistant 90, 198
   see also lime plasters
plastic foam insulation 566
plastic rainwater goods 374, **375**
plasticity **28**
plastics, sunlight damage 169
plumbing 140
   see also water pipes
POE [post-occupancy evaluation] 546
pollutants 171
   chemical attack 156
   from combustion heaters 121
   investigating 249
   monitoring **294**, **299**, 305
   protection from 398
   see also atmospheric pollutants; indoor pollutants
polythene-sheet membranes 184, 186
polyvinylchloride [PVCU] rainwater goods **375**
porous materials 42, 43
   see also permeable materials
porous open-cell foams 424
portières 562
Portland cement *see* cement
Portland limestone 43, *43*

positive-pressure buildings 414
post-occupancy evaluation [POE] 546
potassium salts 157, **158**
powder samples 276, 277, *277*, 280
precast concrete gutters 179, 371
Preliminary Energy Plan 533
pressure testing **528**
Price Brothers, Bristol 125
probes *see* electronic sensors and probes
project development 358–9
protected buildings 353, 542
proxy materials 305
psychrometric charts 42, *251*
pugging boards 102
pull-off tests 271
punkahs 128
putty damage by birds 175, 401
PV [photovoltaics] **592–3**
PVCU [polyvinylchloride] rainwater goods **375**

Q

quartz heaters 428
quinquennial inspections **349**

R

R-values 289
radiant heat exchange, measuring **528**
radiant heat losses 410, 425, 552, 554
radiant heating systems 121, **426**, *426*, 428, 554
   fire risk 475
   radiant heating panels *521*, 552
   thermal comfort *428*, *521*
radiant temperature monitoring **294**
radiation 29, 105
radiation attenuation 274
radiation monitoring **295**
radiative heating 91
radiators (heating) 125, 204
   heat emission *427*
   painted and metallic finishes 430
   positioning 206, 427
   reinstating early models 430
   thermostats 533
radio-telemetry monitoring systems 297, *297*
radon gas 458

rain penetration 74, 76, 76, 164
  remedial work 384–5
rain resistance 74, 76, 76, 164
rainscreen walls 79–80, *80*, 188, 235
  see also curtain walls
rainwater deflection 55, *57*, 68
  see also water-shedding features
rainwater disposal systems 66–71, 72–3
  access for inspection and repair 339
  inspection and maintenance **344**, **345**
  interventions 370–83
  maintenance 193, *194*, 337, 339–42
  surveying 235, 244
rainwater goods
  faulty 179
  materials for 67, **374–5**
  preparing for climate change 377
  repair 370–1, *371*
  replacement 371
  sizing 57, 376–7
  see also downpipes; drainpipes; gutters; hoppers (rainwater)
rainwater handling 55–7
rainwater outlets
  faulty 179, 193
  sizing 377
rainwater resistance *see* rain resistance
rainwater runoff *see* surface water runoff
rammed earth *see* earthen floors; earthen walls
rats 175, 407
reagents 30
reagent indicator strips 270
recording surveys 228, 229
refrigerant dehumidifiers 130
refrigerative air conditioners 438
regulations *see* Building Regulations
Reid, David Boswell 119, *119*
reinforced concrete *see* steel-reinforced concrete
relative humidity [RH] 41–2, 107, 109
  conservation heating to control 429, 554
  monitoring 301
  for mould growth 453
  and salt cycling 440
  and space heating 204, 205, 428, 439
  sudden changes in 152
  and temperature 196, 205, 440
  and ventilation 203, 416
  see also absolute humidity [AH]; humidity buffering
relieving arches 85, *85*

renders
  below-ground walls 90, 390
  inspection and maintenance **348**
  insulating effect 566, 581, **584**
  permeable 384
  problematic 187
  removed in past 195
  replacement 355, 385, 582
  traditional 75, 77
  see also cement-based renders
renewable construction materials 511
renewable energy 588–91, **592–7**
repairs *see* interventions; treatment and repair
repointing 183, 384
reporting investigations 256
  see also recording surveys
resistance meters 252–3, *253*, 302
resonant dampers 424
responsibilities for maintenance tasks 334
Responsible Retrofit Guidance Wheel 543, *543–4*
reverse curves 341
RHeq [equilibrium relative humidity] 107, 157, *159*
'rising damp' 88–9, *89*, 164
  diagnosis **315**
risk assessment and management 216
  disaster management 467
  energy-saving measures 536–8
  fire risk 473–4
rodding points 71, *350*, 379, 380
rodents causing damage 175, 407
Roman cement 187
roof coverings
  care and maintenance 337–8, **338**
  differential movement 63, *167*, 178
  inspection and maintenance **344**, **347**
  measures to discourage theft 487
  rain handling 59–60, 59–61
  repairs 362–3
  and roof pitch 62
  surveying 234
  temporary **489**
  ventilation 59
  'water-resistant' and 'waterproof' 59–60, *61*
  see also metal roof sheets; shingles; slates; thatch; tiled roofs
roof pitch
  and ponding 178
  sizing rainwater goods 376
  for specific roof coverings 62

roof pitch (cont.)
  surveying 234
roof space
  condensation 65, 197, 245, 362, 363
  fire barriers **484**
  inspection and maintenance **348**
  ventilation 65, **65**, 96, *337*, 362, 363, 392
  see also attics
roof voids *see* roof space
roofs 58–65
  boarding 59
  design 62
  design faults 178
  detailing of joints 63
  downpipes discharging onto *57*
  eaves overhang 74
  habitats for animals 175
  insulation 197, 576, **577**, **578**
  pooling of water 234
  protecting openings 64, *64*
  rainwater drainage 66–70
  re-roofing 362–3
  reducing heat losses 576
  supporting structures 58–9
  surveying 234
  U-values **565**
  underlays 59, 197
  vapour barriers 184, 364–5
  see also flat roofs
room heaters 432
roosting sites 403
root barriers 401, *401*
Root, John Wellborn 79
rope access 227
Rose, William 185, 186
'rough cast' rendering 75, 77
routine maintenance 334–44
Rowley, Frank 184, 185–6
rush lights 133, *135*

S

sacrificial plaster 390, **394**
safe access 226
salt contamination 156, 157
  investigating 244
  surveying 238
salt crusts 171
salt crystallisation 152, 156, 157, 158, 270
salt efflorescence *see* efflorescence
salt-jacking 191, *191*, 234, 366

salt-related damage 156, 158, 171
　　chimneys 191, *191*, 234, 366
　　environmental control 440
　　from mosses and algae 173
　　see also sulphate attack
salts and salt solutions 157
　　analysing 285, **285**
　　identification 249, 270, *270*, 285
　　RHeqs 440
　　sampling *270*
　　for setting humidity 284
　　sources of common ions **158**
salvage storage 499
sampling of materials 224, 268
　　moisture measurement 276–85, *277*, *278*, *279*
　　repairing sample holes 278
sandstone
　　permeability 43, *43*
　　rainwater damage 171
sandy soils 8
sash windows 92, 556, *572*
saturation 41
SBS [sick building syndrome] 120, 449
scaffolding 226
scheduled inspections 332
scheduled monuments 353
Scott, George Gilbert 136
sealants
　　break down by sunlight 169
　　rainwater protection 84
sealed buildings 120, 129
　　see also superinsulation
seals
　　curtain walls 288, 342
　　hollow-wall construction 164
　　insulated glazing units (IGUs) 288
secondary glazing 571–3, **575**
　　condensation **316**, 414, 571, 573
　　early examples 92, *92*, *573*
　　openable or removable *573*
　　research into cavity ventilation 420
　　U-values **565**
secret gutters 179
semi-permeable membranes 186
　　see also air and vapour control layers [AVCLs]
sensors *see* electronic sensors and probes
septic tanks 381, **383**
services, building *see* building services
sewage systems 71, 139, *139*, 381, 382, **383**

shading 128, 132, 552
　　see also blinds
sheepswool insulation 566
sheet-metal roof coverings *see* metal roof coverings
shingles 183, 342, 401
shutters
　　energy-saving measures 571, 572, *572*, **575**
　　historical perspective 81, *81*, 132
　　limiting sun damage **397**
sick building syndrome [SBS] 120, 449
signal-generation systems 274–5
significance of building 220, 353, 542
siphonic damp-proofing systems 199–200, *199*, *200*
siphonic drainage systems 373, *373*, 377
skills and knowledge 328
slates
　　care and maintenance **338**
　　inspection and maintenance **347**
smart meters 531
smoke alarms 481, **482**
smoke bays 123
smoke from lamps *135*
smoke hoods 123
smoke testing 286, *286*, 528
smokeless zones 125
Snodgrass, Neil 125
snow
　　meltwater damage 95–6, 168
　　roof design for 65, 95, *95*
snow guards/hooks 395
soakaways 71, *73*, 181
　　blockages 339
　　inspection and maintenance **345**
　　upgrading 379, 380
soakers 63
sodium salts **158**
sodium sulphate 157, 158
Soft Landings 546–7
soil moisture, investigation 243, 260
soil moisture profile probes *300*, 302
soils
　　assessing 260, 269
　　characteristics 8
　　subsidence and heave 165
solar energy *588*

solar films 192, **397**
solar gain 128, *520*
solar heating (natural) 169
solar shading 128, 132, 552
　　see also blinds
solar water heating 555, **592–3**
solid core samples 276, 278, 283
solid fuels 434
solid ground floors 100, *100*, 107
　　concrete replacement 195, 389
　　condensation 100, 204, *205*, **315**, 416
　　insulation 586, **587**
　　limecrete 389
　　moisture problems **315**
solid walls
　　energy performance 516
　　insulation 411–12
　　see also traditional construction systems
soluble salts 157
sound, loads from 34
sound propagation 31
　　see also noise
soundproofing 102, 423, 424
spark arrestors 366, 431
specialist investigations 215, 256–307
　　air exchange and heat loss measurement 286–90
　　building envelope 264–7, **528**
　　building materials 268–85
　　environmental monitoring 291–307
　　groundwater and drainage 259–63, 386
　　indoor air quality 451
　　weather stations 258
　　when required 257
specific humidity 39
splashback 86
spot measurements 251, 272
spouts (rainwater) 68, 69, 72
sprinklers (fire fighting) 485
Stachybotrys 454, 455
stack effect 98, 128
staining **314**
　　at the bottom of windows 205
　　chimney breast 191, 432
　　concrete façade *235*
　　dirt deposition above a heater 35
　　exposed lead 7
STBA [Sustainable Traditional Buildings Alliance] 516, 543

steam heating 125
steel-reinforced concrete
    corrosion 494
    investigation 268, 269, *269*
    repair 385
Stevenson screens 291, *298*
stew stove 127
stonework
    permeability 43, *43*
    pollution damage 171
storm damage 463
    inspection for **344**
storm drains 87
street lighting 135, 142
strength of materials 24–5, **28**
strip foundations 101
stripping out 246, 495
structural characteristics of materials **28**
structural damage 493
structural failure 34, *148*
structural glazing 79, 80
structural load 32–4
structural movement
    monitoring 241, *241*, **295**, 298
    surveying 240–1
Strutt, William 118, *118*, 125
stucco 83, 245, 385, 498
subfloor voids *see* underfloor voids
subflorescences 157
subsidence 165, *165*, 465
subterranean spaces
    dehumidifying 440
    faulty treatment 190, 352
    moisture penetration 90, *90*, 190
    pumping flood water from **471**, 490
    trenches around 101, 386, 393
subterranean walls
    insulation 583
    interior wall finishes 190, 198, 390, 393, **394**
    moisture penetration 90, 243, 386
    treatment 390, 393
    waterproofing 90
Sugg, William 136
sulphate attack 121, 156, 157, 171, 234
    see also salt-related damage
sulphates 157, **158**
sulphur-dioxide fumes 121, 204, *204*
sun-burner luminaire *137*

sunlight
    damage limitation 396, *396*, **397**
    degradation of coatings 189
    filters 396
    light damage *see* light damage
    monitoring 305
    temperature-related damage 155, *167*, 169, 395
superinsulation 568–9
surface finishes
    blistering and flaking *237*, **314**
    reinstatement works 501
    staining *see* staining
    water damaged 498
    see also coatings; paint finishes; plasters; renders; wall finishes
surface spalling 47
surface temperature, monitoring **294**, *298*, *299*
surface tension 37, 45, *45*
surface water drainage 86–8
    see also groundwater
surface water runoff 87, 164, 181
    ground slope 239, *240*, 380
    investigating 261
surface wetness sensors *293*, **294**
survey records 228, *229*
surveying equipment 230
surveys 215
    health and safety 225–7
suspended floors *100*, 101
    inspection and maintenance **349**
    insulation 586, **587**
    soundproofing 424
    U-values 565
    ventilation 101, *101*, 190, 417, 422
    see also floorboards; timber floors; underfloor voids
sustainability, heating and air conditioning 425
Sustainable Traditional Buildings Alliance [STBA] 516, 543
Swan, Joseph 138

T

tanking 190, 390, 393, **394**
tapestries *see* wall hangings
Taylor, John 89
TDR [time-domain reflectometry] 275, 302
temperature
    and air movement 427
    and biological attack 456, 496
    buffering *103*, *104*, *105*, *106*, 196

temperature (cont.)
    dew-point 40, *206*
    dimensional change *see* differential thermal movement
    and moisture 40–2, 94, 416, 440, 541
    and moisture damage 155, *155*, 395
    operative 520
    and relative humidity 196, 205
    thermal inertia 91
temperature control 111, 204–6, 554
temperature measurement 238, 251
temperature-related damage 155, 167–8, 395
temporary roof coverings **489**
tensile roofs 59
tensile strength 25, **28**
terrace houses 328
    fire spread *483*
terrain 7
textiles, light damage 154
thatch 61, 68
    care and maintenance *334*, **338**
    fire hazards 431
    inspection and maintenance **347**
    protection from birds and squirrels 401
    spark arrestors 366
    U-values 290, *290*
thermal breaks 93, 106, 411
thermal bridges 91–3, *93*, 105, 236
    interventions 410–11
    in retrofitted insulation 567–8
    window frames 571
thermal buffering 105–6, *106*, 410–12
thermal comfort 317, 425, 427, 435, 518, 520–1, *520*
thermal conductance and conductivity 36, 565
thermal energy in materials 29
thermal imaging 264, *265*, 267
    limitations 529
    moisture assessment 273, *273*
thermal inertia 91, 105
thermal insulation *see* insulation
thermal mass 106, 563
thermal movement *see* differential thermal movement
thermal paints 411
thermal performance, measuring 288–90, 528
thermal properties 91
thermal resistance 36
    see also U-values

643

BUILDING ENVIRONMENT
INDEX

thermal resistance (cont.)
  measuring 288, 289–90, **528**
thermal resistivity 36
thermal sensors 275
thermal transfer coefficients 36
thermal transmittance *see* U-values
thermistors 298
thermography *see* infrared thermography; thermal imaging
thermostatic radiator valves [TRVs] 554
thermostats 126, 428, *533*
Thompson, Benjamin (Count Rumford) 124
Thompson, J. J. (Lord Kelvin) 45, 46
tile-hanging 77, 183, 342
tiled roofs 61
  care and maintenance **338**
  inspection and maintenance **347**
  mitre valleys 363
Tilehurst Water Tower 140
timber
  decay processes *148*
    fungal decay 160, *160*, 172, 248, **314**, 399, 494
    insect attack *160*, 248
    temperature damage *155*
  microdrilling 268
  moisture content 107, 152, *153*
  moisture measurement 252, *253*
  moisture response 272
  post-flood drying 498
  shrinkage *153*
  silvering *154*, 169
  see also wood
timber dowel method *see* monitoring rods
timber floors *100*, 101
  decay problems 190
  opening up for inspection 246
  soundproofing 424
  underfloor ventilation 190
  see also suspended floors
timber-framed buildings 74
  infill panels 183
  inspection and maintenance **348**
  insulation 583, **585**
  maintenance 342
  moisture problems 243, 245
  vapour barriers 365
  see also half-timbered construction
timber gutters 371
timber joists 102

timber lintels *85*, 192
timber panelling 390, 393, **394**, *412*, *581*, **584**
  fire spread 473
  inspection and sampling behind 277, 361
  thermal performance 552
  ventilation 422
timber roofs 58, *58*, *337*
time domain reflectometry [TDR] 275, 302
time-lapse imaging 293
timelines 219
topography 7, 233
town gas 434, 457
toxic materials 225, 452–3
toxic moulds 454, 455
tracer-gas tests 287
tracer testing, for water problems 259
traditional construction systems 33
  energy performance 516, 520
  energy-saving measures 532, 543
traditional materials 331, 566
treatment and repair 350–442
  assessing interventions 443
  dealing with persistent issues 351–2
  grants for 330
  historic repairs and alterations 352, 355
  interventions on the envelope 362–407
  minor repairs 332, 334
  modifying the interior environment 408–42
  planning interventions 354–61
  selecting interventions 360–1
  see also headings for specific building elements
Tredgold, Thomas 119
tree-related damage 173, 174
tree roots 401, *401*
trees on site 233, 335, 401
trench arches 381, **383**
trenches
  around basements 101, 386
  for drains *378*, 379
trunking, electrical 143
TRV [thermostatic radiator valves] 554
  see also thermostats

U

U-values 36, 289–90, 565, **565**
  insulated glazing units [IGUs] 574
  measuring 290, **528**
ultrasonic humidifiers 439

ultrasonic testing 266, 275
ultraviolet radiation 29
  filters 132, 396, *396*, **397**
  light damage 154, *154*, 169
underfloor heating 126, 207, 435
underfloor insulation 190
underfloor voids 101
  inspection **349**, 495
  moisture penetration 190
  ventilation 101, *101*, 190, 417, 422
underlays, roofing 59, 197
  see also air-and-vapour control layers [AVCLs]
unplasticised polyvinylchloride [PVCU]
  rainwater goods 375
upper floors 102
utility meters 531

V

vacuum panels 566
valley gutters 68, 72
  gradient 377
  inspection and maintenance **347**
  moisture problems 178, *178*
  repair 370, 371
value added tax [VAT] 329
vandalism 464, 487
vapour barriers 183–6, 364–5
  see also air-and-vapour control layers [AVCLs]
vapour pressure 39
vapour transfer 185
  in building materials 46–7
vapourisers 439
varnishes, light damage 154
VAT [value added tax] 329
vegetation growth *see* plant growth
ventilating lamps 137, *137*
ventilation 117–20, 203, 556–7
  air bricks 101, *101*
  air exchange requirements 287, 413
  and air flow 416
  in cavities 417–22
  chimneys and flues 117, 342, 366, 367, 414
    disused flues 369, 416
  for combustion 366, 457
  for control of condensation, mould and rot 120, 190, 203, 362, 392, 417
  controlling 416, 556
  cross-ventilation 128, 437
  energy-saving measures 541

ventilation (cont.)
   and fire control 369, 472, 476
   gas lighting 137
   historical perspective 118–20
   increasing 415–16
   mechanical ventilation with heat recovery [MVHR] 557, **558**
   opening doors and windows **344**, 556, *556*
   passive cooling 128, 554
   and relative humidity 203, 416
   roof coverings 59
   roof space 65, **65**, *96*, 337, 362, 363, 392
   stack effect 98, 128
   underfloor 101, *101*, 190, 417, 422
   walls
      cavity walls 78, 183, 417, 422
      rainscreens 80, 183
   wind-induced 97, 117
   see also air conditioning; air exchange; draughts; natural ventilation
ventilation grilles 190, 417
   for heating systems 436
   inspection and maintenance **346**
vernacular architecture *53*
vibration, loads from 34
Victoria and Albert Museum 137
video recording 305
vinyl wallpapers 186, 207
VIR [vulcanised-rubber insulation] 143
Vitruvius 132
VOC [volatile organic compounds] 459
voids
   condensation in 41, 46
   fire protection measures **484**
   fire stopping **484**, *484*
   flooding 494, *495*
   inspection 266, *266*, *495*
   roof *see* roof space
   in timber 268
   underfloor *see* underfloor voids
volatile organic compounds [VOCs] 459
vulcanised-rubber insulation [VIR] 143

W

wall coatings 102, 186, 189
wall coverings 102
   vinyl wallpapers 186, 207
wall finishes
   basements 390, 393, **394**
   inappropriate 187–9, 190, 198
   traditional *75*
   see also plasters; renders

wall hangings 110, 410, *581*, **584**
wall paintings
   deterioration processes *121*, *203*, *231*, *250*
   environmental control 196, 305
   post-flood drying 501
wall siphons 199–200, *199*, *200*
wall ties 78
walls 74–80
   below-ground *see* subterranean walls
   capillary rise 88–9, *88*
   cavity *see* cavity walls
   cladding 77, 188
   cold 410–12
   condensation in corners 182
   design faults 182–90
   groundwater penetration
      damp-proofing 387–9, 393
      preventing 386
   impermeable finishes 89, 329
   inspection and maintenance 342, **348**
   insulation 106, 197, 581–3, **584–5**
   localised damage 244
   modern construction 78–9
   moisture content measurement 272–83
   moisture content monitoring 300–2, 564
   moisture distribution 279
   moisture problems 164, 182–90
      diagnosis **315–16**
      investigation 243–4, 279, *279*
   moisture profiles 301
   moisture resistance 74
   mortar joints *see* mortar joints
   protective finishes 75, *75*, 77
   rain penetration 74, 76, *76*
      remedial work 384–5
   rain resistance 74, 76, 164
   renders *see* renders
   sampling from 277–9, *277*, *278*, *282*, 283
   solid *see* solid walls
   structural characteristics 283
   surveying 235, 237–8
   thermal buffering 105–6, *106*
   thickness 182
   traditional construction 74–5
   U-values 565, *565*
   vapour barriers 364–5
warm roofs 197, 576, **577**, *578*
waste recycling and reuse 511
waste-water disposal 87, 381, 382, **383**
water absorption 47, 107
   testing 283
water as liquid 44–8
water-borne pollutants 249

water disposal systems
   see ground drainage; rainwater disposal systems
water leakage monitoring **299**
water mist fire-fighting systems 485
water molecules 37–8, *37*, *38*, 44
water pipes
   freeze-thaw damage 168
   leaking 207, *343*
water properties 37–44
water-resistant coatings 107, 186, 198, 361, 364, 386
   see also impermeable finishes
water-resistant plasters 90, 198
water sampling 259
water-shedding features 57, 180, *180*, 192
   effect of external insulation 582
   restoring 385, *385*
water-source heat pumps 126, 589, **594–5**
water supply 139, 140
water table 9, 164
   see also groundwater
water tanks 140
water-tube boilers 433
water vapour 39–42
   humidity buffering 107–8, *108*, **409**, 412
   hygroscopicity 46, 107, 284
   sources of 121, 206, 223
   see also absolute humidity [AH]; condensation; evaporation; humidity buffering; relative humidity [RH]
water vapour pressure 39
weather 5–6
weather stations 258, **294**, 298
weatherboarding 77, *77*, 183
weatherings 63
   inspection and maintenance 338, **347**
   see also metal flashing; mortar fillets
weekly inspection and maintenance **344**
weep holes 8, **346**, 417
weighted sound reduction index [Rw] 267
Weir, William 142
Welsbach, Carl Auer von 137
'wet' 152
wetting of permeable materials 45–7
whirling hygrometers *251*
White, Gilbert *133*

BUILDING ENVIRONMENT
INDEX

whole-house fans 438
wicking *see* capillarity
wildlife issues 336, 401–3
    see also animal-related damage
wildlife protection 247
wind and ventilation 97, 117
wind-catchers 129, *129*
wind damage 166, 463
wind-driven rain 57, 76
wind exposure 166
wind loading 97, *97*
wind turbines **594–5**
window blinds 192, **397**
window cills 84
windows 81–4
    air exchange and ventilation 117, 128, 556, *556*
    design faults 192
    deterioration and damage 166, 175, *189*, 236
        condensation damage *155*, *205*, 232, 237, **315**, **316**
    draughtproofing 413–14, *413*, *549*, 550, *562*
    effect on air circulation 427
    failed coatings *189*
    heat transfer 91–2, 105–6, 410, 520
        reducing heat losses 570–4, **575**
    inspection 236, **318**
    lintels 85
    maintenance 329, 343, **346**
    natural lighting 132
    protection against vandalism 467, 487
    rainwater protection 82, 83–4, *83*
    replacement 572, **575**
    shutters 81, *81*
    U-values **565**
    see also secondary glazing
wiring *see* electrical wiring
wood
    fuels 432
    light damage 154, *154*, 396
    rainwater goods **375**
    see also timber
wood-burning stoves 432, **592–3**
    historical perspective 124, 126, 127
    and thatch 431
wood fibre insulation 566
wood fires 428, 432
wooden dowel method *see* monitoring rods
wooden panelling *see* timber panelling
wooden shutters *see* shutters

work, definition 20

X

X-ray diffraction 285

Y

yield 26
yield strength **28**
York sandstone, permeability 43, *43*
Young, Thomas 24
Young's modulus 24

Z

'zero carbon' *see* low- or zero-carbon [LZC] technologies

ACKNOWLEDGEMENTS & PICTURE CREDITS

ACKNOWLEDGEMENTS

Project Manager: Sally Embree

Picture Editor: John Stewart

Picture Research: Suzanne Williams

Design: Robyn Pender & Tracy Manning

Thanks are also due to HoWoCo for Design Consultancy, 4word for copy editing, Chris Dance for indexing, and Altaimage for colour processing and print preparation. The diagrams in this volume were produced by Simon Revill, Robyn Pender and Iain McCaig (who also provided many of the diagrams in the first series of Practical Building Conservation). The glossaries for all volumes have been produced by David Mason.

All British Standards extracts reproduced with permission from The British Standards Institution (BSI – *www.bsigroup.com*) © The British Standards Institution. All Rights Reserved.

English Heritage and the volume editors would like to thank the peer reviewers of this book: Chris Sanders, Laurie Gibbs, and Trudi Hughes.

We would also like to express our great gratitude to the many individuals, both within English Heritage and without, who generously gave support and assistance, and without whom this book could never have been produced.

PICTURE CREDITS

Ashgate Publishing and English Heritage would like to thank the following people and organisations for their kind permission to reproduce their pictures.

Abbreviations key: t=top, b=bottom, l=left, r=right, c=centre, ct=centre top, cb=centre bottom

Cover picture: Robyn Pender © English Heritage
4: Robyn Pender © English Heritage
7: © Clive Murgatroyd
8: © Clive Murgatroyd
9: © Clive Murgatroyd
12: © Clive Murgatroyd
15: © Clive Murgatroyd
19: © English Heritage
22: Robyn Pender © English Heritage
23: Getty Images/ Steve Bronstein
25: Alamy/ © John Davidson Photos
27: Science Photo Library/ Alastair Philip Wiper (l); Science Photo Library/ Martyn F. Chillmaid (tr); Geoffrey Wallis (cr); Getty Images/ DEA/ G. Dagli Orti (br)
29: © 2000 Jeff J. Daly, Fundamental Photographs, NYC
30: © English Heritage
31: Shutterstock/ © Joshua David Treisner
32: Nicholas Warns Architect Ltd
35: Alamy/ © Shotshop GmbH
37: Robyn Pender © English Heritage
38: Robyn Pender © English Heritage
39: © English Heritage
40: © Tobit Curteis Associates
41: Robyn Pender © English Heritage
42: Robyn Pender © English Heritage
43: © Robyn Pender
44: Robyn Pender © English Heritage
45: Alamy/ © AR Images (tl); Alamy/ © Vladimir Jovanovic (bl); © 1990 Chip Clark - Fundamental Photographs, NYC (r)
46: Robyn Pender © English Heritage
49: akg-images/ Gustave Caillebotte, detail from *Linge séchant au bord de la Seine, Petit Gennevillier*, 1888. Wallraf-Richartz-Museum, Cologne
53: Alamy/ © Martin Bond (tl); Alamy/ © Peter Davey (tr); Alamy/ © Martin Karius (bl); © English Heritage (br)
54: Iain McCaig © English Heritage
56: © Tobit Curteis Associates
57: Robyn Pender © English Heritage
58: © English Heritage
59: © Clive Murgatroyd (t)
59: Alamy/ © Matthew Noble Yorkshire Images (b)
60: Robyn Pender © English Heritage (t); Nicholas Warns Architect Ltd (b)
61: Simon Revill © English Heritage (tl), (br); Iain McCaig © English Heritage (tc), (bl), (tr), (cr)

62: © Clive Murgatroyd (tl), (tr), (bl); Robyn Pender © English Heritage; Robyn Pender © English Heritage, with thanks to the Dean and Chapter of Lincoln Cathedral (br)
63: © Colin Burns. Reproduced with the kind permission of the National Trust (tl); Robyn Pender © English Heritage (tc), (br); © Clive Murgatroyd (tr), (bl), (bc)
64: © Clive Murgatroyd (tl); Robyn Pender © English Heritage (tr), (bl); © English Heritage (br)
65: Robyn Pender © English Heritage
66: © Reproduced by permission of English Heritage
67: © Tyler Bell http://www.flickr.com/photos/tylerbell/4098999939
69: © Tobit Curteis Associates (tl); Robyn Pender © English Heritage (tc), (br); © Peter T. J. Rumley (tr); © Clive Murgatroyd (c); Nicholas Warns Architect Ltd (bl), (bc)
70: Robyn Pender © English Heritage, with thanks to Wing with Grove All Saints, Wing
71: Robyn Pender © English Heritage
72: Robyn Pender © English Heritage. Reproduced with the kind permission of the National Trust (tl); Robyn Pender © English Heritage (tcl), (tcr), (tr), (ccl), (bcl), (bcr); © Tobit Curteis Associates (cl); © English Heritage (ccr); Nicholas Warns Architect Ltd (cr), (bl); © Clive Murgatroyd (br)
73: Nicholas Warns Architect Ltd
74: © Clive Murgatroyd
75: Robyn Pender © English Heritage (tl), (tc); © Clive Murgatroyd (bl), (tr); Brian Ridout (br)
76: © Robyn Pender, with thanks to the National Trust for Scotland (t); © Robyn Pender (b)
77: © Clive Murgatroyd
78: Simon Revill © English Heritage
79: © English Heritage (l); Robyn Pender © English Heritage (r)
80: Simon Revill © English Heritage (l); Robyn Pender © English Heritage (r)
81: © Andrew Plumridge, Peter Scott & Partners (l); © Linda Hall, with kind permission of Historic Royal Palaces (r)
82: Robyn Pender © English Heritage. Reproduced with the kind permission of the National Trust (tl); Alamy/ © DWD-photo (tr); Robyn Pender © English Heritage (cl), (c), (cr), (bl); © Clive Murgatroyd (br)
83: © Clive Murgatroyd, by kind permission of the Warden, Fellows and Scholars of Keble College, Oxford
84: Simon Revill © English Heritage
85: © Rodney Bender, Innovative Glass Products Ltd www.innovativeglass.co.uk (t); Robyn Pender © English Heritage (b)

86: Chris Wood © English Heritage
87: © English Heritage
88: Robyn Pender © English Heritage
89: Robyn Pender © English Heritage
90: Simon Revill © English Heritage
92: Robyn Pender © English Heritage (t), (b); © Clive Murgatroyd (c)
93: Universal Images Group via Getty Images (l); Thermal Images by Linas Dapkus, Infraspection Institute Certified Level 3 Thermographer # 8510, Chicago Infrared Thermal Imaging Inc. (tr), (br)
94: Robyn Pender © English Heritage
95: © Clive Murgatroyd (t); Nicholas Warns Architect Ltd (b)
96: © Tobit Curteis Associates
97: © Jazai Engineering Inc.
98: Simon Revill © English Heritage
99: © Matthew Hall
100: © Crown copyright (2013) Visit Wales
101: © Tobit Curteis Associates
103: © Tobit Curteis Associates, with kind permission of the Dean and Chapter of Canterbury Cathedral
104: Robyn Pender © English Heritage
106: © Tobit Curteis Associates
108: © Tobit Curteis Associates, with kind permission of the Dean and Chapter of Canterbury Cathedral
109: © English Heritage
111: © Tobit Curteis Associates
115: Richard Jack (1866–1952), *The Toast*, 1913. The Bridgeman Art Library/ Private Collection/ © John Noott Galleries, Broadway, Worcestershire, UK. By kind permission of the estate of Richard Jack (tl); © Tobit Curteis Associates (tr); © Clive Murgatroyd (bl); Mary Evans Picture Library/ Grosvenor Prints (br)
116: © Tobit Curteis Associates, courtesy of the Dean and Chapter of Peterborough Cathedral
118: © The British Library Board/ Source: Charles Sylvester *The philosophy of Domestic Economy, as exemplified in the mode of warming, ventilating, washing, drying, and cooking ... adopted in the Derbyshire General Infirmary, etc.* 1819. Shelfmark 536.1.27, frontispiece
119: Getty Images/ Doug McKinlay
121: © Courtauld Institute, Conservation of Wall Painting Department
122: Robyn Pender © English Heritage, with thanks to the Weald & Downland Open Air Museum (r), (bl); © Chris Wood, with thanks to the Weald & Downland Open Air Museum (tl)

BUILDING ENVIRONMENT
ACKNOWLEDGEMENTS & PICTURE CREDITS

123: Robyn Pender © English Heritage, with thanks to the Weald & Downland Open Air Museum•
124: Getty Images/ Alan Copson (l); © The British Library Board/ Source: *Mechanics' Magazine*, October 4, 1834. Shelfmark 536.1.27, frontispiece (r)•
127: © Clive Murgatroyd with kind permission of Sir Osbert de Broilg•
129: Alamy/ © imageBROKER•
130: Robyn Pender © English Heritage•
131: Johann Mongels Culverhouse, (1820–91) *Evening at Home*, 1867, oil on canvas. The Bridgeman Art Library/ Private Collection•
132: Robyn Pender © English Heritage•
133: © National Trust Images/ John Hammond•
134: detail from Claude Monet, *The Dinner*, 1868–9, oil on canvas. The Bridgeman Art Library/ Buhrle Collection, Zurich, Switzerland•
135: Harriet Backer, *By Lamplight*, 1890, oil on canvas, (64.7x66.5 cms). The Bridgeman Art Library/ Private Collection/ Photo © O. Vaering•
136: © The Hereford Mappa Mundi Trust and the Dean and Chapter of Hereford Cathedral•
137: © National Trust Images/ W. Anderson-Porter (tr); © English Heritage (tl); © Christopher Sugg. Courtesy of Victoria and Albert Museum, London (bl); © English Heritage (br)•
138: Science & Society Picture Library/ Science Museum (l); Reproduced by courtesy of the University Librarian and Director, The John Rylands Library, The University of Manchester (r)•
139: © English Heritage•
140: © Wilco Krul•
141: © Clive Murgatroyd•
142: Getty Images/ Fox Photos•
143: Reproduced by courtesy of the University Librarian and Director, The John Rylands Library, The University of Manchester (t); Geraldine O'Farrell © English Heritage (bl), (br)•
147: © English Heritage•
148: Brian Ridout•
150: © Alex Witt/ www.alexwittphotography.com•
151: © Odgers Conservation Consultants Ltd•
153: Reproduced with permission of Rupert Harris Conservation (t); © Tobit Curteis Associates (cl), (c), (br); Brian Ridout (cr), (bl)•
154: Brian Ridout•
155: Robyn Pender © English Heritage (tl), (bl), (br); Tobit Curteis Associates (tr)•
156: © Tobit Curteis Associates•
159: Robyn Pender © English Heritage•
160: Brian Ridout•
162: Robyn Pender © English Heritage, with thanks to the PCC of Coombes Church, West Sussex•
165: Rex Features/ David Bagnall•
166: Arthur McCallum © English Heritage•
167: Robyn Pender © English Heritage•
168: © Clive Murgatroyd (l), (tr); © Nicholas Warns Architect Ltd (tc); Iain McCaig © English Heritage (br)•
169: Robyn Pender © English Heritage•

170: Robyn Pender © English Heritage•
171: Robyn Pender © English Heritage (l); Robyn Pender © English Heritage, with thanks to the Dean and Chapter of Norwich Cathedral (r)•
172: Brian Ridout•
173: Robyn Pender © English Heritage (tl), (tc); Brian Ridout (tr), (cr), (bl); Rex Features/ EDPPICS/ S Finlay (br)•
174: Robyn Pender © English Heritage•
175: Chris Wood © English Heritage•
176: Tim Allen © English Heritage•
177: © David Martyn•
178: Brian Ridout•
179: © Clive Murgatroyd•
180: Robyn Pender © English Heritage•
181: © Tobit Curteis Associates•
182: Robyn Pender © English Heritage (l); © Courtauld Institute, Conservation of Wall Painting Department (r)•
185: By permission of Steven J. Bostwick, Bostwick Forensic Architecture•
187: Nicholas Warns Architect Ltd•
188: © Clive Murgatroyd•
189: Robyn Pender © English Heritage (l); Reproduced with permission of Rupert Harris Conservation (r)•
190: Andrew More © English Heritage•
191: © Clive Murgatroyd•
192: Robyn Pender © English Heritage•
193: Robyn Pender © English Heritage•
194: Nicholas Warns Architect Ltd (tl), (tc); Brian Ridout (tr); © Tobit Curteis Associates (bl), (br); Robert Gowing © English Heritage (cr)•
196: © Crown copyright. English Heritage (tl); © Tobit Curteis Associates, with thanks to the Courtauld Institute, Conservation of Wall Painting Department (tr); © Courtauld Institute, Conservation of Wall Painting Department (bl); © Tobit Curteis Associates (br)•
198: © Tobit Curteis Associates•
199: © Tobit Curteis Associates•
200: Louise Brennan © English Heritage•
203: © Tobit Curteis Associates•
204: Brian Ridout•
205: © Tobit Curteis Associates (t); Brian Ridout (b)•
206: © Tobit Curteis Associates•
209: © Tim Jenkinson•
213: Robyn Pender © English Heritage, with thanks to the Rector of St Thomas, Salisbury•
217: Robyn Pender © English Heritage•
219: Mary Evans Picture Library/ Francis Frith (t), (c); © Skyscan Balloon Photography/ Skyscan.co.uk (b)•
223: GSS/DJA, www.djaweb.co.uk•
224: © Tobit Curteis Associates•
226: Robyn Pender © English Heritage•
227: Robyn Pender © English Heritage•
231: Robert Gowing © English Heritage (tl), (tr); © Tobit Curteis Associates (cl), (bl), (br)•
232: Brian Ridout•
233: Robyn Pender © English Heritage•
234: Robyn Pender © English Heritage•

235: Robyn Pender © English Heritage•
236: Robyn Pender © English Heritage•
237: © Tobit Curteis Associates•
238: © Tobit Curteis Associates•
239: © Clive Murgatroyd, with thanks to the PCC of Coombes Church, West Sussex (t); Simon Revill © English Heritage (bl), (br)•
240: © Tobit Curteis Associates, courtesy of Guernsey Museums and Galleries•
241: © Tobit Curteis Associates, courtesy of the Dean and Chapter of Canterbury Cathedral (tl); Robyn Pender © English Heritage (tr); © Tobit Curteis Associates with thanks to GB Geotechnics (bl); © Tobit Curteis Associates, courtesy of the Dean and Chapter of Canterbury Cathedral (br)•
247: Robyn Pender © English Heritage•
248: Brian Ridout•
249: © Tobit Curteis Associates•
250: © The Wall Paintings Workshop (t); © Tobit Curteis Associates (b)•
251: Robyn Pender © English Heritage, with thanks to Pedro Gaspar•
253: © Odgers Conservation Consultants Ltd•
254: © Tobit Curteis Associates, courtesy of Guernsey Museums and Galleries•
255: Robyn Pender © English Heritage•
258: © Tobit Curteis Associates, courtesy of the Dean and Chapter of Canterbury Cathedral•
260: Sarah Pinchin © English Heritage (l); © Tobit Curteis Associates (r)•
262: Master and Fellows of Trinity College Cambridge•
265: © Tobit Curteis Associates (tl); © Tobit Curteis Associates, with kind permission of Historic Royal Palaces (tc), (tr), (c), (cr); © Tobit Curteis Associates (cl), (bl), (bc), (br)•
266: © Sean Wheatley – Plastering Specialist•
269: © Sandberg•
270: © Tobit Curteis Associates (t); Alison Henry © English Heritage (b)•
271: Reproduced with permission of Rupert Harris Conservation (l); © Patrick Baty (r)•
272: © Tobit Curteis Associates•
273: © Tobit Curteis Associates•
276: © Tobit Curteis Associates (t); © English Heritage (b)•
277: Sarah Pinchin © English Heritage•
278: © English Heritage•
279: Robyn Pender © English Heritage•
280: © Odgers Conservation Consultants Ltd•
281: © John Stewart•
282: Robyn Pender © English Heritage•
286: Robyn Pender © English Heritage•
290: Alamy/ © Guy Edwardes Photography•
291: © Tobit Curteis Associates•
293: Chris Wood © English Heritage•
297: © Tobit Curteis Associates•
298: © Tobit Curteis Associates•
300: © Tobit Curteis Associates•

303: © Tobit Curteis Associates, with permission of Westminster Cathedral and St Ann's Gate Architects•
304: © Tobit Curteis Associates, with permission of Westminster Cathedral and St Ann's Gate Architects•
306: © Tobit Curteis Associates•
311: Robyn Pender © English Heritage (tl), (tr), (bl), (bc); © Clive Murgatroyd (br)•
312: © Clive Murgatroyd•
313: © Tobit Curteis Associates•
314: Alison Henry © English Heritage (t); © Tobit Curteis Associates (ct), (cb); Brian Ridout (b)•
315: © Courtauld Institute of Art, Conservation of Wall Painting Department (t); © Tobit Curteis Associates (ct); Robyn Pender © English Heritage (cb), (b)•
316: © Tobit Curteis Associates (t), (ct); Robyn Pender © English Heritage (cb), (b)•
323: Chapter of Durham Cathedral•
327: © Nicholas Warns Architect Ltd (tl); © Tobit Curteis Associates (tr), (cl), (bl); Iain McCaig © English Heritage (br)•
330: © Nicholas Warns Architect Ltd•
334: © John Letts•
335: © Clive Murgatroyd•
337: © Nicholas Warns Architect Ltd•
339: © Nicholas Warns Architect Ltd•
340: © Clive Murgatroyd•
343: Brian Ridout•
350: © Tobit Curteis Associates•
352: © Nicholas Warns Architect Ltd (tl); Brian Ridout (tc), (br); Robyn Pender © English Heritage (tr); © Clive Murgatroyd (bl)•
355: © Tobit Curteis Associates•
357: Robyn Pender © English Heritage•
360: © Clive Murgatroyd•
363: © Clive Murgatroyd (l); Robyn Pender © English Heritage (r)•
365: By permission of Steven J. Bostwick, Bostwick Forensic Architecture•
369: Robyn Pender © English Heritage•
371: Chris Wood © English Heritage•
372: © Tobit Curteis Associates•
373: Simon Revill © English Heritage•
376: Robyn Pender © English Heritage•
379: © Nicholas Warns Architect Ltd•
380: Simon Revill © English Heritage•
384: © Mike Wye & Associates Ltd•
385: Robyn Pender © English Heritage•
386: Simon Revill © English Heritage•
389: S & H Hanna•
391: © David Hackney courtesy St John's Smith Square•
392: © Tim Floyd•
396: Laurie Gibbs © Historic Royal Palaces•
399: © Tobit Curteis Associates (tl), (bl); Robyn Pender © English Heritage (tc), (cl); © Nicholas Warns Architect Ltd (tr); Brian Ridout (cc), (br)•
401: Alan Cathersides © English Heritage, with kind permission of Historic Royal Palaces (l)•
403: Robyn Pender © English Heritage•

404: Iain McCaig © English Heritage•
405: © Clive Murgatroyd (t); © Bird-B-Gone, Inc. (c); Robyn Pender © English Heritage (b)•
406: PestFix, www.pestfix.co.uk (t); Getty Images/ Daniel Berehulak (c); © English Heritage (b)•
407: Nature Picture Library/ © Steve Packham•
411: Iain McCaig © English Heritage•
412: © English Heritage•
413: © Clive Murgatroyd•
415: Robyn Pender © English Heritage (tl), (bl); © Tobit Curteis Associates (tc), (br); Elizabeth Ridout © Ridout Associates (tr); Brian Ridout (cl)•
418: © Sean Wheatley – Plastering Specialist•
420: © Tobit Curteis Associates, with kind permission of the Dean and Chapter of Canterbury Cathedral•
423: Alamy/ © age fotostock•
427: Robyn Pender © English Heritage•
428: © Tobit Curteis Associates•
430: © J. Michael Barber (tl); Andrew More © English Heritage (bl); Geraldine O'Farrell © English Heritage (r)•
431: Essex County Fire and Rescue Service•
433: Andrew More © English Heritage•
436: © Clive Murgatroyd•
437: © English Heritage•
448: © The British Library Board/ Source: *Punch*, 1850. Shelfmark P.P. 5276.(3.)•
450: Robyn Pender © English Heritage•
452: © Kenneth and Edwards Limited (Chartered Building Surveyors and Asbestos Consultants), with kind permission of Swindon Borough Council•
457: © Tobit Curteis Associates, with thanks to Clemmie Curteis•
458: Tom Gretchman•
462: © East Anglia Daily Times•
465: Parkinson, Dodson & Cheung•
466: © English Heritage•
469: © Clive Murgatroyd•
471: As supplied by Caro Flood Defence Systems, www.carofds.co.uk (l); Floodgate Ltd (r)•
474: Image courtesy of Donald Insall Associates•
476: Courtesy of FPC (UK) www.fpc-uk.com•
477: Robyn Pender © English Heritage•
478: © Cavendish Press•
483: Deadline News/ © Katielee Arrowsmith•
486: © Steve Howe•
487: Robyn Pender © English Heritage•
488: © Karen Roe•
491: Reproduced by permission of MOLA (Museum of London Archaeology), photographer Maggie Cox•
500: Elizabeth Ridout © Ridout Associates•
504: Getty Images/ Maremagnum•
506: English School, (17th century), *The Frost Fair of the Winter of 1683–4 on the Thames, with Old London Bridge in the Distance*. c.1685 (oil on canvas). The Bridgeman Art Library/ Yale Center for British Art, Paul Mellon Collection, USA•
507: Robyn Pender © English Heritage•
509: Robyn Pender © English Heritage•

511: © English Heritage (t); Getty Images/ Benjamin Howell (b)•
512: Charles Mertens (1865–1919), *Tailors*, oil on panel. The Bridgeman Art Library/ Private Collection/ © John Davies Fine Paintings•
513: Robyn Pender © English Heritage•
514: Hotmapping.co.uk and Horton Levi Ltd•
517: Alamy/ © travelib prime•
518: © Tobit Curteis Associates, with thanks to Gabriel Curteis (r); © Tobit Curteis Associates (l)•
520: Iain McCaig © English Heritage•
521: Robyn Pender © English Heritage•
526: Robyn Pender for English Heritage, based on data supplied by Parity Projects Ltd•
529: © Tobit Curteis Associates•
530: © Clive Murgatroyd•
532: Robyn Pender © English Heritage•
533: © Clive Murgatroyd•
535: Iain McCaig, Robyn Pender © English Heritage•
537: Robyn Pender © English Heritage (t)•
543, 544: These images are used with permission from STBA and the Department of Energy and Climate Change (funders of the Guidance Wheel and Knowledge Centre). Please see www.stbauk.org and www.responsible-retrofit.org/greenwheel for more information•
549: © Quattro Seal•
551: © Tobit Curteis Associates, courtesy of the Dean and Chapter of Peterborough Cathedral•
553: Getty Images/ olaser•
555: © Tobit Curteis Associates•
556: © English Heritage•
562: Alamy/ © Elizabeth Whiting & Associates (l); © Clive Murgatroyd (r)•
564: Iain McCaig © English Heritage•
567: © Historic Scotland•
570: © Clive Murgatroyd (tl), (tr), (c), (bc), (br); © Clive Murgatroyd, with thanks to the PCC of Coombes Church, West Sussex (tc); Robyn Pender © English Heritage (cl), (cr), (bl)•
572: © Linda Hall, with kind permission of Historic Royal Palaces (l); Robyn Pender © English Heritage (r)•
573: Robyn Pender, with kind permission of the Dean and Chapter of Carlisle Cathedral•
574: Getty Images/ VisitBritain/ Daniel Bosworth•
579: Alamy/ © National Geographic Image Collection•
580: Livingroofs.org•
581: © Crown Copyright reproduced courtesy of Historic Scotland. www.historicscotlandimages.gov.uk•
584: © Clive Murgatroyd•
588: Robyn Pender © English Heritage, with thanks to Bradford Cathedral•
590: JN Bentley Ltd (tl), (tr), JN Bentley Ltd/ Morgan O'Driscoll Photography (b)•
598: O-Facelift (GB) Ltd•

651

BUILDING ENVIRONMENT
ACKNOWLEDGEMENTS & PICTURE CREDITS